EDMONTON: THE LIFE OF A CITY

Paul Kane's painting of Fort Edmonton. He visited the fort in the fall of 1846.
(ROM 912.1.38)

EDMONTON
THE LIFE OF A CITY

BOB HESKETH AND FRANCES SWYRIPA, EDITORS

Canadian Cataloguing in Publication Data

Main entry under title:

Edmonton

ISBN 1-896300-02-2

1. Edmonton (Alta.)—History. 2. Edmonton (Alta.)—Biography.
I. Hesketh, Bob, 1950- II. Swyripa, Frances, 1951-
FC3696.3.E36 1995   971.23'34   C95-910881-5
F1079.5.E3E36 1995

Editor for the Press: Satya Das
Cover photographs:
street scene: Provincial Archives of Alberta PA BL 1015/7
back cover: Jim Cochrane, *Edmonton Journal*

NeWest Press gratefully acknowledges the financial assistance
of The Canada Council; The Alberta Foundation for the Arts,
a beneficiary of the Lottery Fund of the Government of Alberta;
and The NeWest Institute for Western Canadian Studies.

Printed and bound in Canada by Best Book Manufacturers

NeWest Publishers Limited
Suite 310, 10359 – 82 Avenue
Edmonton, Alberta T6E 1Z9

To all Edmontonians who have shared

in the life of this great northern city.

CONTENTS

BOB HESKETH AND FRANCES SWYRIPA

PREFACE

Two fairly simple ideas led to the creation of *Edmonton: The Life of a City*. First, there was no up-to-date book about Edmonton. James G. MacGregor's survey, *Edmonton: A History*, first appeared in 1967. At the same time, 1995 marked the two hundredth anniversary of the founding of Edmonton, so what better occasion for a book. Second, we wanted to bring together the different perspectives of academic and popular historians. Each article in *Edmonton: The Life of a City* is written by an expert on a particular aspect of Edmonton's history. Some authors are academics, some are popular historians. They have bridged the gap between their two worlds.

We have accumulated a large number of debts that we wish to acknowledge. Many of the histories here were first told at the conference, Edmonton's Bicentennial: Historical Reflections, held 11-4 May 1995 at the Edmonton Convention Centre. The conference was co-hosted and funded by the Edmonton and District Historical Society (EDHS) and the University of Alberta Department of History and Classics. Major sponsors included the Alberta Foundation for the Arts, the Alberta Historical Resources Foundation, the Canadian Imperial Bank of Commerce, CKUA Radio, the *Edmonton Journal*, Heritage Estate & Retirement Consulting, Luscar Ltd., Northwestern Utilities Limited (An *ATCO* Company), the Social Sciences and Humanities Research Council of Canada (SSHRCC), Syncrude Canada Inc., and the University of Alberta. The conference could not have taken place without the hard work of the volunteer members of the conference planning committee, particularly its chair, Sean Moir.

Funding for this book was provided by the Edmonton Community Foundation, SSHRCC, the EDHS, and the Historical Society of Alberta. Among the institutions that helped with the pictures, the Provincial Archives of Alberta, the City of Edmonton Archives, the Glenbow Alberta Institute, the University of Alberta Archives, and the Royal Ontario Museum deserve special mention.

We are grateful to NeWest Press for their sustained belief in this project. Satya Das, the editor for NeWest, made valuable editorial suggestions. The anonymous referees provided prompt and insightful analysis. Every article has benefited from their work. The authors responded rapidly to our requests and often put other projects on hold. Many authors also donated pictures from their personal collections. Finally, Bob Hesketh would like to thank Betty Matwichuk and Andy Hesketh for their enduring patience while he worked on this project. ∾

GILBERT A. STELTER

WHAT KIND OF CITY
IS EDMONTON?

Muttart Conservatory and downtown skyline, Christmas 1978. (PAA J.4364/1)

*D*oes Edmonton have a unique character? Have its natural resources and ethnically diverse population created a distinctive community? Or is it much the same as other North American cities, such as Toronto or Phoenix? These are some of the questions Gilbert Stelter answers in this witty and perceptive overview of Edmonton's history.

Stelter is a former resident of Bruderheim who as a child came to the big city of Edmonton. He graduated with a PhD in History from the University of Alberta in 1968. Since then he has gone on to distinguish himself as a pre-eminent Canadian urban historian. With dozens of articles and edited books to his credit, he has earned an international reputation for his scholarship.

Drawing on his memories of the city and his training as a scholar, Stelter looks at Edmonton's growth from fur trade settlement to the cosmopolitan community of the 1990s.

THE CITY, ACCORDING TO THE GREAT FRENCH ANTHRO-
pologist Claude Levi-Strauss, 'is both natural object
and a thing to be cultivated; individual and group; something lived and something dreamed; it is *the* human invention, *par excellence*.'[1] His poetic description should remind
us that *cities* and *civilization* have usually been equated
since the beginnings of human recorded time; that we
can't understand our society, our civilization, without
knowing these objects, these concentrations of people,
that hold such a central place in it; that we can learn to
read these objects, these entities, making sense of them
even though they might often seem to be chaotic or formless; that cities are not just created but can also become
creative, collective entities with per-
sonalities and directed behaviour;
and that we never really know these
objects, these communities, without
knowing their past, any more than we
can know a person without knowing
something of his/ her background.

Cities have long fascinated me
perhaps because they are something
exotic and not natural to my personal
background. My first experience of a
city was as a child when my family
came into Edmonton for shopping or
business. I was born and raised in the
Edmonton district on a farm near
the village of Bruderheim and was
awestruck by the crowds, the traffic,
and the tall buildings. And I was
especially impressed by modern urban
marvels such as the flush toilets in
the washrooms at Eaton's. I have
explored cities as foreign and strange
territory ever since. After college in Pennsylvania, where
I got to know New York and Philadelphia, I returned
for a PhD at the University of Alberta and worked on
the subject of western American cities, particularly
Cheyenne, Wyoming. And I married an Edmontonian,
Sally Shortliffe, who remains passionately loyal to
Edmonton even after thirty years of residence in Ontario. I
have spent most of my professional life working in the field
of Canadian and international urban history and am still
trying to come to grips with elusive concepts such as
'urban' and 'city.' My favourite cities are those in France
and Italy and I have been particularly influenced by the
French and Italian approaches to urban history. Unlike
the English, they tend to look at cities in a holistic way,

As members of a community,

we must have a strong, shared

sense of our collective past

if we are going to make wise

decisions about the future

directions of our communities.

conscious of how much image and perception can be a
significant part of total reality.

It is difficult not to be critical of how most urban history
has been done in Canada, and elsewhere for that matter.[2]
The academic study of cities tends to be a pretty colourless,
lifeless affair, with most scholars apparently never dreaming
of actually going out and looking at the places about which
they write. In fact, if cities were as dull as most urban history, nobody would live in them. Local historians capture
some of the excitement of urban life and write about real
people, but they often lack a sense of a larger context or
they are local boosters who manage to make mountains out
of what are really molehills.[3] I do not wish to suggest that
local history has no value. Quite the
contrary. I believe we should encourage and celebrate localism and not
always assume that the really important things in life happen somewhere
else. The point is that we should
combine the best qualities of local
and urban history. This involves
more than history for its own sake,
legitimate as that is. As members of a
community, we must have a strong,
shared sense of our collective past if
we are going to make wise decisions
about the future directions of our
communities.

There are many Edmontons,
perhaps as many as there are people
who think and experience and write
about it. I will look at Edmonton in
the context of national urban development, which involves explaining a
complex set of relationships. I will
examine these by setting out a 'city-region' explanation of
the settlement process. By this I mean a process whereby
cities like Edmonton serve as nationalizing, standardizing
agencies for the transmission of established power structures, organizational procedures, and culture to any specific region. Paraphrasing Fernand Braudel, a city is a city
wherever it is.[4] On the other hand, we now recognize that
regions tend to act as localizing forces, making the urban
place more like the countryside. As one scholar has put it,
'the urbanization of the countryside involves a subsidiary
ruralization of the city.'[5] As a city, Edmonton therefore has
a lot in common with Toronto, Winnipeg, and many
United States cities. But is there not also a measure of distinctiveness based on its western Canadian setting and on

its close connection with an agricultural and resource-based hinterland?

There has been a good deal of discussion about Canadian city-region relationships, some of which misses the point, I believe. There are several levels of relationships, and these need to be distinguished if we are to make any sense of these links.[6] At the highest level, an international system is dominated by great world cities such as New York, London, and Tokyo. A second level is that of the nation-state's urban system, in Canada's case dominated by two or perhaps three places. A third level involves the regions within a nation-state, such as the eastern, central, and western regions of Canada, with smaller divisions at provincial boundaries also possible. And a fourth level is a city and its local region or hinterland (or district, the term used in the Edmonton case).

In the following pages I will examine three specific elements of these relationships by looking in turn at the nature of urban systems, at the shape or look of the city, and finally, at urban culture.

∾ THE NATURE OF URBAN SYSTEMS

By world standards of city size, Canadian cities do not rank very highly. Toronto is in sixty-second place, Montreal seventy-first.[7] Sheer size, of course, is not always a good indicator of power, but the trends are obvious—cities in Asia and South America are growing in significance as well as size. Historically, our world has been dominated by London, Paris, and New York. A kind of 'aesthetic metropolitanism' prevails, with fashions such as architectural styles and ways of organizing space spreading from the centre to the outer fringes of the system. Examples would be the Victorian revival styles of the nineteenth century or the Beaux Arts classical tradition of the turn of the century. At this international level, regional variations exist: it is possible to talk about a North American approach to city-building in contrast to the European approach. North American cities are generally younger, without the depth of historical layers going back to the medieval or even the ancient world, as in Rome or Athens. And they are usually much more spread out, much more the product of the automobile.

At the second level, that of the nation-state as an urban region, the question arises: is there such a thing as a Canadian city, different from cities in the United States, for example? Do national borders make a difference? It has been persuasively argued that different value systems in the United States and Canada in the areas of political culture and social life have led to substantial and important differences in cities and urban life in such areas as racial composition and relations, criminal behaviour, and ethnic mix.[8]

The time factor—when a city was founded—has major consequences for the nature of the system in which it operates. The national system Edmonton hoped to join was decisively centred in central Canada, headed by the older established cities of Montreal and Toronto. Neither of these is a primate city in a national sense—that is, a city which completely dominates a country's system, as in the case of London in Britain or Paris in France. The Canadian system more closely resembles that of the old Soviet Union, of the United States, of Brazil, and perhaps of Australia—all cases of countries with huge land masses and where two or three cities dominate, reflecting the power structure of those societies. Montreal and Toronto were the key organizing centres that focused the views of the complex central region dominating the country. By the turn of the century, with Montreal at about 267,000 and Toronto just over 200,000 people, they had grown to be three and four times as large as the next cities below them in the system. A massive structural change had taken place in the system just below the two leaders in the previous thirty years with the opening of the West. The relative status of the Maritimes cities was in sharp decline, with the initiative taken by two new western upstarts, Winnipeg at 42,000 and Vancouver at 27,000 people.

The emerging metropolitan system had several characteristics that had a direct bearing on the status of any new entrants like Edmonton. Westerners do not have to be told that national systems do not resemble a level playing field. As described most effectively by J.M.S. Careless, the metropolitan relationship between cities was a feudal-like chain of vassalage, with Winnipeg, for example, tributary to Montreal, but serving as the metropolis of a large region of its own in the prairie West. This unequal relationship between cities and regions is as old as human civilization and is something of a natural process, but certainly the political economy of Canada accentuated the unequal character of the relationship. Federal legislation, such as the Canada Bank Act of 1871, centralized banking into a few large banks with many branches instead of adopting the American system of many independent banks. The result was the concentration of financial control in Montreal and Toronto. For a quick education in the reality of financial power, I recommend a walk along Bay Street in Toronto, where the five big banks and some of the major trust companies are located. Actually, these are not just huge buildings—soaring skyscrapers—but each is also a giant complex in its own right, with stunning modern lobbies featuring modern sculpture, and the whole edifice topped by massive towers symbolizing the bank's place in the Canadian economy. An urban skyline dominated by bank towers is very much a Canadian phenomenon. In American cities, where banks are smaller and localized, it is corporate towers that dominate the skyline, as in Chicago, for example, where the major skyscrapers are named Sears, Standard Oil, and John Hancock.

In the area of industry, the key to most urban growth from about 1850 to 1950, the National Policy of 1879 centralized economic power in the cities of central Canada by accentuating the earlier development of industry in a corridor from Montreal to Hamilton. One of the characteristics of this early phase of industrialization in central Canada was a close association between a family-owned firm and a local community. Individual entrepreneurs equated their prosperity with that of the community in which their firm had been established. Western cities, and particularly Edmonton, however, only became established toward the end of this phase of industrialism. From the turn of the century, the trend was to large industrial conglomerates that had no loyalty to any particular community.[9] We are now witnessing the next phase in this process, with another national policy, the two recent free trade agreements. Corporations have been freed from any national, regional, or local responsibilities, and the result is a rapid deindustrialization of many places, particularly in Ontario.

The West emerged late in the nineteenth century, even as the Maritimes declined, with the boom towns of Winnipeg and Vancouver leading the way.[10] What was western about the West's cities? They were very young and, like their region, were subservient economically and culturally to distant metropolitan centres like Montreal and Toronto. Their settlement and development is generally described in the context of transportation technology—the railways—and staples production—wheat. One could point to the environmental setting, the climate, the resource pattern, and the distance from established centres of population. In some respects, in the early twentieth century Canada's western cities were going through a phase that its central cities had experienced a century earlier. Their urban fortunes depended on the development of local agricultural and resource-based hinterlands. But urban growth led the development of the region. Within twenty years, by 1921, remarkable changes

had taken place in this urban system, with Calgary at 63,000 people in ninth place, and Edmonton, with 58,000 in tenth. What had happened was that both of these cities had become metropolitan centres in their own right, organizing their respective regions of Alberta, focusing the views of these regions, and dealing with outside forces on their behalf.

In recent years, the older Canadian and western systems have been transformed almost beyond recognition. Edmonton now stands fifth in the country in population, after Toronto, Montreal, Vancouver, and Ottawa-Hull. Edmonton is thus a solid member of the second tier of Canadian cities also made up of Vancouver, Ottawa-Hull, Calgary, Quebec City, and Hamilton. And further changes are certainly in the works, for new political arrangements such as free trade have accentuated the old north-south attraction. Vancouver's connections with California and Alberta's with the American Sun Belt threaten the traditional east-west connections that have characterized the Canadian system.[11]

In one respect, Edmonton's regional position has been and still is unusual in the Canadian context. The Canadian norm is for one place to dominate a province, as in the case of Winnipeg and Vancouver, and in the cases of all of the other provinces except Alberta and Saskatchewan. Edmonton has been one of a pair of siblings, not a favourite, only child. It has had to share the province with Calgary; in fact, one can't explain either of these cities without constant reference to the other, although the historians of each seem quite willing to ignore the other. These two cities are not exactly twins, but the comparable ages are difficult to determine. Edmonton obviously is older if you count the trading post days, but Calgary was established earlier as an urban place. The relative parity between the two since has been the product of an intricate series of actions at the national, provincial, and local levels and fortuitous circumstances which have usually been locally defined as opportunities successfully exploited. Calgary got the transcontinental railway, Edmonton the provincial capital and the university. Calgary chanced upon Turner Valley and became the centre of the oil industry. The sibling rivalry continues, from professional sports teams to the hosting of international sports events and the sponsoring of major cultural activities. This intercity rivalry seems to be one of the defining characteristics of urban life in Alberta, not present to the same extent elsewhere in the country.[12]

Any explanation of Edmonton's success has to involve an examination of its local region, which eventually extends to the larger North itself. In this respect, Edmonton as an urban place took over the extended network that had been established by the fur trading post.[13] The broadening function from trading post to city is an old Canadian tradition, including especially Quebec City and Montreal, but also Fort Frontenac at Kingston and even Fort Rouille at Toronto. In some cases Natives had already recognized the strategic and commercial values of a particular site long before the arrival of Europeans.

Those who laid the foundations for the modern city of Edmonton in the late nineteenth century—entrepreneurs like John A. McDougall and especially Frank Oliver of the *Bulletin*—did not think in terms of building a little local village. In the mould of the great city-founders of previous generations, Champlain at Quebec City, Cornwallis at Halifax, and Simcoe at Toronto, Edmonton's pioneers thought in terms of a city and its regional hegemony long before a realistic demographic basis for such a claim existed. As early as 1890, when the town's population was only about 500, Edmonton's aggressive young Board of Trade published a pamphlet entitled *The Edmonton District of Northern Alberta* that pictured Edmonton as the commercial, communications, and legal centre of a huge territory, extending from the Red Deer River in the south to the Athabasca River in the north and from the Rockies in the west to the provisional provincial boundary in the east. Of

other places, Fort Saskatchewan, St Albert, and Clover Bar were mentioned, but not as potential rivals. As for the weather, locals had already learned to emphasize the positive. The Board observed: 'The summer temperature seldom goes above 85 degrees while in winter 40 below is uncommon. Calm weather without a suspicion of wind always accompanies low temperatures.'[14]

By 1922 the Board of Trade's description of its local district was sub-titled 'Canada's Richest Mixed Farming District,' a territory equal in size to that of England or American states such as Illinois, Iowa, Michigan, or New York. The weather had apparently improved, for the Board now boasted 'it is doubtful if there can be found a more desirable winter climate in the whole of the prairie region . . . blizzards are unknown.'[15] The greater North was now also regarded as a part of the city's hinterland. With a population close to 60,000 and no less than ninety-five wholesale and jobbing houses engaged in the city's distribution trade, Edmonton was now said to hold the 'key position geographically to about one quarter of the area of Canada, comprising the Valleys of the Saskatchewan, Peace, Athabasca and Mackenzie Rivers, and the great hinterland of North-West Canada.'[16]

Regional horizons continued to expand with the growth of the city. By 1944, during the war boom, with a population just over 100,000, Edmonton had become the

Legislature building under construction, 1912, before the addition of the dome. (PAA B.3387)

The grand design of Percy Nobbs for the University of Alberta campus, 1912. Much of the plan was never realized. (UAA 73-124)

'Crossroads of the World.' With the advent of air traffic, the Chamber of Commerce emphasized Edmonton's strategic location for polar routes, making the city the gateway to the north in a global sense. In case anyone questioned these claims, the Chamber concluded on a belligerent note: 'These are the facts. Anyone who doesn't take them into account is like the majority who in Columbus' day did not realize the earth was round.'[17]

To a remarkable extent the dreams of the promoters have been realized with the entry of Edmonton into the big leagues of Canadian cities. But boom and bust cycles are part of the normal life of any city, even New York. Identifying a community's status, however, with the success of professional sports—the City of Champions—is a risky business as Montreal has also discovered recently. Local pretensions of other kinds can be dashed just as quickly. In the late 1980s at the height of Toronto's self-romance, its citizens constantly referred to their 'World Class City.' The deep recession since then has changed the nature of local discourse there—Toronto is now desperately looking for ways to avoid becoming the hole in the donut as the communities around it siphon off much of the economic and population growth. Edmonton's other recent title—Official Host City for the Turn of the Century—is in line with some of its earlier slogans, but seems to have a somewhat sinister apocalyptical tone.

∾ URBAN FORM

To the casual observer, the shape of Edmonton seems quite similar to what you would see anywhere in North America. Here is the same equivocal, languishing downtown with its anonymous glass towers, the strip malls, and the sprawling suburbs. Is there nothing Canadian, or western Canadian about the place? The differences may well be in the details rather than in the general scheme. The prevailing form of North American cities at the turn of the century was the core-periphery type, a compact central business district surrounded by suburban rings. While early Edmonton's central core amounted to a rather scattered settlement, the general North American urban pattern was eventually established. What was western about it was a popular predisposition to low-density settlement, accentuated probably by a desire to escape the Hudson's Bay Company survey and develop cheaper land. The whole city became suburban in character, with the annexations of 1904–14 more than tripling the city's area. By the 1940s, when Edmonton was the least densely populated of any Canadian city, it had 1,000 miles of streets, of which 63 were paved and 138 gravelled.[18] The remaining 800 miles of streets alternated between mud in wet weather and dust in dry, a condition with a long life in some parts of the city.

The city's shape has obviously been affected by its location on a major river. The river and its valley—a substantial gorge—offer spectacular views but have made communication up and down the 160-foot banks relatively difficult. Although the river was crucial to fur trade communication and steamboat traffic was considerable in the pre-railway era, Edmonton never was a river port like Quebec City and Montreal on the St Lawrence or Old World cities like London on the Thames or Paris on the Seine. The North Saskatchewan is a quite ordinary river for most of its length, but at Edmonton it is both a river and a great valley—a valley that has been the site of human habitation for several millennia. With the recent development of a series of walking and biking trails, the valley has become one of the city's most positive physical amenities.

Urban development depended on the coming of the railways, and even though Edmonton's layout north of the river was not determined by a railway, as in the case of most western places, its shape has been affected. It would probably have developed primarily north of the river had not the Calgary and Edmonton Railway created a separate, supposedly replacement town, Strathcona, on the south side. Similar policies had worked for the Canadian Pacific Railway in Brandon, Regina, Calgary, and Vancouver, where the central cores of fledgling townsites had to be moved to correspond to where the company located its station. The development of a competitive townsite on the south side meant that the two sides of the river were developed in more equal fashion than might otherwise have been the case.

Much of Edmonton's early layout was the product of aggressive developers who laid out subdivisions at a furious pace far beyond actual demand until about 1914.[19] Before the end of this feverish expansion, Edmontonians discussed the currently fashionable planning approach, the American-based City Beautiful Movement, that had captured the thinking of leaders in Montreal, Toronto, and especially Ottawa. Like the grandiose proposals in these central Canadian cities, Edmonton thought about the creation of an elaborate park system and even a dramatic civic centre in the Beaux Arts style usually associated with the great public buildings during the City Beautiful Movement. Calgary went even further by having a spectacular plan drawn up in this manner by the flamboyant British planner, Thomas Mawson. When planning was officially instituted, however, with the Alberta Act of 1913, the results were something less exciting. Like other provinces that selectively imitated a British act, Alberta put in place a regulatory system that applied only to undeveloped land on the urban fringe, not to any areas already subdivided. Of course, the greatest land boom in Edmonton history was already over by the time the act came into effect.[20]

The built environment is perhaps the best indicator of Edmonton's relative youth among cities in Canada and elsewhere. The layers of successive building, like geological formations, are few and of very recent origin. The early building phase in Edmonton does not seem to have been as distinctive as that of Calgary, where Stephen Avenue buildings in sandstone from the nineteenth century gave a special local touch. Early Edmonton more closely resembled other smaller places in Alberta with their one- and two-storey wooden buildings. Edmonton did not get started soon enough to take part seriously in the Victorian era that defined so much of North American urban form. Thus there are no streets lined with Queen Anne, Italianate, or Second Empire houses, nor of course is there anything of the earlier Georgian, that formed the basis for the cities of central and eastern Canada. But Edmonton was clearly created in a new wave of classicism at the turn of the century, a notable aspect of which was the Beaux Arts style. In this regard Edmonton was like other Canadian cities at the time, for the currently popular styles were imported from elsewhere, usually the United States. In what I have termed 'aesthetic metropolitanism,' Edmontonians tended to look to Montreal for an interpretation of what was currently in fashion. It could be argued, therefore, that if Edmonton has a past, it is a past that happened somewhere else.

Two examples of this process will be cited. The first is the design of the provincial Legislature building (1908–13). This was apparently modelled on some influential American state capitols, especially the one in

The McLeod Building was typical of pre-First World War commercial architecture. (PAA BL.784)

Providence, Rhode Island, designed by Allan Jeffers who just happened to have become Alberta's provincial architect. Alberta had appointed an advisory committee headed by Percy Nobbs, an Englishman who had recently been appointed to head McGill's architectural faculty. Nobbs objected to the American character of the designs and, according to his biographer, drew up the final designs in order to make them slightly more British—whatever that meant.[21] Regardless of the details of the design, the juxtaposition of this large, elegant stone structure, representative of current cosmopolitan taste, and the shabby logs of old Fort Edmonton huddled next to it symbolized the changes taking place in the city and in the city's perception of itself.

Nobbs was also directly involved in revising Jeffers's plans for the fledgling University of Alberta. Here the Montreal connection was more obvious for the University's president, Henry Marshall Tory, had been a colleague at McGill. Nobbs became involved in 1909 and then joined with Frank Darling, a well-known Toronto architect, to produce a 'General Building Scheme' for the campus in 1912. Nobbs was not known for any Beaux Arts proclivities, for his favourite styles were based on the English Arts and Crafts Movement, yet his design for the Alberta campus looked remarkably like currently fashionable projects being put forward in Toronto and Montreal, based on American precedents. And it certainly presaged the elegant plans that Thomas Mawson drew up for Calgary and Regina a couple of years later. In the Alberta plan, a wide central avenue was terminated by a Parisian-style 'Place' with a central monument, and near the river a great Convocation Hall, never built. Nobbs also took over from Jeffers the design of the first academic building, the Arts Building, and, according to him, did it in 'modified English Classical.' After the war he designed the Medical Building in similar fashion.[22]

Other landmarks from the pre-First World War era also were designed in the current styles, illustrating the extent to which Edmonton was being integrated into the Canadian cultural system. For commercial architecture, the best example was the nine-storey McLeod Building (1913–15) in the Chicago Commercial style, by an American architect, John Dow. Bigger versions of this kind of building dominated the commercial hearts of Montreal, Toronto, and Winnipeg. And in what became a recognizable Canadian national chateau style, the Macdonald Hotel (1913–15) was designed by Ross and McFarland of Montreal, who had also done the Chateau Laurier in Ottawa and the Fort Garry in Winnipeg.[23]

Edmonton is not a great city for churches in architectural terms, even though it has often been referred to as a city of churches. The major Protestant churches—First

With a commanding view of the river valley, the Macdonald Hotel has offered elegant dining and accommodation since its construction at the start of the First World War. This view is from 1953. (PAA BL.2126/2)

Presbyterian, McDougall United, Knox Presbyterian, and Robertson United—are all rather dull interpretations of early twentieth-century types more suitable in a small Ontario town. More interesting are St Joachim's and St Josaphat's cathedral and the finally completed St Joseph's basilica. But there is an absence of any truly outstanding example of church architecture of the quality that graces many major cities.

Edmonton's outstanding architectural feature, the West Edmonton Mall, is a more fitting metaphor for the city's current version of modernism. It is widely regarded by urbanists as the exemplar of the most powerful, and disturbing, trend in contemporary city-building, the privatization of public space. The critics who point to the artificial, derivative, placeless character of the mall have some valid points. Yet it must be understood that the older European tradition of providing public space to promote social encounters or to serve the conduct of public affairs never really caught on in North American cities. In other words, the social world of cities that was represented by the town square never became our tradition, and so it appears that only our desire to consume can force us into something vaguely resembling a public realm.[24]

Residential architecture, at least that for the elite, represented the same kind of borrowing so common in other cities. Certainly this applies to some of the older mansions in the Groat Estate, Old Strathcona, and the Highlands. Examples from the Groat Estate include the Georgian Revival Gibbons House (1911) and the Tudor Revival Cornwall House (1912).[25] Current architectural guides give little indication of the more modest, ordinary homes that constituted the bulk of the city's built environment. From my own experience, the basic types seem similar to those in other North American cities: the pre-Second World War 'minimal traditional,' carpenter-built houses that omitted most of the detailing of earlier styles, the 'Ranch' style, and the 'split-level.' What is distinctive is the use of stucco on all of these types. To what extent has this been a product of a rural influence, brought to the city by generations of migrants from the farms and villages of the district?

∾ URBAN CULTURE

Cities have always acted as agencies of cultural transmission to a new region. I am defining culture here in the large sense of the word, as the collective values, beliefs, and behaviour of a society—perhaps also defined as character. High culture is only one element of this bundle of characteristics. In this respect, early Edmonton's culture was largely derivative, for the basic social institutions and ways of organizing society—from municipal government to education, religion, and entertainment—were not original but reflected the cultural baggage of those who created the early town.[26] Of course, the same could be said about any early city, anywhere. But eventually this nationalizing

The Delmar Bard House, built in 1912, is still one of the most imposing houses in Old Strathcona. The basic 'four-square' style was very common for modest houses in this era in North America, but here it is dressed up with features such as a conservatory and a carriage house. (GILBERT STELTER)

character of the city was affected by the culture of the surrounding district as people migrated to the city.

It is difficult to characterize Edmonton in this regard, compared to Calgary, which has a more clearly defined image. The travel writer Jan Morris found Edmonton more than she could handle after a week's visit in the late 1980s. She usually encapsulates a community's culture or character in a few pages or phrases but had to admit that she was never able to get a fix on what made Edmonton tick.[27] That difficulty won't stop me from trying to outline some of the local cultural norms by looking in turn at the economic structure of the city and the changing ethnic composition of the population. In each case, Edmonton's image may become slightly more discernable if compared to Calgary, for I believe that the differences between these two communities are more than skin deep.

What a city does for a living is a vital part of its culture. Early Edmonton was closely tied to its agricultural district, which specialized in mixed farming, and it therefore developed a commercial leadership in the areas of wholesaling, transportation, and the processing of agricultural produce.[28] Early Calgary became the centre of large-scale ranching enterprises and the alliance of ranchers and business elites left a lasting imprint on that city's personality. The early development of Alberta's oil resources at Turner Valley made Calgary the centre of that industry and this arrangement continued even after the discovery of oil at Leduc. Head offices continued on in Calgary, which prides itself on being a 'brief-case' rather than a 'lunch-box' city.[29] A strong American connection is reflect-

ed in a conservative, free-enterprise ideology. Edmonton, looking north and northwest, has been more government- and education-oriented in its employment base, and its political ideology seems less anti-Ottawa, or at least more 'small l' liberal.

Some of the differences between the cities are reflected in the ethnic composition of the population. Edmonton's population has never had as large a proportion of people of British background. In 1901, for example, those of British ethnic origin made up 61 per cent in Edmonton, compared to 80 per cent in Calgary and 92 per cent in Toronto. Edmonton's did reach a high of 72 per cent in 1921 but has declined rapidly ever since, like most Canadian cities, to about 45 per cent in 1971, about ten percentage points lower than in Calgary. Those of French and German background vied for second place in Edmonton until almost 1931, when German and Ukrainian became roughly equal at 12 per cent, similar to the ratio in Winnipeg. The French and Ukrainian ratios of Calgary have always been considerably lower. The ethnic balance has changed with post-Second World War immigration, although those of Italian background are not nearly as numerous in prairie cities as in Toronto, nor are the Asian and Caribbean populations. As Toronto has been transformed in the twentieth century from the most British to the most ethnically cosmopolitan city in the country, its population make-up has become quite different from that of the cities, towns, and countryside of southern Ontario. To what extent is this also happening in Edmonton and Calgary in relation to their districts?

Certainly the ethnic composition of the populations of Edmonton and Calgary's local districts were quite differ-

Several examples of the 'minimal traditional' carpenter-built houses, popular around the time of the Second World War. (GILBERT STELTER)

ent. To what extent have the values of these rural people, many of whom have migrated to the cities, affected the character of the cities themselves? Some examples of local communities in the region of each city offer some possible clues. The foothills communities of Bragg Creek, Priddis, Millarville, and Kew were settled primarily by individuals of British origin. Among other things, they brought their cricket, tennis, and polo with them and used these sports to create effective associations between people of the foothills. They were closely tied to Calgary for urban amenities, and Calgarians were in turn attracted to foothills sporting and social activities.[30]

A world away, in many respects, are some of the small communities founded in the Edmonton district, based on Ukrainian or German ethnic origin. One example was Bruderheim, founded in 1895 by ethnic Germans from the Russian empire who were associated with the Moravian Church, followers of John Hus, the pre-Reformation reformer. They also formed little church-centred, rural communities in other locations nearer Edmonton; Bruderfeld, New Sarepta, and Heimtal. The village of Bruderheim became a religious, social, and commercial focal point for the farmers of its district.[31] And so we come full circle, with the smallest villages having their place in a system headed by the biggest cities. For the past century, residents of this and hundreds of other rural communities have been migrating to Edmonton, bringing with them their rural values and customs and changing Edmonton itself in the process.

ω In conclusion, what kind of city is Edmonton? It is obviously necessary to go beyond the fact that Edmonton is 'one of the northernmost big cities on earth, and one of the coldest,' as Jan Morris puts it,[32] although that feature has to be incorporated into any portrait of the city. In many respects cities become what they admire most. Toronto has always wanted to be New York; Winnipeg wanted to be Chicago. Early Edmonton looked to Montreal for a model of how to create a far-flung empire. More recently Edmonton has become more like Toronto.

But any portrait has to be drawn subtly, for Edmonton is a complex community. Like Canada itself, it is difficult to define. Arguably, it has become the most Canadian of Canadian cities. Two general characteristics of the city may explain what I mean. First, Edmonton is a *comprehensive* community, one with a balance of major features. There is a judicious mix of aggressive business ambition and a concern for the quality of life. Central to both is the notion, now generally under attack, that it might be necessary to take collective action for the common good, economically and socially. Second, Edmonton is a *cosmopolitan* community. It is cosmopolitan in its ethnic diversity and in its sense of decency and respect for differences, which is at the heart of Canada at its best. And it is cosmopolitan in its cultural dynamism, which has become one of the driving forces of the city's being. Comprehensive and cosmopolitan. Perhaps these characteristics don't make for catchy slogans. But they have made a good city. ω

JOHN FOSTER

JAMES BIRD, FUR TRADER

Paul Kane's painting of Fort Edmonton. He visited the fort in the fall of 1846.
(ROM 912.1.38)

*F*or centuries, Alberta's parklands were Indian lands. The first Europeans ventured into the West only in the 1700s. The community of Edmonton came into being just over two hundred years ago, when the first fur trade forts were built near present-day Fort Saskatchewan.

The establishment of these forts required cultural adaptation and adjustment between Euro-Canadians and Natives. These exchanges took place on an individual level or within a family context. But they also had wider implications and contributed to the nature of the fur trade itself and the formation of the Métis nation.

When James Bird of the Hudson's Bay Company took the position of Chief Factor of Edmonton House in 1799, he followed the custom of the country and took a 'country wife.' The fur trade was then largely dependent on Natives for many things, from food to furs. Both groups viewed these marriages as beneficial to their trade relationship. During Bird's tenure at Edmonton, lasting until 1816, the Northwest Company and the Hudson's Bay Company battled for the fabulous fur wealth of the Athabaska Country. The struggle would be significant not just for the two companies but also for Natives and Edmonton.

The eventual victory of the Hudson's Bay Company would solidify Edmonton's position as a supply centre for the northern fur trade. In the decades after Bird's tenure at Edmonton House, fur trade society would change forever as a result of the depletion of the fur-bearing animals, the impact of disease on Natives, and the arrival of the first missionaries.

University of Alberta historian John Foster is well known for his volunteer work in the community with local genealogical societies and the Edmonton and District Historical Society. He brings more than two decades of research into fur trade, Native, and Métis societies to this carefully drawn portrait of James Bird.

*I*N THE AUTUMN OF 1788 JAMES CURTIS BIRD, BORN in Acton (now a part of London), England, was close to fifteen years of age when he disembarked from the Hudson's Bay Company's annual supply ship, anchored off York Factory on the west coast of Hudson Bay.[1] Enlisted as a writer, young Bird would be employed for the next four years in hand-copying the Factory's business papers: correspondence, journals, and accounts, before they were sent to the Company's Governor and Committee in London. This experience coupled with his own mental quickness would provide Bird with an excellent schooling in the fundamentals and the particulars of the Company's fur trade on the Saskatchewan River during the closing decade of the eighteenth century. Bird's years at York Factory and later at such posts as Cumberland House, South Branch House, Nepawi, and Carlton House, all in the 'Saskatchewan Country,' would prepare him for his service as the officer-in-charge at Edmonton House from 1799 to 1816. In this crucial start-up period for Edmonton, Bird would lay the foundation for the Post to emerge as the Company's foremost entrepôt on the Saskatchewan River. Known as Fort Edmonton, or Fort des Prairies after 1820, Edmonton would prove to be one of the few fur trade posts to become a major urban centre in the succeeding era of settlement.

We know little of Bird's background. He was born to James Bird and Elizabeth Curtis shortly after their marriage in 1783. He was the eldest of five boys and two girls. None of his younger brothers were apparently employed in the fur trade. We know nothing of his schooling except to note that his correspondence in later years reflected an excellent grasp of writing as a means of communication, permitting him to make sophisticated analyses of fur trade problems and recommend insightful solutions. As well he was most effective in using the written language to ingratiate himself with, and to persuade, superiors. Such skills imply middle class origins for his family. A possible connection to Thomas Bird who served the Hudson's Bay Company (HBC) as an officer a generation earlier, while in line with middle class origins, also suggests the family lacked sufficient prominence to unlock similar opportunities in England. Throughout his career Bird would demonstrate an inordinate interest in his own social consequence and advancement.

Bird may well have been close to his mother. He chose to give her name to one of his native 'country wives,' a not uncommon practice among fur traders. Similarly he gave his mother's surname as a first name to his youngest son, born to his last wife, an English-born school mistress, after his retirement to the Red River Settlement. Bird's contact with his natal family may well have suffered the exigencies of time as his service record demonstrates only a single furlough to England, two years before he retired to the Red River Settlement in June of 1824, when he was almost fifty years old.

From his 'schooling' while at York Factory and later at posts westward through the Saskatchewan Country, Bird would learn that the fur trade was conducted in circumstances dominated by two intertwining factors. The first factor, figuring most prominently in the Company's business correspondence, was the competitive rivalry with Montreal-based traders, particularly the emerging giant in the fur trade, the North West Company (NWC). The second factor was the mutual adaptation of Euro-Canadian traders and parkland-prairie Indian bands to each other's presence. Fur trade rivalries and Indian-Euro-Canadian relations would constitute a major part of the stage-setting within which Bird would try to conduct a fur trade profitable to his employers and, thus, rewarding for himself.

The fundamental feature of the fur trade rivalry at this time was the NWC's de facto monopoly of the fur trade of the Athabaska Country, the 'Eldorado' of the fur trade.[2] Ten years previous to Bird's arrival at York Factory, Peter Pond, for his NWC partners, had penetrated into the Athabaska Country. There he found beaver in number and quality unequalled elsewhere and at prices that heightened profits. Quickly the partners of the NWC realized that, if they were to keep this trade to themselves, they would have to preoccupy their rivals elsewhere with an energetic and provocative opposition. If necessary the NWC was prepared to trade at a loss in the Saskatchewan Country and in the Winnipeg region. Their objective was to direct their opponents' attention away from the Athabaska Country.

The Saskatchewan Rriver posts were of much importance to the NWC. Northern posts such as Fort Chipewyan frequently faced scarce game returns, and the abundant fisheries in the area were seasonal and could fail in any given year. Provisions from outside the Athabaska Country were essential to the success of this fur trade. Provisions were also essential for the annual fur brigades making their way from Fort Chipewyan to Grand Portage (later Fort William) on Lake Superior and returning during the seasons of open water. These brigades did not have en route, since to have done so would have been to risk freeze-up short of their destination and, possibly, starvation. Supplies of provisions along their route of travel were necessary for their success.

Surplus provisions such as pemmican were available from the Saskatchewan Rriver posts and, farther to the south and east, from posts along the Red and Assiniboine rivers. Pemmican was usually made from dried buffalo meat, pounded into a coarse powder, mixed with melted fat and various dried berries, and, when cooled, sewn into buffalo hide bags of ninety pounds. If kept dry and cool the resulting product could last for years. The posts of the NWC on the Saskatchewan River had as their primary task the acquisition of provisions for the manufacture of pemmican for shipment to posts bordering the route of travel of the northern Athabaska brigade. A failure of the provision trade on the Saskatchewan could threaten the viability of the NWC's Athabaska trade, a possibility if the Plains and Parkland Indian bands failed to appear as expected.

While the NWC emphasized provisions in posts along the Saskatchewan it welcomed fur as well. The Company's interest was beaver as a staple fur, but fancy furs, such as marten, fisher, and others, were quite acceptable. Such valuable fancy furs, however, were found to the north and west in the boreal forests. Along the Saskatchewan less valuable furs, including wolf, coyote, kit fox, and bear, were drawn from the prairie lands to the south. This fur trade together with the provision trade brought contact with distant prairie bands such as the Peigan and Atsina as well as the Plains Cree, Sarcee, Siksika (Blackfoot proper), and Kainah (Blood) who lived in the more immediate regions of the post. The Peigan, particularly, were suppliers

of beaver from the foothills of the Rocky Mountains in this period.

The HBC with its shorter transportation route to York Factory and lesser number of personnel did not have, initially, the same need for provisions as did the NWC. It soon appreciated, however, the importance of provisions, both in supplying its own efforts to break into the Athabaska Country and in tying particular Indian bands and their furs to its interests.

The presence of fur traders in numbers on the Saskatchewan River began a quarter century before the founding of Edmonton House.[3] The presence of so many traders altered the relationship between Euro-Canadian traders and Indian bands as well as altering relations among the bands themselves. In the previous one hundred years the HBC had been content to 'sleep by the frozen sea' on Hudson Bay, leaving the conduct of the fur trade in the interior in the hands of Indian trade chiefs—who functioned as middlemen between the traders in the coastal factories and the hunting and trapping bands in the interior. Trade chiefs were band leaders who excelled in negotiating favourable terms with European traders. At other times of the year their bands differed little in nature and size from other parkland bands. But when the trading season approached others would join these trade chiefs, acknowledging their reputation as trade-negotiators. Such trading bands had few women and children with them, as they were left in the interior. During the French period the La Vérendrye family pushed into the interior, enfilading the

HBC's posts on Hudson Bay. While their presence disrupted relations for the Company, Indian trade chiefs still led their canoe flotillas down from the interior for the annual ten- day to two-week trade fair at the coastal factory. Only after the conquest of French Canada did 'pedlars' succeed in mounting a commercial rivalry from Montreal which led in a decade to the formation of the NWC with its experienced *canadien* work force. In 1773 the HBC responded by abandoning its century-long coast factory system, and penetrating the interior. The Company was ill equipped in terms of transportation craft and experienced personnel to mount an effective opposition. As well with the HBC penetration of the interior, the Indian trade chiefs and their bands were no longer needed in the fur trade, while the hunting and trapping bands found better prices for their wares now that they no longer had to deal through the trading bands for European manufactured goods.

The chaotic circumstances on the Saskatchewan in the closing decades of the eighteenth century encouraged various bands to experiment with new relationships to enhance their opportunities and security.[4] The military consequences of the gun were not lost on the Indian. Such a tool, however, required a continuity of supply in terms of shot and powder. Some Cree bands in the parkland had apparently ensured the continuity of their supply by involving themselves more intimately in the lives of the traders.

Indian bands did not separate their commercial interests and activities from those of a social and political nature. It can be said they preferred to conduct business with family; that is, their confidence in the trader and his wares increased when the trader was a kinsman. This relationship was inaugurated through a country marriage involving a prominent woman of the band as a country-wife to the trader. Such a social relationship ensured the band's trading loyalty as well as tying the trader to its interests. While more study of this topic is required, evidence suggests that some Cree bands used their relationship with trader kinsmen to facilitate their movement westward.[5] Bird apparently acquired his first country wife (possibly Oo-menahomisk) when he was posted into the interior in 1792, to Cumberland House. He may have had country wives polygynously. As his career during the 1790s progressed and he was posted westward, the bands of his country wives would have seen him as an assured base of support enabling them to leave their own traditional areas and try more westward opportunities. Their kinship with Bird and the guns and ammunition he could supply would enable them to assert their interests over other bands who might express a traditional claim to a particular area.

When Bird reached Edmonton House in 1799, much change was already underway. At the time of first contact with Indians on the Upper Saskatchewan very sparse evidence suggests the Beaver Hills (centred by Elk Island park today) were frequently home to the Sarcee Indians.[6] References in their folklore to events at Buffalo Lake (near present-day Stettler) suggest that at the time they were in transition from their ancestral people, the Beaver of the boreal forest in present-day northern Alberta, to hunters in the parkland-prairie. No doubt their move southward was hastened with the appearance of the horse in what is today southern Alberta in the 1730s. The Blackfoot peoples (consisting of the Siksika, the Kainah, and the Peigan), whom the traders had encountered in the Eagle Hills (to the south of Battleford in present-day Saskatchewan), were similarly involved in using the gun to challenge the hegemony of horse-mounted Indians. Within less than a generation, the Sarcee and Blackfoot peoples would become horse-mounted themselves. Behind them—supported by their close relations with traders—Cree, Thickwood Assiniboine (Stoneys), and a few Saulteaux bands would become dominant from the Eagle Hills to the Beaver Hills and then southwestward towards the foothills of the Rocky Mountains in the vicinity of where the trading post, Rocky Mountain House, would appear.

Among the Siksika two distinct trading strategies would emerge.[7] Those residential bands of Siksika who looked to Painted Feathers (later taking his father's name, Old Swan) as their spokesman expressed a policy of consensus and cooperation. This policy contrasted sharply with those Siksika who looked to Le Gros Blanc or the Fatt Man or Big Man for leadership. This physically striking leader, who rode a large white mule, had a mercurial manner, coupled with what appeared to be a disdainful attitude towards his own safety. His style with the traders was confrontational; apparently he resented the close trading alliance between all the traders and the Cree, which enabled the Cree to assert their presence farther westward and southward. Big Man and some of his bands joined with the Atsina, who were equally resentful of Cree intrusions, in attacking the Pine Island posts in 1793. A year later, when Bird was the officer-in-charge, the Atsina attacked South Branch House killing several of the inhabitants. The NWC post repelled the attack, killing one of the leading Atsina chiefs. Fortunately for Bird, he and most of the complement of the HBC post were absent at the time of the attack. Bird's superior, William Tomison, who had risen from the position of servant to be the officer responsible for the Company's affairs on the

Saskatchewan, resisted the pleadings of his junior officers and would not sanction joint action with the NWC against the attackers. Perhaps Tomison was right for within two years the Blackfoot led by Big Man had made peace with the traders, although their trading style remained confrontational and uncooperative.

Evidence suggests that Old Swan's bands may have sought a special relationship with the traders as Homeguard or House Indians. In the HBC tradition these terms were used to describe Indian bands who had close social ties to the traders and servants, who functioned as provisioners and couriers, and who rendered other services as they were required. It would appear that the continuing assertive presence of the Cree who were accompanying the traders westward denied Old Swan's Siksika this opportunity. Nevertheless, he and the bands associated with him would continue to be identified with a trading policy very different from that of Big Man and his bands. At Edmonton House, Bird was most disturbed with consequences for the provision trade at the time of Old Swan's death in 1814. It is significant that this division among the Siksika continued until after the time of the numbered treaties in the 1870s.

Bird entered the fur trade at a particularly difficult time for the HBC. Britain's war with France, beginning with the Revolution and extending to the demise of Napoleon at Waterloo in 1815, required manpower for the fleet and made the recruitment of servants increasingly difficult. Experienced servants, aware of their employer's difficulties, demanded improved wages and working conditions. Some would refuse to work unless they were granted their demands. Tomison, the officer-in-charge, was an Orcadian or Orkneyman.[8] Younger officers like Bird felt that Tomison was much too accommodating to these older rebellious servants, most of whom were also Orcadians. They would have preferred him to react far more aggressively. Yet the historical record would suggest that Tomison was right. On the Saskatchewan, Tomison was out-manned and out-financed by the Montreal traders, particularly the NWC. He held his Company in the competition, however, enabling it to solve its transportation problems with the York boat and to gain valuable experience in running a fur trade in competitive circumstances. Through Tomison, the Company sustained a presence on the Saskatchewan at a time when the wars with France rendered commerce difficult. As well it matched the Montreal traders fort for house as they leap-frogged westward up the Saskatchewan River. When Tomison finally retired, much of Bird's activity as the officer-in-

charge at Edmonton House suggests that he had learned well from Tomison's example.

Taking command at Edmonton House in 1799, Bird would be given a critical role in the HBC's attempts to launch a competitive trading adventure into the Athabaska Country.[9] Initially, however, Churchill and York factories on Hudson Bay were feuding over the issue of who should lead the thrust into the Athabaska Country and how and where it would be done. In the meantime Bird assertively established his presence in the Edmonton region. He immediately pushed westward to supervise the construction of Acton House to compete with the NWC at Rocky Mountain House. At the same time he directed Peter Fidler's push northward to Lac La Biche to establish Greenwich House. Bird's bosses in London found his efforts 'most pleasing.' When Tomison finally left the fur trade in 1803, Bird was placed in command of the Hudson's Bay Company posts on the Saskatchewan River. Still undermanned and underfinanced he was expected to lend his support to the attempt to mount a successful competition in the Athabaska Country. With Tomison's retirement the main opposition within the Company's ranks to a major effort was supposed to be gone. Yet, surprisingly, difficulties remained in coordinating efforts from Churchill and York. At the turn of the decade, when William Auld emerged at Churchill with responsibility for the project, Bird was better able to coordinate his efforts with those of Auld, including the supply of provisions to the HBC traders attempting to make their way to the Athabaska Country. The reasons for repeated failures until 1818 cannot be placed at Bird's door as he was vigorous in moving his provisions north, even in particularly difficult if not dangerous circumstances.

Bird did not limit his competitive efforts to moving provisions northward. In the immediate neighbourhood of Edmonton House he attempted to remain competitive with his opponents at Fort Augustus. When they established outposts farther west Bird responded in so far as his resources would permit. As well he attracted the services of freemen, formerly working with the Montreal traders, to hunt and trap for the HBC. Among the freemen temporarily housed in Edmonton House in this period was Jean Baptiste Lagimondire and his *canadienne* wife, Marie Gaboury, the grandparents of Louis Riel.[10] It was Bird who personally thwarted an attempt by a Blackfoot woman to kidnap their infant son known as 'La Prairie.'

Social interchange with his NWC rival at Fort Augustus as well as intelligence from freemen and Indians made Bird aware of David Thompson's exploits west of Rocky Mountain House in the Columbia country. It was

This photo is of an Indian encampment outside Fort Edmonton in the 1890s. The Big House, built by Hudson's Bay Company factor John Rowland, can be seen in the background. (PAA B.6626)

not until 1810, however, that Bird was able to send Joseph Howse on a similar venture. Unfortunately Bird's resources were such that he was unable to sustain Howse's efforts. European wars and timid management in London would deny him the funds and personnel needed to mount an effective opposition in this far western region.

Bird's attention was not devoted to the Montreal-based traders alone. As his tenure at Edmonton began it was evident that relations among neighbouring Indian bands were becoming more tense, with increasing incidents of confrontation and violence. The circumstances that had provoked the violence in 1793 at the Pine Island posts and the next year at South Branch House were repeated at Chesterfield House in 1801 when the Atsina wiped out a party of ten Iroquois trappers and two *canadien* freemen. The Cree and their allies were pushing towards the southwest where previously their presence had been more limited. In this period as well the Cree and the Assiniboine were coming to appreciate the value of the horse in war as well as on the hunt. But there was a problem. The parkland areas inhabited by the Cree took a terrible toll of horses most winters. Enduring cold, deep snow, and wolves were the major factors. Bird had difficulty protecting hay mows from the depredations of wild game, such as elk, and from Indians and freemen, who had not found good wintering areas for their horses. In such circumstances young men from the Cree and Assiniboine looked to the horse herds of the Blackfoot peoples to replenish their stock.[11]

While some horses were traded, the preferred route of access was theft. The Blackfoot became increasingly hostile. Violent confrontational incidents in the Upper Saskatchewan country reached their height in 1806. Cree peoples abandoned the Saskatchewan River valley while Blackfoot peoples remained south of the Battle River. Finally in the closing months of the next year Old Swan of the Siksika appeared at Edmonton to establish a peace among the warring groups. In spite of Old Swan's peace, however, tensions remained high and provocative incidents on both sides continued to occur. Even the death of Big Man in 1810 did not change the course of events.

As a result of the violence few Indians were appearing at the Edmonton posts. The provision trade was very much in jeopardy. By 1810 in concert with his junior officers in the region, Henry Hallet and John Peter Pruden, Bird came to an agreement with Nor'Westers James Hughes and Alexander Henry to attempt to separate the Cree and Blackfoot for purposes of trade. Fort Augustus and Edmonton House would be abandoned and new posts constructed sixty miles down river at White Earth River, in hopes of attracting only the Blackfoot peoples. Other posts for both companies would be abandoned in favour of new posts at La Montee (NWC) and Carlton House (HBC) for the Cree. At White Earth the posts of both companies were included within a single stockade.

The White Earth experiment, in attempting to separate the Cree and Blackfoot for trading purposes, failed.

Indians packing furs, 1901. The fur trade continued to be important in the twentieth century. (PAA B.900)

At this time Indians may have been advised and encouraged to undertake a particular course of action—but they could not be told. Young men particularly could not resist the reputation that would accrue from a trading adventure into the trade centre of an enemy. Thus, the efforts of Bird and his NWC rivals to keep the two separated frequently came to naught. In 1813 White Earth was abandoned with both companies moving to what would become the site of present-day Edmonton and building on the Rossdale flats before, in time, moving to what are now the Legislature grounds.

In part Bird and his NWC rivals were drawn westward by events transpiring in the south of Blackfoot territory. These events to the south were problematic for both Bird and his rivals. A hostile encounter between Captain Merriweather Lewis of the American Lewis and Clarke expedition and a small party of Peigan in 1805 had heralded the presence of American traders on the upper Missouri River. In time Mountain Men (trappers) would appear in the Rocky Mountains. The Blackfoot, particularly the Peigan, would war with the Mountain Men; but the traders on the Missouri were another matter. They offered the Blackfoot peoples an alternative market to the traders on the Saskatchewan. Now the Blackfoot had the opportunity to play one group of traders against the other. These advantages were not lost on the Blackfoot.[12] The traders on the Saskatchewan had to be prepared to extend special prices and privileges to the Blackfoot peoples if they would keep their commercial loyalty.

Little scholarship has been directed at the nature of the society that emerged in Edmonton House during the foundation years. Studies of similar posts elsewhere suggest a face-to-face community in which individuals (from our perspective) were inordinately concerned with status.[13] One might think that, given the relatively small numbers involved in trading post communities, there would be a tendency to blur distinctions of social rank, but such was apparently not the case. The cultural tie to Great Britain and the previous one hundred years of experience in posts on the coast of Hudson Bay underlined the values of social hierarchy and authority in regulating social behaviours. As a result individuals were very conscious of the rights and privileges appropriate to their particular occupation and social rank. They emphasized the obligations they were owed and the obligations they owed to others. In effect the society incorporated systems of patronage that in time were augmented by kinship.

In terms of Edmonton House, Bird would have occupied the pinnacle of the social system. Yet he devoted much time to his position in trading post society at large. His correspondence reflects the gossip that was the chief means of competition in such a social system as well as his attempts to ingratiate himself with his superiors.[14] At the same time there was apparently a shared sense of discretion in terms of keeping personal family matters out of the Company's documents. More than one officer had more than one country wife at the same time. While the Governor and Committee were not unaware of the families arising from country marriages they appear to have avoided detailed inquiries. In time several of Bird's sons from these marriages would hold clerkships in the Company's service until the full weight of 'modernization' after 1821 made itself felt in the Company's service. Bird's sons, who lacked their father's education, would be 'retired' from the Company's service. Denied the opportunities their father had enjoyed, they would become embittered men—particularly after their father chose to ignore them in his will and to bestow most of his estate on his two children by his English wife.

When Thomas Douglas, the fifth Earl of Selkirk, bought control of the HBC in 1809, he acquired a fur trade company that had been bested in the fur trade competition.[15] To an extent the chaos of war had disrupted recruitment and the marketing of furs. Yet the NWC faced similar if not identical problems. The HBC's Governing Committee, dominated by Selkirk's supporters, was highly critical of the costly sinecures established by many of the Company's officers at their respective posts. Practices that assured the officer's position atop the social hierarchy of the trading post often added appreciably to the costs of the trade. Selkirk's new broom, in the person of the Governor and Committee, responded with policies and regulations that modernized the Company's commercial practices. In this process the enthusiastic support of the officers in the field was expected.

Initially the Company looked to William Auld to head its efforts in Rupert's Land. Bird had cooperated with him extensively in attempting to mount a trade into the Athabaska Country. Auld, however, proved to be less than enthusiastic with respect to the colonizing efforts at Red River, launched in 1811. In London in 1815, he called into question the experience of the Governing Committee; his services were immediately ended and the Committee turned to Bird as an interim successor.[16] Bird appears to have responded with enthusiasm. He was appointed a justice of the peace for the 'Indian Territories' in 1815 and that same year he was appointed to the Council of the Governor of Assiniboia (the Red River Settlement). Bird remained at Edmonton House as his foremost responsibility remained the Company's trade on the Saskatchewan.

By 1815 the Governing Committee of the HBC had implemented the reforms necessary to ensure that the trade would be carried on profitably. The Committee then supported another attempt to mount a successful trade into the Athabaska Country, but the mismanagement of the expe-

dition's leader, John Clarke, led to failure. Clarke had not secured adequate provisions. As a result over twenty men lost their lives. But the Governor and Committee were not prepared to acknowledge defeat, and planning began anew for another challenge to the NWC's 'El Dorado.'

The effective steps taken by the HBC increased the commercial pressures on the NWC. Internal dissension within the NWC, between younger wintering partners in the field and the older partners in Montreal, surfaced. Increased tension in the interior burst forth in violence in the Red River Settlement when on 19 June 1816 a mixed group of HBC servants and Selkirk settlers challenged a band of Métis moving pemmican out of the settlement for the NWC.[17] More than twenty servants and settlers, including Governor Semple, were killed. Only one of the Métis died. Bird was called to act for Semple until a successor could be found. Keeping responsibility for the Saskatchewan trade, Bird left Edmonton House for Carlton to be nearer the Red River Settlement. The next year William Williams replaced Bird as Governor and initiated a final and successful assault on the NWC trade in the Athabaska ountry. Already in his late forties Bird found these developments unsettling.

It was becoming increasingly apparent that the new HBC required a different type of officer to carry out the directives of the Governor and Committee.[18] They expect-

Hudson's Bay Company fur train leaving Fort Smith for Athabaska, 1901. As in the early nineteenth century, the furs would then be transported to Edmonton. (PAA B.2932)

In the early years of the fur trade, Euro-Canadians in the West learned many survival skills from the Indian population. Indians, in turn, adapted to the technology they found in centres like Fort Edmonton. (PAA B.764)

ed a relatively high level of education and a high degree of professionalism. This was not the world that Bird had known. Neither he nor his sons would be eligible for employment in such a commercial enterprise. In 1819 a fellow officer noted that Bird had 'more knowledge of the internal arrangements of this country than all the officers put together.'[19] Yet Bird felt increasingly out of place. He apparently became suspicious of colleagues and petty in his criticisms. By the time of the amalgamation of the HBC and the NWC in 1821, with the HBC emerging victorious, it was apparent that Bird would not be a part of the new company. He was given a leave home in 1822–3 and, to facilitate his retirement, was placed in charge of the Upper Red River district for 1823–4.

In his retirement, as a 'principal settler' in the Red River Settlement, he would remain active. On the death of his native wife Elizabeth he married Mrs Mary Lowman, a governess in the 'Female Seminary' at Red River. His two children by her, Eliza Margaret and Curtis James, inherited the bulk of his estate. Bird was not a popular member of Red River society during his retirement. Others found him pretentious and insensitive. He physically chastised an old servant and ill used an errant serving maid. For many he represented misplaced privilege.

The emerging Victorian era in Red River was passing James Bird by. Yet the closing years of his life in the Red River Settlement should not detract from his significant accomplishments on the Saskatchewan, particularly at

Edmonton House. Bird had learned quickly and effectively when he was introduced as a youth into the fur trade. For most of his career the HBC would be number two in the fur trade competition and frequently not particularly effective at trying harder. Bird appears to have clearly understood the limitations that impinged on his efforts. Yet he continued to mount an effective commercial presence for his employer at a time when Indian animosities in the region were intensifying. Circumstances dictated the dominance of the NWC. But Bird served up an effective opposition in his employer's interests. His relations with Indians recognized the paramountcy of their views of local circumstances without sacrificing his employer's interests and those of the people under his command. Inordinately ambitious he would use his position to enhance his family's interests. And while in many ways his ambition and pursuit of social advancement would be his undoing, such could not detract from Bird's very real achievements while commanding at Edmonton House. ✑

ESTABLISHING AN ANGLICAN PRESENCE

Canon William Newton, 1896. (PAA B.9560)

For almost fifty years, the name Lewis Gwynne Thomas has been synonymous with writing the history of the Canadian prairie West, especially in academic circles. Born in southern Alberta to British immigrant parents, Thomas has called Edmonton home for most of his adult life. Two of his enduring interests have been the city's Anglican community, of which he is a long-time member, and the University of Alberta, where he received his BA in 1934 and taught in the Department of History, with a few breaks, from 1938 to 1975.

Thomas's historical and Anglican interests mesh in this chapter, parts of which he describes as 'an historical artifact.' The section on William Newton, the first Anglican missionary in Edmonton (arriving in 1875), was first written almost forty-five years ago at the encouragement of Bishop Walter F. Barfoot, anxious that Newton's contribution to early Edmonton not be forgotten, and presented to a meeting of the Historical Society of Alberta, then in the process of revival after

virtual dormancy during the Second World War. In retelling the story for today's audience, Thomas not only brings one of Edmonton's colourful pioneer figures to life but also demonstrates the importance of British values and British institutions to the city's foundations as it passed from fur trade post to urban settlement.

Thomas notes that the influence of the Anglican church waned after the First World War claimed so many of the young men who had been its backbone—in an era when all churches increasingly had to contend with the challenges posed by industrialization, urbanization, and secularization. Over forty years of activity by Anglican clergymen, the Anglican church as an institution, and individual members of the Anglican communion had, however, left an enduring mark on Edmonton's development and character.

CANADIAN HISTORIANS, AT LEAST THOSE WRITING IN English, have been reticent about identifying themselves with particular religious denominations. In their explorations of Canadian historiography, they have shown little disposition to examine the religious convictions of their predecessors and contemporaries or to estimate the influence of their own beliefs, if any, upon their thinking about history. Perhaps this reticence is Canadian politeness, a sense that it would be improperly intrusive to venture into such private realms.

As I have grown older, I have become increasingly sceptical about the scholar's pursuit of objectivity, at least in the writing of history. It seems to me a worthy goal but I think we should beware of thinking we have attained it. Rather we should acknowledge bias, in ourselves and others. It therefore seems to me appropriate to affirm here that I am a 'cradle' Anglican and write and speak as a committed churchman. My interest in the Anglican church and its history in Canada, especially in the West and North, and my sense that Anglican records have much to offer not merely to the church historian in the narrowest sense but also to the secular historian, especially when their interests lie in social, economic, cultural, and intellectual development, have not diminished with the years. I find it very difficult to separate my experience of Anglicanism from my experience of Anglican documents, and I am sure my thinking and writing provide plenty of evidence of Anglican bias. Whether this should exclude me from the mainstream of Canadian history is a question I feel I must leave to others.[1] I have come to see the Anglican church, and early missionaries like the Reverend William Newton, as a major means for the transmission of values seen as English or British to Canada, and especially to western Canada.

Although there may have been Anglican services held in Edmonton (or its vicinity) in the preceding one hundred years, and although there certainly were Anglicans among the population of the Fort Edmonton area, Anglican work was not formally established until the arrival of the Reverend William Newton (1828–1910) on 28 September 1875, the eve of St Michael and All Angels.[2] Newton came with the support of the Society for the Propagation of the Gospel, the English missionary society that concerned itself especially with the religious needs of overseas settlers. He would stay in Edmonton until 1901.

Norfolk born of humble parentage, Newton remains a somewhat shadowy figure. He himself was reticent about his early years and his family generally, but he does seem to have confided in his friend of later years, the Reverend Robert Connell, who left this most illuminating account:

> He [Newton] did say that he was the son of very poor parents and that, even as a child, he was small of stature. One day, during his childhood, he was playing by a bridge when two ladies came along in a carriage and . . . stopped to speak to him. Dr. Newton did not say who they were but conveyed the impression that they were wealthy, of Portuguese origin, and connected with a wine importing firm. At all events they got in touch with his parents and undertook to provide for his education.[3]

There is little firm evidence as to the nature of that education except for Connell's statement that it trained Newton for the Unitarian ministry. There is firmer ground for believing that he exercised that ministry among the Congregationalists.

Newton made his first of two marriages to the daughter of a Spanish family, probably a woman of means, and, sometime before 1870, the couple and some of their nine sons immigrated to Canada, settling at Lindsay, Ontario. Newton was ordained an Anglican deacon by Bishop Bethune of Toronto on 8 October 1870 and priested in 1871. His name is associated with the parish of Rosseau in the Muskoka country—already a popular summer resort and in winter a focus for the lumber industry—where he was long and warmly remembered. In 1874 Newton answered the appeal of the Right Reverend John Maclean, recently consecrated first Bishop of Saskatchewan, for men to work in his diocese. The following spring he began the trek west, leaving his wife and sons to enjoy the superior amenities of Lindsay.

With the timely assistance of Government surveyors, who sometimes teased him but were always ready to help, whether in the hazards of the road or in finding a place to hold Sunday services, Newton was able to reach Winnipeg before the end of May. There he camped near Fort Garry and made preparations for the journey to Edmonton. The prairies at this season appealed to his nature-loving eye, but Winnipeg, with its plague of locusts, its grog shops, and its traders who rivalled the locusts in their appetite for the money of strangers did not impress him.[4] He was persuaded to acquire a Red River cart and two horses, as well as provisions enough not only for the journey but also to keep him on arrival at Edmonton. He finally left Winnipeg in early July. Newton's most memorable adventures on the last leg of his trip were a painful accident with his Red River cart and an encounter with some Indians, 'adverse to the passage of white men through their territories.' Just south of Fort Pitt, an Indian messenger, speaking for a band of Cree, ordered the party to return eastward. Newton despatched a message to the chief that he had been sent 'by the great chiefs of the English Church' to 'teach the people around Edmonton the way of the true Christian religion,' and must, therefore, go on with his journey, but he wished to meet with the chief and his people. The party tried to evade the Cree, but without success, and finally a meeting was held at which Newton appeared 'arrayed in all possible finery, and first gravely distributed plugs of tobacco to all who were seated in the nearest circles.'[5] Newton convinced the band that it was unreasonable to expect him to turn back and persuaded them to give him, as his friends and brothers, all help within their power. From this point there was no more trouble. Later in the journey, Newton turned aside to go twenty miles to hold a service for the Cree of the White Fish Lake band and was rewarded by his first and only sight of a buffalo herd. These episodes are of particular interest, for they mark the beginning of Newton's extremely happy relations with the Indians, a people for whom he had the warmest sympathy and who, he believed, reciprocated his affection.

The Fort Edmonton to which Newton came was still little more than a Hudson's Bay Company (HBC) trading post, remote from the central provinces of the new Dominion of Canada and with few genuine settlers. Most of the population in the vicinity—whether Native, European, or mixed blood—depended directly or indirectly on the fur trade. Edmonton had always been an important point in the industry's network for collection and supply, commanding as it did the water routes of the Saskatchewan, the Athabasca, and the Peace. Although the fur trade was by 1875 in relative decline, the HBC was still a potent force in the post-Confederation West and an important component of the new order the new Canadian government sought to establish in what it saw as an essential hinterland for the developing economy centred on the St Lawrence and the northern shores of the Great Lakes.[6] Already, beyond the agricultural activity related to the needs of the Company, there had begun a trickle of settlement that looked to a wider agricultural future and that saw Edmonton as a centre for the development of the rich resources in land, forest, mine, and, ultimately, manufacturing and commerce, to which it promised access.

Such dreams in the North America of the time depended upon railways, and Edmonton's dreamers confidently expected that the first Canadian transcontinental, the essential foundation stone of the Dominion, would generally follow the established water route, including the North Saskatchewan. Such a railway would make use of the recommended Yellowhead route, relatively familiar to the fur trade, with its comparatively moderate and therefore economical gradients. Such a railway would also give intending farmers access to the parkland of the fertile belt, leaving the virtual deserts of the Palliser triangle to the aborigines and the buffalo, with the promise of grazing leases on intermediate lands that could be controlled to exclude intrusive Americans in favour of British subjects.

The prospects for the future of Edmonton were a factor in Bishop Maclean's decision to send Newton to the fort. Maclean was also influenced by the arrival of the North West Mounted Police at nearby Fort Saskatchewan to the east as part of the northward movement of the force from its base near the American border. The spiritual needs of the police became one of Newton's primary responsibilities from the beginning. Although the outlook for settlement appeared reasonably bright when he first arrived in Edmonton, the decision to build the Canadian Pacific Railway (CPR) on the southern route dashed the hopes of the handful of pioneers who had gathered around the Hudson's Bay post. No railway arrived until 1891 and then it came to a halt on the south side of the North Saskatchewan, where the CPR developed a rival centre of population at Strathcona. Thus, the community to which Newton ministered grew very slowly, and for sixteen years, in a territory as large as England, he was the sole priest of the Anglican communion. After 1890, with the arrival of a curate, Charles Cunningham, Newton devoted himself to the rural mission work he had developed beyond the Edmonton settlement.

The Church of England in its missionary aspect fitted

The Fort Edmonton to which Newton came was still little more than a Hudson's Bay Company (HBC) trading post, remote from the central provinces of the new Dominion of Canada and with few genuine settlers.

neatly into the visions of the Conservative governments of Canada's immediate post-Confederation years. Its hierarchical structure and its inclusionary ideal—where every element in the population, aboriginal or immigrant, could have at least the opportunity to be an Anglican—were not inconsistent with the creation in the western interior of a peaceful and orderly society. That society would be very different from what men like Macdonald saw as chaos and violence south of the 49th parallel, in a nation recently divided by a savage and prolonged civil war. In the United States, they believed, menacing democratic elements dangerously challenged lawful authority.

From Newton's point of view, the religious situation at Edmonton was not encouraging. The Roman Catholic church had a chapel within the walls of the fort, but its main establishment was nine miles away at St Albert, where a Métis settlement flourished; a subsidiary settlement existed at Lac Ste Anne. The McDougalls, long effective missionaries in the area, had built a Methodist church and parsonage not far from the fort and the leading people there were zealous in their support. The Methodists also had a successful mission at Victoria (now Pakan), some distance northeast of Edmonton. The few Anglicans were in the habit of attending the Methodist services, and Newton was put in the embarrassing position of appearing to have 'come to upset Methodism and to introduce religious strife into a distant, and not very devout community.'[7] His position was not made easier by the report of the Methodist chairman of the district to the conference in Ontario that he had seen the sad sight of the Church of England clergy at Prince Albert and Edmonton 'working day and night, not so much to call sinners to repentance, as to make Ritualists of Presbyterians and Methodists.'[8] The alarm of his Protestant fellow workers is not too diffi-

cult to understand. Newton, although scarcely an Anglo-Catholic in the later sense of the term, had undoubtedly been strongly influenced by the Tractarians, and his churchmanship was of an order more advanced than was general at that time in the Church of England in Canada. If the cassock that he wore so consistently upset the Methodists of Edmonton, the white gloves in which he is said to have preached would have caused even more perturbation among many of his fellow churchmen in eastern dioceses. Newton's relations with the Roman Catholics were rather more cordial, for shortly after his arrival he visited St Albert on the occasion of the reception of the Bishop's nephew into the priesthood. He lunched with the Bishop and seems to have found him most congenial.[9]

Judging from his writings, Newton had a strong sense of community and some appreciation of the contribution made by the various elements within it. His parishioners were certainly a mixed bag, a reflection of the elements from which the Anglican congregations of central Alberta, and to some degree the Alberta 'establishment,' were formed. From his own account, those who attended his services included 'officials in the Hudson's Bay Company service . . . glad to renew old church associations . . . camps of surveyors [seeking] a little Sunday rest, and change from the monotony of their life on the prairies . . . Mounted police . . . just come into the country . . . Children . . . collected for instruction.'[10] Newton also visited the Indian tents.

As a place of worship, Newton initially used the upper story of the house he had rented from Chief Trader Hardisty of the HBC. 'We have a simple altar place, which I have covered with blue and red cloth and which looks as nice as we could expect.'[11] As long as the weather was fine, this arrangement worked, but when the snow came, as the building was unfinished, it was less comfortable: 'Often on Sunday mornings we had to use shovels to throw the snow out of the window; then when the fire had melted the snow on the open rafters the wet came down on our heads, and caused discomfort at the services.'[12] The problem of accommodation was a serious one, for although Newton had spent almost two hundred dollars to make his dwelling habitable, he had no security of tenure. When the owner suddenly informed him that he would require possession the following morning, he was in an awkward position. A suitable house with some land had been available at the reasonable price of a thousand dollars, but Newton had been unable to secure this sum from the church authorities to whom he applied. In these circumstances, he decided to homestead and chose a spot about seven miles down the North Saskatchewan from the fort, opposite Clover Bar. There, in mid-December 1876, he took up permanent residence in the Hermitage, whose name has since been perpetuated in an Edmonton suburb. Although the Hermitage eventually became quite an elaborate structure, framed by 'some of the finest lilacs' Robert Connell 'had ever seen,'[13] it was originally a small house for which Newton brought in the lumber and shingles himself at great expense and with great difficulty. The property also held two cabins, one to entertain Newton's 'native friends,' the other 'kept as a very plain and simple chapel, its chief ecclesiastical marks being the little Holy Table and the red cloth that decked it and the wall behind.'[14]

Although Newton had many critics and often annoyed bishops (including Maclean, who certainly had doubts as to his capacity as a missionary), he did establish an Anglican constituency not only in Edmonton but also in the surrounding area to the north and east.[15] And he gave this congregation a focus in All Saints' Church, built on a site at what is now approximately 121 Street and 103 (Victoria) Avenue. The need for a church had become crucial after Newton lost his first house near the fort as he was obliged to hold services wherever a room could be obtained. But the difficulties in the way were many. Money was almost non-existent. Where were building materials to be found? How was the ground upon which to build to be secured? The last was a particularly perplexing problem. Surveys had not been made and no man knew where his homestead was or would be. A Hudson's Bay officer, who claimed ownership of lots, refused to give or sell a site and the Company itself, through Donald Smith, later Lord Strathcona, regretted that it had no power to grant land for such a purpose. Finally, Malcolm Groat, a

The interior of All Saints' Church, 1897, decorated for Christmas. (PAA B.9494)

settler west of the fort and a former Company employee, allowed five acres from his claim, for which Newton paid five dollars to seal the bargain. Groat's five acres became nine when the survey took place and extended from the brow of the hill overlooking the North Saskatchewan up to the present Stony Plain Road along the west side of 121 Street.[16] The construction of All Saints' Church proceeded slowly, but it was ready for Newton to hold the first service sometime between June 1878 and June 1879, and by 1882 Newton could tell the Society for the Propagation of the Gospel that it was free of debt. 'Although the little church is modest enough,' he writes, 'it looks pretty to some of us, transformed by the trouble and self-sacrifice it has cost.'[17]

Newton became devoted to the little church and held services regularly, driving there from the Hermitage. Unfortunately, the town of Edmonton grew up to the east and not to the west of the fort and the congregation found the location inconvenient. When Bishop Maclean visited Edmonton in September 1883, he acted with his usual decision, called a meeting, and organized a second congregation (St Michael's), which obtained permission to hold evening services in the public school. At first the services, whose location varied, met with an excellent response and attendance averaged about fifty. A good choir was also organized and Newton delighted in the new opportunity to influence the young men of the community. Then in spring 1884 attendance began to decline, and, as money was scarce, the services in the east end of the town were reluctantly discontinued in favour of an evening service at All Saints'.[18] In 1891 All Saints' Church was moved nearer the centre of settlement to the northwest corner of what is now 106 Street and 99 Avenue, with the Reverend Charles Cunningham (who had just been ordained deacon) in charge of the parish.

As Edmonton developed, Newton never forgot the Indian and mixed blood population. In 1878, for example, the church warden translated his sermons into Cree.[19] Newton liked the French Métis and was extremely critical of the Canadian government and the HBC for their failure to take their interests into consideration at the time of the transfer of Rupert's Land. During the Riel Rebellion in 1885, he was much annoyed by the unwillingness of any of the settlers to guide him to the sick bed of an Indian girl who had sent a message begging him to visit her. During the same excitement, he worked in his garden at the Hermitage, quite unaware that a band of Indians encamped nearby watched him constantly. Afterwards, they told him that they had discussed his fate, should the massacre begin, and had decided that they might take his mare if they were pressed for horses, but 'would not meddle with the little white robed priest, for I had not been bad to the Indians.'[20]

Working in virtual isolation from his fellow clergy, Newton created a rallying point for those of European background who had been nurtured in an English tradition. This tradition did not distinguish itself sharply, if at all, from what came also to be seen as the British tradition, rooted in notions of class and racial superiority, that was carried from the mother country to all parts of the globe where the British had settled or acquired a dominant managerial and cultural role. These attitudes played a role in establishing an acceptable level of comfort in the fluid and almost formless society of the Canadian post-Confederation West. Newton, of humble but impeccably English origin, used his education and considerable natural abilities to enter, through his Anglican ordination, into what may be seen as the influential minority in the changing western polity. No matter how sceptically one may view his academic attainments, he was certainly a man of wide-ranging curiosity with an insatiable appetite for intellectual novelty and a strong desire both to share his interests and to elevate the cultural level of society. People, however, did not always appreciate his efforts. Newton's sermons and his occasional public lectures do not seem to have aroused universal enthusiasm; and his attempt with his sister Eliza, a registered nurse associated with Queen Charlotte's Hospital in London,[21] to establish a school for girls did not succeed. Nor, incidentally, did Eliza's efforts to make use of her nursing training, when she advertised in the *Edmonton Bulletin* that she would receive women patients for their confinements at the Hermitage and was available for consultation on the diseases of women and children.[22]

Newton did his best to assert the values of law and order in an environment where the popular mood was often in favour of more direct action against the offender. He himself suffered from the chaos that attended the postponement of adequate land surveys and here his influence appears to have had some effect upon government. He was a man of unusual complexity of character—reserved to a degree, often querulous and annoying to a good many people, yet capable of profound friendships and easily roused to anger by any injustice, real or suspected, to his friends. As an Anglican priest, his reputation as a ritualist came at time when standards of churchmanship in the Canadian church were by no means high, especially on its pioneer fringes. Newton recounts an incident that occurred when

First meeting, Anglican Diocesan Women's Auxiliary, circa 1910. Women were often the backbone of the church's work in the community. (PAA A.1796)

he ventured to wear, at a children's Christmas party at All Saints', some 'special vestment' and a small white cross. This greatly annoyed one of his flock, who promptly circulated a petition to the Bishop for his removal. The petition, however, got short shrift. 'It came to me,' a Roman Catholic friend of Newton told him, 'but I took care to place it where it will give no more trouble to anybody.'[23] Newton did try to introduce more seemliness into his services, as his report to the Society for the Propagation of the Gospel at Christmas 1884 suggests:

> We have a good organ paid for and a young gentleman from the Mother Country gives his services and makes himself very useful in helping us to render our common chants and hymns more worthily. A large number of our people had been trained to sing in the manner of the Orkney Islands, and it has required the patient management of years to change their ideas of music so as to make our church music acceptable to their sense of devotion. In this matter we have much improved without jarring the feelings of the people, and we hope to hasten slowly in this direction.[24]

Newton's comments do not sound much like those of a tactless and opinionated priest trying to force unwelcome innovation upon a reluctant congregation.

Newton was pensioned by the Society for the Propagation of the Gospel in 1899 just as the Anglican church was about to enter a new era of rapid change in the West. By that time, the pace of settlement across the prairies had accelerated and it would continue under the immigration and railway policies of Laurier and the Liberals, proudly proclaiming the twentieth century as Canada's. Demographic factors too complex for examination here—for they were continental and intercontinental, national and international, in their scope—precipitated the new province of Alberta into an unprecedented period of growth, ending with the outbreak of war in 1914.[25] In a time of pronounced optimism, no speculation as to the future, no matter how intrinsically absurd, was seriously questioned. As settlers poured into the province, expectations of extravagant profit from real estate brought projects for expansion that were often no more than fantasy. Railways were built and many more projected, and along them, cities and towns, some mere figments of the speculative imagination, were forecast in most unlikely locations. Out of this frenzied activity emerged the structure of a new Alberta, jerry-built, as time was to prove, but at least in outline the basis for an organized agricultural society with some prospects for development of other industries, especially forestry and mining. The rapid

All Saints Church, Edmonton, Alta.

Built in 1896 on 103 Street south of Jasper Avenue, the second All Saints' Church shown here was destroyed by fire on 20 December 1919. (PAA ACE 3)

increase in population, and the prospect that it would continue in the foreseeable future, was the basis for institutional development, indeed appeared to dictate a rapid institutional expansion based upon an assured future. The Christian churches responded to the best of their ability.

Edmonton shared in the growth of the two decades before 1914, and, with increasing immigration from the United Kingdom and increasing migration from the English-speaking regions of central and eastern Canada, its Anglican population grew. Although Presbyterians and Methodists were more numerous among settlers from the easterly provinces, nominal Anglicans probably predominated among arrivals from the United Kingdom, their ecclesiastical allegiance as much cultural as doctrinal. It should be remembered that in these years, and often long afterwards, the building in which Anglicans worshipped was called 'the English church.' This ethnic reference, which later generations were to try, although perhaps not very hard, to jettison, was not in pre-1914 Edmonton altogether a disadvantage. 'The English church' did act as a rallying point and a comforting support for those who saw themselves as inheritors of an English, or, perhaps more properly, a British tradition. An analysis of Anglican congregations might quite often reveal that a substantial number of the most dedicated members were ethnically Irish, the descendants of immigrants who had been adherents of the United Church of England and Ireland. Many immigrants from Wales and Scotland similarly found themselves relatively at home in Anglican congregations,

especially if they were isolated from others who shared their old-world denominational attachment.

The parish system of England, where churches were by-and-large within walking distance of their parishioners, transplanted somewhat uneasily on the prairies, particularly among rural homesteaders. It was easier to organize parish life in an urban centre like Edmonton, which became the centre for a new phase of Anglican institutional growth. The diocese of Edmonton was established in 1913 and the following year received its first bishop, Henry Allen Gray, a man who left a lasting imprint on the development of Anglicanism in Alberta.[26] Around 1886, when he would have been in his early twenties, Gray, like so many young Englishmen of his time, came to Alberta to ranch. He soon became active in the church life of the diocese of Calgary. From 1892 to 1895 he studied at St John's College in Winnipeg and in 1895 was licensed as deacon to Holy Trinity, Strathcona, the pioneer parish on the south side of the North Saskatchewan. Ordained priest in 1896, he was inducted into the parish of All Saints', where a new church (subsequently destroyed by fire on 20 December 1919) had been dedicated on the site of the present cathedral on 103 Street south of Jasper Avenue. Gray and his family fitted easily into the life of the city, with All Saints' as its Anglican heart, and he gave leadership in the wider community as well as the church. He served as judge of the juvenile court and participated in the development of the social institutions—whether the courts, the police, the school, or the hospital—whose health he saw as a major responsibility of the church. Although Anglicans in the early years of the century were a minority, they were relatively youthful, comparatively literate, economically not particularly disadvantaged, and, in spite of occasional differences over churchmanship, reasonably cohesive. Gray used his authority as successively parish priest, archdeacon, and bishop to make his flock, if not a dominant element, at least an effective influence in a community that was still in a malleable stage of its movement from an isolated outpost to a minor metropolis.

Like other episcopal pioneers in Anglican Canada from Halifax to Vancouver Island, Gray depended almost completely for money and missionaries alike upon external support. This support came largely from Britain, for the church in eastern Canada had little to spare for work beyond its provincial borders and, like the Anglican remnant in the United States, had to engage formidable missionary challenges on its home ground. Not for a generation were dioceses like Edmonton able to think realistically of total self-support, not to say substantial missionary enterprise abroad. The expansion of the Anglican community in central Alberta was a function of the pressures of population in the United Kingdom and the well-advertised attractions of early twentieth-century western Canada, but that community could scarcely have survived, let alone prospered, without backing from the church in the mother country. The magnitude of this support and its importance for the diocese of Edmonton is effectively illustrated by the impact of the Archbishops' Western Canada Fund.[27] Edmonton was one of three centres of mission supported by the Fund, and the arrival in 1910 of the Reverend W.G. Boyd, 'a former chaplain to the Archbishop of Canterbury . . . [and] a prime mover' in the Fund's establishment,[28] was critical in the development both of the diocese and of the city and rural hinterland it served. An infusion of money and workers—men and women, lay and clerical, who were committed not only to Anglicanism but also to the culture it reflected—brought new vigour to the church and to the community.

Among the many projects the mission affected was an Anglican college within the new University of Alberta. This project was the special responsibility of J. Burgon Bickersteth, a young lay worker with excellent connections in ecclesiastical and educational circles in the United Kingdom.[29] He had enlisted the support of his wealthy and influential Oxford college, Christ Church; some money had been raised and more promised; and a young historian of outstanding ability (Keith Feiling) had been chosen to take up the chair Christ Church was prepared to finance.

Meanwhile, in the intervals of his work as a lay missionary on the railway lines being built west of Edmonton towards Vancouver and Prince Rupert, Bickersteth had used his considerable social and intellectual gifts to commend his project to the university community and its allies among Edmonton Anglicans. The university, although committed to the non-sectarian and secular ideal acceptable to Canadian governments, was receptive to the idea of denominational colleges—especially to one like the Anglicans' proposed St Aidan's, which was oriented towards providing residential accommodation rather than theological training. The university faculty, in an environment where post-secondary education had a scarcity value, soon formed ties of friendship with the mission workers, men and women alike, who found the campus community socially congenial. Eventually, this project for an Anglican college was a casualty of the First World War.

Bishop Henry Allen Gray, circa 1915. He was an effective leader of his church until his retirement in 1931. (PAA A.9989)

The years immediately preceding the war were a kind of golden age for the Anglican church in Edmonton, in which Bishop Gray came to assume a position similar to (if not of quite the same mythic proportions) that of Lacombe for Roman Catholics, the McDougalls for Methodists, and McQueen for Presbyterians. As Edmonton changed from a small frontier town, isolated at the end of steel, into a provincial capital and regional railway centre, the multiplication of the British and Anglican population markedly affected every aspect of life—from politics to sports and pastimes, from religious exercises to reading habits. Often young, ambitious, and with their way to make in a new world, settlers from the United Kingdom gave a unique impulse to the development of not just Edmonton but all central Alberta. Although in the practical business of agriculture they were all too often not as well equipped as their contemporaries with North American experience, they reinforced the attachment to cultural values, identified by an earlier generation with a peaceful and orderly society, that were seen as British rather than American. In this process the Anglican church played a vital part and few were more enthusiastic advocates of these values than the missionaries who came under the auspices of the Archbishops' Fund.

Alberta seemed well on its way to being, if not quite as British as British Columbia, at least not radically different from, if less developed than, Ontario or Manitoba. The outbreak of war in 1914 changed everything. Less than two decades old, the province's institutions had developed on a less mature substructure than those of its immediate neighbours, Saskatchewan and British Columbia. The Anglican population, given the presence of so many young men with strong sentimental attachments to the United Kingdom, was particularly affected. Britishimmigrants enlisted and died in such numbers as to be close to catastrophic for a church that saw them as its present and future constituency. Forced to contend not only with the appalling casualties of war but also the fact that immigrants from the United Kingdom no longer dominated the demographics of central Alberta, recovery for the Anglican community in Edmonton following the war would be difficult. But the foundations laid by Newton, Gray, and the men and women who worked with them were strong enough to survive the troubled twenties and thirties and in the years after 1945 permit a new period of consolidation and growth signalized by the episcopates of Walter Foster Barfoot and Howard Hewlett Clark. ॐ

JOHN PATRICK DAY

DONALD ROSS, OLD-TIMER EXTRAORDINAIRE

Donald Ross's Edmonton Hotel, 1903. (PAA B.4315)

*D*uring the last quarter of the nineteenth century, settlement was moving outside the walls of Fort Edmonton. Increasingly prominent in the emerging town were institutions like the church, school, and clubs; would-be entrepreneurs; and a local boosterism mentality that expressed the ambitions of community leaders anxious to put Edmonton on the map. Among the growing number of new-comers who gave the town its shape, young men dominated by far. One of these young men was Donald Ross, arriving in 1872 via the gold fields to the west.

A transitional figure between the old and new eras, who eventually found himself marginalized as another generation took over, Ross was nevertheless typical of the age. Never content with single-mindedly devoting their energies to one project or goal, and practical enough to realize that specialization was impossible if they wanted to make a living in a frontier settlement, he and his contemporaries were city builders in a broad sense. They became the driving force behind a wide variety of activities—political, cultural, and economic—encompassing all aspects of Edmonton life. It would be difficult for any one individual to duplicate their feat today. Ross's economic interests alone ranged from mining to hotelkeeping to horticulture to real estate to communications. Already in his lifetime recognized by his fellow citizens for his contribution to their common community, Ross became Edmonton's old-timer extraordinaire.

John Day is an independent scholar with particular interests in the history of Edmonton.

I N NOVEMBER 1881, WHEN THE LAND RESERVE OF the Hudson's Bay Company (HBC) at Edmonton was being surveyed into town lots, the Edmonton Hotel, owned and operated by Donald Ross, was discovered to extend nine feet into HBC property. 'Mr. Ross,' the *Edmonton Bulletin* quickly reported, 'has notified the Company to move their land from under his hotel as it was put there without his knowledge or consent.'[1] This characteristic response is a useful indicator of the difficulties posed in considering Ross's significance to Edmonton's history. He himself worked hard to promote an image of a rough-hewn, outspoken pioneer who embodied the spirit of early Edmonton. It is easy to fall into his trap and important not to do so, if only because an accurate picture of the man and his activities remains to be drawn. In cultivating his legend, he seemed to think that his career was too familiar to require discussion; as a result, subsequent generations knew little about him beyond a handful of his favourite anecdotes. Yet Ross was too prominent a player in Edmonton's early development for his impact to be ignored.

Donald Ross was born on 17 June 1840 in Dumfriesshire, Scotland.[2] His father was a gardener, originally from the county of Ross and Cromarty, while his mother came from Fife county; the family consisted of at least two boys and one girl. In later years, Ross's Scottish roots were reflected in his love of Scottish songs; his presence at St Andrew's Society meetings; his commitment to education; and his prudence as a businessman. Ross also considered himself to be Presbyterian. It would be a mistake, however, to make more of his Scottishness than he did; at least one of his children believed him to be English by birth. The Ross family moved to Cumberland, England, in 1846. Here Ross learned his father's trade and picked up what he called a 'rudimentary' education. He left school at age thirteen and entered domestic service as a page boy to Dr Archibald Tait, then Dean of Carlisle and later Archbishop of Canterbury. When Tait became Bishop of London in 1856, Ross went to work for a retired industrialist.

In 1857 the seventeen-year-old Ross hired on as a cabin boy on a transatlantic steamer. Either he always saw this position as a way to earn passage to America or he dis-

Donald Ross, 1904. (EA-10-669.2)

liked the new job, for after two trips he elected to stay in New York. A local judge found him a job as a waiter at the Astor Hotel; he worked here for thirteen months, before going briefly to the Fifth Avenue Hotel, also in New York, and then to the National Hotel in Washington. Ross arrived in the capital in time to attend President James Buchanan's New Year's Day levée of 1859. Twelve months later he witnessed the return of the Virginia troops following the execution of John Brown and, fearing imminent civil war in the region, decided to relocate somewhere safer. On New Year's Day, 1860, Ross left for Yuba County, California, where he tried his luck as a prospector for the next eighteen months. He also cast his vote for Abraham Lincoln in the 1860 presidential election. In 1861 Ross moved to Carson City, Nevada, and then to the silver mines of Virginia City, gathering a rich fund of stories (later retold at the Edmonton Hotel) together with expertise in gunpowder blasting.

By 1870 the mines of Nevada, as well as elsewhere in the western United States, were in decline, and a number of miners, Ross among them, concluded that British Columbia offered brighter prospects. Unimpressed with Victoria, Ross joined a group of miners who eventually reached Lightning Creek in the Omineca River area, but once there they found provisions to be scarce and expensive and decided to push farther east. Ross later recalled:

> We had heard in the gossip of the camps and had gathered from the stories of guides and Indians that there was a great river on the other side of the mountains in a country kept as a great fur reserve for the Hudson's Bay Company, where the yield of gold was such that men had never known before . . . a party of us made up our minds to cross the great divide . . . We found gold on the Peace River, as you will find it on all mountain streams, but not in such quantities as we had imagined. For months we toiled at gold-washing, but eventually tired and drifted southward to St. Albert . . . and then to Fort Edmonton.[3]

Ross gave the date of his arrival in Edmonton as 20 August 1872. Although he had not completely given up the idea of living on the Peace River,[4] he would reside in

Edmonton for the remaining forty-three years of his life. As Ross explained in his ballad 'Pemmican'—first performed on New Year's Day, 1873—he was tired of not being sure of three square meals a day.[5]

Ross's personal circumstances changed in either 1877 or 1878 when he married Olive Blewitt. A woman who jealously guarded her privacy, she claimed to have been born in London in 1850 and to have lived in Toronto, Hamilton, and Rochester, New York, before moving with her family to Battleford and then Edmonton. For the wedding ceremony at the Methodist church, officiated by the Reverend Mr Walton, Ross obtained some gold from two of his mining friends and got the HBC blacksmith to make a ring. The couple's first home was Ross's log house next to one of his coal mine shafts. The marriage eventually produced three children: James (b 1879), whose severe deafness was possibly genetic; Olive or Dolly (b 1881), who trained as a nurse in Montreal but practised in Edmonton; and Donald Jr (b 1883), a quiet, studious youth who studied electrical engineering at McGill University before becoming the Macdonald Hotel's first electrician. The Rosses were a close family and a private one.[6]

But if Ross protected his personal life from scrutiny, he quickly acquired a public profile as Edmonton passed from fur trading fort to commercial settlement. How did someone who arrived without money or useful connections come to play a prominent role in Edmonton's economy? Most men, unlike salaried HBC officers (or miners who wrested sufficient gold from the North Saskatchewan River), found it difficult to produce their own business capital. A more realistic route for local residents was to 'sell' their talents to vested interests—like the HBC, the federal government, and church missions—that furnished the capital for specific enterprises. The HBC, for example, increasingly contracted out functions formerly filled by indentured servants. Even if they became successful businessmen, the individuals who chose this course were frequently dismissed as crude and unsophisticated by a new self-proclaimed 'elite' that was descending on Edmonton. These men—from urban and often professional or commercial backgrounds—obtained their capital through 'grubstaking' by backers in eastern Canada, Britain, or the United States wishing to invest in undeveloped territories. Ross was most closely identified with the second group as a cultural reality, and his apparent lack of urban polish seems to have caused difficulties with the aspiring elite associated with the third group. However, he recognized the value all three avenues to economic power and moved freely among them as the occasion demanded.

Entrance to Ross's coal mine on River Lot 6. Ross is standing to the immediate right of the entrance. (EA-10-1180)

Although Ross is best remembered for the Edmonton Hotel (est 1876), the first operation of its kind between Portage la Prairie and Barkerville, he came to Edmonton as a miner and worked at washing gold from the North Saskatchewan until the late 1870s.[7] He and his generation of miners stopped short of advising newcomers against trying to make a living from the river, but they recommended an additional source of income or support such as a garden. Ross himself appears to have done less well than many of his contemporaries, never making more than $10 in any one day (1874, when he averaged $7.50 per day, was his best year).[8] He had given up on gold in an active sense by the time of his marriage, although he continued to give advice, retained a wealth of stories, and put up old mining friends who could no longer look after themselves at the Edmonton Hotel.[9]

Ross's interest in mining shifted to the coal seams readily visible in the high banks of the North Saskatchewan. The *Edmonton Bulletin* credited him with the first commercial use of Edmonton coal; and if Mrs Ross's recollections of her wedding day are accurate, Ross may have been shipping coal downriver already by 1878.[10] He acquired an important partner and backer in Captain Henry S. Moore of Prince Albert, who saw the upper reaches of the North Saskatchewan as a source for the lumber and coal needed at Battleford and Prince Albert. Moore also had good political credentials. By 1883 an even bigger name—John Stoughton Dennis Jr, son of the Surveyor-General of Canada—had joined the partnership.[11] Ross and Moore each worked their own diggings: Moore upriver on a claim on Big Island, and Ross, during winter 1879–80, a seam on the bank opposite his buildings and farm. By November

399 — VEGITABLES FROM D. ROSS'S GARDEN EDMONTON (1902)

PHOTO BY C. W. MATHERS EDMONTON

1880 he was extracting two tons a day and by April 1881 employed three to six men who could produce between two to four tons a day. In its first two years the mine yielded some 500 tons of coal. Success attracted competitors and by 1896 an unknown number of self-employed miners and an estimated six mines employing 20 to 40 men operated in the area.[12]

In spring 1883 Ross lost interest in these drifts, possibly because they produced less than the 825 tons of coal he had anticipated, and that autumn he turned his attention to the high bank north of his hotel. This mine seems to have operated until 1898, when it and other mines in the vicinity were closed by agreement between their owners and Town Council to prevent further destabilizing of the high river bank and the buildings it supported.[13] Just because Ross no longer operated coal mines did not mean he abandoned the business altogether, however. Coal continued to be sold or delivered from the Edmonton Hotel until spring 1905.[14]

Ross never put all his eggs in one basket. References in 'Pemmican' and other stories to him protecting the HBC potato patch against a Blackfoot trading party suggest that he might have done casual work for the Company as early as 1872. Ross clearly had an arrangement with the HBC during winter 1873–4, as he was residing in the Fort the following April.[15] That fall he agreed to operate the Company's farm for three years in return for a substantial, albeit unidentified, fee. Ross himself described the farm as 'cropped for many years and run down' when he took over management from William Leslie Wood, who was being posted to the Bow River area.[16] The fact that the land lay outside the surveyed HBC Reserve subsequently sparked considerable controversy, as after a year Ross understood that he owned the land outright in return for waiving his operator's fee and opened a hotel on the property.[17] Over the next fourteen years he devoted much energy to his garden—growing onions, potatoes, cabbages, cauliflowers, carrots, parsnips, mangold wurzels, turnips, and peas. He considered all these plants, most of which were already being cultivated, to produce reliable crops.[18] With varying degrees of success, Ross also attempted to grow cucumbers, citrons, pumpkins, corn, and tomatoes.

Ross's horticultural efforts had a far-reaching impact. Beginning in 1879 the *Edmonton Bulletin* and *Battleford Herald* regularly received news, if not the actual products, of his garden. Ross himself corresponded with other agriculturalists and received plants from Ottawa's Central Experimental Farm for trial at Edmonton. He also attracted the attention of the celebrated American botanist, Luther Burbank, who visited him in 1894 and sent plants for experiment.[19] In addition, gardening had obvious advantages for a hotelkeeper, and as the settlement developed a more urban character after 1881, there was a certain demand for vegetables among local residents who did not grow their own. By 1893 Ross had begun to sell vegetables either through retailers in the developing business centre, by delivery, or at 'Edmonton under the Hill.' By 1895 he had expanded into the floral business; that same year he duplicated the experiment of Frank Mariaggi of the Alberta Hotel and opened a greenhouse.[20]

In 1904 Edmonton Town Council recorded its appreciation of Ross's work 'for Edmonton and district in the cultivation of vegetables of fine quality from year to year, and thus advertising the productiveness of the soil.'[21] Much of that publicity had come through agricultural fairs and societies. Edmonton held its inaugural fair on 15 October 1879, when Ross was elected a director of the newly-formed Agricultural Society. He also won firsts for his carrots and parsnips and third-place ribbons for his potatoes and overall vegetable display; in a rare public appearance, Olive won two first prizes.[22] After public apathy led to the collapse of the Agricultural Society, it reorganized without Ross's input on the executive; thereafter, except for a brief period as vice-president between 1885 and 1887, he long limited his involvement to being an exhibitor.[23]

Ross resumed a prominent role in Agricultural Society work in 1900. The following year he joined the board of directors of the Edmonton Exhibition Association and took charge of the fair grounds; in 1902 he oversaw the construction of a new grandstand, exhibition hall, and race track. In 1903 he was elected president, serving a two-year term.[24] Ross's stewardship of the Edmonton Exhibition Association received good reviews, including reluctant praise from Bob Edwards of the Calgary *Eye Opener*: 'One cannot but admire Edmonton folk for the tact and savvy they display on occasions of public importance. Their annual fairs, for example, are models of good management and consequently are always a success. Their unlimited nerve, of course, has a good deal to do with it.'[25] Ross also helped promote Edmonton produce at fairs elsewhere in Canada, with prize-winning exhibits of grains and vegetables in Winnipeg, Calgary, and Toronto. In 1903, at the request of the Dominion Experimental Farm at Indian Head, he assembled a collection of Edmonton grasses and grains for the St Louis exhibition in Missouri.[26]

If the needs of his hotel encouraged Ross's interest in gardening, feeding his guests also led him to experiment with commercial meat packing. Until the Edmonton Hotel temporarily closed in 1892, Ross kept a large number pigs (although not within town limits after incorporation) and cured his own bacon and ham for the hotel. By fall 1895 he had established 'an extensive hog ranch' which housed the Edmonton Pork Packing Company that operated over the winter. Although the company soon reorganized without Ross's direct involvement, he maintained his interest in the hog industry. The old hotel was still in use as a packing house in 1898, and Ross was still operating the hog ranch in 1899.[27]

During its lifetime the Edmonton Hotel—already enlarged by 1878 (probably due to marriage)—served a variety of functions. It was home to Ross and his family until 1884, when he built a house on the HBC Reserve opposite.[28] The men who worked in Ross's coal mines could also receive room and board as part of their wages. Moreover, the hotel played a significant social role in the infant settlement, hosting community events like the New Year balls of 1879 and 1880.[29] Ross also made the hotel's icehouse available as a printing office for the publication of the first issue of Frank Oliver's *Edmonton Bulletin*. 'The matter of sticking type,' Ross later wrote, 'was confided to one of my coal miners, Collins by name, who considered himself well paid . . . [at] . . .$5.00 per issue.'[30] The emergence of an urban nucleus on top of the river bank introduced competition, but Ross met the challenge in a number of ways. He had installed Edmonton's first billiard table by September 1880; his new coal-burning stoves that consumed the output of his own mine made good advertising; and the worried traveller of more sophisticated tastes

Rossdale after the 1882 addition to the Edmonton Hotel but before Ross's home was completed in 1884. The building at the far right is probably the first printing and editorial office of the *Edmonton Bulletin*. (EA-10-602)

was assured that 'pemmican and dried meat has long been a stranger at the table, . . . its place taken by substantives more in keeping with the onward march of civilization.' A major addition to the hotel in 1882 met North American standards of the age. Business was sufficiently good to justify opening the Eureka saloon, complete with billiard table, in 1887; it was rented as a bank when the hotel closed its doors in summer 1892.[31] The premises continued to be used for occasional events, like the founding banquet of the Northern Alberta Old-Timers' Association in 1894. By 1899 Ross was once again taking boarders, and in November 1901 the Edmonton Hotel reopened.[32]

The hotel's fluctuating fortunes are significant. It would be too simple to ascribe its closure to the setback on the north bank when the Calgary and Edmonton Railway failed to cross the river and its reopening to the renewal that attended the arrival of the Edmonton, Yukon, and Pacific line. What happened to the hotel mirrored a larger crisis in Ross's life characterized by contraction and then resumption of activities in a number of areas. There are several possible reasons. First, Ross may have been in poor health. He had experienced eye trouble in 1887 that required specialized treatment in Montreal; he missed at least one public appearance, apparently due to illness; and

he is known to have broken a rib after slipping on ice.[33] Second, neither Ross nor his wife was young, and by 1890 they had three children, aged eleven, nine, and seven; quite conceivably, family priorities diverted time and energy from both hotelkeeping and public affairs. Finally, Ross's ego might have been bruised. In 1891 he was one of the citizens who pressed for the incorporation of Edmonton as a town, and he sat on the committee that determined its boundaries. But when he stood in the first election for Town Council, he was not merely unsuccessful but badly thrashed and came not far from finishing dead last.[34] It was a shockingly poor result for one of Edmonton's oldest, most visible, and most colourful residents.

Ross's relations with the Edmonton Board of Trade and the Northern Alberta Old-Timers' Association suggest that public rejection might have been a major factor behind his retreat in the 1890s. Established in 1888, the Board of Trade was reorganized in 1894.[35] Ross, still too important an economic force to be ignored, had been a founding member, but, aside from an ongoing seat on the board's agricultural committee, he played no important or visible role in its affairs. One is tempted to conclude that the commercial elite which emerged in the 1890s saw him as a marginal player and did not pay him more attention

The Edmonton Hotel barroom, 1903. Ross is at the far right. (PAA B.4322)

than necessary. At the same time, Ross's high profile in the Northern Alberta Old-Timers' Association gave him a public role and enabled him to redefine himself as part of the new age. He was a popular entertainer and in 1895, to wide acclaim, performed 'Pemmican,' his great hit of 1873, at a reception for Sir John Schultz. As the association's second president, he represented the group at meetings of such 'national' bodies as the St Andrew's Society and the Société St Jean-Baptiste. Ross's presence of mind, and his repertoire of songs, also quelled an acrimonious row featuring Edmonton's leading politicians at the Old-Timers' second annual banquet.[36] Just possibly, Ross began to see that the town saw some connection between itself and the settlement that preceded it and that there might be a role for him after all. Whatever crisis Ross might have had, the reopening of the Edmonton Hotel early in the new century symbolized his recovery.[37]

One other area of Ross's business activities—his real estate dealings—merits attention. A major controversy erupted between Ross and the family of the Reverend George McDougall on behalf of the Methodist mission over ownership of River Lot 4, to which Ross thought he had obtained clear title from the HBC. Ross ultimately got more or less what he wanted in this conflict north of the

river in what became known as Rossdale flat, just as he did in a similar conflict south of the river involving parts of River Lots 17 and 19 where he had been digging coal. Ross seems to have resisted momentary temptations such as land booms, and, unusually for an Edmonton landowner, he did not subdivide any of his land until a year after the Calgary and Edmonton Railway had reached Strathcona. He subdivided River Lot 17 only in 1900 and River Lot 19 (if at all) only in 1901.[38] Ross believed that the river's proximity and a possible railway crossing earmarked his land for industry rather than housing.

Nonetheless, a substantial residential area did emerge in Rossdale, and a smaller one in Ross's southside properties. The southernmost corner of Rossdale had been a camping ground for parties trading at the Fort at least since Paul Kane's time. Other residential development in Rossdale accompanied the various industries established there and declined into respectable poverty after they closed or relocated after 1915. Hoping for a higher grade of residential settlement on the western bank of River Lot 17, Ross subdivided the area into one acre 'villa lots.'[39] The plan proved unrealistic, as an industrial area, including two packing plants, grew up east of Centretown, and the Edmonton, Yukon, and Pacific Railway passed right by the lots. This area is still residential, but resembles Rossdale prior to the latter's recent gentrification.

Industry, besides the three different coal mines worked by Ross, did develop on both sides of the river. The Edmonton Electric Light and Power Company built its first station just upriver from the Low Level Bridge. In what seems to have been a customary practice, Ross provided the site in return for part of the company; his twenty-five shares amounted to a 3 per cent interest when the town acquired the company in 1902. Other Rossdale enterprises launched in the 1890s included the Edmonton Brewing and Malting Company, the sales yard for a limestone quarry, the Edmonton Sawmill Company, Frederick Mayerhofer's dye works, John Dowling and Philip Ottewell's flour mill, and John Walter's second sawmill.[40] Industrial development also proceeded south of the North Saskatchewan. In 1901 Ross sold an area on River Lot 17 immediately west of Mill Creek to Peter Anderson, who started a brick factory; within two months, Anderson also opened a coal mine under the grade now known as Connors Road. And the meat packing plant that Cornelius Gallagher had taken over from Ross and relocated south of the river was soon joined by a second plant operated by Joseph Hehsdorfer.[41]

Ross early realized that if he was to earn maximum profit from his land, Edmonton had to acquire both a railway and a bridge to carry it across the river. He made his priorities abundantly clear in a rare public speech following Edmonton's incorporation in response to the arrival of the Calgary and Edmonton Railway in Strathcona. 'Donald Ross,' reported the *Edmonton Bulletin*,

> said he had voted for incorporation as a means of getting a bridge. He did not wish to cast any slurs, but he thought too much had been done on the streets and too little had been towards a bridge. He was willing to chip in and help to pay for a bridge. He had seen the rise of Edmonton and wanted to see it go ahead still further. A bridge would be to our benefit. An attempt had been made to steal our town, our name, our business, and our land office. The name of his Hotel had been stolen. A bridge would prevent anything of the kind in the future and he was in favour of a bridge.[42]

Ross presented a resolution to Town Council in which Edmonton would offer the federal government 25 per cent of the cost of a traffic bridge connecting River Lot 17 and River Lot 8.[43] This route, already among the frontrunners for a rail line into Edmonton, crossed from a property Ross claimed to own to a spot immediately adjacent to land he

definitely owned, and he undoubtedly saw great personal advantages in pressing it. Fortunately, the interests of Ross and Edmonton coincided. The other two routes under consideration (at Fort Saskatchewan and the mouth of Whitemud Creek) would bring little benefit to Edmonton and could not easily take advantage of the existing Calgary and Edmonton Railway. It would prove somewhat ironic that Ross's relative financial importance declined with the entry of the railway into Edmonton and the development of the commercial centre on Jasper Avenue.

Under Mayor Matthew McCauley the municipally-owned Edmonton Street Railway Company was incorporated to run electric trams across the river and connect with the Calgary and Edmonton track. McCauley's successor, H.C. Wilson, favoured a separate railway company that would run lines as far as Athabasca Landing. A new Edmonton District Railway Company (EDRC) received its charter early in 1896, and Ross was handily elected to its board of directors.[44] Ottawa agreed to pay the full cost of a traffic bridge, and the EDRC to cover the remaining costs to upgrade the bridge for trains. Edmonton would issue debentures to help raise this additional sum, provided that any railway company could use the bridge. The EDRC's active pursuit of business ended in April 1897, when the company voluntarily dissolved, and the debentures were transferred to the federal government.[45] However, several New Brunswick entrepreneurs, backed by Mackenzie and Mann of the Canadian Northern Railway, saw the EDRC charter as way to obtain a rail line to the Yukon, and the street railway scheme was separated from the EDRC,

Ross, driving the first train into Edmonton, 28 October 1902, is the 'Old-Timer' featured in the cartoon. (PAA B.6208)

which became the Edmonton, Yukon, and Pacific Railway. The directors of the EDRC continued to be involved in negotiating terms between the railway and Edmonton. Ross himself donated a strip of land on River Lot 17 and purchased a similar strip from the McDougall Estate in order to provide approaches for the railway at either end of the bridge.[46] The street railway maintained a separate existence, and the directors of the EDRC from time to time were drawn into discussions that did not conclude until 1908. It was Ross's last active corporate involvement.

While private gain was one impetus behind taking part in Edmonton public life, Ross had a long record of public service, especially in the field of education. His hotel hosted the meeting in late 1881 that created the first School Committee (predecessor of the present Edmonton Public School Board). Shortly thereafter Ross performed in a minstrel show to raise funds for the school, and he sat on a committee seeking the support of householders to levy school taxes. He was eventually elected to the School Committee itself and was reelected in the last general meeting prior to the erection of a school district under the terms of the new NWT School Ordinance of 1885. Ross played a prominent role in the lively plebiscite held to obtain the approval of the prospective ratepayers for the change, and, after Edmonton Protestant Public School District No. 7 was proclaimed, became a trustee. He sat on the board until the end of 1889, serving as chairman in his last year.[47] Despite the visibility that elected office thrust upon him, Ross appeared to know his shortcomings. When once asked for his comments, he reportedly 'remarked that too much good could not be said or done in a good cause, but that he knew enough to know that he could not make a speech.'[48] In fact, he rarely attempted to make one, preferring to express his opinions through ballads and anecdotes.

Yet Ross possessed qualities that made others turn to him for leadership. The earliest recorded instance occurred in March 1875, when he chaired a settlement meeting that sought to persuade the North West Mounted Police to reconsider locating its barracks at Edmonton rather than Fort Saskatchewan. In 1885 Ross again sat in the chair as the Edmonton settlement debated how to organize its defence during the second Riel uprising. He was also one of five members named to the Committee of Defence that functioned as the local authority until General T.B. Strange's military force arrived.[49] Ross's leadership role in the community began to decline after 1885 and came to an end by 1888.

Retreat from the limelight perhaps reflected that Edmonton was beginning to think of Ross as part of its past rather than as part of its present or future. And perhaps it was Ross's adjustment to this perception, together with Edmonton's realization that its past was an integral part of its identity, that led to his return from the shadows. In this process, the founding of the Northern Alberta Old-Timers' Association played a crucial role. It put Ross back into public circulation, and he began to be seen as the personification of a settlement that had faced and conquered formidable impersonal forces. Ross—whose memories of thirty years at Edmonton were either well recorded or well remembered, who had absorbed the legends and traditions of previous residents, and who regaled visitors to the Edmonton Hotel (where he was the primary entertainment) with his stories—was ideally suited to represent the settlement's spirit. And Edmonton recognized him as its eldest son. In 1905 Ross was invited to drive the last spike in the 'loop' linking the Canadian Northern and the Edmonton, Yukon, and Pacific railways. In reporting the event, the *Edmonton Bulletin* recalled how it had been Donald Ross who carried the first telegraph line across the North Saskatchewan River; Donald Ross who drove the last spike in the Calgary and Edmonton Railway; Donald Ross who drove the first spike making the connection with the Edmonton, Yukon, and Pacific Railway; Donald Ross who drove the first spike in the latter line on the north side of the river; Donald Ross who pounded in the last rivet in the eagerly awaited bridge; and Donald Ross who piloted the first engine across it.[50] When he died on 20 December 1915, Edmonton lost a man synonymous with the major symbolic moments in the life of the city. ❧

LAURENT GARNEAU (POEMS)

Laurent Garneau. (EA-10-2606)

*I*n 1881 the CPR decided to take a southern route through the Rocky Mountains. For decades, Edmonton's growth and population would lag behind the chief Alberta beneficiary of the CPR's decision—Calgary. Even the river traffic on the North Saskatchewan decreased. Still, Edmonton did grow.

Gradually, the new settlers—often of British stock from Ontario—threatened the position of some of the original inhabitants, particularly the French Métis and Natives. Nevertheless, some Métis went on to win a place in the emerging settlement society. Laurent Garneau was a mixed-blood farmer, who had fought alongside Louis Riel in the 1869 Red River Rebellion, then went on to homestead above the North Saskatchewan River opposite Fort Edmonton. When Riel led a second uprising in 1885, the frightened inhabitants of Fort Edmonton suspected Garneau was too sympathetic. Shunned in his own time, his contribution as an early settler and community activist is today preserved, among other places, on a commemorative plaque erected in the district that bears his name.

The poet Gerald Hill is a University of Alberta PhD candidate studying Canadian historical novels. Active in public poetry readings, Hill sees history as more than factual text; art can provide an important and different perspective.

In 1953 the City Fathers wrote
the words for a man
who'd left his name on twenty city blocks,
a bakery, school, theatre, highrise
and church (a United Church
although he was Roman Catholic)—
the man is Laurent Garneau.

And the City Fathers considered their words.
Do we call him Larry?
Was he halfbreed or Canadian?
Do we call him a Métis patriot?

And they voted not once but twice.
They voted not to mention his Métis blood
or the power of his sixty
years in the north-west.
They voted to forget
Garneau was jailed for six weeks in '85
as a treasonous supporter of Riel
by the Edmonton Home Guard.
And the City Fathers in 1953 wrote
their words on a plaque on a fieldstone cairn:

> *This part of the city (Garneau, River lot 7) was*
> *named after Laurent (Larry) Garneau, farmer,*
> *community organizer and musician, who acquired*
> *the property in 1874. His original home was on*
> *the lane at the rear of 11108 90th Ave. A maple*
> *tree planted by him still grows there.*

A short time later
an unknown driver turned
sharply onto 89th Avenue and crashed
his '49 Ford into Garneau's cairn,
cutting it in half

except it wasn't *his* '49 Ford,
it had been stolen
from a frat house party
in a place now known
as North Garneau.

not Larry or Lawrence
not John Walter
not English or the Hudson's Bay Company
not the South Edmonton Protestant School Board
not the Loyal Order of Orange #1654
not the 14-piece Strathcona brass and drum band
not the north side of the North Saskatchewan river
not the Edmonton Home Guard or the NWMP
not a squatter on a road allowance
not a claim jumper
not a vendor of buffalo bones
not white, Ontario, Presbyterian, Methodist
not the *South Edmonton News*
not the township survey system
not a candidate for district seat on N.W.T. Council
not the C. & E. Railroad
not Ojibwa, Sioux, Cree or Blackfoot
not a halfbreed rebel
not a spy for Riel

(after an editorial by Frank Oliver, *Edmonton Bulletin*,
November 5, 1881)

Seeding general by next week.
Wild ducks lighting on chimney tops.
Ice on the river breaking in front of town.
Flocks of ducks and geese seen flying over town.
A greater acreage of wheat will be sown this
   season than last.
Prairie fires raging have destroyed a great deal
   of willow and brush.
Roads from Red Deer south wet on account of
   the melting of a recent snow.
Cow belonging to McKernan of the south side
   gave birth to two fine heifer calves on
   Tuesday, cow and calves doing fine.

The people have taken up unsurveyed land,
have built on it and made their homes there,
have supplied the necessities of life to Government survey
   parties and treaty Indians,
have shown by practical text the capabilities of this country,
have pioneered the land for the thousands that will people
   it in the near future,
have fuelled the joint pursuit of the CPR Syndicate and
   the government with the products of their toil,
they have done all that and now,
in the innocence of their hearts,
they imagine that the land is theirs.

They think that when the Government surveys are made,
they will receive the title.
Whether they will or not
remains to be seen.

Statutory Declaration

born Pentangueshene, Michigan,

age 43

married, three children

came to Manitoba from Michigan 1861, to Edmonton 1875

occupation: trader, cooper, farmer, herdsman for the H.B.C.

first settled on homestead claim in 1876, lived continually
on claim since then, done some freighting for Indian Dept.

20' x 16' log house, thatched roof, worth $150

25–30 acres broken and cropped, 6 acres broken per year

byre and stable $100, fencing $200

7 horses, including colts, 3 cows, 5 head of yearlings

signed,

Laurent Garneau
July 22, 1884

A Mare, *Edmonton Bulletin*, July 5, 1885

A mare belonging to L. Garneau
committed suicide on Wednesday last.
She had been suffering from the epizootic
for some time, and on this occasion
walked deliberately into the river,
which is very swift and deep,
and was carried away
without making the least effort
to save herself.

Her colt followed,
but as it had no suicidal intention
soon struck for shore
and got out safely.

Northern Alberta Threshing Company claims Garneau executed a promissory note for $80.00 but did not pay.

Garneau says there was a later note.

Garneau claims that George Beeler owes him $40.00 for 65 acres of cutting and binding of crop, $5.00 for the use of 3 cows, and $.75 for the use of 1 spade for atotal of $45.75.

Beeler says he paid him $13.00 and only owes $32.75.

Garneau as Chairman of the South Edmonton Roman Catholic Separate School Board signs a contract with Elizabeth O'Higgins, $500.00 for the January to June school term.

O'Higgins says the Board still owes her $91.00

Hudson's Bay Company says Garneau owes $33.40 for goods, wares, and
merchandise.

Settled out of court.

J.M. Bannerman claims Garneau and five others did remove and destroy a shanty in the course of construction, did lift it from the ground with their hands, it being a small shanty 1/4 the size of this courtroom, place under the building a pair of bobsleighs, fasten the shanty with a rope or chain, attach a team of horses, haul it about a 1/4 mile,hurl it over the high bank overlooking the river, with the resultto the shanty of total destruction, $825.00.

Not guilty.

Spring.
Snow gone.
Weather fine.
Roads muddy.
Trees budding.
Creeks lowering.
Cattle feeding out.
Hay enough, but scarce.
Mail a week behind time.
Stock generally in fair condition.
Police pay three months in arrears.
Gardening commenced on Saturday.
McCauley's pig fell down the stable well,
    was fished out none the worse.
Last day of issue of rations to the destitute
    halfbreeds at Edmonton and St Albert.

THE DANGER OF LETTERS

1

May, 1885, a halfbreed from Battle River
is arrested on suspicion of spying for Riel.
Upon hearing he might be shot
he implicates Laurent Garneau.

2

Riel had taught Garneau the power to write
or be written, to claim
who you are, where you stand.

From exile Riel's letters
arrived like the fall of leaves
on the house of his old friend Garneau.
Suncook, New Hampshire; Worcester, Mass.;
  Carroll, Montana.
Albany, Washington, New York, Québec. Riel
wrote every day
his unusual flights of words.

3

The Edmonton Home Guard crosses Walter's ferry,
climbs the south bank to get Garneau.
Seeing them approach,
Eleanor runs inside,
gathers the bundles of letters from Riel,
throws them into her washing
and scrubs the evidence to bits.

TO THE EDITOR OF THE *EDMONTON BULLETIN*, JULY 1, 1882

Sir,

A letter written from Edmonton which I have seen lately in The Toronto Daily Globe wherein Laurent Garneau is stigmatized as a Red River rebel is both false and cowardly and I consider the writer no better than an assassin that will stab a man in the back without giving him a chance to defend himself. This reply I think is as much as the coward and sneak is entitled to.

L. Garneau

P.S. Please Mr. Coward next time you write to the Toronto Daily Globe state your name and address that the rustics of Edmonton may know what kind of snake in the grass you are.

L.G.

NOTES OF WARS AND RUMOURS, *EDMONTON BULLETIN*, SPRING 1885

1

Saddle Lake: plunder and burn.	Lac Ste. Anne: plunder and talk like Bonaparte.

Fort Edmonton

Battleford: slaughter.	Battle River plunder and blood

So the circle
draws around us.

When the Indians will rise
is only a matter of days
with what result in loss
of property and life
may be imagined.

2

The halfbreeds in Edmonton organize
secret meetings to plan
action of some kind.

Trouble is expected at once.

3

Fort Edmonton is a fort no longer except in name? Five general stores stand utterly exposed, and a large population of men, women and children live distant from the fort. Our businesses collapse but for the great demand for buckshot just now. The settlement at large has lived on ragged edge for days.

Let us order night patrols near the fort. Women and children from the south side must be brought in at once. The south wall is to be strengthened, the cannon tested, the bell to be tolled in case of attack. Issue arms to the families at the houses of Walter and McKernan. See that the grade on the south side of the river opposite the fort is put in a state of repair to facilitate passage of troops and supplies.

And let us arm the Edmonton Home Guard.

Cattle fat.
Hop vines loaded.
Nights getting cool.
Cranberries reddening.
Nearly all the rafts are down.
Shower of rain Thursday night.
Butter still plentiful. Eggs scarce.
Mosquitoes and flies less troublesome.
Roman Catholic chapel built on Garneau's property,
    26' x 30', 12' walls, finished inside and out.

first steamship into Edmonton, the *Northcote* 1874,
the very boat that eleven years later during its attack
on Batoche was decapitated by the cable of Gabriel
Dumont's ferry

first maple seedling, brought from Manitoba by
Garneau, planted at his homestead, growing there still

first cable ferry west of Winnipeg, the *Belle of
Edmonton*, flat and open, 33' long, room for six loaded
carts with animals

first land survey of river lots around Fort Edmonton,
10 to 20 chains river frontage, a mile deep, Surveyor
M. Deane, Department of the Interior

first Roman Catholic Church on the south side,
Ste. Antoine, same name as the mission at Batoche

first locomotive into Strathcona, the northern-most
railroad terminal on the continent

first train wreck, eight cars derailed and a bridge
destroyed, ten miles south of Strathcona, many
photographs taken

first hockey game against the Edmonton Thistles,
December '95, the south side lads, numbers on their
arms, attacking with plentiful vigour but failing to
provide adequate defence of their own goal,
goalkeeper Timmons' robust presence all for nought

first steam-operated steel rollers in any western
Canadian mill,

first paddock built to display a moose in a zoo

Plowing.
Damp weather.
Upper ferry running.
Slight snow fall Saturday night.
Ground entirely clear of snow on Thursday.
J. Kelly's raft of lumber come to grief up the river.
Joseph Macdonald, south side freighter, is seriously ill.
Ice running, upper ferry can't be used, but river forded.
Indians camping around town ordered to their reserves
     by police.

Garneau plays a Shadow-Caster
fiddle brought from Winnipeg
on the railroad
to the new town.

In the brick building that W.E. Ross
built near the station in '94, Garneau
'the best fiddler in the district' plays
jigs and reels until sun-up many times—
the fiddle-glory of the *Bois-brûlés*—
and the settlers, Orangemen, most of them, dance
and shake their boom-town facades.

A few years later, the Orangemen
in their 'Glorious 12th' parade
bigger than Dominion Day
march west on Whyte Avenue,
bitter in their hatred of halfbreeds
(since Riel executed an Orangeman
twenty-five years before), they march
toward the far edge of town.

Garneau sits outdoors
in a fragment of breeze and plays
to the uncertain future
a Manitoba reel.

∾ Epilogue: Laurent and Eleanor at Niagara Falls

The year the Great Blondin crossed
Niagara on a tightrope, Laurent Garneau hid
from a Sioux war party, was found
by buffalo hunters nearly starved to death
and taken to Fort Garry.

By the time Guillermo Farini duplicated
all of Blondin's feats and added
a 200' descent from his tightrope
to the *Maid of the Mist*, Garneau
met Louis Riel and a Scottish woman,
Eleanor Thomas, whom he married.

Marie Spelterina crossed the gorge with baskets
on her feet the year the Métis
dispersed from Manitoba, Laurent and Eleanor
to the far north-west, 1874,
to River Lot Seven, south
of the North Saskatchewan River.

By 1901 when Annie Taylor plunged
over Horseshoe Falls in a barrel, Garneau
had already sold dozens of pieces
of his south Edmonton land.

And the patriarch of 'Garneau Estates'
in west Strathcona and 'Garneau Village'
in St. Paul—father of ten, merchant,
herdsman, freighter, activist, Métis patriot—
travelled by Great Western rail
with his bride of nearly fifty years
to Niagara Falls to sit
for a photograph near the gorge.

Everything was behind him now—
his survival, his fight for land. He'd outlived
the buffalo, Riel, two children, the spread
of a Protestant town.

And everything was ahead of him—
he'd made sure to tell
his stories, write his letters and leave
his name.

A formal portrait of the Garneaus. Laurent was 'the best fiddler in the district.' (EA-58-3)

JANNE SWITZER

EDMONTON'S FORGOTTEN MAN
—ALEXANDER TAYLOR

Alexander Taylor. (PAA B.3890)

*I*f Donald Ross became 'Mr Old-Timer,' Alexander Taylor, according to Janne Switzer, has never received the public recognition he deserves. Settling in Edmonton roughly a decade after Ross, Newton, and Garneau, Taylor was another individual who participated actively in all facets of Edmonton life. He was, among other things, an avid Presbyterian churchman, sportsman, supporter of education, meteorologist, and gardener. But undoubtedly his greatest contribution to the city came in the field of communications. Taylor was responsible for the first telegraph and first telephone service in Edmonton and instrumental in the founding of the first newspaper, the Edmonton Bulletin. He also brought

neighbouring St Albert and Fort Saskatchewan into a new communications network centred on Edmonton, in which modern technology supplemented existing trails and water routes. Taylor's fascination with technology and its potential also led him to experiment with linkages to places as far away as Battleford and Winnipeg, cutting into Edmonton's physical isolation and underlining its position as part of an interconnected system of urban communities. Alexander Taylor made it possible for Edmontonians to play checkers with Winnipegers.

Janne Switzer is the museologist at Fort Edmonton Park.

Edmonton has lost one of its most prominent citizens, one of the actual founders of the city proper and one who has been identified with practically every movement, from its days of villagedom down to within a few years ago, making for its advancement and welfare. He was a citizen in the best sense of the word.[1]

Mr. Taylor's wisdom and influence assisted in the up-building of practically every organization of this city, and his council has always been eagerly sought and considered valuable in the affairs of any of the institutions here.[2]

PERHAPS THESE WORDS, WRITTEN AT THE TIME OF Alexander Taylor's death in 1916, seem exaggerated, out of respect for a well-liked and highly regarded old-timer. Those who knew him, however, have since echoed those sentiments, painting a picture of a modest and private man who never sought personal recognition and who never received the credit he deserved for his role in Edmonton's development.[3] Taylor's daughter-in-law called him one of the finest men she ever knew: generous, selfless, brave, sentimental, intelligent, and uncomplaining despite the paralysis that inflicted him in later life.[4] Yet he could also be surly if challenged, and he resented interference in his affairs, telling his family that his work was 'none of their business.'[5] Today, Alexander Taylor is remembered for the inner-city school that bears his name; otherwise his activities have been largely forgotten. But in the 1880s and 1890s, this seemingly private gentleman occupied a prominent place in the Edmonton community, involved in everything from agricultural fairs and experimentation, communications development, and meteorology to sport and social clubs, the Presbyterian church, and education. So who was Alexander Taylor and what legacy did he leave his adopted city?

Born in the Ottawa area in 1854 to a railway engineer and his wife, Taylor came from a family of four boys and four girls. Sometimes the boys accompanied their father on his Ottawa-Prescott run and on one particular trip, left to their own devices, they passed the time by chiselling their initials into the carriage woodwork. Years later, two of Alex's brothers were taking the Calgary and Edmonton Railway north to visit him when one remarked that the coach seemed familiar. The two men looked at each other, then down, and there, perfectly preserved, were the initials they had mischievously carved so long ago.

Taylor himself arrived in the Edmonton area well before the above reminder of his youthful pranks.[6] He left Ottawa for the west in 1879 at age twenty-five, having been hired by Richard Fuller, a government telegraph contractor, to go to Hay Lakes to relieve the local operator. The previous year, eager to increase their links with the outside world, the residents of Edmonton had petitioned the federal government to relocate the telegraph office to their community, promising to clear a right of way, supply the necessary poles, and provide a building. Ottawa agreed, and no sooner had Taylor settled in Hay Lakes than he was obliged to move. By the end of January 1880 he had set up temporary quarters on John Walter's property; three months later he crossed the river to his permanent office inside Fort Edmonton.[7]

Edmonton was then a small hamlet of approximately 300 people grouped in several small settlements around the Hudson's Bay Company (HBC) fort. Homesteading, in strips back from the North Saskatchewan River, had supplanted the fur trade as the main economic activity. Many retired HBC employees, both European and Métis, had taken up homesteads and would later develop building industries along the river flats. Among a throng of newcomers, mostly single men in their twenties and thirties, were a few individuals who came to Edmonton via the gold fields farther west. Others, attracted by the anticipated railway boom and driven by an entrepreneurial spirit, came from Ontario and Manitoba as prospective businessmen. They soon established an embryonic commercial core east of the fort between present 95 and 101 streets. Physical isolation and a small population hindered specialization, so that in order to survive many of these men diversified into multifaceted enterprises—like Frank Oliver's cartage and dry goods supply or Matt McCauley's livery, cartage, and butcher shop. Despite dashed hopes of a railway in 1882, these entrepreneurs joined with a handful of professional men and civil servants to begin creating the social, educational, religious, and political foundations integral to a small western town. As the decade progressed, the young men who had initially lived above their businesses became more firmly established, married brides from 'back east,' and settled down to raise families in new residences apart from their places of work. Alexander Taylor typified this trend.

Between 1880 and 1882 Taylor seems to have been involved in various occupations, temporarily leaving his telegraph job to homestead and perhaps to work as a clerk on the steamboat, *Lily*.[8] During this period, he also helped found the settlement's first newspaper, the *Edmonton Bulletin*. While still telegraph operator, he had hired T. Walsh of Winnipeg as a weekly news correspondent to wire national and international news stories to Edmonton.

The first tamarack
telephone poles on
Jasper Avenue, 1890.
(PAA B.5537)

Taylor and John Alexander Mitchell copied the stories out in longhand to be distributed to local subscribers. Although there are conflicting accounts as to who first thought of a newspaper and who actually bought the first printing press, Taylor's initiative served as a catalyst for the *Bulletin*, with Taylor and Frank Oliver as partners. Legend claims that when the banner type for the first issue on 6 December 1880 was lost in transport, a resourceful Taylor carved the masthead with his pen knife on a piece of dry birch. This birch heading was used for several issues until Mr Laurie of the *Saskatchewan Herald* donated some large type.[9] Taylor remained Oliver's partner until summer 1881, when he apparently lost interest in the newspaper business and concentrated on his homestead at Fort Saskatchewan. For the next thirty years, however, he remained a figure of interest to the *Bulletin*, and its reports of his activities constitute one of the most valuable sources on Taylor's public life.

Taylor resumed his job as telegraph operator in April 1882. Over the next decade he became increasingly involved in the fledgling community and initiated several improvements in the communications sphere. In 1883, for example, he used his influence and contacts to secure telegraph lines for St Albert and Fort Saskatchewan, giving them more sophisticated links with the larger settlement at Edmonton. The following year, to provide a common and reliable time signal for the town, he acquired a cannon from the HBC and began firing it daily at noon.[10] Taylor's telegraph office also became something of a resource and social centre. He frequently displayed outstanding samples of local garden produce or spring wheat, and customers, friends, and others were welcome to drop by for a visit. On one occasion, an anticipated evening game of 'long-distance' checkers between J.A. McDougall of Edmonton and J.W. McLean of Qu'Appelle drew a large crowd of townspeople. The game failed to materialize, however, when the telegraph operator at Battleford cut in on the line, making the signal from Edmonton too faint. A week and a half later, technology triumphed with a successful game played between Miller of Edmonton and Dunlop of distant Winnipeg.[11] Taylor's office also served official functions: for example, it was used to count ballots during the 1885 Territorial election (Taylor was the returning officer) and occasionally became Justice Roleau's chambers.[12]

Taylor's fascination with technology led to perhaps his greatest contribution to communications in the Edmonton area. In 1884 he ordered two telephones from the Consolidated Telephone Construction and Maintenance Company of London, England, installing one in W. McKenny's new store in St Albert and the other in his telegraph office, now located just outside the fort on 98 Avenue and 106 Street. The first telephone call in Edmonton was made on 3 January 1885 at four o'clock in the afternoon. Acknowledging the solemnity of the occasion, Taylor shouted a severely formal greeting, structured like a telegraph message: 'Edmonton 3 of January 1885. The Reverend Father Leduc of St. Albert—We wish you all a very Happy New Year, Alex Taylor.'[13] Taylor continued to experiment with the telephone and on 1 November 1887 succeeded in talking to the telegraph operator at Battleford, three hundred miles away. Shortly thereafter his office became a concert hall as he and his cronies played music through the telephone hooked up to the telegraph line to Battleford.[14] Taylor's telegraph office served as the telephone central for Edmonton from 1884 to 1891. By 1887 an increasing number of Edmontonians were requesting telephones and Taylor soon turned the demand into a business opportunity. He ordered telephones from the Bell Telephone Company in Montreal and devised a subscription system to rent them out for an annual fee while his company maintained ownership rights.[15] The telephone was a novelty whose mysteries neither Edmontonians nor the surrounding population understood, giving the initiated a powerful tool with which to play pranks on the unsuspecting. The unfortunate target of one such prank was an important HBC Native customer who out-stayed and out-smoked his welcome after trading in the fort; he received the shock of his life when he was called to the telephone and Taylor had someone deliver a message in Cree, 'This is God, get the heck away from there now!'[16]

Whether out of necessity or ambition, Taylor was a versatile man and seldom devoted himself to only his telegraph and telephone service. From 1886 until his death he served as Deputy Clerk of the Court, Edmonton division, and later the Supreme Court; the court sat infrequently enough that his duties (which included processing marriage licenses) did not interfere with his other activities.[17] More time consuming was Taylor's meteorological work. From the beginning, the job of meteorologist was tied to that of telegraph operator. George Slack Wood, Taylor's replacement as telegraph operator in 1881, began reporting the weekly weather to the *Edmonton Bulletin* and Taylor continued the practice in a regular 'Meteorological' column when he returned in 1882. Affectionately referred to by the newspaper as 'the gentlemanly meteorological observer' and the 'lightning manipulator,' he provided data on minimum and maximum temperatures, wind velocities, precipitation, and barometric conditions. Taylor attached his weather instruments to the roof-tops of his various telegraph offices, first at John Walter's, then at the fort, then in one of Dr Wilson's buildings outside the fort, and finally in his home.[18] Initially, Taylor had to climb up a series of ladders to read the instruments indicating the speed and direction of the wind, but by 1887, according to the *Edmonton Bulletin*, he had installed 'a long shaft anemometer and wind millvane combined' which allowed readings to be 'taken from two dial plates fixed on the wall just over the desk.'[19]

Taylor's business portfolio acquired another new dimension in December 1891 when the Edmonton

The Edmonton telephone switchboard, 1896, located in the Post Office Block, before being moved to Gariepy Block. The structure on top holds the insulators which connected each line to the switchboard. (PAA B.1523)

Electric Light Company began operation with 700 lamps. Taylor was a founding member and sat on the board until the town took over the company in 1900; in 1893 the *Edmonton Bulletin* described him as manager.[20] His position certainly gave him an excellent opportunity to exercise his knowledge of electrical engineering, and, for the most part, he proved a valuable influence in the company. It was his eye to improvements for the future that led to bringing in Earl's Air and Steam Injector to save on the expense of burning solid coal.[21] Attached to the furnace of the engine running the generator, this apparatus took coal slack that was then converted into fuel for the furnace.

Taylor resigned as telegraph operator and meteorologist in 1893, although he remained Deputy Clerk of the (by then) Supreme Court and became the town's postmaster. Within a year he had instituted a Post Office Savings Bank and moved the post office itself to a new block housing the telephone switchboard and Electric Light Company offices. He was postmaster until 1906. In 1893 he had incorporated the Edmonton District Telephone Company (EDTC) and arranged a ten-year franchise agreement with Town Council. As Edmonton grew, so did the telephone system. It reached St Albert in 1901, to bring the total number of telephones in the area to 150, and by 1904 included Fort Saskatchewan. In 1904, however, the EDTC franchise expired, and, with opposition from Bell Telephone Company making it difficult for the EDTC to implement improvements, Taylor and his shareholders decided to sell. The Edmonton Board of Trade recommended that the newly incorporated City of Edmonton buy the EDTC and the voting public supported the move. Taylor asked $25,000 but accepted Mayor William Short's counter offer of $17,000 rather than see his company go to the rival Bell Telephone Company, which had entered the only other bid, for $12,500. As the EDTC's equipment was by then mostly outdated and often second hand, Taylor really had few hopes of realizing a higher price.[22]

One final economic activity, again illustrating the diverse nature of Taylor's talents, merits mention. Since his arrival in Edmonton, Taylor had sustained an avid interest in plants and animals suitable for the region, and he soon earned a reputation as an innovative agriculturalist and horticulturist. His Fort Saskatchewan farm was only one of several he owned over the years, arranging to have his crops put in on shares. One hired man kept his own stock with Taylor's, and whenever an animal died, strangely enough, it always seemed to belong to an unquestioning Taylor.[23] Taylor's kind and generous nature—and ability to be had—also came to light over a real estate deal in North Edmonton. Some time before 1910, unaware that Swifts was looking to buy land in the area for a meat packing plant, he and his mother bought a farm from an old man anxious for a quick sale. Soon, however, a prominent lawyer came to say that the man was sorry he had sold out and wanted his land back. A sympathetic Taylor returned the property for the price he had paid. When the dust settled, the lawyer and his sister emerged as the owners of the farm and ultimately sold it to Swifts for a tidy profit. Thereafter, the lawyer was widely known as 'Crooked Bill.'[24]

The *Edmonton Bulletin* described Taylor as 'one of the most practical farmers in Western Canada' whose farm was a fine example of mixed farming methods. The article went on to say that Taylor's pioneering contribution to the cattle industry in the Edmonton area 'before the rush of immigration and the coming of the packing houses and government aid to agriculture cannot be measured in mere dollars and cents. . . . It is doubtful if there is a better flock of Oxfords in the West than these on the Taylor Stock and Dairy farm.'[25] They were so fine, in fact, that Superintendent Craig bought a few for foundation stock at the government's Vermilion demonstration farm. Taylor also experimented in grains, shrubs, and flowers. His garden was famous for its variety, and he pioneered the growing of such plants as dahlias, sweetpeas, and white currant bushes in the area. His garden also contained flowers ranging from mignonette, candytuft, and pansies to lilac bushes, lupin, carnations, marigolds, and wild chrysanthemums.[26] His lovely yard was popular for social gatherings, and Christina

Taylor played an active role on numerous community organizations, including the public school board and the Presbyterian church, pictured here. (PAA B.454)

McQueen McKnight, who lived at the manse across the street as a child, later remembered it as a scene of lively parties, often complete with Japanese lanterns.[27]

In addition to his work, Taylor also played an active role in the development of Edmonton social and community life. He became a director of the Agricultural Society in 1882 and sat on the committee investigating the possibility of acquiring a permanent site for the annual exhibition. In 1885, responding to the fear of widespread unrest and rebellion, Taylor joined the Edmonton Volunteer Company and was elected corporal. He belonged to the fledgling Literary Club and in 1886 was elected president (a decade later he would become vice president of the new public library). Taylor served as secretary of the farewell committee for HBC Chief Factor Richard Hardisty, in 1883. He was prominent in the Presbyterian church, holding numerous executive offices in addition to lending his talents for the Sunday School entertainment (on one occasion he gave a magic lantern show).[28] He helped draft the proposal for the establishment of the Edmonton Cemetery Company as a joint stock company and in 1889 became its auditor. That same year he became a founding member of the Edmonton Board of Trade and the following year was elected treasurer. He also served as secretary treasurer of the Edmonton Building and Investment Company, which financed the town's first curling rink.

Not long after the Riel Rebellion had been put down, Taylor's bachelor days ended. On 29 July 1885 he married Harriet Thomasina March, the daughter of Archdeacon Marsh of London, Ontario, who had arrived in Edmonton in fall 1883. Following their marriage in All Saints' Anglican Church, the couple lived in J.A. McDougall's old house until they built their own home two years later across from the Presbyterian Church. Taylor's attachment to his young wife is reflected in the fact that two months after the wedding he added a branch telegraph office to their residence. Mrs Taylor's health and welfare remained a priority and in 1886 she went East to have her first child (Eleanor). Returning to relatives and guaranteed professional care for childbirth was a common practice, that is, when the family could afford it; although the following two children (James and Walker) were born in Edmonton. The first of many personal tragedies struck Taylor on 20 November 1891 when Harriet died; he never forgot his 'Tommie,' as he affectionately called his wife, and talked of her often in subsequent years. Harriet's maiden sister, Eleanor, soon moved to Edmonton to manage the household and look after the three small children, the youngest only a year and a half old. Two years later, while attending the Canadian Electrical Association convention, Taylor and Eleanor slipped away to London 'to tie the knot'; apparently the idea was hers. Within a year of his second marriage, Taylor began laying a stone foundation for a new house on 104 Street.[29]

The second Mrs Taylor was well liked, and, like her husband, played an active role in the community. She became first president of the Edmonton branch of the National Council of Women in 1895 and was known as a gracious hostess who could throw a party for forty guests without so much as 'the bat of an eye.'[30] Towards the end of 1898, however, Eleanor died suddenly of illness, leaving Taylor once again to raise his three children. His widowed mother—a formidable woman who kept her grandchildren strictly in line—soon arrived to take over the household

Taylor with friends (left-Tom Stevens, right-Dr H.C. Wilson) on front porch, circa 1905. Taylor wore the cape to disguise his paralysis. (PAA 70.218/40)

duties. Dressed in a widow's cap and veil, she could often be seen tending her lilacs or roses in the garden.[31]

Another tragedy beset the family in 1899 when both of Taylor's arms became paralyzed. In the years that followed, he consulted doctors across the country and was finally diagnosed at the Mayo Clinic as suffering from a slipped disc, but medical technology was not yet sufficiently advanced for corrective surgery. Inevitably, illness forced Taylor to curtail some activities, particularly the sports—golf, cricket, curling, bicycling, and rifle shooting—he had both enjoyed and played proficiently. But by all accounts, he adapted to the new situation and cheerfully carried on as best he could. Tony Cashman has referred to a treadle contraption that Taylor rigged in his office to allow him to answer the telephone. When a call came through, he would step on the treadle and a system of levers lifted the receiver to his ear. Taylor also had a custom stamp made so that when his signature was required, he could make his imprint.[32] Illness did not stop Taylor from participating in his clubs—the Edmonton Club (he was one of the founding members and served as president in 1902), the Saskatchewan Masonic Lodge (of which he was also a charter member), St Andrew's Society, and the Northern Alberta Old-Timers' Association. In addition, just prior to his paralysis he was elected chairman of the public school board; he held this position continuously for ten years until 1909, a testament to the esteem in which his fellow trustees, impressed by his earnestness and impartiality, held him. In 1907 the Alex Taylor School was named after him, giving Taylor the distinction of being the first trustee to be so honoured while still an elected official.[33]

Paralysis made it difficult for Taylor to put his arms into the sleeves of his overcoat. His solution was to adopt a black cape that not only kept him warm and concealed his limp arms but also came to symbolize his courage and fortitude. Sam Dickenson, a local lawyer, always said that it was an honour to put Taylor's cape on for him.[34] Although Taylor relied on others to dress and feed him, he still walked twice a week to the bathing facilities behind a local barbershop, to be effortlessly lifted in and out of the water by the Black attendant. Perhaps one of the most amusing stories of Taylor's resilience, ingenuity, and sense of humour is told by Christina McQueen McKnight. One day her mother went to answer the doorbell to discover Taylor standing there alone. When she incredulously asked how he rang the bell, he replied that he had used his nose.[35]

Alexander Taylor died of pleurisy in his home at the age of sixty-two on 12 February 1916. Although it is believed he had accumulated a small fortune in his time, he did not die a wealthy man, and, ironically for one who had held so many offices as treasurer, his business affairs were found to be in a mess. Perhaps his paralysis caused him to neglect to keep records and perhaps his pride and love of privacy kept him from accepting help. Harry Hyndman, Taylor's secretary for years after he became disabled, had offered to look after his books for nothing but Taylor refused, saying he could do it himself.[36] Alexander Taylor has often been called 'Edmonton's forgotten man,' and indeed he figures rarely among the politicians and wealthy businessmen heralded as pioneer leaders of the city. But many less celebrated individuals also played vital roles in Edmonton's development and Taylor should be numbered among them as a model citizen who did much for his community. ❧

WILLIAM C. WONDERS

EDMONTON IN THE KLONDIKE
GOLD RUSH

Ready for the Klondike. T. Denhardt, pictured here
1898, captures the romantic ideal of the rush for gold.
(PAA B.5348)

*T*he allure of the North has been part of Edmonton's makeup for more than a century.

From the time the CPR was routed through Calgary, Edmonton boosters, like Frank Oliver of the Edmonton Bulletin, looked to the North as a resource hinterland. Edmonton would be the conduit through which supplies would flow to—and resources would be exported from—the North. Thanks to the fur trade, the town already had trade contacts and established trade routes to the North. But for the dream of the boosters to come true, improved water and land routes—ones less subject to seasonal changes—were needed. In a word, rail connections were imperative. Although a CPR branch line did reach Strathcona in 1891, Edmonton remained isolated—and Edmonton's boosters frustrated—until the Low Level Bridge was completed in 1902.

In 1897 the Klondike Gold Rush offered Edmonton an important new opportunity to assert to the world the town's claim as supply centre to the North. Local businessmen wanted the large financial rewards of the outfitting and transportation business. The Klondike was about to enter into Edmonton mythology.

William C. Wonders brings to this chapter a lifetime interest in frontier settlement in northern regions—including those in Canada, Scotland, and Scandinavia. He first came to the University of Alberta in 1953, where he developed Geography into a separate department and served as founding chairman of the Boreal Institute for Northern Studies. Now retired to Victoria, he continues to study, write, and publish articles and books about the North.

GOLD DISCOVERIES HAVE PLAYED A PROMINENT part in Edmonton's two hundred year history. American prospectors from the Midwest, on their way to the Fraser River gold rush in the late 1850s, first recorded gold in the North Saskatchewan River gravels.[1] That same gold persuaded some 1862 Overlanders to remain at Edmonton instead of continuing to the Cariboo. Discovery of gold, silver, and copper in the West Kootenay and Border country of British Columbia in the early 1890s and the development of mining communities there expanded the market for the growing agricultural output of the Edmonton area. Meanwhile, gold discoveries in the Northwest, in the Stikine, Omineca, and Cassiar districts, culminated in the Klondike Gold Rush, with dramatic impact upon Edmonton. In the twentieth century, gold discoveries and development along the western margins of the Canadian Shield to the north brought economic benefit to Edmonton.

Of these, the Klondike Gold Rush proved the most memorable. Despite the short time span, it had great importance for a young frontier community as it changed from a fur trade centre to a service centre aspiring to meet the needs of an expanding geographic area. Edmonton House had been a major centre of the Hudson's Bay Company (HBC) in the fur era, but it was the Klondike Gold Rush that first brought Edmonton to the attention of most Canadians and Americans as a potential jumping-off point for the gold of the Yukon. Those who actually assembled here for 'the great adventure' included some of the most colourful and bizarre individuals to participate in the Rush (tales of their adventures and tribulations continue to fascinate readers to the present day[2]). They relied on Edmonton as a supply centre for their trek to the Klondike.

In the transcontinental fur trade system developed by Sir George Simpson, Edmonton's orientation was dominantly east-west. Having personally experienced the difficulties of the Beaver River and Portage La Biche route to the Athabasca River in 1824, he accepted Chief Factor John Rowand's plan of replacing it with an 80-mile horse trail northwest from Edmonton House to Fort Assiniboine on the Athabasca River.[3] The fur trade posts of the far Northwest were then served primarily from Fort Chipewyan, not from Edmonton House, by way of the Methye Portage.

The pack-road to Fort Assiniboine was often so plagued by mud and dangerous river crossings that freighters refused to travel at time.. Accordingly, in 1874 Chief Factor Richard Hardisty at Edmonton initiated a preliminary survey of the 100-mile route northwards to the 'elbow' of the Athabasca River. Hardisty won over Company officials to the project and in 1876 the Athabasca Landing Trail was completed, displacing the Fort Assiniboine Trail as the main route to the upper Athabasca River and to the Peace Country.[4] (The latter district was reached by a cart trail from the west end of Lesser Slave Lake.) After the Canadian Pacific Railway (CPR) reached Calgary, HBC shipments through Edmonton and along the Trail increasingly replaced those over the Methye Portage route. Until completion of the Calgary and Edmonton Railway in 1891, these were hauled from Calgary to Edmonton and then forwarded to Athabasca for distribution north, giving rise to 'hopes for a dazzling metropolitan future for Edmonton, based on its northern hinterland . . .'[5] The Klondike Gold Rush would provide local optimists with an opportunity to convert such hopes into exhilarating reality.

In 1897 Edmonton was a town of about 1,500 population, compared with Calgary's 5,000. According to the *Edmonton Bulletin*, the previous decade had been one of 'disappointment and stagnation' for Edmonton.[6] Nevertheless, a group of capable and visionary businessmen worked vigorously to promote the community, in 1889 establishing the first board of trade west of Winnipeg and in 1892 successfully bringing about incorporation of Edmonton, with a population of about 700, as a town.[7] The Calgary and Edmonton Railway had stopped on the south side of the North Saskatchewan valley, giving rise to 'South Edmonton,' a separate new community of 500 or 600 people by 1897. Still, the greater accessibility of Edmonton by railway was a significant advantage for gold seekers on their way to the Klondike by what came to be known as the Edmonton Route. The town had problems from its earlier expectations of boom conditions: in early 1896 some 900 town lots were put up for sale for unpaid back taxes.[8] Overvaluation of town properties resulted in such high assessments later that year that the town council was inundated by complaints. A special meeting in October forced the resignation of the mayor, Dr H.C. Wilson, and led to an overall 20 per cent reduction of the entire assessment of the town.[9] Little wonder that the potential economic benefit to be derived from the Klondike Rush was so attractive.

George Cormack made the original discovery of Klondike gold on 17 August 1896. In late 1896 William Ogilvie, in charge of the Canadian boundary survey, advised Ottawa of the significance of the new discoveries, but his findings were not made public until June 1897, when the Canadian government issued a pamphlet entitled 'Information Respecting the Yukon District.' Hard evidence of the rich new goldfield did not reach the outside world until July 1897, when the first successful miners disembarked from ships in San Francisco and in Seattle. The story was sensationalized by newspapers across the United States and by cable to most European cities.[10]

The earliest local news of the Klondike goldfield had appeared earlier, on 3 May 1897, in a brief report in the *Bulletin*, headed 'Trouble in the Yukon.' It noted that a large number of American 'toughs' from Circle City on the Alaskan side of the boundary had gone to the 'immensely rich placer mines now being opened' on the Klondike to try to take over many of the claims from Canadian miners whose rights were backed by the North West Mounted Police (NWMP). The report stated that the 'Klondyke river is on Canadian soil,' but in the previous sentence referred to the 'Klondyke river, Alaska'—doubtlessly reflecting the report's origin in Tacoma. Just three days after this first report, the *Bulletin* carried a very full account of the new goldfield as provided by a former Saskatchewan stage driver, recently come 'outside' from Fortymile, Yukon. Expanding on his account, the *Bulletin* suggested that 'the question of a commercial route to that region entirely through Canadian territory arises.' After pointing out that the HBC formerly serviced its post at Fort Selkirk by way of the Liard and Pelly river,s which could be reached overland from Peace River, it ventured 'that the Canadian government should take steps to open a wagon road to the Yukon along this route, to be followed ultimately by a railroad, should the development of the gold fields warrant.'[11] Edmonton had joined in the economic war for the lucrative Klondike trade!

Prospectors and fur traders had been active on the Yukon River and its tributaries since the 1870s, with the first significant goldfield at Fortymile on the Yukon immediately east of the 141st meridian International Boundary. To serve these activities, American steamboats, supplied mainly from Seattle, had operated on the river from its mouth at St Michael since 1869.[12] The shorter, but more arduous, access route from the coast through the Coast Mountains by way of the Chilkoot and White passes was long denied to the whites by the Chilkat Indians, jealous of their ancient trade route. In 1864 or 1865 they delivered a HBC employee from Fort Selkirk to a coastal ship by this route, but it was prospector George Holt, crossing to the interior over this route in 1878, who led the way for others to follow.[13] In 1896 it was reported that 900 miners had gone into the Yukon during the year though the route was not specified.[14]

By the final decade of the nineteenth century, several transcontinental railways provided direct access to such major United States west coast cities as San Francisco, Portland, Tacoma, Everett, and Seattle, each of which vied to attract the Klondike trade. In Canada, Vancouver offered similar access by way of the CPR, while Victoria stressed its advantages as the provincial capital with long experience in providing for northbound travellers. To gain the trade, each city and the railway serving it flooded the public, both national and international, with advertising pamphlets and special 'Klondike editions' of local newspapers trumpeting the advantages of their city. Seattle, for example, sent a copy of the 'Klondike edition' of the *Post-Intelligencer* to postmasters in the United States (70,000), to every public library (6,000), to every city mayor (4,000), to the Great Northern Railroad (10,000), and to the Northern Pacific Railroad (5,000).[15] Newspapers like

Figure 1, The Northwest in 1898. (GEOFFREY LESTER)

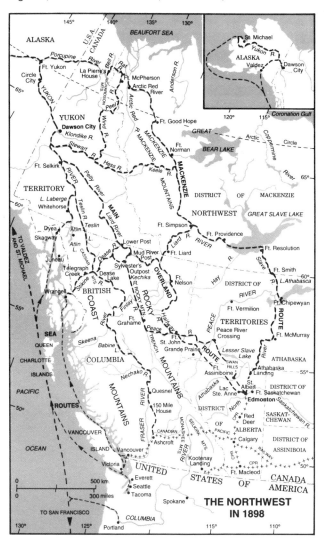

Curious Edmontonians gathered to watch prospectors readying for their trek to the Klondike, 1898.
(PAA B.5172)

the *Edmonton Bulletin* contributed much to the momentum of the Klondike Rush.[16]

Travel to the Klondike from these Pacific coast cities had the advantage that all or much of the distance could be traversed in relative ease by ship. A disadvantage for Canadian prospectors at least was that it required passage through American territory in Alaska and American customs duty on their outfits. The all-water route by ship to St Michael and then by sternwheeler up the Yukon (2,750 miles from Victoria to St Michael and 1,700 miles upriver to Dawson City) was time consuming (six weeks being average time) and expensive.[17] Most prospectors favoured the shorter, less expensive route from the head of the Lynn Canal in the Alaskan Panhandle at Skagway and at Dyea. The main difficulty on the 30- 40-mile passage to the headwaters of the Yukon River and a down-river float to Dawson City was the arduous climb to the 2,900-foot White Pass or to the more favoured 3,700-foot Chilkoot Pass through the Coast Mountains. It was 1,600 miles from Victoria to the Klondike by this route.

Two lines of approach lay mainly within British Columbia—the Stikine Route and the Ashcroft Route. The Stikine River had been an important route into the interior since fur trade days, when the HBC rented Wrangell (750 miles north of Victoria), at the river mouth in the Panhandle, from the Russians. It was the main route to gold discoveries on the Stikine in 1861 and in the Cassiar District in the 1870s.[18] Telegraph Creek, the head of navigation, lay 150 miles up the Stikine River and from there it was another 150 miles overland to the head of

Teslin Lake and then 600 miles downstream to the Klondike. An estimated 5,000 people landed at Wrangell in the winter and summer of 1898; about one-half got as far as Telegraph Creek, and possibly only 200 or 300 actually reached Dawson City.[19] Once the CPR was completed, Ashcroft in south-central British Columbia replaced Yale as the main inland supply point for the Cariboo. Like the Edmonton Trail, the Ashcroft Trail was an all-Canadian land route. It utilized the Cariboo Road north to 150-Mile House, continued along the Fraser River to Quesnel, and then followed, so far as possible, the track of the old Collins Overland Telegraph line, a total distance of about 650 miles. At Telegraph Creek it joined the overland, northwards continuation of the Stikine Route. The muskeg, large rivers, and timbered nature of the northern sections defeated most would-be prospectors. One who completed the trip reported that, of the more than 1,500 men and 3,000 horses that left Ashcroft, only six men and no horses reached the Klondike.[20]

By 1897 Edmonton already had well-established business ties with fur traders farther north. The HBC was still important, but an increasing number of free traders, many from Edmonton, were competing with the old company. Richard Secord, 'Edmonton's premier fur dealer,' had numerous fur posts and agents over a wide span of the North, from Peace River Crossing to Isle-à-la-Crosse and Athabasca Landing to Fort Smith.[21] In the winter of 1895 the *Bulletin* noted the presence in town of fur traders, from Slave Lake and Peace River, to conduct business.[22] Increasingly such men pushed still farther north down the

Athabasca-Mackenzie system. In the winter of 1895–6 Colin Fraser had his main trading post at Fort Chipewyan but also operated satellite posts at Fond-du-Lac at the east end of Lake Athabasca and at Little Red River up the Peace River. Alphonse Boileau was at Fort Smith, and Ed Nagle had a post at Fort Resolution on the south shore of Great Slave Lake. James Hislop was in his third year at his post some 16 miles north of the HBC post at Fort Rae, on the north arm of the same lake.[23] These traders commonly came south with dog teams in late winter to purchase goods for the following season in Edmonton, remaining there until they could return north when the rivers opened. In addition to the fur trade business, Edmonton supplied most of the needs of the missions that had been established along the waterways to the mouth of the Mackenzie River.

In November 1895 the reported value of freighting for the HBC from the South Edmonton railhead north to Athabasca Landing was 'many thousands of dollars every year.'[24] Freighting by horses and oxen, mainly to Athabasca Landing but also to Peace River and Fort St John, provided employment for many Edmontonians. In the previous decade the HBC had greatly improved its northern transportation facilities by placing three shallow-draft steamboats on the waterway north from Athabasca Landing to the mouth of the Mackenzie River.[25] Growing demands from non-Company individuals in the North were an increasing burden for the HBC, however, and clearly there was a need for change. Up to the mid 1890s the Company provided a northern mail service to its posts twice a year and also carried general non-Company mail. When the Company discontinued the latter service because of the increased volume—much of it for competitors—the *Bulletin* pressed for the government both to provide a weekly mail service to Athabasca Landing in summer and fortnightly in winter, with monthly service to Lesser Slave Lake and Fort Chipewyan, and to extend government telegraph lines to Athabasca Landing.[26] The government did assume responsibility for providing a northern mail service, but not adequately enough so far as Edmonton was concerned. The Town Council passed a resolution urging increased mail service owing to the 'growing importance of the trade of the Athabasca River and Mackenzie River Country.'[27] Another major concern of Edmonton was the 100-mile long Athabasca Landing Trail, constructed by the HBC in 1875 and improved at Company expense in 1885. Through heavy use it had deteriorated and was nearly impassable in rainy weather.[28]

The first woman, Mrs Garner, to leave from Edmonton for the Klondike, August 1897. (PAA B.5241)

That it was a privately owned road was seen as hampering its improvement in Edmonton, prompting the Town Council to add a clause to its motion calling on the Government 'to have the trail from the Sturgeon River to the Athabasca Landing surveyed and declared a public highway.'[29] This the young North-West Territories government did in 1898.[30]

Athabasca Landing had come into being in 1877 when the HBC had constructed a log storage building for goods waiting for transport by river scow. In spring, Métis labourers and boatmen were temporary residents, awaiting breakup of the ice. In 1894 the building was upgraded to a trading post with a permanent trader in residence. Several additional buildings, including a large freight warehouse, were later added. In 1887–8 the HBC built its 162-foot-long SS *Athabasca* here to serve its needs on the central Athabasca River between Mirror Landing and Pelican Portage. In order to protect its interests as newcomers were attracted by the growing business opportunities, the HBC purchased one square mile (640 acres) of land from the Dominion government in 1888 to create a Company Reserve. By 1896, on the eve of the Klondike Rush, Athabasca Landing had developed into a true community with four groups of permanent residents: Company employees, Anglican missionaries, policemen, and independent traders.[31]

Much of this fur trade infrastructure could be used by Klondike-bound prospectors. From Edmonton, there were two main routes to the Klondike. The more eastern route was largely all-water, while the more western involved both land and water travel. In addition, there were places where other rivers made it possible to cross from one route to the other.

The eastern, or Mackenzie Route (also known as the Water Route) from Edmonton to the Klondike was 2,600-2700 miles long, including 90–96 miles of the Athabasca Landing Trail at the start. Because of the low transportation costs once the waterway was reached, it also was known as the 'poor man's route.' Except for about 350 miles it was all downstream, utilizing the Athabasca, Slave, and Mackenzie rivers to the Peel River at the head of the Mackenzie Delta, the Bell and Porcupine rivers northwestwards to the Yukon River, and then a 300-mile upstream passage on the Klondike. HBC posts were dotted along the waterway from Athabasca Landing to Fort McPherson on Peel River. Portages were necessary around rapids on the middle Athabasca and Slave rivers and at the watershed between the Peel and Bell rivers. Three types of boats were used by Klondikers on the Mackenzie

route—the flat boat, the sturgeon head, and York boat. Many were constructed at Athabasca Landing.[32] Indians and Métis along the way usually were hired to assist in passing hazardous sections of the waterway. Depending partly on the type of boat used, the *Bulletin* reckoned that the Klondike could be reached by the Mackenzie Route in about two months—in the same season if a start was made between 20 May and 20 July.[33]

The western or Overland Route from Edmonton to the Klondike was only 1,400 miles long, including 400 miles of navigable water on the Pelly and Yukon rivers. Promoted as the All Canadian Route, it completely avoided passage through United States territory, unlike the west coast routes. As advocated by the *Bulletin* it trended northwest from Edmonton to Fort St John on the Peace River and then by way of the Liard and Pelly rivers to the Yukon at Fort Selkirk and on to the Klondike. A wagon and cart road existed from Edmonton over 70 miles by way of Lac la Nonne to the Athabasca River, but the former 100-mile pack trail beyond to the west end of Lesser Slave Lake had been abandoned when the HBC constructed the Athabasca Landing Trail. A 70-mile wagon road existed from Lesser Slave Lake to Peace River Crossing, with a 150-mile cart and pack trail continuing on to Fort St John. A shorter route to the latter point existed by way of Lac Ste Anne, Sturgeon Lake, Smoky River, and Grande Prairie, but it was mainly a pack trail, with only the first sector to Lac Ste Anne a wagon road.[34] Beyond Fort St John the *Bulletin*'s description was very general, but nevertheless confident that the terrain posed no serious obstruction to construction of a 'good pack trail if not a wagon road,' even where the Liard cut through the Rocky Mountains.[35] An alternative used by some parties was to cross the Rocky Mountains, either by the Peace River or over the Laurier Pass at the head of Halfway River, into the Rocky Mountain Trench and proceed northwards along it via Fort Grahame and Sylvester's Post to the upper Liard River. In addition to its relative shortness and location entirely within Canadian territory, the Overland Route offered a potential outlet for sale of cattle and horses. The *Bulletin* also pointed out that the route was 'within reaching distance' of the known goldfields of the Omineca and Cassiar districts of northern British Columbia and that the Peace, Liard, and Pelly rivers themselves were gold-bearing.[36]

In order to compete effectively with other centres, Edmonton had to make its existence, location, and advantages as a jumping-off point for the Klondike much better known to the world-at-large. At the same time, it had to press for improvements to its routes, particularly the

The Mackenzie or Water Route to the Klondike measured some 2,700 miles. This picture shows the Clarke party leaving Athabasca Landing, 1898. (PAA B.5200)

Overland Route. To these ends local businessmen and the Town Council subsidized special 'Klondike editions' of the *Bulletin*, explaining Edmonton's advantages for Klondike-bound prospectors, which were distributed widely to cities in Canada and the United States. In addition, the Town persistently lobbied territorial and federal governments for route improvements. Public meetings in August 1897 in St Albert and Edmonton urged the Dominion government to undertake improvements to the Overland Route.[37]

Although Edmonton boosters confidently promoted the Overland Route, they conceded that 'information as to the country (north of Peace River) not immediately along the banks of the rivers is very meagre and fragmentary.'[38] Accordingly, the Board of Trade hired P.D. Campbell and J.R. Brenton, both of whom had first-hand experience in the North, for a reconnaissance trip overland to Pelly River. Their trip was a failure as they had to return to Edmonton when they were unable to obtain necessary supplies at Peace River. Edmonton's political pressure for a road to the Yukon did lead to the Territorial government sending surveyor T.W. Chalmers to investigate the route for a road through the Swan Hills from Fort Assiniboine, which resulted in the project's being undertaken in the winter of 1897–8. The Dominion government sent Inspector J.D. Moodie with a NWMP party to Edmonton

at the beginning of September 1897 to explore an overland route to the Yukon.[39] His subsequent discouraging assessment of the route did not sit well with Edmontonians!

When Edmonton learned that the Dominion government was supporting a railway between Telegraph Creek and Teslin, the *Bulletin* opined that it would do little to reduce American dominance of the Klondike trade: 'The straight answer to the question: How will this railway advantage Canadian trade at the expense of that of the United States, is that it will not give it any advantage. . . . Geographical considerations make the United States master of the trade of the Yukon by any possible coast route.' It again stressed that 'the only route whereby Canada can absolutely control the Yukon trade is that by way of the Peace and Liard rivers, from the present terminus of the railway at Edmonton.'[40] Despite the disappointing result of Campbell and Brenton's trip, Edmonton finally persuaded Ottawa to provide one thousand dollars to underwrite the cost to the Town Council of a new survey by W.P. Taylor of Lac Ste Anne for a road route between Peace River and Pelly River. Blazing his trail as he travelled, Taylor set out from Edmonton in late February 1898 and reached Pelly River in May by way of Fort Nelson, returning by way of Fort St John (the better route). In a remarkable achievement, he had covered over 2,000 miles in 157 days, but, as James G. MacGregor has noted, 'his blazes upon trees did not necessarily mean that anyone following them was taking the best route.'[41] He also was unencumbered by the large loads of supplies and equipment carried by the Klondikers.

The sale of supplies and equipment and the promise of profits interested the businessmen of Edmonton. Each Klondiker needed to take supplies for a year and perhaps two, depending on the route. Using the daily allowance for a member of the NWMP as a guide, the *Bulletin* estimated that a year's supply of food, clothing, and basic equipment (tent, cooking utensils, carpenter's tools, shovels, picks, gold pans, medicine chest, rifles, and ammunition, etc.) for one man would weight from 1,500 to 2,000 pounds.[42] McDougall and Secord, the town's leading general merchants along with the HBC, set out a detailed list of essentials along with their costs, totalling $200, in a half-page advertisement in the newspaper.[43] Their outfitting business reportedly amounted to several hundreds of thousands of dollars a year.[44] The HBC put out an attractively printed folder, with a large map showing the location of their posts and routes to the Klondike and a list of outfitting needs for a year costing $190 to $220. Under a headline 'This Way to the Klondyke!,' the South Edmonton newspaper noted: 'Many Parties Outfitting

Here. Thousands of Dollars Being Spent in Edmonton for Supplies.'[45]

The influx of Klondikers created an unprecedented demand on the services of many Edmonton businesses besides the general merchants. Blacksmiths, saddlers, tent makers, meat packers, hardware merchants, druggists, and clothiers all enjoyed boom times. The much increased wheat harvest of the Edmonton area in the autumn of 1897 swamped the transport capabilities of the Calgary and Edmonton Railway but the Klondikers' needs for flour from local mills provided some solution at least.[46] New businesses came into existence, a tent factory and a new restaurant among others. Bossange's Bookstore not only offered Klondike literature for sale but also advertised a new popular song, 'The Spirit of the Klondyke,' and urged potential customers, 'Hear it. Buy it. Sing it. For it brightens all the journey to that far distant land.'[47] In light of their subsequent tribulations, one can imagine the reactions of most northbound travellers if one of their number had burst forth with this song! The Edmonton Methodist Church minister preached on 'The Manly Klondiker' by special request to a 'crowded audience of Klondykers and citizens' and the sermon was carried in the *Bulletin*.[48] The newspaper did not however, report on the Town Council's 29 December 1897 motion 'that the Clerk be instructed to inform the

The Overland Route was only 1,400 miles long, but the journey was arduous. Note the flags of Britain and the United States carried by this party. (PAA B.5236)

W.C.T.U. [Woman's Christian Temperence Union] that the Town has a By Law dealing with houses of ill fame, and that this Council recommend the careful attention of the Council of 1898 to the matter in question.'[49]

Long-time boat builder John Walter could scarcely keep up with the demand from those planning to use the Mackenzie Route, and numerous other Edmontonians, such as lumberman W.H. Clark and K.A. McLeod, also went into the business. Walter particularly favoured an adaptation of the traditional York boat as best suited overall for the varied water conditions on the Mackenzie Route. The boat was 25 feet long, 6 feet beam, 2 feet 9 inches deep, sharp at both ends, and rigged with mast and sail, two sets of sculls, and a sweep. It weighed 800 pounds, could carry over three tons, and cost $60.[50] Besides the boats constructed in Edmonton and then hauled north to Athabasca Landing, several other boat-building yards came into existence at the Landing itself, employing both locals and Edmonton residents. Local freighters on the Landing Trail were hard pressed to meet demands for their services.

Klondikers heading north on the Overland Trail required wagons, buckboards, and jumpers (low, short, strong sleighs). The City Carriage Works turned out 320 'Klondike Flat Sleighs' for use by Klondikers during the winter of 1897–8, and John Walter completed an equal number.[51] Thomas Bellamy advertised that he would have one carload of ox or pony carts available for use on the Klondike Trail before 1 March 1898.[52] Large numbers of horses were needed by these overland parties for saddle, draught, and pack purposes, providing a welcome market for local ranchers and farmers. The *Bulletin* placed the cost of a ten-horse pack outfit for one year's trip at $340 per man.[53] One large party alone bought 120 horses by the time it started off.[54] Still others bought dog teams for winter travel.

The Klondike was seen as an important market outlet for cattle from plains ranches and this was a major reason for Edmonton's incessant pressure for opening up an overland road or failing that, a cattle trail to the Yukon. Cattle were driven successfully to the Klondike, but all via North Pacific ports.[55] An overland drive from the Chilcotin in interior British Columbia had similar results to those from Edmonton.[56] At least three parties consisting of 4–6 men each, set out to drive cattle overland from Edmonton— G.W. Lang, of San Antonio, Texas, with 65 head of cattle purchased in southern Alberta and 40 horses; another American party, Geddis-Harris, with 50 cattle and 26 pack horses; and H.Y. Jones of Swift Current, Saskatchewan,

with 75 head of cattle from there.[57] A pioneer Peace River rancher, C. Bremner of Spirit River, also announced his intention of taking 100 head of cattle through to the Yukon in the spring of 1898.[58] None of the parties reached the Klondike, but skilful handling of the herds along the way, despite the ruggedness of conditions, resulted in most of the animals being taken safely through the mountains to Fort Graham. Lang and Jones then drove their herds north down the Kechika River to its junction with the Liard River at the Mud River Post where the animals were slaughtered and the meat sold to local miners in the 1898-9 winter. Geddis had bad luck with his herd at McDame Creek when winter storms and starvation killed all but 6 of his 46 cattle.[59] There was no report on the fate of the some 1,800 horses, most brought in over the Edmonton Trail, that were wintered the same year between McDame and Telegraph creeks.[60]

Much of the success or failure of overland parties depended on whether they secured the services of competent guides. They were particularly critical for the cattle herds as pasture was often in limited supply in the more heavily wooded sections. The favoured overnight stopping places soon became denuded of good pasture. Knowledgeable guides could provide alternative locations, reducing the suffering and death of animals as well as the hardships for prospectors and the time taken in the trip. Many experienced Edmonton 'frontiersmen' found a ready demand for their services, and the same was true in such nearby communities as St Albert and Lac Ste Anne.[61] Still other locals were taken on as cooks and boatmen by some outfits.

The influx of hopeful goldseekers in Edmonton swelled over the summer of 1897, reached its peak in late winter/ early spring of 1898, and then fell off rapidly by the following summer. In May 1898 a southbound freighter on the Athabasca Landing Trail met 129 teams northbound.[62] As soon as river ice permitted, boats and scows headed north from the Landing. An Edmonton river pilot estimated that, by 21 June, 130 boats had gone through the Grand Rapids.[63] Six hundred men had passed Fort Smith, northbound, before 24 June that year.[64]

Winter permitted overland transportation by sleigh and with a relatively mild winter that year, there was little seasonal slackening of the pace of activity. By early February 1898 nine parties had proceeded overland by sleigh to Peace River and twenty-seven others were preparing to do so.[65] In early March the *Bulletin* gave a vivid picture of the Rush's influence on Edmonton:

The rush over the snow to the Yukon by the Edmonton route is at its height. Parties are arriving by twenties and thirties on every train and hurrying to take advantage of the last snow which is gradually, but steadily disappearing. The main street is now in a state of semi-slush and the strings of loaded flat sleighs travel along the side in preference to the centre where the travelling is heavier . . .

So numerous are the pilgrims who are pouring in that it is practically impossible to keep track of the many different parties. Some immediately upon arrival go to the hotels, some remain for a few days at the south side, all available rooms and shanties are occupied by 'batchers', and the great majority leave the train and go immediately into camp. A walk through the bluffs in the vicinity of the HBC and McDougall and Secord's stores reveals the fact that literally 'the woods are full of them'. Around the bluffs are clustered tents and teepees while bare patches on the ground, from which the snow is thawed, show where some passing pilgrim had made his transient home. In the open all is activity and life. Loaded flat sleds are everywhere and the work of packing and collecting their outfits is being pushed by every party with all possible speed. The open space offered by the race track is utilized for breaking horses, both to ride and drive, and the scene it offers is not only lively, but amusing to the spectator.[66]

Another source of amusement for Edmonton residents was the preconceived notions many would-be Klondikers had of their needs. One person wrote to Edmonton asking if he could get through to the Yukon on his bicycle, and another wanted to know if there were good boarding houses on the way. Still another brought his own hay with him by rail, unaware that it could be easily purchased in the Edmonton area. The newcomers included many inventive individuals promoting companies that promised dramatic new methods of overland transportation to the Yukon. Particularly noteworthy was C.L. 'Barrel Smith' from Houston, Texas, whose early version of an all-terrain vehicle based on whisky barrel rollers disintegrated before he reached St Albert. An Iowa company wrote to the City Carriage Works to ask if it could supply sleds with axle and wheel attachments so the sleds could be changed into carts when the snow melted. A Chicago company constructed a steam sleigh in Edmon-ton to travel over snow and ice pulling four enclosed sleds, but after a formal send-off the vehicle gave up the ghost and the remains were sold to K.A. McLeod.[67] The mass of luxury supplies, including cases of champagne, gourmet foods, and dinner jackets, of the aristocratic British

Expedition, Col. O'Brien's party, was the subject of widespread local commentary and entertainment.[68]

Edmontonians themselves were not immune to 'Klondike fever.' The earliest report in the *Bulletin* was of J. Shand and M. Velgue who departed with N. Atkinson and P. de Wolf of Pine Lake on 9 June 1897 to Athabasca Landing on their way to the Liard River. The newspaper's summary of the parties that had left Edmonton for the Yukon to the end of August 1897 listed 102 individuals, of whom 39 were from Edmonton and vicinity, 27 from other parts of Canada, and 36 from the United States. Significantly, 77 of the total, including all but one Edmontonian, were using the water rather than the overland route.[69] By and large, however, Edmonton residents preferred to make their money from the sale of their goods and services to the Klondikers rather than joining in the rush for distant gold.

The *Bulletin* reported on the places of origin of many Klondikers passing through Edmonton, but not consistently and with no final summation. Surviving reports[70] tend to confirm MacGregor's estimates that 'over half came from the United States, mainly from the eastern half, with especially heavy contingents from Chicago, where some of that city's businessmen put on an extensive advertising campaign. Perhaps fifteen per cent of the total number of Klondikers were from the western states. Eastern Canada supplied about one-third of the total, and these were mainly from Ontario, with a heavy representation from Hamilton. Several parties came from Winnipeg and the prairies.'[71] The success of the northbound Klondikers from Edmonton depended upon many variables—the route chosen, the time of year the trip was undertaken, the appropriateness of their transportation equipment and supplies, the experience of the parties in northern travel or the reliability of their guides, the dedication of individuals to achievement of the goal, and just plain luck.

Prospectors travelling the Mackenzie Route benefitted from improvements on that route. The Athabasca Landing Trail was improved and an increased number of freighters used it. A weekly stage service operated between Edmonton and the Landing from 1 March 1898, increasing to twice a week by the tenth of May. Edmonton businessmen and politicians urged the federal government to improve navigation conditions at Grand Rapids on the Athabasca River. When the government refused, the Board of Trade launched a private subscription to cover the cost of removal of several boulders from the navigation channel by an Edmonton team. The project, though completed, was not entirely successful.[72]

Several navigation companies, usually organized by Americans, proposed steamboat transportation on the various waterways, and a few of these actually placed such boats in service. By the autumn of 1898 the *Alpha*, 7.50 tons (Alaska Navigation Company), and the *Daisy Bell*, 65 tons (Albertan Jim Wallwork), had joined the *Graham*, 359.48 tons (HBC), and the *St. Alponse*,24.94 tons (Roman Catholic Mission), on the Athabasca and Slave rivers. The HBC's steamer, *Athabasca*, which since 1888 had provided service on the Athabasca River above Grand Rapids unfortunately had been so damaged in 1897 that it was not worth repairing.[73] In autumn 1898 the Alaska Navigation Company's *Edmonton*, 50 tons, was in service on the Mackenzie River, along with the HBC's *Wrigley*, 130.19 tons, and the Roman Catholic Mission's *St Joseph*, 29.91 tons. On the Athabasca River, en route to join the Mackenzie boats were G.T. Leitch's *Sparrow*, 49.28 tons, and trader W. Connor's *Upas*, 16.71 tons. Besides these, the government steamboat inspector reported five other steamboats, ranging from 4 to 10 tons, owned by prospectors then on the Mackenzie River and bound for Peel River, and a sixth that already had passed up that river.[74]

Northbound trips on the water route often were delayed by ice. Though the more southern middle Athabasca River permitted a relatively early start, downstream progress was often delayed by ice jams and, particu-larly, the late ice breakup on Great Slave Lake. The Athabasca River rapids cost some lives as well as boats and cargoes when they were run by inexperienced crews. Low water conditions in the same river late in the season also caused problems. Even after Great Slave Lake cleared of ice, storms and high winds often delayed passage. While the York boats sailed on this large lake, most other boats were towed by the steamboats, at a charge of $10 to $40 depending on their size.[75]

Although the *Bulletin* reported that two months were needed to reach Dawson from Edmonton, again much depended on the variables. In 1895 an early 'tourist,' who simply wanted to experience the midnight sun, made the trip on his own by canoe from Athabasca Landing to Peel River in 64 days. After a 9-day stay, he returned to the Landing in 43 days, travelling part way by steamer on the return.[76] In 1898 the Lamoureaux party from Fort Saskatchewan reached Fort McPherson in a record 49 days from the Landing.[77]

If Klondikers did not leave the Landing until after the first of August, they invariably had to winter somewhere along the water route. Many did so at one of the trading posts, in comparative comfort. Others occupied primitive dug-outs on the river banks, perhaps trapping over the winter. Still others threw up simple shacks, clustering in temporary new 'settlements' that were abandoned the following spring—for example Little Chicago on the Mackenzie River, Destruction City near the junction of Rat River with Peel River, Shacktown at McDougall Pass, and Wind City on Wind River about 8 miles above its junction with Peel River.

Prospectors travelling the Overland Route undoubtedly faced the greatest difficulties, despite the *Bulletin's* best efforts to promote the route and the limited improvements that were effected in parts of it. Heavy forest, muskeg, and snag-strewn tangles of burned-over land made passage difficult. Mountainous terrain in the northwest added to these problems. Though the river network provided pass routes through the mountains, they proved to be not as easy a solution as suggested by the simple patterns shown on very general maps. It was one thing for an experienced frontiersman to cover such a route on his own, but very different for a party of 'greenhorns' burdened down with their necessary animals and supplies.

One of the most troublesome areas of the Overland Route occurred near the very beginning, in the Swan Hills. Notorious before the Chalmers road was opened, it continued to be the source of much complaint even afterwards. Frank Walker, of Fort Saskatchewan, succeeded in reaching Dawson City three months after setting out on the Overland Route from Edmonton on 8 March 1898. He recalled:

> One of the most heartbreaking hills which tried all the skill and ingenuity even of the old timers who were on the trail, was at the crossing of the north side of the Athabasca River, near old Fort Assiniboine. The hill is a very long one and a great deal of the difficulty was experienced by the tenderfeet in handling the horses up this grade. The hillside was littered with broken boxes, smashed sleighs and harness, and practically every tree on the lower side of the grade was blazed and the owners of the outfits gave vent to their feelings in epitaphs upon the trees . . . [Beyond], at the Swan Hills [the journey] became simply awful. Even the party that I was connected with, who . . . were accustomed to travelling in the western country, were simply appalled at the hills that they had to go up and down. I never could understand why the man who chose this route should ever pick such a terrible one.[78]

Similar tests of endurance awaited the overlanders as they continued northwards, though not all outfits found them equally discouraging. When Inspector Moodie of the NWMP condemned as impracticable the trail which he followed from Edmonton to Fort Graham and beyond, the *Bulletin* intimated that perhaps he did not really want to get through to the Pelly and that he was at fault for not following the recommended route farther east, through Fort Nelson and up the Liard River.[79] The latter route had significant tribulations of its own, of course, particularly in the 'Grand Canyon of the Liard.' The hardships and dangers of this 30- to 40-mile stretch of river above appropriately named 'Hell Gate,' had so discouraged the HBC that it had abandoned this supply route to its northwest trading posts.[80]

Like Klondikers on the Mackenzie Route, most overlanders had to winter along the way, often suffering the effects of scurvy. Little wonder that many gave up. Some preferred to try their luck in gold-bearing streams closer at hand, for example the upper Liard; some just wanted to return home and headed west to follow the Stikine Route to the coast; and some straggled back to Edmonton, where, nearly destitute, they appealed to the Town Council to help them secure rail transport home. The town clerk wrote to the traffic manager of the CPR in Winnipeg: 'Yet another case of Klondyke failure has turned up in the town and I am instructed to ask if you can see your way to grant the same rate you were good enough to give us in the previous cases, i.e. 1¢ per mile from here to Detroit. The man's name is M.E. Welch and Major Edmiston is satisfied the case is deserving.'[81]

MacGregor has estimated that the total number of Klondikers who passed through Edmonton was 1,560, of whom 775 followed the Overland route and 785 the Mackenzie Route, with a further 100 originating at Prince Albert and joining the latter route at Fort McMurray. Only 160 of the Overlanders reached the Yukon compared with 565 who followed the water route. Twice as many (580) of the former either turned back or remained in the country as compared with the latter (285), and probably 35 died on each of the routes.[82]

❧ The Klondike Gold Rush through Edmonton was a short-lived phenomenon. By the time it was underway locally, all the most promising creeks in the Klondike, so far as individual prospectors were concerned, already had been staked. The *Bulletin's* first report of northbound parties was in mid-July 1897; by 20 March 1899 it was referring to 'the now historic Klondike rush.'

The significance of Edmonton's role in the Rush is seen very differently with the passage of time. MacGregor writes that 'for magnitude, daring and adventure, this year-long migration of prospectors over routes which varied in length from 1,500 to 2,500 miles is unparalleled in

Canadian history.'[83] Most writers however, pass it off as a minor blip in the grand spectacle of the Klondike Gold Rush. Certainly in comparison with the numbers of Klondikers who moved through Pacific ports, both American and Canadian, those passing through Edmonton were very few. The *Bulletin* reported proudly that 289 had passed through Edmonton in 1897;[84] in comparison, 8,000 had passed through Seattle the same year![85] An American historian finds it remarkable that even these few should have chosen the Edmonton routes: 'It seems strange that the Edmonton routes lured argonauts in preference to the comparatively easy and well-known Yukon routes from Skagway and St. Michael.'[86] A Canadian historian explains it as the result of a 'strange mixture of patriotism and economic self-interest' and refers to 'Edmonton's civic greed.'[87] Quoting John W. Dafoe, Pierre Berton has written that 'to doubt the practicability of the Edmonton trail "was regarded as a species of treason.." '[88] To these latter factors might be added the widespread promotion by the *Edmonton Bulletin* and its aggressive editor and local Member of Parliament, Frank Oliver.

Certainly, Edmonton benefitted financially from the passing Klondikers, with the *Bulletin* estimating $250,000 to $500,000 from the trade in the spring of 1898 alone.[89] Heady figures indeed, for a town 'of little significance on the edge of settlement.'[90] By mid-April 1898 the town's population had reached 2,500,[91] a 67 per cent increase in one year! Most of this increase was due to newcomers, some of whom had arrived as Klondikers but, already discouraged, had decided to take employment locally, and some of whom had been drawn to start new businesses in what seemed a promising location.

The publicity and promotion linked with the Rush made the name 'Edmonton' widely known, not only in North America but also in Europe. Reports on the rich agricultural potential of the area by Klondikers and visitors reinforced the efforts of government authorities and the railway company to encourage increased homesteading in the area. Even in the exhilarating days of the Rush, the *Bulletin* reported on these matters, including the progress of such new ethnic settlers as the Ukrainians east of town and the Scandinavians southeast of Edmonton. For their part, town businessmen and the council actively encouraged a widened economic base through advertisements pointing out the advantages for the establishment of 'water works, flour and woollen mills, machine shops, tanneries, and other industries within the town.'[92] The Klondike Gold Rush above all else, dramatically marked the start of a new era in the history of Edmonton. ∾

The Klondike Gold Rush is remembered in Edmonton's annual Klondike Days celebration. Here, Bob Breen as Klondike Mike, 1976. (PAA J.2604)

R.G. MOYLES

COURTING SALLY ANN

The Salvation Army's first Red Shield drive in Edmonton, officially launched on 18 March 1919 at the corner of 101 Street and Jasper Avenue. (SALVATION ARMY ARCHIVES)

*A*t the turn of the twentieth century, the frustrations of Edmonton boosters with the community's slow growth gave way to unbounded optimism.

First, thanks to the immigration policies of Prime Minister Wilfrid Laurier and his minister of the interior, Clifford Sifton—and to the lack of better land elsewhere—the Canadian prairies became the destination of choice for tens of thousands of European immigrants starting in the mid-1890s. Second, Edmonton gained its first transcontinental rail connections, the Canadian Northern in 1905 and the Grand Trunk Pacific in 1909. It was named capital of the province in 1906; nearby Strathcona beat out Calgary as site of the University of Alberta in 1907; and in 1912 Edmonton absorbed Strathcona (suddenly, the much smaller community). Community leaders gloried in the promise of the future. Surely Edmonton would continue to prosper, perhaps becoming the dominant metropolitan centre of western Canada.

Yet if the future held the promise of progress community leaders worried about some of the less attractive aspects of mod-ern society that they could see in the larger, more developed cities in eastern Canada, Britain, and the United States. More than 70 per cent of Edmonton's population was of British origin. How were the new immigrants, many from eastern Europe, to be taught 'Canadian' values? Would problems of crime, drink, and prostitution inevitably grow as Edmonton grew? Longing to be part of the modern world, Edmonton now worried about how to deal with the problems of that world.

In these years, across Canada, there was growing experimentation with alternative religions and secular reform movements that promised to cure society's ills. Many of the groups were committed to social work and social reform and often featured women in prominent roles. One such group, the Salvation Army, arrived in Edmonton in 1893.

Gordon Moyles has published numerous books on aspects of Canadian history, from settlement in the Grande Prairie region to the first trials of Inuits under white man's law. He is a professor of English at the University of Alberta and the official historian of the Salvation Army in Canada.

I N 1865, WHEN WILLIAM AND CATHERINE BOOTH commenced what they called the East London Christian Mission, the British public barely noticed. It was, most people thought, a passing fad—one of many such religious eccentricities of English life. They came, and they disappeared, as did a new fashion from Paris or a new opera song from Milan. The Christian Mission was therefore dismissed as just another sectarian flash-in-the-pan, unworthy of much concern or interest.

In 1878, however, the British public was jarred into awareness. The Christian Mission changed dramatically— it became The Salvation Army. 'From the moment the Army received its title,' wrote W.T. Stead, 'its destiny was fixed. The whole organization was dominated by its name.'[1] Unorthodox religious worship was augmented by pseudo-military display: 'officers' and 'soldiers' marched through the streets with bands and flags and tambourines. They sang 'war songs,' adhered to 'Orders and Regulations,' saluted commanding officers, and generally formed themselves into military units called Corps. Using female preachers to flamboyant advantage, the Army 'invaded' pub territories and engaged in a scheme of social-reclamation that upset traditional notions of poor relief.

Believing that it was pointless to preach salvation to hungry people, William Booth launched, as the popular phrase has it, a 'soup to salvation' mission. Content at first merely to offer free breakfasts to any who would stay for prayer, Booth was soon immersed in a variety of activities aimed at the amelioration of social ills. His 'slum sisters' patrolled London's streets, welcoming any female willing to be helped to one of several Salvation Army Rescue Homes. Working-men's hostels offered places of rehabilitation for the unemployed and starving. A Poor Man's Insurance Society, a Safety-Match factory, 'farm colonies' (at home and overseas), and a host of other agencies met social needs in a manner not previously attempted by either Church or State.[2]

By such innovative daring, William and Catherine Booth not only attracted a committed following—at least fifty thousand soldiers and almost six hundred Corps by 1882—but also acquired a notoriety beyond even their expectation. English newspapers and magazines vied with each other to unveil the secrets of this new religion. From the prestigious *London Times* to the lowly *Morning Advertiser*; from the *Graphic* to *St Stephen's*; from the *Pall Mall Gazette* to *Blackwood's Magazine*; indeed, from London to Karachi, the Salvation Army was lampooned, cartooned, debated, described, dissected, and denounced. To some observers, such as W.T. Stead, William Booth

was perhaps the greatest religious reformer of the nineteenth century and his Salvation Army an exemplar of practical Christianity. For others, especially those among the established upper-classes, the Salvation Army was a social anathema; one of several (like trade unionism, suffragism, and democracy) that threatened to undermine upper-class domination of British society. According to the *Saturday Review*, an outspoken advocate of the status quo and a virulent critic of the Army, the organization represented a 'loathsome disease on the body politic,' deserving of every denunciation and brickbat thrown its way. The Army was, judging by contemporary commentary, an organization to be loved or hated; but it certainly was not one to be ignored.

❧ As this brief introduction should make plain, early Salvationism had a distinctiveness that caused it to become, in the words of G.M. Trevelyan, 'a permanent feature of modern British life.'[3] The Salvation Army also enjoyed such public prominence that, by the time the Army expanded into Canada in 1882 (into Alberta in 1887 and Edmonton in 1893), its reputation for religious flamboyance tempered by good works had been firmly established and preceded it wherever it went. Even before it arrived in Edmonton many citizens of the small fort-cum-town would have known of its confrontational methods—of its clashes with Skeleton Armies—and the prominence of its female ministry—its 'Hallelujah Lasses.' This was so not only because some Edmontonians had encountered the Army before they came West, in England or Ontario, but also because Salvation Army activities often made front-page news. In 1885, for example, the *Edmonton Bulletin*, owned and edited by Frank Oliver, had reported on the Army's involvement in England's famous 'Maiden Tribute Affair' and in 1891 had publicized Booth's 'Darkest England' scheme, his panacea for England's social ills.[4]

Though Oliver had an eye for news, and probably would have featured the Army stories had he not sympathized with its work, the fact is he was, as journalist and politician, temperamentally in league with William Booth. Oliver was, one might say, a kind of Salvationist himself. He was somewhat of an exhibitionist, an anti-establishmentarian, outspoken in his defence of the down-trodden; yet he was a staunch believer in Anglo-Saxon virtues and the settlement of the West by British citizens. One can sense from Oliver's editorials that he and William Booth would have seen eye-to-eye on many issues. And, in actual fact, they did. So much so that, when the Army decided to invade Edmonton in 1893, Oliver became one of its staunchest supporters.

Eleven years earlier, when British immigrants brought their Salvationism to Toronto in 1882, forcing William Booth to send out officers to take charge, Edmonton was still a tiny fur trading post (though beginning to become a town), away out there in the District of Alberta, North-West Territories. Like most towns west of Ontario it was of little interest to a city-bred, slum-oriented, religious-rescue organization like the Salvation Army. In fact, even in 1887, when the Army finally turned its eyes westward and sent out a 'Northwest Brigade to reconnoitre the North-West Territories,' its report back to headquarters suggested that, while Winnipeg, Calgary, and Victoria had some semblance of civilization—i.e., enough sin and social ills to warrant Salvationist intervention—the tiny fort-town of Edmonton, already occupied by Reverend McDougall, was simply not sinful enough to require an Army purging. Captain Arthur Young, western scout for the Army, saw the place for himself, and was not impressed:

I am [he wrote in May 1877 in the *War Cry*, the Army's official newspaper] in a little place called 'LONGPINE,' about 60 miles from Calgary on the Edmonton Trail . . . We left Calgary on Thursday at about eight o'clock for a drive of 218 miles across a vast prairie to Edmonton. The trail is a rough beaten track marked out by small mounds of soil, in the centre of which is an iron rod. These mounds are placed so that you can see the one in front and the one in the rear, and without which it would be difficult, and at times impossible, to find the way . . . So far nothing has opened up; in fact in the five places visited there are no buildings of any size except churches, and few people at Calgary. I have already travelled on a wagon over land (sometimes on horseback) over 520 miles, and I suppose the outside number of human beings I have seen have been one hundred. Nearly all those I saw at Calgary.

Concluding that Edmonton, without a railway line, would not—indeed could not—grow as fast as Calgary, Young struck the town from his list of possible Army invasions. After a brief rest, he was off to the equally unpromising town of Battleford.

But Young, though perceptive in his positive assessment of the West, was clearly wrong in his negative opinion of Edmonton. Contrary to the prevailing view that settlements in the south—places like Medicine Hat— would attract the bulk of new immigrants, Edmonton, as gateway to the North, soon began to assert itself. In 1891 a railway connection with Calgary accelerated the town's growth (even though the rail terminus was on the south side of the river); and in 1892 the town was incorporated, its 1200 citizens electing Matthew McCauley as their first mayor. As evidence of progress (and no doubt as a mayoral duty) McCauley could cite the facts that Edmonton now had two flour mills, a brickyard, a saw mill, a furniture factory, a school, a glee club, and a Literary Society.[5] And it was, no doubt, a place that soon would have the kinds of social problems the Salvation Army loved to tackle.

In 1893 the Army was back, the advance guard this time, not men but attractive Hallelujah Lasses. As William Booth had done in the toughest towns in England, so in Canada the Army sent its 'best men'—young female officers—to secure the West. They carried out their invasions in pairs, cracking what the Army called the 'toughest nuts' and winning (as no man could) the support of even the most obdurate opponents. In their attractive poke bonnets, and long tight-fitting blue dresses (often adorned with Hallelujah sashes), possessing a courage that had taken some of their English sisters into London's worst slums, they had successfully 'opened fire' on Winnipeg, Calgary, Vancouver, and Victoria. In some cases they had become local heroines. Captain Abby Thompson, for example, who opened the Corps at Kingston, Ontario, 'was so popular that soap manufacturers named their products after her.'[6] An English MP who visited Calgary in 1888 wrote that 'it would evidently fare ill with any cowboy or idler who ventured to say a rude word to any of the Hallelujah lasses.' With little money, and only the uniforms they wore, but with plenty of faith in their mission, these early female officers went boldly into unfamiliar (often unfriendly) towns and soon were in charge of thriving Hallelujah Corps.[7]

The Salvation Army commanders, with typical exaggeration, used to call these Corps openings invasions. And, to be fair, some of them, notably in England and Europe where opposition was strong, had some of the characteristics of a military skirmish. The officers, braving missiles aimed at their heads, used loud musical instruments, even cowbells, to attract attention; they sometimes turned cartwheels in the streets or donned outlandish costumes or carried large billboards announcing the imminent defeat of the Devil. But that was not the case in Edmonton. Captain Marie Kadey and Lieutenant Hattie Scott more-or-less drifted into town on the afternoon train from Calgary on 29 June 1893 and began their salvation campaign in a manner not altogether outrageous. Rather disappointingly, perhaps, they went quietly about their business, renting the old Methodist Church—built by the McDougalls in 1873—and beginning their hallelujah services on the evening of 6 July.

It is not too speculative to suggest that Kadey and Scott did not need the usual Army circus-like methods to attract attention. For on one thing they could rely: they would be noticed, without any supporting theatricals. Edmontonians, prompted by advance notices in the *Bulletin*, were anxious to see Salvationists in the flesh and were especially intrigued by the female attire of the two young officers. Large poke-bonnets, with ribbons, and tight-fitting long-skirted uniforms, sometimes with red sashes, were a novelty and enticement few could resist. Indeed, in a town largely comprised of males, it would have been remarkable had they not been noticed—for sheer good looks, as their photos attest, these two young 'lassies' were unrivalled.

So, on that warm Thursday evening, fifty people filled the little wooden church, most merely curious, some seriously interested, to experience the 'new-fangled' religion with its emphases on joyful singing (of religious songs and choruses to music-hall tunes), 'instant' conversion, 'red-hot' testimonies, and open-air evangelism. On the Sunday more than eighty-five turned out, and during the following week, with meetings being held every evening (after open-air marches through the streets), a total of three-hundred Edmontonians—some obviously more than once—flocked to hear the Hallelujah Lasses. Quite an impressive beginning had been made, particularly when one learns that they were competing against the Reverend James Woodsworth, Superintendent of Methodist Missions, who was conducting meetings in the new Methodist Church; the Big Bonanza Vaudeville Company, in town for several shows; and the Toronto Ideal Concert Company, that was playing to a packed house in Robertson Hall.

The key to the Salvationists' success, however, lay not so much in the novelty of their meetings or poke bonnets, but in their zeal and hard work. In the first week alone Kadey and Scott visited some thirty-five Edmonton homes, making their presence and their message known. By the end of that week also, with great confidence, they ordered one hundred copies of the *War Cry*. And every week thereafter, when not at their 'open-air corner' near Jasper Avenue and 103 Street., they could be seen selling their *War Crys* at all the local establishments (their customers included most merchants) and always at the editorial office of the *Bulletin*.

Frank Oliver made no bones about it: he liked the Salvation Army and its lasses. Almost every week his

'Hallelujah lasses' Lieutenant Corlett and Captain Kadey, 1893. They avoided the circus-like theatrics of some Salvationists. (PAA B.9553)

Bulletin was promoting a Salvation Army event—a 'banquet at the barracks,' 'limelight views' of Booth's Darkest England scheme, kaleidoscopic musicals, Self Denials and lantern slides, and special speakers from Winnipeg and missionaries from abroad. He 'boomed' the War Cry and reported rather facetiously on some of the Army's more 'profound' moments:

> The case of the Salvation Army vs Morley was tried before Mayor McCauley on Tuesday. This was a case of disturbing religious services, the disturbance consisting of singing out of harmony with the congregation in a manner that was annoying to the worshippers. Some of the witnesses swore that they were obliged to leave the meeting on account of the inharmonic noises made by the defendant, while others swore that his singing was disagreeable to them. The weight of evidence seemed to prove that Mr. Morley's voice was not melodious upon this occasion, and the mayor thereupon imposed a fine of one dollar, disallowing all witness fees.[8]

Well-known Edmonton photographer C.W. Mathers's portrait of the first Edmonton Salvation Army congregation with its officers, 1893. (PAA B.4017)

When the time came to say farewell to Captain Kadey, Oliver was magnanimous in his praise:

> At the time of her arrival it did not appear that there was a very good opening for any work here. Edmonton is a town of churches with a very large proportion of church-goers amongst the population, and a comparatively small proportion of the element upon which the Army chiefly directs its artillery. The Army in Edmonton has now quite a long muster roll, and it is not difficult to point out a number of formerly hard cases for whose change of living the Army must be given credit. But this is the smallest part of the work done. There is no doubt that the influence of the Army is felt beyond the individuals who have joined it and that it has been a leaven of good to all that part of the public that does not usually attend church . . . That this has been the result of the work of two young women during some ten months is good evidence as to the talent, energy, and devotion to the salvation cause of Captain Kadey and Lieutenant Corlett who has been her assistant since September last.[9]

Oliver, however, was not the only known admirer of the Salvation Army.

Edmonton's early, brilliant, and ubiquitous photographers, C.W. Mathers and later Ernest Brown, were also enamoured of salvationism—at least of the colourful externals if not of the message itself. Mathers has left us more than a dozen photos—of Kadey and Scott, Kadey and Corlett, all later officers, Harvest Festival events, and of the early soldiers themselves. In February of 1894, for example, Mathers photographed the Corps contingent on the occasion of its second 'enrolment of soldiers.' Kadey, Corlett, and one brave female soldier (a Miss Graham) are surrounded by a phalanx of seemingly protective males: young Albert Fraser and William McKay staring earnestly into Mathers's camera; Archibald Dipon holding a 'Soldier's Song Book' seemingly ready to burst into song; William White, his guitar ready to accompany such an outburst; James McConnell, James Dinner, Alex McDonald, Joe Hay, Pete Campbell and four Prices—James, Will, George, and Tom the Fiddler.

Later there would be individual portraits of such new converts as Willie Groat and Frank Kiel, and together they provide a photographic record of local Salvationism more extensive and diverse than can be found anywhere else in Canada. And, when Ernest Brown arrived in 1904 and commenced his photographic history of the West, he not only acquired many of Mathers's photos but also continued to 'snap' every Salvation Army personality and activity. From the first Corps-built Salvation Army barracks on 98 Street (1903) to the then-magnificent brick Citadel on 102 Street (1925), Brown recorded the Army's progress. He made his admiration of the Army publicly known in 1912 when he presented to the Corps, on the death of William Booth, a magnificent painted portrait of the founder as a memorial tribute.

It would, of course, be naive to suppose that this evident admiration and support was always universal, uninterrupted, or sustained throughout the Army's sojourn in Edmonton. For example, Frank Oliver himself, though an admirer of the Army's religious fervour and practical social work, had grave doubts about one of Booth's social plans. In July 1895 Commandant Herbert Booth, son of the General, visited Edmonton to investigate the possibility of establishing an overseas colony—a 10,000-acre farm on which to locate some of England's rehabilitated slum-dwellers. A farm colony had been created by the Army at Hadleigh, near London, at which young men, once society's outcasts, were re-trained as farmers and mechanics. Booth's plan was to create a series of overseas colonies to which these men could be sent to begin new lives.

Understandably, there were many opponents to the farm colony scheme, especially in the colonies themselves. It was, they felt, just another means by which Britain could unload its poor and lazy on them; it was not, they averred, in the best interests of the colonies, nor was it a practical means of colonization. 'Do not send us your poor,' they pleaded; 'rather send those with some means of support and with other skills than farming.'

Among the critics was Oliver. Though supportive of the Army's work in general, he had grave doubts about this particular scheme: 'When the Army is endeavouring to improve the material as well as the spiritual condition of the unfortunate,' he wrote, 'it will have such support as the *Bulletin* is able to give. . . . But in the opinion of the *Bulletin* the work of caring for the wreckage of a congested civilization is one thing and laying the foundation of a new colony or country or kingdom or nation or empire— as you please—is another.'

> And while it is the business of the Army to raise the fallen by such means as they can, it is no less the business of those who as citizens are the legislators of this country to secure and select the best materials, and only the best materials, out of which to build a strong and vigorous and prosperous nation. To keep clean is not less a duty whether private or public or religious than to make clean, and is particularly desirable in laying the foundations of a new country where the influence of one man is equal to the influence of ten or of a hundred in an old and populous country. Taking the spokesmen of the Army at their word, the class of people for whose benefit the proposed farm is to be established are not the strong characters, either mentally, morally or physically, who lay the best foundation of society; they are not the class who have so far built Canada.

Such rhetoric—labelled by Booth as 'selfish and ignorant

prejudice'—was obviously effective (and was perhaps shared by more Canadians than Lord Aberdeen, a promoter of the scheme, had anticipated). No offer of land was made by the Canadian government and, though the Army did sponsor a few bloc settlements in places like Tisdale, Saskatchewan, the overseas colonies plan was largely abandoned.

Almost two decades later, in 1912, the mutual admiration that had characterized the Army's relationship with Edmontonians was again briefly interrupted by what seemed to be a bit of bureaucratic bungling. On 21 June of that year City Council, as part of its plan to relieve congestion on city streets, passed by-law 418, 'For the Regulation of Streets and Traffic Thereon.' The third paragraph stipulated that 'no persons shall stand in groups . . . so as to cause any obstruction to the free use of streets and sidewalks' while the fourth expressly prohibited 'street preaching' on certain streets including the Army's favourite open-air stands on Jasper and Whyte avenues.

The Salvation Army, considering the by-law rather inoffensive, in that no one was likely to believe their street

The first Salvation Army Barracks on 102 Avenue and 98 Street. (PAA B.4019)

meetings were causing obstruction, left well enough alone. Nor were they molested for almost a year. On 24 April 1913, however, an over-zealous policeman from the South Side precipitated a civic furore when he arrested six members of the Edmonton Corps for obstructing pedestrian traffic on Whyte Avenue. 'Salvation Lassies in South Side Jail' screamed the *Edmonton Journal* headlines (though only two were females). And, in true Army fashion (enjoying a new kind of publicity), they made the most of incarceration:

> The first few minutes after their committal they spent singing in the cells well-known hymns . . . Vigorously they used their lungs, and treated with disdain the efforts of a policeman, who was endeavouring to sleep after being on night duty, to silence them by throwing two nickles on the concrete floor which surrounded their new quarters. When they first entered the courtroom some minutes before the court opening this morning [26 April] they played the piano there, sang hymns and gave a few addresses to the expectant crowd which had congregated to hear the result of the action.[10]

Magistrate Downes, not anticipating obstinacy, found the Salvationists guilty of obstruction and fined each of them $1.00 or ten days in jail. Naturally enough, given the publicity, the Salvationists chose the latter. They would, they declared, stay in jail until the by-law was altered—in spite of the judge's pleading that they pay the fines and even of a policeman's offer to take up a collection to do so. No, they would make their point. Though they would not, so the *Journal* playfully suggested, go as far as the English suffragettes and go on a hunger strike. 'For it was to be noticed that through the kindness of others, tea and sandwiches were joyously partaken of, which were handed to them by a sympathetic constable through the bars of the cell.'[11]

After some public intervention, six of Edmonton's leading clergymen having been to see the attorney-general, the Salvationists were released. This action did not entirely satisfy the Army's lawyer, Mr Charles Grant, and he immediately asked the Supreme Court to rule on the case. On 30 April Chief Justice Horace Harvey did just that, quashing the conviction on the grounds that obstruction had not been proven; and he ordered the City to pay the costs of the preliminary and Supreme Court hearings.

The whole affair was, though very much a tempest in a teapot, a boost for the Salvation Army. In the *Bulletin*'s opinion the Army would not suffer 'either in repute or usefulness,' but would rather gain in those regards by the

The Salvation Army Citadel, built in 1925. Edmonton's Citadel Theatre began in this building and adopted its name. (PAA BL.528)

proof they gave of their willingness 'to go even to prison through zeal to do good.' City Council, far from turning against the Army, lamented the ill treatment they had received, claiming that the by-law was never intended to prohibit their street meetings, and chided both the policeman and magistrate for having wrongly interpreted a law merely intended to prevent congestion. Clearly, no policeman would again risk such censure and, just as clearly, the Army, not wishing to bite the hand that partially fed it, let the matter drop. The by-law remained in effect, becoming by-law 23 in 1917, but was not, as far as is known, used again to stop the Army from preaching on street corners.

ꙮIn the years since Frank Oliver gave the Salvation Army editorial encouragement, the citizens of Edmonton have on the whole continued to be very understanding and supportive of the Army. They have not joined it in large numbers, but have been aware that the impact of its mission has exceeded its size—a fact neatly summed up by the well-known maxim that 'it is not big armies which win battles; it is the good ones.' In Edmonton, as elsewhere, the Army's effectiveness is judged not merely by its evangelistic outreach but by its social welfare work.

Almost from the moment Kadey and Scott opened fire in Edmonton, the Army began its social outreach. At first this outreach consisted of free weekly meals for new immigrants and the unemployed. Later, a woodyard, established next to the Citadel, allowed transient and out-of-work men to redeem work for free meals. In 1914 this program became the nucleus of the Army's present-day social work: a Metropole (working man's hostel) was opened at 534 Frazer Avenue (just east of 98 Street) with sleeping accommodation for seventeen men. In 1915 this unit was enlarged to include an 'Industrial' Home, Wood Yard, Store, and Warehouse all on 97 Street. And in the later 1920s, aided by the generous gifts of unused buildings by the City, the Salvation Army opened a Maternity Hospital in the Ross Flats and a Eventide Home for men in Bonnie Doon.

Perhaps the greatest prominence accorded the Salvation Army as a social service organization in Edmonton was during the Second World War. Soon known as 'Sally Ann,' the Army erected its first Red Shield hut in September of 1939, a marquee that eventually was replaced by a large canteen/auditorium on the Prince of Wales military encampment. March of 1943 saw the opening of the War Services Hostel at 10128-98 Streeet, with accommodation for two hundred men, open to all enlisted men of the allied nations. The *Journal* in that year named Sally Ann the 'soldier's best friend.' 'Perhaps it really is so,' suggested

Packing Christmas hampers, 1974, the Salvation Army continues its long tradition of community service. (PAA J.1637/1)

the reporter, 'for wherever he goes he leaves her, and no matter where he arrives he finds her. No, she isn't beautiful or attractive, just an ordinary wooden military hut, but the soldiers love her dearly.' And, though it is well-nigh impossible to quantify the 'good work' of Sally Ann during those years, the continued praise and goodwill of ex-servicemen testify to a spiritual and physical comfort that will never be forgotten.

In the midst of all that social work, and inextricably involved, the Edmonton Corps of the Salvation Army continued its evangelical outreach, its bands and flags, and the large brick Citadel on 102 Street, visible signs of their presence. They had been there to help some besotted gold-seekers on their way to the Klondike in 1897–8; they shared Edmonton's celebration of Alberta's entry in Confederation in 1905; some of them took part in the Hudson's Bay Company land sale in 1912; so that, by the 1920s, Salvationists were an integral part of Edmonton society and counted its history their own. Many of them, in fact, were among the English immigrants who helped build the city—the Groats, the Holmes, and the Battricks—and whose children (among them Kenneth Blatchford, a later mayor; and Judge Stevenson) have maintained the pioneering spirit. ꙮ

PÁDRAIG Ó SIADHAIL

KATHERINE HUGHES,
IRISH POLITICAL ACTIVIST

Katherine Hughes. (NAC C-8785)

The Edmonton to which Katherine Hughes moved in 1903 was predominantly British in character. Of Irish origin, born in Prince Edward Island, educated and intelligent, she moved easily among the social and political elite. She was a respected journalist, a biographer, and soon to be provincial archivist and private secretary to Alberta's Premier Rutherford. A devout Catholic, she was chosen to write Father Lacombe's biography.

Like other ethnic groups, emigrants from the different regions of the British Isles brought old world loyalties, political ideas, religious beliefs, values, and disagreements with them when they came to Canada. When Hughes embraced political

self-determination for Ireland as the cause of her life, she would be treated as an outcast and traitor by an unsympathetic public.

Like Hughes, Pádraig Ó Siadhail is of Irish background. Born in Derry City, Northern Ireland, he studied at Trinity College, Dublin, and since 1987 has held the Chair of Irish Studies at Saint Mary's University, Halifax. A novelist, he has written a history of the Irish-language theatre and is currently working on a biography of Piaras Béaslaí, the founding father of the Irish Free State. He is also working on a full-length biography of Hughes.

IN SPITE OF HER FASCINATING AND COLOURFUL career, former Edmonton resident Katherine Hughes remains a little-known figure in Canada. Biographical sketches portray a quiet, undistinguished journalist, public servant, and biographer,[1] but these clash sharply with descriptions of Hughes by a Toronto Orange journal as 'one of the greatest trouble makers in the West'[2] and, later, by an Irish-American organization as one who had died 'worn out with the work she had done for the cause of Irish independence.'[3] Linking the disparate threads of her life in order to present a more complete account of Katherine Hughes and her accomplishments is a major challenge. While Hughes's achievements during her short and exceptionally active life can be listed and described, understanding what motivated this enigmatic figure is less easy as she left little personal documentation.

Hughes's checkered career from her early days as lay missionary and teacher to the political activism and idealism that dominated the final decade of her life brought her into contact with a wide range of contemporary issues including the position of Native people, attempts by women to establish themselves in the male-dominated field of journalism, the development of western Canada, and the cause of Irish independence. Through her work, Hughes came face to face with prominent players in these spheres, figures as diverse as Albert Lacombe, the Oblate missionary; Sir William Van Horne of the Canadian Pacific Railway; Arthur Sifton, remier of Alberta; Pádraic Ó Conaire, the noted Gaelic writer; and Eamon de Valera, the Irish nationalist leader and future prime minister and president of Ireland. Far from leading a sedate nondescript existence, Hughes led a life of active service in both her professional career and personal activities.

Hughes emerges as a complex character. Despite the different occupations and the ease with which she crossed social, cultural, and political divides, Catholicism was the cornerstone of her life and the source of her social activism, colouring her perception of the issues of the day. Katherine, when she took up a cause, adhered to it loyally, nay doggedly. The *Edmonton Bulletin* noted after her death that she was 'always filled with enthusiasm for any cause which had enlisted her sympathy . . .'[4] Though Hughes was a Catholic activist and crusader who believed in service, it is difficult to argue that she had a clearly defined social reformist agenda—however, her exposure to and involvement with Irish politics would force her to reassess her political beliefs.

Throughout her career, Hughes displayed a wide range of seemingly contradictory traits: wildly romantic and emi-

nently sensible, hardheaded and naive, radical and conservative, social worker and social climber. The most intriguing of these contradictions concerns her attitude to women. An outspoken opponent of female suffrage in 1913, Hughes only supported it at a late stage, once it had become a respectable cause.[5] Despite her own non-traditional lifestyle and her contacts through the Canadian Women's Press Club (CWPC) with prominent social reformers such as Emily Murphy and Nellie McClung, there is little evidence that Hughes viewed her achievements as gains in the struggle for political and economic equality between the sexes.

Club members figured prominently in social reform campaigns, especially the struggle in support of suffrage. The opposition to suffrage by Kathleen 'Kit' Coleman, first president of the CWPC, and by Hughes attests to the fact that there was no uniformity of thought within the CWPC. Hughes's deliberate decision not to fight for suffrage likely came from her own remarkable success in obtaining position and prestige without access to the franchise and from a belief that a woman's strength lay in her ability to work behind the scenes within the existing system in order to influence those in power. Throughout, Hughes preferred to remain in the background, writing, organizing, and lobbying, although, when called upon during her years as an Irish activist, she emerged as a fine public orator. Moreover, while Hughes had much in common with other female professionals as regards solid middle-class background and upbringing, and as a young energetic journalist shared many of the concerns and interests of her female colleagues, her strong Catholicism, rooted in the rich cultural soil of Ireland and Prince Edward Island, separated her from her peers, largely of Anglo-Saxon Protestant stock, who promoted a social reform agenda.[6] Hughes's volunteer activities, practical in a material sense and purposeful in religious terms, found expression in efforts on behalf of Catholic relief causes under the aegis of her Church,[7] just as her literary work found expression in biographical studies of major Catholic role models.

Extremely close to her family, Hughes appears to have had few lasting intimate friendships. In referring to her as 'Katie' Hughes, the *Edmonton Bulletin* suggests a degree of informality and frivolity that contrasts with the austere public persona of 'Miss Hughes,' the energetic, humourless, and exceptionally capable organizer and administrator. But her success in adapting to new challenges in a wide range of locations demonstrates that Hughes was a flexible individual who seized career opportunities as they arose and earned the trust and confidence of men of importance. Hughes, who never married, seems to have been comfortable with older men to whom she could look up, but, when the occasion demanded, she refused to be intimidated by men or to accept meekly the role they had decided upon for her. Though Hughes parted company with her former colleagues in the CWPC on the question of suffrage, she never viewed a woman's position as submissive to that of men. It was merely different.

◐ Katherine Angelina Hughes was born into a strong Irish Catholic community at Emerald Junction on Prince Edward Island on 12 November 1876. If her father, John Wellington Hughes, a 'Merchant, Magistrate and Postmaster,' possessed social status within his community,[8] his wife, Annie Laurie O'Brien, sister of Cornelius O'Brien, Roman Catholic archbishop of Halifax from 1883 to 1906, was the real power in an aspiring middle-class household in which the females were the strong characters.[9] However, John Wellington was active in Conservative party circles on the Island[10] and passed on his love of politics to Katherine.

The third-youngest of nine children, Katherine appears to have benefited greatly from the O'Brien connection. Not merely did she inherit their self-confidence and assertiveness but the O'Brien name opened the doors of Notre Dame Academy in Charlottetown for her. Hughes completed her education at the Prince of Wales College and Normal School in Charlottetown from which she graduated in 1892 with a first-class Teacher's License.[11]

There is no record of Hughes having taught on Prince Edward Island. Although she reportedly 'did mission work among the Indians of Eastern and Central Canada,'[12] her whereabouts and activities for much of the following decade remain vague. In the summer of 1899 she was appointed as a teacher at the Native school on the Mohawk reserve at St Regis (now Akwesasne), which straddles the Canadian and American international border and the provincial borders of Ontario and Quebec.[13]

In published short stories based on her experiences, Hughes's sympathy with the plight of the Natives is mani-

She never viewed a woman's position as submissive to that of men. It was merely different.

fest.[14] Her involvement with the establishment of the short-lived Catholic Indian Association in 1901—though secretary, she is described as 'the originator of the movement'—demonstrates not only that she was keen to ensure that Catholic Natives remained faithful to their Church but also that she was an advocate of the cultural assimilation of Natives, a position that would contrast starkly with her actions later in support of Irish cultural and political independence. Through providing employment outside reserves to graduates of the Indian school system, Catholic Indian Association literature declared, the Natives 'will thus acquire the habits of the white man, and the Indian problem will disappear because the Indians will have become Canadians.'[15]

Hughes remained at St Regis until she resigned, apparently due to ill-health, in March 1902. She speculated about going off as a teacher to Africa[16] but instead opted for the 'literary work' to which she was turning increasingly.[17]

From 1903 to 1906 Katherine Hughes was employed as a member of the editorial staff of the *Montreal Star*.[18] In 1906 she published her first book, *Archbishop O'Brien: Man and Churchman*, 'a simple study' of the 'beautiful life' of her recently deceased uncle.[19] The most important outcome of this period was that her work with the *Montreal Star* introduced her to prominent women journalists who were attempting to make advances in a field dominated by men. On 16 June 1904 a group of 16 female journalists, including Hughes, departed from Montreal to attend the St Louis World Fair and visit Chicago on a trip sponsored by the Canadian Pacific Railway. In the course of this journey the ladies established the CWPC.[20]

In June 1906 when the CWPC held its annual gathering in Winnipeg, Hughes was appointed recording secretary of the club.[21] She was among the journalists who journeyed from Manitoba for a tour of the West under the auspices of the Western Canadian Immigration Association.[22] The recently established provinces of Saskatchewan and Alberta were actively seeking to attract settlerss from eastern and central Canada and from abroad and thus wished to encourage favourable reports from the women journalists. The week-long railway trip took Hughes and her fellow writers as far as Banff, Alberta.[23] Katherine's reaction to the West was positive, and shortly afterwards she left central Canada to move to Edmonton where her brother, Alfred, was living.[24]

Hughes quickly made her mark when she arrived to work at the *Edmonton Bulletin* in November 1906. Her responsibilities with the *Bulletin* included the special Christmas number from 1906 to 1908,[25] the society page,[26] and representing the paper in the press gallery of the Alberta Provincial Legislature during its working sessions.[27] Her work at the *Bulletin* also brought her into contact with the paper's publisher, Frank Oliver, a prominent Liberal politician. Despite her family's traditional allegiance to the Conservative party, Katherine easily adapted, especially in this new province where old party labels were less clearly defined.

In June 1908, when the Government of Alberta announced the setting up of the position of provincial archivist, Hughes applied for and was appointed to the position with a salary of $1000 per annum.[28] The *Bulletin* released Katherine 'with no small measure of regret.'[29] Within months of commencing her responsibilities as first provincial archivist of the newly established Bureau of Archives, Hughes had contacted all the post offices throughout the province, seeking to interview 'old-timers,' early settlers of Alberta when it was still a district of the North-West Territories. 'I should like to get from them, if possible, portraits of the early settlers, buildings, fairs, banquets or any striking incident connected with the old times,' she wrote.[30]

Hughes also prepared a comprehensive report on the work, organization, financial needs, and future plans for the Archives that was presented to Alexander Cameron Rutherford, the first premier of Alberta, in February 1909.[31] She had contacted the Dominion archivist for advice on the scope of the material she should collect and had set about obtaining records relating to Alberta's past from a wide range of sources, including the Hudson's Bay Company Archives, the North-West fur traders, the national Archives in Ottawa, the Manitoba and Saskatchewan governments, and the Oblate missionaries, in addition to the 'old-timers' already mentioned.[32]

Hughes was well aware of the richness of material that could be obtained from the Oblates, for by 1909 she had started work on the biography of Albert Lacombe, the famous priest in western Canada, at his request.[33] For Hughes, Lacombe likely personified the power and the potential of the Church militant to do good by 'uplifting'

the Natives on both a corporal and a spiritual level. Drawing on their shared experience as Catholic missionaries among the Natives and her interest in and preoccupation with the early days of settlers in the West, in which Lacombe had played such a significant role, the two became good friends. Letters from Hughes to Lacombe combine a business-like quality—usually she sought information or clarification from him—with a genuine note of tenderness.[34]

At the end of June 1909 Katherine travelled from Edmonton to the little-explored Peace River and Athabasca districts of northern Alberta to secure material for the Archives and to visit and interview 'old-timers' who might aid her research for the Lacombe biography. The *Canadian Magazine* described her trip:

> About eight years ago Miss Hughes made the trip from Fort Vermilion, on the Peace River, down to Fort Chipewyan, on Lake Athabasca, in a small canoe with two Indians, shooting the Vermilion rapids on the way. The voyagers camped out at night, and throughout the eight days of the journey they met human beings but once—at the little Red River trading post. During the greater part of the whole trip she was the only woman among the travellers, who were mostly traders and trappers and mounted police, excellent travelling companions and finely chivalrous, as all north country men are toward all women.[35]

Back in Edmonton, Hughes continued her amazingly active life. In 1909 she was elected vice-president of the CWPC with responsibility for the British Columbia and Alberta region. The following year, she began a three-year stint as the club's historian[36] and in 1911 became literary secretary of the Women's Canadian Club of Edmonton, which Emily Murphy had established.[37]

Hughes's work as archivist was soon interrupted when she was seconded to the office of Premier Rutherford in mid 1909. Although she officially retained her position as provincial archivist, she remained in the premier's office, later serving Rutherford's successor, fellow Liberal Arthur Lewis Sifton, as his private secretary from May 1910 to 1913. Hughes was reportedly the first woman to be private secretary to a Canadian provincial premier.[38] It was a job for which she was eminently qualified on account of her experience as the *Bulletin's* Legislative correspondent and her proven ability to organize her work efficiently.

Meanwhile, Hughes pressed ahead with the Lacombe biography. She sought and received the *imprimatur* of Lacombe's old friend and benefactor, Sir William Van

Hughes became Alberta's first provincial archivist in 1908. By 1909 she was seconded to the office of Premier Rutherford as his private secretary. Here she is shown in Alberta, circa 1909. (NAC PA-082240)

During her years in Edmonton, Hughes continued her Church-related missionary work when she became involved with Eastern-rite—Ukrainian Catholic immigrants—and with a group called the 'Catholic Women's Auxiliary.'[41] As in her activities with the Catholic Indian Association, Hughes's motivation was twofold: a desire to assist the needy and a concern about strengthening the Ukranians' connections with mainstream Catholicism in the face of fears of corruption by socialists and proselytizing by Protestants.[42] This volunteer work culminated in November 1912 when Hughes founded the Catholic Women's League of Edmonton to coordinate care for Catholic immigrants.[43] Although the Catholic Women's League of Canada was not established as a national organization until 1920, the Edmonton group was the parent league of this network. Hughes became secretary of the Edmonton group but her decision to leave Canada soon after finished her active involvement with the Edmonton league. Whereas Hughes's connections with the CWPC ended with her departure from Edmonton—and subsequently she was to elude chroniclers of the organization, including the Edmonton-based Miriam Green Ellis[44]—she was never to lose interest in or contact with the Catholic Women's League, and she retained a strong affection for 'the healthy acorn of 1912' that would grow into the 'big oak' of the Catholic Women's League of Canada.[45]

By 1913 Katherine Hughes was a prominent figure in Edmonton. She had a secure profession in journalism to which she could return, should political fortunes change. Her parents and family members had joined her out West. She was highly respected personally and professionally. She was well connected not just politically but with the Catholic authorities in the city. Yet at this juncture, she decided to leave Edmonton.

Hughes loved travelling and one senses a wanderlust in her which may well explain her departure. That decision may have been influenced somewhat, however, by dissatisfaction with her life. She was now in her mid thirties and unmarried. At this time, she was friendly with Paul A. von Aueberg, a civil engineer in the Edmonton City Engineering Department. Katherine clearly hoped that their relationship would blossom.

Unfortunately, the only correspondence between the two that has survived is several letters from von Aueberg to Hughes. These letters give a rare and fascinating glimpse of the private individual behind the public persona, 'Miss Hughes.' Von Aueberg, an intelligent, humorous man who was very much Katherine's intellectual equal, is frank and enlightening about her prejudices: 'You

Horne, in the form of a preface.[39] Published in 1911, *Father Lacombe, The Black-Robe Voyageur* met with positive critical response.[40] Certainly, the Lacombe biography is a finer work than *Archbishop O'Brien: Man and Churchman*. As in the earlier work, there is a large element of eulogy, but overall, the reader is given a glimpse of the multi-faceted personality of the Oblate, as well as an account of his multifarious doings. Unlike the rather wooden and hagiographical portrayal of O'Brien, Lacombe emerges in all his contradictions as missionary and colonizer; trusted friend of the Natives and confidant of major capitalists; simple churchman and wily old politician.

certainly are a snob. After I knew you 2 months you told me that the only two occupations worth while, in your opinion, were politician or literary man. These were the "polite" occupations.'[46]

Hughes emerges from this admittedly one-sided correspondence as a strong, willful individual. Certainly, these are characteristics which she demonstrated throughout her relatively short life. In addition, she comes across as an inveterate social climber, as a lady full of airs and graces, a view of her that, while conflicting somewhat with her image as the selfless and unstinting worker for Catholic causes, merely points to one of the contradictions in her personality. Hughes liked to see herself as a woman of substance. In describing her as a 'royal woman,' her fellow writer and journalist Kate Simpson Hayes succinctly summed up how Hughes saw herself and how she liked others to see her.[47]

The lack of success with von Aueberg may well have influenced Katherine's decision to leave Edmonton. In the summer of 1913 Premier Sifton returned to Alberta after a trip to England where he had established the Office of the Agent General for Alberta, with John A. Reid as agent general and Hughes as assistant and secretary.[48]

The decision to leave Edmonton was to prove a watershed in Hughes's career. Her stay in Alberta had honed her writing skills, affirmed her interest in politics, and demonstrated her capacity as organizer. To date Hughes's Church-related activities—her 'uplifting' work among the Natives and the missionary efforts on behalf of immigrants in Alberta—were motivated by religious and social factors. The persona of Miss Hughes, the public servant, remained largely detached from that of Hughes, the Catholic activist. Soon her life would be transformed and the personal and professional would merge in a crusade of 'self-sacrifice.'[49] Hughes left Edmonton a successful writer and political insider. She would return a maligned and marginalized figure.

Katherine commenced her duties in London in September 1913. She was based in the new Office of the Agent General for Alberta at Trafalgar Building, 1 Charing Cross. The office had been established as a focal point for the promotion of trade between Britain and Alberta, to encourage immigration into Alberta, and to deal with general enquiries about this new western Canadian province. Unfortunately, the earliest records for the agent general's office have not survived, but as John A. Reid's administrative assistant and secretary, Hughes probably handled much of this routine work.

As part of her official duties, Katherine visited Ireland for the first time in the summer of 1914.[50] In Dublin she had lunch and tea with the Marquis Aberdeen, Lord-Lieutenant in Ireland, and his wife, Lady Aberdeen.[51] In Ireland and back in London, Hughes also met prominent activists involved in the Irish cultural revival and in the political separatist movement.[52] The latter were to cause Hughes to reconsider radically her opinions about Ireland. Formerly a 'Home Ruler,' a supporter of limited self-government for Ireland within the British Empire,[53] Hughes became a staunch advocate of a fully-independent Ireland. She later explained this shift:

> I want to tell you why I changed from a Canadian Imperialist to Irish—a proper Irish person . . . No matter how much we know of the old history of Ireland, we know nothing of the conditions in Ireland till we go there by ourselves, and when I was sent over there in a position for our Government some few years ago, and saw things for myself, I was appalled at the conditions—a country made up of the very old and the very young. . . .[54]

There were few young adults, Hughes declared, for most had emigrated or gone off to join the British Army due to the lack of opportunities at home.

Hughes with the Roman Catholic priest, Father Albert Lacombe. Her biography of Lacombe was published in 1911. (PAA OB.8466)

Hughes started learning the Irish language in London, where she collaborated on a play, *The Cherry Bird*, with Pádraic Ó Conaire, the foremost Gaelic writer of his time.[55] Katherine Hughes, or Caitlín Ní Aodha as she now styled herself on occasion, had 'discovered' Ireland, a sense of Irishness, and her roots. With the certainty, conviction, and complete lack of self-doubt that marked all her undertakings, she took up the torch of Irish independence from the British Empire. This issue would dominate the remainder of her life.

Apart from the collaboration with Ó Conaire, Hughes had begun researching material for a book on political, social, and economic conditions in Ireland; however, she had not lost contact with her Canadian connections. As she explained in a letter to Lacombe, she had met Sir William Van Horne in London in the summer of 1914.[56] It was during this meeting that the ailing Van Horne, who had been impressed by the Lacombe biography,[57] discussed collaborating on several volumes about the Canadian Pacific Railway. The two sketched out their plans in a series of letters during the summer of 1915.[58] When the financial arrangements were to her satisfaction, Katherine resigned her position with the Government of Alberta in August. She intended to leave London at the end of September and sail back to North America, but prior to her departure Sir William died in Montreal on 11 September, causing doubt about Katherine's future. In an exchange of letters, Richard Benedict Van Horne, son of the railway magnate, agreed that Hughes would write his father's biography: 'My mother tells me that Sir William told her shortly before he left St. Andrews [New Brunswick, where Van Horne had a summer home] for the last time that there were only two people whom he would care to have write his biography and his preference was for you, and I may add that I quite share his opinion. So, if you still desire to undertake this work, we will be glad to have you do so.'[59]

Based in Montreal after her return from London, Hughes set about her new tasks with her customary zest. Yet in spite of the tremendous amount of effort that she expended in researching and writing the biography, a draft

In a Canada gripped by wartime jingoism and aware of attempts by the 1916 Irish insurgents to obtain weaponry from Germany, being pro-Irish independence was synonymous in the establishment press with being disloyal, treacherous, and pro-German.

of which she completed and presented to R. B. Van Horne in August 1918, Ireland and major events there—including the Easter Rising of 1916 and the subsequent executions of its leaders by the British—forced her to act. '1916 has shaken me out of a good deal of laissez-faire,' she wrote.[60] Already to the fore in promoting the cause of Irish independence through the publication of her monograph *Ireland*,[61] Hughes lectured on the subject in Canada. The hostile reaction that she garnered from a *Saturday Night* columnist demonstrated that in a Canada gripped by wartime jingoism and aware of attempts by the 1916 Irish insurgents to obtain weaponry from Germany, being pro-Irish independence was synonymous in the establishment press with being disloyal, treacherous, and pro-German.[62]

Hughes's trips to pro-Irish independence gatherings in the United States brought her into contact with activists there. She attended and addressed the Irish Race Convention, organized by the Friends of Irish Freedom, in New York City in May 1918.[63] Impressed by the potential for advancing that cause in the United States, she later referred back to the 1918 Race Convention as the occasion on which 'I . . . asked the privilege of myself coming to work where there was a field worth working in.'[64] As soon as she had completed in draft form the Van Horne biography, she headed to Washington, DC, to work fulltime as a propagandist for the Irish cause in the office of the newly established Irish National Bureau. Over the following thirty months, using all her organizational skills, Hughes became an important and highly respected figure in the pro-Irish publicity machine in the United States. After her testimony before Congressional hearings in December 1918, the *Gaelic American* declared: 'Miss Hughes differed from the other women speakers in this, that she marshalled her facts like a trained lawyer and had very complete command of them. She is an encyclopedia of Irish knowledge.'[65] Apart from lobbying and organizing, Hughes assembled a compilation of press reports, *English Atrocities in Ireland*, describing British military activities in Ireland.[66] She also lectured extensively throughout the southern States, explaining the origins of the guerrilla war being waged by the Irish Volunteers (or Irish Republican

Army [IRA] as they were now known) against the British administration in Ireland and organizing supporters in advance of the arrival of Eamon de Valera, the Irish republican leader. The *Gaelic American* reprinted a laudatory report from the Richmond *Virginian* of late June 1919 of Hughes, 'Woman Champion of the Irish Republic,' silencing a heckler at a meeting in Richmond, with the unnamed reporter (clearly male!) describing her as 'a young woman of slender build, with bright blue eyes, a mass of soft light-brown hair and finely-chiseled features . . .'[67] Yet Hughes had to overcome problems with male colleagues. Commenting on the personal difficulties that she, as an independent and spirited woman, had with the bureau's director, Daniel T. O'Connell, she noted: 'I believe he gets along well with many men—but women have no reason for existence with him except as wives, mothers, schoolteachers and very docile stenographers.'[68]

By mid 1920 there was a well-organized pro-Irish lobby in the United States. Now it was decided to coordinate Irish republican supporters in Canada. While the Self-Determination for Ireland League of Canada and Newfoundland was formally under the leadership of Lindsay Crawford, a former Orangeman, Katherine Hughes moved from Washington to Montreal in May 1920 as provisional national organizer of the league.

Between 2 July and mid-October 1920 when the league held its first national convention, Hughes travelled from St John's, Newfoundland, to Vancouver organizing and lecturing on her 'Facts about Ireland Tour.' Hughes was extremely successful in organizing the local Irish and supporters of their cause, but, by the time she reached western Canada in late July, she was attracting the attention of opponents. Branded in Regina as 'repeatedly guilty of treasonable utterances,'[69] she was dismissed by Kennedy H. Palmer, commissioner for the Society for British and American Friendship, when he lectured to Orangemen in Calgary, as 'simply an agent in Canada for De Valera.' He added, 'our fight is not with the fair maid who only slightly stirs up the stream of our Canadian life with a camouflaged propaganda. The fight is with the hogs wallowing in the creek above, muddying the stream of the Empire.'[70] Attacked in a nasty editorial in the *Calgary Herald*,[71] Hughes also had to contend with official hostility. The Criminal Investigation Bureau (CIB) of the newly renamed RCMP—whose reports, ironically, were presented to Arthur Sifton, now federal secretary of state —was wary of collaboration between the league and 'other disturbing elements,' especially the One Big Union and 'the foreign population' in the Winnipeg area.[72] And

Canadian Military Intelligence was keeping a close eye on the alleged connections of prominent Leaguers with the Irish Republican gun-running chain that extended through the United States to Canada and on to Ireland.[73]

Hughes's old paper, the *Edmonton Bulletin*, reported that news of her lecture in Edmonton on 15 August aroused such interest that 'large crowds . . . thronged the sidewalk at the Pantages Theatre before 8 p.m., while when the doors opened half an hour later every seat in the big building was filled while the aisles and space around the walls accommodated large numbers.' At one stage during Hughes's address, 'the interruptions were violent and frequent,' and, according to the *Bulletin*, 'the mention of De Valera's name brought a storm of hisses and cheers . . . .'[74] The following evening, Hughes presided over the official launching of the Edmonton Branch of the Self-Determination League, with 267 Edmontonians joining.[75]

Despite Hughes's personal success, the league's drive during the summer of 1920 aroused unease among quite a number of Canadians—generally Irish or Catholic, and frequently Irish Catholics—who felt uncertain about their status and position within the country. Faced with the disapproval of the establishment press and justifiable worries about the close scrutiny of the CIB and Military Intelligence, these people felt vulnerable to charges that they were supporting IRA violence, were being manipulated by Bolshevik agitators, and were subverting the British Empire. Henry O'Leary, the Prince Edward Island-born Catholic archbishop of Edmonton and a supporter of the league, was implored by unnamed Catholics to ban a league meeting scheduled to be held in a church-run school. These Edmonton Catholics declared:

We, as Catholics, have lived through trying times in Edmonton during the last few months and since Miss Katherine Hughes was allowed to speak here on Ireland and Sinn Feinism.

Just as we are trying to live down and bury the insulting things she shamelessly told us about our wonderful soldiers, along comes another Anarchist . . . [a Mr Latham who] was going to speak to-night on Ireland and Self-Determination in our Separate School . . .

We all know that Sinn Feinism is only a form of Bolshevism which we should stamp out in its infancy in this country and it is such an easy thing to stir up an agitation of any kind at the present time.

These Catholic Edmontonians also stated: 'Among Women's Organizations in Edmonton, there is the bitterest feeling—loyal *vs* disloyal and it is a very common thing to hear that of course Catholic and Sinn Fein is [sic] one and the same thing.'[76]

Despite hostility, threats, and predictions of dire consequences, over seven hundred delegates, representing the league's 25,000 members, attended its first national convention in Ottawa in October. Keen to remain in the background, Hughes was finally introduced 'as the woman who had done more than any other for the cause of Ireland in Canada.'[77] Nor was there any respite for Hughes. Once the convention broke up, she returned to the United States where de Valera's obsession with controlling the Irish-American network was rapidly leading to an inevitable split with the Friends of Irish Freedom.

While Hughes, somewhat blindly, pledged her allegiance to de Valera and his new organization, the American Association for the Recognition of the Irish Republic, her attention was focussed on her next mission: to organize supporters in New Zealand and Australia. In addition, Hughes had heard in New York, following the Canadian campaign, that her Van Horne typescript was to be published immediately, having been prepared for publication by Walter Vaughan, a former Canadian Pacific Railway (CPR) employee. He alone would be credited as author of the book. She contacted R. B. Van Horne seeking clarification and what she referred to as 'an equitable settlement' for her labours in writing the book.[78] In addition, she explored the possibilities of seeking a court injunction to prevent publication of the book under Vaughan's name.[79] Though the publishers, the Century Co. of New York, suggested a compromise whereby both her and Vaughan's names would appear on the book, Hughes wrote later on that R. B. Van Horne was not interested in compromise:

> I felt that Mr. Van Horne would not alter his apparent objection to my name on the book, because I am an advocate of Irish Freedom—an 'Irish agitator' I have no doubt he would term it.
> I learned from the best possible authority in New York that Mr. Van Horne did strongly object to my political views and open advocate [sic] of Ireland's cause.[80]

The Life and Work of Sir William Van Horne was quickly published, solely under Walter Vaughan's name. In the preface, Vaughan acknowledged Hughes's involvement with the project, though ingeniously managing to distance himself and the final product from her by claiming he had adapted her rough narrative. Hughes admitted that the typescript she had submitted to the Van Horne family for examination needed cutting and pruning.[81] To that extent, her version may be termed a 'rough narrative.' However, if one studies both published work and typescript in tandem, one realizes the extent to which Vaughan not merely drew on her material but used it in his version, frequently just altering words or phrases.[82] He certainly shortened the text, leaving out whole incidents or anecdotes or transferring passages to tighten it up. His role was that of editor not author, however, for the book in its final published form remains substantially the work of Hughes, as researched and written by her.

Until her death, Hughes remained bitter about this matter. For financial reasons, she was never able to mount a court challenge. In the fall of 1920 she had to put aside her anger and concentrate on her new assignment. Unlike Katherine's work in the United States and Canada, her mission in Australia and New Zealand would be more secretive. Being a Canadian citizen was a valuable asset in gaining admission to the sister dominions (which would have been less easy for an American), but Hughes still had to be careful not to draw attention to herself lest she might be refused entry or deported as a trouble-making alien. For this reason, Hughes's activities and her movements from one centre to the next, from one country to the other, are difficult to document and track.

The earliest located reference to her is in the Melbourne Catholic paper the *Advocate*, which reported in February 1921 that 'Miss Katherine Hughes, a lady well known in the American literary world, is at present on a visit to Melbourne.'[83] Branches of the new Self-Determination for Ireland League of Australia began to appear in Sydney at the end of February and, following Katherine's visit to it, in Melbourne on 1 March.[84] Working quietly and effectively in the background, Hughes provided the expertise in establishing branches, laying plans for state conventions, and building a coalition of Irish groups. Openly acknowledged later by Irish Australians as 'the founder in Australia' of the Self-Determination League, Hughes was extremely successful in convincing small groups that they should merge with the new League.[85]

She travelled from Australia to New Zealand, probably in May 1921, as branches of the Self-Determination for Ireland League of New Zealand were founded on both the North Island, including Wellington, and the South Island, including Dunedin, during this period.[86] The Wellington Irish, notes Richard Davis, 'were inspired' by her visit.[87]

Katherine's last great mission of coordinating the Irish World Race Congress, scheduled for Paris in January 1922, was a logical follow through of her work in North America and Australasia.[88] The Anglo-Irish Treaty of December 1921 and the acrimonious debate that ensued in Ireland transformed what was intended to be a major propagandist vehicle for the Irish republican cause into an irrelevant and embarrassing sideshow. Hughes, dejected by the lack of unity among Irish republicans who were soon to turn on each other in a nasty civil war, returned to North America, where the Irish support networks in Canada and the United States had been decimated by the new internecine strife in their homeland.

Marked as an agitator and troublemaker in Canada, Katherine Hughes spent the final three years of her life in the New York area, residing with family members. It is not clear that she had any steady employment. While still a member of the now infinitely weakened pro-Irish republican lobby, she withdrew virtually completely from public politics but continued to advocate the need for unity among the Irish at home and abroad.

Katherine Hughes died of carcinoma of the stomach at the age of forty-eight in New York on 26 April 1925.[89] The New York *Irish World* stated that news of Hughes's death 'caused profound regret, not only in the city itself, but wherever she was known over the United States by her kindly and unsparing efforts in [sic] behalf of the cause so dear to her heart. Her funeral . . . was of imposing dimensions. . . .'[90]

An old friend and colleague, Peter Magennis, provides another version of the 'imposing dimensions' of the funeral and a testament to the ultimate irony, if not tragedy, of Hughes's life. She had sacrificed her career and status as respectable literary figure and political insider in support of an unfashionable political stand. If she compensated for this loss by finding a cause to which she was able to devote herself intellectually and emotionally, her loyalty and commitment were ultimately in vain on both a professional and personal level. Ireland was partitioned. And Hughes's funeral was unofficially boycotted by her colleagues in the Irish republican movement on account of her obsession with grandiose and unrealistic plans to unite the Irish worldwide at a time when the overthrow of the Anglo-Irish Treaty was deemed the primary tactical goal. Writing in the Dublin *Catholic Bulletin*, Magennis quotes a fellow priest: 'Poor Catherine [sic] Hughes has passed away; she died lonely, and her funeral was remarkable for the number absent from it. Surely she deserved more, and from the Republicans, too.'[91]

Katherine Hughes is buried in an unmarked grave in St Raymond's Cemetery, The Bronx, New York. Though her death was noted in the *Edmonton Bulletin*,[92] the 'Royal woman' was soon a forgotten figure.

❧ Maligned at the time on account of her unpopular stand in support of Irish self-determination and overlooked since by historians of women's experience and of Ireland, the winsome and dynamic Hughes remains something of an enigma. Despite the major obstacles in the path of the advancement of women, Hughes was successful not only in obtaining positions of prominence and of influence but in fulfilling her responsibilities in an exceptionally effective and competent manner. She demonstrated a capacity to adapt to her surroundings, whether on Native reserves, in western Canada, or among Irish political activists, without sacrificing or compromising her strong religious faith. Indeed, much of her strength and self-confidence likely came from her family's commitment to Catholicism whereby, as illustrated by the life of her uncle, Archbishop O'Brien, service on behalf of the Church was highly rated.

While Hughes's career implied that she was a supporter of social reform, if one searches for evidence that her crusades were part of a more extensive personal social and political consciousness, the evidence is scant. She stood as an example of a woman who refused to be confined to her proper sphere but the issue of collective women's rights did not figure prominently with her. She laboured on behalf of Natives and the Irish but she did not develop a critique of society and power structures based on her Native and Irish experiences. The American social reformer, Jane Addams, stated: 'I do not think we are put into the world to be religious, we have a certain work to do, and to do that is the main thing.'[93] Addams believed not just in service, however, but in social change. While this quote summarizes much of Hughes's life and career, her vision, likely influenced by her Catholicism, was less expansive than Addams's or that of other reformers. Ultimately, Hughes's faith was both her major strength and weakness. ❧

JARS BALAN

UKRAINIAN THEATRE: SHOWTIME ON THE NORTH SASKATCHEWAN

Edmonton *Journal* ad for three January 1915 performances by the Ukrainian theatre company.

*B*ritish immigrants and Anglo-Canadians from Ontario and the Maritimes were not the only people to seek out Canada's prairies for adventure, new economic opportunities, or simply a fresh start. Ukrainian peasants fleeing poverty and political oppression in Europe flocked to 'free' homesteads in western Canada, settling in blocs that perpetuated their institutions, practices, and beliefs. Some Ukrainian immigrants also went to urban centres (particularly Winnipeg) where, as unskilled labourers digging sewers, paving streets, and working on construction projects, they helped city boosters realize their goals.

A few better-educated Ukrainians infiltrated the fringes of Anglo-Canadian society as small businessmen or school teachers. They also assumed the leadership of the Ukrainian community and led the resistance to demands that Ukrainians assimilate to so-called superior British ways. Contrary to much popular Anglo-Canadian opinion, Ukrainians possessed a vibrant grass roots peasant culture, a rich religious tradition, and an active public life in which theatre enjoyed great popularity. As Ukrainian society became increasingly politicized along old world lines, theatre mirrored the tensions. Among a semi-literate people, drama was not simply entertainment but also a vehicle for propaganda. The staging of plays became occasions for demonstrating and asserting influence.

Relatively few Ukrainians lived in Edmonton through the First World War, but they, too, developed a theatrical tradition, and it, also, reflected the tensions in the larger Ukrainian community. Jars Balan is an Edmonton-based writer and poet who researches the history of Ukrainian-language literature and theatre in Canada. He explores the evolution of early Ukrainian drama in Edmonton, including attempts to reach out to the non-Ukrainian-speaking public.

MAJOR CULTURAL ENDEAVOURS BY UKRAINIANS IN Canada before the First World War marked an important step in the process by which they became truly 'landed' immigrants. In establishing large performing ensembles the pioneer generation signalled that it was building a society ready to meet some of the emotional and intellectual needs of its community. No longer simply preoccupied with everyday survival, or satisfied by informal and sporadic get-togethers, New World Ukrainians sought more structured pursuits to express their creativity and to occupy their leisure.

The advent of theatre was especially significant because of the high degree of cooperation, planning, and commitment required to mount a drama successfully on the stage. Actors had to be recruited and a rehearsal site arranged before a director could begin the difficult task of breathing life into a script. Next, costumes, props, and backdrops needed to be made or obtained and a suitable space secured for the performance. Lastly, the event had to be effectively advertised, if the investment of time and energy was to be rewarded with an appreciative, paying audience. In short, theatre demanded the existence of a rudimentary infrastructure to present plays to the public.

In many respects the unfolding of Ukrainian-language theatre in Canada points to some of the more subtle developments taking place within the broader community. Besides indicating that a settlement attained a critical mass capable of supporting theatrical undertakings, the birth of the first dramatic ensembles revealed that immigrants had achieved a measure of cultural sophistication and were motivated to become participants in and patrons of the arts. Similarly, the shift of performances from occasional events to regular occurrences was a sign that a community was achieving relative stability in the conduct of its affairs. Even improvements in the quality of productions and the expansion of repertoires were obvious benchmarks of progress, gauging on the one hand the technical advances made by the performers, and, on the other, the aesthetic or intellectual refinement of the audience. The introduction of plays written by immigrant authors, for instance, announced that the theatre was acquiring an indigenous character and not just importing its content from the Old Country. Likewise, the addition of contemporary titles and recent translations to playlists was evidence that drama was starting to engage and challenge audiences, instead of simply pandering to their nostalgic yearnings. The history of early Ukrainian theatre, therefore, sheds important light on the psychological breakthroughs made by the pioneer generation in becoming acclimatized to Canadian reality.

The inception and early years of Ukrainian-language theatre in Edmonton provide a fascinating illustration of how a transplanted culture struggles to take root in unfamiliar soil, adapts, and begins to flourish in its new environment. At the same time, the evolution of the local performing arts scene in the opening decades of the twentieth century serves as an indicator of the social and artistic progress that urban Alberta Ukrainians were making as a distinct community. Finally, the story of Edmonton's pioneer Ukrainian theatre shows how foreign-born Canadians could idealistically reach out for mainstream acknowledgement and approval, yet meet with almost complete indifference from their fellow citizens.

Although Ukrainian immigrants began passing through Edmonton as early as 1892 en route to homesteads east of Fort Saskatchewan, almost six years went by before any of the newcomers settled permanently in what subsequently became the capital of the province of Alberta. The first Ukrainian to take up full-time residence in the city was a twenty-three-year-old bachelor named Michael Gowda (1874–1953), who arrived in Canada sufficiently fluent in English to find immediate work as a commercial interpreter. Upon disembarking at Strathcona station on 18 May 1898, he was quickly hired by the Bellamy Agricultural Implement Company (located on Jasper Avenue at 100A Street) to negotiate and promote sales with the swelling tide of Slavic farmers. Besides translating for settlers when they came into town to purchase equipment and supplies, Gowda also met incoming trains from Calgary so that he could assist new arrivals as they prepared to set out to begin homesteading.

The educated son of a Greek Catholic cleric, Gowda had been instilled from youth with the progressive, community-oriented values of the Galician Ukrainian populist movement. As such, he was firmly committed to helping his fellow countrymen better themselves materially, socially, and educationally. His interpreting jobs—initially in the farm implement business and then with the Dominion Land Titles office—enabled him to play a pivotal role in the development of Ukrainian life not only in the burgeoning colony of rural east central Alberta but also in Edmonton during its formative years. Indeed, a strong case could be made that he deserves recognition as the 'founding father' of Ukrainian Edmonton.[1]

Given Gowda's position at the very hub of immigrant affairs in turn-of-the-century Alberta, it is not surprising that he figured prominently in the inauguration of organized Ukrainian cultural activity in Edmonton. In late

1901 he helped to establish the first reading society (*chytalnia*), named after Taras Shevchenko, Ukraine's great poet.[2] The Taras Shevchenko Chytalnia is said to have been responsible for mounting the first Ukrainian play in the city, staged, appropriately, under the direction of Michael Gowda sometime in 1907. At that time, there would have been some two to three hundred permanent Ukrainian residents in Edmonton, mostly young women working as domestics and hotel maids. We do not know any details about this symbolically auspicious event—neither where the performance took place nor the name of the play—and curiously Gowda makes no mention of it in any of his autobiographical writings.[3] Despite the fact that the production seems to have been an isolated effort of no lasting consequence, it does suggest that by 1907 the nascent Ukrainian element in the new provincial capital was starting to crystallize into a more cohesive and dynamic ethnic force.

Because the Ukrainian presence in Edmonton before the First World War received scanty attention in the contemporary press, and has as of yet been poorly researched by historians, we have only a fragmentary picture of the embryonic period of immigrant institutional growth. Thus, there is no evidence of theatrical enterprise for five years following the debut production in 1907, with one notable exception: in 1909 a local amateur group apparently staged Ivan Kotliarevsky's classic comic operetta, *Natalka Poltavka* (Natalie from Poltava). Since an extant photograph of the cast members was obviously taken in the late summer or early fall (judging from the attire of the participants and the foliage on the trees in the background), the play was probably presented around that time. Of course, the possibility also exists that the drama claimed to have been mounted in 1907 was actually the *Natalka Poltavka* performance of 1909. Interestingly, one of the actors was Sophia Gowda-Kotyk, a sister of Michael Gowda.[4]

It was not until 1912 that Ukrainian-language drama in Edmonton finally became launched on a more consistent basis. That year an amateur theatrical circle was organized as part of the fledgling Boian Society, an independent musical and dramatic club that had began in 1911 with the establishment of a choir. Named in honour of an eleventh-century Kievan bard, this society was modelled after similar performing ensembles spawned throughout Ukrainians' native Galicia and Bukovyna in the late nineteenth and early twentieth centuries by the Rus'ka and Ukrains'ka Besida associations. In their first year of operation, the Edmonton Boian players presented three stageworks, heralding a modest but solid beginning for Ukrainian-language drama on the shores of the North Saskatchewan. Henceforth, theatrical undertakings increased in frequency, audiences grew in size, and productions became more varied and ambitious.[5]

Nevertheless, compared to other immigrant centres in Canada, Ukrainian theatre developed relatively slowly in Edmonton. In Winnipeg, for example, where the first play was presented in 1904, fourteen different stageworks had been mounted by the end of 1907, and there were almost forty verifiable productions by the end of 1912. Over the same time span, multiple performances had also taken place in such cities as Fort William, Port Arthur, Vancouver, and Montreal, and there were signs of theatrical endeavour in rural and resource frontier settlements from Manitoba to British Columbia. Indeed, the Alberta hinterland had been the site of the earliest Ukrainian drama production in Canada (a play was put on in the Beaver Creek colony near Lamont in 1901–02), and between February 1910 and December 1912 amateurs in Vegreville had offered no less than four evenings of native-language theatre.[6] Clearly, Edmonton was not in the vanguard of Ukrainian immigrant drama in the initial phase of its New World development, although the city soon made great strides in boosting its theatrical profile.

In 1913 the amateur players with the Boian Society doubled their output from the previous year, putting on a total of six plays and earning an impressive $534.60 in gate receipts. This money was put towards the building of a National Home (*narodnyi dim*) which would provide a much-needed facility for Boian and other cultural, social, and educational organizations. Until the National Home was erected in 1917, Ukrainian theatre groups made use of various venues, ranging from makeshift community-owned spaces to the Separate School Hall on Third Street.

One of the early performances at the latter venue was particularly memorable because it coincided with the first visit to Edmonton of the newly-appointed Greek Catholic prelate for Ukrainians in Canada, Bishop Nykyta Budka. As part of the festivities held in his honour, a reception at the Separate School Hall on 2 March concluded with the staging of *Pobida svitla nad t'moiu* (The victory of light over darkness) by O. Vasylevych. The event was covered by a reporter for Edmonton's English-language press, who described how 'six hundred Ruthenians' or Ukrainians gathered at the hall 'to welcome the ecclesiastical head of their church' with flowers, speeches, songs, and recitals. Among the local dignitaries present was His Grace Archbishop Legal of St Albert. The article's mention of an unidentified 'moral drama' put on as part of the program marked the first time that the new immigrant theatre came to the attention of non-Ukrainians in the city.[7]

One of Boian's 1913 offerings was *Natalka Poltavka*, presented on 6 November at the Ukrainian student residence located at 10628–96 Street. A promotional notice about the play placed in the local Ukrainian newspaper, *Novyny* (The news), somewhat unusually announced that this Eastern Ukrainian classic was being directed by a native of Kiev. Possibly the sponsors were implying that this interpretation of the play would be more authentic than the one staged earlier, no doubt under the leadership of a Galician director. Since most Edmonton Ukrainians emigrated from Western Ukraine, they would have required some coaching to capture the proper accent and other regional nuances of *Natalka Poltavka*.[8] Although the advertisement promised that the work would be 'better than all of the preceding plays' put on by Boian, an unfortunate incident marred the evening for the capacity audience.

According to a report published two days after the show, the production was successfully staged and well received by the public, although the quality of the acting was characterized as being uneven. Afterwards, the Boian choir sang three songs, which the reviewer ambiguously described as having been very capably rendered 'given the local circumstances.' In fact, the proceedings were disrupted by a 'drunken hooligan' who forced himself among the theatre-goers and let loose a torrent of abuse, resulting in his prompt eviction. Fifteen minutes later, in an apparent gesture of protest, someone further spoiled the mood by shattering a window with a rotten potato. The unexpected attack sent a wave of panic through the crowd, nearly triggering an exodus that would have sabotaged the dance scheduled to end the evening. The anonymous *Novyny* reporter blamed the antics on an unnamed individual who had 'taken his "courage" ' in a nearby bar, but the heading of the review tellingly labelled the whole affair a 'Hooligan-like demonstration by Moscophiles.'[9]

The reference to Moscophiles is significant because by mid-1913 a rival theatre group had been established in Edmonton by pro-tsarist Ukrainian adherents of the Russian Orthodox church. Called the 'Russka' Drama Circle, it staged its premiere production—*Satana v bochtsi*

The reference to Moscophiles is significant because by mid-1913 a rival theatre group had been established in Edmonton by pro-tsarist Ukrainian adherents of the Russian Orthodox church.

(Satan in a barrel) by Vasyl Dmytrenko—at the Separate School Hall on 21 June 1913.[10] Three weeks later, this one-act comedy and a second play were taken on the road to rural Russian Orthodox parishes in Vegreville and Shandro.[11] The two-day excursion into the adjacent Ukrainian bloc settlement marked the first time that an Edmonton production toured the surrounding countryside, a practice subsequently adopted by other theatrical ensembles. On 27 December 1913 the Farmer's Drama Circle from Mundare blazed a trail in the opposite direction when it brought Antin Nahoriansky's comic operetta, *Okh, ne liuby dvokh!* (Oh, don't love two at once!) to the city.[12] Although it made sense to give repeat performances because of the cost and effort involved in staging a drama, the logistics of moving a show around, as well as the difficulties inherent with poor roads and unpredictable weather, understandably limited the frequency of such travel.

By 1913 Boian also faced competition from two other aspiring theatre groups. One of these was a drama circle sponsored by a society called Postup (Progress), which staged *Yasni zori* (Bright stars) by Borys Hrinchenko in mid-June.[13] Unfortunately, this company seems to have disbanded after just a single play, leaving few clues about its existence. While Postup's name suggests that it may have been sponsored by socialists (or perhaps Protestants), it was more likely the creation of a prominent local activist and businessman, Roman Kremar (1885-1953). Kremar had founded the newspaper *Novyny* in January 1913, after having only recently undergone a striking political transformation from a leading Edmonton socialist into a successful land speculator and Conservative party supporter with latent Catholic sympathies. This metamorphosis probably explains an article that appeared in the left-wing Winnipeg publication, *Robochyi narod* (Working people), which mocked Kremar for allegedly starting a drama group to promote his newspaper.[14]

Of greater import was the debut production of the Ivan Franko Drama Circle of Edmonton on 9 October 1913. Entitled *Torhivlia zhemchuhamy* (Trade in pearls), by Hryhorii Tsehlynsky, it proclaimed the appearance of an

Advertisement from the Ukrainian-language newspaper *Novyny* for an 11 June 1914 production of Marko Kropyvnytsky's drama, *The Captive*.

ensemble that joined Boian as a dominant and durable force on the pioneer Edmonton Ukrainian theatre scene.[15] This sudden proliferation of theatrical troupes in 1913 paralleled the changes then taking place within the immigrant community in general, as political and denominational differences were rapidly dividing Ukrainians into fiercely competitive camps. While unfortunate in some respects, this rivalry had a beneficial effect on the performing arts, because it spurred theatrical ensembles to exert themselves more vigorously and to raise the quality of their presentations.

In sum, at least thirteen Ukrainian play performances, by four different amateur groups, were staged in Edmonton in 1913—and there were probably several more, given the gaps in the available newspaper record. But while a solid foundation had been laid for further growth, it would take several more years before circumstances permitted Ukrainian-language theatre in Edmonton to reach its full potential.

Only ten performances are documented for 1914, but it is unlikely that this figure reflects the actual total. As fewer than 10 per cent of the issues of the Moscophile Edmonton newspaper, *Russkii golos* (Russian voice), have survived for this year, documentation for theatre activity in the pro-Russian sector of the Ukrainian community is woefully lacking. It is noteworthy that while Boian's theatrical productivity dropped from six to four shows (which with the help of two concerts realized $660.26 in admissions), one of these was the five-act melodrama, *Ubiinyky* (The murderers), by the Protestant minister and Ukrainian immigrant activist, John Bodrug (1874–1952).[16] Staged 10 January 1914 at the Separate School Hall, this Canadian work with an Old Country setting featured an impressive twenty-two-member cast.[17] Meanwhile, the Ivan Franko Drama Circle also presented at least four theatrical evenings during the year, including two performances of a popular play by Ivan Tohobochny, *Zhydivka vykhrestka* (The baptised Jewess).[18]

A new group of players, the Ukrainian Youth Circle, presented a musical tableau by Petro Nishchynsky called *Vechornytsi* (Evening revelries), and a visiting troupe from Mundare appears to have put on the first Edmonton production of the comedy, *Svatannia na Honcharivtsi* (Matchmaking at Honcharivka), by Hryhorii Kvita-Osnovianenko. The latter play went on to become one of the staples of the New World repertoire, being performed in immigrant settlements throughout North America over several decades. The fact that the proceeds from both above productions were slated for the Red Cross illustrates how Ukrainians were becoming more integrated into mainstream Canadian society.[19]

By 1915 Ukrainian theatre in Edmonton had generated considerable momentum and was ready to expand its horizons. That, at least, was one of the assumptions behind an unusual venture with the laudable aim of fostering appreciation of Ukrainian culture across ethnic and linguistic lines. Conceived by a small circle that included Roman Kremar and his *Novyny* editor, Myroslaw Stechishin (1883–1947), the project was partly intended to improve the image of Ukrainian immigrants by showcasing the richness of their artistic heritage. However, the secrecy with which this ambitious undertaking proceeded suggests there was also another agenda behind the planned theatrical coup.

Without any fanfare or even an appeal for volunteers in *Novyny*, so as not to alert the rival *Russkii golos* that something was afoot, late in 1914 a group of more than thirty young people began quietly rehearsing three plays simultaneously under the direction of I.K. Dorosh.[20] Their aim was to present the works in quick succession to the non-Ukranian-speaking public early in the new year, thereby impressing Edmonton theatre-goers with the vitality of Ukraine's ethnographically-based musical theatre. Besides trying to influence mainstream opinion, the daring move must have also been intended as a surprise manoeuvre in the ethnic political arena by Kremar and Stechishin. Since the emerging nationalist wing of the Ukranian community was then locked in a bitter struggle with the Moscophile camp (which in 1913 had successfully elected Andrew Shandro as the Liberal MLA for Whitford), any bid to promote specifically 'Ukrainian' awareness would at the same time strike a blow against those propagating a pro-Russian orientation.

Having booked the spacious Empire Theatre on Jasper Avenue and hired the house orchestra to provide musical accompaniment, the backers of this covert enterprise placed an ad in the New Year's day edition of the *Edmonton Journal*, announcing that a 'Ukrainian Theatrical Company' would be presenting 'Dramatic and Operatic Gems in the Native Language' for three nights beginning 4 January.[21] No details were provided about the dramas being offered and there was no other advance publicity about the company or its objectives, effectively keeping everyone—and not just *Russkii golos* supporters—in the dark about the performances as well as the performers.

The first show in the planned run was an operetta written by Mykhailo Starytsky, a translator of *Hamlet* and the author of more than thirty stageworks. Entitled *Oi, ne khody, Hrytsiu, tai na vechornytsi* (Oh, don't go to the party, Hryts), this perennial favourite of Ukrainian audiences featured colourful costumes, beautiful songs, and exciting folk dances, which the sponsors evidently believed would make it broadly accessible and entertaining despite being in the Ukrainian language. The *Edmonton Journal* critic sent to cover the performance seems to have been genuinely impressed with the story, the production values, and the overall quality of the acting. He likewise noted the auspiciousness of the occasion in the lead paragraph to his detailed account of the show:

> Dramatic history was made last night at the Empire theatre when for the first time in a Canadian theatre a company of Ukrainians produced a play in their own language. In their old home the drama is well developed and they have many playwrights and actors who take a high rank. But though it is now some years since they began to come to the Dominion in large numbers, they have had to give such constant attention to everyday occupations that there has been no time for bringing out their artistic talent. Last night's play is accordingly an important milestone for them.[22]

The reviewer was especially taken by the performance of the female lead—E. Lastiwka, in the role of Marusia—whom he singled out for praise as having both 'charm' and 'real dramatic instinct.' He encouraged others to attend the two follow-up presentations by the company, suggesting they would be interesting and enjoyable to anyone whose curiosity had been stirred by the people who were 'now so large a part of our Western Canadian population.'[23] Ominously, the reviewer appears to have been the only 'non-ethnic' at the show, and he did not take his own advice by coming to the second performance.

Nor did his enthusiasm have any visible impact on *Journal* readers, who took no notice of the unique opportunity being offered to them. Attendance at the first performance was sparse and confined almost exclusively to Slavs, while the turnout for the second show, on 5 January—when Marko Kropyvnytsky's operetta, *Perekhytryly* (Outwitted), was staged—seems to have been even more dismal, and comprised entirely of Ukrainians. The disastrous situation led the patrons of the amateur company to relocate the third play, *Beztalanna* (The hapless maid) by Ivan Tobilevych, to Paul Rudyk's much less costly and more familiar Ukrainian student residence.[24]

The complete failure to attract the targeted audience was a humiliating and costly lesson for all those involved in the Ukrainian Theatrical Company, who were ultimately undone by a combination of their naïvety and their questionable promotional strategy. Adding insult to injury, for all its kind words, the *Journal* review had confusingly used 'Little Russia' and 'Russian' interchangeably with 'Ukraine' and 'Ukrainians,' either consciously or unknowingly undermining the political purpose of the company's calculated intervention. Significantly, when translating the article for their readers, the editors of *Novyny* consistently used the word 'Ukraine' and placed 'Little Russia' in brackets. A *Novyny* article on 9 January also tried to put a positive spin on the fiasco by suggesting that the initiative had a beneficial side and may simply have been premature, but the author of the carefully-worded piece (probably Stechishin) was unable to hide the pain of rejection in his acknowledgement of defeat.[25]

Not surprisingly, the affair prompted delighted jeers from *Russkii golos*, which gleefully described Kremar as having burst into tears while speaking at the Ukrainian student residence presentation of *Beztalanna* on 7 January. The same article also pointed out that the opening night performance of *Oi, ne khody, Hrytsiu!* had concluded with 'God Save the King' instead of the Ukrainian national anthem, disingenuously implying that the orchestra's unfamiliarity with the hymn somehow proved the patriotic folly of an independent Ukraine.[26]

The Ukrainian Theatrical Company attempted to recoup some of its losses by resolutely taking the show on the road. In the following weeks and months the plays were successfully re-mounted with accompanying choral concerts in a series of nearby and distant Ukrainian settlements: Mundare (14, 15, 16 January), Vegreville (19, 20, 21, 22 January), Coleman (20 February), Medicine Hat (1 March), Moose Jaw (6, 8, 9 March), and finally, Regina (circa 10 March). Other presentations were announced for Camrose, Wetaskawin, Red Deer, and Calgary, but there is no documentation confirming playing dates at these locales.

Notwithstanding the bitter disappointment incurred in the setback experienced by the Ukrainian Theatrical Company, nationalist community support for Ukrainian-language theatre in the Alberta capital remained undiminished. Thus, in 1915 the Boian players went on to produce a total of five dramas, the most notable being the comedy, *Odruzhiinia* (The marriage) by the famous Russian-language author, Nikolai Gogol.[27] A native of the Poltava region in Eastern Ukraine, which he celebrated in several of his prose works, Gogol's father, Vasyl Hohol, was a pioneering Ukrainian-language playwright. While the Ivan Franko Circle seems to have been less active in 1915, judging from the available sources, a local Moscophile group reappeared on the scene after an apparent period of dormancy.[28]

A new drama group also contributed to the theatrical fare available to Edmonton's wartime Ukrainian community, adding yet another dimension to the organizational rivalry played out within the performing arts. On 5 April a freshly-established chapter of the Ukrainian Social Democratic Party (USDP) presented the appropriately political *Straik* (The strike), a play by a radical priest named Mykola Strutynski which depicted economic

unrest in an Old Country village.[29] Although the Edmonton local of the USDP soon collapsed and was only revived after a lapse of almost two years, a core group of left-wing theatre enthusiasts remained intact during the interval, forming the nucleus of a drama group called the Samoobrazovanie or Self-Enlightenment Society. Its early efforts are not properly documented, but within two years it had emerged as a major force on the Edmonton Ukrainian stage.[30]

In 1916 the growing Ukrainian student community in Edmonton became more theatrically active, starting with boarders at the Ukrainian student residence, who, together with an organization called Samopomich (Self-Help), put on two January performances of *Verkhovyntsi* (The highlanders) by Jozef Korzeniowski.[31] Students also mounted Borys Hrinchenko's *Nakhmarylo* (It has become cloudy) in mid-February and the recently-written *Rozladdie* (Disorder) by Dmytro Nykolyshyn in March, expanding the range of the Ukrainian-language repertoire while injecting some of their infectious enthusiasm.[32] Boian's output for the year was a total of six dramas, netting $441.40 for the planned National Home.[33] While there are no documented performances for the Ivan Franko Drama Circle in 1916, it most likely continued to be a vital presence on the theatre scene.

By now an integral and vibrant part of community life, Ukrainian-language theatre in Edmonton enjoyed a banner year in 1917. The Boian Drama Circle once again set the pace by giving ten performances, while the Ivan Franko players are known to have contributed at least two stage-works to the dramatic roster. One of these, *Pimsta za kryvdu* (Revenge for an injury), deserves special mention, because its author, Vasyl Kazanivsky (b. 1889), was himself an immigrant renowned as a theatre activist in Winnipeg. The Greek Catholic Markiian Shashkevych Society and some visiting teachers and students from Vegreville each added productions to the theatre calendar,[34] while amateurs affiliated with the resurrected USDP branch presented no fewer than five evenings of drama, including a performance in the working-class suburb of Beverly.[35] Further strengthening the left-wing representa-

By now an integral and vibrant part of community life, Ukrainian-language theatre in Edmonton enjoyed a banner year in 1917.

tion in this diverse organizational mix were three play productions credited to the rapidly rising T. Shevchenko Samoobrazovanie Society.

But by far the most significant development in 1917 was the official opening of the new Ukrainian National Home (located at 9645-108 Avenue) on 29 September, when Boian and the Markiian Shashkevych Society jointly staged the opera, *Kateryna* (Catherine) by Mykola Arkas, as part of the inaugural festivities.[36] The building was specifically designed to serve as a venue for the performing arts, and it became the focus of Ukrainian theatre in Edmonton as the pioneer era drew to a close with the arrival of a second wave of immigrants in the early 1920s.

An appreciation of the National Home's cultural importance can be garnered from the fact that in 1918 it was the site of fifty-one play productions and three concerts, earning a much needed $1,678.58 for the organization's coffers. Children's drama groups like the Ukrains'ka Ditocha Hromada, and student companies like the one sponsored by the Adam Kotsko Society, made use of the new facility, alongside established ensembles like Boian and the dynamic new Samoobrazovanie players. Clearly, little more than a decade after its tentative beginnings, Ukrainian-language amateur theatre in Edmonton had come of age and was in full stride. In a relatively short time span, it had accomplished a remarkable evolution from a sporadic grass-roots effort to a viable cottage industry. ∽

CHRISTOPHER SPENCER

THE SQUIRE OF SYLVANCROFT

Harry Evans, 1945 at age 69. (PAA B.6831)

*B*usiness and city boosterism went hand in hand in the years preceding the First World War. It seemed that what was good for business was good for Edmonton and what was good for Edmonton was good for business. City streets buzzed with real estate speculators as the combined population of Edmonton and Strathcona shot up from some 4,200 in 1901, to 31,100 by 1911, and over 70,000 by 1913.

Then the Edmonton real estate boom went bust. It started with declining agricultural prices in 1912 and gained frightening momentum as Europe prepared for war. The Hudson's Bay Company, for instance, had followed its usual policy of holding land off the market in the hopes of maximizing prices. When real estate prices suddenly tumbled, it lost money on its 3,000-acre reserve in Edmonton.

Edmonton's population actually dropped to 53,800 by 1916. And the city acquired tens of thousands of lots through tax defaults and soon teetered on the edge of bankruptcy.

Edmonton would not fully recover until the Second World War. Unbridled boosterism and speculation had their costs.

The man chosen by the business community to save Edmonton from financial ruin was H.M.E. Evans. He had arrived in Edmonton in 1907 and quickly became a prominent local businessman. He was connected to British capital and, like many Edmonton businessmen, involved in speculative enterprise. As Europe moved towards war, the British investment house for which Evans worked collapsed, very nearly taking Evans with it. Yet, backed by business, Evans ran for mayor in 1917 and was elected on a platform of strict fiscal responsibility.

This chapter is more than a simple account of a businessman-mayor. The author, Christopher Spencer, is a grandson of H.M.E. Evans. He provides an intimate portrait of life inside Sylvancroft, Evans's home overlooking Groat ravine.

THE RAVINE WAS NAMED GROAT, AFTER THE pioneer who had built the first of the grand homes in the area and in whose honour James Carruthers, a real estate speculator of Scottish descent, had donated the land to the emerging city of Edmonton in 1909 for a public park.[1] Its ecosystem supported an assortment of wild creatures—beavers, coyotes, foxes, deer, and, living in the brush, unpopular skunks and porcupines. Overlooking the boisterous stream that tumbled noisily into the North Saskatchewan River, pine, poplar, and birch trees, tall and steadfast, protected an undergrowth abundant with clusters of wild roses.

The rushing water was audible in the great dwellings that towered above the ravine: the homes of Edmonton's incipient aristocrats—Ramseys, Cornwalls, and Crosses—and, on the west bank, Government House, the residence of the lieutenant-governor. Perhaps, on bare November afternoons, looking north and east across the ravine, His Honour could see the impressive abode of one of his neighbours: a brick and stucco house, designed by Roland Lines, replete with mullioned windows, and, to shelter the front entrance, a porte-cochere.[2] The domain, including stables, gardens, a tennis lawn, and, in winter, a skating rink, went by the name Sylvancroft.[3]

Here, servant and master woke before six bells, pushed aside the lethargy of sleep, and moved towards the beginning of the new day in darkness. The squire of Sylvancroft, whose unconstrained energy established the pace for everyone in the house, set his purpose every morning without reprieve on the ritual of bathing in his tub. He did not soak languorously, retracing faded dreams while his body slowly absorbed the water's warmth. Harry Marshall Erskine Evans, politician and businessman, son of a Methodist minister, father of five children, mayor of Edmonton in 1918, and recipient of the Order of the British Empire in 1946, always set the temperature of his bath to just a few degrees above freezing. This practice, he believed, was healthy; best to shock the body awake, to focus one's powers of concentration on the new day. All obstacles to progress, he affirmed, could be vanquished through the power of a disciplined mind.[4]

Evans would live to be 97. Although he converted to Anglicanism and was a founding member of Christ Church in 1909, throughout his life he maintained his father's prohibition against cigarettes and alcohol. His health was excellent; every day he exercised and, whenever possible, indulged his passion for riding horses. 'Give a man an hour a day on horseback,' he was fond of saying, 'and you can't break him down with work.'[5] At Sylvancroft he was his own groundskeeper; other servants, kitchen, parlour, and nursery maids, attended to the house.

Harry Evans was not born into wealth; he earned his money through a combination of happenstance and perseverance. John Evans, a deaf Methodist minister, was operating an orphanage in Davenport, Ontario, when his wife, Mary Jane Vaux, gave birth to her fourth child on 17 August 1876. By his thirteenth birthday, the child himself was an orphan. Only the patronage of a powerful uncle, Senator W. E. Sanford, allowed Harry Evans to continue

South view of Sylvancroft, 1913, secluded in trees above Groat ravine. (COURTESY EVANS FAMILY)

with his studies.[6] In 1893 he graduated from the Hamilton Collegiate Institute with the highest grade average in Ontario, receiving a scholarship to attend the University of Toronto. There, he earned a gold medal in natural sciences. He worked as a mineralogist before moving west, where his brother, named Sanford after their uncle, had become editor of the *Winnipeg Telegram*.[7] Harry worked as business manager with the newspaper until he was fired in 1904 in a shake-up aimed at checking Sanford's increasing civic influence. Next Harry signed up as a geologist for the Manitoba Lands Commission and then in rapid succession homesteaded as far south as Mexico and as far north as Churchill.

In 1907 Harry moved from Churchill to Edmonton at the behest of John Butchard, an American businessman who that year had purchased a large parcel of land near the Pembina River. Commissioned to survey for coal deposits, Evans reported that the Pembina region promised a sizable lode. On his own initiative, he had plans drawn up for a town site on the western bank of the river capable of accommodating a small mining community. He also became the local agent for Royal Trust. Established in business, Evans searched for and soon found a suitable wife.

The friends of Edith Isabel Jackson, daughter of William Shutt Jackson, a classics teacher at Upper Canada College, forewarned her to expect desolation and winter's constant chill when she moved to Edmonton as Harry's new wife in 1910. Nevertheless, Isby—Harry's preferred name for his wife—quickly adapted to her household duties and became one of the city's most popular hostesses. A formidable antidote to Harry's dour Methodist upbringing, she insisted that her house should be alive with music and dance.

Harry's coal enterprise took further shape in 1910 when the land was sold. Boasting £2,500,000 in paid-up capital and £1,500,000 in debenture issues, the Canadian Agency operated as an umbrella organization under which English financiers could speculate in the Dominion's real estate markets. In 1906 the agency had purchased 500,000 acres of agricultural land from the Canadian Pacific Railway. Seeking to expand the company's holdings in Western Canada, in October 1910 chairman Arthur Grenfell arrived in Edmonton with a mandate to acquire large tracts of land in central Alberta. The Pembina Coal Company soon became affiliated with the Canadian Agency, with Evans appointed Edmonton manager for the combined business interest. To provide impressive lodgings for the English businessmen Harry began to entertain (and to ensure that they would not have to endure the indignity of the King Edward Hotel), in 1911 he built Sylvancroft, three storeys and thirty rooms in all.

The Western Canada Land Company, part of the Canadian Agency conglomerate, sold parcels of land to colonists settling in rural Alberta. Seeking additional investors, Grenfell had Evans publish a summary of the company's intent in the *Edmonton Bulletin*:

> In order to discourage speculation in land as distinguished from colonization of it, the Western Canada Land Company sells only to those who intend to cultivate . . . Lots are purchased as desired by the customer, houses built to his plans and specifications. He pays 10% of the total cost as a cash payment, but is given ten years to pay for the balance.

An investor in the Western Canada Land Company could expect to become a millionaire, and quite quickly, too—on paper. In truth, any profit depended upon the continuing expansion of the real estate market.

When Grenfell returned to Edmonton with a party of Canadian Agency investors in September 1912, the local economy seemed as if it would expand forever. Real estate offices could be found all along Jasper Avenue. A trolley conductor and a motorman operated a flourishing enterprise from their streetcar, a map of the subdivision they were selling displayed in the motorman's compartment. Another entrepreneur sold land from his office in an ice cream parlour.[8] The combined population of Edmonton and Strathcona multiplied by more than 60 per cent in just one year, rising from 31,000 to 50,000.[9] Beyond the city limits the pace of expansion was even more dazzling: with the introduction of Marquis wheat to replace Red Fife in 1909, the Alberta grain acreage swelled by 608,800 in two years, an annual growth rate of 162 per cent.[10] Declared Grenfell: '[I have] absolute reliance in the city of Edmonton, and I think I may safely say that you will see myself and my associates taking even a more active interest in this part of the country.'[11]

Pushing west through Edmonton, the Grand Trunk Pacific and Canadian Northern railways built steadily toward British Columbia. As both lines crossed the Pembina River near the site of Butchard's old mining interest, Evans suggested that the time to develop the new town site had finally arrived. After a quick inspection of the locale, Grenfell pledged one million dollars. Proclaimed the *Bulletin*, 'It will not be for the lack of money if the new mining town which will spring there will not go ahead.'[12] In London, the directors of the Canadian Agency decided to name the town *Evansburgh*.

The developers' optimism did not take long to dissipate. Even Edmonton, among the most remote outposts of the British Empire, was not exempted from rumours of war. By 1914 the pace of economic growth had stumbled, halted, and then reversed towards recession. Fortunes were depleted; paper millionaires were unable to pay their property taxes; real estate values plummeted. Initially, the Canadian Agency benefited from the misery of others, acquiring Anglo-Canadian Lands and the Edmonton Land Syndicate at bargain prices. Then, diverting funds from Chaplin, Milne, and Grenfell, one of the most respected financial houses in London, Arthur Grenfell attempted to purchase the Grand Trunk Pacific Railway for the Canadian Agency. The endeavour was unsuccessful; it was also illegal, as Grenfell did not hold a majority of shares in the financial house. His partners had barely enough time to fire their disgraced colleague before irate investors assailed the company's doors. One day later, on 8 June 1914, with Arthur Grenfell's reputation irretrievably tarnished, the Canadian Agency followed Chaplin, Milne, and Grenfell into receivership.

Harry Evans learned from an *Edmonton Journal* reporter that the Canadian Agency had failed. No, the suspension would not affect local operations, he calmly assured the newsman.[13] It was not true. The next morning, the Bank of Montreal forbade Evans access to the Canadian Agency's Edmonton accounts. To avoid insolvency, he pledged his own credit at the bank and met payments out of his pocket. 'With the failure of the Canadian company,' he later recalled, 'I was left with a huge debt and my savings lost. I had them in a joint account with the Canadian Agency. It was a terrible business and Sylvancroft as yet not paid for.'[14] One week after the collapse, Evans, now desperately in need of financial support, wrote to the London liquidator, Sir William Plender, complaining that he had received no instructions.[15] On 17 June, Plender replied in a coded telegram: Evans had been retained by the liquidator and was authorized to sell all real estate holdings of the Western Canada Land Company and of the other Canadian Agency affiliates. As a creditor, a portion of what Evans could salvage of the assets would default to him. The terms of receivership enabled Evans to convert land holdings into cash.

Able to retain his personal financial security and ruled medically unfit for the armed services due to old age—he was thirty-eight, Evans began to devote more time to civic duties. He served on several municipal committees, most notably, city planning. The absence of so many able-bodied men thrust him into further positions of civic leadership. He ran the Victory Loan Campaign for northern

Alberta and in 1916, still sorting out the mess left behind by the failure of the Canadian Agency, became chairman of the Board of Trade and undertook responsibility for public welfare.

Though he disliked the competitive nature of politics, he became a candidate for mayor. 'I am being put up for mayor chiefly by the business interests,' he wrote in 1917, 'and my friends assure me that I shall be elected.'[16] The consequences of land speculation for Edmonton had turned out to be a crushing municipal debt and declining revenues due to unpaid property taxes.[17] By the end of 1917, Edmonton would have one million dollars in debt past due and about three million ready to come due.[18] The city was on the verge of bankruptcy.

Whatever small role Evans had played in encouraging real estate speculation, he now ran for office on a platform of fiscal responsibility and austerity. His campaign literature promised 'even greater reductions of civic expenditures, rearrangement of civic finances, broadening the basis of civic taxation, reducing interest charges on temporary loans and passing on some of the civic debt burdens to posterity . . .'[19] With a respectable successor in sight, William Henry, mayor since 1914, was only too glad not to seek re-election (having run in 1916 only at the importunings of the west-end business lobby). Both city newspapers supported Evans. The *Bulletin*, though suspicious of his ties to the Conservative party, recommended him 'as a candidate whose election would be a straight declaration that the city's debts must be paid and faith with its creditors kept to the absolute limit.'[20] With 4134 votes of a total poll of 7887, on a cold December day, Harry Evans became mayor of Edmonton.

As mayor, Evans could claim to represent the best interests of all Edmontonians. He established his independence from the business lobby by prodding prosperous citizens to settle their arrears with the city. At one point, shortly after his election, he asked Rotarians to shame their neighbours into paying, thereby generating over $500,000 on past due accounts.[21] Council went so far as to consider taxing churches but settled instead for special powers from the province to introduce a personal income tax and a graduated business tax.[22] But many Edmontonians simply had no money to give; over a three-year period beginning in 1918, the city became the unwilling owner of 44,348 forfeited lots.[23]

Evans was unable to reduce the municipal budget by any significant measure. Urban expenditure had already dropped by more than half from 1913 to 1915.[24] By 1918 the mayor of Edmonton had no room to manoeuvre, as the largest portion of revenue was allocated to pay interest on the existing capital debt. His task was to increase earnings while diminishing, if possible, direct government participation in the economy. The only policy he could pursue under these circumstances was vigorous taxation. Consequently, municipal services were poorly maintained. Finally, in response to labour discord and wartime inflation, Evans had to curb his austerity program by authorizing pay increases of up to 16 per cent for civic employees.

Evans suffered another reverse when, foreshadowing the labour strife that would roar across western Canada one year later, seventy members of the Firefighters' Federal Labour Union went on strike to protest the appointment of a chief from outside of the department. City Council authorized the hiring of a new brigade and sought the support of the citizenry in a plebiscite. The campaign started poorly for Evans: the *Journal* reported sixteen false alarms in one four-hour shift, and R.G. Davidson, the new fire chief, publicly complained that his replacement workers were refusing to cross picket lines.[25] The plebescite was decided when fire swept through the Lines-Brake Automobile Company and spread to the Maryland Hotel, destroying both buildings. By a count of 6539 to 2330, the ratepayers instructed council to rehire the old brigade and dispose of the controversial fire chief.[26]

In his last major decision as mayor, on 18 October, fearful that the Spanish influenza epidemic would spread to Edmonton, Evans ordered all schools, churches, and theatres to close. The next day forty-one cases were reported; before the disease completed its grim tour, 445 Edmontonians had died.[27]

In the first month of peace, as the next election loomed, the business interests, now organized as the Citizens' Progressive League, recruited Charles Wilson, the finance committee chairman, to succeed Mayor Evans, who absolutely refused to seek a second term. Succumbing to influenza, Wilson was unable to campaign and narrowly lost the election (by 487 votes) to Joe Clarke, a populist politician and former alderman who drew his support from labourers and the unemployed. 'Edmonton is better off than a year ago,' the *Edmonton Journal* announced in a 21 December 1918 editorial reviewing Evans's mayoral record. His administration had succeeded in reducing the city's debenture debt by one million dollars and had ended with a surplus in general revenue accounts.[28]

Relegating his political career to memory, Evans fixed his attention on business. H.M.E. Evans and Company (a descendant of one of the Canadian Agency affiliates,

Western Homebuilders, that Evans had managed to salvage) was christened on 2 April 1919. Evans could no longer rely on investors from Britain for his company's well-being. Their enthusiasm for Empire had vanished in the trenches of Ypres and Vimy Ridge. American investors were becoming more important, but, as a Conservative, Evans supported the British Empire, maintained contacts with European investors, and opposed American expansion into the Canadian marketplace. To achieve true progress, he believed, Canadians had to act independently of their southern neighbours.

Learning from past mistakes, Evans vowed to diversify his portfolio and avoid spectacular risks. Real estate, once the focus of all his energy, became just one aspect of his diversified holdings. Moving into new quarters on the north side of Jasper Avenue, he operated the CPR building on behalf of the railway. Later his services were acquired by a prominent European client, the *Frères Revillon*, to manage their Edmonton interests.

As a further bulwark against bad times, Sylvancroft was almost self-sufficient. In addition to home-grown vegetables and eggs—collected from the chicken coop in defiance of predatory weasels—the family enjoyed fresh milk with their breakfast, much to the chagrin of the medical health officer, who in 1927 lamented 'the large number of private cows scattered from one end of the city to another.'[29] The size and elegance of the large house, modern when constructed, was no longer in style by the end of the First World War, but Evans continued to live in it for the rest of his life.

Between the wars, the vigour of the local economy depended in large part upon agricultural prices, which, in the three years following the Armistice, declined by 42 per cent.[30] Many Edmonton firms lapsed into bankruptcy, but, steadied by diversification, Evans and Company continued to expand. In the relative stability of the late 1920s, Harry Evans realized profits he had not seen since the collapse of the Canadian Agency.

By then, marriage had brought five children, daughters Sylvia, Louise, Anne, and Honor, and finally, in 1924, a son, Vaux. The growing children were schooled at home, not, as the neighbours suspected, because the children were mentally deficient, but because the public school ignored that one indispensable ingredient that nurtured the young mind like none other: sunshine. 'Boys and girls ought not to be indoors all day,' Harry Evans would pronounce. 'They ought to be outside playing.'[31] After lunch—the largest meal of the day at Sylvancroft—the

The Evans family, 1936, from left to right, Sylvia, Honor, Vaux, Isabel, Harry, Sarah Jackson (mother-in-law), Louise, and Anne.
(COURTESY EVANS FAMILY)

teacher, often Mrs Evans herself, dismissed her small class so the children could play in the ravine below. But despite the limited hours for education, the Evans brood were formidable students, as their father was before them. Fond of reading poetry aloud, Harry introduced his children to his favourite Victorian, Robert Browning, and to other authors of classic literature.[32]

Isby loved to entertain, and an invitation to appear at a Sylvancroft soirée was the most coveted piece of paper in all Glenora. Yes, functions at Government House were consequential, a favourite of social climbers, but for pure fun nothing could match an evening at Sylvancroft. Excuses for a celebration were readily discovered. Formal balls, complete with dance cards and fancy dresses, demarcated the arrival of a long weekend. Not all evenings were so elaborate, of course, but the aspect of a party never left the house. Charades and pantomimes were favourite activities. The children arranged their own theatrical productions, often coached by the finest actors in the Dominion, including Dame Emma Albani, Canada's first renowned prima donna. (The big house was open to any theatre troupe passing through the capital city.) *Aladdin or The Genie with the Light Brown Hair* was a smashing success, inspiring a second production, *Cinderella or Stepmother, What Have I Done?*[33]

Any sense of security Evans may have enjoyed soon faded, however, with the coming of the Great Depression and then, in 1935, the election of William Aberhart as premier. Aberhart's unorthodox monetary policies held that private control of credit creation was responsible for a perpetual insufficiency of mass purchasing power. In Aberhart's eyes Evans must have seemed a curious incongruity: a bankers' toady with impeccable western credentials. Furthermore, Evans was not helped by his association with the ousted United Farmers of Alberta government; in addition to acting as chairman of the coal commission in 1925, he had served as a financial advisor to Premier Brownlee in the early years of the Depression. As a real estate agent, Evans was subject to Aberhart's moratorium on debt collection; as an Albertan, he could not benefit from the Dominion Housing Act, as not one loan was made in Alberta while

To journey into a realm of chaos from the structured, innocuous world of Sylvancroft was, for the Evans children, simply a matter of strolling along the trails behind their house.

the Province defaulted on its bond payments. Annual profits at H.M.E. Evans dwindled from $43,896 in 1928 to an average of $1,568 during the last five years of the depression.[34]

Nevertheless, Edmonton was not an unhappy place for the Evans children during the Great Depression. The sudden expansion of 1912 followed by the collapse of 1914 had left pockets of undeveloped wilderness throughout the metropolitan area. Unemployed men lived in dug-outs and small cabins in the ravine below Stony Plain Road; along the south bank of the North Saskatchewan River, Indian campsites were frequent curiosities.[35] To journey into a realm of chaos from the structured, innocuous world of Sylvancroft was, for the Evans children, simply a matter of strolling along the trails behind their house. Though the family lived in comfort, poverty was literally just around the corner. Even the richest residents of Glenora were conscious of the need for austerity.

Before the tides of economic hardship had subsided, Edmontonians were again at war with Germany, and Evans diverted his attention from his personal business concerns to enlist in the collective effort to defeat totalitarianism. Though sixty-six years old, in 1942 he reclaimed his old position as chairman of the northern Alberta Victory Loans Campaign. The war affected him personally: Louise had moved to London in 1938 and Sylvia was serving in the Royal Canadian Air Force, where she had attained the unprecedented rank (for a woman) of Squadron Leader. At home, Sylvancroft was converted into a hostel for 'guest children.' The Evans were the first family in Edmonton to shelter war refugees.[36]

Across Canada the Victory Loans campaign succeeded beyond government expectation, with total cash sales of $12 billion by the end of the war.[37] Evans's own contribution was considered extraordinary: not only was he well connected to the region's wealthiest businessmen, during his term as mayor he had acquired a reputation as Edmonton's most ruthless collector of overdue debts. He knew how to manipulate money out of a miser's wallet. On 2 July 1946 King George VI made Harry Marshall Erskine

Evans an Officer of the Order of the British Empire 'for meritorious service in war work.'

Evans did not retire after the war, though he was in his seventies and wealthy beyond his needs. He continued to work part-time, with no detail of the business escaping his attention. In 1966 Isby, predeceased by her beloved son Vaux, who had died of an intestinal ailment in 1956, passed away after a long illness. Occasionally, as the city's oldest surviving mayor, Harry Evans was called upon to preside over award ceremonies or to greet distinguished visitors. Every year on his birthday he attracted the attention of the *Edmonton Journal*. 'How do you account for your longevity?' the reporter inevitably asked. 'Exercise and clean living,' Evans replied, year after year after year.[38]

On 24 March 1972 Sylvia Evans officially opened Evansdale School in Edmonton's north end, the city's tribute to one of its oldest and most prominent citizens. Severely crippled by arthritis in his later years, Harry Evans died on 21 September 1973 at the age of ninety-seven, survived by four daughters, a daughter-in-law, and their children and grand-children.

❧ The landscape around Sylvancroft has been drastically altered since the house was built. In 1954 the Groat ravine was obliterated, its source redirected into the city sewer system and its path superseded by a winding, four-lane road. (Sylvancroft itself survived modernity's wrecking ball. Currently it is the home of Sylvia and Louise Evans, the late mayor's oldest daughters.) Curiously, Harry Evans had not opposed the construction of Groat Road. Although he was fond of nature and preferred an unsullied landscape,[39] he had a passion for progress. Nevertheless, in his final years he had acquired a new perspective on his old belief that the human mind could overcome all obstacles. The cycles of boom and bust, of luxury and austerity, of good fortune and personal hardship, continued perpetually throughout his age, and repeated backward through the expanse of history and forward into the foreseeable future. Said the former mayor on his ninetieth birthday: 'People have always thought the same. The punch always used to taste better. But it never did—it was always about the same.'[40] ❧

MICHAEL PAYNE

EDMONTONIANS AND THE LEGISLATURE

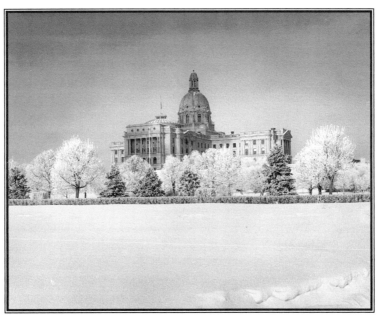

A majestic view of the Legislature building on a frosty winter's morning.
(PAA BL.330/2)

*W*hile Edmonton was still busy attracting the men and women who would establish the social, cultural, political, and economic institutions that define an urban community, the young city was named capital of Alberta. Over the next several decades, this role as seat of government shaped Edmonton's self-image, provided jobs for politicians and civil servants, and acted as a magnet for much of the rest of the province. Towering over the North Saskatchewan River, the Legislature and its park-like grounds were familiar to generations of Edmontonians, and the building itself came to symbolize what they felt about their city as provincial capital. Gradually, however, for reasons Michael Payne suggests in this photographic essay, a 'reciprocal process of the separation of the Legislature from the city and the retreat of the city from the Legislature' occurred.

Michael Payne is currently head of the Research and Publications Program of the Historic Sites Service of Alberta Community Development. He first became interested in the history of the Alberta Legislature and its changing relationship with Edmonton in the 1980s, while working on the Legislative Assembly Interpretive Centre slated for the new underground Pedway Mall, built in conjunction with the massive redevelopment of the Legislature grounds.

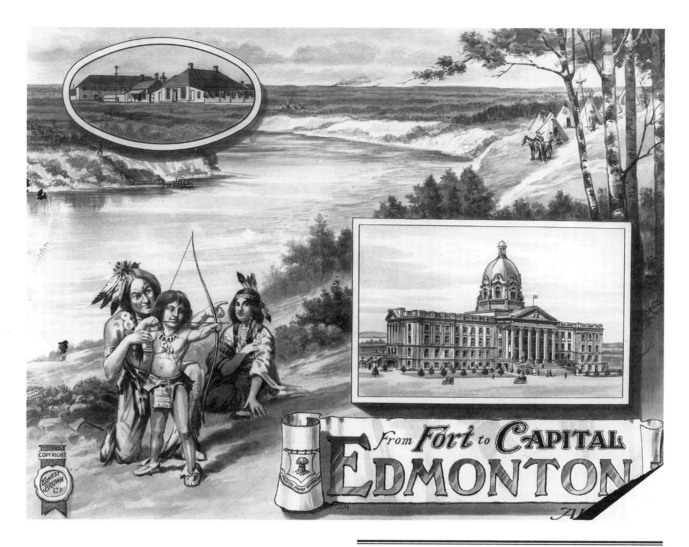

From *Fort* to *Capital* EDMONTON

On 1 September 1905 Edmontonians took to the streets to celebrate the creation of the new province of Alberta. They, of course, had reason to celebrate the event with greater enthusiasm than other communities. Thanks to Frank Oliver, Edmonton's representative in the federal cabinet and a tireless city booster, and to the election of Alexander Cameron Rutherford, from adjacent Strathcona, as head of the first provincial government, Edmonton had won the coveted prize of provincial capital. Nothing—including such later claims to distinction as 'Gateway to the North' and 'City of Champions'—would be as crucial in shaping its future development.

The importance of having their city named capital was not lost on Edmontonians. Photographer Ernest Brown, clearly entranced by the idea of progress, created this somewhat romanticized promotional postcard linking Edmonton's historical past as a fur trade post to its bright future as a capital, symbolized by the Legislature building. (PAA B.3402)

Work on the foundations of the Legislature building began in 1907—intriguingly, before there was even a final design. Indeed, architectural drawings indicate that changes were being made until 1912 when the structure was finally completed. (PAA B.3356)

Alberta's first Legislative Assembly opened in Thistle Rink before moving to McKay Avenue School for its sessions. But these were temporary quarters only, and once Edmonton was confirmed as the capital, the Rutherford government set about acquiring a suitable site for a Legislature building. In 1906 it struck a deal with the Hudson's Bay Company to purchase twenty-one acres, at a cost of $4,000 an acre, on the bank of the North Saskatchewan River just west of downtown. The last Fort Edmonton still stood on the site.

Most of the work on the design was done under the direction of A.M. Jeffers, the provincial architect from 1907 to 1911, but his successor, R.P. Blakey, made significant amendments, and the Montreal architect, Percy Nobbs, also contributed to early sketches. (PAA A.5307)

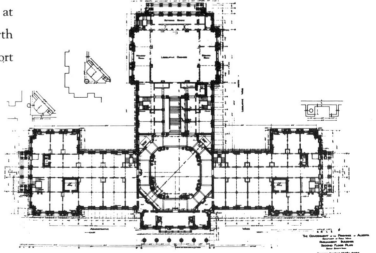

Although the proximity of the Legislature building to
the old fur trade fort underlined a Whiggish connection
between Edmonton's supposed past and anticipated future,
not everyone was enthusiastic about the new completely
sweeping away the old. The Canadian Club of Edmonton
and the Historic Landmarks Association of Canada were
two groups involved in a plan to dismantle Fort Edmonton
and reconstruct it as a museum just west of the High Level
Bridge on the site of the present Enzio Ferrone Park.
Nothing came of the idea, but timbers from Fort Edmonton
were stored by the bridge for several years. Most were eventually burned, but some may have been reused and others
were acquired by the Provincial Museum of Alberta as part
of its permanent collection.

COPYRIGHT
ERNEST BROWN.
2760

EDMONTON FROM THE SOUTH SIDE, 1912.
SHOWING H.B.CO'S OLD FORT.

Booth

As if in subconscious recognition of the relationship between Edmonton's growth and prosperity and the construction of the Legislature, amateur and professional photographers took picture after picture of the building as it rose on the banks of the North Saskatchewan River. The pylons to the west are for the High Level Bridge. (PAA B.3409)

As the most visible symbol of Edmonton's status as a capital city, the Legislature building not only symbolized provincehood but also became a source of civic pride and identity. There was good reason for this. A significant portion of the boom Edmonton experienced in the years up to approximately 1912 is attributable to the massive investment in infrastructure that followed the city's selection as capital. The final cost of the Legislature certainly exceeded the initial estimate of $1,250,000 and may have been as high as $4,000,000. The bulk of this money was expended in Edmonton-Strathcona—even by conservative estimates, an expenditure of more than $100 for every man, woman, and child then living in Edmonton-Strathcona. It is not entirely surprising, then, that the end of Edmonton's property boom coincided with the completion of the Legislature, the High Level Bridge, and other projects.

Remarkably few photographs documenting the construction of the
Legislature actually show anyone working on the site. Why is a
matter of conjecture, but it would seem that the idea of the building
and what it represented was much more engrossing for photographers than the physical labour involved in seeing it become a reality.
This photograph is something of an anomaly in that it shows proud
workers posed alongside their handiwork. (PAA A.2348)

Over the years the Legislature has provided employment for significant numbers of Edmontonians—from gardeners and cafeteria workers to pages and Hansard reporters—as well as for politicians and their staff drawn from across the province. The role of the Legislature as a community focal point was established early. When Governor General Earl Grey laid the cornerstone for the building on 1 October 1909, Edmonton turned out in force to celebrate the occasion. A ceremonial arch with the pithy motto, 'We Reap—We Sow,' graced the grounds, and Hardisty Cartage Company provided wagons to transport 1,600 children around the site. The Legislature and its grounds quickly became a preferred location for celebrations of all sorts: Royal Visits, parades, concerts, and anniversaries. Of course, not all events at the Legislature have a celebratory function. It also serves as a focus for political statements and demonstrations, even when they have little to do with provincial powers. Disarmament rallies, protests against drug laws, demands for changes in gun control laws—all wind up at the Legislature, which has become the symbolic centre of government of all sorts in Edmonton.

Alberta's Golden Jubilee stagecoach leaving the Legislature grounds with an RCMP and military escort on 27 June 1955. There are hundreds of photographs like this preserved in archival collections, reflecting how central the Legislature became in the ceremonial life of both Edmonton and the province. (PAA PA.480/3)

While many of the political causes publicized outside the Legislature affected all Albertans equally, some were particularly important to Edmontonians. Here civil servants protesting stalled contract negotiations picket the opening of the Legislative Assembly on 11 October 1973. (PAA J.1104/1)

For most Edmontonians, the most significant and enduring civic purpose of the Legislature building and grounds has been as a downtown park. The parcel of land purchased from the Hudson's Bay Company far exceeded what was needed for a building and early maps show the surrounding grounds as one of the few public park areas in Edmonton, particularly the centre core. The location of the Legislature, close to the heart of civic life, with residential housing and the street railway system coming almost to the front entrance, made it unique in the prairie provinces. Neither of its prairie counterparts—in Regina, situated on the edge of the city, and in Winnipeg, erected in the midst of an already developed office and commercial district—was as easily accessible to the city's citizens. In Edmonton the park-like quality of the grounds behind the Legislature was consciously enhanced by the creation of formal gardens and walkways that offer a vivid contrast with the natural vegetation of the river valley below. The grounds have also been used for more organized recreational facilities—such as tennis courts, more recently a skating rink, and the famous bowling greens which still sit more or less right on top of the site of Fort Edmonton. Although the river valley parks system has now assumed some of these recreational functions, the Legislature grounds continue to enrich the leisure hours of Edmontonians.

Legislature building and south-facing grounds, 1929. (PAA BL.22/1)

The reciprocal process of the separation of the Legislature from the city and the retreat of the city from the Legislature culminated in the massive redevelopment of the north side of the grounds in the 1970s and 1980s. (PAA J.4752/2)

The relationship between the Legislature and Edmonton has never been static. Although little came of plans commissioned as early as 1910 to redevelop approaches to the building, after 1928 successive governments bought up property between 107 and 109 streets, north of the existing grounds. Gradually, as buildings like the Bowker and the Haultain were constructed, a distinctive government office district began to emerge around the Legislature, physically divorcing it from the rest of the city. This process was further encouraged in the 1950s by the rapid growth of municipal, provincial, and federal government functions. Edmonton city politicians and planners joined forces to discourage the development of government offices in downtown locations they wished preserved as commercial areas. The relocation of the proposed Federal Building from a site on Churchill Square to 107 Street is a good example. By the time the building opened in 1958, it was almost totally surrounded by provincial government offices (ironically, the Churchill Square site was never developed commercially and today houses the Edmonton Public Library).

In 1974 plans were drawn up to divert traffic on 97 Avenue, which ran past the main entrance of the Legislature, through an underpass beneath the adjacent grounds. The scheme also called for the erection of a large plaza, complete with fountain and reflecting pool, in front of the Legislature and an underground pedway linking nearby office buildings. The plan provoked considerable controversy, which delayed the start of construction until 1979. A price tag of approximately $62,000,000—roughly fifteen times the original cost of the Legislature building—reflected the times, but so too did the concept. The redevelopment completed the symbolic separation of the Legislature building and grounds from the city and marked a profound change in Edmonton itself. Huge office and commercial developments along Jasper Avenue, evidence of oil-based economic prosperity, had transformed Edmonton's skyline and dwarfed the Legislature building. Edmonton is no longer just a capital, and the Legislature, once a central symbol of Edmonton's civic identity, is now almost invisible from most vantage points in the city. ❧

BOB IRWIN

WHOSE RAILWAY WAS IT?

Alberta Great Waterways Railway crossing the muskeg
near Fort McMurray, 1919. (PAA A.4000)

The Peace River country was the last great settlement frontier in North America. Edmonton boosters saw a guarantee of future wealth if the city
could become the supply centre for this northern agricultural
paradise. To achieve their goal, these Edmonton promoters had
to compete against Vancouver to finance a viable railway to the
Peace. Their dream found a curious counterpart in the ambitions Peace River boosters had of a rail outlet for the region's
agricultural wealth.

In this carefully drawn study we learn what happened when
provincial politicians responded to the demands of boosters by
issuing charters and providing bond guarantees for not one but
three railways to the Peace country. One of those railways,
Bob Irwin tells us, ran so slowly that the editor of the Peace
River Record sarcastically remarked that 'the crews have been
issued with calendars to take the place of stop watches.' The
story is about not just government ineptitude in sponsoring railway development but also how other communities in the
province saw Edmonton.

Bob Irwin recently completed his PhD at the University of
Alberta on regional identity in the Peace River country.

*I*N THE EARLY 1900S PEOPLE IN ALBERTA BELIEVED that the Peace River country represented a potential source of tremendous wealth for the province. Edmontonians saw the region as the city's natural hinterland. Exploiting and developing that region would make the city prosperous. The problem, of course, was how to realize the potential. Trails encouraged the most ambitious pioneers to enter the Peace River region, but true development and prosperity required better modes of transportation. Railways—the primary transportation and communication system of the industrial age and the symbol of progress and economic development for early twentieth-century Canada—had to be constructed. By 1910 fifteen railways had already been given charters to build into the Peace River region and both the Canadian Northern and Grand Trunk Pacific (GTP) had considered building their transcontinental lines through the region, but no promoters exercised their charter options. The government of Alberta therefore looked at other ways of providing the north with railway lines. In entering the railway promotion field, however, the government faced a difficult problem. How could it satisfy Edmonton's persistent merchant and booster community, fulfill the expectations of Peace River settlers, and protect the provincial treasury at the same time? It turned out to be an insoluble problem.

The Liberal administrations of premiers Alexander Rutherford (1905–10), Arthur Sifton (1910–17), and Charles Stewart (1917–21) proved especially inept. Rather than develop clear strategies for railway construction that could be implemented cautiously, they reacted to immediate conditions, creating deals that in the end served only the interests of promoters and speculators. Hoping to convince railway promoters to exercise their charter rights and build the desired lines, the Liberal governments turned to the long-abused system of bond guarantees. Using the credit of the Province to support the capital demands of the railway builders without actually giving them any money seemed like the perfect solution for cash-strapped provincial administrations. Problems had emerged from previous examples of this style of financing: promoters did not risk losing their own capital investments; the railways they built began their commercial life with heavy debt burdens; and the bond guarantees encouraged promoters to exaggerate costs and sub-contract work to subsidiary companies. With no capital invested, the promoter could declare the railway bankrupt, take the construction profits, and leave the guarantor with the rail line and the debt. These problems were forgotten or ignored by the Liberal administrations.

The province's first northern railway venture, the ill-fated Alberta and Great Waterways (A&GW) scheme, came in response to rumours of oil discoveries in the tar sands around Fort McMurray in 1909. The Edmonton business community and the Liberal MLAs from northern Alberta, many with development interests in the region, clamoured for a rail link. As a result the Province entered into an agreement with the Kansas City-based Clarke syndicate. The government guaranteed $7,400,000 of A&GW corporate bonds at such generous terms of interest that the promoter sold the bonds at a 10 per cent premium and pocketed the profit without ever laying a rail along the route. The ensuing scandal fractured the Liberal party, forced the resignation of Premier Rutherford, and left a bitter taste in the mouths of Alberta taxpayers. A royal commission in 1910 discovered that the government was not crooked but merely naive.[1] Rutherford's actions, unfortunately, set the stage for the Sifton government's foray into the railway business.

Undaunted by the failure of the A&GW project and the lengthy investigation it inspired, the Edmonton business community continued to clamour for northern railways. The *Edmonton Journal*, angered by rumours that the Sifton government would use the A&GW money for non railway purposes, remarked 'what Edmonton wants and what the whole province desires is that the north country should be tapped by the railway at the earliest possible moment.'[2] Frank Oliver, always a promoter of northern development, attempted to quell dissent by emphasizing the needs of Peace River pioneers, but he also linked that development to the aspirations of the city:

> It is the peopling and utilisation of the vast and undefined extent of territory which lies beyond [Edmonton] to the west, the north-west, the north, and the north-east, which is looked upon as the most potent agency in making this a city of more than ordinary proportions and importance . . . Into this undeveloped region there are now projected no less than eight lines of railway radiating from Edmonton . . . Everyone of these eight projected railways will tap country for which Edmonton is the logical and necessary metropolis . . . The north-westerly line will bring to the city the trade of thousands of settlers who have in the last few years pushed out in that direction in confidence that so goodly a district could not long remain cut off from the world.[3]

The Edmonton Board of Trade relied on the traditional booster technique of threatening competition from other urban centres. The president, J. McGeorge, noted:

The railways projected and approved towards Fort McMurray and Peace River are not yet commenced, with every evidence of the former having been abandoned for the present. The lines, if constructed, would open a vast amount of valuable territory tributary to Edmonton, and upon which the early development of our city largely depends. I notice a charter is being applied for to build a line from Prince Albert through the Athabasca country to Fort McMurray. If this line is built and in operation before one is constructed and operated from Edmonton, all traffic originating in that vast territory would be diverted to the Province of Saskatchewan instead of through Alberta, which is its natural outlet.[4]

Concerned with rebuilding the Liberal coalition in the immediate aftermath of the A&GW scandal, Sifton temporarily ignored these pleas. Unfortunately, he did not use this time to plan a rational railway strategy.

The situation changed dramatically late in 1911. While early competition for metropolitan domination of northern Alberta involved Edmonton and the smaller, although ambitious, Saskatchewan communities of North Battleford and Prince Albert, Vancouver soon emerged as Edmonton's true rival. Following the completion of the GTP line to Fort George, the trade of northern BC naturally flowed along the line to Edmonton. Vancouver's business community immediately perceived the threat posed to its own metropolitan aspirations and demanded the provincial administration connect this region with the lower mainland. In 1911 the government responded by giving charters for seven new railways from the west coast to the Peace River region.[5] One newspaper noted:

There has been a distinct movement in Vancouver latterly towards a broader view of Vancouver's relation to the province as a whole . . . There is a strong movement being organised in favour of building a railway from Vancouver via Pemberton Meadows and Fort George to the Peace River districts. It will be greatly to the advantage of the coast if Vancouver can get her grip on that famous and undeveloped interior which is looked on as having fabulous wealth. The opening of the Panama Canal should see the linking up of the northern interior, even perhaps as far as Dawson, with Vancouver and a steady stream of raw materials, agricultural, mineral and vegetable, flowing to the coast.[6]

As Professor Morris Zaslow has correctly surmised, Vancouver's business community was larger and wealthier than Edmonton's and just as politically influential. The city was also a major coastal trading centre.[7] Its business elite was a serious threat to the northern aspirations of Edmonton boosters. As the earliest indications of large scale settlement in the Peace River region appeared in the winter of 1911–12, the Alberta and British Columbia provincial governments responded to the pressure from Edmonton and Vancouver boosters.

In December 1911 premiers Sifton and McBride both announced their support for a Peace River railway, and in February 1912 both guaranteed the bonds for railways into the Peace River country. The Alberta government guaranteed the bonds of the Edmonton Dunvegan and British Columbia Railway (ED&BC). An obscure railway chartered by the Dominion in 1907 and under the control of GTP contractor J.D. McArthur, it was given a $20,000 per mile guarantee for 350 miles of line between Edmonton and Dunvegan, via the south shore of Lesser Slave Lake.[8] Not yet satisfied, the government also guaranteed the bonds for two branch lines of the Canadian Northern Railway, giving it a $15,000 per mile guarantee for 100 miles of line between Athabasca and Peace River Crossing, via the north shore of Lesser Slave Lake, and a $20,000 per mile guarantee for a line between Onoway and Grande Prairie and on to the British Columbia boundary.[9] The British Columbia government, not to be outdone, granted the Pacific Great Eastern Railway (PGE), controlled by another GTP contractor, Foley, Welch, and Stewart, a $35,000 per mile guarantee for a line between North Vancouver and Fort George with the proposal to continue the line into the Peace River region.[10] Thus, in February 1912 not one but four railways were sponsored into the region. Of these, the Northern's Onoway to Grande Prairie route best served the combined interests of Alberta, Edmonton, and Peace River. It offered the shortest direct connection between Edmonton and the Peace country and, if continued through the Rocky Mountains, would also open the region to the coast. Unfortunately for all parties, Mackenzie and Mann were too busy completing the Thompson River sections of their main line to concern themselves with this branch line. Only a few miles were completed.

The ED&BC and the PGE lines instead became the focus of building activity. The ED&BC had the worst route of the three Alberta lines (few railways, however, could claim a more difficult route than the PGE), but McArthur, unlike so many other railway promoters, seemed determined to build his railway. He purchased land for his terminals six miles north of the city (undoubtedly avoiding expensive city real estate while attempting to

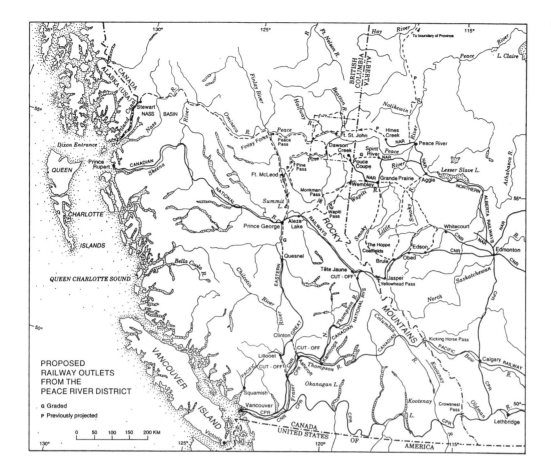

Figure 1, Proposed
Railway Outlets from
the Peace River District.
(GEOFFREY LESTER)

maximize his own profits by selling warehousing lots) and quickly commenced construction. By January 1914 the line reached the Athabasca River (130 miles) and the new town of Smith was established.[11] The pace of construction did not meet the expectations of the guarantee, but most observers were simply happy to see construction crews at work. McArthur soon cut off the territory tributary to the proposed Canadian Northern lines, receiving a provincial charter and $2,400,000 bond guarantee for the Canada Central Railway (CCR) to serve as a branch line into Peace River Crossing, and later obtaining a federal subsidy to build a branch line from Spirit River to Grande Prairie.[12] Finally he both solidified his position as the dominant northern railway promoter and thrilled the provincial administration by assuming the A&GW charter and guarantees in September 1914. McArthur's efforts seemed to fulfill all the province's goals: the Peace River country had a railway access thus ensuring large scale settlement and commercial agriculture; Edmonton's connection with the northern hinterland had been realized; and the province had committed no money to the deal. Unfortunately, neither had McArthur.

Although Sifton's policy and the construction of the

Dunvegan line appeared to redeem the Liberal government's earlier bond guarantee fiasco, the problems so obvious in the bond guarantees quickly emerged. McArthur's rail lines were poorly constructed. He used light sixty-pound rails, untreated ties obtained in the local market (often soft wood such as spruce), and insufficient ballast throughout.[13] The landscape through which the railway travelled, the Athabasca country or the land of muskeg, required extra, rather than less, sturdy construction techniques. As a result, the rail bed often heaved as the train travelled the route; the cars rocked back and forth and often leapt from the tracks. The rails, furthermore, sometimes separated as the ties failed to hold the spikes in place, leading to more serious derailments. To avoid such problems, the train trip between Edmonton and Grande Prairie took as long as 37 hours for an average speed of eleven miles per hour. During one settler's journey to Grande Prairie in 1919 the train never exceeded ten miles per hour.[14] The editor of the *Peace River Record* sarcastically remarked that the crews 'have been issued with calendars to take the place of stop watches.'[15]

McArthur had exploited the bond guarantees and the provincial government's gullibility in financing the railway's construction.[16] His subsidiary construction companies overcharged for clearing, grading, and ballasting the rail line. They also obtained funds on fraudulent grounds. The most glaring example occurred as the railway approached the town of Peace River. The Dunvegan lines faced two significant obstacles along their route into the Peace River region. The deeply incised valleys of the Peace and Smoky rivers were a railway builder's nightmare. In the case of the Peace, two viable routes existed. The railway could descend to the town of Peace River slowly, following the North Hart River valley for fourteen miles. This route provided an easy grade of 1 percent but required 64 bridges as the railway snaked back and forth across the North Hart River. The second route, keeping high on the plateau until the railway reached the junction of the Peace and Smoky rivers and then descending Judah's Hill, had steep 2.2 percent grades but offered cheaper construction. McArthur decided upon the gentle grades of the North Hart route and received guarantees to fund this expensive venture. Unable to sell the CCR bonds because the Great War had interrupted the world's financial markets, he convinced the province to lend him $2 million against the unsold bonds. Once the money had arrived, he quickly shifted the line to the cheaper Judah's Hill route.[17]

In the aftermath of the war, McArthur's railway, like so many others in Canada, collapsed.[18] His poor construction techniques and inability to maintain the line resulted in the breakdown of communication. In 1919 service between Edmonton and Grande Prairie stopped entirely. The unballasted rail bed between Spirit River and Grande Prairie had become unusable. The onset of winter and the freezing of the rail bed led to a temporary restoration of train service, but a shortage of rolling stock meant the ED&BC could not move the Peace River harvest out of or supplies into the region. Then, in the spring of 1920, the nine-mile descent into the Smoky River valley and the steeper, but shorter, descent into the Peace River valley both washed out.[19] McArthur tried to blame his problems on the postwar settlement boom. He lamented the full trains along his lines: 'The Railway is at its wits end to accommodate new settlers for this country. Trains leaving Edmonton are crowded to capacity with the best type of settlers. Four or five Hundred people are packed on the trains and it is impossible with our present equipment to cope with the question of feeding them. If this type of immigration continues, something must be done at once to relieve the congestion.'[20] The railway promoter's dream, full utilization of the railway, had become his nightmare.

Financially, the ED&BC was bankrupt and in default by 1918, and it was clear that Sifton had neither provided Peace River with viable railway service nor protected the provincial treasury. The province was forced to draw money from the unused North Hart valley construction accounts to pay interest upon the bonds, but it continued to back McArthur. Sifton supported a plan to have the ED&BC incorporated into the newly-formed Canadian National Railways and obtained support from the *Bulletin* which called upon the Dominion for a 'square deal.' Patience with McArthur and the provincial government had clearly frayed in the Peace River region, however. The editor of the *Record* wrote:

> The McArthur railways should get a square deal. The Alberta government has been the banker and Mr. McArthur the stool long enough. Both have bluffed the game through for the past six years, and the people of this province are becoming unanimous in the opinion that the time has come for a show down . . . By all rights, and to give a square deal both to the McArthur interests and the people, the government should have exercised its rights in foreclosing the road before it went further into the hole . . . Instead, the province has paid defaulted interest repeatedly, and when conditions are now becoming intolerable both for the province and the railway, the cry is raised that the Dominion government should also be called upon to pour money into the railway sinkhole that has resulted from the cupidity of McArthur and the extravagant stupidity of the Alberta government.[21]

While the Peace country, unlike the government or the Edmonton boosters, had given up on the McArthur lines and would begin to search for alternatives, the consequences of this division of opinion were hidden as the Province's plans fell apart. A Dominion engineer sent to investigate the line's potential discovered that McArthur, in order to maximize revenue, had delayed and deferred normal maintenance along the line. He estimated $950,000 was needed to upgrade the lines and an additional investment of $3 million to complete the bonded mileage for the system.[22] Facing a $47 million loss on the CNR system in 1919, the Dominion turned down the opportunity to purchase another poorly constructed, money-losing railway.

The failure of negotiations with the Dominion forced the provincial government, now under the leadership of Charles Stewart, to act.[23] Although the ED&BC had declared an operating surplus in 1919, the $1 million deferred maintenance charges and the defaulted interest on bonds left the railway with a loss of $1.4 million. In 1920 McArthur defaulted on his bond payments and the Province of Alberta, as guarantor of the bonds, took control of the line.[24] The province did not intend to operate the railway as a public utility, nor could it shut down the line and threaten Edmonton's connection with the Peace River region. Since the federal government refused to consider buying the line, Stewart approached the CPR. Before it would lease the line, the CPR demanded the government pay for the deferred maintenance charges and improvements on the line required to meet minimum operational standards. The province invested another $2.5 million and leased the road to the CPR.[25]

The Stewart government's policy of leasing the line looks reasonable at first glance. Although no fee accrued to the government, the revenue from the lines was to go to ordinary maintenance and then to interest on the bonds and government loans—anything left over went to the CPR. The CPR gained all traffic to and from the lines in return. To appease the residents of the Peace region, the rail lines were extended from Peace River to Berwyn and from Grande Prairie to Wembley, with the province paying for the construction costs under CPR management. In Edmonton, the *Bulletin* reported: 'It will be good news to the people of the north that the CPR is undertaking to operate the ED&BC . . . The Company is financially inter-

ested in exerting on behalf of northern development the active influence it has hitherto exerted to secure the settlement and cultivation of the land along its lines in the southern part of the province.'[26] Grande Prairie was more cautious. The first train of the summer arrived there in September and was greeted warmly, but Grande Prairie boosters were not entirely pleased.[27] They had hoped the collapse of McArthur's railway would result in the extension of the Canadian National line through Whitecourt. Any construction along the Whitecourt route would now add to the liabilities upon the government's books.

Stewart's government was soon dissatisfied with the leasing arrangement. The terms of the lease required significant extra money from the provincial treasury. The ED&BC, CCR, and A&GW railways cost the provincial treasury $4,750,000 in 1921 out of a total expenditure of $13 million. That same year, the UFA replaced the Liberals as the governing party in Alberta. The new deputy minister of railways, John Callaghan, quickly discovered further problems in the leasing arrangement. The CPR, he argued, charged exorbitant amounts for rentals on locomotives and rolling stock, collected rent on unused rolling stock, spent the deferred maintenance charge on ordinary maintenance, and charged the government nearly $34,000 per mile for construction costs on the Berwyn extension when similar lines were being built for under

An Edmonton, Dunvegan & British Columbia Railway car derailed, circa 1914. (PAA A.2232)

$20,000 per mile.[28] At the same time, the government realizsed that the CPR had made a $300,000 profit on traffic originating along the Dunvegan lines.[29] Confirming the government's complaints about the CPR, a report by two Dominion engineers noted 'that the Railway properties have not been brought up to a reasonable standard of efficiency as intended by the Agreement and that the present state of the ED&BC track efficiency would not compare favourably with a skeleton track as laid on ordinary new grade without ballast.'[30] The UFA government concluded that the Stewart lease policy was no longer satisfactory.

Problems with the lease arrangement were complicated by the changing interests of the Peace River booster community. The region was totally dependent upon the outlet through Edmonton following the 1918 failure of the PGE project. During the postwar recession, as farms in the region failed and farmers left, the region's boosters blamed the provincial government, Edmonton, and the Dunvegan lines for their problems. There was little doubt that the operation of the Dunvegan lines by the CPR was a marked improvement over the original management. While the government complained that the CPR failed to provide adequate maintenance, the trains began to run on schedule and fewer breaks in service occurred. Peace River resentment focused instead upon exorbitant freight rates and limited branch line construction. The region's boosters believed that neither Edmonton nor the province shared their concerns with these issues.

Freight charges on the ED&BC were a source of contention from the beginning of the railway service to the region. McArthur had obtained the right to set freight rates at double the prairie scale in 1917 and continued to advocate further increases in the tariffs.[31] The rate from Peace River to Edmonton therefore compared with the rate from Edmonton to the Lakehead. McArthur's failure to negotiate freight rate agreements with either of the transcontinentals, moreover, meant all products shipped beyond Edmonton faced a higher two-line haul charge. The Dominion government's desire to ship grain through the Lakehead added further charges to Peace River farmers since grain shipped from the region rarely reached the port before freeze-up, forcing them to pay winter storage at the terminal. The farmers therefore fought for better freight rates and shipment of grain through Vancouver during the postwar recession. The district received some relief in 1924 and 1925, but the campaign continued into the 1930s.[32]

The delays in extending the ED&BC from Grande Prairie towards Lake Saskatoon merely exasperated residents in the Peace region. The provincial government wanted to mortgage the lines in order to finance the construction but found itself in a confrontation with McArthur's primary commercial lender, the Union Bank. Although the government controlled the railway, McArthur and the Union Bank refused to turn over the outstanding shares in the ED&BC. The government, therefore, had to obtain the bank's permission to construct the new lines. The bank eventually agreed, but the lengthy negotiations regarding its interest in the line were not completed until 1925. The Province finally purchased the bank's claims against the Dunvegan lines for $1,250,000, thus increasing its investment in the railway.[33]

High freight rates and delays in construction of branch lines refocused attention on the Edmonton boosters' greatest fear, a rail link between the Peace country and the coast. The failure of the PGE had dampened hopes for the early construction of a coast outlet railway, but the dream remained. Neither the Alberta nor the British Columbia governments had the jurisdictional authority to provide an inter-provincial railway to the coast. An enquiry into the PGE debacle, furthermore, concluded that building into the Peace River country could not be justified financially.[34] Despite these problems, the pleas for a shorter outlet railway to the coast intensified as farmers in the region continued to pay high freight rates, the condition of the Dunvegan lines remained in question, and the region suffered the effects of the postwar recession.

By 1923 the Canadian National Railways' interest in opening the Hoppe Coal fields at the headwaters of the Smoky River offered a solution acceptable to Edmontonians. The line to access this field from the Canadian National mainline at Brulé could be viable if it was extended into the agricultural territory of the Peace country.[35] The CNR President Sir Henry Thornton was determined to build the line. He informed the federal minister of railways: 'From the point of view of agricultural development and interests, there are reasons why the line should be constructed as soon as possible, but from the point of view of coal and other mineral developments, the necessity is even more pressing.'[36] Rumours that the CNR was interested in the Brulé cut-off were greeted by intense lobbying from the Peace country.[37] As a result, in 1923, E.M.M. Hill surveyed the route, and the CNR prepared to construct the line.[38]

The Alberta government did its best to support the aspirations of the Peace River country because it hoped that the Brulé cut-off would lead to an eventual CNR takeover of the Dunvegan lines. Edmonton boosters, buoyed by the prospect of opening another productive coal producing area in the city's hinterland, also joined in the campaign. Thus both provincial governments, metropolitan boosters, and Peace River residents all advocated building the line.[39] But the Brulé cut-off — later referred to as the Obed line — was not a true coast outlet railway for most areas of the Peace country. It did shorten the distance from the region to the west coast considerably over the circuitous ED&BC route, but it did not breach the Rocky Mountains. Instead, it called for a direct southern route to be constructed from Sturgeon Lake to the Athabasca watershed and then to the CNR Yellowhead mainline. While it served the interests of the Grande Prairie district, it required all rail traffic in the other districts of the Peace River country to accumulate at the southeastern corner of the district before beginning the route to the west coast ports. Farmers at Beaverlodge went so far as to argue the only cut-off option Brulé provided to the area was the 'right as a tax-payer to cut-off their heads by financing the route.'[40] The districts to the north and west of Grande Prairie preferred alternative routes through the mountain passes that had been surveyed by the GTP and PGE projects.[41] No less than five routes would be considered.

Fearing that the CNR would cut the CPR out of a possibly lucrative new district and that its lease on the Dunvegan lines would become worthless, the CPR provided the opponents of the Brulé line with hope for an alternative. It sent R. James and C.R. Crysdale to perform reconnaissance surveys through the Peace River and Pine passes in 1923. Rumours soon spread that the CPR had interest in developing the Hudson's Hope coal field and building a line to Naas Bay and the Portland Canal.[42] The *Record* reported that the CPR appeared ready to purchase the PGE railway from the British Columbia government and provide the Peace River region with the 'true' coast outlet railway through Peace Pass; it lobbied strongly for this solution.[43] The divisions within the Peace River region created problems for the provincial government, but the Dominion government's refusal to commit to an outlet route allowed it to postpone any decisions.

Finally, when faced with the expiration of the CPR lease arrangement on the ED&BC, Premier Greenfield took the initiative on the coast outlet issue. At his request

Farmers at Beaverlodge went so far as to argue the only cut-off option Brulé provided to the area was the 'right as a tax-payer to cut-off their heads by financing the route.'

the premiers of Alberta and British Columbia, the federal minister of railways, and the presidents of the CNR and CPR met on 9 January 1925. At this meeting, Greenfield and Oliver made every effort to sell their railways. Although no real progress was made, there was agreement that joint study of the coast outlet issue by CNR and CPR engineers should be conducted.[44] The engineers from the companies met 16 January and prepared a draft proposal by 26 February. This report, eventually tabled in the House of Commons in 1926, contained a devastating critique of the coast outlet proposals.[45]

The report discussed the Obed, Wapiti Pass, Monkman Pass, Pine Pass, and Peace Pass routes from the Peace country and concluded that the Obed line was the cheapest, easiest to construct, and most cost effective. Even this route, however, was dismissed. To make any outlet railway sustainable, significant branch line development was needed to move traffic to a central location. The expense of constructing the branch lines, when combined with the construction costs of the outlet itself, made the coast outlet economically impractical. Although Sir Henry Thornton called the report 'unduly pessimistic,' the CNR Bureau of Economics suggested it might be considered optimistic. The Bureau concluded that the Obed line would lose $1 million per year even if it received two-thirds of all the traffic connected to the district.[46] The traffic from the Peace River region simply did not warrant two railways. Any coast outlet railway, consequently, would necessitate the abandonment of the Edmonton Dunvegan and British Columbia rail line. Even this action, the report noted, would not ensure the success of the coast outlet, and it would increase settlers' costs and make shipping goods into the Peace River region from Edmonton more expensive.

Alberta's new premier, J.E. Brownlee, clearly understood the ramifications of the coast outlet report. Alberta had supported the Peace region's coast outlet aspirations, but these could no longer be reconciled with the Province's financial or Edmonton's commercial interests. Brownlee's government moved quickly to implement a new railway policy that placed the financial interests of the Province at the forefront of the decision-making process. Since Greenfield had been unable to secure a better lease arrangement with either the CPR or CNR, Brownlee decided to sell the Dunvegan lines.[47] His preferred purchaser would be the Canadian National Railways. The sale would win him support in Edmonton, a CNR divisional centre, which would benefit from the additional railway connections. More important, however, may be Brownlee's perception of the coast outlet issue. A coast outlet would ruin the ED&BC and the Obed route, the cheapest and most likely to be constructed, was tributary to the CNR system. If the Province sold the Dunvegan system to the CNR, any construction on the Obed route would undermine its own rail line.[48] Hence, selling the ED&BC to the CNR would ensure the Peace River region remained connected to Edmonton.

The province had queried the two transcontinentals about purchasing the Dunvegan lines during the coast outlet debate; it now began a concerted effort to sell the railway. The Premier offered the railway to the CNR with no conditions for approximately $14.5 million, much less than the government's $17,472,994 valuation of the physical assets. The Dominion government's rejection of this offer forced Brownlee to become creative.[49] In order to strengthen his bargaining position with the railways and give the Dominion a better appreciation of the value of the Dunvegan lines, Brownlee terminated the lease arrangement with the Canadian Pacific Railway, assumed operation of the railway, and entered into a traffic sharing arrangement with Canadian National Railways. The Alberta government estimated the CNR made $758,636 from this arrangement.[50]

The boom in the Peace River country which began in 1926 also helped Brownlee. By keeping operating and maintenance charges at a minimum, the increased traffic allowed the Alberta government to generate exceptional revenue to expense ratios along the Dunvegan system. The railway thus increased in value. Since the CNR had made no satisfactory offers, Brownlee approached the two railways about a joint ownership proposal. It seemed to make the most sense as Grande Prairie and Peace River boosters divided on which railway should control the ED&BC.[51] Moreover, both railways feared a competitive construction boom in the district thus limiting the value of the line. The CPR had rejected earlier efforts by Alberta to negotiate a joint ownership arrangement, but Beatty now responded favourably. Thornton, however, remained opposed to any co-operative venture, and by November 1927 the CNR had made an independent offer that Brownlee promptly rejected.[52]

Rumours of a proposed sale led to swift responses from Edmonton and the Peace River region. Edmonton's boosters preferred a Canadian National purchase but would accept any solution that maintained the existing system. The Journal noted: 'The taking over of the ED&BC by the CNR has been frequently urged . . . The Province, which owns the railway, is prepared to offer reasonable terms, though it sees no reason why it should sacrifice its investment entirely . . . With northern Alberta's resources, a similar outcome is assured for the ED&BC, no matter who controls it.'[53] Sentiment among Peace River residents now coalesced around the CNR as the preferred purchaser as well.[54] The coast outlet issue dominated their perspective. They blamed the CPR and its desire to avoid the cost of constructing such an outlet for the failure of this issue to emerge in the negotiations. Unlike Edmonton, however, the Peace country also feared a joint ownership proposal. Such an arrangement, and the consequent end of any hope for a coast outlet through competitive railway building, was especially threatening.[55] Regional boosters called the failure to discuss a coast outlet a 'crime against the North.'[56]

The pressure from Edmonton and Peace River had little impact on the premier. He told Thornton that his responsibility lay with the province as a whole and his government would act in the provincial interest. Furthermore, he would reject any offer that did not include the purchase of the A&GW line as well as the now profitable Dunvegan system.[57] The joint offer he sought was made 16 January 1928. It amounted to $17,420,000 for the Dunvegan system (the government's 1927 valuation of the physical assets) and an independent CNR offer for the A&GW amounting to $5 million paid over ten years. It also promised construction of forty miles of branch lines.[58] Edmonton interests supported the new offer. The Board of Trade recommended the government accept the deal, and the editor of the Journal suggested 'if price were the only consideration, the joint offer . . . must be regarded as reasonably satisfactory.' Further branch line development seemed to be their only concern. When the railways improved the terms of payment and promised to build 100 miles of branch lines, even these modest objections disappeared.[59]

Brownlee's bargaining position had continued to improve in early 1928 as the traffic along the Dunvegan lines reached record levels. Confident that the two railways would compete for access to the booming Peace River region, he rejected the joint offer and asked for $25 million the ED&BC, the CCR, and the A&GW.[60] In September, following a visit to the Peace River region to assess its potential, E.W. Beatty independently offered $25 million for the Alberta government lines. Fearing Thornton's response, however, he offered to include the CNR in the purchase if that railway desired. The government accepted Beatty's offer.[61] This proposal suited Edmonton's business interests. They understood the importance of the CNR and Edmonton's role as a divisional point in the purchase. At a meeting at Edmonton's city hall on 21 November they passed a resolution that: 'in the interests of the Canadian National railways, the city of Edmonton and the north country in particular, in order that the benefit of through rates on both railways may be obtained, we urge this [joint purchase] upon the railway and the government authorities.'[62] After unsuccessfully attempting to convince the federal government to allow his railway to build a new line into the Peace River region, Sir Henry Thornton agreed to the joint purchase and the new Northern Alberta Railways corporation was created.

Although Edmonton was completely satisfied with the arrangement, protest from the Peace River region did emerge. Many feared the joint ownership proposal and its negative implications for a coast outlet and resented the lack of consultation regarding the project.[63] The quick action of the NAR in pressing forward the promised extensions from Fairview to Hine's Creek and Wembley to Dawson Creek alleviated many of these concerns. Brownlee finally appeared to have solved the northern railway issue; and, ironically, the solution emerged when he focused only on the provincial aspect of the issue.

Attempting to fulfil both Edmonton's desire to become the 'Gateway to the North' and Peace River's need for rail connections had been a costly adventure for the Province of Alberta. Despite Brownlee's efforts to extricate the Province from its costly northern railway debacle, the provincial auditor calculated it lost $10,000,000 and assumed an ongoing yearly loss of $460,572 after all sums had been paid.[64] Moreover, the provincial government had postponed and cancelled several other public works projects as it struggled with the ongoing financial obligations it assumed after 1920. The issue is even more complicated when the significance of the rail link to Edmonton and to the Peace country is assessed. The years 1910 to 1926 never generated the wealth in Edmonton or the Peace River country that boosters, settlers, and speculators had envisioned, and the railway failed to generate a return on investment throughout this period. Indeed, the railway had probably been built fifteen years too soon. The ED&BC, CCR, and A&GW stand out as monuments to government extravagance, Edmonton's dreams of grandeur, and the speculative economy of western Canada during the settlement era. ∾

PAULINE PAUL AND JANET ROSS KERR

A PHILOSOPHY OF CARE:
THE GREY NUNS OF MONTREAL

The heart of French Edmonton, St Joachim's Roman Catholic parish, 1902. The
Grey Nuns' General Hospital was about a block away. (PAA B.3757)

hat do the Grey Nuns of Montreal have to do
with Edmonton? As Pauline Paul and Janet Ross
Kerr of the Faculty of Nursing at the University
of Alberta show, the Sisters of Charity, or Grey Nuns of
Montreal, have contributed immensely to the quality of life
in Edmonton since they arrived in the area over a century ago
to work among the Métis and Native populations. A French
Catholic religious order devoted to nursing service, the Grey
Nuns made the necessary adaptation to become one of
the pillars of community health care, putting the needs of
patients before purely economic considerations. Their General
Hospital, one hundred years old in 1995, was the first such
facility in the city.

The Grey Nuns represent two additional threads in
Edmonton's history. One concerns the public role played by
organized women and institutions like the church to make
Edmonton a better place to live. The other concerns the role
played by Franco-Albertans in what is often perceived as an
Anglo-Canadian city. There has been a strong French presence
in the Edmonton area since the days of the fur trade: a person
has only to visit the bedroom communities of St Albert, Legal,
and Morinville to be reminded. In Edmonton itself, the Grey
Nuns and their hospital, only a block from St Joachim's Roman
Catholic Church and rectory, formed part of a distinctly French
cultural and linguistic community that not only served the city
but also had ties to much of the province.

THE YEAR 1995 MARKS NOT ONLY THE BICENTENNIAL OF the founding of Fort Edmonton but also the centennial of Edmonton's oldest health care facility. That the Edmonton General Hospital was established, owned, and operated by a French-Canadian Roman Catholic order—the Sisters of Charity, or Grey Nuns of Montreal—had roots deep in the history of the fur trade. In 1639 the Ursulines and the Augustinian Hospitallers had been the first female religious orders from France to settle at Quebec, providing educational and other services to the Native and European populations. Founded in 1737 by Marguerite d'Youville, a Canadian-born widow well connected with the fur trade and governing establishments of New France who dedicated her later life to the poor and sick, the Grey Nuns were indigenous to Canada. They took over the administration of the Hôpital Général de Montréal in 1747. As an uncloistered order, they were also able to provide community services outside the hospital walls, from the outset visiting the sick in their homes. By the mid-1800s the Grey Nuns were sufficiently strong to expand outside Quebec's borders.

The establishment of a mission at St Boniface in 1844, at the request of Bishop Provencher, marked the beginning of the order's activities in western Canada. In 1859 three sisters answered the call of local French-speaking missionaries to come to Lac Ste Anne, north and west of Fort Edmonton, to provide health care and educational services to the European fur traders and to the Métis and Natives. By 1894 the Grey Nuns had provided health care in the Edmonton area for thirty-five years, the last thirty-one at nearby St Albert. It is not surprising that when five Edmonton physicians decided that the town was sufficiently large to merit a hospital, they turned to these experienced and respected sisters.[1]

The Grey Nuns' philosophy of care would shape the services provided at the Edmonton General Hospital after 1895, while the French-Canadian origins of the order and the majority of its members would contribute to the distinct character of the institution.[2] The hospital's provision of charitable services, its care of epidemic victims, tuberculosis patients, and the elderly, and its role in the Franco-Albertan community would all reflect these two overriding influences. The Edmonton General School of Nursing (1908 to 1973) would also play an important role in educating nursing students, including many French-Canadian young women.

As members of a Roman Catholic nursing religious order, the Grey Nuns share a long tradition of caregiving based on the belief that the body and soul are equally integral parts of a human being. This belief gave rise to the conviction that patient care must account for spiritual as well as physical needs. According to Bishop Legal of St Albert, nursing sisters had a two-fold mission. 'The service of our sisters, in hospitals, is even more precious,' he wrote in 1916, 'since while working towards the cure of bodies they can powerfully assist the priest in the sanctification of souls.'[3] The tenet that patients must be treated in a holistic manner has always been central to caregiving at the Edmonton General. For example, in 1917 Sister St Augustine maintained that 'we must speak with patients about their physical and spiritual needs. We must fulfil the needs which arise from their physical and spiritual state, we must console them, encourage them and provide them with instructions.'[4] In her memoirs, Alvine Cyr Gahagan, a 1932 graduate of the hospital's School of Nursing, described a similar philosophy:

> The importance of 'communicating' with our patients became a common treatment. We got to know our patients well and vice versa, as we mostly took care of the patient for his or her whole stay at the hospital . . . in the three years, we had learned much about the human being, medicine, and life in general, and also about ourselves. In our profession, we must have a high Christian character, as there is a great demand for respect of Life and Death in our line of duty.[5]

The following definition in use at the Edmonton General in 1957 provides additional evidence of this belief. Nursing, it stated, 'includes an understanding of the sick person and his needs and a real attempt to help him disentangle his problems whether they be economic, social, physical or spiritual, in the light of all the best available knowledge.'[6]

Owing to religious belief, the owners of Catholic hospitals usually insisted that poor people should not be refused treatment because of their financial status. Furthermore, the religious mission of the sisters included assistance to those in need even if they were not hospital patients. In the case of the Grey Nuns, assisting the poor was one of the order's fundamental objectives and part of the legacy of its founder. It is important to note here that the Grey Nuns understood 'poor' in its broadest sense— referring not only to economic poverty but also to people made vulnerable because of a variety of problems such as ill-health or isolation. Mother d'Youville devoted her life and the

The first General Hospital built in 1895. (PAA B.3770)

lives of the women in her order to the service of all poor, which explains the emphasis on the provision of charitable services by her spiritual daughters. When d'Youville was beatified by the Roman Catholic church in 1959, Pope John XXIII proclaimed her 'Mother of Universal Charity,' officially recognizing the centrality of charity to her conception of religious life. This title was directly conferred at d'Youville's canonization in December 1990.[7]

The principle of providing care to all those in need was clearly enunciated by the Grey Nuns in the admitting policies of the Edmonton General made public in January 1896:

> Be it well understood that the hospital has nothing to do with paying the medical men; all patients, who have not the means of paying a Doctor, will be under the care of the Physician of the month; all who pay, can have any Doctor they may choose . . . To . . . [the Grey Nuns] alone belong the right to determine the different offices to be filled by the Sisters and employees, to engage the necessary help and to watch over the perfect working of the Hospital. The Hospital . . . is open to all patients without distinction of belief, religion or nationality.[8]

This same statement specified that non-Catholic clergymen were welcome to visit patients of the same faith. Providing services regardless of the economic, denominational, or ethnic background of the recipients came to characterize the work of the Grey Nuns at the General—although abiding by this philosophy was occasionally arduous.

The most significant administrative issue faced by the Grey Nuns in the General's first decade surfaced in 1899 when a conflict arose between them and the physicians associated with the hospital. The seeds of the controversy lay in the admitting policy of 1896, whose unambiguous rules the medical men had originally accepted. However, on 30 January 1899 the *Edmonton Bulletin* reported that doctors Wilson, Harrison, Braithwaite, and McInnis had resigned from the General. The same issue of the newspaper also announced the establishment of a committee to consider the creation of a civic hospital and seek popular support for the project.[9] The Grey Nuns responded publicly three days later. 'The fact is,' they wrote, 'that the medical directors have resigned the obligations which they had voluntarily and kindly taken upon themselves to attend pauper patients for the space of a month alternatively. Such being the case, the hospital authorities will see that pauper patients are not neglected, but rather be received and cared for in the hospital as before; at least as long as the Sisters of Charity have the means to do so.'[10]

The situation obviously interested the local English- and French-language press. On 9 February both the *Edmonton Bulletin* and *L'Ouest Canadian* carried the Grey Nuns' six point explanation for the physicians' departure. Their evidence showed that while the doctors had requested the transfer of admitting authority from the Grey Nuns to themselves, the directives of the Superior General of the order in Montreal unequivocally gave the Superior of the Edmonton General total control over the admission of all patients, including poor ones.[11] It must be understood that the Superior General, assisted by her General Council, had ultimate authority over all Grey Nun institutions. Although the Superior of a hospital controlled its daily administration, important decisions required the approval of the Provincial Superior and her council (in this case, the Province of St Albert). In critical matters, the Province had to seek approval from the Superior General. It must also be stressed that the Grey Nuns, being under canonical law, reported directly to the Vatican, which meant that local bishops did not have authority over the sisters' administrative decisions. The authority of the local bishop was limited to strictly religious issues.

From the physicians' point of view, the conflict amounted to a power struggle over a matter that they considered to be within their domain and normal responsibilities. In lay hospitals, which were usually administered by men, control over admissions lay with the medical profession. Thus, it is not surprising that some of the Edmonton General physicians sought similar arrangements. One might suspect, however, that monetary issues were also an important factor. Having to serve as physician of the month was far from lucrative and, in fact, meant a reduced income since patients had to be treated free of charge. Once again the General's philosophy was contrary to the practice of lay hospitals. The sisters decided not to back down and relinquish their authority over patient admissions.

By the time the Grey Nuns had published their articles in the press, the physicians in the dispute and members of the local Protestant clergy had spearheaded the establishment of the Edmonton Public Hospital as a 'non-sectarian' institution.[12] The use of the term 'non-sectarian' is most intriguing. While the Edmonton General was a Roman Catholic hospital, it had always accepted patients of all denominations: in 1896, for example, 494 Catholics and 450 Protestants were admitted.[13] In addition, the composition of the board of directors of the Edmonton Public Hospital suggests that this institution was as Protestant as the General was Catholic. It is also significant that the Masonic Lodges, which did not sympathize with Catholicism, were among the first to offer financial assistance to the Edmonton Public.[14] Father Leduc's letter to the *Edmonton Bulletin* in April, supporting both the right and the obligation of the sisters to provide universal health care, further indicates that the conflict had taken on religious overtones.[15] Most likely, a combination of religious and cultural values was involved. That the two French-Canadian physicians (P.S. Royal and P. Roy) remained at the General shows that they did not oppose the sisters' authority.[16] Both men were from Quebec and had studied medicine in that province (all hospitals affiliated with French-speaking medical schools were owned, controlled, and operated by Roman Catholic sisterhoods). In contrast, the dissidents were probably more familiar with the dominant model of English Canada, in which hospitals tended to be operated by municipalities and male boards of directors. For such men, authority resting with an entirely female administration would probably have been difficult if not impossible to accept.

Given the financial climate of the late 1890s, the creation of the Edmonton Public was a blow for the Grey Nuns, who certainly did not need competitors. To add to their problems, Edmonton Town Council informed them

The sitting room in the General Hospital.
(PAA B.3775)

that beginning January 1900 they would have to pay taxes like any other private business.[17] In the long term, however, the existence of the Edmonton Public was positive for the Grey Nuns. First, physicians who elected to practice at the General had an alternative if they clashed with the sisters' views. Second, and more importantly, physicians who chose to pursue a long career at the General possessed similar values to the sisters and thus did not constantly question their authority, particularly with respect to providing charitable services and holistic care.

Ironically, it took the smallpox epidemic of 1901 to restore the sisters in the 'good books' of Town Council. Without the four Grey Nuns—assisted by Dr Royal and a lay nurse from Misericordia Hospital (another Catholic institution, founded in 1900, that handled maternity cases), those affected by the disease would have had no medical or nursing care. Probably fearing smallpox infection, the staff at Edmonton Public refused to have anything to do with these patients. Throughout the epidemic, which lasted from 21 February to 20 May, the Grey Nuns cared for smallpox victims not in their own thirty-bed hospital but in a small house rented from the Hudson's Bay Company, to avoid the risk of contagion for patients hospitalized for other problems. The number of persons treated during the epidemic was not recorded, but it is known that for several weeks as many as forty-five patients were under the Grey Nuns' constant care.[18]

In the wake of the epidemic and no doubt in recognition of the sisters' contribution during that crisis, Town Council revised its position on property taxes and gradually began to offer financial assistance to the Edmonton General.[19] Although the amounts were small, they were appreciated; at the same time, the Grey Nuns' autonomy was much more important than money from the city. Indeed, a few years earlier, the Superior General had cautioned the sisters in Edmonton about the dangers of accepting large grants from any municipality which could then try to impose its views. She had written: 'We are in our house, we will stay independent and continue to be the masters of this house. We do not need a board of directors to rule and control us . . . We must keep our rights. When Protestants have a foot in a place, soon they will have both feet in, with all their boards of directors and visitors.'[20]

The services rendered to Edmontonians during the smallpox epidemic of 1901 are only one example of how the sisters consistently attempted to serve the most needy. Over the years, the assistance the Grey Nuns and the staff of the Edmonton General provided hospital patients took three forms: free consultations, free treatments, and free prescriptions.[21] In 1918, for example, a record 1,089 patients received free consultations, while in a later period, an average of 1,172 free drug prescriptions were donated annually between 1952 and 1957. Free meals, especially during economic downturns, constituted the main charity offered to people who were not patients of the hospital. The highest number dispensed in a single year occurred in 1931, during the Great Depression, when a phenomenal 9,000 free meals were distributed; the lowest number occurred in 1960, when only fifty-two meals were served.[22]

The activity of the Edmonton General during the Spanish influenza of 1918 was also remarkable. From the outset of the epidemic, the hospital was filled with influenza victims. At this time, it had slightly fewer than 100 beds, but space was found to accommodate at least 150 patients by transforming every available space into patient-care areas. In the absence of efficient curative measures for Spanish influenza, good nursing care constituted the essence of treatment. An internal document, probably written in December 1918, stated:

> The nursing staff has been doing its bit with a smile and they have been very successful. Of the 192 patients admitted to date—and some were received in critical condition—10 died, 150 remain in different stages of convalescence and 32 have been discharged permanently recovered. A patient stay is on average ten days. A few nurses have contracted the disease, but none have been seriously ill.[23]

The Edmonton General's response to tuberculosis, more than any other infectious disease, made it unique in the city. In fact, the role played by the General in respect to this disease could alone testify to the fact that it offered different services than other hospitals. Although not as 'spectacular' as the influenza epidemic of 1918, tuberculosis remained an important—if not the major—public health concern until the 1950s. Provincial mortality rates for the disease were as high as 53.2/100,000 in 1921, still stood at 41.3/100,000 in 1941, and finally dropped to 7.4/100,000 in 1955.[24] As early as 1932 the Grey Nuns proposed to the province that the General be permitted to transform a section into a specialized tuberculosis service. Considering the upheaval this step would have caused—as the hospital let other specialty areas go, and its employees risked contracting the disease (sanitorium workers regularly became infected)—volunteering this type of service was unusual. The deputy minister of health rejected the offer.[25] Four years later, however, the new Social Credit government took proactive measures in the area of tuberculosis care. Its Tuberculosis Act (1936) guaranteed free hospital and diagnostic services for sufferers of the disease.

The Edmonton General's offer was reconsidered, and from 1936 to 1952 the hospital was the most important provider of tuberculosis care in Edmonton. Significantly, because of the city's location, the Edmonton General also became the treatment centre for the population of northern Alberta. On 1 July 1936, after receipt of the TB contract, the hospital set aside sixty-five beds for tuberculosis patients.[26] The University of Alberta and Royal Alexandra hospitals were also assigned tuberculosis beds, but they numbered fewer than twenty. A year later the province showed its satisfaction with the General by requesting an additional forty beds. Although the sisters decided to comply because of the great need for tuberculosis beds, the decision must have been difficult since finding the necessary space required a reorganization of patient services. In particular, the number of pediatric beds had to be reduced, and the sisters had no choice but to eliminate the maternity service.[27] The closure of the latter was not without consequences, as the director of the hospital's School of Nursing had to find an affiliating agency for the obstetrical experience of nursing students. Nonetheless, the sisters accepted the challenge of tuberculosis care and offered an essential service to Edmontonians, without losing sight of the importance of maintaining a good nursing school (without whose students, of course, it would have been difficult to operate the hospital). Finally, it is important to mention that the involvement of the Edmonton General in tuberculosis care was not restricted to in-patient treatment. The hospital directly contributed to public health efforts against the disease. In 1943, for example, the school children of Edmonton and St Albert were all received at the Edmonton General for screening tests.[28]

At another level, the role of the Edmonton General Hospital School of Nursing in preparing future nurses contributed significantly to the health of Edmontonians and Albertans. Of the school's 1,999 graduates, an estimated 15.9 per cent were French Canadians (at least 75.8 per cent of these were Franco-Albertans), 29.6 per cent came from other provinces and even countries (10 individuals), and almost two-thirds of the Albertans came from outside Edmonton, from all regions of the province.[29] Clearly, the Edmonton General played a province-wide role in nursing education. Why it attracted so many non-Edmontonians is less clear, but perhaps local parish priests publicized the school; the French nature of the institution would also have been an important factor for the French-Canadian population. Other data show that the Edmonton General's

nursing school was constantly at the forefront of developments in nursing education.[30] Part of the reason undoubtedly lies in the fact that the Grey Nuns were better educated than nurses in Canada generally; approximately one-fifth of the sisters at the General who were also nurses had acquired university education.

The opening of the Youville Memorial wing in 1982 further illustrates the unique character of the Edmonton General. This 280-bed facility was designed to provide needed auxiliary beds in the city and to improve the care and treatment of the elderly and chronically ill, with emphasis placed on rehabilitative services.[31] From the beginning, the Youville Memorial wing also offered a geriatric day hospital program, one of the first such programs in Alberta, and it continues to serve as a model in this area of care. In the 1990s new initiatives directed at seniors included a unit for the care of elderly Chinese, where services are provided in their mother tongue, and a unit for older members of Catholic religious orders, many of them French Canadians, in need of long-term care.

The Grey Nuns' sensitivity to cultural needs may well be related to their own experiences as members of the Franco-Albertan minority. Addressing the response of the Grey Nuns to the needs of Edmontonians would not be complete without discussing the links among them, the hospital, and Franco-Edmontonians. Between 1895 and 1970, 222 sisters worked at the General; fully 181 (or 86.6 per cent) of the 209 on whom data is available were French Canadian.[32] Thus, it is not surprising that the Edmonton General maintained close ties with the Franco-Albertan community. The chronicles of the hospital, which were written in French, show that the Grey Nuns celebrated French-Canadian holidays, socialized primarily with other French-Canadian sisters, and regularly participated in Franco-Albertan festive events.

The sisters observed the important events in the French-Canadian calendar—Christmas, New Year's Day, Epiphany, Saint-Jean Baptiste day, and St Catherine's day—in the traditional French-Canadian way. During the entire history of the hospital, they followed the popular Quebec custom of *Réveillon*, consisting of a full Christmas dinner and celebrations lasting into the night long after midnight mass. New Year's Day—traditionally a time when the entire extended family rejoiced together—was particularly meaningful for French Canadians in western Canada. The fact that most of them had left dozens of relatives in eastern Canada probably explains why, until the 1950s, they coveted the honour of being the first to wish other members of their community 'Happy New Year.'[33]

Based on the chronicles of the Edmonton General, it appears that Franco-Edmontonians cherished that tradition and visited the Grey Nuns after New Year's mass. Until the practice disappeared after 1960, the French-Canadian parishioners of St Joachim church (located a few blocks south of the hospital), the Knights of Columbus, and French-Canadian physicians returned year after year to give their seasonal wishes.[34] Like their ancestors from France, French Canadians celebrated Epiphany by hiding a dry pea and a dry bean in a special cake; the two individuals who found the pea and bean in their pieces of cake were proclaimed queen and king and given the privilege of establishing the evening's agenda. The association between royalty and Epiphany came from the three wise men, referred to in French as 'kings.' The sisters followed this tradition but added a religious dimension. Pieces of paper bearing the name of each sister were put in a hat and the sister whose name was drawn received 'charity'— meaning that at the mass of the following day the other sisters all prayed for her well-being and happiness.[35]

French Canadians have always celebrated Saint-Jean Baptiste day by burning ritual bonfires, but during the political turmoil of the 1830s the celebration began to take a new meaning.[36] On 24 June 1834 Ludger Duvernay, a patriot, founded *La Société Saint-Jean Baptiste* to protect French-Canadian institutions, language, and laws, and proclaimed St John the Baptist the patron saint of French Canada. After 1867 the society began to expand outside Quebec. A branch was created in Edmonton in 1894 and for the next three decades *La Société Saint-Jean Baptiste* was a key association for Franco-Albertans.[37] St Joachim parish hosted the annual celebration, with typical activities including a mass, a banquet, and a play.[38] The Grey Nuns participated in these activities and collaborated with the Oblate priests in charge of the parish. In 1928, for example, the sisters helped prepare the menu for the picnic on 24 June and the hospital kitchen was used to cook the hams purchased by the *Société*.[39] The first French settlers in New France also brought the custom of celebrating St Catherine's day (25 November), the feast of all women still unmarried after their twenty-fifth birthdays. In

the 1660s Marguerite Bourgey, founder of the *Congrégation de Notre-Dame*, which was devoted to the education of children, established the tradition of making molasses candies as part of the festivities. Since then, every year on 25 November, elementary school children learn how to make *la tire Sainte-Catherine*. The Grey Nuns followed the custom of making *la tire* and, as single women, they found the day particularly relevant to their status. The chronicles often referred to it as the sisters' birthday.

Records of the Edmonton General show that, in addition to French-Canadian nursing students, French-speaking physicians often held leadership positions and the hospital employed a number of Franco-Edmontonians.[40] As late as 1954, for example, three of the six physicians on the medical executive committee of the hospital were French Canadian. Although the exact number of Franco-Albertan employees is unknown, evidence suggests that they were numerous. The hospital chronicles regularly mention their marriages, deaths, and the births of their children, while a partial staff list from 1969 shows at least seventy-five workers of Franco-Albertan origin.[41] French Canadians were also routinely hired for construction or renovation projects, and the sisters usually had French-speaking legal advisors and insurance agents.[42] Older Franco-Edmontonians still refer to the Edmonton General as 'their hospital,' which indicates the importance it has had in their lives. The Grey Nuns consistently made efforts to provide services to the Franco-Albertan community in the French language, and Edmonton was always the hub for the province's French population. In 1914 there was an active population of 3500 Franco-Edmontonians among the city's 72,516 residents. Until the 1920s Franco-Edmontonians were sufficiently numerous in proportion to the rest of the population to play a highly visible role in commercial, professional, and political activities. Store owners such as J.H. Picard and J.H. Gariépy, physicians such as J. Royal and A. Blais, and lawyers such as W. Gariépy and L.A. Giroux were well known and participated in the life of the larger community. Picard, for example, served on Town Council from 1893 to 1907 and from 1914 to 1917, Gariépy was a long-time Member of the

The Grey Nuns consistently made efforts to provide services to the Franco-Albertan community in the French language, and Edmonton was always the hub for the province's French population.

Legislative Assembly, and Blais sat in the Senate for a number of years.[43]

The provision of French-language services at the Edmonton General was not always appreciated by the English-speaking majority. The fact that most French Canadians were Roman Catholic and most Anglo-Canadians belonged to Protestant denominations magnified tensions, as did the different visions of Canada held by each group. In addition, as elsewhere in Canada, tensions existed between French and Irish Catholics, especially with respect to Catholic schools and language of instruction. For example, when Ontario agreed to permit separate schools, bitter disputes erupted between the two Catholic linguistic minorities, aware that only one language would be adopted.[44] Tensions spread beyond problems related to language of instruction, and in Alberta were particularly acute in the 1920s when the Irish Archbishop O'Leary succeeded the French Bishop Legal (who had died) as head of the Edmonton diocese. The subsequent massive replacement of French Oblate priests with Irish priests was certainly the most salient source of discord and reflected a power struggle.[45]

No evidence has been found that the Grey Nuns engaged in these conflicts originating in the male hierarchy of the church. The sisters probably thought it wiser to keep a low profile. As well, they must have realized that their position in the province was fairly secure and that they could not be replaced as easily as parish priests. In particular, any search for an English- or Irish-Canadian sisterhood would have been difficult since most religious orders were French Canadian. The Grey Nuns also owned their institutions and were under the authority of their Motherhouse. Lastly, as the General's open admissions policy testifies, they refused to be embroiled in ethnic conflicts. During the Seven' Years War which led to the conquest of New France by Britain, Marguerite d'Youville had provided the example, caring for wounded British soldiers even though they were the enemy.

When directly attacked, however, the Grey Nuns reacted and used the power of their order to do as they saw fit. Such was the case when a conflict linked to language—in which Archbishop O'Leary unsuccessfully attempted to impose his views—embroiled the nursing school in 1929. That spring the Grey Nuns decided to transfer the director of the school, Sister O'Brien Laverty, to another hospital. The decision was not unusual in that she had been in her position for the customary three years. However, in March alumnae of the school made their opposition to the transfer known in a letter and petition to

the provincial superior. Archbishop O'Leary also opposed the transfer, and on 28 July the provincial superior informed him that the order would not grant his wish of seeing Sister O'Brien Laverty remain in Edmonton. The controversy culminated in September when nursing students threatened to go on strike. According to the *Edmonton Journal*, they sought the reinstatement of three classmates recently dismissed from the school.[46] In the end, the students did not go on strike, and on the surface their revolt would appear unrelated to the departure of Sister O'Brien Laverty. Other evidence suggests a strong link between the two events. In a letter in October to the assistant general of the Grey Nuns in Montreal, the superior of the Edmonton General wrote:

> Here in June, some had decided . . . that the competent authority would direct the ship. It did not happen, but they did not accept defeat; at all costs they had to find the means to penetrate the administration. They pushed some students to act about a matter which they did not understand; change immediately, at 7 p.m. tonight, the method by which students are released and establish an arbitration committee made of the Archbishop and two physicians . . . I intend to rely on the advice of the Provincial Superior of the Oblate Priests: not to accept any new types of meeting, not to provide any explanations about our internal discipline.[47]

The fact that Irish/French issues were at play is apparent from the alignment of the Oblates with the Grey Nuns against the archbishop. Significantly, an article in the French newspaper *La Survivance*, owned by the Oblates, directly linked the students' threat to language issues:

> The student nurses say: 'Since in this country the majority of nurses do not understand French and SINCE ENGLISH IS THE OFFICIAL LANGUAGE, we request that the sisters in charge of nursing units be able to speak English' . . . This mention of being in an English country stinks of fanaticism. Let us say here that all nuns, but one, speak English very well . . . , the sisters are graduate nurses. This shows that they are competent. The only thing left is the question of race and language, this internal crisis is fed from external fanaticism.[48]

The ethnic nature of the conflict is further revealed by a letter sent to the Grey Nuns' provincial superior by the reverends McGuigan, O'Neil, and Retchen. Appointed by the archbishop to make recommendations, they requested the replacement of the superior of the Edmonton hospital, the appointment of a board of appeal (which would include the archbishop's representative), and the nomination of sisters of English origins in leadership positions.[49] On 11 November 1929 the superior general of the order and her council reiterated that the administration of the Edmonton General would not be changed, that the competence of a sister was not a function of being French or English, and that the system of appeal would not be modified. The preamble to her letter confirms the Grey Nuns' views of conflicts rooted in ethnicity: 'We shall love our beautiful French language and we must protect her faithfully; but it would not be proper for a Sister of Charity to be conducted by the spirit of nationalism; we must see in all beings the children of our Eternal Father, thus our brothers. It is the example left by our Venerable Mother.'[50]

The 1929 episode was not an isolated case, since in 1937 Archbishop MacDonald pressured the sisters to recognize the Edmonton General as an English-speaking institution. They refused, so as not to impose restrictions on the still common use of French.[51] As years passed, ensuring French services at the Edmonton General became a challenge tied to the difficulty of finding French-speaking personnel, but ethnic issues remained alive. 'Even if fifty per cent of the patients of the Edmonton General were French Canadians,' the provincial superior of the Oblates wrote to the superior general of the Grey Nuns in 1945, 'the sisters are about the only ones who speak French since the majority of the employees are English speaking, protestations do occur on both side[s] of the population [English and French].'[52] The words of Dr L.P. Mousseau at the inauguration of the 1953 hospital wing confirm that tensions related to language persisted: 'Personne ici ne devrait s'étonner que je prenne la parole en français, ce serait le contraire qui serait étrange, car l'oeuvre des Soeurs de la Charité des Territoires du Nord Ouest tel que son nom l'indique est une réalisation canadienne française.'[53] In that the Grey Nuns always based their actions and administrative decisions on the premise that all should receive the best possible services, it is not unreasonable to conclude that in order to serve the needs of Franco-Edmontonians, offering services in the French language, when possible, was part of quality care giving.

After the new Grey Nuns Hospital opened in Mill Woods in 1988, most acute care services were transferred there from the General, which continued to offer a variety of rehabilitative and support services. In 1995, with the restructuring of health care in Alberta, the future of the Edmonton General might seem uncertain, but the hospital has a proven record of meeting challenges, adapting to new circumstances, and responding to the societal needs of the time. Even if the nature of its activities is once again altered, the General will surely continue to offer unique services to the residents of Edmonton and Alberta. Even if few sisters now work at the hospital, the Grey Nuns still own the institution and their philosophy of care continues to inform the creation and delivery of patient services. This legacy of care belongs to Edmontonians. ✌

SHARON RICHARDSON

STAFFING THE HOSPITALS:
EDMONTON'S NURSE TRAINING PROGRAMS

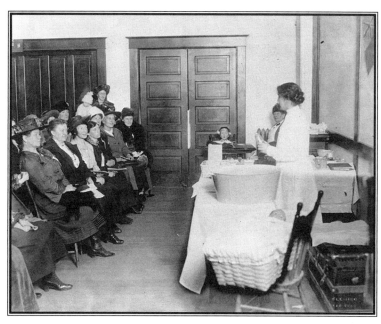

In the 1920s, if they had further training, graduates of Edmonton's hospital nursing programs could sometimes find employment as public health nurses. Here a public health nurse is conducting a child welfare clinic. (PAA A.6949)

*A*s a growing city, Edmonton had need of modern hospital facilities, doctors, and nurses to take care of the ill and injured. Behind these immediate needs, there were other worries.

In the large cities of Britain, the United States, and eastern Canada, modern urban industrial society brought with it problems of run-down tenements, inadequate sewage systems, contaminated water supplies, infectious diseases, and high infant mortality rates. Edmontonians knew the seriousness of these problems and hoped they would be spared. As the germ theory of disease became more widely accepted, improved standards of sanitation and health care offered much hope.

By the start of the First World War, Edmonton had four hospitals with schools of nursing. The city would play a leading role in providing hospital care to Albertans. Yet even in that day, the tension between the quality of patient care and budgetary considerations affected hospital policy.

Sharon Richardson teaches in the Faculty of Nursing at the University of Alberta. She argues that the nurse training programs at the Edmonton Public (Royal Alexandra), Strathcona Municipal (University of Alberta), Misericordia, and Edmonton General hospitals were administered to provide cheap labour for the delivery of patient care. Education of pupil nurses was secondary to their service to the hospital.

PROVIDING FOR THE ILL AND INJURED WAS A MAJOR challenge in Alberta's frontier communities around the turn of the twentieth century. Many single men, in particular, had no family to help them through periods of sickness. The need to care for ill and injured town residents, homesteaders, and immigrants soon led to the establishment of hospitals. Even before incorporation as a city in 1904, Edmonton had three hospitals to serve its 8,000 people.[1] They were the 36-bed Edmonton General Hospital, owned and operated by the Sisters of Charity, more commonly known as the Grey Nuns; the Misericordia Hospital, owned and operated by the Misericordia Sisters; and the 25-bed Edmonton Public Hospital (later renamed the Edmonton City and finally the Royal Alexandra Hospital), incorporated as a public institution in 1900. In 1904 Edmonton City Council opened an Isolation Hospital to treat patients suffering from infectious diseases such as smallpox, scarlet fever, measles, tuberculosis, and erysipelas. Across the river, the small Strathcona Hospital started in 1906 as a 15-bed general institution.[2] Shortly after the amalgamation of Edmonton and Strathcona in 1912, ownership of the Royal Alexandra Hospital was transferred to the City of Edmonton, and the Edmonton Hospital Board was created to administer the Royal Alexandra, the Strathcona, and the Isolation hospitals.[3]

Each hospital required staff—in particular, nurses to care for patients and assist the physicians. In the non-sectarian hospitals a Lady Superintendent or Matron, always a nurse, was needed to manage the institutions on a day-to-day basis. Other trained nurses for the Edmonton Public and Strathcona were originally recruited mostly from central Canada, or less frequently from other Alberta non-sectarian hospitals such as the Galt in Lethbridge and the Calgary General.[4] These nurses rarely stayed more than one to two years and often left after only a few months. The two Catholic hospitals were managed by the Sister Superior who reported to her respective council and motherhouse. Because of their committed sisterhoods, the two Catholic hospitals had a more stable nursing force (augmented by a few lay nurses) in these early years than the three non-sectarian institutions.

Both sectarian and public hospitals established nurse training programs to ensure they had adequate staff—the Edmonton Public in 1905, the Strathcona in 1906, the same year it opened, the Misericordia in 1907, and the Edmonton General in 1908. The Strathcona Hospital School shut down in 1916 when the hospital was leased to

The Edmonton Public Hospital later became the Edmonton City and then the Royal Alexandra Hospital. The first building occupied by the hospital, shown here, was later converted into the Astor Hotel; it was demolished in 1977. (PAA A.2994)

the Military Hospitals Commission to treat soldiers returning from the First World War. It was replaced in 1923 by
the University of Alberta Hospital diploma program.[5]
Sponsoring hospitals regarded the pupil nurse's labour *during training* as most important. Hospital boards were not
concerned about the number of trained nurses they prepared, nor about where or how these trained nurses might
be employed after graduation. They wanted a reliable,
numerically sufficient nursing labour force to ensure continued operation of the hospital. Pupil nurses comprised
the bulk of this labour force.

These four early hospital nurse training programs established a pattern of training for nursing that continued
until well after the end of the Second World War, profoundly influencing the development of nursing work and
education in north central Alberta. In particular, these
training programs established the preeminence of hospital
service over education, reinforced the perception of nursing as a vocation, and, by the interwar years, produced an
oversupply of trained nurses.[6]

At irregular intervals, early Edmonton hospitals admitted women—only women—who wished to become trained
nurses.[7] Date of admission depended upon when the hospital wanted to accept a new pupil and when the prospective
pupil could arrange to move into the hospital. There were
few admission criteria beyond a willingness to submit to
the authority of the Lady Superintendent or the Mother
Superior, a freedom from family responsibilities, and sound
character and health.[8] Sound character was usually attest-
ed to by a clergyman and one other responsible individual,
while evidence of health often required a statement from a
private or a hospital physician. Although hospitals preferred pupils with high school education, prior to 1918 at
least some likely had only grade school education, especially if they came from rural areas.[9]

Pupil nurses enrolled in an initial probationary period
of from one to six months during which the hospital
assessed them for suitability to continue in training.
Probationary pupils began immediately to work on the
hospital wards, often under the direction of another pupil
who might be her 'senior' by only a few months.[10] The bulk
of the probationer's time was spent in housekeeping tasks
such as cleaning patient equipment and the operating
room and preparing hospital supplies. With probation successfully completed, the pupil graduated to bathing and
feeding patients and making beds. In a relatively short
period of time, she might even find herself on night duty
with seriously ill patients. Hospital needs dictated the
assignments of pupils rather than their readiness to assume

Nurses at Edmonton Public Hospital, 1909. (EA-500-119)

responsibility as reflected by time in training or amount of
instruction received.

Pupil nurses (and graduate nurses) worked on the hospital wards six and one half days a week, twelve hours a
day (7:00 am-7:00 pm or 7:00 pm-7:00 am).[11] They were
permitted a half day off on Sundays and one late leave per
month. On day shift, they were given one or two hours off
in the afternoon if all work was completed, but on night
duty there was no mid shift break. During the day, the hospital would usually be staffed by the Lady Superintendent
or Mother Superior (supervisors who did not provide
direct patient care), a graduate nurse on each floor or unit,
and the pupil nurses. During the night, the pupils staffed
all units, with a graduate nurse as Night Supervisor to
assist them.

The hospital's reliance on pupil nurses for patient care
is evident. For example, in 1905 three graduate nurses and
four pupil nurses provided care to between 26 and 52
patients at the Edmonton Public Hospital. Since one of
these graduate nurses was the Lady Superintendent, one
graduate and two pupil nurses likely cared for all patients
on each of the two shifts. In 1910, with an average monthly census ranging between 33 and 42 patients, five graduate (the Lady Superintendent, the Assistant Superintendent, the Night Supervisor, and two head nurses) and
seven pupil nurses delivered care on two shifts. By 1912,
six graduate nurses (now including one more head nurse)
oversaw the care given 70 to 74 patients by 22 pupil nurses, distributed over day and night shifts.[12] Similar gradu-
ate/pupil and nurse/patient ratios existed prior to the First
World War at the Medicine Hat General Hospital and the
Calgary General Hospital.[13]

Prior to the First World War, the city's sponsoring hos-

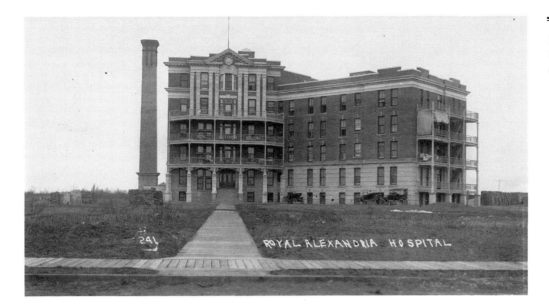

Royal Alexandra
Hospital, 1915.
(PAA B.3794)

pitals offered formal instruction to pupil nurses on an ad hoc basis. Physicians provided formal lectures in all four hospital training programs on such subjects as anatomy, physiology, pharmacology, medicine, surgery, gynaecology, pediatrics, and, later, obstetrics. Usually they delivered these lectures in the evening, after pupil nurses had worked a full day shift,[14] with content and sequencing apparently at the physician-instructor's discretion. There is no indication of standardization of these lectures within or between Edmonton hospital training schools. As permitted by their other duties, the Lady Superintendent or the director of the Catholic schools gave additional formal classes in patient care; however, this practice may have been omitted at the Strathcona Hospital, where 1916 graduate Annie Berggren recalled learning nursing techniques while 'apprenticed' to a senior nurse but did not remember taking any classes from the Matron.[15] Most learning took place on the wards, sometimes under the supervision of graduate nurses if they had time and sometimes under the direction of other, more 'senior' pupil nurses. This pattern of instruction was similar to that provided in other Canadian nurse training programs.[16]

The content of ward learning was dictated by the illnesses, age, and number of patients, so pupils learned about nursing the type of patients most common to their institutions. Unlike at the Misericordia, maternity cases were infrequent at the Edmonton Public, Strathcona, and Edmonton General hospitals,[17] so nurses had little opportunity to develop or demonstrate knowledge and skills associated with birthing and infant care. Surgical skills, on the other hand, were in high demand in these hospitals as the number of in-hospital operations increased dramatical-

ly once the move was made to specially designed buildings.[18] Nurses readied equipment and supplies and set up the operating room, prepared patients for surgery, assisted the doctors during operations, and sometimes administered anaesthetic. Post-operative care took place back in the ward, requiring continuous observation by one nurse until patients were fully conscious.

Hospitals tested pupil nurses only infrequently to determine what they learned and how well they knew it. In 1907 at the request of the Matron of the City Hospital Training School a Medical Board of Examiners comprised of three physicians was appointed to act as examiners for the final year of the program.[19] How long this examining board remained active is not known. Standardized examinations for pupil nurses in Alberta were not set up until 1919, and they were not compulsory. A nurse was considered 'trained' if she completed the time required by the hospital, with time missed for reasons such as illness made up before graduation. As a result, the actual length of time spent in the training school often exceeded three years.[20]

Over the years rules and regulations for pupil nurses became more strict as class sizes increased to meet the growing staffing needs of Edmonton's hospitals. All pupil and graduate nurses lived in the hospital or in a nearby nurses' home operated by the hospital, making enforcement of late leave, days off, and other similar regulations relatively easy. The ringing of a loud bell regularly woke pupils on day duty at the Royal Alexandra; they were expected to report for breakfast and prayers, before marching in order of seniority to the wards. Often, pupils were inspected by the Lady Superintendent or her designate for compliance with rules about length of uniform and hair.

They were punished by cancellation of late leaves for such infractions as not arriving on wards on time or failing to retire at the prescribed bedtime.[21] They could be suspended or even dismissed for infractions of other rules, such as one at the Royal Alexandra Hospital restricting ill pupils to medical care given by physicians appointed by the training school.[22]

Pupil nurses experienced a variety of sleeping and living arrangements in the accommodation provided by Edmonton hospitals. The worst conditions may have been experienced by the first two pupils of the Strathcona Hospital, who reportedly slept with the hospital's laundress and cook in a tent throughout the winter of 1906-7, one of the coldest ever recorded in western Canada. In their second year, they moved to slightly better accommodation in a prefabricated hut. Later, Strathcona Hospital housed pupil nurses in the hospital and in a rented house, before moving them for a very short time in 1916 to Pembina Hall, the women's residence of the University of Alberta.[23] The Strathcona Hospital training school was disbanded in 1916 and pupil nurses completed their training at the Royal Alexandra Hospital in Edmonton, and in Regina and Vancouver.[24] Misericordia and Edmonton General pupils apparently lived in their respective hospitals, as did pupils at the Edmonton City-Royal Alexandra Hospital.[25] About 1913, a nurses' residence was completed for the Royal Alexandra. It boasted a large dining room, furnished reception rooms, a suite for the Lady Superintendent, and rooms for graduate and pupil nurses.[26] This tastefully decorated residence was likely the most comfortable accommodation for pupil nurses in the city at the time.

Attrition among pupil nurses was high throughout the three-year training period. For example, although the Edmonton Public Hospital admitted four probationary pupils in 1905, only one graduated in 1908; it admitted five first-year pupils in 1908 but only two graduated in 1911.[27] The situation had not improved at this hospital by the beginning of the First World War. In 1912, the hospital admitted twenty-six pupil nurses on probation, with nineteen eventually being accepted, and ten graduating in 1915. The exact reasons for such a high attrition rate are not documented; however, dissatisfaction with the nursing role, fatigue associated with prolonged hours of work, marriage, and illness are known to have contributed to high attrition rates after the war and were likely causes in these years as well.[28]

By 1918 at least 155 nurses had graduated from the four Edmonton hospital training schools (76 from the Edmonton General, 51 from the Royal Alexandra, 22 from the Misericordia, and at least 6 from the Strathcona—that hospital's records were lost or destroyed when the training school was disbanded).[29] While 155 may seem an impressive number of graduates available to provide care to Edmontonians, hospitals only hired a limited number of single women—so graduates who married were essentially unemployable. Graduate nurses in hospitals worked six and one half days a week, twelve hours a day and lived in the hospital or its nurses' home. Such employment conditions precluded married graduate nurses working on hospital staff, even if home and family responsibilities had permitted them to do so. Employment in private duty was usually not an option for married graduates; it required

The University of Alberta Hospital, which began as the Strathcona in 1906. (PAA A.3863)

twenty-four hour attendance for the duration of the case in whatever geographic locale the patient lived. In any case, few people could afford private nurses. Although no accurate figures exist, a significant majority of Edmonton graduates can safely be assumed to have soon married and 'retired' from salaried nursing work. They might be available to aid family, friends, and neighbours in need of nursing on an ad hoc basis.

ᖰ The pattern of training for nursing work established by the Royal Alexandra, Edmonton General, and Misericordia continued essentially unaltered until after the Second World War. The implications were significant for nurses and for health care delivery in Edmonton—and in the province. The city's programs served as models for training programs in northeastern and central Alberta, such as those established at the Lamont Public Hospital in 1912, St Joseph's Hospital, Vegreville, in 1915, the University of Alberta in 1923, and St Mary's Hospital, Camrose, in 1924.

The service needs of a hospital continued to take precedence over improvements in education so long as that hospital attracted sufficient pupil nurses to operate with a limited number of graduate nurses. The hospital's initial and overriding reason for establishing a training school was to acquire a nursing work force. From the hospital's perspective, a pupil was given the opportunity to learn how to nurse in exchange for service to the institution, room and board, laundry, and a stipend once probation was completed.[30] From the pupil's perspective, a minimal initial outlay for uniforms, shoes, and incidentals enabled participation with like-minded women in a program that could provide a socially sanctioned way of earning a living and geographic mobility. Nurse training was one of the few options for advancement open to less affluent women from rural and urban Alberta. Edmonton hospitals continued to attract a large number of pupil nurses between the two world wars; some 1500 nurses graduated during these years (435 from the Edmonton General, 607 from the Royal Alexandra, 310 from the Misericordia, and several hundred from the University of Alberta).[31]

The hospital training programs also reinforced a public perception of nursing as an extension of altruistic women's work, requiring dedication and the perceived feminine virtues of caring and compassion—but not intellectual rigour. Nursing was seen as a vocation rather than a developing occupation. The seclusion of pupil nurses within institutions that provided both working and living environments reinforced this view. Pupils were believed to be obedient, willing workers, subservient to physicians and the head nurse, following carefully detailed regulations, and deferring to those in authority. The fact that almost all 'retired' from nursing upon marriage fit readily into this public image. Nurses and the general public alike viewed nurse training as an admirable preparation for marriage and motherhood.

The hospital's reliance on pupil nurses for their labour supported an environment heavy with the rules and regulations believed necessary since inexperienced pupils were providing patient care with minimal supervision. Extensive rules and regulations substituted for direct supervision and ensured a degree of patient safety and a minimum standard of care. But this environment stifled individual initiative and independent decision making and reinforced the public perception of the nurse as physician's handmaiden. The development of an independent role for nursing was retarded.

Hospital training programs also perpetuated the retention of many housekeeping and domestic duties by nurses. As suggested, through the First World War much of the routine cleaning of patient utensils and rooms was performed by unpaid probationary pupils. A 1930 national survey of Canadian nurse training programs by George Weir confirmed that much of the probationer's time was still spent in housekeeping tasks, not nursing activities.[32] Hospitals had no incentive to increase the number of ward maids and other housekeeping staff when pupils did the work at much less cost. Hospital and nursing literature is replete with reminiscences of graduate nurses regarding the excessive time they spent on domestic cleaning when they were pupils.[33]

The staffing of hospitals almost exclusively with pupil nurses contributed significantly to the paucity of salaried employment for graduate nurses in hospitals. Because pupils provided virtually all nursing care to patients, the only salaried positions requiring graduate nurses were head nurse and supervisor. As has been shown, to the start of the First World War a very limited number of these supervisory positions were available in Edmonton hospitals, and many trained nurses, upon graduation, found themselves with no place to go and hard pressed to earn a living.[34] Almost as soon as war was declared, graduate nurses began volunteering for military service abroad and at home. The first to go were usually hospital-employed nurses who were perceived by the military as most useful in casualty clearing stations and other active treatment centres. The positions these nurses vacated in Edmonton became available to other graduates. As a result, unemployment problems for graduate nurses were deferred to the end of the First World War. Between the wars, hospitals became an increasingly significant component of the health care delivery system, creating a need for increased nursing staff. But hospitals met this need by increasing their pupil nurse labour force. The result was significantly more graduate nurses in a market that was already unable to employ the available supply.[35] Graduate nurses also had to compete with so-called 'practical nurses' and other untrained attendants who cared for the sick for a lower fee. As a result, underemployment and unemployment of graduate nurses became endemic.

The only employment option open to a significant majority of graduate nurses was private duty. The extent of the underemployment of private duty nurses was documented in 1930 by Weir, who reported that 60 per cent of the nurses actually practising were engaged in private duty. He found that in Manitoba, Saskatchewan, and Alberta, the average private duty nurse worked only twenty-six weeks out of fifty-two and had a median annual income of $920.[36] That employment security was a major concern for private duty nurses is evident in letters and articles published in the interwar years in the *Canadian Nurse*, the journal of the national nursing association, and in Alberta hospital alumnae and provincial nursing association newsletters. Although able to 'scrape by' financially, many private duty nurses worried about what would happen to them as they aged and became less able to withstand the rigours of their occupation. Most private duty nurses surveyed by Weir saw little prospect of saving sufficient money to provide for their old age; since 90 per cent of these women were unmarried, their concerns seem justified.

Through the interwar years, Edmonton hospitals graduated far more trained nurses than they hired. What had begun as a practical solution for hospitals—namely establishing nurse training programs as a way of staffing their institutions—had created a surplus of graduates who suffered from chronic unemployment. Hospital nurse training programs also slowed the development of nursing as an independent profession. ∾

FAYE REINEBERG HOLT

MAGISTRATE EMILY FERGUSON MURPHY

Emily Ferguson Murphy. (EA-10-2024)

aye Reineberg Holt is a Calgary writer and editor. She has published non-fiction, fiction, and poetry and is working on a full-length biography of Emily Ferguson Murphy.

A strong supporter of the franchise for women, Murphy is now perhaps best remembered for her role in the Persons Case. She had been appointed to the bench in 1916. Alberta lawyers protested that neither she nor Alice Jamieson, a juvenile court judge in Calgary, had the right to sit on the bench. Their argument was based on the terms of the British North America Act which did not clearly include women as 'persons.' Later, when Murphy's name was suggested for the Senate, the same challenge was raised. In 1927 Murphy, Henrietta Muir Edwards, Louise McKinney, Irene Parlby, and Nellie McClung demanded that the federal government decide the issue. Eventually, their case went before the Judicial Committee of the Privy Council in London. They won, but the first woman summoned to the Senate was not Murphy but Cairine Wilson in 1930.

Here Holt looks at a less well-known though fascinating aspect of Murphy's life—her career on the bench.

With the immigration boom, Edmonton had acquired the trappings of modern society—industry, telephone communication, railways, urban growth, and, by the 1920s, an increasing number of automobiles. While virtually everyone approved of 'progress,' few were comfortable with the social inequality and value changes that accompanied this more secular society. Social gospellers attempted to solve problems of urban slums, harsh working conditions, and political corruption by applying practical Christian teachings to the reform of society. Their attitudes to immigrants, Natives, and people of other races, however, often revealed the prejudices of their Anglo-Saxon middle-class background.

To social gospellers then, cities like Edmonton might be bellwethers of progress, but they were also nesting places for crime and sin. Such concerns were not entirely misplaced. In her job as magistrate and through her involvement with women's clubs, Murphy turned her reformist energies to rescuing young people from prostitution, drugs, juvenile delinquency, and crime.

I N 1916 THE ALBERTA GOVERNMENT RESPONDED TO lobbying and a shift in public opinion regarding women's roles by appointing prominent author and social activist Emily Ferguson Murphy as "Magistrate for the Province of Alberta with Jurisdiction in the City of Edmonton." The first woman magistrate in the British Empire, Murphy was confronted with the objection that she had no right to sit on the bench in her first days in court.[1] In Calgary, the same scenario was enacted before Judge Alice Jamieson. Defence lawyers claimed that under the British North America Act (which was written using the pronoun 'he') women were not legally persons but should be classified with children, criminals, and the insane. The ensuing dispute eventually would lead to the famous Persons Case appeal by Murphy, Henrietta Muir Edwards, Nellie McClung, Louise McKinney, and Irene Parlby to the British Privy Council. Today Murphy is justifiably remembered for her role in that struggle and for her equally famous 'Janey Canuck' books. Her career as a magistrate is less well known; however, it provides a fascinating glimpse into her character and social activism as she confronted a darker side of Edmonton in the early decades of the twentieth century.

∾ Emily Ferguson Murphy's upbringing, religion, and experience predisposed her towards the social gospel movement. She was born in Cookstown, Ontario, on 14 March 1868. The daughter of an important landowner, she was not raised in a family of social activists, but her privileged childhood helped her to develop a sense of confidence and an understanding of politics that would serve her well in later years. One uncle was a cabinet minister while another uncle and her Irish grandfather had served as members of Parliament. When she was a youngster, Prime Minister Macdonald reportedly dined at her family's home. In belief, she embraced Christian values, cooperative endeavour, and the work ethic. Privileged members of society, like herself, had a duty to better the community and to educate the less fortunate. In personality, she was straightforward, determined, and pragmatic. Though widely read, her role in social reform movements would be pragmatic rather than philosophical. At eighteen, she married Arthur Murphy, an Anglican minister eleven years her senior. His success as an evangelist took them from rural Ontario to Europe. Then illness forced Arthur to make career changes. He moved his family to Swan River near the Saskatchewan-Manitoba border where they had purchased a timber limit and where he continued a part-time ministry.

In these years, under the pseudonym of Janey Canuck, Murphy became recognized as a successful writer, especially in England where her biographical and travelogue style, sensitivity, and Canadian perspective had tremendous appeal. Her early writing was filled with witty tug-of-wars between her and Arthur, ones sometimes related to women's roles, often solved through laughter, and generally reflecting marital compatibility. Concern with poverty, dysfunctional families, and poor working conditions were also evident. Often accompanying her husband in his duties as minister, she witnessed the problems poor families faced.

In 1907 the family moved to Edmonton. The city was to become Murphy's real home, a place she would love deeply and whose people would bring her a mature understanding of the successes and tragedies inherent in the human condition. As a new resident Murphy quickly imbibed the spirit of boosterism then typical of the city. In 1910 writing in *Janey Canuck in the West*, she marvelled at the unlimited possibilities of her new northern home, its hospitable, big-hearted residents, and its modernity and progressive air: 'the first thing that strikes you about the city is its up-to-dateness. It is not wanting in any good thing that makes for the commonwealth or the common-health . . . Few cities in the world afford better opportunities for the investment of capital and push.'[2]

Murphy quickly became a well-known figure on the executives of local women's clubs. For the most part, her club associates were middle- and upper-class Christian women. Most were conservative and born in Canada, the British Isles, or the United States.[3] Although some considered her pushy, Murphy fit in readily.

In 1908 the Edmonton Local Council of Women was re-instated as a club.[4] For many years Murphy would serve as its convenor of the Committee on Laws for the Better Protection of Women and Children, in which position she would focus on the legal status of Alberta women. One problem women faced was the possibility of being left destitute if their husbands chose to gamble away or sell the family homestead. A husband could choose to will their land and possessions to sons or other male relatives. When the Married Women's Relief Act passed second reading in the Legislature, as Convenor on Laws Murphy conveyed the Local Council's concern. The bill offered widowers the right to petition the courts for one-third of the homestead. The premier had suggested that eventually his government's intention was to do better for women. The reform-minded, however, wanted the legislation to provide for an absolute one-third share. Murphy wrote:

I am instructed by the Edmonton Local Council of women to make protest on their behalf against a bill which has passed two readings of the Legislative Assembly, which bill is known as 'The Married Women's Relief Act.' It has been stated on the floor of the House that this bill meets the wishes of your petitioners concerning the matter. This statement is wholly incorrect. The bill, in no particular[,] meets the approval of your petitioners.[5]

After significant amendments, the bill was passed in December 1910, and it became a step towards future concessions.[6]

Not surprisingly, Murphy and other Local Council law committee members were introduced to the lifestyle of women accused of crime. To see how the defendants were treated, the women from this committee and from the Standing Committee on Equal Moral Standards and Prevention of Traffic in Women attended court cases involving women. When a police sweep brought forty prostitutes into court, the judge warned the female observers the case would not be pleasant but approved their presence. A prosecuting attorney, however, said he would give evidence 'no decent women would care to hear.'[7] Murphy

and the Local Council women were not ordered to leave but rather embarrassed into withdrawing from the courtroom.

Murphy prompted them to lobby to have a woman appointed to the bench. The Social Service Home, Beulah Mission, Salvation Army, Children's Aid, Good Shepherd, YWCA, Travellers Aid, and the Catholic Women's League were all doing good work to help delinquent girls. Yet their efforts seemed futile to Murphy when 'the last spark of modesty, decency and self respect is stamped out of [the girls and women] in the manner of their trial.' As a result, the 23 March 1916 committee report recommended 'immediate steps be taken for the establishment of a Woman's Court in Edmonton, as the first step toward stamping out Traffic in Women.'[8] In fact, by this time, Murphy had already been approached by Attorney General Cross and asked to accept an appointment as magistrate for the City of Edmonton.[9]

Though without formal legal training, Murphy was a realistic choice. She was well known for her community and social activism. She had been the only woman member of the Charter Committee of the City of Edmonton (1914), the first president of the Women's Canadian Club of Edmonton (1911-13), and the first woman member of the Hospital Board of the City of Edmonton (1910).

Murphy, front and centre, with officers of the Women's Canadian Club of Edmonton, 1911. The King Edward Hotel, where this meeting took place, was still under construction and Murphy had to stand on an apple box to be seen when she delivered her presidential address. (UAA 73-171-2)

Believing education was essential to creating a better quality of life for upcoming generations, in 1911 Murphy, on behalf of the Local Council, had appeared before a royal commission supporting what today is known as vocational training and technical institutes.[10] The teaching of useful skills, as curriculum, would be a safe-guard against vice-dominated lives for those not academically inclined. She had inaugurated a movement for public playgrounds in Edmonton (1911) and another for the Victorian Order of Nurses in the city (1909-10).[11] In early 1916, she had worked with the superintendent of neglected children on proposed revisions to Alberta's Child Protection Act.

The time was also right politically for Murphy's appointment. On 1 March 1916 the second reading of the provincial women's suffrage bill had passed—virtually guaranteeing it would become law. Murphy, Nellie McClung, Alice Jamieson, Henrietta Muir Edwards, and Irene Parlby had been key activists. The attorney general knew Murphy had pored over law books, researching and drafting proposals for suffrage and property rights legislation. The ground-swell of public opinion and the support of the United Farmers, Local Councils of Women, and the Woman's Christian Temperance Union for women's rights indicated the community wanted women to have more power and responsibility as citizens.

Reflecting this attitude, the *Edmonton Bulletin* reported on Murphy's appointment: 'Edmonton has its first woman police magistrate and Alberta has taken another step in the path of social reform, leading every other province in the Dominion . . .'[12] On 16 June Murphy was also made a commissioner under the Child Protection Act and on 30 July 1917, a police magistrate for Alberta. With these appointments, she automatically was judge of the juvenile court.[13] Her first task was to learn more about the law and the civic, provincial, and national social service programs available for defendants. She later wrote that not knowing every law or procedure had been little problem; as long as a magistrate was studious and had a teachable spirit, she would 'find the clerk of the court, crown prosecutors, Deputy Attorney General, his solicitors, the librarian at the Law Courts, and nearly all the barristers in the city, ready to help and advise.'[14]

The backgrounds of those who came before Murphy were varied. There were the respectable women who did not pay their driving tickets and dog taxes or who allowed their children to skip school. Murphy wrote, 'These ladies are highly indignant and take a long time to get over what they consider a personal and unpardonable affront.'[15] Most cases, however, were far more serious. There were the dis-

advantaged, some of whom had taken one or two wrong turns in their lives and some of whom were hardened criminals. Although the defendants included men, most of the cases involving women were scheduled on her docket—which became known as Women's Court. As judge of the juvenile court, Murphy also saw the problems of Edmonton and northern Alberta's youth. She dealt with the seamy underworld of crime, child neglect, prostitution, and family violence, as well as drug and alcohol abuse.

Murphy had studied many of the attendant social problems but pronouncing judgements or finding realistic solutions for individuals was a different matter. From her position on the bench, Edmonton was not the bright and cheerful city of boosterism described in *Janey Canuck*. She now saw a more intimate view of Edmonton life:

> A police magistrate is closer to the human side of his city than anyone in it—or ought to be—and sees all phases of its life. Added to this . . . his findings and opinions are recorded constantly by the local papers, so giving him a continuous access to the public conscience . . . And pray how many of us come out publicly in favour of temperance enactments or a campaign against venereal disease, or against the exploitation of girl-children for immoral purposes? For some reason, all of us are strangely silent about these things, concerning which we have intimate knowledge, when it is our plainest duty to warn the public.[16]

Soon Murphy was speaking her mind, and some considered her blunt, abrasive, egotistical, and aggressive.[17] Already in 1919 she felt alone and overworked. She sensed city women were uninterested in the court work. Then, she learned that women in Edmonton churches were praying for her.[18] Over the years, she had read extensively about world religions; she had experienced scepticism and a time when she could not pray. Ultimately, she affirmed the Apostle's Creed, but maintained the right to interpret the terms.[19] Prayers were certainly appreciated, yet the reassurance that women valued her work as a spiritual force in the community was most meaningful to her.[20]

In her work as magistrate Murphy was not immune to the prejudices of the day. In contrast to today's attitudes, her support for sterilization of the insane and mentally handicapped was considered forward-thinking.[21] Also unacceptable today are descriptions that would be considered racial slurs. An anecdote in *Open Trails* recalled a Negro man who referred to himself as a "nigger." The incident was retold in a review in *The Bookman* of August 1914 to illustrate the warmth of Janey Canuck. Murphy also used the word "blackie." Such slang was common,[22] but we would now brand the references as prejudicial. In fact, whether she possessed prejudices that affected her judgement as a magistrate became an issue in her own day.

In *The Black Candle*, the first book on drug abuse written for lay people in North America, Murphy wrote of Chinese involvement in both the drug and white slave trades. She also told of how the police and legal systems were manipulated by whites:

> In certain houses and hotels—both rural and urban—the users of the pipe borrow the 'lay-out' belonging to the Chinese cook. Should the noisome, insinuating odour escape, no one is suspected but Ah Sin. Should the place be raided, Ah Sin is apprehended for being in the unlawful possession of opium. He pays the fine, this sallow, unsmiling Oriental, and says nothing for, after all, he loses nothing but his inconsiderable reputation.
>
> 'The Boss he pay back, allee light. Boss he hophead allee samee China boy.'
>
> Do you say this thing is abhorrent and hardly credible?
>
> Sirs and Madames, on such evidence we, ourselves, have issued orders for search and warrants for apprehension.[23]

In 1924 an application for an order of prohibition to prevent Murphy from hearing drug charges against two Chinese defendants was filed. Passages from *The Black Candle* were presented in support of the application. The judge ruled: 'There is nothing here to lead me to think the magistrate is biased against the two accused. I am biased against those who unlawfully deal in narcotics . . . but that is not enough to prevent a fair trial.'[24]

Curtailing illicit drug use became a crusade for Murphy. To her, the problem was not limited to the streets. The system was failing. She insisted seized drugs should not be donated for hospital or scientific use but

> should be destroyed as the Act provides, and in view of their dangerous nature, it is not too much to ask that the magistrate sees to it personally. Any good court-house keeper who would preserve an unvexed and gladsome mind, must have a care that no poisons are left lying around loosely.
>
> Having said this, we are conscious that our view may be publicly stigmatized as 'domestic,' 'merely feminine,' and quite unbefitting the dignity of a stipendiary magistrate.[25]

Her response might be labelled maternal feminism, a

classification allocated to many of the feminists of Murphy's time—a classification frequently implying the adjective *merely* because many maternal feminists saw their first obligations as care-givers, wives, and mothers. In fact, as serious as she was about women's rights and social conditions, Murphy objected to labels. 'Don't be an *ite* or an *ist*. When you label your faith, you limit it,'[26] she noted in one of her many Canuck mottos.

Murphy had discovered the world of Edmonton's back streets. In court she heard little-known stories of cocaine abuse on Edmonton streets. Limpy Lill's was one of them:

> A young half-breed woman tells me that she and her pal, Mildred, sniff between them from thirty to forty 'decks' [of cocaine] a day. She robs persons at night—in her words 'frisks them'—and has no ridiculous delicacy in telling of it. As a criminal, Limpy Lill is capable of all that her looks imply.
>
> Often these girls divide the money with their 'steadies' who are without funds—that is to say those black-hearted, iron heeled fellows who live basely upon these earnings . . .
>
> Limpy Lill would have me understand that Mildred is a person of no common clay in that she can absorb much whisky even while 'lit up' with cocaine. Mildred has used so much cocaine that she is getting 'the saddle nose'—a nose that has width at the bridge as though it were broken, and which is not uncommon with 'coke' fans . . .
>
> Limpy Lill keeps to 'coke' herself, because it is 'love medicine,' at least she has been told it is, and further she tells me in expression both immoderate and unholy, how she hopes all the police officers may die soon . . . [27]

Another girl, seventeen year-old Maxine, was charged under the Insanity Act. In her magistrate's notebook, Murphy wrote:

> Persistent thief. Since 13 has been co-habitating with her step-father. Twelve children, mother and step-father live in two rooms on homestead. Girl has two venereal diseases. Runs away from any home in which she is placed to lead an immoral life. Extremely nervous. Needs eye glasses. Suffers a good deal. Cried in court and promised to 'make good.' Struck me as a victim of her environment rather than insane—needs care & teaching [28]

Murphy did not convict her, but placed her in the Social Service Home working to help rehabilitate youth in Edmonton.

Murphy did convict many others. She took it as her duty to help those who were unfortunate, redirect those who could be rehabilitated, and punish those who had become incorrigible. Her idea of justice might best be compared to the present concept of tough love; however, sentencing in her courtroom was not necessarily the end of the relationship between Magistrate Murphy and the convicted women. Commonly, letters were exchanged between Murphy and women prisoners. On 5 June 1921 a young woman named Margaret, serving time in the Provincial Gaol at Fort Saskatchewan, wrote to her:

> I have come to the conclusion I had been a bad girl but will be a good girl when I get out.
>
> Mrs. Murphy please don't order any more whippings for me. Sargent [sic] gave me such a hard whipping I shall never forget it.
>
> I like the matrons very much. I am crocheting a yoke for one . . .
>
> Well, Mrs. Murphy I must say goodby hoping to hear from you soon with lots of love from your little girl Margaret. [29]

Murphy replied on 16 June:

> I was glad to get your letter of June 5th, and to hear that you were being a good girl. I did not order you that whipping which you mentioned; but if you got one, I have no doubt in the world but that it was well deserved as apparently you are behaving yourself better.
>
> Dr. Orr was speaking to me about you the other day and said you were giving no trouble. I am wondering why you are so bad in Edmonton and so good at the Fort . . . At any rate you will be back here shortly and we will hear all about it . . . [30]

Murphy also corresponded with women in the community who might help released prisoners or girls in trouble. To one Edmonton woman she wrote:

> I hope you will be a big sister to [the prisoner] and see that she gets a letter frequently, as she has requested, and perhaps a place of refuge when she comes out. Her father is a V.C. (May) and was killed in Flanders. Her mother and sister have disowned her. She lost all her organs from venereal diseases a couple of years ago. I am of the opinion that she is not very strong mentally and so will be easily led; but, on the other hand, she is very anxious to make good.[31]

At the end of this letter, Murphy added a request to keep the girl's name private.

Knowing of problems and doing nothing was an unacceptable alternative to Murphy; she pressed for improvements to conditions within jails. The jail of the Provincial Police Headquarters was located in the basement of the Edmonton Court House. After a visit to the cells in April of 1918, Murphy was adamant changes be made, and she wrote to the provincial police commissioners. During the previous session of the court, fifteen people had been held in custody in just three cells. Only one bed was in the cell available for the female prisoners; another was in one of the two cells for male prisoners; and the third was in an unlighted hall next to the vaults beneath a courtroom. Murphy also protested the rule that forbade insane persons, being held pending admission to the mental hospital, from looking out the window. In her opinion, they should be made happy and comfortable and encouraged to look out windows as part of the recovery process. The lavatory situation was also deplorable. Incarcerated women were expected to use the lavatory in the men's hallway. It was open and in full view of anyone in the hall or passing though it. She wanted a *closed* pail in the women's cell. In contrast, she commended the City for conditions in the city police station, at the time located in the Civic Building. There, twenty-two cells were available. Food was prepared on site, and it 'permits preparing of hot tea if required say in the case of any feeble minded or insane patients who may need refreshments.'[32]

In time Murphy became proud of steps taken locally to address the special needs of females in contact with the police and legal system. As early as 1919, there was a very experienced female orderly in Woman's Court, and Edmonton had appointed two women constables to assist the morality squad and for late night patrols of the dance-halls and streets. Also, women probation officers for the Department of Neglected Children held constabulary powers. The Local Council of Women even lobbied to have Murphy appointed as police commissioner, but Murphy declined their nomination.[33]

Magistrate Murphy recognized the legal system was not the answer to all the ills of the needy. She believed the government was responsible for providing public heath services, and, in speeches across the country, she insisted both public health and public education were vital. In both fields, Edmonton was progressive. The University of Alberta Out-Patient Clinic offered medical, surgical, obstetric, orthopaedic, psychological, pediatric, and venereal disease treatment to women and children. Services were free and therefore available to the poor. To Murphy, this clinic was an example of important and effective community service.

Networking with social services and health care com-

munities at the civic, provincial, and national levels was extremely important to Murphy. Nationally, she became vice-president of the Social Service Council of Canada (1920-31), vice-president of the Canadian Association of Child Protection Officers (1921-25), vice-president of the Canadian Social Hygiene Council (1921-31), director of the Canadian Council of Child Welfare (1923-27), and member of the National Board of Directors for the Canadian Committee of Mental Hygiene (1918-25).[34] As a result, she was in a position to try to influence social policy and programs across Canada.

Certainly not all of Murphy's contributions to community life were centred on the needy. She became Patroness of the Edmonton Branches Army & Navy Veterans and of the Royal Life Saving Society. She was Vice President of the Edmonton Branch of the Canadian Authors Association (1923-24),[35] and she supported the work of the Extension Department of the University of Alberta. Edmontonians also knew Judge Murphy as a friendly, down-to-earth woman with a fine sense of humour.

Eventually, however, the sheer number of tragedies to which Murphy was privy became disheartening. By the end of 1929 she hoped to broaden the sphere of her reform influence in the Senate. However, she did not receive the first female appointment for Canada nor the next appointment from Alberta. On 14 June 1930 she wrote to long-time friend, reformer and one-time Edmontonian, Nellie McClung:

> I have just been trying to identify a young half-breed girl at the undertaker's who died in a store here from haemorrhage . . . A pretty little girl, almost white, who wore 'whoopee' trousers, a gay cap, silk underwear and lovely slippers . . . all of these soaked with her life's blood. She had been round the city, I believe, serving the taxis, and here she is at the end of the road, and no one knows her name. She had a heart—a lovely crimson heart—and some roses tattooed on her arm. Poor child! 'Only a half-breed.' I'd like to tell the world some of the things I know about 'superior men'—but I've just got to keep the heartbreak of it all to myself.[36]

In 1931 Murphy retired as magistrate but kept her designation as judge of the juvenile court to hear cases if needed. With retirement, she began the process of returning to her life as a writer, translating her life experiences into words so others might understand. During the 1920s Arthur had lived in the rural community where he served as minister, but in 1932 he was appointed rector of St John's and moved back to their Edmonton home. Emily

Rear view of Murphy's house, now a historical site on the University of Alberta campus.
(FAYE REINEBERG HOLT)

was to have little opportunity to adjust to her new lifestyle, set new goals, or enjoy semi-retirement. On 26 October 1933 she had a heart attack and died. Present at her funeral were politicians, judges, magistrates, police officers, women's leaders, journalists, prostitutes, clergy, and the ordinary men and women of Edmonton.

Strangely foreshadowing her own contributions, Murphy had written in the final chapter of *Janey Canuck in the West*: 'It is good to live in these first days when the foundations of things are being laid, to be able, now and then, to place a stone or carry the mortar to set it good and true.'[37] Her strength lay in discerning the needs of individuals and groups, especially the needs of women and children; then she did something about those needs. Sometimes she prescribed deserved punishment. Other times she wrote or made speeches—both locally and nationally—about sensitive issues such as drugs, social diseases, and mental illness in order to bring the problems to the public's attention so that solutions might be implemented. Still other times, she brought about change as a member of civic and provincial committees reporting on hospital and prison conditions. Often, she protested conditions by writing letters to appropriate officials. Throughout, her response remained deeply human and personal. With all her meetings, responsibilities, and status, she never lost touch with the lives of common people.

In her scrapbooks, there are countless letters suggesting these people saw her as someone who would find solutions to their troubles and who would not dismiss them as unimportant. To Emily Murphy, that kind of connection with the needs of citizens meant a community could be built on solid foundations whatever the future might bring. ✎

REBECCA PRIEGERT COULTER

PATROLLING THE PASSIONS OF YOUTH

The rehabilitation of youth—the state's view.
Before. (PAA A.5637) / After. (PAA A.5638)

*B*y the 1920s the problems of modern industrial society were the target of voluntary groups and growing numbers of professional social workers. The need for proper guidance and uplifting, instructive activities for young people, particularly in light of what were seen as evils of the age (tobacco, alcohol, dancing, moving pictures, and the legacy of lax supervision during the Great War) had become a major preoccupation of both churches and secular youth-oriented organizations. Surrounded by a broad expanse of prairie and farming country and hundreds of miles from urban giants like Montreal, Toronto, or New York, Edmonton might seem to have been immune from the 'passions of youth.' But the nature of the age, with rapid advances in mass communication and

their homogenizing effects on popular culture, ensured that young people in Edmonton were exposed to the same influences as their counterparts across the continent.

Rebecca Coulter of the Division of Educational Policy Studies in the Faculty of Education, University of Western Ontario, has written extensively on youth and related issues in early Edmonton. She examines how adult Edmonton—through groups like the Public School Board, Boy Scouts, and Canadian Girls in Training—attempted to impose its values on the city's youth. She also shows how young people had their own ideas about what was good for them.

W HEN W.G. CARPENTER, EDMONTON'S SUPERINTEN-dent of schools, returned to the city in February 1922 after meeting with his western Canadian colleagues, he found that the school board was being asked to allow dancing at Grade 12 class parties. Carpenter opposed the request, claiming that 'a wave of immorality involving young people' was sweeping the country and that dancing was precisely the type of amusement that demonstrated the problem.[1] He also noted that his counterparts in Calgary, Regina, and Brandon harboured deep concerns about the moral condition of high school boys and girls, particularly in relation to their social activities. Edmonton trustees expressed similar concerns, especially about house parties among a 'certain set.' While he was not against young people having a good time, Frank Scott declared, he hated 'the contemptible thing that they call dancing around here.'[2]

The above controversy situates Edmonton within the North American and western European debates of the time. As Joseph Kett observes, 'to speak of youth in the 1920s was to speak of their behaviour'—of their rebellious-ness, promiscuity, and passion for a good time (dancing, drinking, smoking, and joy riding).[3] In addition, the

media's publication of instances of youthful transgression sparked outbursts of more widespread moral indignation and outrage, which youth workers seized upon to promote their own activities and organizations. Such anxiety was, of course, not new. 'Young people have always suffered from the envious criticism of their elders,' and scholarly and popular literature has dwelled on the 'allegedly wild moral values' of the young for centuries.[4] By the 1920s, however, growing numbers of young people were experi-encing 'modern' adolescence, a period of life defined by delayed social responsibility, prolonged economic depen-dence on the family, and increasingly more time in school.[5] The spread of new technologies—the radio, the moving picture, and the automobile—and the rapid com-mercialization of popular culture encouraged the develop-ment of a new and separate world where teenagers could escape adult supervision. These factors contributed to adult perceptions about new types of youth behaviour that had to be managed and controlled. Previously, much of the concern about immoral and unruly behaviours had focused on neglected and dependent children and working youths. Now concern shifted to the middle class, where young people were beginning to create a youth culture

Looking for action in Edmonton in the 1920s?
(EA-160-728)

around the social life of high schools and the consumption of the products of the new mass culture.

Adults responded to the new social relations of age in a number of ways, but most visibly in the continuing work of organizations, agencies, and groups designed specifically for youth work. In Edmonton, a growing cadre of professional youth workers joined volunteers in re-creating the institutions and organizations of older cities in Canada, the United States, and Great Britain. The derivative nature of youth work in Alberta should not be surprising, since many of the people engaged in helping and supervising teenagers had migrated from central Canada or the United States, bringing the ideological baggage of middle-class social reformers and child savers in those two areas.[6] However, while ideas about the nature of youth work were not home-grown, Albertans often prided themselves on

Young girls experimented with cigarettes; some even smoked in public or dared to record their transgressions for posterity. (PAA FE.355)

fine-tuning approaches adopted from elsewhere.[7]

The dominant ideology of child and youth work in Edmonton in the early twentieth century is epitomized by R.B. Chadwick, Alberta's first superintendent of neglected children. Originally from Ontario, he worked with the Boys' Club in New York and the Boys' Department of the Young Men's Christian Association (YMCA) in Toronto and Edmonton before assuming the provincial post in 1909.[8] Chadwick's annual reports as superintendent, produced between 1909 and 1915, include discussions of adolescent psychology and the social problem of youth. They illustrate how many adults in Edmonton would continue to think about teenagers in the context of youth work until well into the 1930s.[9]

While Chadwick and his colleagues used both 'adolescent' and 'teenager' sparingly and were more inclined to speak of the 'third age of childhood' or 'the boy and girl problem,' it is clear they were popularizing and disseminating G. Stanley Hall's ideas about adolescence.[10] In 1911, for example, Chadwick singled out the stage of life from the ages of thirteen to seventeen as one fraught with danger. Echoing Hall, he said: 'During this period the child is up against the most serious time of its life. Rapid physical and mental growth, lack of knowledge of how to conduct itself under new conditions and circumstances, the ambitions and desires of men and women with the experience of children to carry them through this trying time, are a few of the many trials to which the child is subjected.'[11] By 1912 Chadwick had extended this 'dangerous' period for boys to the ages of ten to eighteen and tied it to sexual awakening and the need to assert independence. Adolescence, said Chadwick, was marked by physical and mental restlessness and impulsive behaviour. The adolescent boy found 'no emotion . . . too deep, no song too gay for him to participate in. He is explosive and submissive, varying in turn with a speed that is most ominous to those who are not familiar with boy life.'[12] Because teenaged boys were seen as acting on impulse and desirous of excitement and immediate gratification, often within the context of 'gang' activity, their lives were considered to be in need of constant supervision by responsible adults.

Despite this analysis of the behaviour of teenaged boys, there is an inescapable note of wistful ambivalence—a sense of longing for their own youth—in the discussions of male adolescence by male social reformers. Even delinquent behaviour was often excused as the unintended result of 'the desire for fun' or 'mischiefmaking.' The claim was made, for example, that 'the average boy gets into trouble because there is not much else provided for him to

get into' and hence 'undirected energy' found 'an outlet along the lines of mischief.'[13] On these grounds, the goal of 'boy work' became the proper guidance of adolescent males as they struggled towards self-reliance, self-discovery, and independence.

The adolescent girl was considered separately and differently. Here the central concern was not the guided development of self-reliance and independence. Indeed, independent and self-reliant young women were the source of much annoyance to Chadwick, who railed about girls who would not enter domestic service but sought employment in restaurants and factories. The latter gave them free evenings and the money to rent their own rooms, however humble, where they could entertain friends of both sexes without the supervision of parents or other responsible adults.

Working girls were condemned for their perceived love of good times and nice clothes, while daughters of the 'better' class were criticized for failing to set a good example for other young women. Chadwick found the female offspring of the wealthier elements of the population most exasperating: 'Those little girls think it smart to be spoken to by young men, and thereby expose themselves unwittingly to conditions that lead to the midnight supper, the "joy ride", and later to the girl's [sic] downfall.'[14] The real worry was the sexuality of young females, for their independent behaviour threatened the dominant patriarchal concept of ideal womanhood, which encouraged dependency on a protecting male—first the father and then the

husband—and emphasized pre-marital chastity.[15] While Chadwick had some idea of a developmental psychology of male adolescence, which he saw as having a base in science, he offered no counterpart for females and the 'problem of the girl' was seen largely in terms of morality. This bifurcation between what was understood as a normal adolescence for boys as opposed to girls had significant ramifications for the ways in which youth workers treated young males and females.[16]

If Chadwick's ideas about adolescence seem simplistic, it must be remembered that the social sciences, from which most of our current theory is drawn, were still in their infancy. Furthermore, in a city which was still, in important respects, a frontier community composed of people from elsewhere, citizens eschewed theory for the more practical approach of 'getting things done.'[17] This was evident in a concern for the more pragmatic aspects of what was termed 'the boy and girl problem' and in practical work in such areas as youth groups and the juvenile court system. A closer examination of some of these activities and the ways in which they were rationalized and justified provides a more complete picture of what adults thought youth was all about.

Edmonton in the 1920s had a full complement of youth groups, especially church-sponsored ones. Boy Scout and Girl Guide troops existed throughout the city: the Canadian Girls in Training (CGIT) was active; the YMCA and the Young Women's Christian Association (YWCA) sponsored boys' and girls' clubs respectively; young people's groups functioned in many churches; and community leagues and other organizations established various sports teams or activities.[18] In most cases, these youth groups were part of a national or international organization, with the same programs and same goals as youth groups throughout Canada, the United States, and Britain.[19]

While surviving records of youth groups in Edmonton are at best spotty, a fairly good indication of how boys' work (and, to a lesser extent, girls' work) was understood and implemented can be gleaned. The most complete outline of the purpose and practice of boys' work, as explained to adults, is found in the pages of the *Western Catholic*, which described the role of Edmonton's Knights of Columbus as part of its coverage of boys' work undertaken by the church in North America. Roman Catholic involvement in youth groups like the Boy Scouts is significant because, of all the mainstream Christian denominations, the Roman Catholic church most constantly emphasized the key role and responsibility of parents in the education and preparation of youth. By the 1920s, however, Catholic leaders were realizing that in a modern urbanized and industrialized society parental supervision, especially *paternal* supervision, was increasingly rare, and they wholeheartedly recommended boys' groups to fill the gap left by parents' inability or unwillingness to supervise teenagers.[20]

The main Canadian spokesperson for this work was Brother Barnabas who, at various times, was vice-president of the Canadian Council on Child Welfare, an international Boy Scout leader, and secretary of the Knights of Columbus Boy Life Bureau.[21] Brother Barnabas visited Edmonton on several occasions and spoke to many groups about the ways in which youth work should be handled. In particular, he spent time talking to the Knights of Columbus both from an educational and a motivational perspective.

Like so many of his social reform colleagues, Brother Barnabas adapted and popularized Hall's ideas about adolescence by presenting them in a way that justified involvement in boys' work. Like Chadwick, he emphasized the importance of the ages twelve to eighteen as central to character formation. In a particular Canadian analogy, he compared the boy to Niagara Falls: 'The wind will blow and the water will dash along, do what we will. But the wind which plays havoc in the garden turns the windmill industriously, and the power of the water which upsets the boat may be harnessed to run an engine. The boy's restless energy, if directed, may be guided to useful pursuit and wholesome ideals.'[22] Barnabas went on to argue that where once boys had received the necessary guidance at home, urbanization and industrialization and the resulting complexity of life militated against parents being able to provide full-

Girl Guide camp, Sylvan Lake, 1927. (PAA A.12024)

time supervision of their offspring. Furthermore, since low wages had driven men out of the teaching profession, leaving only women in the classroom, boys were denied strong male models in school, too. The time had come, Brother Barnabas suggested, for the development of a program of directed activity for all boys during their leisure time and for the professional training of men who would take on the establishment and running of such programs.

The case for this method of attack was made on the grounds that boys, even those attending school, had eight hours of leisure each day during which their future lives would be made or broken. Given the view that teenaged males had natural needs for the companionship of their own kind and for heroes to worship, it seemed appropriate to create a cadre of young, educated adult males with high moral standards to provide role models and leadership for younger males and to organize and manage the volunteers engaged in boys' work programs. The goal, of course, was to prevent delinquent behaviour and to build not only the character of the boys but also, through them, 'the character of the world tomorrow.'[23]

So seriously did the Knights of Columbus in North America take the task of 'boyology,' the study and guidance of boy life, that a two-year MA program in Boy Guidance was established at Notre Dame University, with the first class graduating in 1926. Cyril Burchell of Edmonton was a member of that class; he had been sponsored by the local Knights of Columbus, who expected him to return to Alberta to practise his new 'profession' as a boy worker.[24] Year One was devoted to foundational work in the liberal arts, with special emphasis on the psychology of adolescence and a course entitled 'The Principles and Theory of Boy Work.' This course studied 'every phase of boy activity . . . its history . . . its development and its everyday practice, in order that the students when placed in the actual working field may evolve the best procedures depending on the circumstances in which they find themselves.'[25] During the summer semester, students spent two weeks studying the Boy Scout program and woodcraft and six weeks working in boys' camps. Year Two stressed the administration of boys' work and included a compulsory practicum and the preparation of a thesis on some practical aspect of boys' work. Graduates were considered well prepared to work not only in boys' clubs, community centres, and the Boy Scout movement but also as juvenile court probation officers, camp directors and counsellors, directors of municipal recreation departments, playground supervisors, and recreational officers of large industrial concerns.

Unfortunately, no record has been found to indicate the nature of the tasks Burchell assumed on his return to Edmonton, although it is clear that the Knights of Columbus continually put most of their efforts into organizing and maintaining Boy Scout troops and that Burchell assisted with this work during his summer practicum between the first and second years of his training.[26] There is no written evidence to suggest that Edmonton's Roman Catholic community was uncomfortable with participating in a youth group that originated in the imperial sentiments of Lord Baden-Powell, although the implicit militarism and English tone of the Boy Scout movement perhaps troubled at least some Franco-Albertans. Attempts to establish the Columbian Squires, the youth wing of the Knights of Columbus, in Edmonton might be seen as evidence that not all Catholic men favoured the Boy Scout alternative.[27]

Roman Catholic Boy Scout troops, like all others, engaged in activities that emphasized the outdoor life, games playing, woodsmanship, and other occupations and skills that utilized what were seen as the primitive urges of boys for action and excitement. The distance from the lofty heights of Brother Barnabas's conviction that the survival of a civilized world depended on the proper supervision and guidance of adolescent males by university-educated professionals to the trifling mundanity of knot-tying and occasional camp-outs illustrates only too well the gap between the ideology and the practice of boys' work.

That this gap was not as wide in girls' work reflects the more limited role assigned to women in Canadian society in the 1920s.[28] The emphasis on chastity and the view that all girls were destined to be wives and mothers meant that groups for young females tended to focus on tasks suited to training the next generation of housewives, mothers, and church and social service volunteers. For example, while the aim of the Girl Guides was to develop good citizenship, citizenship was defined as teaching girls 'services useful to the public and handicrafts useful to themselves; promoting their physical development; making them capable of keeping good homes and of bringing up good children.'[29] This philosophy made the Girl Guides a suitable female counterpart to the Boy Scouts for the Roman Catholic church. In 1923 Edmonton's archbishop provided a similar vision of women's purpose in life:

A woman should be like the sun, shedding warmth and brightness everywhere. The sun beautifies the earth, gives to the fruits their varied hues, and causes the little birds to sing. So should a woman fill her home with joy and happiness and make her influence felt by all with whom she comes in contact. All this she can prepare to do by cultivating her mind, acquiring habits of thrift, developing her talents and thus produce the flowers and fruits of kind words and good actions.[30]

While the Knights of Columbus were busily engaged in boys' work through the Boy Scouts, the Catholic Women's League was being urged to establish Girl Guide companies 'for the general welfare of the Catholic womanhood of Canada' and to help solve the 'tremendous problem in the safe-guarding and protecting of young girls, in the preservation of their Christian Faith and Morality.'[31] More specifically, adults were to

assume the responsibilities of helping these younger citizens develop a sound mind in a sound body, and assist them in every way to face life equipped with moral stamina, at least a fair measure of practical knowledge of the usual arts of home-making, handicraft, hygiene, and a careful development of the instincts which are natural to childhood, but which must be developed or repressed as the case may be, by prudence and loving supervision.[32]

If the Girl Guides were seen as non-denominational, the CGIT was strictly a Protestant group. Its objectives were somewhat less traditional than those of the Girl Guides, for although the CGIT continued to train girls for motherhood, it also concerned itself with teaching political citizenship and asked girls to learn about the Canadian government, women's struggle for the vote, and women's influence on legislation.[33] Girls 'should know what injustices prevail, and should be taught to feel responsible for the happiness and well-being of all their fellow citizens,'[34] leaders were told. The CGIT encouraged its members in 'a quest for the four-fold life': the development of the physical, intellectual, spiritual, and social aspects of existence embodied in the motto, 'cherish health, seek truth, know God, and serve others.'[35]

How these objectives were actually implemented can be seen in the 1921-3 minute books of a CGIT group in Edmonton affiliated with the McDougall Woman's Missionary Society. Attendance at this group, the 'Alberta Vistas,' varied from five to twelve girls. Over the course of two years, members took first aid lessons; debated the resolution, 'that the factory system is more beneficial to both the manufacturer and individual than the Domestic system'; studied the life of Bliss Carman and read his poetry; made toy furniture for hospitalized children; gave impromptu speeches; planned a 'physical night' of bedmaking, chang-

ing sheets, and bathing patients but had a skating party instead; engaged in Bible study through reading 'Lives Worth Living,' a description of the friendship of Mary, Martha, and Jesus; explored the lives of hymn writers and how hymns came to be written; joined other CGIT groups for a talk on growing bulbs by Mr Markham of Walter Ramsey's Floral Company; grew bulbs to give to hospitals and decorate the church; attended the CGIT all-city rally; heard a woman missionary talk about her work; made a quilt; gathered donations for Christmas gifts and for a farm mother of eight who wrote asking for clothes; read favourite Bible verses to one another; discussed dress, speech, reading, and the use of slang; saw movies of missionary work; sewed; read sections from the 1922 church missionary report and talked about a section from 'Canadian Girls' Ideals.'[36] The group's leader clearly tried to build on the four-fold concept of life and conscientiously organized a wide range of activities for the girls in her care.

In the end, most youth groups had a transitory or unstable existence. Part of the reason lay in the fact that formal youth groups such as the Boy Scouts and Girl Guides were organized and led by adults, most of them volunteers, so that the fortunes of each club depended to a large extent on their dedication, commitment, and sustained interest. The many comments in church bulletins and reports indicate that adult involvement was often only temporary[37] and that all too frequently the burden of organizing activities fell on the shoulders of a handful of over-extended, though dedicated, church workers. As a result, the attention paid to work with teenagers tended to ebb and flow, possibly suggesting that, ultimately, most adults were less concerned than a few activists with supervising and controlling youth's leisure time. In yet another indication of lukewarm commitment to youth work, even where full-time youth workers were employed, their job security was so low that they did not know from month to month whether they would actually be working with youths.[38] The only real exception is found in the continuing work of the paid staff of the YMCA and the YWCA.

The annual reports of churches, which assumed responsibility for most of the work with young people, indicate that membership in youth groups fluctuated considerably from year to year. Because the statistics are very incomplete, it is impossible to calculate how many teenagers belonged to any one organization at any given point in the 1920s. However, those records which do remain show very small memberships, usually from five to twenty-five individuals, making it unlikely that a majority of Edmonton teenagers were active and continuing participants in any adult-supervised youth group. The limited impact of youth work can be seen in the 1929 report of the Edmonton District Girl Guides. That year only 223 Guides, 30 Rangers, and 141 Brownies were registered in the entire district; even fewer girls (sixty) qualified for badges. These numbers are minuscule compared to the approximately 8,000 girls, aged seven to sixteen, who lived in Edmonton at the time.[39] Comparable figures for the Boy Scouts in Edmonton cannot be found, although in 1929 there were 4,700 registered Boy Scouts throughout Alberta, earning 819 badges.[40] During the 1920s the Edmonton YWCA claimed between 400 and 500 boy members a year, many of whom took gym and swimming classes but few of whom enrolled in Bible classes.[41] It would seem that while the rhetoric of youth work argued for the constant and thorough supervision of teenagers by responsible adults, the reality was much different.

As already noted, the discrepancy between theory and practice was partly due to the unwillingness or inability of adults to volunteer as leaders for youth groups. There is, however, another important consideration to be taken into account in trying to understand the failure to translate the ideology of boys' and girls' work into practice. The argument of labour and women's historians that all human beings are active creators of their own history should be extended to youths as well.[42] The evidence in Edmonton points quite clearly to the conclusion that boys and girls made conscious decisions about their involvement in youth groups. For example, when youth groups sponsored social events such as dances, attendance was much higher than for lectures on character formation; and planned activities like week-long summer camping trips to lakes outside the city attracted far more interest than study sessions on religious books. The most continually successful of all adult-sponsored activities were the organized sports teams, physical education classes, and military cadets.

Baseball, basketball, hockey, gymnastics, swimming, and the like obviously offered young males, especially, something they wanted, so they chose to participate in large numbers. McDougall Methodist Church, for example, reached 2,000 boys through its baseball clubs, but only 800 ever attended Sunday school and then on an irregular

When youth groups sponsored social events such as dances, attendance was much higher than for lectures on character formation; and planned activities like week-long summer camping trips to lakes outside the city attracted far more interest than study sessions on religious books.

basis.[43] YMCA statistics tell a similar story. In 1921, 200 of 425 boy members took gym classes but only twenty enrolled in Bible study. In 1926, of 397 boy members aged twelve to seventeen, eighteen attended lectures and talks and thirty-nine Bible classes. In 1928 the staff stopped reporting enrolments in Bible study classes, possibly because the figures were so discouraging or because such meetings were discontinued for lack of participation.[44] The YWCA found that girls, too, were attracted to swimming and gym classes, and also gathered at the building for friendship and camaraderie.[45] Local newspapers recorded large attendances of youths at sports programs and fairs of all sorts, in direct contrast to the much smaller enrolments of teenagers in organized youth groups. It appears that young people simply resisted many activities designed for their moral uplift. As a result, historians who uncritically accept enrolment figures provided by adult leaders as evidence of the success of youth groups in inculcating moral standards and promulgating their world views are likely misinterpreting the experiences and motives of young people and confusing intended with actual outcomes.[46]

Organized, and increasingly professionalized, youth work represented one approach to patrolling the passions of youth. However, an alternate way of engaging in youth work was found in community leagues like the one in Norwood. Community leagues brought families together for social and political purposes. For example, through the organizing medium of community leagues, parents argued for their children to stay within local districts for Grade 9 rather than be forced to attend high schools farther from home. They wanted their teenagers to be within a neighbourhood where people 'looked out for one another.'[47]

Many community leagues operated teen groups, where the young organized and implemented their own programs. That is, they were given relative freedom within a broader framework that allowed adults to supervise in a 'gentler way' reminiscent of the 'natural' overseeing that occurred in an earlier period when age-mixed groups congregated in village squares or at community festivals and celebrations. A specific instance of this approach can be found in the

Braxton's Moonlight Syncopators, 1927. Community leaders feared that modern music and dance oozed with sexuality, threatening the virtue of youth. (PAA A.20840)

community league solution to the dancing question. In 1925, as the school board continued to refuse permission for students' unions to hold dances in the schools, the community leagues intervened and assumed responsibility for organizing school dances. When the Ministerial Association expressed its unanimous opposition, one community league member retorted: 'If the Ministerial Association studied dance in the city, it would find more people dancing than going to church.'[48] W.C. Deane, speaking for the Edmonton Federation of Community Leagues, was less inflammatory. He indicated that he personally opposed dancing, but as the father of seven children ranging in age from sixteen to twenty-three, he had a problem in his own family. He felt that teenagers were going to dance whether adults liked it or not, and thus it was better that they be allowed to dance in their own communities, where they could be supervised in social situations with family and friends, than in downtown cabarets and dance halls. Closing public schools to dancing, he argued, would cause young people to drift downtown and conditions would get much worse.[49]

If adult-organized and -supervised youth groups were less than totally successful in attracting the attention of continuously large numbers of teenagers, other recreational activities did not suffer the same fate. Besides sports, physical education classes, and dances, one other leisure activity was taking Edmonton's teenagers by storm in the 1920s and causing adults a great deal of worry. Movies were becoming a major factor in the lives of large numbers of teenagers. J.C. well remembers the warm June night he

took a girl to see *Svengali* and stayed out until 1:00 AM, an experience that illustrates both how dating was becoming linked to movie-going and why adults might have serious reservations about the influences of this new form of mass entertainment.[50]

The importance of movie-going as a leisure activity for teenagers is confirmed by a 1933 study conducted in Edmonton and Calgary by a graduate student completing a Master of Arts degree in psychology. His sample of 661 students included 432 students from the McKay Avenue, Queen's Avenue, Rutherford, Westmount, Eastwood High, and Strathcona High schools in Edmonton. The students ranged from Grades 6 to 10 and in average age from twelve to sixteen. Of the total sample, 36.4 per cent attended movies once a week; another 9.1 per cent of the boys and 8.8 per cent of the girls attended more often. An additional 20.7 per cent of the boys and 17.6 per cent of the girls saw movies at least twice a month. Clearly, movies were an important amusement. When asked why they did not go even more frequently, teenagers identified lack of money and time as the most significant reasons. The majority of young people went to the movies with friends of the same sex, although attending with siblings was also common and many boys (but not girls) went alone. Most of the sample made their own choices about what movies to see, although girls were a little more closely supervised than boys in the selection process. Further gender differentiation was evident in the types of movies preferred, with boys showing an appreciation for war pictures and movies involving airplanes, boats, trains, cars, and motorcycles and girls liking love stories and shows about children. While 56 per cent of the teens responding to the questionnaire thought that the movies taught them 'to be honourable and do right,' 23.6 per cent of the boys and 15.2 per cent of the girls felt that movies taught them how to do wrong without getting caught.[51]

It was precisely this last view that was shared by many adults engaged in teaching, social service work, and church work. They were convinced that movies had a bad influence on the young because they showed a range of immoral practices—including gangsterism, adultery, and smoking—and made those practices seem attractive. Movies joined and then exceeded cheap literature and the vaudeville stage as entertainment forms to be soundly condemned.[52]

Movie censorship became a hot issue in Edmonton as elsewhere. The debate assumed increased urgency as adults tried to understand why teenagers from well-to-do backgrounds turned to crime. Middle-class people could understand why children from poor and immoral homes would do so; they could not grasp why young people from good, solid homes would engage in vandalism, drunken brawls, thieving, and other delinquent activities. In 1921 the Social Service Council of Alberta investigated the case of two boys from good homes who were well supplied with all the necessities of life and yet committed criminal acts. The inquiry convinced council members that the boys had been motivated to turn to anti-social behaviour through the influence of moving pictures and their 'insidious immoral propaganda.' As a result, the council called on the provincial government to censor and control both movies and advertising for movies in order to protect the young from 'irreparable damage in the moral sense.'[53] The council also called on other groups to follow its example. The Edmonton Public School Board did, passing a motion asking the government to exercise strict censorship to eliminate

> indecencies in act or speech that tend to pollute the public mind and lower the moral tone of the social order [and moving pictures which show] incidents that tend to emulate crime and make heroes of criminals, to glorify vice and give respectability to immoral acts or in any way ridicule or depreciate the sanctity of home, and the dignity of the law, whether a moral law or a law of the State.[54]

The government responded by pointing out that the Association of Provincial Motion Picture Censors already had a set of standards that were applied to all movies shown in the province.[55] Alberta's Board of Censors 'condemned' pictures that dealt with 'white slavery,' the seduction of women, assaults upon women for immoral purposes, common-law marriages, adultery, abortion, and venereal disease. Pictures containing gruesome and distressing scenes of violence or scenes of gross drunkenness were also condemned. The board 'disapproved' of moving pictures that dealt with the use of drugs; showed how to com-

Capital Theatre, 1924. If music and dancing were bad, Hollywood movies were worse.
(PAA A.8714)

mit criminal acts; were set in the underworld; portrayed the abuse of children or animals; ridiculed a race, class, social body, or religious group; or displayed vulgar scenes 'burlesquing' morgues, funerals, insane asylums, hospitals, or houses of ill-repute. Also meeting with disapproval were bathing scenes, lewd and immodest dancing, sensuous kissing, women in their night dresses or underclothing, vampire scenes, and women in bed together.[56] Thus, from January to September 1922, for example, movies were condemned for being 'too sensuous,' 'grossly suggestive,' 'immoral,' 'very offensive,' and 'vulgar' as well as for portraying a 'suggestive sex story,' 'a story of a vampire,' 'the life of an immoral woman,' 'a burlesque on clergymen,' and 'a burlesque on missions.'[57] The Board of Censors felt that it was protecting the youth from improper and immoral movies, but the debate on movie censorship persisted throughout the 1920s, with some community elements arguing that the application of standards was too liberal and others that it was too restrictive.[58] Young people, however, continued to attend the movies in large numbers, an indication that commercialized mass culture was making an impact on teenagers and helping to create the image of what sociologists call youth culture.

If teenagers' interest in movies and dancing raised the ire of adults, so did certain other activities. Adults complained about hockey on Sunday, bands playing for Sunday afternoon skaters (a practice said to keep the young from church), and teenagers spending too much time on sports and on other 'distractions' and not enough on studying.[59] Edmonton experienced something of the 'jazz age' and teenaged girls, in particular, were the subject of adult condemnations because of their hair styles and manner of dress. J.C. remembered that 'girls dressed very impractically in short skirts, etc.' and claimed this caused young men like him often to be in a state of sexual arousal. He also noted that young men 'needed a car to make it with girls,'[60] which suggests that the motor car had started to become the now-ubiquitous escape from adult supervision of courting and sexual activities.

Of course, the older generation has always criticized the younger one and accused it of a wide range of crimes, from slothfulness through stupidity to immorality. At the same time, youths have been seen as the hope of the future and the source of cultural continuity.[61] Adult Edmontonians carried on this tradition of ambivalence, for while a distinct strand of fear about what the young were becoming runs throughout the historical evidence, so, too, does a sense of optimism that the future could be made better by youths who were well educated and trained in

'right living.' It was for this latter purpose that many adults applied themselves to patrolling the passions of youth. Through their work, these adults both publicized new ideas about adolescence and attempted to establish and control standards of behaviour. They achieved some success in the first task, but in the second they met resistance from teenagers, encountered indifference from many other adults, and faced stiff competition from mass-marketed forms of entertainment such as movies and spectator sports.[62] Occasional episodes of moral indignation and condemnation notwithstanding, ultimately the majority of Edmonton's adults probably agreed with the editorial writer who declared

we still have the profoundest faith in our youth in the mass. We are not blind to the fact, of course, that some of our teen age boys and girls are straying far from the straight and narrow way of right living and high thinking. [But] we think, and we have good reason for thinking, that our Canadian boys and girls, our Canadian young men and women, compare very favourably with the best in any country and of any generation.[63] ❧

CATHERINE COLE

GARMENT MANUFACTURING IN EDMONTON

GWG advertisement, *Edmonton Free Press,*
4 October 1919. (PAAA.18996)

or decades, GWG (Great Western Garment Company) was synonymous with Edmonton. Labourers wore their uniforms, farmers their overalls, and teenagers their jeans. The company got its start in 1911. GWG soon became an important part of the city's small industrial base.

Most Edmonton manufacturers then served the immediate agricultural hinterland. If they wanted to trade further afield, they had to compete with Winnipeg, Canada's third largest city and the dominant supply and distribution centre for the prairies. It was an unequal battle. Winnipeg was a major rail centre, enjoyed superior freight rates, and had an established base of manufacturing industries and wholesale houses. For Edmonton's manufacturers, the real threat was that cheaper goods manufactured in or distributed from Winnipeg would

force them out of business. One way of meeting that threat was to lower the wages of labourers in order to remain competitive, but such action could create a radical work force—particularly in the garment industry which was notorious for terrible working conditions.

Catherine Cole argues, however, that garment workers in Edmonton were less radical than their counterparts in Winnipeg; indeed, they were quite conservative. The explanation lies in the example GWG established in its relations with labour and in its influence on government legislation respecting the rights of labour. Cole is a museum consultant and pursuing a doctorate in Museum Studies from the University of Leicester, England.

Most Canadian garment manufacturing industries were centred in Montreal, Toronto, and Hamilton until 1900, when Winnipeg and, to a lesser degree, Edmonton established a number of firms that produced men's work clothes, women's housedresses, and uniforms for the western market.[1] Compared with these other centres, the garment manufacturing sector in Edmonton was smaller and later to develop, with a delicate balance among management, labour, and government.[2] To some extent, the balance achieved in Edmonton may be explained by the fact that the industry developed largely in a climate of economic uncertainty. The Great Western Garment Company (GWG), the leading firm in the province, unionized in its first year of operation and set the standard for working conditions, hours, and wages. As elsewhere, the vast majority of workers in Edmonton's garment industry were women, but Edmonton's workforce was generally more conservative. Neither juveniles nor a particular ethnic group were exploited in Edmonton. Alberta's labour legislation, enacted when the industry was in its infancy, benefited from lessons learned elsewhere and struck a balance between the demands of management and labour. Perhaps as a result of these factors, Edmonton did not experience the militancy shown in Winnipeg, Toronto, or Montreal, where the garment trades were the focus of a series of strikes in the 1920s and 1930s.[3]

Although numerous independent dressmakers, tailors, and milliners had set up shop in Edmonton before 1910, few could be considered clothing manufacturers. Such companies appeared with the rapid expansion Edmonton experienced between 1911-13. By the 1920s more manufacturers and fewer independent businessmen and women could be found.[4] This shift paralleled developments in factory production in central Canada, where the predominance of custom dressmakers had passed by 1910 with the increase in popularity of the simple housedress, encouraging the rise of mass production by the 1920s.[5] Constructed later, Edmonton's garment factories were built as factories, whereas in cities like Winnipeg garment factories were often located in converted warehouses, a situation that resulted in inadequate light and air circulation and contributed to the dissatisfaction of the workforce.

In Edmonton, the garment manufacturing district lay between 95 and 97 streets and between Jasper and 105 avenues. Independent dressmakers, milliners, tailors, shoemakers, furriers, and others working in related businesses, such as dry cleaning and retail clothing, also located their businesses in this district. LaFleche Bros. 'high-class' tailoring firm was founded in Strathcona in 1906 but moved to Jasper Avenue following the amalgamation of Strathcona and Edmonton in 1912. By the 1920s the company had a staff of 40 and business interests in Calgary, Vancouver,

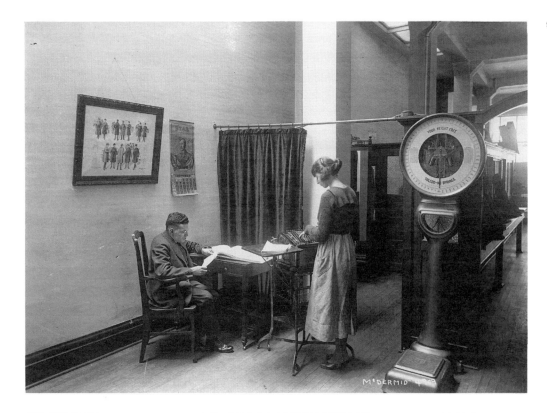

LaFleche Bros. store interior, 1920.
(GAI NC 6.4909)

and Montreal. GWG, manufacturers of men's workwear, was established in 1911 and moved several times in the 1910s and 1920s as the firm expanded rapidly, partially due to wartime contracts. GWG's staff reached 300 by the 1920s. In 1913 Emery Manufacturing was established, initially as a manufacturer for James Ramsey & Co., a major department store; but the firm became independent the following year, possibly as a result of the depression of that year or of the owner's growing political commitments. Emery employed 50 to 75 women by the 1920s. James B. McCormack, a hosiery manufacturer, was in business briefly from 1912-13. Kays Overall Manufacturing operated from 1914-19. Courtney Manufacturing, another overall firm, was established in 1916 and was in business manufacturing a variety of goods until the late 1930s. North Western Manufacturing produced shirts and overalls from about 1922 to 32 and employed over 75 workers. The Edmonton Knitting Co., producers of sweaters and hosiery, operated from 1919-27. The Reynolds Manufacturing Co., established in 1928 as manufacturers of uniforms and hospital gowns, is still in business in Edmonton today. As well, there were several short lived firms established in the 1920s, including the Alberta Garment Manufacturers Ltd. in 1929, the Economy Commercial Co. Ltd. in 1921-22, and the Grace Lingerie Co. in 1921. General Whitewear was established in the late 1930s.

In spite of the substantial number of firms, GWG played a predominant role when it came to relations with labour. With only seven employees, the minimum required to get a charter, the workers of GWG formed Local 120 of the conservative United Garment Workers of America (UGWA) the same year the company was established, 1911. The *Edmonton Journal* reported that 'the employers were desirous of using the union label on their products, and the employees experienced no difficulty in launching their local union.'[6] The union label, promoted by UGWA, was useful from the firm's perspective because it attracted sales from other unionized occupations. Although GWG was the only garment manufacturing firm in the province to unionize during this period (an American journeyman tailors' union included tailors working for a number of different firms), it influenced the wage scale and standard of working conditions in other, non-unionized firms in the West. A 1914 *Journal* article captured the importance of GWG: 'the company is so absolutely keeping up the quality of its output that they have made it impossible for a sweatshop ever to be established in this line in Edmonton. They pay the union scale of wages and keep expert help in all departments.'[7] In 1927 a union organizer from the United States used GWG as an example of a firm with excellent working conditions when trying to organize garment firms in Vancouver.[8] Working conditions and wages were com-

GWG first workroom, 1911. Note that cutting, sewing, finishing, and storage were all done on the same floor. (GAI NC 6.62221)

parable because there was a lot of mobility among firms, as operators made overalls one week and tents the next.

The labour force was generally conservative, grateful to have a job in hard times, and prepared to work with dedication. Management expected a lot from its staff but, at the same time, expressed appreciation for loyalty by providing bonuses or having get-togethers. Cooperation between employers and labour was particularly important in maintaining industrial growth in the early years. In contrast to Winnipeg, which experienced a number of strikes in the 1920s and 1930s, the only strike vote taken by Local 120 of the UGWA during this period was in 1919, when organized labour throughout the West went on strike in support of the Winnipeg General Strike. The vote was 52 for and 91 opposed to the strike, and GWG was one of only 4 unions (out of the total of 38) in the city to stay at work.[9]

Women formed a large proportion of the labour force in garment manufacturing, a generally low-wage, highly competitive industry. Division of labour along gender lines was a force in sustaining the low wages paid to women.[10] Men were managers, salesmen, shipping clerks, cutters, and machinists; women were sewing machine operators. The only management position usually open to women was that of forelady. Fewer in number and requiring different strengths and expertise, men's positions were better paid. Technological advances that simplified jobs or reduced the physical demands placed upon operators resulted in women

replacing men and the subsequent decline of wages. Mercedes Steedman argues that the gap between the lives of women and men in the needle trades in Canada resulted first from 'the social view that [women's] ultimate destiny as wives and mothers made them peripheral to the paid work world' and second from the lack of support from 'male workers and trade unionists who saw women's entrance into the work force as a threat to their jobs.'[11]

Employees at LaFleche Bros. were predominantly males. In 1931 the firm noted that tailors were generally men because it was not worthwhile to train women in highly skilled positions because they usually resigned when they married.[12] LaFleche's attitude was typical of employers who considered women temporary employees. In fact, former employees in interviews indicate that most women who worked for LaFleche did not continue working after they were married or started their families. Because of the degree of handwork required and the level of skill of those working in fine tailoring, it was not as easy for women to move in and out of work at LaFleche Bros. as it was at such firms as Emery (a ladieswear firm), Reynolds (a uniform manufacturing firm), or GWG.

The low wages paid to women factory workers had implications for the wider community. When the issue of women's inability to support themselves was raised in 1913, the City of Edmonton considered providing a grant to subsidize rooming houses for women from rural areas to prevent them from turning to prostitution or other desperate measures, as they did elsewhere, to pay their rent. The Trades and Labour Congress opposed this move, arguing it would condone the low wages paid to women.[13] In spite of evidence demonstrating that women supported themselves and frequently their families, their wages were considered by politicians and employers to be supplementary rather than essential to their survival. A 1921 *Alberta Labour News* article about GWG stated that a number of the women working for the firm were 'mothers of large families, who in some cases entirely support them and in others help materially.'[14] Young, single women were often daughters of men unable to support their families on their wages alone. Former employees recall that during periods of general unemployment men often had more difficulty finding jobs than did women.[15] One former GWG employee notes that she worked throughout her marriage taking as little as two weeks off to have a baby. Her husband, a printer by trade, was often unable to find work of any sort and would stay home to care for the children.[16]

Contributing to the conservative nature of the Edmonton garment industry work force was the uniform ethnic background of the workers. In Winnipeg many of these women were Jewish, Ukrainian, Polish, German, and Russian. Company owners in Winnipeg were frequently Jewish or Eastern European and hired friends and relatives. In contrast, most manufacturers in Edmonton were English. No exploited immigrant group worked within the trade in Edmonton. Former garment workers recall that Ukrainians from the St Paul region of Alberta were encouraged to move to Edmonton to work at GWG, but there was not a disproportionate number of Ukrainians on staff, nor were Ukrainians brought in to work for lower wages or to allow the factory to discharge other workers.[17]

Labour legislation governing the garment industry reflected a give and take between management and labour, as each tried to see its position established in law. Perhaps because of the later development of the garment industry in Alberta, labour legislation developed alongside the industry. A number of firms were established in the years 1906-16; the Factories Act was introduced in 1917. The act applied only to the cities of Calgary, Edmonton, Medicine Hat, and Lethbridge, where legislators thought that it would protect homeless girls.[18] It was similar to other labour legislation in Canada at the time, with the exception of the child labour and minimum wage clauses which stipulated the ages, hours of work, and salaries of workers. These were the clauses that generated the most discussion in the legislature and that were the most significant.[19] The act also governed the physical environment of workers, such as construction and layout of factories, safety of machinery, regulation of elevators, ventilation, and drainage, and it stipulated that the employer had to provide fire protection. Thus, the government was able to provide protective legislation for workers early in the industry's history in the province.

The Department of Labour indicated that the act was also designed to protect the public from the dangers of homework that had been experienced in other garment manufacturing centres. In fact, sweating and homework had been in decline in Toronto and Montreal since the 1910s; outwork, the prime cause of sweated labour, was not practised in Edmonton, nor was industrial homework carried on to any extent in Alberta beyond independent dressmaking, millinery, and tailoring.[20]

Other clauses in the act applied specifically to women. One specifying that women should be allowed to use a seat while working was derived directly from Ontario's legislation, designed to protect working women from harm to their reproductive organs brought on by extended periods of standing up. Other clauses indicated that women working in factories had to secure their hair to prevent it from coming in contact with machinery, shafting, belting, or material being handled and that they were not permitted to clean machinery while it was in motion. Later, Walter Smitten, secretary of the Alberta Federation of Labor

GWG advertisement, *Alberta Labor News,* 16 October 1920. Advertising the union made label was good business. In similar ads, GWG boasted that it was working 'hand in hand with Labor in the service of the great masses of the people.' (PAA A.18999)

(AFL), suggested the government had been insincere in adopting these measures since they were never enforced.[21]

When the Factories Act was revised in 1920, the minimum wage clauses were removed. Labour argued for stronger enforcement of the act and the formation of a minimum wage board. In 1922 the Minimum Wage Act established the Minimum Wage Board, which determined periods of employment, or shifts, as well as wages. Judging from the records of the Minimum Wage Board, the act was written largely for women in garment manufacturing. Labour initially greeted the establishment of the board with enthusiasm, but its effectiveness was immediately questioned and the *Alberta Labor News* referred to it as 'a huge joke.' The AFL continued to lobby for the extension of the Minimum Wage Act to cover men as well as women and proposed an increase in the minimum wage to $14 per week, the minimum 'required to provide a proper living for a female worker who was dependent on her own earnings.'[22]

Most of the records of the Minimum Wage Board from the 1920s and 1930s concern garment manufacturing and GWG in particular. The board divided manufacturing into two main divisions: needle trades and other industries. In fact, garment manufacturing was considered such a significant aspect of the Minimum Wage Board's role that the representative of employees was the president of Local 120 of the UGWA, Harriet J. Ingram. The *Alberta Labor News* applauded the appointment: 'It was almost essential that the workers' representative be a woman and it is doubtful that one more qualified for the position could have been found than the president of the largest women workers' union in the province.' Lillian Morris, who succeeded Ingram as president of Local 120 of the UGWA, was also appointed to the three-member Minimum Wage Board between 1925 and 1934.[23]

Even in garment manufacturing, where most firms paid piece-work, women had to be paid at least the minimum wage per hour. In some firms, bonusing and piece-work were used in an attempt to avoid the minimum wage. Women were paid x amount per buttonhole rather than x amount per hour. The more they accomplished, the higher they were paid; however, if production increased greatly, the price per buttonhole would go down and they would have to work harder to maintain their previous salary. Still former employees comment that piece-work was preferable to being paid by the hour because if a dressmaker was particularly skilled or hard working she could earn more than the minimum wage. One woman commented that she was sorry to have been taken off piece-work and moved to inspecting because she would earn less money on the weekly rate.[24]

Women working in garment manufacturing earned wages at least comparable to those paid to women in other manufacturing industries and considerably more than those paid in other female-dominated occupations, such as the service industry, where the minimum wage was usually the maximum they could expect (see Table 1). Wages are difficult to interpret because records are incomplete and factory inspectors sometimes had difficulty getting accurate information. In 1935, Margaret A. Hamilton, chief factory inspector, noted the difficulty inspectors faced because false information was given to them by employees in order to protect their positions.[25] As well, factory inspections only occurred once a year and there were not sufficient Inspectors to be effective in enforcing legislation. Unfortunately, few reports of factory inspectors remain with the Department of Labour's files and those do not refer to garment manufacturing firms.

TABLE 1

Weekly Wages of Employees in Garment Manufacturing Compared to Those in Other Manufacturing Positions, 1925-1928 (Wages in $)

| | 1925 | | 1926 | | 1927 | |
	garment	other	garment	other	garment	other
Men over 18	23.39	27.74	28.46	26.95	30.02	27.66
Men under 18	8.55	11.44	9.55	11.50	11.00	12.17
Women over 18	15.14	16.10	16.93	16.52	17.15	16.31
Women under 18	9.55	10.62	12.00	10.69	12.00	11.28
Apprentices	7.89	13.89	8.46	12.86	11.37	12.84

Source: The Annual Report of the Commissioner of Labour, 1926-1928

Comparisons between Alberta's minimum wage and wages paid in the other western provinces were regularly used either by labour, to support increases, or by management, to oppose increases. For example, in arguing against an increase in the minimum wage in 1933, Charles A. Graham, president of GWG, explained the significance of the wage in the competition for markets:

> The great volume of business that we compete for is western Manitoba, all of the Province of Saskatchewan, Alberta and British Columbia[;] because it is more convenient to ship west, rather than East, Manitoba has by this influence and more favorable minimum wage legislation developed a substantial volume of business[;] we have thirteen direct competitors in the City of Winnipeg, who are working at a minimum of $10.80, rather than our $12.50, and I submit that unless we are put on a parity with Manitoba, we must of necessity lose the bulk of business, with consequent reduction in employment.[26]

To remain competitive, garment companies also wanted the ability to move employees from one machine to another and to handicap employee wages. GWG claimed that the ability to move employees from one machine to another on the one hand allowed the company greater efficiency in meeting changing supply and demand and on the other offered employees an opportunity both to earn more money on a machine requiring greater skill and to maintain constant employment. Companies applied to the Minimum Wage Board for permission to handicap employees from 10 per cent to 25 per cent, meaning the company would pay that percentage less than minimum wage. For example:

> Miss Critchley who was employed as embroiderer at Emerys Garment Works had been informed by her employer that, unless she could get a permit from the Board to work for the amount she could earn at rates paid by this firm for this class of work, her services must be dispensed with. Miss Critchley has been employed for four years with this firm and is able to make more than [the] minimum amount on [the] average run of work but, on certain classes where the amount of work is out of proportion to the amount of remuneration can not make minimum. The Board decided that there were no reasons why Miss Critchley should be considered handicapped.[27]

No doubt, where garments required particularly extensive or intricate embroidery Miss Critchley had to take more time to get the work done. Emery did not want to pay extra for this additional time. Unfortunately, Miss Critchley was the loser as she was then out of a job.

In addition to handicapping due to a change from one machine to another or from one class of work to another, manufacturers often requested a handicap when, due to personal illness or hardship, the employees were not able to work as hard as they had previously.[28] GWG described to the Minimum Wage Board the circumstances of ten women it wanted to handicap, some of whom were widowed and most of whom were supporting children and, in some cases, parents or husbands as well. The brevity and matter-of-fact approach in presenting these cases ('had trouble with her husband recently, was abused and he finally threatened to shoot her'; 'husband at present in Mental Hospital in Ponoka; woman is rather frail and is worrying'; and 'just returned to work after an absence of 5 months due to illness; husband suffering from cancer') suggests they were not considered extreme.[29] In response to GWG's request, Lillian Morris sought further information about how many employees were falling behind the minimum wage in order to determine how many handicaps should be offered and to be able to address each case individually. She wrote:

> I am convinced that if we granted handicaps to the ten mentioned in your letter, within a month that many more, and some of them even older, and with as bad disabilities will also be asking for handicaps.
>
> For the handicap to be of any benefit to the ten mentioned, it will have to be the difference between what they make and the minimum wage as the Company have made it quite clear they will not make these operators up. I am quite sure a 25% would be required for all of these women. It should be remembered, if they make over the handicap as allowed them they receive it anyway.[30]

Juvenile labour was another important issue in the competition for markets, yet it is difficult to get an accurate impression of the extent of juvenile employment in the province. Only juveniles in the age 15-17 bracket could work in factories following the 1917 passage of the Factories Act. However, enforcement of provincial regulations was not always rigorous. For example, a boy could state his age and if he 'had the height' the employer did not question him. Two interview subjects recall that they started working for GWG at age 14. A former employee of LaFleche Bros. also started under age.[31]

Throughout the 1920s and 1930s the Minimum Wage Board was concerned with ensuring a fair rate of pay for learners who were working on piece-work basis. Apprentice labour was considered when the Factories Act was written: "There was a factory in Edmonton in which 250 girls were employed at an average wage of four dollars per week, and the object of the bill [the apprenticeship clause thereof] was to prevent girls being employed for a period of one year and then being discharged when they asked for an increase.'[32] At the 1920 hearings, the Vogue Hat Shop of Calgary expressed concern about a six-dollar minimum wage for apprentices, saying:

> It did not pay the milliner to employ more than one or two such girls in her business, that it was cheaper for her to pay an experienced worker at $22 a week than to let a green hand at $6 spoil material. Miss Steel claimed that if the old apprenticeship plan of working without pay for one year were adopted, more help would be taken into local shops, their working capacity would be increased and the women of Calgary would be able to buy cheaper hats.

A similar argument was raised by a dressmaker named Mrs Ryan, who felt that 'a girl learning the dressmaking trade should not expect a wage for the first three or four months.'[33]

The Minimum Wage Act limited the number of apprentices who could be hired, but companies could request permission to hire a greater proportion of apprentices. Garment manufacturing firms, including Hatchwear, Caldwell Knitting, Emery Manufacturing, LaFleche Bros., and the Edmonton Knitting Company, all requested permission to hire additional apprentices. Although the Board frequently agreed to such requests, each application was considered individually. In 1926 permission was refused to the Edmonton Knitting Company. The board was concerned about operations at the firm and 'agreed that this matter [should] lay in abeyance until a full investigation has been made and complete record of the firm's activities during last year be presented to the Board.' The results of this investigation are not preserved. The company was in serious difficulty at the time and perhaps the Board's decision was a factor in the company's subsequent failure.[34]

In 1926, when a new Factories Act was introduced, the government established a three-member commission to consider the 48-hour work week. It searched the records of the Bureau of Labour, sent notices to all factories, and held hearings in Medicine Hat, Lethbridge, Calgary, and Edmonton that December. The Canadian Manufacturers Association joined companies, boards of trade, and merchants' associations in opposition to the proposed legislation. J.A. LaFleche, who employed 40 men working 54 hours per week, wrote protesting the 48-hour week on the basis of competition, production, and the welfare of employees. He argued that LaFleche Bros. would not be able to compete with the prices of garments manufactured by eastern firms that did not have similar restrictions and that employees would be hurt if they could not take advantage of the inherent seasonal nature of tailoring by working longer hours in the busy season. He argued that the 48- hour law would lead to piece-work and, ultimately, sweat-shop methods. Interestingly, LaFleche also sent a letter to Premier J.E. Brownlee outlining the same objections but also including a petition signed by his employees stating they were in opposition to the 48-hour week. LaFleche switched to the piece-work system shortly after writing this letter. No doubt the thought of being laid off in the off-season encouraged the employees to sign. Fred White, a Calgary Labour member who spoke in favour of the new legislation, said that petitions from employees who were not in favour of the proposed act were obtained by coercion.[35] The only garment manufacturing companies heard from at the hearings were non-union shops that employed primarily men rather than women.

The majority report submitted by Judge A.A. Carpenter and Norman Hindsley concluded, to the disappointment of organized labour, that a further reduction of hours of work was not required at that time. Out of 10,683 employees in factories in the province, 7,262 were already working 48 hours or less; of these 1,200–1,400 were women whose hours were limited by the minimum wage legislation. The commission noted:

> In some industries the hours of labor, largely through the organization of employees, are fairly uniform throughout the whole Dominion. Thus, in the manufacture of clothing, statistics from the Dominion of Labor Department show that a forty-four hour week is widely prevalent throughout the country and the effect of this is seen in the comparatively short hours of labour in this industry in Alberta.[36]

This conclusion was limited to those protected either by union contacts or existing legislation and did not apply to outworkers, knitters, or tailors whose hours were not limited.

The 1920s and early 1930s were years of determining how to apply legislation to garment manufacturing. Complex issues such as payment of apprentices, movement of employees from one department to another, handicapping, and hours of work were addressed. Legislation was sometimes modified to accommodate labour (e.g., the introduction of the 54-hour week in 1917 and the establishment of the Minimum Wage Board in 1925) and sometimes modified to accommodate manufacturers (for example,. maintaining the 54- hour week in 1926 rather than introducing the 48-hour week, although most garment manufacturers were already working the 48-hour week).

By the beginning of the Great Depression, Edmonton boasted a number of well-established firms, including GWG, Emery, LaFleche Bros., and Reynolds Manufacturing. Many more short-lived ventures had passed from the scene. The need for compromise became more overt during the depression. Slowdowns and layoffs in one season, then overtime the next, were part of the nature of garment manufacturing—but their effects became more pronounced during the depression. The union label again became an important selling feature, as GWG encouraged other unionized trades to buy GWG clothes to support a unionized manufacturer. Annie Stephenson, president of Local 120, UGWA, requested the support of the Edmonton Trades and Labor Council through endorsement of the union label. Lillian Morris wore men's overalls during a trip with representatives from management to

Drumheller to appeal to miners to wear only GWGs. Daisy Houck, a member of the board of the UGWA from California, spent two weeks in Edmonton developing a systematic working schedule to streamline operations.

The challenge brought by the depression was met with ingenuity. GWG introduced several new lines in 1931 in an attempt to diversify. The firm also looked to homesteading in the Peace River district as a new market for its goods. Finally, management and labour continued to co-sponsor the annual picnic which boosted morale.[37] In these difficult times, the delicate balance between management, labour, and government continued, with each lobbying to improve its own position but at the same time respecting the other's position. ∾

ANNE NOTHOF

MAKING COMMUNITY HISTORY: THE RADIO PLAYS OF RINGWOOD AND GOWAN

CKUA Players, with Gowan at her desk. (UAA 70-89-4)

*C*anadians first started listening to radio in the 1920s. Most of the stations were located in the United States. The public generally listened to the radio for entertainment, but cultural and political leaders worried that the radio was also a powerful tool for influencing the masses. Radios imparted knowledge and values. So long as Canadians listened to American stations, radio would teach American values and spread American influence. These concerns led to the formation of the Canadian Radio League which lobbied the federal government to regulate broadcasting through the establishment of a public broadcasting system like the British Broadcasting Corporation. In 1932 the government agreed and set up the Canadian Broadcasting Commission (by 1936,

Corporation). A strong national culture was the best defence against American influence.

Edmonton's first radio station, CJCA, began broadcasting in 1922. CKUA went on the air in 1927 as a way of taking the 'university to the people.' Gwen Pharis Ringwood and Elsie Park Gowan wrote plays for CKUA and the CBC. Many of them were pioneering works of Alberta cultural and social history.

Anne Nothof teaches English at Athabasca University and hosts 'Theatre on the Air' on CKUA. She has published numerous articles on Canadian and British playwrights and on Canadian radio drama.

HE PLAYS OF GWEN PHARIS RINGWOOD AND ELSIE
Park Gowan are preoccupied with community and
with the lives of the individuals who characterize a
community. In Ringwood's folk plays and community
pageants, the intersecting rituals and customs of individuals from diverse cultures and countries make up the unique
matrix that she identified as small town Alberta. Gowan's
epic radio plays and pageants comprise a social history of
Edmonton and Canada, a history that she dramatized with
ironic affection. Her intention in writing was to give to her
audience a sense of belonging and participation in the life
of the community, a spirit of unity. She portrayed history
from the standpoint of the 'minor' characters—particularly
the women whose lives were affected by the choices made
by their political leaders, but who also participated in these
choices. Both playwrights recognized and celebrated the
diversity of cultures within Canada and the distinctive
contributions of individuals who were ignored in 'official'
histories. More than a chronology of events, history
for Ringwood and Gowan was a record of social exchange
and change.

Both women believed strongly in the pedagogical
potential of drama, and their personal histories testify to
their commitment to education as a force for community
building. Yet both felt the hindrance of juggling their
writing careers with their other obligations. Looking back
in 1975 Ringwood wrote to Gowan that she regretted she
had never devoted herself wholly to her writing: 'Damn—I
wanted so much to write a truly fine play—but I wanted to
be a mother, wife, housekeeper, gardener, mrs. doctor, adju-
dicator, teacher too . . . so I nibbled at them all.'[1] Gowan's
response was equally frustrated: 'Know what you mean "nibbled at them all." Was lately asked to write my biography
for something called "Women's Who's-who" and when put
down, its a very confoosing [sic] read. What AM I? Teacher
. . . radio writer . . . playwright . . . lecturer etc. etc.'[2]

ᖆ Ringwood was born in Anatone, Washington, in 1910.
Her family moved to a farm near Barons in southern
Alberta in 1913 and then to Magrath, where her father
taught in the local school.[3] Growing up in small towns on
the prairies, she developed an appreciation for the distinctive nature of each community. Ringwood would later say
that her mother, who was of Pennsylvania Dutch and
English-Irish origin, believed staunchly in 'Education as
the Key to Upward Mobility, that somewhere in a book
one finds the answers to everything—how to keep house,
how to write, how to make a life.'[4] Ringwood pursued her
own education at the University of Alberta in an Honours

English program, working part-time for the Department of
Extension's director of drama, Elizabeth Sterling Haynes,
and acting as registrar for the newly established Banff
School of Fine Arts. In 1937 she was awarded a Rockefeller
Foundation Fellowship to study at the Department of
Dramatic Art at the University of North Carolina. While
there she wrote the first draft of what became her best-
known play, 'Still Stands the House,' a domestic tragedy set
during the Great Depression on the prairies. In 1939, following her marriage to Dr John Brian Ringwood (they had
met while she was a student at the University of Alberta),
she returned to the Department of Extension as a drama
advisor, keeping her marriage a secret in order to retain her
job. After a few years in Edmonton she lived in Goldfields,
northern Saskatchewan; Lamont, Alberta; and Williams
Lake, British Columbia, thus enriching her experience of
small communities. In Williams Lake Ringwood was particularly active in community theatre and teaching, volunteering her theatre experience to the Cariboo Indian
school while continuing with her own writing.

Elsie Park Gowan was born in 1905 in Helensburgh,
Scotland, and came to Edmonton with her family in 1912.
She obtained a teaching certificate from Camrose Normal
School in 1922 and taught for five years in rural schools.
Her stage play, 'The Hungry Spirit,' is loosely based on
her own experience as a young teacher with the incontro-
vertible need to improve her own education. From 1926 to
1930 she studied history at the University of Alberta,
where she was the president of the Dramatic Society and
the Literary Society, and acted under the direction of
Elizabeth Sterling Haynes. As Moira Day indicates in her
biography of Gowan,[5] between 1930 and 1958 she was
very active in education and community theatre in
Edmonton, participating in the Edmonton Little Theatre
from its inception in 1929. Following her marriage to
Dr Edward Hunter Gowan, a physics professor at the
University of Alberta who was also active in community
theatre, she retired from teaching and devoted herself to
playwriting. Her stage plays include 'Homestead' (1932),
'The Last Caveman' (1938), and 'Breeches from Bond
Street' (1949), but most of her plays were written for radio.

Early in their careers as playwrights, both Gowan and
Ringwood wrote plays for broadcast by radio station
CKUA, which was founded in 1927 by the University of
Alberta Department of Extension to bring education to
remote areas of Alberta. From the onset of their writing
careers, then, their plays were informed by a pedagogical
function. In fact, radio drama in Canada inherited from
BBC radio drama an educational mandate to reach indi-

viduals who might not have access to the cultural resources of urban centres and to encourage a wider audience for theatre. In the 1930s and 1940s, when radio drama was developing rapidly in Alberta through the agency of the CBC and CKUA, radio was also conceived as a means of linking Canadians distributed widely across an empty land. It continued the tradition of the Chautauqua, touring companies of performers and lecturers who provided an entertaining education wherever their tents were pitched. During a period when professional theatre consisted of American or British touring companies offering bowdlerized Shakespeare, farces, and melodramas, the productions of radio drama by the CBC and CKUA provided both a locus for an indigenous theatre and a way of accessing the world. As Ringwood pointed out in a 1979 speech to the Association of Radio and Television History, in the 1930s and 1940s 'for most people on farms and in small prairie villages throughout the West radio was their theatre.'[7] Radio plays could exploit the dramatic potential of history as human interaction.

Ringwood and Gowan were approached to write a series of history plays for CKUA by Sheila Marryat, who had also been active in the University of Alberta Dramatic Society. She was the first paid staff member at CKUA, functioning as radio technician, program director, and on-air host from 1928 to 1939, when she left to take up the position of talks producer for the CBC in Winnipeg. Marryat's conception of radio drama matched that of Ringwood and Gowan, to reach isolated individuals who had little opportunity for education, and to help build a sense of community.[8] She gave all the credit for CKUA's radio productions to engineers, actors, and playwrights. Her reward lay in the belief that she was doing something for 'the women who have plunged into the country life, leaving their music, drama, and friends behind them.'[9] According to radio drama critic Howard Fink, from 1933 to 1939 the CKUA Drama Department under the direction of Sheila Marryat provided a greater 'quality and variety of drama' than any prairie radio station including the national networks, the CRBC and CBC.[10] To perform these radio plays, Marryat founded the CKUA Players, a group of amateurs (including Myrna Hirtle, the

Gwen Pharis Ringwood, University of Alberta *Evergreen and Gold* yearbook, 1934.
(UAA 93-82)

wife of W.O. Mitchell) who acted in Edmonton's Little Theatre, the University Dramatic Society, and the Dickens Society. The plays were live to air, with the sound effects improvised by the cast—once described by Gowan as 'coconut horses, hissing through clenched teeth for wind in the rigging of sailing ships.'[11] According to CKUA operator and announcer, Dick MacDonald,[12] producing historical radio plays at CKUA was very much a communal experience, with the actors doubling as sound technicians to create scenes through soundscapes.

CKUA's broadcasting of historical plays was also very much a result of the energetic proselytizing of Haynes. She had joined the Department of Extension in 1932 and proceeded to take drama to the people throughout Alberta—setting up workshops, lecturing, directing, and adjudicating. Both Gowan and Ringwood were caught up in her enthusiasm for the theatre. Looking back in 1979, Ringwood said of Haynes:

> Her belief that people, unschooled, untried, sometimes without much talent, could help to bring to life fine productions of good plays was unwavering. She set about to teach us how. Her work influenced theatrical production and programs all over Alberta, Saskatchewan, Manitoba and British Columbia.[13]

At that time, the actual plays were still primarily imports. In the years Ringwood worked with Haynes, from 1933 to 1939, she could not recall seeing a Canadian play until the Banff School and CKUA began actively to solicit and develop Canadian works. The series that Marryat commissioned from Gowan and Ringwood, entitled 'New Lamps for Old,' featured the 'great names' in history—individuals 'who had contributed to humanitarian causes or changed the course of history.'[14] Ringwood and Gowan each wrote ten scripts, varying in length from one half-hour to an hour. They were paid five dollars per script. Their focus, however, was not so much on the heroic deeds of 'great' men and women of history as on the details of their social and personal lives—their interactions with the 'ordinary' people of their time, with the plot and action dictated by 'the struggle to achieve what was often an obsessive goal' for the benefit of the community. In Ringwood's play on Socrates, for example, she introduced his 'shrewish wife with some sympathy, realizing that Socrates was a hard man to live with,' and she interpreted Socrates's decision to drink the hemlock as being 'with the hope that the Athenians would change their unjust law.'[15] In other plays she showed how Galileo prodded 'his students to find out the universe,' how Beethoven's audience stood in 'exultant admiration' at the end of the Ninth Symphony, although he could not hear their applause, and how Nansen of the North organized relief to the displaced, the lost, the children who were homeless and hungry after World War I. Florence Nightingale was cast as 'the lady with the lamp whose heroic struggles for cleanliness and organization . . . and compassion for the wounded and dying inform medical services across the world even today.' Unfortunately, Ringwood destroyed her scripts of 'New Lamps for Old' in 1954 during a cleaning binge, embarrassed by what she considered the 'purple passages.' No copies have survived. She later regretted discarding so much of her history, the consequence of undervaluing her own role in the cultural life of the country, yet she did recognize the importance of radio drama which 'brought us from isolation into a global community.'[16]

Elsie Park Gowan. (UAA 79-51-66)

Gowan's scripts for 'New Lamps for Old' also reflected her predilection for community history—the consequences of discoveries, inventions, and innovations for the average individual and for the community. She believed that history could inform the present. Her play on Mary Wollstonecraft, for example, concludes with one of Mary's students wondering whether women will listen to and remember the story of 'the first champion of half of the human race.'[17] In 'The Coming of Power,' which dramatizes the life of James Watt, Gowan showed that his obsessive determination had consequences for his wife, his servants, and the workers in the factory where his steam engine was built. As so often, she included an ironic reference that connected her audience to the historical events, this time a derogatory reference by an English manufacturer to Canada as 'a few paltry acres of snow . . . utterly barren' and destined to be of not the slightest use to Britain.[18]

History, she implied, had demonstrated just how erroneous that assessment was.

Although Ringwood wrote about famous people for 'New Lamps for Old,' her interest was more in community history as interpreted in the stories of the 'folk'—the idiosyncratic and imaginative originality of relatively isolated people. In 1937 when she left Edmonton to study playwriting at Chapel Hill, North Carolina, she learned about the potential of a national folk theatre for developing an indigenous culture. Her writing was heavily influenced by the Irish dramatic renaissance and the plays of John Millington Synge, Lady Augusta Gregory, W.B. Yeats, and Sean O'Casey:

> Here was exciting, important, challenging work that somehow related to the prairie experience. . . Their depiction of the fisherfolk, the farmers, the myth and history and political conflict of the non-urban and non-industrial people had a relevance to my own experience and life that was not apparent in the London and Broadway plays I read. [19]

Her orientation towards the 'folk' was reinforced by Robert Gard, who taught at the University of Alberta and the Banff School from 1942 to 1944 and gave weekly talks on CKUA on Alberta's heritage of folklore, tall tales, and history, as well as writing radio plays himself.

Ringwood's 'folk' plays, written for the stage, are all portraits of Alberta's distinctive communities. 'Still Stands the House' and 'Dark Harvest' portray the tragic lives of isolated prairie farm women with a strong need for an extended community and the amenities of 'civilization.' 'The Rainmaker' shows the divergent reactions of the townspeople of Medicine Hat when an outsider offering a promise of rain during the drought of 1921 inadvertently shows them that they have to depend on their own inner resources to survive as a community. As the young farmer, Tom, concludes: 'I guess if people have to depend on something outside, like a rain, to keep them together, why they just aren't worth saving.'[20]

Through dialect and song, 'Stampede' recreates a cowboy community in southern Alberta, showing the loyalties and conflicts that determine its particular mythology as

CKUA Players, University of Alberta, 1935-6. (EA-137-71)

the cowboys anticipate riding in the 1912 Calgary Stampede—a 'last chance for a souvenir of the old West.'[21] 'A Fine Coloured Easter Egg,' set in Lamont, shows the farcical consequences of an oil boom on a traditional Ukrainian community, when a husband attempts to escape what he believes will be the ravages of wealth, only to learn that his real wealth is in his family—his wife, seven daughters, fourteen granddaughters, and a grandson—symbolized by his wife's 'fine coloured Easter egg.' Although interested in the characteristics of the 'multicultural' society of western Canada, Ringwood tended to stereotype these characteristics from an Anglo-Canadian point of view and to regard them as pervasively humorous. But she also saw such characteristics as culturally enriching, contributing to the variegated coloration of the country:

> Our population is a heterogeneous one and our manners and customs vary greatly from community to community, from region to region. We have villages when speech and action and thought is in the light, quick rhythm of the French. Again a Ukrainian town seems to have a slower, outwardly stolid rhythm but underneath run the deep, passionate undercurrents of feeling and a lusty broad humour. We have towns with the flavour of a quiet English village or a slightly aggressive American town; we have industrious German settlements, mining towns with a preponderance of Latin names, the cow towns when the flavour and play-acting of the ranching industry have

their way, the northern town with its feeling of the fur trade and the dog team. There are towns when the talk is of jumping horses and polo, and towns when the talk is of an historic past. And a few ghost towns—in the desert or at the site of a defunct mine.[22]

Ringwood believed it was time 'to try to interpret the life we know and love to the rest of the world, unless we are content to go down as a people who were blind and inarticulate and afraid, a people who had nothing to say.'[23] Her most ambitious expressions of cultural and social history were the community pageants she wrote for Edmonton and Edson. The Edmonton pageant on Methodist missionary John McDougall and Chief Maskapetoon was staged before a large outdoor audience in 1940 to commemorate the seventieth anniversary of the Methodist Church. In 1961 she was commissioned by the Fiftieth Anniversary Committee of Edson to write a musical play about the early days of the town. She chose the title 'Look Behind You Neighbour' to suggest the interpersonal nature of community history. She brought 3000 people together to evoke the personality of a town through vignettes and songs, highlighting events from 1909 on: the foundations of the community in farming, coal mining, and forestry; the building of the Grand Trunk Railway with the attendant scandals; the construction of the first hotel by a Chinese immigrant; the closing of the brothels; the proud exodus of young men during the

First World War. Its production was the occasion of considerable civic pride. Elsie Park Gowan, who had taught in Edson as a young woman, had a more jaundiced view of the town.

As suggested, unlike Ringwood, who wrote primarily for the stage, Gowan wrote scripts mainly for radio, for CKUA, CJCA, and the CBC—over 200 in all. Following the series, 'New Lamps for Old,' she wrote a more ambitious series for CKUA entitled 'The Building of Canada,' broadcast in 1937 and 1938 and rebroadcast for a national audience by the CBC a year later. This series dramatized Canada's development from its first settlement to its independence as a nation primarily from the point of view of fictionalized 'onlookers' and individuals directly or indirectly affected by political decisions and indecisions, discoveries, and battles—in other words, it was a history of the marginalized. As the *Edmonton Journal* announced,

> In 'The Building of Canada' . . . the dry bones of our political history will come to life, with all the vigour, romance and human struggle that went into the making of our country. . . On the human side, 'The Building of Canada' will trace down the years the 'saga' of Canadian families whose sons' and daughters' lives link together the chapters of our history.[24]

'The Building of Canada' was an attempt to popularize Canadian history and to express Gowan's personal conviction that only through mutual understanding and tolerance could a community or a nation grow and prosper.[25] History was not made only on the battlefields and by governments but also in 'the parlor and the drawingroom where families meet to argue over the impact of these larger affairs on their individual fortunes.'[26] Each historical episode showed the interconnectness of the families whose lives were affected by historical events—the Couillards and Morels of Quebec, the English Grants who intermarry with the Morels, the United Empire Loyalist Steele family, and the Scottish McLeods and McKays. Gowan disrupted the chronological sequence on occasion to show the extent to which the lives of the past have conditioned the present. 'The Men in the News,' the twelfth play in the series, opens in 1939 in the lobby of the Macdonald Hotel, Edmonton. Hanging on the wall of the hotel is a copy of the painting of the 'Fathers of Confederation.' Two newspaper reporters discuss the significance of the Sirois Royal Commission on Dominion-Provincial Relations for the British North America Act. One is Charlie Connor, the great-grandson of the newsman who covered the meetings of Macdonald, Brown,

and Cartier in 1864 and 1867, and a direct descendant of one of the three central characters in the ninth play of the series, 'The Patriots of 37.' The other reporter is the descendant of another of the series' families—the McKays. In the last scene of the play, set in Ottawa on 1 July 1867, the significance of Confederation is noted, not by the 'Fathers' but by the individuals who constitute the new 'community'—a wife, a reporter, and a servant. In the final play, entitled 'No More Heroes,' the descendants of the founding families must also learn to accommodate different cultures and traditions when a new wave of immigrants from Eastern Europe settles in the West. Like Ringwood, Gowan promoted tolerance and cooperation through her work.

Many of Gowan's radio plays were commissioned for particular projects, and these tended to be more obviously formulaic and propagandistic. To promote the Community Chest campaign in 1943, Gowan wrote 'How Big is Edmonton?,' which was performed by the CJCA Players. Composed of 'case studies' of Edmontonians in need, the play shows how their needs were met by agencies funded by the Community Chest, such as the Salvation Army and the CNIB. 'Bigness' is measured not in population, reputation, fame, or fortune, but in generosity. In 1942, for the Canadian Society for the Control of Cancer, Gowan wrote a series of instructive dramas on cancer control entitled 'The Call to Health and Happiness,' based on real-life stories taken from the files of the Provincial Diagnostic Cancer Clinic. 'These are My Neighbours,' broadcast on CJCA and CFRN, was a series of plays designed to increase public understanding of welfare services. She wrote 'Tales from Near and Far' for a joint CBS-CBC broadcast and contributed five programs to a joint NBC-CBC production entitled 'Lands of the Free,' humanizing political subjects such as Dominion status through humour and pathos. 'The Town Grows Up,' a five-part series on the development of a city, showed what individuals could accomplish for their own well-being by sacrificing some personal liberty and cooperating in the growth of an integrated city. 'The People Next Door,' produced by the CBC in Winnipeg and broadcast on CJCA in 1944-45, again dramatized problems that must be addressed through communal cooperation. In all of these series, drama becomes a tool of the educator, a means of vivifying social issues in order to prompt social action.

Like Ringwood, Gowan expressed her interpretation of community history in larger forms: in 1954, she wrote the script for a pageant for Edmonton's Golden Jubilee—

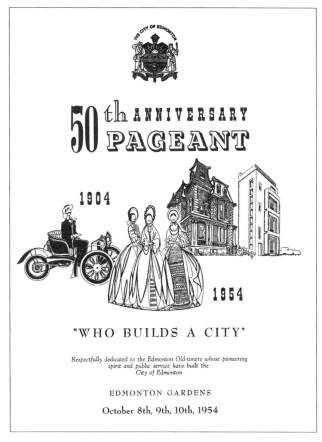

50th ANNIVERSARY
PAGEANT

1904

1954

"WHO BUILDS A CITY"

Respectfully dedicated to the Edmonton Old-timers whose pioneering
spirit and public service have built the
City of Edmonton

EDMONTON GARDENS

October 8th, 9th, 10th, 1954

Playbill advertising Gowan play marking the fiftieth anniversary of
Edmonton's becoming a city. Many of Gowan's plays had historical
themes, often highlighting the lives of ordinary people and using the
past to build a sense of community. (EA)

'Who Builds a City,' produced by Doug Hamersham and directed by Frank Glenfield, with assistant directors Douglas Campbell and Carl Hare. The music was composed, arranged, and conducted by Bob McMullin. The pageant began with the arrival of Edmonton's first family and traced it through three generations. Though not entirely 'history without tears,' the mood of the pageant was primarily celebratory. Included in a section about the Great Depression, entitled 'A Time of Testing,' was a song set to 'After the Ball':

Keep in your hearts the glory
Don't let the brightness fade
Deep in your hearts the memory
So was our history made.
All we had dreamed came true then
Answering the music's call
Proud was our future we knew then
After the ball![27]

And in a section entitled 'Drillers on Our Doorstep,' set in 1954, Gowan showed how a positive adjustment could be made to inevitable change:

There'll be some changes made.
There'll be a change on Jasper . . change at the Mac.
A new town hall for Mayor Hawrelak!
The old cow pasture's going to have a new look.
The south side limits reaching clear to Leduc![28]

In 1956 Gowan devised another pageant—this time for Jasper—and involved most of the community in the production. The three main lines of interest were the history, the community, and family life.

Despite her lifelong interest in dramatizing social history, however, Elsie Park Gowan was not enthusiastic about being a 'source of living history' herself. In 1979 she lamented that she was 'being pestered much these days by archivists who want [her] scrap books' and by 'tape recorders thrust in [her] face for the history of Theatre in Edmonton.' Ringwood responded with a limerick by the CBC radio drama producer, Andrew Allan:

I never saw an Archive, I hope I never see one.
But one thing's sure, while I'm alive,
I'd rather see than be one.[29]

Ringwood's official archives are in the University of Calgary Special Collections, but her plays constitute a living archive—a social history of western Canadian communities and people. Gowan's contribution as an historian was recognized by Edmonton's Historical Board in 1976 and by the Fort Edmonton Historical Foundation in 1979. Her radio plays on the building of nation and community have more recently been recognized by scholars and critics.[30] However, it is unlikely that the radio plays will be rebroadcast: television has superseded radio in the production of 'docudrama' for audiences more oriented to images than language. Moreover, the celebratory tone and didacticism is perhaps too blatant for a more jaded, sceptical contemporary audience. In their time the plays fulfilled an important educational purpose—assisting in the development of a community identity and revisiting the history of a nation from a woman's point of view. Gowan's interpretation of local and national history reflected her conviction that women's voices should be heard and acknowledged; they should not be relegated to the 'supporting roles.' Although many of Gowan's radio scripts survive in the archives at the University of Alberta, the radio productions have been lost or erased, causing her to wonder if her life's work was 'written on the air' and 'its substantial

pageant faded.'[31] In a sonnet composed to fulfil an assignment for one of her own adult writing classes, however,
she expressed a more positive view of the significant
details that comprise a life:

On Growing Old

Be with me, Beauty, that I may enjoy
Sunrise and sunset in the hovering sky.
Now, when I glimpse embracing girl and boy
Memory says, 'Happy, sometime, there went I.'
The trees I planted forty years before
Thrust out, each spring, their seed buds to the sun.
Laughing grandchildren march up to my door,
Challenge of precious lives now just begun.
Some pride in work's accomplishment I knew,
And loving partnership in ripening years.
'Rosemary for remembrance and some rue.'
Help me accept my world, with all its fears.
Thankful for youth, maturity, and age
Let me act bravely on a darkling stage.[31] ❧

JOHN GRIGSBY GEIGER

'WRONG TIME, WRONG PLACE, WRONG COLOUR'

Gysin's artwork, which sometimes drew on his life in Edmonton, can be found in some of the world's most prestigious galleries. Here, *Arbre Généalogique Féminin Accablé par un matin machinal, (Woman's Family Tree Overwhelmed by an Automatic Morning)* 1935. (CENTRE GEORGES POMPIDOU, PARIS)

Famous Edmontonians usually fall into one of two categories. They are born in the city (or come while still relatively young), live in the city, make their names there, and die there. Or, they stop briefly in the city during high-profile careers—long enough to become enduring popular icons identified in the public mind with the best Edmonton represents—before moving on to other places and other opportunities. Donald Ross and Alexander Taylor, for example, are Edmontonians of the first type. Edmontonians of the second type include women's rights activist, Nellie McClung, who spent far fewer years in the city than many people probably realize, and, of course, hockey superstar, Wayne Gretzky.

But there is also a third, albeit far rarer, type of 'famous Edmontonian,'—those who never on their own choose to live in the city (unlike Katherine Hughes) but who end up there anyway, and who soon leave, quietly and unsung. They can acquire national and even international reputations while remaining totally unknown to their former fellow Edmontonians. Brion Gysin, artist and writer, was one such man. Most Edmontonians will never have heard of him, and, in fact, Gysin intensely disliked the place where he spent his childhood. But Edmonton should not be dismissed so easily, for Gysin's memories of that time and that place were to leave their imprint on his creative work.

John Geiger has co-authored the bestselling Frozen in Time and Dead Silence. He is a columnist for the Edmonton Journal. His lively account of Gysin's 'Edmonton exile' is based on his forthcoming biography of the artist and writer.

RION GYSIN WAS AN ARTIST LINKED WITH SOME OF the great movements of the twentieth century. His career as a painter began with a Surrealist exhibition in Paris in the 1930s (before he was expelled from the movement by its leader, André Breton), and his illusionist desert landscapes—now represented in the collections of the Centre Georges Pompidou in Paris, the Museum of Modern Art in New York, and the Musée de l'Art Moderne de la Ville de Paris—were precursors of later calligraphic abstractions. Gysin was a leading creative influence on the writer, William S. Burroughs. Their multimedia collaborative experiments with cut-ups, published as *Minutes To Go* (1960) and *The Third Mind* (1978), which sought to overrun the dividing line between painting and writing, inspired succeeding generations of artists and authors. Gysin has been identified with the Lettristes and his sound-poetry influenced Fluxus. He experimented in Jazz with American great, Steve Lacy, and invented the Dreamachine. He 'discovered' the trance music of the Master Musicians of Jujuka, which had been performed for centuries by tribal players in the hills outside of Tangier, Morocco, and introduced it to the Rolling Stones. Before his death in Paris in 1986, he was made a Chevalier de l'ordre des Arts et des Lettres by the Republic of France.[1] Perhaps Gysin's greatest achievement, however, was to have been all of this—and a product of Edmonton.

There was never any question that Brion Gysin was a remarkable child. As he later described it, no sooner had the phlegm been cleared from his breathing tract than the newborn Brion screamed out ungratefully: 'Wrong address! Wrong address! There's been a mistake in the mail. Send me back. Wherever you got me, return me. Wrong time, wrong place, wrong colour.'[2] It was certainly the wrong time. John Clifford Brion Gysin was born on 19 January 1916 in Taplow House, a Canadian military hospital in Taplow, Buckinghamshire, England. Eight months later, his father, Leonard Gysin, a captain with the 8th Canadians or 'the Little Black Devils,' fell at the bloody Somme, one of the most horrific and futile battles of the Great War. In all, Leonard Gysin had spent eleven days with his son. After the war, Stella Gysin returned to Canada, every bit 'the Widow Woman with her fatherless child in a Western.'[3] The wrong place was Edmonton. Gysin characterized his youth spent in the Alberta capital as his 'exile.'[4] He arrived in 1921 at age five and he put Edmonton and his mother behind him in 1932 at age sixteen. 'He just thought . . . [Edmonton] was awful, nowheresville,' said William S. Burroughs.[5]

Yet the decade Gysin lived on the Canadian prairies

left its mark. Memories of the West crept into his early Surrealist landscapes, with train tracks reaching across empty flat horizons, and into his pen-and-ink sketches of grotesque figures draped in furs. Later, memories of the Canadian prairies influenced his illusionist desert landscapes, which Paul Bowles, who himself captured the vast emptiness in his novel, *The Sheltering Sky* (1949), declared to be the only paintings true to the Sahara: 'To make the dead landscape come alive in a picture, the painter cannot paint what he sees; he must paint what he knows.'[6] Gysin could fill an empty space; it was something he knew from his earliest experience. 'Sometimes at night in the desert under the full moon,' he once commented, 'all the dunes seem to turn into blue snow.'[7] Most significantly, the memories surfaced in his finest novel, *The Process* (1969), which took the form of fragmented autobiography.[8] Tellingly, the chapter devoted to his childhood was called 'She.'

Brion Gysin and William Burroughs, in the courtyard of the Pharmaceutical Institute and Museum, Basel, Switzerland, 1979.
(ULRICH HILLEBRAND)

To young Brion's eyes, Edmonton was a postwar world swarming with ruthless widows on the prowl, where 'eligible veterans . . . banded together for mutual protection.' Even such citadels of male solidarity as Memorial Hall were soon overrun by political ladies in three-cornered hats.[9] 'Cornered' is precisely what Stella's second husband, a fifty-year-old bachelor eighteen years her senior, always claimed to have been. A retired lieutenant-colonel who worked for the federal government as an Indian agent, 'Uncle Billy' married Stella in February 1925. Nine-year-old Brion, swaddled in rank-smelling buffalo robes, travelled to the reception in a cabin outside of Edmonton by horse-drawn sleigh, sailing over the hard, crackling snow with the Northern Lights rustling overhead. The sled stopped at a cabin in a clearing in the wilderness high above a frozen river. Inside the cabin, a Hudson's Bay Company trade blanket was neatly folded on a wooden chest, against which leaned a shotgun. A friend of his stepfather's had built and occupied the cabin, and Brion always believed that the man had wanted 'Uncle Billy' to come and live with him. Now he had gone and got married. The drunken revellers were all outside, around a bonfire, when the friend took the gun, went behind the cabin, and blew his head off.[10] It is little wonder that Gysin saw life in the West as invariably barbarous, something out of a Hollywood shoot 'em up:

> We lived on the reservations with the Indians. A French half-breed trained the dogs for my sled. Indian girls looked after me when I was small and showed me theirs if I showed them mine. There were cowboy shootups Saturday nights. Prominent politicians would be found dead in a speakeasy run by a Ukrainian lady of easy virtue. Everybody was investing and losing their money in oil wells, uranium had just been discovered in the north. Doukhabours [sic] burned themselves in front of city hall.[11]

The marriage was not, however, nearly so wild as might have been implied by Gysin's characterization of frontier culture. It was shortly annulled by the court on grounds of 'the malformation, or frigidity and impotence of his [Uncle Billy's] parts of generation.' For this reason, if no other, any visits to an Indian reservation to see young Brion's stepfather would have been brief. 'We were not asked to stay the night,' Gysin remembered.[12] It was, perhaps, for the best. In his 1977 autobiographical short story, 'FIRE: Words by Day—Images by Night,' Brion observed cryptically that 'Uncle Billy caught wild animals like the silver fox and small boys in his traps.'[13] Stella subsequently said

of her 'unfortunate' second marriage that Brion 'was unavoidably touched by bitterness when very young.'[14] She and 'Uncle Billy' spent virtually their entire marriage apart, with Stella raising Brion in a duplex three blocks off Jasper Avenue, in the least imposing house on an unremarkable street. Later, Stella and Brion moved to the south side, close to Whyte Avenue. Wherever they went, they lived at the pleasure of her spinster sister, 'a houseful of women without men.'[15]

No one perhaps had a more profound impact on Brion than his mother, and nothing more than the absence of his father, who became the commanding but ambiguous figure around which the boy's fantasies revolved. Leonard Gysin homesteaded in 1903 at Castleavery, near Roblin, Manitoba, and by 1909 had accumulated two quarter sections of land, a log house, stables for his four horses, and twenty-five head of cattle.[16] When war broke out in 1914, he enlisted with the Winnipeg Rifles but was later transferred to the 8th Canadians. Gysin met Stella Margaret Martin while stationed in Ottawa, where she worked as a secretary and coyly introduced herself only as Tillie the Toiler, the name of a popular comic strip character. A twenty-one-year-old native of Deseronto on the Bay of Quinte, Lake Ontario, Stella was the youngest of thirteen children and the product of a strict Irish Catholic upbringing. She had learned to type at Loretto Abbey, a boarding school for young ladies run by the Ursulines. Leonard Gysin married Stella in her hometown during a blizzard in January 1915, and when his regiment went overseas, his already pregnant wife joined him in England. Leonard was reported first as missing believed killed, then as killed in action. 'He saw me once before I had my eyes open. I never saw him,' wrote Brion.[17] Because no body was ever found, Stella clung to the forlorn hope her husband was alive, even travelling to Poland to search for him after the war. She shared her delusion with Brion: 'Daddy is said not to be dead. He lost his memory in the explosion. He forgot his own name in the hospital. He is a man with only a number in a Polish prison camp. A long nightmare. When mother gets there, the man has no face and he cannot talk. She goes on dreaming for years that she made a terrible mistake when she turned away from that man.'[18] Stella inherited Leonard's library, and it was in his books that Brion learned how to read. Of the few photographs of his father, one, which showed him posing with his schoolmates while sailing on the Great Norfolk Broads in summer 1902, bore Leonard Gysin's hand-written inscription. Under his own image he had written, 'the one I knew least of all.'[19] It was a fitting epitaph. Even the homestead he built in Manitoba would be submerged by a hydro-electric project, now forming part of the bed of the Lake of the Prairies.

Brion was smothered by maternal instincts. His mother and aunt were 'virtually his only companions' and Stella fretted that 'he had never been in a position to acquire a man's point of view.'[20] His aunt, a teacher, was not only the breadwinner but also the disciplinarian, and sometimes her practical nature got frustrated by the dreaming side of the family. Gysin came to resent his childhood reliance on women, and later in life this resentment developed into full-blown misogyny, although he disputed the label. 'Don't go calling *me* a misogynist . . . a mere misogynist,' he retorted to one interviewer, 'I am a monumental misanthropist. Man is a bad animal.'[21] As an adult, Gysin steadfastly refused to discuss his mother even with his closest friends and once fell into a rage at the memory of his aunt's distant claim of having taught him to swim, something he had taught himself. The Beat poet, Allen Ginsberg, was the only one of Brion's contemporaries to meet his mother, looking her up in the early 1960s while in Vancouver for a reading. Ginsberg concluded that she was a farm girl and that Brion felt shame about his background.[22] Marion Wilson, who knew Stella in Edmonton in the 1930s and considered her a 'mentor,' remembered her differently—as a highly cultured woman who, for a Canadian, seemed very English. Brion put it more crudely, saying his mother had 'pseudo-aristocratic pretensions.'[23]

Stella lived such pretensions to the extent her limited means allowed. When she saw a photograph of a Persian prayer rug in a magazine but had no money to buy it, she made one from scratch. She furnished her home in antique Canadian pine years before it became fashionable. Her interests included gardening, poetry, music, and art, and she supplemented her war widow's pension by working as a story-teller at the Edmonton Public Library for 40 cents an hour.[24] There was a theatrical quality about her that made her stories raise the hair on the back of a listener's neck. Stella was also active in Liberal party circles and in the Catholic Women's League, where she was given responsibility for publicity. 'We were all feminists, way back before

they invented the word,' recalled Wilson. 'Stella was the same way, she believed in women and their ability to do things.'[25]

One thing Stella could not do was to make a manly specimen of her boy. For that she turned to Mr W.H. Nightingale, founder and headmaster of Westward Ho! School for Boys. 'No greater gift could come to this strong, lusty young West,' the local *Saturday News* had declared on Nightingale's arrival in Edmonton in 1908.[26] Many Edmontonians in 1925 remained convinced that the city still needed his kind of school and headmaster, steeped in Kipling and the hallowed traditions of Trinity College, Port Hope, Ontario—not so much for mathematics or the humanities but for manners and the higher ideal. The Westward Ho! curriculum emphasized scripture. Rodney Pike, an old boy who retained a vivid memory of Nightingale reading about Moses going up to the mountain to receive the Ten Commandments, said that he 'always pictured Moses as . . . a man like Mr. Nightingale.'[27] Westward Ho! was rigidly fashioned after the English public school, or as Nightingale termed it, 'the English system of supervision.' The boys played cricket in the spring, rugger in the fall. Discipline was a year-round activity. According to Pike, Nightingale 'did not have the slightest doubts about the efficiency of a sound caning to exact discipline and used the cane to great effect.' Some concessions were made to preserve Canada's cultural identity: in his attempt to tame the lusty young West, 'Moses' used the butt end of a hockey stick.

A group of Irish Catholic hooligans known as the Dawes Gang also carried out a Holy War against Brion. More than fifty years later he still remembered them, 'all properly dressed in ragged knickerbockers, black stockings and running shoes you can smell across the street, across the years.'

Even with the Christian ethic thus deeply imbedded in the students' psyche, the decision of Stella Gysin, a Roman Catholic, to enroll nine-year-old Brion in the Anglican private school scandalized the local Catholic hierarchy. A group of Irish Catholic hooligans known as the Dawes Gang also carried out a Holy War against Brion. More than fifty years later he still remembered them, 'all properly dressed in ragged knickerbockers, black stockings and running shoes you can smell across the street, across the years.'[28] No less a personage than Archbishop Henry Joseph O'Leary was moved to denounce Stella from the pulpit. Still, a mother's humilia-

Westward Ho! School epitomized the worst of Edmonton for Gysin. He is in the back row, fourth from the left. (PAA A.13952)

tion was tempered by the knowledge that Westward Ho! ranked among the finest preparatory schools in western Canada, where budding scholars received a thorough grounding in those subjects deemed essential to their future success: Latin, English, French, grammar, composition, arithmetic, and history. A budding homosexual who later sought refuge and excitement in the free port of Tangier, Brion remembered the school somewhat differently. 'The boys in my class were all two years older than I was, more developed. We did our studies around big wooden tables beneath which we compared cocks and naturally not entirely in my favor. The classroom stunk of nutty young male sex. Our schoolmasters seemed not to notice what we were up to or found some amusement in it.'[29] Perhaps this is what Nightingale meant by the 'English system of supervision.'

The sissy school uniform of cap, tweed blazer, short pants, and knee-stockings proved an ill-fit for Brion, who rebelled against the regimentation. As the only Catholic day boy at an Anglican boarding school, he also found the school itself an ill-fit. More than sixty years later, old schoolmates remembered that he stood out, and 'Moses' himself quickly dubbed the boy 'Trotsky.' Brion's real education came in the valley of the North Saskatchewan River. There, at night, he ran naked to swim the cold and wild current, 'loving myself, loving nature, the gods!'[30] There, he hunted mushrooms and puffballs with the berry-skinned boys who were the progeny of the 'mysterious old moccasin widows of early settlers, sitting silent in dark coal-burning kitchens.'[31] There, while on a hike to

Hogs'back ravine, he found a chain with a cross. The cross was hollow but he refused to open it, saying it contained wood from the Garden of Eden. Brion's view of Creation soon changed. By age fifteen he was an avowed atheist attending St Joseph's Catholic High School. Gerard Amerongen, a fellow Grade 11 student and later Progressive Conservative Speaker of the Alberta Legislative Assembly, remembered Gysin as 'far more intellectual than most of my classmates. We had some very interesting discussions, vigorous arguments. I have always had a rather firm Catholic faith. I had trouble understanding how anyone could be an atheist, although I've since come to know others.'[32]

Gysin obtained his senior matriculation at age sixteen. Hoping to channel his literary tendencies into a sensible calling, Stella encouraged him to enroll in library science at the University of Alberta. Her dream remained unfulfilled, as university regulations precluded direct admission into the program until age seventeen. Fearing the effects of a year of idleness and conscious of the economic climate in 1932, Stella concluded that a year or two of schooling at an English public school would be the best solution. She even found a school—Downside, run by the Benedictines in a monastery dating to the Middle Ages—willing to take Brion for only £50 a term. According to a relative, Downside's reputation as the 'Eton of Catholic public schools' influenced Stella's decision to approach it. But she was also a mother concerned for the direction of her son's interests, particularly his literary aspirations. 'In a former era science may have been the breeding ground for atheism but today I believe it is in literature,' Stella confided darkly to the headmaster in 1932. She elaborated in a second letter: 'I have realized that if . . . [Brion] lived up to the promise of his literary ability his only hope of salvation was the English Catholic atmosphere . . . If he were mechanically or mathematically inclined it might not be so dangerous for him. As he is, his very abilities are his dangers.'[33]

Gysin's last glimpse of his place of exile was of the stockyards of North Edmonton. He had papers showing two boxcars of cattle were to be shipped east in his charge. The journey proved to be more ordeal than adventure, with stark images of the depression—a boozy brakeman staggering down the narrow catwalk of the train, swinging his steel hook at a double row of hobos, sending them spinning off into the landscape. Gysin would join them, his papers torn up, thrown off the train into a lethal maze of shining steel tracks and 'one-eyed express trains like Cyclops.'[34] He made it to Montreal, where his mother had arranged a third-class passage on the *Empress of Britain*. Landing at Southampton at midnight one week later, he was greeted by a chauffeur in the headmaster's Daimler, who said, 'late again, Sir. You'll catch it.' Brion laughed, glad to be called 'Sir.' Boys at Downside used to complain of homesickness but Brion preferred life in the dormitory. He never returned to Edmonton from what he called his 'glorious adventure.' Stella was hurt by his decision, and over time her feelings turned into a sense of abandonment. But her friend, Marion Wilson, understood. Brion was an artist, and 'in those days being an artist in Edmonton was about as far out as you could get. It was a small, conservative town.'[35] To Gysin, 'the real world was out there in Europe, waiting for me, for Me.'[36]

On 10 January 1966, while Brion was writing *The Process*, Stella Gysin died in Vancouver. Earlier she had been put in a sanatorium. Now Brion had to go there to settle her affairs. Burroughs asked if it was 'the kind of place with brutal lesbian attendants?' and Gysin answered, 'Yes, I'm afraid it is that kind of place.'[37] With his mother's death, Gysin used *The Process* to return one last time to the long-forgotten places of his youth. Set in the Sahara, the novel is interrupted by evocations of the Canadian prairies, part imagined, part memory. 'He has been dreaming of snow cold as chloroform, winter air heady as ether,' Gysin once said of a character and himself.[38] When one of *The Process*'s central figures, Mya Himmer, remembers a childhood spent partly in Canada's open spaces, she is Brion recalling his own experiences. When Mya sits by a campfire in Hogs'back ravine, the shadows leaping into the woods behind her, she is 'back home.' Her aboriginal origins are also Gysin. He believed he was born with the wrong skin colour, at one point admitting, 'I have never accepted the colour or texture of my oatmealy freckled skin,' and dismissing his complexion as 'bad packaging.'[39] Nostalgia for Mounties in their scarlet tunics and Scottish Hudson's Bay Company factors aside, Gysin's sympathies in the book lie not with the dominant culture but with Alberta's downtrodden Indian tribes. His anger at their humiliating treatment is that of a witness, and he vividly describes the appalling consequences. One character is found 'half-starving and covered with lice . . . the only member of his tribe left alive. All the rest of the Bloods had frozen to death in their cabins . . . been eaten by their own sled-dogs . . . mangled by their own bear traps . . . or they killed each other with axes . . . over a bottle of whisky in a motel.'[40] This is young Brion, returning to his stepfather's reservation.

Each of the central characters in *The Process* is Brion, and yet none of them is. The novel is a cut-up of memory and pure invention. In an allusion to experiments with 'sacred-mushrooms' possessing hallucinogenic properties, Mya Himmer declares, 'Oh, I've been on *trips* in my childhood . . . such trips!' She had learned about the mushrooms from a book at the public library in Edmonton. 'Right from the start of high school, when I first took chemistry, I knew at *once* that chemistry would always be my love!,' she says. As a student at St Joseph's High School, Gysin failed Grade 11 chemistry, receiving a final grade of 33 per cent.[41] In the novel, he combined his own adult hallucinogenic experiences in Tangier—Burroughs's Interzone, Gysin's 'Wild West of the Spirit'—with a childhood recognition that 'I was "other-directed," I think . . . from the start.' The one good thing Gysin remembered about his early years in Canada was the wild open spaces. The 'trips' in *The Process* were taken across the landscapes of memory and the imagery is recognizably western Canadian—the Northern Lights, the smell of pine, the beds of muskeg, but most of all the bald prairie. 'I had all the flat places of Earth in my memory . . . snow fields behind me . . . Asian steppe . . . chains of deserts ringing the planet.'[42] ∾

FRANK PIKE, BANKER AND POET

Frank Pike with his dog, Laddie, 1942.
(COURTESY PIKE FAMILY)

odney Pike was born in Vancouver but grew up in Edmonton, where he married Margaret Sutton and raised four children. In 1915 his father, Frank Pike, had come to Edmonton as manager of the Merchant Bank of Canada (later the Bank of Montreal). By the 1920s Frank was one of the city's most prominent citizens. As bank manager, he entertained visiting investors, actors, and dignitaries. In the community, he was active on the Board of Trade, in the Kiwanis, and as a supporter of the University of Alberta. With his friends, he played bridge—in a group known as the Murderers Club—and hunted. In private and with his family, he indulged his passion for poetry and gardening.

This intimate biography reveals a little known side of Edmonton society, where formal dining, servants, golfing with the lieutenant governor, and weekly evenings at the Macdonald Hotel were an accustomed part of life. Like his father, Rodney Pike has been active in community and university affairs. Now retired, he is a member of a seniors' writing group. His stories are about his early days in Edmonton and his life in the navy.

My father, Frank Pike, was the manager of the Merchants Bank in Edmonton from 1915 to 1922. When Merchants was taken over by the Bank of Montreal, father served as manager of the main branch on Jasper Avenue until his retirement in 1942. I have a portrait taken by Yousuf Karsh, the famous photographer, of my father sitting at his desk. Just as Karsh was about to snap his shutter he paused and said, 'Mr. Pike, I am short of cash. I wonder if you could lend me $10,000.' Snap! 'Thank you that's perfect.' The story of my father's life provides an interesting 'snapshot' of aspects of the business and social life of Edmonton during the first half of the twentieth century.[1]

Father was born in 1878 in Carbonear, Newfoundland, to Captain James Pike and Susanna (née Taylor). He had two brothers, Jim and Fred, and a sister, Maizie. The house in which he was born is now a heritage house because, under a flat grave stone in the backyard, is reputedly buried an Irish princess, the mother of the first Pike born in Newfoundland and the wife of Gilbert Pike, the first lieutenant of Peter Easton, the famous pirate of Elizabethan times. At the end of the nineteenth century the glorious days of the square riggers were over and Newfoundlanders were experiencing hard times. In 1898, promising his mother that he would not take a drink until he returned—Newfoundlanders have a reputation as rum drinkers—my father, with his two brothers, became the first of a long line of seafarers in the family to give up the sea and seek their fortune in Canada.

Father set out for Montreal, carrying with him a letter of recommendation from J.L. Robinson, the colonial secretary of Newfoundland, attesting to his honesty, trustworthiness, and sobriety. There, he found work checking freight car doors in the railway yards as an employee of the Grand Trunk Railway. Shortly after, he apprenticed with the Merchants Bank of Canada in Port Renfrew, Ontario, and was sent out to Portage la Prairie, Manitoba, where he roomed with a young lawyer, Arthur Meighen, later prime minister of Canada. Meighen was also an authority on Shakespeare, and he may have influenced my father in his love of poetry and good literature.

Father had a bound collection of his favourite poems and he recited them at every opportunity. Some of the poems were once studied in school; others were picked out of magazines and newspapers. As can be expected from his heritage, many of his favourites had to do with the sea and the navy. The collection suggests that he believed history was made by daring heroes. He came West not long after Rogers discovered the pass for the CPR and before bush pilots like Punch Dickins, Wop May, and Leigh Brintnell opened up the North. He must have felt that the Elizabethan spirit of adventure was still necessary to develop the West. One poem he often quoted was 'The Adventurers':

They sit at home and they dream and dally
Raking the embers of long dead years
But ye go down to the haunted valley
Light hearted pioneers.
They have forgotten they ever were young
They hear your song with an unknown tongue
But the flame of God through your spirit stirs
Adventurers. Oh, Adventurers.

In 1902 father was transferred to Wetaskiwin, where he roomed over P. Burn's Butcher Store with another young banker, Bob Dinning, later a western leader and chairman of the board of the big conglomerate that P. Burns grew into—Burns Foods.[2] In Wetaskiwin, father began courting Georgia West, the daughter of John Sackville West and Harriet (née McFarlane). They had left Prince Edward Island and opened a store in Wetaskiwin in 1891, the same year the Calgary and Edmonton Railway reached that town. My mother was then nine and she had two brothers, Sackville and Girard, and a sister, Hope. I believe the bank boys were not allowed to marry until they earned what the Bank considered sufficient income to support a wife, and my father and mother did not marry for several years.

What an adventure for a young banker in the West at the beginning of the century! As settlers poured in, the demand for land increased. Railways spread out like spider webs. The steam engines had to stop for water and coal, and red grain elevators were built every six miles, within easy hauling range for a horse and grain wagon. Some of these stops grew into hamlets and others quickly expanded into towns and required banking services. Bob Dinning, I remember, had a story about setting up shop with my father in a hotel, I think it was in Daysland, and using a plank as a counter for making loans and taking deposits. That night they slept in a room above their temporary banking facilities, and, having taken in some money, they kept a revolver by the bed. In the middle of the night they thought they heard someone below and cautiously went down the stairs in the dark, clutching the revolver. As their eyes became accustomed to the dark, a big black form appeared and one of them—they could never agree which one—fired the revolver at it. When they regained their composure and got a lamp lit, they

discovered they had shot a hole in Bob's coonskin coat that had been hanging on a hook.

In 1905, the year Alberta became a province, my father rode out along the right of way of the railway that was opening to the east of Wetaskiwin. He had money in his saddle bags to start a branch of the bank in what was to become the town of Camrose. Thanks partly to my father's memory for poems, he was soon in demand as a speaker and master of ceremonies. A news clipping from the *Camrose Mail* of 19 December 1906 reports on his participation in a popular debate, 'Resolved that Woman's Suffrage is Desirable,' that was staged in the Methodist Church before a crowded and enthusiastic audience. According to the *Mail*, my father's side won, arguing that: 'God and Nature intended that man should be the protector and provider and that women should be the comforter and helpmate, and that women in demanding the franchise, demand that they shall be their own protectors and providers and are usurping the rights and places of their husbands and brothers and sons.' Later, father became a good friend of Nellie McClung. No doubt he had his tongue in his cheek during the debate, but he always seemed to have a gallant attitude towards women. I can remember him reciting from Owen Meredith's 'Lucille':

The world is a nettle, disturb it, it stings
Grasp it firmly it stings not
A woman is too slight a thing
To trample this world without feeling its sting

It's hard to conceive that at that time the pioneer women who had so much to do with building the west were still classed in law as 'non persons.'

In Camrose, my father founded the Agricultural Society, the Chamber of Commerce, and the Canadian Club, which had its own building. In 1910 the Merchant Bank put up a brick building on Camrose's main street across from the CPR station (today, there is a brass commemorative plaque on its side). That was the year my father married my mother and they set up housekeeping over the bank. The next year he was transferred to Saskatoon and then to Vancouver, where he managed the Hastings Street Branch. The Merchants Bank provided a home at 1663 Burnaby Street, where I was born on 21 March 1912. Three years later, in May 1915, he was again transferred, to Edmonton.

In 1915 there must have been many bad loans in the Edmonton Branch of the Merchants Bank. The city's booming economy, marked by the amalgamation with Strathcona and the completion of such landmarks as the

High Level Bridge, the Tegler Building, and the Macleod Building, had gone bust a couple of years earlier. Lots reverted to the city for taxes and for years the centre of Edmonton was made up of fields and bush. My father did not like what he saw and asked to be returned to Vancouver. His request was not granted by the general nanager who wrote in July 1915 explaining what the bank expected of its young managers:

> I want you to devote yourself to the Edmonton office closely and particularly I do not think I will send you back to Vancouver.
>
> Personal inclinations cannot always go hand in hand with the best interests of the bank.
>
> What we want is the cultivation of energy, firmness and the capacity to see straight, stripping proposals of side issues, converging on the heart of things. This is the business of the banker, with as much goodwill and manners thrown in as each particular situation calls for.
>
> I know perfectly well I am not sending you to an easy job. Some of our men, having made a little money have become softer and easy going; it has taken the ambition out of them. You have in you to do good service for the Bank and in this direction I want to use you.

My father accepted his fate. In the coming years he did not make too many bad loans. He also learned to turn down, with goodwill, prospective borrowers who had insufficient resources to back their loans. One old-timer told me he got turned down for a loan and came out with a poem instead. Others told me they got their start because he took a chance on them.

Bankers' salaries were modest even for those times, but to enable them to attract the wealthier clients and create good will for the bank the perks were good. In the bank building, like a small Greek temple, on the corner of 100A Street and Jasper Avenue, my father had a large wood-panelled office with a fireplace. He was also provided with a large three-storey yellow stucco house overlooking the river valley on Victoria Avenue and 118 Street and memberships in the Edmonton Club, Edmonton Golf and Country Club, Mayfair Golf Club, Glenora Skating Club, Granite Curling Club, and Edmonton Saddle Club.

Community activity was expected by the bank, which suited my father's inclinations, and he became a very active community worker. He promoted Edmonton as a vice-president of the Board of Trade and as an early shareholder in the Edmonton Exhibition Association. He watched over the city's finances as chairman of the Sinking Fund Board. Critical of government spending and municipal misman-agement, he helped persuade the mayor and council to hire a city manager, who turned out to be a friend of my father's. Much in demand as a public speaker, my father received plenty of newspaper coverage. His friends John Imrie, the publisher of the *Edmonton Journal*, and Balmer Watt, the editor, reported some of his talks verbatim and even made some the subjects of editorials. Father was also chairman of a committee that raised money to build the Memorial Hall for returning veterans. I remember when the Prince of Wales came to Edmonton in 1919 for the opening of the Memorial Hall, my father sported a silk top hat. The roof of the Overland Ninety was too low to wear the hat in the car, however, so when the prince went by my father stuck his head out and put on the hat. Father always seemed to be raising money, whether it was for the Salvation Army or for a blind boy who had been kicked by a horse.

In 1919, when the Calgary Kiwanis came to Edmonton to recruit members for an Edmonton club, my father was impressed by the calibre of the recruits. He joined the Edmonton Kiwanis and ended up as the first president. The national motto of the Kiwanis Club is 'We Build,' but my father set out his own idea of what the objectives of the Club should be. The *Journal* ran what you might call his creed:

THE THINGS THAT COUNT
(By President Frank Pike)

In days of old, Ponce de Leon and his followers set sail for the Western Seas, in search of the Fountain of Youth, little realizing that all that was necessary for the rejuvenation of man and the deferring of old age, was to join a Kiwanis Club, where, with an ever-widening circle of friendship, a man is given an opportunity of getting away from the lone trails of selfishness and exclusiveness, and on to life's broad highway, where he can rub shoulder to shoulder with his fellowmen and get the right perspective of the important things in life. . . .

When considering nominations for membership in our Club, we are not much interested in a man's wealth or social position, his religious or political views, providing he is a good citizen of undoubted integrity, who believes in his God and is loyal to his Country, to his Flag, and to the great British Empire.

We recognize the importance of getting as far away as possible from bigotry and narrow-mindedness, and we look for, and expect from our members a broad spirit of magnanimity and good-will.

We believe it is entirely a matter of a man's own personal opinion, and no concern of ours, whether he likes his beverages mildly flavored, even as low as two percent, or perhaps a little stronger concoction; whether he risks a dollar occasionally on a pari-mutuel machine, or raises the ante with a four card flush, providing he is a good loser, is temperate in all things, and never guilty of conduct unbecoming a gentleman. These are the things that count. The other matters are comparatively unimportant.

We preach no pious platitudes. There is, to some extent, a growing spirit of artificiality and hypocrisy abroad in the land, which is entirely at variance with our rugged, wholesome, Western character. Hypocrisy is the unpardonable sin.

The Kiwanis Club strongly emphasizes the importance of 'Playing the game,' in our business, professional, social, and personal lives. We know what it means; it is not always easy.

In a word, our motto is 'Play up school, and Play the game!'

After the structured hierarchy, expected proper marks of respect, and obedience due the general manager within the bank, membership in a service club where members called themselves by their first names must have been a welcome change.

In 1919, as the fear of Bolshevism spread through the western world following the Russian Revolution, headlines in the *Edmonton Journal* read 'Kiwanis will assert loyalty at all meetings,' while a subtitle stated 'National Anthem will be sung at all Gatherings and Flag displayed.' The local club pledged to study and support 'our British and Canadian traditions and institutions.' I do not know what was accomplished in this regard, but the club did stage Gilbert and Sullivan plays in the new Empire Theatre to raise money for a home for neglected children. My father helped raise funds and, together with his chief banking competitor, G.R.F. Kirkpatrick of the Imperial Bank of Canada, even played minor roles in the plays. They took their roles very seriously.

Regular church attendance was expected of bank managers, but my father failed the test. I do not know to which church my grandparents belonged in Newfoundland. My father did not openly express his faith. We did not say grace at meals. My mother taught me to say my prayers before going to sleep. Father began attending church more regularly after Reverend Hugh McLeod came to Robertson United Church and recited poetry in his sermons. He even organised a men's club and invited prominent citizens to speak about famous people in history. McLeod was delighted to have the husbands take an interest in the church and said to my father, 'You are not what we would describe as a holy man, but you're doing a good service to the church.' I think the religious group for which my father had the most respect was the Salvation Army. He remembered the work it had done in Newfoundland, and when I was a little boy he would take me downtown to listen to the bands play on the street corners.

For their most senior managers, banks sometimes provided substantial homes so that they could entertain important customers and visiting members of the elite. Here, Frank Pike's home at 10242 Connaught Drive provided by the Bank of Montreal. The house became an important centre for hosting Edmonton's social elite. (COURTESY PIKE FAMILY)

For relaxation with friends my father played bridge and poker. He and some friends (Bob Dinning, chairman of the board of Burns Foods; S.W. Field, lawyer; R.K. Gordon, professor of English; H.R. Milner, K.C., chairman of the board of Canadian Utilities; S.W. McQuaig, lawyer; J.G. Nickerson, bank manager; N.C. Pitcher, dean of Mining; A.C. Rankin, dean of Medicine; G.H. Steer, K.C., lawyer; Edouard Sonet, professor of French; C.W.H. Scott, heart specialist; E.D.C. Thomson, accountant; J.M. Taylor and Hugh Pearson, Taylor & Pearson; Egerton Pope, professor of medicine; Balmer Watt, editor of the *Journal*; Bob McLaughlan, lawyer; W.D. Ferris, physician) formed the Murderers Club, so named because they murdered bridge. They took turns holding the meetings at each other's homes. They tried to outdo one another and had a wonderful woman named Florrie in to help with the meals. They wore dinner jackets. Father also belonged to a poker club composed of Walter Pitfield, John Dobell, and John Calaghan, general manager of Northern Alberta Railways. Calaghan was a bachelor and lived in the Macdonald Hotel. They played in his suite and the hotel chef outdid himself with the meals he provided. My father would come home and make our mouths water with his descriptions of such things as pheasant under glass.

In 1922 the Merchants Bank was amalgamated with the Bank of Montreal. The Edmonton Branch, under seven years of my father's management, seemed to have made a profit and he was promoted to take over the main branch of the Bank of Montreal at the corner of Jasper Avenue and 101 Street (to make sure he got the job he had letters of recommendation from people like Arthur Sifton, former premier of the province and then in the federal Cabinet, the attorney general, the chief justice, and John Brownlee, a future premier of the province—the bank was after government business and was naturally influenced by the opinion of its customers). Ensconced in his corner office, you might say he became a fixture of the life of Edmonton for the next twenty years.

The Bank of Montreal was equally generous with its perks. We moved to a house on Connaught Drive on Groat Ravine and then farther along the drive to 10242, at the time a bare, three-storey brick house with a veranda on the front and another on the side. When my father later had a chance of moving into a still larger house on Victoria Avenue between 116 and 117 streets (the bank had apparently acquired a number of properties as a result of the pre-World War I bust), he convinced the bank instead to invest in a weed-filled vacant lot next to 10242 for a garden.

This prize rock for Frank Pike's garden came from the 'dismantled wall of old Fort Prince of Wales on the mouth of the Churchill River.' (COURTESY PIKE FAMILY)

My father loved his gardens. The Dunne brothers who had planted the garden at Government House were engaged to landscape the new lot. A grass tennis court was seeded and large spruce trees were brought in from an old home on Capitol Hill and planted all around both lots, spaced far enough apart so they could fill out and with white birch planted in between in the meantime. Father never stopped planting or moving trees—his friend, Norman Pitcher, suggested he should put his trees on rollers so they would be easier to move. Later my father got a real old English gardener named Downie. Hops were planted at the end of the veranda and they provided a cool, shady place to sit after they grew. All along the sides of the veranda, beds were built up for roses, gladioli, and dahlias, and every spring boxes of annuals were brought in.

Father's pride and joy, however, was his rock garden and lily pool. Whenever we went for a drive we picked up rocks for the garden—one time we got in trouble for taking them off the riprap on a culvert. The rock garden was filled with alpine plants and the pool with lily pads and goldfish. My father wanted to have a waterfall at the top, but the bank drew the line at the expense of installing the plumbing. When he had visitors he wanted to impress, father would have Downie hide behind the trees at the top of the rock garden with the hose. Father's prize rock was a piece from the dismantled wall of old Fort Prince of Wales on the mouth of the Churchill River, the terminus of the Hudson Bay Railway. Father had been invited to go in a private car with W.A. Brown, superintendent, Western Division, Canadian National Railway, and John Calaghan to the opening of the new grain terminal. There, he had persuaded a teamster to haul the rock across the tracks and into the private car for transport back to Edmonton. When Major Ashley Cooper, the thirtieth governor of the Hudson's Bay Company, and P.A. Chester, the general manager, visited Edmonton, my father got the 'waterfall' running and had a ceremony placing the rock in the garden. His garden won many prizes.

As a western bank manager, father played a role in helping to attract capital and to create goodwill by entertaining important visitors from Britain, France, and eastern Canada. Sir Frederick Williams-Taylor, the general manager of the Bank of Montreal, who had been knighted for his achievements in attracting British investment to Canada while he was the bank's representative in England (and no doubt for a generous contribution to the Conservative party), would detail his expectations in formal letters written on excellent quality stationary and addressed to 'Dear Mr. Pike' rather than 'Dear Frank.'

> You will presently have a call from Lord Cranworth and I have told him that you will be good enough to assist him in making arrangements for duck shooting.
>
> He and Lady Cranworth and Mr. Banks Senior will arrive in Edmonton on the twenty-eighth and you will be good enough to see that rooms with bath are engaged in advance.
>
> He and his wife are very good golfers, so that if the season is not too late perhaps they would like a game.
>
> You will find them most charming people, and if you put yourself out as a guide, counselor and friend while they are in your neighbourhood, it will be highly appreciated by them.

Williams-Taylor added a postscript: 'The Lieutenant Governor would probably like to know of their arrival and perhaps might like to dine with them.' I am sure my father had no trouble arranging a duck shoot. In the winter our upper back porch was covered with ducks and prairie chickens. My father was not that great a golfer and seemed to play mostly with two clubs, a putter and a jigger, but he probably arranged for someone like Tommy Morrison at the Mayfair to get some better golfers from among the lieutenant-governor's best friends.

Williams-Taylor also travelled like royalty. When he and Lady Taylor planned a visit, the bank's western superintendent wrote, explaining the detailed arrangements my father was to make. 'Reserve two bedrooms and two baths and a sitting room at the Macdonald Hotel, flowers to be put in both the bedroom and the sitting room, a decanter of Scotch whiskey with ice and soda water.' Sir Frederick wished to avoid a large dinner party and preferred dining with a few 'representative' men—the lieutenant-governor, the premier, the president of the university, the publisher of the *Edmonton Journal*, the chief justice, and some of the bank's best customers, like John Gillespie of the Gillespie Grain Company. The western superintendent even explained how the place cards were to be filled out and the seating arrangements. Taking the initiative, my father invited some of his 'not so important friends'—as was his usual practice. His arrangements pleased Sir Frederick and the next year father was asked to propose the toast to the bank at its annual general meeting in Montreal—quite a compliment to my father, a 'Westerner.' I wonder at the thoughts of the would-be sailor who had left Carbonear, Newfoundland, not so many years before.

In those days, a banker's wife really had a full-time job because important customers and visitors were often entertained in the banker's home. My mother not only knew a lot more about harnessing the horses than my father but also had learned how to cook from her mother and how to run a household at a ladies' finishing school in Toronto. My mother always had a maid; over the years many of them were Scottish girls who had immigrated to Canada and gone into service as part of the bargain to pay their way. Our maids lived on the third floor and were allowed out on Thursday afternoons. There were bells arranged strategically around the house to summon them. We also had an Irish washerwoman, a gardener, and a Scottish handy man. For larger affairs, special staff was brought in, and Florrie became a regular member of the establishment.

I was allowed to participate in these affairs so long as I observed the rule 'that children are to be seen and not heard.' I can remember parties for a visiting opera company, for the actor Sir John Martin Harvey, for Sir Hubert Wilkinson, and for a charming lady, la Marquise des Brontes, who owned a champagne company. Two wealthy American visitors became close friends, John Bowditch, who became a partner in the Kleskun Ranch, a Peace country cattle ranch in which my father had shares, and Curtis Munson, who lived in Edmonton six months of the year to manage his coal mine on the Coal Branch. Father always used these occasions to entertain his friends. He served cocktails although he did not drink them himself (he had kept his promise to his mother and had not taken a drink until he returned to Carbonear with his new bride in 1911, after which he drank moderately, enjoying vintage wines). I can still smell the dry martinis he made in the butler's pantry. He would chop a chunk of ice off the large block in the ice box, put it into a bowl, pour gin over it with a dash of vermouth, and then pour the mixture, undiluted by melting ice, into the cocktail shaker. The meals were served in separate courses with different wine glasses for each course, white wine with the soup, red wine—usually Burgundy—with the rare roast beef, and sometimes champagne with the dessert. The women would retire to the living room for coffee in small demitasse cups, and the men would go to the den for brandy and Havana cigars. Looking back, despite the Westerners' claim to have an unstructured society and disdain for the pompous superior Englishmen, successful Westerners emulated that way of life.

Under my father's management, the Bank of Montreal made good profits through the 1920s.[3] Each year George Riach, the proprietor of the Motordome, would go into my father's office, take his car keys, and give him the keys to a new Chrysler car. In those days Chrysler numbers indicated maximum miles per hour. We got up to a big Chrysler 77 with a 5 speed transmission.

Then, in 1929, the stock market crashed and things started to dry up on the prairies. Many farmers could not pay their debts and the monetary and bank systems came under a considerable amount of criticism, particularly when Social Credit came into government. Jackson Dodds, who was then the general manager of the bank, spent many hours before a federal banking commission explaining the banking system and my father arranged for him to meet the Alberta Social Credit Cabinet. No matter what the occasion, father quoted the inscription from the Boston Library: 'The Commonwealth required the education of the people as the safeguard of order and liberty.' In reaction to Social Credit, father preached 'that only education will counteract the pernicious fallacies and half-baked doctrines that we hear from many sincere but pedantic theorists who are stirring up class hatred and causing disunity.' I took political economy in the 1930s, and father got quite upset when I told him my professors taught that banks were not dependent on savings accounts but could create credits. He became even more upset when he discovered that his brother, Jim, was helping write speeches for the Social Crediters. Solomon, the Indian workman who lived at the end of Moonlight Bay and was helping father plant trees at our cottage at Kapasiwin, could not be depended on either.

And while they planted trees he would ask my father what he thought of Social Credit . . . Every now and then he would put the shovel down and exclaim, 'Jesus Christ, Frank, twenty-five dollars a month for everyone.'

He and my father became friends. He called my father 'Big Pike' or 'Frank.' Like just about everyone else, Solomon listened to Social Credit leader William Aberhart's Sunday broadcasts, and while they planted trees he would ask my father what he thought of Social Credit. He had a lot of children. Every now and then he would put the shovel down and exclaim, 'Jesus Christ, Frank, twenty-five dollars a month for everyone.'

My father's faith in education made him a great supporter of the University of Alberta. In response to the criticisms voiced by some Edmonton businessmen of provincial government spending in this area, father had formed a group called the 'Friends of the University,' creating a structure within which businessmen without university degrees could meet with university professors and learn something about the role of a university. In October 1935 he was elected honorary president of the Faculty Club and invited to give a short address, then introduce the new premier and minister of education, Aberhart. The task was not easy when you consider that the banks had been the prime target of the Social Credit movement and that father was a staunch critic of Social Credit. He planned his speech carefully. To help overcome his own feelings of inferiority at not having a university education, he went down to the Mayfair Golf Club where many of the professors played and looked up their handicaps, finding that many were higher than his own. To avoid having to discuss the economic situation in front of Aberhart, he told the story about the policeman who, while guarding the High Level Bridge, saw a man about to jump over and asked why he contemplated suicide. The man replied, 'Economic problems,' so the policeman said, 'Come with me to the police station and we will talk it over for half an hour.' At the end of the time they returned to the High Level Bridge and they both jumped over. What father needed was a neutral topic. With some trepidation he chose to tell his audience about his collection of poetry. To get off to a good start with his critical audience he began with the poem, 'Northward,' written by Dr Broadus, the head of the English Department. No doubt some of the English professors questioned some of father's selections that night, but poetry was his tool and he always seemed to be able to find a poem that expressed a thought better than he could himself. Though a success on this occasion, sometimes his recitations backfired.

Dr Sonet, head of the French Department, was the chairman of a meeting of the Philosophical Society when a Mr Brockington gave a talk on humour. Sonet had asked my father to thank him. My father said, 'Mr. Brockington, in the language of your fellow country man, the Welsh poet, "a rainbow and a cuckoo song may never come together again," such a chairman and such a speaker may never come together again.' Mr Brockington rose, bowed and replied, 'On behalf of the cuckoo, I thank you.'

With the Great Depression, the moratorium the Social Credit government soon placed on debts, and its default on Alberta bonds, eastern financial institutions faced millions of dollars in potential losses. The 'Eastern Interests' sent out a man wearing a Homburg hat to tell off the provincial government and inform the farmers about the sanctity of contracts. His approach did not go over too well with hard hit farmers. My father suggested a different approach for the Bank of Montreal. He wrote to his general manager that he believed that 90 per cent of westerners were honest and would repay their debts when things improved, given half a chance. He also persuaded the 'East' to hire Bob Dinning to go around and quietly explain to people that one cannot just default on debts and expect to borrow money in the future and that the bond default would ruin the province's credit standing. He also tried to sell the creditors on providing seed grain, and making other debt adjustments, if they didn't want to lose their investment altogether. He was able to nurse many of his mixed farmer customers through the depression.[4]

By the late 1930s, the economy in Alberta was starting to improve but the situation in Europe was looking ominous with the rise of Hitler and Mussolini. When Mr Chamberlain came back from Munich and boasted that there would be 'peace in our time,' my father sent him a letter of congratulations. Peace was not to be, however, and I was called up to the navy in September of 1939.

During the war my father and I developed our own code for communicating with one another. Remember the posters we had then, 'Careless Talk Costs Lives,' and the warnings that the movement of His Majesty's ships was Hush! Hush! I had to be careful about what I wrote to him because he would read my letters to all his friends. Before I went off in the navy, father had his secretary prepare me copies of his poems. I used them as a code to tell my father where we were. For example when we were up in the

Miches looking for U-boats off Scapa Flow, I picked out the 'Canadian Boat Song' (the author is unknown but it was originally published in *Blackwoods Magazine* in 1829):

From the lone sheilling of the misty island
Mountains divide us, and the waste of seas
Yet still the blood is strong, the heart is highland
And we in dreams behold the Hebrides

Despite my attempts to disguise our whereabouts my father read my letters to everyone up and down Jasper Avenue. Fortunately, with the time delay in the mail, the information was of no value to Donetz's U-boats if any spies were listening.

By the war years my father was close to retirement. His enthusiasm had switched from community involvement to his cottage, his garden, and his friends in the Murderers Club and Poker Club. He resisted retirement, however, and pleaded to stay on with the bank. He tried many different tactics—to act as an advisor to the bank, to be a plenipotentiary extra-ordinary to keep the Alberta Cabinet on the right track, to entertain visiting dignitaries—but all to no avail. Mr Dodds wrote that they had several managers in their forties ready to move up and that there was only one man in the whole organisation older than my father. The best he could do was to get his retirement postponed from June to September 1941. In October 1941, 102 customers and friends put on a dinner in his honour at the Macdonald Hotel. His old friend, Dinning, spoke of his kindness of heart, buoyancy of spirit, and unfailing courtesy and respect for all his customers. The Murderers Club presented him with a silver chafing dish engraved with the names of the those still living.

In 1945 he moved to Victoria where he could garden all year round, taking the rock from the old Fort Prince of Wales with him. He missed Edmonton and would often go to the Empress Hotel and the Union Club looking for old western friends. When he died, at his request, I had the rock engraved as his flat headstone in the Royal Oak cemetery where his grave overlooks the sea: 'Frank Pike, Born June 1878, Died June 1947, "He lived in between." ' ∾

SLOPES AND SHAFTS

The James Stewart Mine Co. showing the slope entrance, trestle, miners, mine cars, coal chute, and the barge into which the coal was gravity loaded, 1903. (PAA B.1626)

The coal industry and railways developed side by side in Canada. If railways were the engine of progress, coal fired that engine. Thus, when the CPR built through Calgary and southern Alberta in the 1880s, coal mining became an important industry in Lethbridge and the Crowsnest Pass. The new transcontinental railways that passed through Edmonton in the first decade of the twentieth century encouraged coal mining farther north, in the Coal Branch, and at Jasper. It was at this time, for instance, that the companies that eventually amalgamated to form Edmonton's Luscar Ltd. staked claims on their first mines. Edmonton also had its mines.

Europeans started burning the coal that could be found locally along the banks of the North Saskatchewan in the late eighteenth century. By the early twentieth century there were

more than two dozen mines within the city. Edmonton coal heated many of the city's homes and public buildings. The industry was an important contributor to the local economy, employing men and buying from local merchants. As Geoff Ironside tells us, however, the industry may have had its greatest impact not on the city's economy but on 'the development of the built-up-city'—that is on the stability of some of its river banks and major streets, including the land under the Convention Centre. A geographer at the University of Alberta since 1963, Ironside researches regional and rural development in hinterland areas.

RECOGNITION AND USE OF RESOURCES OCCURS WHEN humans first inhabit an environment. In what became central Alberta, Indian settlements made use of vegetation and animal resources. Later, the establishment of sedentary settlement in the area, represented by the fur trade forts and the houses, businesses, and homesteads around them, encouraged the use of a wider range of local resources. There was a gradual expansion of gardens, homestead farming, and coal mining first in the river valley and then farther away. Though less well known than farming, coal mining was a necessary condition of permanent settlement in Edmonton, providing a cheap and efficient source of energy. Initially, the coal resource was extracted through the development of the slopes, drifts or 'gopher hole' coal mining. Later, with changes in technology and the market place, larger commercial shaft coal mines appeared. The Edmonton coal industry suffered from several disabilities in competition with coal from other areas, but it was the physical effects upon the development of the built-up city that eventually curtailed the economic contribution of the industry to the local economy.[1]

The coal deposits of the North Saskatchewan district were well known by the Indians as 'burning rocks,' so named because exposed seams sometimes were ignited through spontaneous combustion or by grass and forest fires. The Indians did not recognize coal as an energy resource and were astonished when Europeans began to use it in their own fires. The first white person to observe coal (brought downstream by the river) was Edward Umfreville, who was in charge of the North West Company's western-most post on the North Saskatchewan river in 1786.[2] The first definite reference to the use of coal occurs in the Edmonton House Journal for 1 October 1798 which states that a party had collected a boat load of coal from sand bars for the use of the blacksmith.[3] Colin Robertson, Factor of Edmonton House in 1823, and John Rowand, Chief Factor in 1824, mentioned the coal seams in the area when they reported to the Hudson's Bay Committee in London, England. Acknowledging the significance of coal deposits for the future, Donald H. Smith, Chief Commissioner of Hudson's Bay Company (HBC), later wrote Richard Hardisty, Chief Factor of Edmonton House: 'I trust you have secured for the Company some of the best coal deposits at and near Edmonton or other parts where it exists. This I consider to be of importance and if not already done you ought to do so without delay.'[4] In the selection of land holdings the HBC would receive as compensation for rights ceded to the Canadian Government in 1869, coal was clearly a major guideline. Yet if the impor-

tance of coal was recognized, the resource itself was little used until after 1874 when John Walter brought a stove to Edmonton capable of burning coal, thus allowing its use for cooking and heating. The tedious chore of cutting firewood for the winter continued until such stoves became commonplace.

Commercial mining in Edmonton probably started between 1875 and 1880. In December 1880 the Edmonton Bulletin began publication and recorded that three or four small mines were operating that winter. These were small untimbered slope mines run in 50 to 100 feet on the river bank and allowed to collapse when abandoned. They provided coal for the steamer Lily, a fifty-horse-power steam saw, and a grist mill under contract to the HBC.[5] The coal mined in 1880–81 came mainly from the south side of the river and was transported by sleigh across the river ice. In December 1881 William Humberstone developed a slope on the north bank and built a road up it so that coal could be hauled to customers in the town at any time. The scale of development of this early coal mining is suggested in a Bulletin editorial of 28 January 1882 (also see Figure 1).[6]

Six different coal drifts have been worked in a distance of about a mile and a half along the banks of the river on each side of the Fort. The furthest up is on Mr. Groat's property on the north side of the river, the coal from which was used by Dr. Verey and Ed McPherson last winter. The next is on the same side of the river . . . at the new steamboat landing. This never was worked much however, a little having been used in the Fort blacksmith shop—The third drift was opened last fall directly under the town by Mr. Humberstone and the coal from it is considered the best from any of the drifts near town . . . on the south side of the river . . . [Donald] Ross opened two drifts last winter having kept a gang of six men employed. Both the upper and lower seams were worked but although the coal of the lower seams was of a firmer quality than that of the upper one, it could not be worked to as good advantage on account of the seam dipping below the level of the river . . . The other two drifts were worked last winter to get coal for the H.B.C. steamers and are on opposite sides of a small creek on the south side of the river opposite the mill and were each carried in about 100 feet . . . Besides these there is a seam about four miles down the river which has been worked and the coal found to be of good quality.

In 1881 coal was expensive relative to firewood, but a ton of Edmonton sub-bituminous coal produced about 50 per cent more heat than a cord of wood.[7] It cost $4 per ton at the mine and $4.50 delivered. The Edmonton Milling Company was paying $1.50 per cord of wood delivered. Nevertheless, an extensive local market for coal was growing. As the distance travelled to timber supplies increased, the time taken to stock domestic and business timber piles also increased. With the development of early industries and, later, large institutional buildings, coal became the more efficient source of energy. Initially it was used for domestic cooking and heating, to provide power for saw and flour mills, to raise steam on the river boats, and by William Humberstone to fire a kiln for brick making. In response to market demand, more slopes were opened in the winters of 1882–83 and 1884–85. This increased competition temporarily forced the price down to $3 per ton delivered. In the winter of 1885–86, however, the price rose to $3.75, encouraging the HBC to mine its own coal from a seam almost directly below the fort. In 1886 production at a rate of approximately one ton per man day amounted to a total of about 1,200 tons from five mines within the town limits.[8] The Fraser and Company's saw mill took 300 tons, 100 tons was barged to Battleford, and the remainder was used in the town. The RCMP detachments at Edmonton took 75 tons in 1885–86 and 300 tons at Battleford in 1887.[9]

By 1889 the phase of slope mining was ending. By 1910 all of the slope mines between the High Level Bridge and 92 Street in Edmonton and Strathcona had been abandoned. Most had been located where a seam was exposed on the river bank. Many had lasted only a season. Some had been subject to flooding in shorter, milder winters, and many would collapse after abandonment, causing river bank slumping. Until the Dominion land surveys conducted in the late 1880s none of the settlers had title to land they claimed and on which slope mines were worked.

In 1889 Donald Ross initiated the first modern mining technique by digging an air shaft from his slope to the surface, thus turning it into, arguably, the first all season mine in the Edmonton area. Ross was typical of the early entrepreneurs in Edmonton who developed coal mines. They were all successful businessmen and most invested capital produced by cash flow in other businesses. Ross had originally panned gold and farmed on a lease from the HBC. He then sold his farm implements, stock, and part of his crop to the Company to pay off his debt of $3,900. 'In 3 weeks Ross had all his debts paid and $800 cash to his credit with the Hudson's Bay Company as well as part of the crop.'[10] He built a log house then and, with his hospitality 'overtaxed by miners,' decided to charge them 50 cents for meals. There was a market opportunity for accommodation and meals so he built the Edmonton

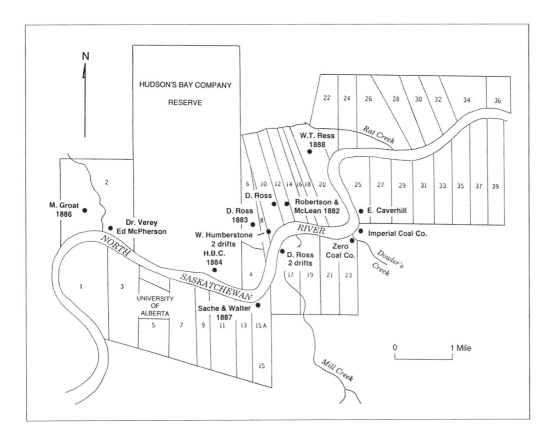

Figure 1. Some early coal mines of Edmonton 1880-1892.
(MICHAEL FISHER)

Hotel (and Feed Stables) in 1876, the second building out-side the Fort. In 1881 he opened two slope mines on the south bank of the river and in 1883 one under the present Holiday Inn on the north bank. His own hotel expanded three times and could advertise 'genuine coal fires for guests.'[11] It became an important public meeting place.[12]

The completion of the Calgary and Edmonton Railway in 1891 made possible the expansion of the number of mines, in particular shaft mines. Greater production became possible as mining ventilation, drainage, underground track, and mine cars were installed. Tipples were constructed, the Strathcona Coal Co. mine being typical. John Walters, boat builder and wholesale timber merchant, developed that mine near the south end of the present High Level Bridge in 1905. Premier Rutherford and W.E. Ross, a hardware merchant, were partners in the venture which unfortunately experienced the worst disaster in the history of Edmonton coal mining when fire killed six miners in 1907.[13]

At the beginning of this modern phase of shaft mining the industry became overdeveloped. In 1895–96 the price of coal delivered sank to $1 per ton. In that year 35 men were employed by 9 mines. The local market comprised a population of 1,670.[14] By 1908 there were 30 mines. With an expanding town, tenders could be offered by the mine operators to schools, the fire hall, and the general hospital. The city power plant, the University of Alberta, the Provincial Legislature Building, and the Macdonald Hotel all became large consumers. Mine output varied. Typical of a smaller operation, the Edmonton Penitentiary mine (1909–20) was worked by inmates and provided coal for prisons in Edmonton and St Albert. At first it was a slope mine but then a 250 foot shaft was sunk to the Clover Bar seam. During its years of operation it produced only 20,000 tons. But its successor, the privately operated Penn Mine Coal Company, produced in 1929 alone 17,200 tons of coal. Similarly the Humberstone mine at Clover Bar could produce 800 tons a day, employing 200 men.[15] The largest, longest operating mine was the Black Diamond, where the Strathcona Science Park is now located (Figure 2). It last-ed 49 years and produced three million tons or an estimat-ed 22 per cent of all the coal mined in Edmonton.[16]

As shaft mines developed, smaller operators were bought out by larger mines though profit margins were gen-erally low.[17] Output increased to a peak of 533,000 tons in 1920 but then started a gradual decline falling to 332,000 tons in 1931. The number of mines and their output decreased during the interwar years for several reasons. The nature of the coal mined, the failure to penetrate markets elsewhere, the decline in the local market after 1923 when natural gas became available, and the effects of mining subsidence on the infrastructure of a growing Edmonton all merit closer examination.

The coal was sub-bituminous, low in ash, and with ease of firing, but it burned too fast and was not suitably sized, being delivered in either large lumps or slack.[18] An advantage was a low sulphur content with no acid waste problem from old workings. The coal was satisfactory for domestic heating. But its burning qualities made it unsuitable for the locomotive market though station houses were supplied. Unfortunately, when exposed to weather it was prone to slacking or break-up as the moisture content decreased and oxidation occurred. These characteristics made it difficult to stockpile unless under cover, which led to shortages during severe winters.[19]

To resolve the problem of stockpiling, mine owners resorted to reducing production or even closing the mine in the summer. Men had to be let go, but they could find other work in that season in farming, construction, and transportation. Coal dealers waited until fall to place their orders with the mines. Unfortunately at that time of year there was competition for transport, particularly for railway cars, from grain shipments, limiting sale of coal to other provinces. Shipments to Saskatoon, for example, frequently took a month to arrive. Extensive, but largely unsuccessful, efforts were made by the coal mine owners to persuade customers, particularly local domestic consumers, to order their coal early and store it in their basements.[20]

The nature of the coal made it uncompetitive with the better quality mountain coals that became available after the completion of the Crowsnest Railway in 1898. Edmonton coal was about the same quality as the coals from the Drumheller and Lethbridge fields, but one central fact placed it at a disadvantage: the relative isolation of Edmonton and as a consequence the higher costs of delivery to markets elsewhere. Before the Calgary and Edmonton Railway reached the city in 1891 the only transportation available was by wagon or by river steamer, both unusable in certain seasons. With coal having such a low value to weight ratio, freight costs made wagon transport beyond the immediate area impossible. While attempts were made to reach downstream markets such as Battleford and Prince Albert, the North Saskatchewan River was never a truly navigable waterway because of its shallowness and sandbars. Typical was a report in 1882 of a flat boat shipment by Donald Ross to Battleford. It drew 25 inches of water when loaded with 50 tons of coal and 7000 feet of timber. Starting out on 19 July it arrived on

11 August 'with all the lumber and part of the coal she started with.'[21] Later, smaller barges carrying less coal were used, but freight rates were $12 per ton of coal.[22]

Trial shipments by rail to Calgary began immediately in 1891. On 2 August the *Bulletin* reported that D.C. Robertson shipped a car load from Ross's coal mine to the Calgary Cartage Company. Robertson's shipments by December were two car loads or 60 tons per week to Calgary. The freight rate to Calgary was $2.30 per ton in the 1891–92 winter. Coal sales increased as rail extensions developed into northern Alberta, Saskatchewan, Manitoba, and British Columbia. In 1923 a trial shipment was made to Ontario at $7 per ton delivered. Like Alberta coal in general, however, the delivery price of Edmonton coal was too high because of freight costs relative to other producers in or near the markets. By 1928 U.S. Pocahontas Coal from West Virginia was delivered to cellars in Toronto at $10.50 per ton, compared to $13.25 per ton for Alberta coal.[23] At no time were sales of Edmonton coal outside Alberta more than 25 per cent of output. This proportion was recorded in 1916 with total sales of 487,864 tons of which 75 per cent was sold in Alberta.[24]

The availability of natural gas from 1923 inevitably heralded a decline in the local market for coal. Initially, natural gas was vigorously opposed by the mine operators.

Figure 2. Major Historic Coal Mines. (MICHAEL FISHER)
The edge of the river valley and the line of geological section A-B (Figure 3) are shown.
Mine locations: 1. Beverly, 2. Black Diamond, 3. Old Bush, 4. New Bush, 5. Clover Bar, 6. Dawson, 7.Fraser-McKay, 8. New Humberstone, 9. Kent, 10. Marcus, 11. New Ottewell, 12. Penn, Chinook, 13. Premier, 14. Red Hot, 15. Standard, 16. Twin City, 17. Whitemud Creek, 18. Strathcona.

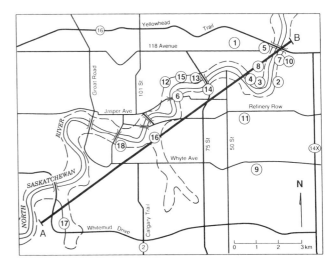

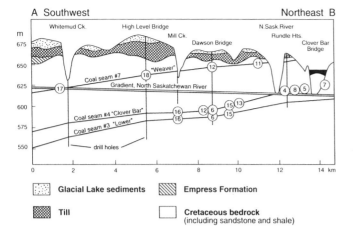

A Southwest   Northeast B

Figure 3. Geological Section A-B (see Figure 2) showing the three main seams and major coal mines. (MICHAEL FISHER)

Because of the importance of coal mining to the city economy, the city rejected offers from Northwestern Utilities Limited in 1924 and 1926 to supply gas to the city power plant. Gas was supplied from the Viking field, however, to south Edmonton and north Edmonton west of 99 Street. By 1927 out of 15,000 homes, 8,000 were using gas.[25] A resulting market loss of 150,000 tons was incurred by the mines, with all the summer coal trade eliminated. Through technical innovations and low prices, the coal operators maintained a reduced market share until the severe winter of 1942–43, when some public buildings were closed because of a lack of coal in the bins to heat them. Conversion to a more reliable fuel supply was thus encouraged and by 1961 there were virtually no households using coal.[26]

The key factor in closing the mines located within city limits, however, was their effect on the built environment of the city—on buildings, sidewalks, roads, water, and sewage lines. Figure 3 shows the geology of the 10 major coal seams. While some were discontinuous, several were up to three metres thick and dipped with sandstones and shales on average two metres per kilometre to the south west.[27] For the purposes of individual mines the seams were horizontal. Most of the coal mined was from three seams: Lower or No. 3, Clover Bar or No. 4, and Weaver or No. 7. Of 13 million tons produced in 100 years of local mining, 95 per cent came from the Clover Bar seam. The shallow unconsolidated overburden and the weak clays and shales of the Edmonton formation were a considerable advantage to the industry, most of the mine shafts being less than 200 feet deep. Mines used the room and pillar method which did not lend itself easily to mechanization. Roof falls in the main tunnels were common and strong

timbering was necessary. Rooms usually were allowed to collapse or 'cave' after being worked out, 100 to 200 tons being extracted from each room. In 1937 the Kent and Banner mines began using the more efficient longwall system of mining with face conveyors.[28] It was also used by the new Penn Mine at Carbondale[29] and in 1946 by Beverly Coal Company mine No. 1366. The problem with the longwall system was its dependence on the strength of the roof. The gain in coal extracted was offset by the extra timbering cost incurred. It did not prove to be a successful method of mining, therefore, in the Edmonton industry. Over the years, the consequence of the extensive use of the room and pillar method of mining was subsidence of the surface land of large areas of Edmonton as well as adjacent communities such as Beverly.

Two other important physical features of mining contributed to the impact of subsidence and slumping. One feature was the presence of water in the mines. While some early slopes were flooded because of the river rising in the spring, more often flooding was caused by meltwater percolating down through the clays and shales that were not good aquifers and accumulating in worked out areas or in adjacent old mines. Another feature was the composition of the clay. As early as 1858 the geologist James Hector of the Palliser Expedition, describing the coal seams stated: 'In the middle of the 6-foot seam, there occurs a layer 5 to 8 inches thick of magnesium static clay which works up into a lather like soap and is used by the women at the Fort for washing blankets.'[30] This clay was later found to be the montmorillonite which is now used as an active component in drilling muds for the oil industry.[31] Montmorillonite acts as a lubricating layer in water soaked strata and when cou-

Figure 4. The City Mines, 1930. (MICHAEL FISHER)

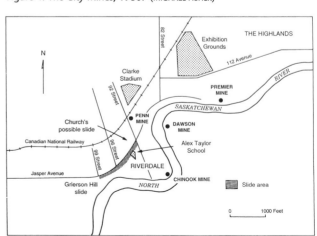

pled with subsidence can cause slumping such as has occurred historically in the case of the Grierson Hill area of the river bank between 95 and 98 streets.

As early as September 1899 the Edmonton Town Council became sufficiently concerned about subsidence and slumping to purchase all the coal rights on river lots 4 to 14 to end slope mining along the river bank and under the town.[32] But until evidence of extensive damage to city property had accumulated, subsequent City Councils were not concerned about ongoing mining subsidence. In 1923 a firm proposed mining a five foot seam 248 feet below the surface on either side of Jasper Avenue between 91 and 92 streets. The City engineers reported there was no danger to the surface.[33] Only five months later, however, in May 1923, the City prepared an appeal to the Province to prohibit mining under roads without permission from the Utilities Board. A rash of ruptured water mains and pavement breaks had alerted the City engineers to the costs of such mining for the City. Overall, coal companies were mining beneath 406 acres of city land with a further 327 acres possibly subject to future mining.[34] A City engineer had concluded that 7 miles of sewers, water mains, and services and 20 miles of city streets were liable to damage. An engineering study by Stirling-Drinnon-Pitcher in 1923 noted the possibility of a slide if all the coal south of Jasper Avenue were mined and stated that it would 'be inadvisable to extend public utilities under the Penitentiary Reserve or to erect buildings on the Reserve,'[35] an area of some 129 acres (located south of the CN tracks and the river) that included the present Exhibition grounds and Clarke Stadium (Figure 4).

Another engineering study by J.H.A. Church in 1926 again documented serious damage to public utilities.[36] Private property owners were suing the coal companies for damages and demanding that the City Council stop mining entirely. Since the City did not control mineral rights, it was powerless and efforts to persuade the Province to stop mining within urban limits again failed. By the fall of 1929 Riverdale residents had extensive property damage. Undermining of Jasper Avenue and 93 Street had caused water main breaks. The discovery of cracks in the walls of the final sedimentation basin at the number one sewage disposal plant had temporarily put the plant out of service. J.H.A. Church was appointed by the City as a consulting engineer and given the powers of an Inspector of Mines by the Province. He reported that undermining could lead to a river bank slide and that all buildings within 150 feet of the edge between 92 and 94 streets, including the Alex Taylor public school, were threatened. He was also the first to

mention the danger of gas leaks from gas lines strained by subsidence. Almost coincidentally with his warning, a home was severely damaged by a gas explosion. At this point the City went to court seeking damages and, again, to the provincial government to restrict mining in the city.

The Penn Mine and the Chinook Mine were most in legal dispute with the City. In an engineering report to the City Commissioner in 1930 Ronald Watson wrote:

> It is contended by the City that much damage to their property and interests have [*sic*] resulted from the operation of these two mines and that the City has been deprived by the actions of the Coal Companies of the natural support of the ground supporting their streets, lanes, water lines, sewers, pavements et cetera to which they are justly entitled, and have suffered thereby considerable loss and are still in receipt of continued suffering and loss from the same cause.[37]

The Penn Mine was working a 128 acre lease on the old Penitentiary property. The Chinook mine, owned also by the Penn Mine Company in Riverdale, was only 90 feet deep. Unfortunately, while jurisdiction over mining rested with the provincial government, the federal government owned the land on which the Dominion Penitentiary was located, preventing effective action. In 1931, both mines were finally closed by the Company because of legal action, public hostility, and the possibility that the City would no longer place contracts with them. Just over a year later, on 29 February 1932, the Urban Mining Act (Coal Mining Within City Limits) was proclaimed by the Province.

One remaining subsidence issue involved Grierson Hill, an area encompassing the old Humberstone Mine that extended 500 feet under the bank ending at Jasper Avenue. The worked out area totalled more than 100,000 square feet, providing a large area for water collection. Saturation of the clay subsoil caused recurrent slumping, damaging the road and threatening buildings near the edge of the riverbank. As early as 1901 slumping damaged seven buildings and the Humberstone mine (which operated until 1911). There were further problems in May 1910 when a whole block of houses facing on Grierson Road slid 30 feet down the hill.[38] In 1915 another 9 buildings were damaged. The Ross mine severely undercut the College Avenue School (now MacDonald Drive), which had to be demolished after it was abandoned in 1911.[39] In 1949 City Council decided to pave Grierson Hill Road. To reduce the slope at the east end, more fill was needed, and this work triggered a slide. To resolve the problem caused by a combination of the mined out areas of the Humberstone mine, water collection, and Hector's 'soapy clays,' Dean Hardy of the Faculty of Engineering at the University of Alberta recommended drainage of the old mine workings with wells and a gravity drainage tunnel.[40] Between 1953 and 1957 some three million gallons of water were pumped out. In addition, impermeable landfill to seal the surface finally stabilized the slope. Nevertheless, the later construction of the Convention Centre at the west end of the slide area required more than its weight removed during excavation of this river bank site to eliminate any remaining instability.

Generally within the city little evidence of past mining can now be found. The Light Rapid Transit tunneling occurred in the surface overburden. A small drift mine was found in the fall of 1988 by the city's crew while tunneling a 2.344 meter diameter sanitary sewer through the Capilano Ravine.[41] The mine fortunately coincided with the centre line of the tunnel and thus no problem arose. Several mine sites identified by surface slumping in Rundle Park were backfilled with filler grout in the early 1980s at the request of the Alberta Department of Environment.

The movement of the coal industry eastward to Ottewell, Beverly, and Clover Bar and south along the Whitemud Creek led to subsidence reports in these areas. Edmund Dale observes that 'Beverly was not suited to residential development . . . The land was pitted with subsidence from old coal workings, and was suited more to the development of parkland'.[42] The city annexed areas including the lower Whitemud Creek in 1912 and 1964. Subsequently, in 1971 subsidence problems under new homes occurred at 142 Street and 48 Avenue.[43] There were also 7 cave-ins during the spring of 1971 on fairways of the Highlands Golf course, the largest being 10 feet in diameter and 7 feet deep.[44]

The economic impact of the coal mining industry is much harder to unravel than the historical record of mines opening and closing and the subsequent physical damage to city buildings and infrastructure. There were Mining Commissioners' reports for Alberta in 1910 and 1925 and royal commissions on the Alberta coal mining industry in 1907 and 1935, but there were no specific studies of the impact of the industry on Edmonton. Therefore, we must rely on more sparse and sometimes subjective evidence.

While coal was expensive relative to wood during the slope mining years, it supplanted wood once appropriate stoves were acquired and provided welcome winter employment for many settlers who worked their homestead farms during the summers. If the harvest was late in the fall, the coal industry suffered from a shortage of labour. Gradually, as the city grew and as shaft mines appeared, coal allowed the heating and maintenance of large public institutional and commercial buildings. For example, by 1929 the Penn Mine Coal Company had contracted to supply 30 tons of coal a day to the University of Alberta central heating plant and about 25 tons per day to the Macdonald Hotel.[45] The Provincial Legislative building took 30 tons per day and the Tegler Building, 12 tons. City Council's appreciation of the significance of the coal mining industry to the city economy was manifested in the way the City placed coal orders. For example, in 1925 an $80,000 order for 30,000 tons of coal for the powerhouse was divided, with 20,000 tons purchased from the lowest bidder, a mine outside the Edmonton District, and 10,000 tons distributed among local mines.[46] The same policy applied to tenders to supply some 10,000 tons a year to the public and separate schools. By 1936 the city power plant required 95,000 tons of slack and 'mine run' (unscreened) coal annually. This need for coal gave the City some market clout and the Finance Committee recommended that the City should buy from any local operator who would meet the City price rather than contract with individual producers.

Perhaps the fullest, though questionable, estimate of the value of the industry to the City was provided in the *Bulletin* of 10 November 1922.[47] The coal mines of the Edmonton District were stated to be producing 12,000 tons a day and employing 3,600 men at an average daily wage of $5, for a payroll of $18,000 a day or more than $100,000 a week. Estimating an average value of $3.50 per ton on mine cars at the pit, the daily value of output was $40,000, or $250,000 a week. With rail freight of $1.50 per ton, the freight charge would be $100,000 a week to the rail companies. Overall, the coal industry was worth a million dollars every three weeks to the local economy. The mines included in these calculations were located on, or adjacent to, the main line of the national railways both east and west as well as within the city.[48] Unfortunately, what mars this account is the inaccurate data base used for the calculations. Sally Hamilton points out that the Mines Branch Report for 1923 recorded a labour force and daily coal output one-third of the estimates by the *Bulletin's* reporter.[49] Nevertheless, the employment totals are still impressive for a city with a population of about 60,000.

A further idea of the significance of an individual mine's contribution to the local economy is provided by the *Bulletin's* description of the Humberstone mine in 1912. Again it is not possible to verify the exact accuracy of the details. William Humberstone was perhaps the epitome of a successful pioneer developer of coal mines in Edmonton (the family business spans the history of mining in Edmonton).[50] Humberstone opened the first slope on the north side of the river in 1880. In 1902 to develop a shaft mine he moved six miles to the northeast to Clover Bar on the river bank. This mine was connected by a private rail spur to the Grand Trunk Pacific railway in 1910.

In 1917 the mine had 250 employees and 10 staff officers with a payroll of $20,000 per month in winter. Employees included miners, skilled mechanics, electricians, carpenters, machinists, blacksmiths, engineers, clerical office staff, farm hands, boarding house chef and staff, and travelling salesmen. The cost of food for men boarding at the mine was some $5,000 per year. Food was also produced by the farm near the mine. Supplies for mining, worth some $45,000 per year and including pipes, steel rails, nails, fittings, hardware, iron for upkeep of mine cars, trainloads of timber and lumber, mechanical and electrical fixtures, and tools, were all bought in Edmonton.

In 1918 the technological development of the mine was advanced. There were two shafts 120 feet deep for hoist and ventilation to work a seven foot seam. A rope haulage system was supplemented by eight horses stabled underground. Four coal cutting machines run by compressed air allowed a capacity of 1,000 tons a day. Two hundred and fifty mine cars were used underground. A private telephone system and five pumps to drain the mine provide additional evidence of a state of the art mine of the day. Humberstone's interests in sawmilling with John Walter complemented the need for timber for his mine. A three month supply was kept in the mine yard, some 50,000 linear feet from Humberstone's own timber limits.

The delivery of coal to customers by wholesale dealers, first by cart and later by rail and truck, was also important to the local economy. Jack Starky was one of the most important coal dealers and haulers. In his early twenties, he bought the first truck in Edmonton used to deliver coal and founded the Crown Coal Co.[51] As the local market grew, the mines in and around the city could not meet the low price that Starky was willing to pay for wholesale coal. The solution was to develop his own mine, so, when the Edmonton Penitentiary decided to relocate, he leased the mine for a royalty of 50 cents a ton. Gradually he developed other mines—the Chinook on the river flats below the Macdonald Hotel, the Kent on Cooking Lake Trail, the Kel-Star at Namao, and the Star-Key to the north of the city.

In addition to the coal mines, he developed Penn Motors, a White truck and Graham dealership. After going bankrupt in the depression, he formed Fitzgerald and

1880.   1916.

The First Load of Coal Ever Delivered in Edmonton.

HUMBERSTONE
COAL

Humberstone Coal has satisfactorily supplied the demand for high-grade coal for steam and domestic use for over 35 years.

Sold by Ton, Load, or Carload.

BEST LUMP COAL,
per ton **$3.75**

BEST KITCHEN COAL,
per ton **$3.00**

Single Ton Deliveries . . . . .25c Extra

Humberstone Coal Co.

9981 JASPER AVE.

Phones   2248—1492

Advertisement of the Humberstone Coal Co. in the *Edmonton Bulletin*, 17 June 1916. Note the oxcart used for delivery at this time. (EA)

Starky, a gravel contracting business with 50 trucks, and he paved roads in Edmonton, Calgary, and Jasper. He later built several hotels, the Wainwright, the Picture Butte, the Stampeder in Calgary, and the Cromdale in Edmonton.

After 1945 the Star-Key was an underground operation with modern mechanical cutter, loader, locomotive, conveyor, and hoisting equipment. Starky sold the mine to his employees for a dollar in 1961. At the time, it was one of the last two producing mines in the Edmonton Coal Mining District; the other was the Egg Lake Coal Company, northwest of Morinville. The Star-Key mine closed in 1977 but still holds a producer's permit. The Egg Lake mine is still in operation.[52]

Strip mines in the Edmonton area also benefitted the Edmonton economy. Most were near Morinville and Cardiff where the Clover Bar horizon is very close to the surface. Homeowners have been known to dig down to the seam from their cellars to mine their own coal illegally.[53] Strip mines in the Edmonton District are first referred to in the Mines Branch Report for 1913. Through the First World War and the 1920s they were known as 'wagon mines,' delivering their coal to local customers or dealers in horse drawn wagons. The Alberta Coal Commission Report of 1925 criticized these producers for contributing to overcapacity and unstable prices by underselling the established producers.[54] In 1944 the relative output for strip and underground mines was 15,247 tons and 374,083 tons. By 1954, their peak year, six strip mines were producing nearly double the underground mine output (158,000 to 82,000).[55] Lower labour costs, two or more times the productivity per worker, and lower prices gave the strip mines an advantage over the underground mines for a time until the more accessible coal was extracted and oil, natural gas, and electricity entered the market.

In conclusion, coal was not a determining factor in the location of Edmonton but it was a welcome bonus for the growing number of settlers and businessmen who located in the town. Coal provided fuel for heating and cooking and employment in the winter season for the farmer-miner. Gradually, as shaft mining commenced, businesses sprang up to provide supplies for the industry. Coal mining was thus an important but not crucial industry to the development of the community. It went into demise after Edmonton had become a large diversified wholesale trade and service centre so that its passing did not have serious economic repercussions on the local economy. In later years, the most important legacy of coal mining has been the effect of subsidence and slumping on surface infrastructure and buildings. ∾

Penitentiary workers in the Penn Coal Mine, 1933. The mine was later purchased by Jack Starky. (PAA BL.152/4)

THE CITY MARKET

Untitled sketch of Edmonton's City Market, circa 1940s, by Calgary artist Illingworth
H. Kerr. The sketch was the base for a painting that was never undertaken.
(ESTATE OF I.H KERR)

*K*athryn Merrett is fascinated by Edmonton's City Market. The City established the Market during Edmonton's boom years before the real estate collapse of 1913. Merrett suggests that the Market symbolized a civic commitment to a prosperous business community. She writes of the Market as a place 'where commerce and community joined in an atmosphere that resembled street theatre.' It was a place that evoked—and helped to determine—Edmonton's political culture, its agrarian identity (until the Second World War, Edmonton's economic fortunes rose and fell with the fortunes of local farmers), and its cultural values as new immigrant groups diluted British influences. Above all,

Merrett writes of the family-owned businesses that operated at the Market, of people like Joe Bre-Win, the Granstroms, Flore Hinse, and Mary Sernowski.

Merrett, an architectural consultant and sometimes lecturer at the University of Alberta, plans to continue researching city markets. Such institutions have customarily been ignored when economic and business history is written. She believes, however, that they have much to teach us about how communities function—economically, politically, and culturally.

THE EDMONTON TOWN COUNCIL AT ITS FIRST MEETING of 1893 charged a newly chosen Town Hall and Market Committee with finding a suitable site for a public market.[1] In December 1900 the selected site—part of the block bounded by Rice (101A Avenue) on the south, Elizabeth (102 Avenue) on the north, McDougall (101A Street) on the west, and Queen's (99 Street) on the east— opened for business.[2] Simply appointed by a public weigh scale and a fence, it was to be supervised by the newly hired Market Clerk, Ernest Grierson.[3] Thus, inauspiciously began a City-run institution that, though rarely mentioned by historians, figured as a compelling feature of Edmonton's urban landscape for 65 years. Until moving to 97 Street in the spring of 1965, the City Market (or Rice Street Market) attracted Edmontonians to the heart of the city by providing a colourful commerce amidst opportunities to meet and speak with friends and acquaintances. As a place where commerce and community joined in an atmosphere that resembled street theatre, the City Market has animated the imaginations of those who frequented it and is still, almost 100 years after it opened, a part of the personal histories of many Edmontonians. An examination of the retail, market garden, and farm-based businesses that rented stalls at the City Market can provide insight into the complex relationship between local commerce and culture.

The businesses that developed at the City Market, all family-owned and family-operated and nearly all informally constituted, fall into three categories. First, a small number of retail businesses—expanding from 8 in 1916 to 14 in 1933—occupied permanent stalls, paid weekly rents, and gave the City its most predictable income.[4] The retail stores, which sold fish, meat, fruit and vegetables, health food, and confectionary, operated as any small retail operation; owners bought their products wholesale, sold 6 days a week, and employed staff as needed. Many of them were long-term businesses, staying in operation for as long as 60 years under the same name. Their growth on the site was limited by space, but a few expanded by setting up outlets in other parts of the city.

Bre-Win's Meat occupied retail space at the Market from 1933 to 1971. Begun by Howard Bre-Win, who came to Edmonton from Staffordshire in 1912 and worked many years for Burns and Company, Bre-Win's was one of six retail operations chosen by the City to open a 1933 addition to the Market building. 'Starting up and running a business in the thirties was pretty tough,' said Howard's son Joseph, who began to work full time with his father in 1939 after being refused entry into the armed forces. 'You would buy your meat from the suppliers on a Thursday and hope you sold enough on Saturday to be able to pay them on Monday.' During the 1930s much of the meat and poultry sold by Bre-Win's was bought directly from farmers. The carcasses were transported by Joe and his brother Harold to the shop, where they were inspected before being butchered. During this time Bre-Win's began a long-

Market Square, circa 1920. Note the produce brought to market by horse and wagon. (EA-10-207)

Vendors and customers at City Market, 1925.
(EA-122-66)

standing tradition of supplying the Sisters of the Precious Blood with a large box of meat at the end of each Saturday. The business survived the Great Depression and World War II and was taken over full-time by Joe in 1956 after the death of his father. It moved to the 97 Street site in 1965 and closed in 1971 when Joe decided to amalgamate his space with his wife's vegetable store.[5]

Second, market gardeners often paid in advance to occupy the largest of the open stalls in the Market building. The largest of the direct-sales businesses, the market garden outlets were supplied from greenhouses in or outside the city limits. Besides selling at the City Market, they often sold from their greenhouse locations and to wholesale outlets such as hotels, restaurants, and grocery warehouses. Some became complex businesses employing a large number of seasonal workers. Market gardeners bought from one another and from other places. They fostered horticultural progress, as Robert Simonet's success in propagating double-flowering petunias particularly illustrates.[6] Unlike the farmers, who tended to represent themselves individually, the market gardeners usually represented their interests collectively through the Edmonton and District Market Gardeners and Florists Association, whose executive officers were almost invariably vendors at the City Market.

The capacity of market gardens to become large and established enterprises on the basis of local trade is well illustrated by Virginia Park Greenhouses, which sold at the City Market continuously from 1929 to 1993. Virginia Park, first located at 7534–110th Avenue, was bought in 1928 by Marius and Pete Granstrom, two brothers from Denmark.[7] Marius, who had come to Canada in 1909, married a young Danish wife, Kathrine, in 1929. They sold their first bedding plants at the Market in the spring of 1929 and in the fall of that year bought their first supply of tulip bulbs from the Dutch supplier the business would continue to use. This investment in bulbs was the beginning of a specialization in flowers, although, like many market gardeners and farmers in Edmonton, the Granstroms rented land from the City—in this case extending from the greenhouse east to Concordia college—and turned it into a large vegetable garden. They sold their produce at the Market (in the spring, six days a week), to bulk buyers such as the RCMP, and wholesale and direct from the Greenhouse; but their business was founded on the Market and its steady customers. Over the years they grew to know their customers, recognizing them as coming from all over the city. For the Granstroms, the Market provided stable cash flow and on-going, inexpensive advertising. Not until 1993, when they closed their 110 Avenue Greenhouse to concentrate on their newer Ellerslie Road facility, would they feel comfortable about leaving the City Market. The business is still operated by Kathrine and Marius Granstrom's son, Ray and his wife. Several family members, including 89-year old Kathrine, are among its many staff.[8]

The third and smallest category of business found at the City Market was farm-based and non-specialist, sell-

Mary Sernowski, vendor, City Market, 1985. (EDMONTON JOURNAL)

ing produce from stalls rented on either a casual or a long-term basis. Farmers, or more frequently their wives, came from farms or acreages both in and around the city to sell produce. Renting on Saturdays only, except perhaps in the spring and fall, they often resisted the City's administrative regulations. Such farmer-operators sold seasonally at the City Market and directly to hotels and restaurants.

Mary (Chipil) Sernowski began taking produce from St Albert to the City Market some time in the late 1930s or very early 1940s. Belgian neighbours told her about the opportunity, which she might otherwise have missed as she does not read or write. An emigrant from the Polish Ukraine who worked in northeastern Alberta as an itinerant farm worker between 1928 and 1933, she married and started her career as a stallholder after a grave farm accident drove her to the city to find help. Marriage gave her the chance to work for herself and her family. The Market, which she sometimes attended six days a week when she got older, let her become a fully contributing member of society: it validated her hard work more than it paid the bills.[9]

Occasionally what began as a simple and non-special-

ized farm-based operation grew into a large, complex, and specialized venture. Flore (Bilodeau) Hinse began selling butter and cream at the Market with her mother in the mid 1920s after the early and unexpected death of her father. Raised on a farm near Beaumont, she learned her first English selling the jars of cream and 150 pounds of butter that they brought to town in the democrat every week. This experience gave her the idea, as a young married woman circa 1930, to start a business at the Market. 'The time was real hard. So, I decided to make butter from my Mother's cows and I bought some eggs from my Mother's neighbours who had chickens and I made a few cents, you know. So, it was good for me and ambitious.' She began raising chickens herself and 'built up our business so that we were taking 200 to 300 chickens per week. We raised a lot of them but we began to buy them from our neighbours.' According to Flore, 'We paid everything with the Market.' The business still operates, now out of retail space at the City Market as well as stall space at the City and other local markets. It is run by her son Denis and grandson Gerry who contract out much of the poultry raising and run a processing plant of their own.[10]

Whether a Market business was retail, market garden, or farm-based, individuals and families tended to re-define their businesses from time to time, in response either to an opportunity (like the chance to rent some land for cultivation or to acquire a greenhouse) or to changed family circumstances (such as the death of a family member which might mean contraction of a business or the coming of age of a child which might entail expansion). Sidelines were added at appropriate times of the year—for instance, Christmas trees in December or hand-painted eggs at Easter.

The scale of the City Market as a commercial venue was limited by the number of stalls available. At any one time, 70 to 100 or more small businesses—in addition to the approximately 12 retail outlets—sold at the City Market. In 1962 the City's Land Department carried out a utilization survey that extended back five years and reported: 'The interior section of the Market is divided into 68 greenhouse and vegetable stalls, each 7' wide, and 141 farmers' stalls, each 3' wide. The 68 greenhouse stalls are rented to 34 permanent stall holders, with 141 farmers' stalls rented to 51 stallholders. Of the 85 permanent stallholders 53 reside within the city limits and the balance are from surrounding country points.'[11] The survey's analysis of selling space and its profile of vendors seem to obtain for the decades before 1960. Likewise, its suggestion that the commercial opportunities at the Market were fully utilized in the late 1950s and early 1960s appears to hold true for the preceding decades.

Market businesses have played a role in the material life of Edmonton, creating jobs and contributing to the circulation of goods and money. Unfortunately, there are no micro-economic studies that isolate the economic impact of the Market over the years. An examination of the Market as a cultural agent can be more fruitful. Market businesses—designed to be responsive to local demand—are uniquely placed to draw from and contribute to their urban culture. Three aspects of the relationship between local commerce and culture will be examined: the city's political culture, the ongoing centrality of agrarianism to the city's identity, and the shift in values from those defined by a British-Ontario elite to a pluralism more in harmony with a multi-cultural population.

The history of the City Market offers insight into Edmonton's political culture, in particular showing how the City's commitment to a public market (implying an acceptance of the City's role as a facilitator of private business) was limited by the counter-position (that government should not interfere in the economy). Conceived as a public service in 1893, founded as such in 1900, and maintained by the City through to the present day,[12] the City Market was not—in itself—a business. Rather, it was designed to foster and regulate business opportunities for residents of the city and its environs. Although the Market developed from a rudimentary open public space to a roofed-in physical structure, the City took a minimalist approach to its administration and a restrained attitude to facility maintenance and expansion. Market facilities and services were kept basic, minimising operational and capital costs. A small staff—never more than four people—performed basic supervisory and janitorial duties. A Superintendent rented stalls, collected revenue, reported to the City, and ensured that the various sets of by-laws were upheld.[13] The records show that until 1965, the year the Market was moved to its present location on 97 Street, the City rarely ran an operational deficit: it usually broke even or realised a small surplus.[14]

On the one occasion in 1914 when the City Council

Throughout the depression the City used the Market to create work. It ensured that whenever janitorial positions came open, even when they were summer relief positions, they were given to jobless city taxpayers with families to support.

was deflected from its minimalist policy, spending a large sum for a new building on 101 Street and 107 Avenue, vendors and customers so firmly resisted the move that the City was forced to return the Market to Rice Street. The incident conveyed two messages to civic leaders: that Market vendors and customers valued the central location of the Market above the prospect of modern facilities and that they were fearful of a situation in which business costs would edge out small producers. The fact that customers and vendors continued to endorse the City's minimalist policy is demonstrated by the fact that the 'temporary' quarters, erected on the Market site in 1916 and extended in 1933, endured until 1964 when this shed-like and weather-permeable structure was demolished to make way for the downtown branch of the Public Library.

The Great Depression of the 1930s illustrates how the City used the Market to regulate the economy and to stimulate local commerce without implicating itself in the economic successes and failures of the Market businesses. In terms of work creation, rental, and relief policies, the City's management of the Market simultaneously upheld the interventionist and non-interventionist models of government. Throughout the depression the City used the Market to create work. It ensured that whenever janitorial positions came open, even when they were summer relief positions, they were given to jobless city taxpayers with families to support. The Market Superintendent was constantly reminded when hiring relief janitors to take economic conditions into account. The boldest work-creation initiative undertaken by the City in the depression was its decision, based partly on the belief that City revenue would benefit, to add a major extension to the Market building. 'The idea,' wrote Mayor Knott in a letter to J. Martland, City Architect and Building Inspector on 27 January 1933, 'would be primarily to provide work for those unemployed home-owners who are unable at present to discharge their tax arrears.' The entire project was planned and carried out as a make-work project. The City became the primary contractor, ensuring that the labour was supplied by citizens unable to pay their taxes and accepting sub-contractors' bids only from firms in financial difficulty. The project finished, the City found that, besides having created construction work that was in short supply, it could offer retail space to six of the many aspiring entrepreneurs who applied, one of whom was Howard Bre-Win.

In addition to using the Market in job creation schemes, successive mayors bowed several times between 1929 and 1936 to individual and group requests 'owing to present conditions and the prospects of the coming season' to lower stall rents. On 17 February 1930 Fred Wagner, a Spruce Grove farmer, wrote to the Mayor warning: 'If City People who live largely from Trading put to much Difficultys against the farmers when they come to Edmonton to buy and sell, then the farmers will put there Heads together and improve there Position by buying Co-operatively . . . Be fair to the farmers and put no unnecessary obstackles in the Way of a free Flow of Trade.' In these years, retail, market gardeners', and farmers' stall rentals were reduced several times, each reduction occurring after negotiations initiated by the businesses involved.

Finally, the City involved the Market in its relief program during the Great Depression by making relief vouchers redeemable by Market vendors. Joe Bre-Win provides a comic insight into the conflict between interventionist and non-interventionist political philosophies in his account of the intricate barter system that affected the City's relations with small business at this time. His father, unable to pay his weekly stall rental, was told to vacate his premises at the Market. Instead, Howard Bre-Win went to the City Commissioners to convert the relief vouchers that the City was unable to redeem into free rent.

While the City used the Market to assist in the circulation of community wealth during tough times, its interventionist stance never extended to a willingness to absorb financial risk. Stalls were fully rented throughout the period, including the overflow space on the Market Square that could be used only during the May through October season. Revenues continued to exceed expenditures, and stallholders who did not pay their rents were asked to 'vacate the premises, as several others are waiting to get the opportunity of securing these stalls.'

The second aspect of local commerce and culture to be explored rests in the idea that urban life was most fully achieved when it existed in an interdependent relationship with the agricultural hinterland. Over the years, the Market reinforced the agrarian content of Edmonton's urban identity.

The emphasis placed by Edmonton's founding citizens on the role that agriculture would play in building the city can hardly be exaggerated. This emphasis was partly dictat-

ed by the National Policy of the Dominion Government which sought to settle the west on the basis of agricultural potential. Yet, Edmonton's early development was restrained by failure to secure a direct rail-link to outside markets. This failure partly explains why mixed farming was promoted so vigorously, as an article in the 27 November 1888 edition of the *Edmonton Bulletin* illustrates:

> The Farmers as a class are doing well, and have always had a ready market for their surplus stock and produce. Most of them are engaged in mixed farming, as it is more profitable than by making a speciality of any one line. The supply has never equalled the demand, in flour, butter and meat . . . The prosperity of the community is seen in new buildings and fences, and by the purchase of agricultural machinery, there being $8,000 expended this year in implements alone. A phenomenally deep, rich soil, good water, plenty of timber for fuel and building purposes, nutritious grasses, and a climate second to none make this a most favored country for farming.

The emphasis on mixed farming and the diversity of the agricultural economy, as reflected particularly in the pages of the *Edmonton Bulletin*, helped determine the institutional life of the city and the cultural horizons of Edmontonians. The column devoted to local news in the *Bulletin* kept its readers informed about products available and agricultural conditions:

> Raspberries are ripe.
> Heavy rain on Sunday last.
> New potatoes are in general use.
> Hogs are scarce. Butter plentiful.[15]

Reported at length were plans for, and results of, the Agricultural Association exhibitions, held annually from 1882 onwards. On 26 October 1889 the *Bulletin* reported that R. McKernan's Butcher Shop was demonstrating 'a hive of honey containing two frames full of solid comb, filled with very thick honey of a most delicious flavor.' Precisely one year later the *Bulletin* reported on the 'great success which has attended the Canadian butter and cheese exhibit at the Paris exhibition,' and on 19 November 1900 an article commented that 'T. Daly, of Clover Bar, has received notice from Paris that it was his oats in the Canadian exhibit at the great exposition which were awarded the Grand Prize.' The dominant impression conveyed by these and other reports is of the diverse potential of the region's agricultural economy.

One reason the City Market was endorsed by Edmonton's 1893 Council and retained as a City responsibility was that it was deemed to be good for business. Contemporary arguments in favour of instituting a public market suggested both that it would stimulate agricultural enterprise while making good quality local produce accessible to consumers and that it would bring the farmers' business to city merchants. So argued Philip Heiminck, the City Market's most vociferous promoter, in a letter to the *Edmonton Bulletin* on 6 May 1900: 'We claim that there is no greater impetus to the growth of any town than a well established market especially to a place like Edmonton whose location is unrivalled in the Dominion of Canada.' Heiminck saw in the Market an opportunity for local producers to support themselves while developing export capability and, at the same time, predicted benefits for urban consumers who would no longer be limited to 'ranky butter.'

Variations on Heiminck's argument were made at regular intervals over the following decades, usually in connection with one of the many debates over location and facilities. On 1 February 1911, for example, an *Edmonton Bulletin* editorialist wrote in support of improved facilities:

> A good market, with moderate fees charged and reasonable conveniences afforded is the best means the city has of holding trade against the competition of other towns where such favorable conditions exist. It is the strongest inducement the city can offer for getting the farmers of the district to produce the dairy, poultry and other products needed by the townsman and for making the farmer a frequent visitor to the city and a more liberal patron of the city stores.

From its founding, the City Market became an important vehicle for bringing town dwellers face-to-face with this agricultural diversity in a commercial setting, thereby contributing to the city's agrarian identity. Meat, poultry, eggs, butter, cream, cheese, vegetables, fruits, honey, plants, and cut flowers were only some of the products sold. As customers, citizens provided economic support to producers. As consumers, they expressed preferences and opinions as to the quality of their purchases. As amateur gardeners, they took an interest in the development of new or hardier plant varieties. The Market also continuously provided incentive to vendors to develop new plants, new products, and new ideas for marketing and presentation, an incentive informed by the direct customer feedback they receive. Most important were the Saturday morning markets, always described by local newspapers in extravagant terms that heightened the quality and diversity of the produce. Significant, too, was the fact that for decades—beginning in the 1920s—annual horticultural and poultry shows were held in the Market building, displaying the importance of agriculture in a central urban location. Joe Bre-Win's first acquaintance with the Market—and with its cultural messages—occurred when, as a student at Alex Taylor School, he was taken to see the annual poultry show with his class. Many of the Market vendors took pride in exhibiting their produce and occasionally, as in the case of Robert Simonet, in developing new plant varieties.

That Edmontonians continued to value Edmonton's agricultural identity into the 1960s is demonstrated by

When the City Market expanded in 1933, Bre-Win's was one of six new retailers to find space in the addition to the Market building. (A94-43)

letters written to the *Edmonton Journal* to protest a proposed closure of the Market. These letters, published in September 1962, called Edmonton an 'agricultural city' and a 'farmer's city' and expressed the belief that the 'Civic Centre should acknowledge the fact.' One suggested 'our heritage has long been allied with the soil, the Market renews our acquaintance with its fruitfulness,' while another urged 'we must continue to have a spot where city and country meet in a friendly human atmosphere.'[16] Buying and selling at the City Market between 1900 and 1965 reinforced, with every transaction, the idea of the urban as a place close to fertile and productive fields.

The third aspect of local commerce and culture to be explored is the transition in officially sanctioned values from 1900, when, despite the varied ethnic origins of many of its citizens, British values were upheld, to 1965, when pluralism had gained more acceptance as a model of community.

Although the City Market was created as a framework for business, it was also made to reflect the social values and preoccupations of its founders. Their vision of Edmonton was informed by cultural models imported largely from Ontario. The founders' cultural imperialism, which assumed English to be the language of commerce and assimilation of minorities to be society's goal, influenced the operations of the Market for generations. The power of the assimilationist model and its capacity for exclusion may be recognized in the stories of many early vendors and in scraps of archival evidence. When a teen-aged Flore Bilodeau began to sell at the Market with her mother in the mid-1920s, she had never spoken English; nor had she

pondered the consequences of not learning to speak the dominant language.[17] In 1927, when an aspiring Chinese vendor was denied a stall 'on the Market' on account of his race, he obtained an official admission that a mistake had been made, but he never secured a stall. Clearly, the culture of assimilation was also the culture of exclusion.[18] In the 1930s, as war in Europe threatened, the Oppelt family, whose farming and gardening business revolved around the Market, stopped speaking German. The younger children, some of whom founded their own businesses at the Market, did not learn their parents' tongue.[19] When Peter Lupul, after being demobilized in 1946, bought a butcher shop at the Market, he conformed the shop to the tastes of his 'better class' customers. Raised on a farm near Vegreville and proud of the quality of his Angus beef, Lupul eschewed selling garlic sausages.[20]

The rise of the model of cultural pluralism and social diversity was advanced by the historical agency of the Market site. Its location in the geographical, political, and commercial heart of the city made the Market Square accessible and desirable to all cultural groups, regardless of social or political standing in the community. Social intermingling attended Market trade and the square's centrality and public status defied any single set of cultural standards. If the square was often conscripted as the martialling yard for annual Remembrance Day Parades, with their cultural associations of British imperialism, it was also open to left-leaning groups such as the Labour League for the infamous Hunger March rally of December 1932 or for the large May Day parades that took place during the 1930s. If the fashionable West End supplied a regular, devoted troop of cus-

The Market Square was often the focal point for community celebrations and demonstrations. Here, the Hunger March of December 1932. (PAA A.9217)

The Great Depression heightened the militancy of workers and unemployed alike. Here, the May Day Parade leaves Market Square, 1 May 1937. (EA-160-1240)

tomers to the Saturday morning markets, others came from humble dwellings in the North East, and vendors travelled from Beaumont to sell live fowl to Asian buyers. If commercial and political leaders often traversed the square in the course of the work week, the horse trough was patronised as often by local eccentrics in search of a public bath. In the final analysis, the commercial transactions taking place in the Market Square and the cultural meanings they embodied displaced the cultural codes of the Market's founders: custom and conduct defied assimilation. Homogeneity gave way to social pluralism, yielding a new community identity.

Since 1900, the Edmonton City Market has provided a specific local context for business, but it has not been the only context within which small business has operated. In fact, its striking atypical features (which include public sponsorship, flexible accommodation, and retail combined with direct selling operations) make it difficult to generalize based on the above analysis. Nevertheless, this attempt to uncover the cultural meanings conveyed through the history of the City Market as a commercial venue points to a need for further work along these lines. Business cannot be explained simply in terms of itself, and small business, so often ignored or subsumed within the more conceptual discipline of economic history, must be viewed as a rich source of information about local culture. ∿

BOB GILMOUR

THE HOMEFRONT IN THE SECOND WORLD WAR

As should be plain from this advertisement for war savings certificates showing the bombing of Edmonton, Albertans took the danger of enemy attack seriously. (PAA P.6567)

In the history of nations, peoples, and even cities, certain events often stand out as pivotal turning points. Their impact extends from the economy and politics down to the collective psyche and everyday life. Such events include the Civil War for the United States, the Holocaust for the Jews, the 1919 General Strike for Winnipeg, and the invention of the birth control pill for women. In twentieth-century Edmonton, two things, the one profiting from the foundation laid by the other, changed the city profoundly: the first was the Second World War, the second the discovery of oil, with Leduc No. 1, in 1947. Alberta's postwar petroleum industry fostered widespread economic growth, expanded the functions of government, and increased the profile of both the province and its two major centres, Edmonton and Calgary. As the backdrop to these developments, the war had provided Edmonton with a unique legacy. The cities of central Canada

might have reaped most of the profits from munitions and related contracts, but Edmonton's location as Canada's northernmost city made it strategically attractive to the United States with the escalation of the war in the Pacific. The Americans made the city their base for large-scale defence projects undertaken in the northwest, injecting huge amounts of money into the economy and helping to reinforce Edmonton's self-image as 'gateway to the north.' Other changes were less dramatic but equally significant to those they touched.

Bob Gilmour brings twenty-two years of experience as a journalist with the Edmonton Journal, *where his news beats have included coverage of military and veterans' affairs, to this pictorial presentation of life on the Edmonton homefront during the Second World War.*

Crowds line Edmonton's streets to catch a glimpse of Their Majesties, King George VI and Queen Elizabeth. The royal visit in June 1939 sparked an outpouring of pro-British sentiment that the Second World War reinforced. (PAA BL.473/4A)

WHEN WAR BROKE OUT IN LATE SUMMER 1939, Edmontonians were still basking in the glow of the recent visit of King George VI and Queen Elizabeth to their city. The royal visit to Canada, the first by a reigning sovereign, had gone ahead despite high-level concerns over whether Their Majesties should risk a transatlantic voyage with war clouds looming. Like all Canadians, Edmontonians remembered only too vividly the horrors of the last conflict and they greeted Canada's declaration of war without the innocence or euphoria of 1914. Yet the Second World War, even more than its predecessor, changed Edmonton forever. Over six years of hostilities, the city was transformed from a remote prairie capital reeling from the Great Depression to a bustling, prosperous centre with expanded ties to much of the world.

Edmonton's per capita enlistment was among the highest in Canada, with the army, navy, and Royal Canadian Air Force (RCAF) all active in the city. Volunteers jammed the air force recruiting office when it opened, with some 15,000 men eventually enlisting. Johnnie Caine, a pilot with the 418 City of Edmonton Intruder Mosquito Squadron, became the RCAF's third highest scorer in enemy aircraft kills in Europe. The Loyal Edmonton Regiment drew 450 of its original strength of 800 infantrymen from the city. When it left for overseas on 15 December 1939, 10,000 Edmontonians gathered at the CNR station to bid it a collective farewell. Even the city's

naval reserve unit, HMCS Nonsuch, which trained in the old Hudson's Bay Company horse delivery barns in Rossdale, was initially swamped with applications; over the course of the war, it served as a basic training ground for more than 114 officers and 3,582 ratings. Hundreds of Edmonton families lost loved ones fighting in Europe, North Africa, and the Pacific. Of 840 former students of Strathcona High School who enlisted, for example, only 732 returned. But Edmonton's military function went beyond that of a recruiting centre and collection point. Several developments gave the city a key role in the Canadian and Allied war effort.

Planes and hangar, belonging to the RCAF No.2 Air Observers Training School, August 1943. (PAA BL.605/16)

The British Commonwealth Air Training Plan, which prepared Canadian and foreign aircrews for combat, made Edmonton one of the biggest air training centres on the prairies. Blatchford Field, now the Municipal Airport, was transferred to federal control, and, after new hangars and runway extensions, could accommodate the largest Allied bombers and fastest fighters. As Edmontonians watched training pilots practice in their Tiger Moth biplanes or looping (and sometimes stalling) their yellow Harvards, they occasionally complained about noise and low-flying, but were told to 'thank God they're our planes.' Aircraft Repair—built by the Department of National Defence as part of the air training plan, but operated by a civilian firm, Mackenzie Air Service—became one of the city's major war industries, and at its peak employed 3,000 workers. The plant repaired and overhauled damaged aircraft engines and airframes, and by the war's end could handle everything from service checks to major crashes on twenty-five to thirty different types of plane. The RCAF opened its No. 2 Air Observers Training School in August 1940, under bush pilot Wop May; No. 16 Elementary Flying School opened in November. In 1941 Ottawa leased the Exhibition Grounds (for the first time, cancelling the annual fair in 1942 and 1943) to house No. 3 Manning Depot, which prepared novice recruits for specialized instruction in various air force branches.

At the peak, there were 33,000 Americans in the northwest. Altogether over 48,000 US civilians and military personnel either passed through or lived in Edmonton, and at one point, Americans comprised an estimated 10 per cent of the population. With the arrival of the Americans, city streets became busy with newer cars, jeeps, and green army trucks with white stars on the doors, and hundreds of vehicles sporting the logo, 'Canol.' The Americans' favourite haunts were the Jasper Avenue movie theatres, Memorial Hall, and the Danceland Ballroom; American baseball and basketball teams also competed in city leagues. (PAA BL.456/1)

In the wake of the Japanese attack on Pearl Harbor in December 1941, which brought the United States into the war, Edmonton experienced a 'friendly invasion' of American civilians and army and air force personnel. The United States made the city headquarters for its vast war construction projects in northwest Canada, and the Canadian and American governments spent nearly half a billion dollars on huge projects like the Alaska Highway, the Canol pipeline and refinery, and the Northwest Staging Route. Buildings, tents, Nissan huts, and offices sprang up almost overnight; the Americans also leased space not already taken by the Canadian military, including fifty-two downtown sites (among them the Tegler and McLeod buildings and the Empire Theatre). A US Army base, with the Stars and Stripes flying overhead, was established at 127 Street and 114 Avenue; a $2-million army hospital sprawled over several blocks to the east and north; and massive hangers were built at Blatchford Field once

the necessary land was cleared of brush. An estimated 25 per cent of Edmonton's labour force went to work for American military and civilian contractors, who paid almost double Canadian wages. US military police, who kept American soldiers and airmen in line, patrolled the streets alongside short-staffed city police, hurt by defections in part to more lucrative war construction jobs.

Blatchford Field became a strategic link in the American reinforcement of Alaska against Japanese attack as well as a refuelling stop for US-built war planes on their way to the hard-pressed Soviet Union under the Lend-Lease program. On 29 September 1943, in what is believed to be a one-day North American record, 860 American Lend-Lease planes passed through Edmonton. Blatchford field became one of the busiest airports in North America, and, to reduce the pressure, the United States built the giant military air base at Namao, which opened in September 1944.

The Americans, together with trainee airmen from the British Commonwealth, Belgium, Holland, Norway, and elsewhere, gave Edmonton an international flavour. The war also brought politicians, foreign diplomats, high-ranking military officials, and celebrities to the city. The US vice president, Henry Wallace, stayed at the Macdonald Hotel en route to special diplomatic missions to the Soviet Union. Soviet officers watched baseball games in Renfrew Park. Comedian Bob Hope stopped on his way to entertain American troops and workers in Alaska. Joe Lewis, world heavyweight boxing champion, played baseball during a promotional tour in 1943. And New York's mayor, Fiorello LaGuardia, a member of the Canadian-American Joint Board on Defence, was spotted grabbing a hamburger in a Jasper Avenue cafe during a visit to inspect war projects in the northwest.

Edmonton's population grew from 90,400 in March 1939 to 105,400 in March 1943, and by the war's end had reached 111,000. The economic boom pulled the city out of the depression, and by 1943 enlistment, wartime construction projects, and spin-off jobs had reduced municipal relief payments to zero. But the influx of civilians and military personnel also introduced problems, ranging from increased mounds of garbage to damage to the city's dirt and gravel roads due to heavier traffic. The diversion of building materials and manpower to the war effort made housing problems particularly acute. People lived in adapted garages, even tents; basements and second floors were turned into suites; and large family dwellings were converted into apartments and rooming houses, with little regard for zoning or building regulations. The arrival of the Americans stretched scarce accommodation to the limit; rents skyrocketed, often taking more than two-thirds of a family's monthly income.

By early 1944 Edmonton police worried publicly about a rise in juvenile delinquency, a problem found across North America. In 1943 juvenile arrests had risen by 60 per cent over the two previous years, with an alarming jump in more serious offenses, such as burglary and theft. One official blamed 'wartime conditions' of too little supervision, as mothers and fathers spent long hours at civilian jobs or away in the armed forces. In fact, only a small minority of Edmonton youth became delinquents. Hundreds more enlisted for service overseas or, attracted by high wages and patriotic appeals, quit school to work (high school enrolments dropped by almost 30 per cent). Teenagers, forced to grow up quickly and assume responsibilities beyond their years, began to be taken more seriously. At the same time, new opportunities and unexpected earning power encouraged a sense of adventure and independence, so that young people insisted on living more by their own rules.

A female aircraft repair worker and her male colleague at the RCAF No.2 Air Observers Training School,1943. The war not only challenged traditional gender roles in the workplace but also made it acceptable for women to wear slacks, forever altering fashion trends. (PAA BL.529/3)

The war also affected the lives of North American women, as the labour shortage forced society to accept their employment outside the home. In Edmonton, for example, an estimated 1,000 of the 2,400 workers at Aircraft Repair in fall 1943 were women. When the drain of men to the armed forces necessitated hiring women in traditionally male jobs as mechanics, meter readers, street car 'conductorettes,' and postal van drivers, society also had to revise its notions of 'proper' female behaviour. Although at the war's end women were pressed to give up their jobs to returning veterans and to retreat to the kitchen, for many the seeds of discontent and permanent change had been sown. Women also acquired a heightened sense of self-worth and confidence in their abilities: they had proven they could do 'men's work,' they had helped to win the war, and they had earned a place in the public realm. Throughout North America, women's wartime experiences paved the way for the liberation movement of the 1960s and 1970s.

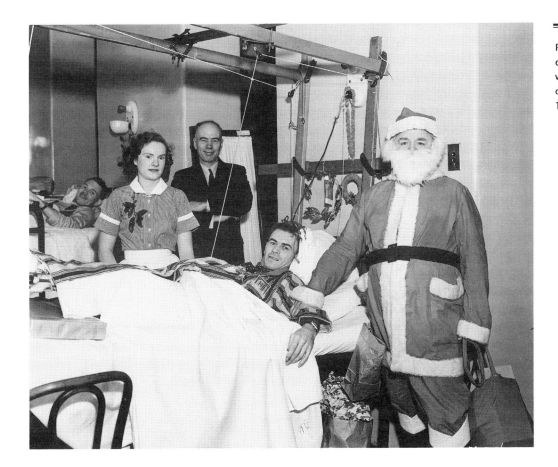

As part of a national campaign to mobilize the homefront, Edmontonians were bombarded with poster and advertising appeals to save, sacrifice, keep healthy, and conserve. They were exhorted to donate blood and to volunteer for war charities. Perhaps the vast majority of citizens made their greatest contribution to the war effort unofficially, within the family or volunteer organizations like the Red Cross. Edmontonians bought and sold Victory Bonds. And after food rationing depleted canned goods on store shelves, they planted Victory Gardens; in 1942 and 1943, for example, tons of vegetables were grown on more than 4,000 vacant lots rented from the Edmonton Horticultural Society. Women worked in servicemen's canteens and rolled bandages, knitted clothing, and collected cigarettes and gum for men overseas. Edmontonians also welcomed lonely Canadian and foreign servicemen into their homes, while community clubs gave time, money, and goods to various causes. The United War Services Club, for example, operated a popular canteen for servicemen in the YMCA, supplying a home atmosphere with Christmas and New Year's turkey dinners.

As goods and raw materials were diverted to military purposes, many consumer items became in short supply. Rationing affected foodstuffs like meat, butter, coffee, tea, sugar, and alcohol. Cars disappeared from the streets because of a shortage of gas, rubber tires and tubing, anti-freeze, and metal auto parts. As this Edmonton shopper in fall 1943 appreciates, the use of nylon and silk in parachutes made women's stockings a scarce luxury. (PAA BL.637/2)

Fat salvage, downtown Edmonton, 1943. Fat and old bones provided glycerine for explosives. (PAA BL.590/1)

The Edmonton Junior Chamber of Commerce began a salvage campaign in January 1942, which grew to cover most of the city. People saved kitchen fat, bones, rags, bottles, wastepaper, glass, rubber, and old tires—all of which could be used in the war effort. They also rummaged through attics, basements, and garages for anything of metal that could be melted down to make guns, tanks, or airplanes. After two years the Junior Chamber of Commerce turned over its campaign, in which it collected eight million pounds of salvage, to the War Services Council of Northern Alberta.

The war effort on the homefront included large-scale aid to Great Britain, the 'mother country' for a majority of Edmontonians. Citizens of all nationalities, however, donated more than 750,000 quarts of milk to British children in bombed out areas in the Kinsmen's Milk-for-Britain campaign. (PAA KS.42)

On 6 June 1944, D-Day, Edmonton ground to a halt for a collective day of prayer. Thousands of citizens prayed en masse for the success of the Allied armies invading Nazi-occupied Europe and for the safety of loved ones. Edmontonians eagerly followed radio and newspaper reports as, over the next year, the Allies slowly claimed victory in theatre after theatre of the war. When peace finally came, men, women, and children poured spontaneously into downtown streets to celebrate.

With peace, fighting men returned to Edmonton and their families in ever growing numbers. Some came home damaged in body or mind. Some just wanted to put the war behind them and make up for lost time. For yet others, the war years would remain the most eventful of their lives. (BL.719/1)

Returning veterans found their city profoundly changed. For one thing, the war had created a new physical infrastructure that could be adapted to civilian purposes. The accommodation crisis, for example, was eased when the Americans turned over their barracks for housing units; the land around the airport, serviced and paid for by the Department of National Defence, was also ready for postwar housing. Edmonton's first commercial aircraft manufacturing industry emerged out of the war as well, as Northwest Industries took over the federal Aircraft Repair plant. Fed by the discovery of oil in nearby Leduc in 1947, the wartime economic boom inaugurated forty years of prosperity that never really ended until the oil recession in 1982. In the short term, Edmontonians were simply glad to see their lives return to normal—with no more rationing, with gasoline and new rubber tires once more available, and with plenty of consumer goods to tempt their pocketbooks. ∾

'LES GIRLS'

Jean Wallbridge, seated, and Mary Imrie, 1947.
(PRIVATE COLLECTION)

One of the changes set in motion by the Second World War concerned women, specifically widespread acceptance of their employment outside the home. Although the return to peace in 1945 brought calls for women to resume their full-time roles as mothers and homemakers, not all did, and single women in particular continued to work for a living. By the 1960s increasing numbers of married women were also entering the labour force. A majority of working women found jobs (as their predecessors had done) in traditionally 'female' occupations like teaching, nursing, and clerical work. But some women, following in the footsteps of nineteenth-century figures like Jennie Trout, licensed to practice medicine in 1875, and Clara Martin, admitted to the Ontario bar in 1897, sought admittance into prestigious professions widely regarded as 'male' preserves. Edmontonians Jean Wallbridge and Mary Imrie, who trained and practised as architects, were two women who made their way in a male-dominated profession in postwar Edmonton.

Erna Dominey of the Historic Sites Service, Alberta Community Development, follows Wallbridge and Imrie's personal lives and professional careers over almost four decades. 'Les Girls,' as they were known, found employment with the City during the postwar construction boom, but they eventually sought the independence of their own architectural firm. Dominey paints a picture of two strong, slightly unconventional women who persevered in the face of professional obstacles, yet did most of their design work in domestic architecture, the field considered most suitable to women's talents.

THAT A WOMAN SHOULD TRAIN AND WORK PROFES-
sionally as an architect is no longer worthy of remark in Edmonton of 1995. During the first half of this century, however, Canadian women who hoped to practise architecture first had to struggle to gain entry to architectural schools and after graduation fight to win acceptance in the profession.[1] Those who did become registered architects were fortunate simply to stay in business.[2] Remarkable it is, then, that at mid-century two Edmonton women, Jean Wallbridge and Mary Imrie—popularly dubbed 'Les Girls'—established an architectural firm that lasted thirty years.

In speaking of the interwar years, Canadian women's historian Veronica Strong-Boag has argued that women were traditionally 'ghettoized' in the Canadian labour force by both gender and class. 'Girls and women possessing the resources and the ability to take extended periods of training,' she writes, 'tended to find jobs in "female" professions such as nursing, teaching, social work, home economics and library science. Only the most intrepid and well-armed penetrated such male monopolies as medicine, law, engineering and theology.'[3] Strong-Boag might easily have added architecture to the latter list.

The first woman architect in Canada, Esther Marjorie Hill, grew up in Edmonton. Her father, E.L. Hill, was instrumental in starting public libraries in Calgary, Strathcona, and Edmonton, and served as Edmonton's city librarian for twenty-four years. Her mother was 'a leader in many fields in the club world and in civic life,' notably the Local Council of Women and Strathcona Baptist Church.[4] Hill enrolled in architecture at the University of Alberta in 1916, but transferred to the University of Toronto two years later, graduating in 1920. Back in Edmonton by January 1921 and denied registration by the Alberta Association of Architects (AAA), she taught at a country school until the prominent Edmonton architectural firm of Magoon and MacDonald hired her as a draughtsman. She worked for them on and off from spring 1922 to 1930. Hill's second application to the AAA in 1925 was successful, thanks to the Minister of Education (also a University of Toronto graduate and displeased that she had been rejected in 1921). He introduced an amendment to the Professional Architects' Act to admit 'any graduate of any school of architecture in His Majesty's Dominion.' This initiative no doubt helped to smooth the way for registration by later Albertan women architects—including Margaret Buchanan (1938), also from Edmonton, Jean Wallbridge (1941), and Mary Imrie (1944).[5] However, like many other architects during the Great Depression, Hill could not make a living. She moved to Victoria with her parents in 1936 and only returned to her profession in 1953, designing 'homes, an apartment house, units for a motel and a garage.'[6]

Similar 'specialization' in domestic architecture characterized the careers of women architects throughout Canada, the United States, and Great Britain. 'By the First World War, patriarchy had squeezed women into what seemed like the smallest, least threatening, least lucrative, least prestigious space in architecture—the design of houses—which was seen as requiring women's "special skills." '[7] Wallbridge and Imrie would be no exception. By far the majority of their architectural projects were of a domestic nature: private residences, apartment buildings, both tract and row housing, and numerous renovations.[8] They began their careers as architects in Edmonton in the early 1940s, and worked in and around the city until 1979. These were

Jean Wallbridge's 1932 presentation to King George V and Queen Mary was commemorated in this portrait from a London photographic studio. (PRIVATE COLLECTION)

tumultuous years in Edmonton's history, during which the housing market responded to both the return of Second World War veterans and the emerging oil industry.[9] Thus, a great demand for housing may have influenced Wallbridge and Imrie's career pattern. But personal factors must also be considered. Both women came from comfortable backgrounds, and as one early client (also Imrie's sorority sister from the University of Alberta) phrased it, 'Mary and Jean didn't have to work for a living.' A fellow architect put it more bluntly: 'They were in the very enviable strategic position, because of their financial independence, in negotiating a commission, to tell a potential client to go to hell.'[10]

Jean Louise Emberly Wallbridge was born in Edmonton in 1912. Her parents, James and Mabel Wallbridge, had come to the city from Belleville, Ontario, in 1902. They began attending Christ Church and joined the Edmonton Golf and Country Club. James was created King's Council in 1913, and, when he died nearly thirty years later, his obituary lamented that Edmonton had lost 'one of its outstanding citizens and the legal profession a lawyer of sound sense and sterling character.'[11] The couple's eldest child, James D. Wallbridge, followed his father into the legal profession. Jean Wallbridge was educated privately in Edmonton (at Lenarthny School for Young Ladies), in Victoria, British Columbia, and in Switzerland and England in Europe. Before she returned home from over-

seas, her mother arranged to have her presented (by Lady Cunliffe-Lister) to King George V and Queen Mary at their third court on 23 June 1932.[12] Wallbridge completed Grade 12 at Edmonton's Victoria High School, played a lot of bridge, and enrolled at the University of Alberta in Architecture, under the tutelage of Scottish architect, Cecil Burgess. He later maintained that his department provided its students with a thorough training in architecture, augmented by classes in the engineering department.[13] According to Gordon Wynn, who graduated in 1936, 'Burgess could talk for two hours about manufacturing lead for lead pencils and be fascinating.'[14]

Wallbridge was one of four women to earn a Bachelor of Applied Sciences degree in the twenty-seven-year history of the program. In 1939, her graduating year, she was awarded a fourth in Class A of the Royal Architectural Institute of Canada (RAIC) Medals. She received a Bachelor of Arts degree the following year, and on 6 February 1941 registered with the AAA. Her first job was with Rule Wynn and Rule, the firm of one of her classmates, Peter Rule. Her next position was with the Town Planning Commission in St John, New Brunswick, during the Second World War. Wallbridge returned to Edmonton in 1946 to work as a draughtsman in the Department of the City Architect and Inspector of Buildings, remaining until 1949, when she entered partnership with Mary Imrie.

Women made a strong showing at the annual convention of the Alberta Association of Architects, 1948. (PAA 88.290)

Mary Louise Imrie was born in Toronto in 1918 to Beth and John Mills Imrie. The family moved to Edmonton in 1921, when her father became publisher of the *Edmonton Journal.* Her mother, who lived to age ninety-nine, was active in Robertson United Church, the Royal Glenora Club, the Edmonton Symphony Society, and the Canadian Mental Health Association. Her father's many pursuits included the Canadian Institute of International Affairs, the Edmonton Council of Social Agencies, the Edmonton Chamber of Commerce, and the Edmonton Museum of Arts. In 1937 he led Alberta publishers in challenging the Social Credit government's Alberta Press Act before the Supreme Court of Canada and the Privy Council in England. The following year, in recognition of his defence of freedom of the press, he received the first Pulitzer Prize ever awarded outside the United States.[15] John Imrie encouraged his only child in her interest in architecture and allowed her to design the family's cottage at Kapaswin Lake when she was only sixteen years old.

Mary Imrie received her education in the Edmonton Public School system, completing high school in 1936. She took a secretarial course and then worked for a year before enroling in Architecture at the University of Alberta in 1938. Upon hearing that the program would end with the retirement of Professor Burgess, she applied to the University of Toronto and was accepted into second-year Architecture in 1940. She spent the summers of 1941 and 1942 back in Edmonton, employed in the office of Rule Wynn and Rule. The three partners were away doing wartime service, and John Rule Sr kept the office going in their absence. A contractor, he had designed many rural exchanges for Alberta Government Telephones and was given a special membership certificate in the AAA.

After Imrie received her degree in 1944, she stayed in Toronto to work with architect Harold Smith on hospital projects. She then moved to Vancouver to work in the office of Charles B.K. Van Norman, 'one of the first of the visionaries' to design modernist buildings in Canada.[16] By the end of 1944 she had returned to Edmonton, joining the AAA on 7 December. Back at Rule Wynn and Rule in 1945, Imrie drafted schools, offices, and industrial buildings. She entered the office of the City Architect and Inspector of Buildings in 1946 and worked there for four years. As Marjorie Hill had done earlier, both Imrie and Wallbridge accepted positions as draughtsmen in the hope that it would lead to advancement. Their boss, City Architect Max Dewar, must have regarded the pair highly, because in 1947 he recommended that they be given

The Queen Mary Apartments in Edmonton, one of Wallbridge and Imrie's earliest efforts in private practice. (ROBERT VAN SCHAIK)

three months' leave without pay to take a study tour of postwar reconstruction and community planning in Europe. The City Commissioners 'found it difficult to understand how your [Dewar's] Department can spare two of its employees for three months of the building season' but gave their assent, as Wallbridge and Imrie would be getting no salary and had agreed to pay all their own travel expenses.[17]

Both women kept diaries and took photographs on this, the first of their many journeys together overseas. Imrie also wrote articles on their various travels, which she submitted to the RAIC *Journal.* The first piece, 'Planning in Europe,' documenting the British leg of their inaugural trip, appeared in October 1948.[18] In England Wallbridge and Imrie met with town planners from London County Council and were impressed by their ideas for the redevelopment of bombed-out areas such as Stepney. As Edmonton was then experiencing a housing boom, both women were also very interested in the concept of the New Towns, like Stevenage, that they visited. At the time of their departure for Europe, the *Edmonton Journal* had noted: 'When they return, they want to make use of all they have seen and done, using it in their work in developing a greater understanding of problems that are being met all over the world and putting into play the progressive ideas being formed in the rebuilding of countries in the wake of the Nazi terror.'[19] Wallbridge and Imrie were the only Canadians chosen for the tour, which was organized through Columbia University and included visits to Paris, Prague, and Warsaw as well as London. Edmonton businessman Sandy MacTaggart later reflected that he had been most impressed with Wallbridge and

A broad expanse of windows lights Wallbridge and Imrie's combined home and office (below the deck), on the banks of the North Saskatchewan. (PAA 88.290)

Imrie's designs for row housing in the early 1950s and he felt that they were among the most advanced architects in the city at that time.[20]

The two women's value was recognized in early 1949 when Dewar recommended that their wages be increased to $3,000 per annum, the rate for registered architects. 'Although these two persons are ladies,' he told the City Commissioner, 'I see no reason why they should be treated differently than male employees.' The City Commissioner's office, however, refused to 'increase the rates for draftsmen,' arguing that the Building Department did not need 'more than two registered architects on its staff.'[21] Dewar then suggested a compromise, with Wallbridge to be given the title of 'Technical Assistant in Town Planning' and Imrie to be known as 'Junior Architect': 'Both these girls, being registered architects, are much more valuable to this department than would be a draftsman who would accept a salary of this amount. I can assure you that it would be next to impossible to replace them with experienced draftsmen in this salary bracket.'[22] Cecil Burgess's column, 'News from the Institute,' in the December 1949 issue of the RAIC *Journal* noted that M.C. Dewar had gone into private practice and that 'two of Mr. Dewar's former assistants, Miss J.L. Wallbridge and Miss M. Imrie, *both of them registered architects* [emphasis added] have resigned from their positions to carry out temporary private researches in South America.' The two women took a full year to make the long drive to South America and back and submitted an article on their travels to the RAIC *Journal* in 1951.

Upon their return to Edmonton, Wallbridge and Imrie opened a downtown office (8 Merrick Block) and began to look for work. Contacts made with the development industry during their years with the City served them in good stead. Imrie knew that projects were often submitted to the Office of the City Architect and Building Inspector without the architect's stamp that was needed to receive a building permit. By contacting developers and offering her services to expedite a permit, she obtained 'three medium-sized apartment buildings of 10 suites each as the firm's first commission.'[23]

Over the next thirty years of practice, Wallbridge and Imrie's firm undertook 224 projects. Of these, sixty-seven were private residences, mostly in Edmonton but also in Calgary, Red Deer, and Lloydminster. The firm designed twenty-three residential additions and alterations, including garages, fireplaces, and recreation rooms—often for houses they had designed originally. Wallbridge and Imrie also did five lakeside cottages and additions to them. Fifty of the firm's projects were apartments, mainly walk-ups but some row housing and what appear in their files as 'garden apartments.' These buildings seem to have been relatively inexpensive structures, and the clients were developers; most were located in Edmonton although eleven were in northern Alberta. Three projects, all coming very late in the practice's life, were apartments for senior citizens in small centres, and the client was the provincial Alberta Housing Corporation. The only other government contracts were for three small-town telephone exchanges (two of which were only extensions) and the Diagnostic and Receiving Centre for young offenders in Edmonton done for the Department of Public Welfare through the Department of Public Works. The firm also designed tract housing for such Edmonton construction and lumber companies as Alldritt Construction, Maclab Construction, and Imperial Lumber.

Wallbridge and Imrie's files list only twenty-three commercial projects. They included two small office buildings, two office alterations, a machine shop, two warehouses (with an extension to one of them), the Alberta Seed Growers' plant (and a later addition), and alterations to two stores and one small shopping centre—all in Edmonton. The two women also designed a radio and television station in Lloydminster, a hotel in Lac La Biche, two motels and a restaurant in Jasper, a burger drive-in and St James Roman Catholic Church (plus a later addition) in Edmonton, and a small museum made of logs (the Luxton) in Banff. The balance of their work consisted of renovations, alterations, and additions to some commercial but mainly residential buildings.

Wallbridge and Imrie's practice—which, tongue-in-cheek, they christened Architects Folles—would appear to conform to the larger pattern of women in architecture described by American architectural historian, Gwendolyn Wright:

> Those few women who were able to take part seldom challenged . . . or competed with the men who dominated architectural practice; instead they took up the slack where they could, performing jobs and concentrating on the services which their male colleagues either put aside or treated only peripherally . . .
>
> A spattering of 'women's fields,' namely domestic architecture and interiors, evolved as areas of specialization where it was permissible for women to practice, since here they were dealing with other women's needs.[24]

According to their colleagues, Wallbridge and Imrie's career path differed markedly from that of the typical (male) architectural firm in the city at the time. 'I would think,' said one male Edmonton architect,

> that most firms starting out would depend on house commissions to some degree but they would broaden their practice very quickly because house design was not a very

lucrative practice. Domestic design doesn't have to be unremunerative. It is in Edmonton because of the circumstances. The houses are small and people are not prepared to pay you what it's worth for the design.[25]

When asked why his firm did not do domestic work, another successful Edmonton architect stated flatly, 'No money in it,' and chuckled, 'We couldn't charge what they were worth. They [the clients] would waste your whole afternoon talking about a kitchen and then they'd change their minds.'[26]

Why did Wallbridge and Imrie do domestic architecture? One client said of the pair: 'I think the one thing about them that architects or all professional people would do well to emulate was their ability to combine business with pleasure. You didn't feel as if they were punching a time clock or charging you $40.00 apiece for every phone call.'[27] Comparing his approach to that of Wallbridge and Imrie, one Edmonton architect said that he 'always . . . put in twice as much as the fee would afford' on a house, but that financial security was not an issue with Wallbridge and Imrie. 'I also think,' he added, 'they were quick to understand what was wanted and able to interpret that architecturally . . . I think Mary and Jean

Wallbridge and Imrie's use of contrasting materials—smooth surfaces with rough textured fabrics, thin metal furniture with rugged ceiling beams —gave their living space a look of simple yet unpretentious elegance. (PAA 88.290)

actually enjoyed doing houses, chiefly because they enjoyed people and I think the two go hand in hand.'[28] Another Edmonton architect, again citing Wallbridge and Imrie's wealth, suggested that a focus on houses was fairly common among small firms; it took many years 'before a client will let you play with his 60 million dollar building and when you get into buildings like that it's not a one man show anymore.'[29] Other former colleagues offered differing views:

> You ask if a residential type of practice was a common pattern for small firms at that time? I don't believe so. As young practitioners, it was generally the hope that one could get their teeth into a real challenge and one was always striving for bigger and better things. I believe that Mary and Jean were no different and I know that they struggled . . . for consideration for more responsible commissions.[30]

In 1954 Imrie made the following observation in a letter to Eric Arthur, her architecture professor at the University of Toronto:

> Our business is still providing a meagre living, although it is not so booming as last year. If only we got more bigger jobs and fewer headachy ones, we would be considerably wealthier and happier. But that is probably one of the disadvantages of being female. People will get us to do their houses, be thrilled with them and go to larger male firms for their warehouses or office buildings.[31]

Wallbridge and Imrie's own house—a combined office and home begun in 1954—is the best example of their work. They moved into the dwelling at Six Acres, named for the size of the property, in 1957. Originally there was just a shack on the site of the living room and they did much of the construction themselves, becoming, in Imrie's words, 'half decent carpenters.' As with many of their houses, their own overlooked the river bank, taking full advantage of the beautiful view. The compact open plan with built-in furniture demonstrates Wallbridge and Imrie's love of simplicity and economical use of space. The open-beamed ceiling and the long horizontal window between the upper and lower kitchen cupboards are also characteristic of their houses. They built the window frames themselves. The unassuming entrance is also typical, as the main living area was located at the rear, oriented towards the view. Their office was located in the basement, which, because of the hill side, was able to have large windows. There was also a guest room, and storage for plans on the lower floor.

Anyone passing one of Wallbridge and Imrie's buildings, with their clean low profiles and lack of pretention, would

The view from their own dining area shows Wallbridge and Imrie's ability to site a house in the best possible location on the lot. (PAA 88.290)

Greenfield Elementary School in Edmonton was designed between 1967 and 1969 by Wallbridge and Imrie on the 'open classroom' principle, around a central courtyard. (PAA 88.290)

see something of the late Modern period in their style. In 1955 Imrie defended Internationalism in architecture, citing three reasons why architecture in Canada 'cannot and should not' be distinctive. First, Canadian lifestyles did not differ greatly from those of other countries; second, the Canadian climate showed greater extremes internally than in comparison with other areas; and third, Canada used relatively the same building materials and equipment as elsewhere. Imrie also referred specifically to her own environment, arguing that 'until the prairie region has some design consideration peculiar to itself, some successful, innovative visionaries to copy, or some economical and peculiarly local building materials or methods, it will not have an architecture that can be called "regional." '[32] According to Wallbridge and Imrie's clients, what set their firm apart from others in Edmonton at the time was their commitment to designing the house the client wanted. 'I think an important thing about them,' commented one customer, 'was that they really loved people and wanted you to be very comfortable and very happy in your house rather than the idea of creating some sort of architectural statement.'[33]

By all accounts, 'the girls,' as they were known, were extremely conscientious about meeting clients' needs and designing a house that would 'fit' and make them happy. Another satisfied customer stated:

> I didn't want any hot shot architect telling me what I wanted . . . There weren't any conflicts with them, they listened and they advised . . . and I was amazed at how they could produce a house that pleased us so well with so little instruction . . . But it was really such a wonderful experience for us and we were so fond of them . . . After 23 years, I would hate to be parted from the house.[34]

In 1977 one of her relatives appealed to Imrie for architectural advice. Her reply reveals much about her attitude towards house design:

> We have both gone over it [the plan], but not with a fine tooth comb or a scale . . . Most lay people consider the details without considering the best relationship of areas with as easy as possible circulation to and from them . . . You could build this house as you have planned it, live in it and enjoy it, and justify the extra steps you had to take in it. And you could never know that you could have had all the things you really want, for less money . . . Good planning can save you more money than it costs you, and can give you a home you will want to stay in for a long time, instead of one that you would get to like less as time went on, because inconveniences get more unbearable with increasing age.[35]

Mary Imrie resigned from the Alberta Association of Architects on 2 October 1979, two days after Jean Wallbridge's death. She finished up a few projects, but essentially retired from the profession. Before her own death, on 11 April 1988, she made a bequest of land and money worth one million dollars to the Province of Alberta for parks. She instructed her executors that there was to be no funeral and to scatter her ashes in the North Saskatchewan River just upstream from her home. Six Acres became the property of the Alberta Recreation, Parks and Wildlife Foundation. Modest and well suited to its owners, Wallbridge and Imrie's house still stands, a monument to their ability to design a house around its occupants and at the same time to integrate it into its physical surroundings. ❧

ALVIN FINKEL

ELMER ROPER:
SOCIALIST, BUSINESSMAN, MAYOR

City Hall, when Elmer Roper was elected mayor of Edmonton, 1959. (PAA G.2543)

usiness and labour share a determination to set the political agenda of governments. In Edmonton labour has been active at the municipal level since the formation of the Edmonton Trades and Labour Council in 1903. In 1919 Joe Clarke was elected mayor with labour's backing. The Edmonton business community, which had been accustomed to controlling the civic political agenda, responded quickly, organizing the Citizens' Progressive League. Through the years, a variety of labour groups (the Edmonton United Peoples League, the Progressive Civic Association, the Civic Democratic Alliance, the Edmonton Labour Council) and a variety of business groups (the Civic Government Association, the Citizens Committee, the Committee for Sound Civic Administration) continued the fight for political supremacy at the civic level.

In 1959, however, most labour and business leaders supported the same man, Elmer Roper. Mayor William Hawrelak had just been ousted—for the first time. Roper was a business-man, a labour leader, and the former leader of the Co-operative Commonwealth Federation. Trusted to bring integrity back to Edmonton municipal politics, he would serve as mayor from 1959 to 1963.

Alvin Finkel is a professor of history at Athabasca University. He has published books on the Great Depression and Social Credit as well as co-authoring a text book on Canadian history. He is currently working on a history of the welfare state since 1945.

WHEN ELMER ROPER CELEBRATED A PERSONAL CENTEN-
nial in 1993, he could take pride in his remarkable
contributions to the development of Edmonton in a variety
of fields: labour, business, politics, media, education, and
community organizations. He is probably best remembered
as leader of the provincial CCF from 1942 to 1955 and
mayor of Edmonton from 1959 to 1963. His contributions
to Edmonton life were possible because of two contradictory forces that shaped his attitudes in the still-developing
frontier Alberta society to which he had moved with his
parents as a lad of fourteen. On the one hand he was an
entrepreneur whose success symbolized the opportunities
available in Edmonton's early urban history; on the other
hand he was a democratic socialist because he was concerned about the tremendous social inequalities that he
witnessed within Alberta. His commercial successes provided him with the time and money needed to pursue his
reformist aims.

Born in Ingonish, Nova Scotia, in 1893, Elmer Roper
was the son of a sea captain and former school teacher; he
attended school in Sydney.[1] His parents moved to Calgary
in 1907 and Elmer immediately apprenticed as a printer at
the Hammond Lithographing Company. During the war
he served as foreman for the press room of both Calgary
dailies.[2] Ironically, for a man who would live to see a second century, young Roper's advancement was aided by his
being rejected for military service as medically unfit; with
many experienced tradesmen at the front, there were considerable opportunities for those left behind.

In 1917 Roper accepted the *Edmonton Bulletin*'s offer to
become foreman of its press room and moved to Edmonton.
By then he was married to the former Goldie Bell, a minister's daughter, and the couple had started a family that
eventually included three girls and one boy. The Ropers
had married in June 1914 and eighty years later, both cen-
tenarians, they would celebrate a rare occurrence: an eight-
ieth wedding anniversary.

Roper had joined the International Printing Pressmen's
and Assistants' Union in 1911 and by 1916 was president
of the Calgary Trades and Labour Council. Before leaving
Calgary, Roper had played a key role in encouraging the
Trades and Labour Council to establish a permanent
Labour Representation Committee whose purpose was 'sup-
plementing our economic activities by political action.'[3]
Once he moved to Edmonton he successfully urged the
Edmonton Trades and Labour Council (ETLC) to follow
suit.[4] Over the next several years Roper was influential in
the movement for a provincial Labour party that would
field candidates in elections at all levels of government.

Like many trade unionists in western Canada, Elmer
Roper had been radicalized by the war. The government's
willingness to conscript men but not to prevent war profi-
teering gave credence to the socialist view that capitalism
would never provide justice to working people. Influenced
by the British Labour Party, Roper and other politically
active, skilled tradesmen took more radical positions than
they had before the war. Gradual nationalization of big
industries became central to their philosophy.[5]

Yet their radicalism can easily be exaggerated. Neither
Roper nor the major leaders of the Alberta Federation of
Labour supported the cause of the One Big Union, the
revolutionary syndicalist movement that emerged in
western Canada in the early post-war period. The ETLC
began to publish its own newspaper, the *Edmonton Press*,
in April 1919[6] and endorsed the British Labour Party's
proposed road to socialism; in almost every issue there
were vicious attacks on Bolsheviks and the One Big
Union. The ETLC half-heartedly launched a sympathetic
strike of Edmonton unionists in support of the Winnipeg
General Strike in late May 1919, but the *Edmonton Free
Press* made clear its preference for collective bargaining
and labour politics over syndicalism.[7]

The ETLC hired Roper as editor of the *Free Press* in
August 1919, paying him half-time while he continued to
work on the *Bulletin*. In September 1920, however, the
Alberta Federation of Labour, keen to have a 'province-
wide medium of expression of Labor views,' decided to
adopt the *Edmonton Free Press* as a provincial paper. They
changed its name to the *Alberta Labor News* and made it
'the official organ of the central body of Organized Labor
in the province.'[8] They also employed Roper full-time as
editor of the expanded newspaper.[9]

The energetic Roper had no intention of simply abandoning his printer's trade for his new life as a journalist,
particularly since the AFL paid him only a modest salary.
While editing the moderate socialist organ of the AFL, he
entered into a partnership with Henry J. Roche, the original publisher of the *Edmonton Free Press*. In 1932 he
bought out his partner and named the firm Commercial
Printers Ltd. Branching out to form Comset Business
Forms and Plastic Platemakers Ltd., this Prairie socialist
could brag in 1948 that he owned 'one of the largest printing establishments west of Winnipeg.'[10]

By the Depression, the AFL could no longer afford to
pay the editor of its house organ and Roper, who claims he
had always enjoyed editorial independence,[11] effectively
turned the paper into a commercial operation, albeit a
money-losing one. Roper, however, remained the provin-

cial secretary of the AFL, a position he held from 1922 to 1934, and the paper continued to advertise itself as the AFL's 'official organ' until 25 January 1936 when Roper renamed it *People's Weekly* and detached it from the AFL, hoping to attract readers who were 'uninterested in . . . a narrow official organ.'[12]

Nine years later, however, Roper turned the paper over to the provincial CCF of which he had become the leader 'so that in Alberta as in all other provinces the CCF paper may become the property of the movement and come under its editorial control.'[13] He continued as editor until 1953, when the paper, scrambling for readers in a province where CCF support was rapidly disintegrating, folded. By then Roper had had a weekly forum for his views that endured for 34 years. Except during the last years of the *People's Weekly* when readership fell staggeringly, the Roper papers had a weekly sale across the province of about 4000 and provided a means of communication and solidarity for socialists and trade union activists that has yet to be replicated.

The views expressed in the newspaper reflected a continuum of social-democratic positions from mildly reformist to near revolutionary. The successes and the campaigns of the Labour parties in Britain and Australia and the Social Democratic parties of continental Europe were dutifully recorded. J. S. Woodsworth, the socialist Member of Parliament from Winnipeg, wrote a weekly column for many years, and the Canadian news gave extensive coverage to left-wing politicians such as William Irvine and Robert Gardiner.

Roper's own views oscillated over the years and often seemed inconsistent from issue to issue and even within issues. One editorial page, for example, reprinted an article from the Glasgow *Forward* denouncing the 'reckless extravagance of Britain's plutocracy,' while a Roper editorial ridiculed those who claimed labour leaders wished to take away cars and chauffeurs from the rich. Without mentioning any rich person in particular, he wrote: 'I wish right now that he would buy a hundred of the biggest cars made and employ an army of chauffeurs to run them.'[14]

Roper was also inconsistent in assessing whether the federal government could solve problems in western Canada. He frequently castigated federal policies such as the tariff that he viewed as benefitting central Canada to the detriment of the West.[15] But he endlessly called on Ottawa to implement a national plan to end the Depression and legislate universal social programs for all Canadians.[16] His socialist beliefs suggested the need for a planned economy in which the state controlled much of the manufacturing sector; but his regional loyalties argued for a free market in manufactured goods that would give Alberta workers, most of whom were not in the manufacturing sector, cheaper goods. Arguably, this contradiction was endemic among socialists in western Canada though they, like Roper, believed that a socialist federal government would be able to reconcile competing regional demands.

In his 1984 interview with this author, Roper suggested, no doubt with some exaggeration, that he got all of his ideas from the British Labour Party. He identified closely with that party as a young adult and believed that it would soon take power in Britain and create a near-paradise through its promised welfare programs and nationalizations. It is clear, in fact, from the articles in the *Alberta Labor News* that the Labour MLAs and leaders in Alberta did not derive their ideas from the same sources as the rural populists in the West. Though they shared the farmers' resentment of the tariff, they devoted far more comment to social insurance proposals, laws governing trade unions, and proposals to nationalize their employers than they did to railway freight rates and tariffs. Their views were, to a large extent, imported from Britain and were urban far more than they were regional. The 'reform' tradition in western Canada cannot be simplified by assuming that both its urban and rural components at all times fit into one pattern. Roper, like William Irvine and a few others, tried to accommodate both labour and rural concerns, but class ultimately was a more potent focus for Roper than region and urban concerns more important to him than rural.[17]

While British labourism may have dominated his thought, Roper was influenced by a variety of British and American thinkers as well as the home-grown socialism of J.S. Woodsworth and other Canadian social democrats. His columns often mentioned Keir Hardie, Eugene V. Debs, and Edward Bellamy. But despite the secular bent of his

Roper, like William Irvine and a few others, tried to accommodate both labour and rural concerns, but class ultimately was a more potent focus for Roper than region and urban concerns more important to him than rural.

thinking, Roper occasionally paid tribute to religious thought as a motivation for his socialist beliefs. In a 1926 editorial, for example, Roper noted that Keir Hardie had obtained more of his socialist ideas from the Bible than from any other source.[18] Yet while Roper was a believer, he was active in almost every area of his community except the churches and made too few references to his faith for one to think religion was a motivating factor in his social activism.

Though he had little formal education, Roper read widely. He also supported a wider extension of formal education to workers and their families and was particularly supportive of the extension program of the University of Alberta.[19] It would be misleading, however, to label Roper an intellectual except perhaps in the sense of being an 'organic intellectual' of the labour movement, in the Gramscian sense. For Gramsci, popular movements threw up their own ideologues whose ideas synthesized the experiences of their exploited members and traced a path that could lead to an end to their exploitation. Their viewpoint reflected their 'organic' connection to the movement and their commitment to social change rather than concern about abstract academic debate of first principles. In Roper's case, inconsistencies of thought were often a reflection of a desire to achieve short-term results, a goal that far outweighed any concerns over abstract principles.

A man of his times, he was not generally a serious critic of either racism or sexism. Yet he did on occasion make commonsense arguments against both. Though his newspaper gave limited coverage to women's concerns, the occasional women's column did raise questions about the pay received by women. Roper also opposed the wholesale firing of women during the Depression. On race issues, the *Alberta Labor News* duly reported anti-Oriental resolutions passed by labour bodies.[20] Roper never editorialized on this issue, but he did denounce spiritedly the Ku Klux Klan which reared its racist head in western Canada in the 1920s and 1930s, largely targeting Catholics for want of a sufficient number of Afro-Canadians to scapegoat for social problems.[21]

Roper always defended democratic socialism against the Soviet Communist model, but he denounced the 'ring of enemy steel around the Soviet state' during the civil war from 1918 to 1921 and joined British Labour in calling for trade with the Soviets.[22] Once the Soviet state was militarily secure, Roper felt few constraints about attacking its economic inefficiency and repression of civil rights. In the 1930s he took a softer line on the Soviets, joining social democrats generally in praising the Soviets' apparent full-employment policies while continuing to reject the anti-democratic character of the Soviet state.[23]

At no time was Roper simply editor of the newspaper and owner-manager of his ever-growing printing establishment. What he may have lacked in intellectual rigour, he made up for in vigour for his many causes. An activist in the Labour Party and later in the CCF, he was often a candidate for public office. He won a Labour Party nomination for the multi-seat riding of Edmonton in the provincial election of 1926 but was not elected.[24] Roper ran again provincially in an Edmonton by-election in 1931 and came a respectable second, winning most of the working-class east end polls but going down to defeat to a Conservative candidate who swept the polls in the south and west ends.[25] There were, however, electoral successes for Roper before he won a provincial seat for Edmonton in yet another by-election in 1942. In 1925 he won the first of two two-year terms on the school board and served as chairperson of the board in 1927.

Roper also began a long period of service in community organizations shortly after arriving in Edmonton, which he maintained even during his terms as leader of the provincial CCF and mayor of Edmonton. He started a lengthy involvement as director and later chairman of the board of Beulah Home in 1922 and a member of the board of the YMCA about the same time. For many years he was a director of St John Ambulance. He served on the Board of Governors of the University of Alberta from 1931 to 1937 and participated in the Canadian Red Cross for a thirty-five year period that included stints as president of the Edmonton branch and president of the Alberta division. In 1922 he was appointed by the United Farmers of Alberta (UFA) provincial government to represent the public interest on the selection committee for plans for the provincial government Homes for Elderly People. During the Second World War Roper served as Alberta member of the Advisory Committee to the Administrator of the Printing and Publishing Industry. Meanwhile, despite having become an MLA and party leader, he found time to take part in the organization of Edmonton's Community Chest in 1943 and to serve on its board of directors, eventually becoming its president. He also was an active Rotarian from 1928 onwards, serving as the Rotary Society's Edmonton president in 1956–7. In 1958 he was appointed to the University of Alberta's Hospital Board. In 1962 he was honoured for his lifetime of community service by being inducted to the Order of St John of Jerusalem by Governor-General Georges Vanier, the Canadian prior of this order, 'the oldest order of chivalry in the Commonwealth.'[26]

Such a whirlwind of activities was only possible for a father of four because he had early on achieved a degree of financial independence and because he had a traditional marriage in which his wife Goldie did all the housework and most of the child-rearing. The Ropers suffered one major tragedy: their daughter, Gwen, who was training to be a nurse, died of a chronic ailment at the age of 21. His other two daughters married Americans and moved away from the city, their weddings dutifully reported in great detail on the women's pages as befitted the daughters of a wealthy and influential member of the community.[27] By the 1940s, with his children grown, Roper had additional family support from his only son, Lyall, who became plant manager of Commercial Printers, leaving his father the time required for his extensive political and community commitments. Lyall Roper served as a business-oriented alderman in Edmonton from 1983 to 1986.

Elmer Roper's 'workaholic' contributions to Edmonton and Alberta public life were motivated by a firm belief in the individual's obligation to his community and the conviction that individuals did make the difference. His view of leadership was nicely summed up in a front-page article in the *Alberta Labor News* in 1931:

> After all, talk as we will about democracy and the ideal of a world wherein the well-being of the masses shall dominate all else, it is the individual and not the mass to whom we look for progress and inspiration. That is why, consciously or unconsciously, we give recognition—by our admiration, or envy, love or hate—to those great men and women whose abilities so transcend our own. I haven't much use for the attitude of the chap who condemns hero worship as a grievous sin against democracy and I have nothing but pity for the self-sufficient individual who sees nothing to admire, nothing to anchor to, in the greatness of one whose intellectual genius or nobility of spirit has lifted him above the prosaic level of the common herd to which the rest of us belong.[28]

Roper's weekly newspaper editorials and commentaries provide a guide to the continuities and changes in his political thinking over much of the period of his public activity. In the 1920s Roper's general perspective shifted between 'labourism' and 'ethical socialism.' On a continuum of reformist thought, labourism usually refers to a desire to have independent Labour political representation but mainly to achieve reforms of benefit to the working class without fundamentally challenging the private ownership and operation of the means of production, distribution, and exchange. Ethical socialism involves a moral rejection of capitalist values and support for socialism as a more just means of organizing an economy. As a successful businessman, Roper's attraction for more moderate reform

is hardly surprising. Yet he remained committed to a longer-term change in the fundamental social structure. In the prosperous part of the decade from 1924 to 1929, however, he, like most non-Communist labour leaders, de-emphasized the need for radical change.

During the Great Depression, despite his continued business success, Roper became more committed to the need for public ownership of large industries (what he thought should be the fate of the printing industry one can only imagine) and large-scale social intervention to insure redistribution of wealth. He was an early supporter of the Co-Operative Commonwealth Federation (CCF) which was formed in Calgary in 1932 and of the CCF's Regina Manifesto, which was approved in 1933.

Despite his own capitalist ventures, Roper rejected the view that ownership of property alone bestowed rights to dispose of that property as one saw fit. As a business owner, he ensured that all his employees, regardless of their rank within the organization, received a share of the profits in addition to their union-scale wages.[29] He often editorialized in his newspapers about the unfairness of shutting much of the population out of industrial decision-making. In May 1920, for example, he commented:

> Industry is now controlled by and for the benefit of those whose capital is invested therein. Capital, money, substance, is practically without exception always given the greater consideration in the conduct of industry. Labor invests humanity, life, in industry and receives an inadequate return in the form of wages. Capital invests substance and receives a return in the form of interest or dividends, but unlike the life investor, capital controls the conduct of the industry. It is doubtful if economic unrest will ever be eliminated until democracy in industry is established and the industrial activities of the nation are conducted for the benefit of the people and not to provide profits for the few.[30]

But, just as Roper combined business success with socialist convictions, he paradoxically embraced both socialism and the non-socialist Farmers' government that ruled Alberta from 1921 to 1935. He argued pragmatically that in a predominantly rural province an understanding between the political arm of the Labour movement and its farmer equivalent was necessary if labour's demands were to receive a hearing. It was not a point of view that won unanimous favour in the Labour Party. Left-wingers in the Canadian Labour Party, particularly Communists, denounced collaboration with the UFA, claiming that it was no more pro-labour than the old-line parties.[31] Roper

CCF convention, Masonic Hall, 1945. Elmer Roper, a longtime labour activist, is second from the right. (PAA BL.1032/1)

defended the gains Labour had made by collaborating with the UFA: improvements in workmen's compensation legislation, a beefing-up of enforcement of factories and safety legislation, a legislated minimum wage for women workers, and legislated maximum hours (54 per week) for all workers. 'I personally wouldn't want to find myself joining the pack that is already yelping at the heels of the Farmer-Labor group in an attempt to defeat the first government of the producing classes of this province,' Roper wrote.[32]

Roper's support of the government may explain why his printshop received lucrative contracts from the government, including Alberta Government Telephones telephone books. Certainly, the Social Credit regime regarded his government contracts as patronage and refused to renew them, having enough supporters of their own to reward.[33] UFA Premier Brownlee was confident enough of Roper's generally supportive attitudes to endorse publicly his candidacy in the provincial by-election in Edmonton in 1931; the UFA did not run a candidate of its own.[34]

Roper emphasized that collaborating with the UFA did not mean sacrificing Labour's long-term aims. In practice, however, Labour's comfortable relationship with the government discredited the former when the latter, during the Depression, proved more concerned about preserving the

province's credibility with creditors than aiding the destitute. Social Credit had as clear a field among workers as among farmers when it denounced those who had done too little to protect the victims of the Depression.[35]

Roper was typical of many Albertans, including Alberta socialists, in being attracted to the social credit notions of British engineer C.H. Douglas. Initially he welcomed cautiously 'Bible Bill' Aberhart's mushrooming movement of social credit clubs first initiated in 1932. But he warned that monetary reform alone would not create a society free of depressions and poverty.[36] As it became clear that Social Credit intended to become a political party and therefore an opponent of the CCF, Roper became more strident in his attacks on Aberhart's simplistic economics and his wilful disregard for the limits of provincial powers in the Canadian constitution.[37]

Social Credit's electoral sweep and Labour's complete defeat in the provincial election of 1935 convinced Roper to change the name of the *Alberta Labor News* and to try to give the new *People's Weekly* a more populist feel. He hired William Irvine as co-editor[38] and the two not only crusaded against the Aberhart regime but also set out painstakingly to build up CCF organizations across the province to replace the moribund locals of the Canadian

Labour Party and the political wing of the UFA.[39] Again, however, Roper seemed drawn to two contradictory positions. On the one hand he wanted the CCF to provide a clear left-wing alternative, emphasizing nationalization and redistribution of wealth, to both Social Credit and the old-line parties. On the other hand he toyed with the idea of having the CCF join with the conservative forces that united as Independents in 1940 in an unsuccessful attempt to defeat Social Credit.[40]

Throughout Canada, the wartime mobilization quickly eliminated the widespread Depression unemployment and encouraged voters to support radical parties such as the CCF. Why, people asked, could such planning not be continued into peacetime so as to prevent the reappearance of a depression after demobilization? When Roper ran in the Edmonton by-election of 1942, he benefited from that sentiment.[41] His fourth-ballot victory was owed to first-ballot Social Crediters whose candidate had been eliminated on the third ballot and whose second preferences had gone overwhelmingly to Roper.[42] Later that year Roper became leader of the provincial CCF.[43]

During his first two years as leader, Roper concentrated on increasing party memberships (they rose from a few thousand to over 12,000 by the provincial election of 1944[44]) and spreading the party message throughout the province. Unlike the Saskatchewan CCF, which emphasized social reforms, the Alberta CCF placed equal emphasis on nationalization of resources and industries.[45] When the party gained a quarter of the vote in the 1944 election but only two of 55 legislative seats,[46] thanks to a fairly evenly spread support throughout the province, some critics suggested the party had presented itself as too radical.[47] Roper responded that he did not wish to be elected on a platform that falsified CCF intentions or to lead a government that did not intend to make nationalization of key sectors of the economy its priority.[48]

Nonetheless, when the post-war depression predicted by socialists failed to materialize, Roper moderated his stance considerably. His party committed itself to public ownership of half of the oil industry which had gained a new life following the Leduc strike in February 1947.[49] Roper's emphasis in the legislature, however, was increasingly on social programs. Though the province's growing prosperity was undeniable, Roper questioned how equally that prosperity was being distributed. While he paid tribute to Ernest Manning's Social Credit government for increasing spending on health, education, and social assistance, he compared its record unfavourably with that of the Saskatchewan CCF government.[50] He pressed, with some results, to have the province pay the costs of indigent relief, rather than leave the municipalities to bear this cost alone, and to assume the full costs of old-age pensions and mothers' allowances.[51]

Though his views moderated over time, Roper was one of the few labour leaders of his generation who maintained his socialist principles during the period of the boom. Alf Farmilo and Carl Berg, his fellow labour leaders of the 1920s and 1930s, had become conservatives in the post-war period, hiding behind non-partisanship and Cold War patriotism to mask their cosy relations with the Social Credit regime and their peace with the capitalist status quo. Berg and Farmilo typified the conservatism of the craft unions that dominated the Trades and Labour Congress of Canada while the socialist Roper, though a member of one of the most elite trades groups and a capitalist to boot, was closer in his views to the leadership of the industrial unions grouped together in the Canadian Congress of Labour.[52]

The Alberta CCF lost ground in every election after 1944 and some analysts have suggested the party was too interested in international affairs and in a purist version of socialism to rally opponents of the Social Credit regime.[53] Roper suggested in 1984 that much of the party leadership, unlike himself, remained enamoured of the Soviet Union in the post-war period. He believed however that the combination of the Cold War and prosperity rather than the behaviour of the CCF explained the party's gradual collapse.[54]

The boom fell on Roper himself in the 1955 provincial election. The Liberals, who had gradually pushed the CCF out of second place in provincial elections, consolidated their position as the natural alternative to the government with a spirited campaign against apparent extensive practices of corruption and patronage.[55] Liberal leader J. Harper Prowse was able to capture votes from former CCF voters whose main aim was to defeat Manning rather than to elect the CCF. Roper, who had topped the polls in Edmonton on his first try in the by-election of 1942, was now unable to place in the top five in the multi-seat Edmonton race. Prowse finished first in the city.

With his party's popular support continuing to crumble, the 62-year-old Roper, for at least the second time in his life,[56] announced prematurely his retirement from active politics. He increased his involvement in community organizations and campaigned to have the CCF join with organized labour to form the New Democratic Party, an unpopular position in Alberta where many socialists mistrusted the labour leaders.[57]

In 1959 Roper began a new political career. Mayor William Hawrelak's turbulent administration of the City of Edmonton had been condemned by an independent commission that forced his resignation. The Civic Reform Association (CRA), a business-dominated federation looking to restore the city's reputation, sought out a candidate for mayor who was both incorruptible and sufficiently populist that Hawrelak's charges that he was the victim of a hostile establishment could be refuted. The CRA settled on Elmer Roper, the successful capitalist and Rotarian who also happened to be a lifelong socialist. It was an ironic choice since Roper had worked in the 1920s and 1930s for Labour coalitions formed to defeat the candidates of such businessmen's groupings. By 1959, however, the Left had no visibility in Edmonton's urban politics, and the CRA was, presumably, confident that Roper would not threaten their interests. The CRA's membership included prominent Social Crediters, Liberals, and Conservatives and its candidates for aldermanic positions in 1959 were a business manager, a lawyer, an accountant, a medical superintendent, and a motel owner.[58]

Roper initially turned down the flattering request that he run for mayor. But the persistence of the CRA paid off and Roper agreed to re-enter the political fray, pledging that as mayor he would restore trust in the management of the City. Perhaps he could not resist going toe-to-toe with J. Harper Prowse, the former Liberal leader whose flamboyance had eclipsed Roper's provincial career. In a four-person race centreing on the issue of who could best restore citizens' faith in the integrity of their civic politicians, Roper became mayor with about 49 per cent of the votes.[59] Shortly after his election, Roper severed ties between Commercial Printers and the city, promising the firm would make no bids for city contracts while he was mayor.[60]

As mayor of a city of 281,000 souls, Roper focussed on city planning. In 1960 city council accepted his proposal for a planning advisory commission charged with determining the 'pattern of the community's future development.' Roper pressed for a new civic centre surrounded by a centre park—the result of which is today's Sir Winston Churchill Square. As he told a planning seminar in June 1960:

> There are lots of places now occupied by derelict structures upon which to erect new buildings. But we have only one area in the centre of our City for a park. And a park it should be and remain. Not a 'keep-off-the grass' series of gardens but a place of people, a place of interest and enjoyment, a place so attractive to young and old that people will be drawn to it, will want to come downtown because of it.[61]

Roper was a popular mayor and in 1961 was re-elected with almost two-thirds of the votes cast.[62] But in December 1962 Roper suffered a mild heart attack following a minor operation. He took two months off from his civic duties

Elmer Roper and J. Percy Page at the official opening of the police headquarters, 1962. (EA-6-8)

and holidayed for three weeks in Hawaii. Vacations and rests of such length, however, hardly suited the energetic Roper and he was pleased to be back at work in late February 1963 with a thousand things to do. Yet he was a man of seventy and he decided that it was finally time to retire from politics. He would serve his full second term but would not run again.

When he left office, the Civic Centre had been built and his efforts to unite the metropolitan region into one entity had achieved some victories with the amalgamation of Beverly into the city and steps taken toward incorporation of Jasper Place as well. In an editorial entitled 'Thank You, Mayor Roper,' the *Edmonton Journal* noted also that his administration had put city zoning on a sound footing for the first time since the Second World War.[63]

In his seventies, Roper continued his whirlwind of community activities. But eventually the Ropers admitted Edmonton's blustery winters were too tough on old bones, and, in 1977, they left the city after sixty years to settle in Victoria. Elmer remained physically active until his early nineties with son Lyall reporting in June 1984 that his father 'takes long walks on the ocean front, and the stormier the weather the better.'[64] Goldie's health, however, had deteriorated, and, in 1986, after she was injured

in a fall, she had to move to a nursing home.

In 1994 a few months before his death, the *Edmonton Journal* interviewed Elmer Roper. He remained lucid but his sight and hearing were diminishing and he needed a walker to take his strolls. Roper looked forward to death: 'It would just be a relief from being not any good anymore. I guess a person who has been as active as I was is inclined to be bored when he's not active anymore.'[65]

Roper's contribution to city life was unique. A successful entrepreneur, he devoted his life to improving the lives of his fellow citizens, particularly the poorest. He helped to create a legacy of labour and left-wing activism in the city that survived Social Credit and the Cold War. Labour organizations, the New Democratic Party, the left wing of the Liberal Party, and community groups that represent the underdog are noticeably more significant in the community life of Edmonton than they are elsewhere in the province. To the extent that organizations that act as a social conscience for Albertans are centred in Edmonton, the legacy of Elmer Roper is a powerful one. Through his political activities, trade union activism, community involvements, and newspapers, he attempted to repay his adopted city for the wealth and comfort it had bestowed upon him. The city in turn owes him a large debt of gratitude. ∾

As mayor, Roper was a visible presence at ribbon-cutting ceremonies. Here he opens a Tilden car rental office in 1962. (PAA WS.465)

P.J. SMITH

PLANNING FOR RESIDENTIAL GROWTH
SINCE THE 1940s

*P*eter J. Smith, a professor emeritus of the University of Alberta in the Department of Geography, is the foremost expert on city planning in Alberta and Edmonton. He has served as the president of the Canadian Association of Geographers and is currently the Canadian representative on the council of the International Planning History Society. Here he tells the absorbing story of how Edmonton coped with the enormous growth in population and area over the last several decades.

In 1941 Edmonton had a population of about 92,000. The city was just emerging from the devastation of the Great Depression. The Second World War was bringing much needed wealth to the city, but labour and materials were in short sup-

ply. The city's infrastructure—housing, roads, sewer systems—was in bad repair. By 1946 the metropolitan population had increased to 120,000. Twenty years later it would stand at 376,000, and by the 1990s at more than 800,000. How could the City cope with such change?

Whether you are interested in why different Edmonton neighbourhoods have different street systems, how communities like Sherwood Park and Mill Woods came into being, or why only some neighbourhoods have walkway systems, read on and you will find the answers.

A LARGE BUT THORNY QUESTION RUNS THROUGH THIS paper: 'Is Edmonton a well-planned city?' For the past 45 years or so, Edmonton can fairly claim to have been one of the most highly planned cities in Canada, with effects that are nowhere more evident than in the extensive new residential areas that have been built since the late 1940s. But attention to planning does not necessarily mean effective planning. People look for different things in their cities and judge them by different criteria, whether they have been 'planned' or not. Moreover, the criteria themselves change over time, just as our notions of good planning do. The question then does not admit of an easy answer.

The situation is further complicated by the fact that planning is not the only force shaping the contemporary city, nor even the most powerful. In our economic system, the effectiveness of planning depends to a large extent on the influence it is able to exercise over the market, an observation that provides this inquiry into Edmonton's residential growth and development with one of its central themes. Planning is an institution that we, as a society, have created to mediate between the market and the community at large (Figure 1). It is a method or 'system' of public decision-making that is now firmly entrenched in the apparatus of community government—most particularly, municipal government—to ensure that the community's

interests in urban development and the urban environment are properly respected. Like any social institution, however, planning is a cultural artifact, a product of its particular time and place. While planners, as professionals, subscribe to ideals and principles that are universal and enduring, the planning *system*, the institutionalized form of planning, can do only what its 'community' is prepared to let it do. This observation establishes a second theme for the paper: the influence that planners' ideals have had on the actions taken by Edmonton's planning system in relation to the power of the market on one hand and community will on the other.

These themes will be explored through a review of the main residential planning principles and policies that Edmonton has pursued since the end of the Second World War. First, however, to set the local context, the key aspects of Edmonton's postwar growth experience will be briefly described, followed by an equally brief description of the evolution of planning as an Alberta and Edmonton institution.

∾ Probably the most basic fact about Edmonton's recent history, from an urban planning perspective, is the sheer scale of the city's growth since the 1940s. Edmonton was still a relatively small city then, one of several at the third level of the Canadian urban hierarchy (Figure 2). Its population in 1941, before the growth surge began, was less than 100,000, placing it tenth among Canadian cities, smaller than places like Halifax and Windsor which it has long since outgrown and significantly smaller than cities at the second level, such as Winnipeg and Ottawa. By 1991 Edmonton's status was utterly transformed. Not only was it a much larger city, with a metropolitan population of 840,000 (Table 1), but it had leapt to fifth place in the national ranking and was clearly established as one of the leading cities at the second level of the Canadian urban system. Its growth was not uniform throughout that 50-year time span, but taking the period as a whole, it was one of the fastest growing cities in Canada. That growth alone presented Edmonton's planning and development systems with their greatest overall challenge.

In fact, the challenge was even greater than the increase in population suggests. Housing need, and hence the demand for residential development of all kinds, is most directly a function of household formation, and the number of households in Edmonton increased even more rapidly than population. The cause was a substantial reduction in average household size, from 3.8 persons per household in 1941 to 2.7 in 1991. The total number of house-

Figure 1. Conceptual diagram illustrating the role of planning as a social institution. (MICHAEL FISHER)

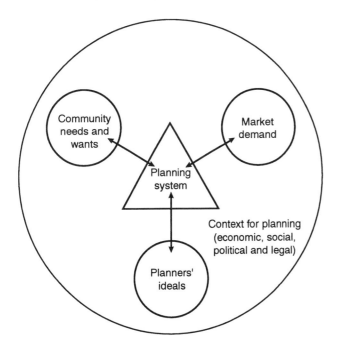

Community needs and wants

Market demand

Planning system

Context for planning (economic, social, political and legal)

Planners' ideals

holds increased from 25,000 to 300,000 over the same period, indicating that the 1941 city had to be enlarged twelvefold to meet the demand for new accommodation.

TABLE 1: Population changes in Edmonton 1941–91

census	metropolitan area population	percentage increase by decade	city population	as percentage of metropolitan population
1941	98,000	—	94,000	96%
1951	176,000	90%	160,000	91%
1961	338,000	92%	281,000	83%
1971	490,000	45%	434,000	89%
1981	657,000	34%	532,000	81%
1991	840,000	28%	617,000	73%

Another vital aspect of Edmonton's growth was its territorial expansion and the degree to which that expansion kept pace with population increase. Generally, across North America, cities have grown far beyond their original boundaries, which have long since been permanently frozen. To mention just one example, the City of Toronto held no more than 15 per cent of Toronto's metropolitan population by 1991. Table 1 shows that Edmonton's share of its metropolitan total has also been slipping since 1941, indicating a steady shift of development into the surrounding communities.[1] Although Edmonton has been able to annex land from its rural neighbours when it has run short, there are many people who prefer to live outside the city and would resist any move on Edmonton's part to absorb them.[2] This resistance was made abundantly clear in 1979–80, when Edmonton attempted to annex St Albert and Sherwood Park, its two largest dormitory suburbs.[3] The city did win an extremely large expansion at that time, yet its share of metropolitan population continued to fall, a clear sign that more and more people were 'voting with their feet.' Residential development is therefore a metropolitan issue as well as a city one. Coping with that reality has been another major challenge for Edmonton's planning system —one to which it has repeatedly had to adapt as the patterns of metropolitan growth and development changed.

The institutional bases of planning have also gone through many changes. Like all aspects of municipal government, the authority for planning is expressly derived from provincial legislation, which goes back as far as 1913 in Alberta's case. Cities were then given the power to adopt a special kind of plan known as a 'town planning scheme.' Its purpose was to facilitate the careful planning and design of new residential areas, thereby supplanting the unimaginative, standardized grid subdivisions that the landowners of the day were laying out with heedless abandon.[4] Unfortunately, the new powers came too late. The great real estate boom was collapsing even as the enabling legislation was enacted, and it would be another 50 years before the land already subdivided around Edmonton would be fully built up.

In the meantime, the Alberta planning system was modified substantially. The most significant changes occurred in 1929 when a new statute was adopted and the town planning scheme, which was a British device, was replaced by contemporary American instruments such as the official city plan and zoning.[5] Once again, however, the legislation was ill-timed. It had little practical effect in the short term, though Edmonton did enact a zoning bylaw in 1933 and appointed a town planning commission to administer it.[6] The commission remained active until 1949, when it was replaced by the first full-time professional planning officer, Noel Dant, and the beginnings of a permanent planning establishment.[7] Since then, planning has been a key function of Edmonton's municipal government, and all residential development has been closely regulated by the local planning authorities. The first step in the creation of a metropolitan planning system also occurred at this time, with the establishment of the Edmonton District Planning Commission in 1950.

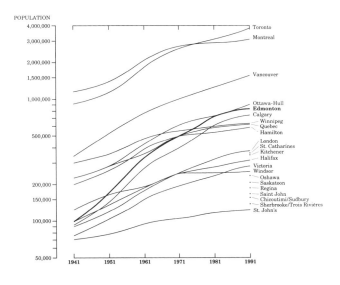

Figure 2. Population growth rates, 1941-91, of the largest urban centres in Canada in 1941 (including St John's Newfoundland). In 1941 Montreal and Toronto formed the first level of the Canadian urban system, while Vancouver, Ottawa-Hull, Winnipeg, Quebec, and Hamilton made up the second level. (MICHAEL FISHER)

These early actions were taken under the general authority of the 1929 Planning Act, though that act merely provided the legal framework within which planning could occur. It did not oblige Edmonton to set up its own planning system and so does not explain why highly developed planning procedures were instituted in such short order. That explanation rests rather in the new mood with which Edmonton, like cities all across the country, was confronting its future in the late 1940s. It was not just that most Canadian cities were experiencing a refreshing outburst of growth and renewed optimism after years of depression and restraint. These were certainly important, but there was also a sense, reflected in the reports of the federal government's Advisory Committee on Reconstruction and Alberta's Post-War Reconstruction Committee, and in the establishment of the Canada Mortgage and Housing Corporation, our first national agency with any responsibility for urban development, that a magnificent opportunity had opened—the opportunity to build a better future, to build better cities and a better society, and, in the process, to redress past ills and overcome past mistakes.[8] In Edmonton's case, where the municipal government was still paying off debts accumulated during the first land boom, when street car tracks and water and sewer lines had been laid across miles of empty land,[9] there was a special determination not to fall victim again to speculative madness. It was in the community's interest to ensure that the new boom—which, in the event, went on much longer and brought much greater growth than anyone could reasonably predict in 1949—would be better managed. The urban planning system provided some of the most important growth-management tools.

In the decades since 1949 planning has continued to evolve in both Edmonton and Alberta. The provincial legislation has been amended many times and was completely rewritten in 1977, when the Alberta planning system was given its current form.[10] The city and metropolitan systems have gone through numerous changes as well, sometimes in response to provincial government dictates (as in 1982 when the metropolitan planning authority was reconstituted as the Edmonton Metropolitan Regional Planning Commission) and sometimes leading them. In 1977, for example, the Planning Act gave municipalities the authority to enact bylaws adopting two new kinds of plans known as 'area structure plans' and 'area redevelopment plans.' These have become extremely important tools of residential planning, but they both sprang from earlier practice in the cities of Edmonton and Calgary. The larger implication is that residential planning has been a central

concern of urban government in Alberta for a long time, and successive provincial governments have given the cities a strong base of planning powers to work from. Whatever planning has been able to achieve in Edmonton owes much to that fact.

In its institutional role as the medium through which the community, the market, and professional planners relate to one another, planning, in theory, should be used to govern three general features of residential development: its amount, its location, and its physical character.[11] These features are highly interdependent and hence difficult to separate in their practical effects, but they provide a convenient framework for reviewing residential planning policies and practices in Edmonton and the larger metropolitan area. Of necessity, the review has to be quite selective, but it will cover the major planning initiatives of the past 50 years and attempt to put them into historical perspective.[12]

The *amount* of residential development is fundamentally market driven in Edmonton. It follows, in more or less direct proportion, the need for new housing generated by population growth and the increased number of households. 'Accommodating' market demand has always been the ruling principle for the local planning system, which has played its part by ensuring that suitable land was available whenever it was needed. Beyond that, the planning system's main responsibility has been to regulate the density or intensity of development, which has given it some control over the amount of land actually used for residential purposes.[13]

At the most general level, when determining how much land should be provided for future development, planners have to choose between two approaches. The first, once again, is to accommodate market demand, meaning that the density standards used for planning purposes will reflect the patterns of development that consumers and developers actually prefer. If the market preference is for detached houses on large lots, for example, that is what the planning system will deliver. The alternative is for the planning system to try to direct the market into a new pattern of development, usually a more intensive pattern. Intensification is a complex and contentious issue, however. It has never been widely supported in Canada, though it has gained strength in recent years from the environmental movement and the linked notions of 'green' and 'sustainable' cities.[14]

In Edmonton, where city councils have generally taken the view that the community should not interfere in the residential land market, the planning system has made only two serious attempts to manipulate the amount of residential development, one by increasing the amount of land available and the other by raising the city's overall density. The first intervention originated in the late 1960s, which was widely regarded as a time of housing crisis in Canada—a crisis of affordability.[15] Housing prices had risen sharply and high land costs were seen as an important contributing factor. If cheaper land could be made available, it was argued, and speculative land trading eliminated from the housing-cost equation, houses could be constructed for a segment of the population that had been squeezed out of the home-ownership market.[16] The mechanism of choice was the public land bank, which depended on some public authority being able to assemble a large block of land relatively cheaply and then to sell it to builders at or near cost, on condition that it be used for housing low-income families.[17]

Edmonton applied this concept in Mill Woods, a site of almost 9 square miles that was acquired at agricultural prices in the late 1960s. At first, the development of Mill Woods proceeded in accordance with land banking theory, but then the emphasis began to shift.[18] For one thing, the feeling of urgency, of national crisis, had faded; for another, Mill Woods was taking on a most unwelcome image—the image of the ghetto, in both economic and ethnic senses. Not only was this image socially undesirable but it also threatened the City of Edmonton's investment in the land bank and land sales were a valuable source of revenue. The City's marketing policy therefore changed from deliberately keeping prices low to selling lots at their full market value. Even in Mill Woods the market ultimately prevailed, and it became an essentially middle-class suburb, like most of the others in Edmonton.

The second attempt at planned intervention received official sanction in 1980, in the general municipal plan of that year, which put forward a long-range vision of a higher-density city.[19] Not a *high*-density city, it should be emphasized, but one in which some growth would be diverted from suburban areas to the inner city, through selective redevelopment. The suburbs, too, were to be developed more intensively, mainly by increasing the proportion of housing in multi-family projects of various kinds, a pattern that was already well established in Mill Woods and other recent communities.[20] Several factors contributed to this trend in the 1970s, but the single most important was the great demand for rental accommodation during a period of rapid population growth. In the two previous decades this kind of demand had been met largely through redevelopment, a combination of high-rise apartments, most heavily concentrated in the Oliver and Garneau districts, and walk-up apartments elsewhere in the inner city.[21] By the 1970s, however, these kinds of redevelopment had virtually ceased. Again, several factors were involved, but the one of greatest importance in the long run, especially with respect to the goal of intensification, was the growing opposition of local residents. Edmonton's first plans for inner-city neighbourhoods were prepared in the 1970s, and the one motive they had in common was the desire to limit, if not prevent, further redevelopment.[22]

In light of these circumstances, suburban locations provided the only alternative for the construction of higher-density forms of housing. Yet even that trend was short-lived. When the energy-driven boom collapsed in the early 1980s, the market for new rental accommodation collapsed with it. Many of the sites that had been allocated to multi-family housing development were no longer needed; they have since been rezoned to allow detached houses to be built instead. The effect has been to return the suburban housing mix closer to the low-density pattern that prevailed in the 1950s and 1960s.

To the present, Edmonton has not been able to pursue an effective intensification strategy. On the contrary, at a time when other Canadian cities, such as Toronto and Vancouver, have accepted the necessity for more intensive development, Edmonton is acting on the presumption that it is not feasible in the foreseeable future.[23] The current version of the general municipal plan, which was adopted in 1990, maintains a wistful kind of ambivalence towards the issue. On one side, it is still considered desirable to encourage the development of 'heterogeneous communities' by planning for a diverse mix of housing types in new suburban neighbourhoods. On the other, says the plan, 'the current strong market pressure for single-family dwellings and the relatively weak demand for multiple-family dwellings in the suburban areas is inevitable and must be accommodated.'[24] The most the plan can offer is a compromise, in hope that the market will adjust in time. Sites have to be set aside for multi-family housing, but they must be designed so that they can be subdivided into single-family house lots later, if needs must. The designated single-family sites are developed first, to allow the decision to subdivide to be deferred as long as possible.

As far as inner-city neighbourhoods are concerned, the idea of increased density disappeared entirely in the 1990 plan. The plan recognizes that a certain amount of redevelopment would be desirable in the interest of revitalization and aims to increase the inner-city housing supply,

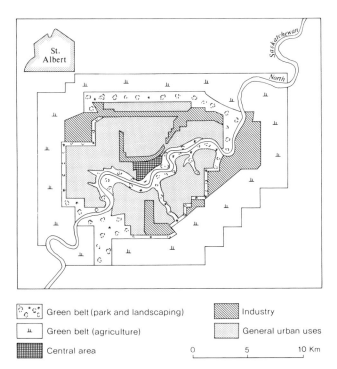

Green belt (park and landscaping)

Green belt (agriculture)

Central area

Industry

General urban uses

0   5   10 Km

Figure 3. The earliest version of Edmonton's first metropolitan plan as it appeared in the second annual report of the Edmonton District Planning Commission in 1952. A later, somewhat altered version can be seen in Noel Dant, 'Edmonton: Practical Results of Planning Measures since 1950,' Community Planning Review 4 (1954): 32. (MICHAEL FISHER)

but this policy is directed at vacant sites, such as those left by the relocation of railway tracks and the abandonment of old industrial premises. In well-established residential areas, where the main development trend is the renovation and upgrading of existing houses,[25] the plan's greatest concern is to 'maintain stable, secure and attractive inner-city communities which recognize residents' aspirations.'[26] Needless to say, these aspirations do not include higher-density redevelopment. In this respect, the planning system has acted against market pressures to give local communities what they want, though at the cost of forcing developers to continue to concentrate their activities in the suburbs.

An implication of even more general importance emerging from this discussion is that attitudes towards intensification affect the *location* of residential development as well as its amount. In practice, deciding where development should occur is a fundamental planning responsibility, and one over which municipal governments can exercise much control, if they choose to do so. For one thing, modern planning systems have strong regulatory powers to call on, including the lawful authority to restrict

development to approved locations while prohibiting it everywhere else. For another, all residential development depends to some degree on public services being made available, especially services to land such as sewerage, water supply, and road access. Municipal governments, as part of their capital budgeting procedure, can decide when and where to provide these services, giving them a direct means of control over the location of new development.

In Edmonton, both kinds of control have been used to good effect since about 1950. They are merely tools, however, which means they have no real *planning* value unless they are used to carry long-range policies into effect. Here Edmonton's record has been more problematic. Long-range plans there have certainly been, and clear intentions to direct development to definite locations, but other factors—both market and political—have also had an important bearing on the evolving development pattern.

Throughout the postwar period, one of the greatest planning concerns in the Edmonton area has been to secure a well-structured metropolitan form in the face of strong tendencies to fragmentation and dispersal. Even in the 1940s development was spilling beyond Edmonton's municipal boundaries, especially westward into Jasper Place, which exploded from next-to-nothing in 1939 to a population of more than 30,000 in 1961. The spectre of urban sprawl and wasteful, uncoordinated development outside Edmonton's jurisdiction was very real in 1949 and led City Council to seek advice from two planning professors, John Bland and Harold Spence Sales, whose report identified the essential dilemma of metropolitan planning everywhere[27]—a dilemma that bedevils Edmonton to this day. On one side rests the need for unitary or centralized control if an efficient, well-integrated development pattern is to be achieved; on the other rests the desire for autonomy on the part of the individual municipalities, including, as one of their most important considerations, the authority to make their own urban planning decisions. In the face of this conflict, Bland and Spence Sales resorted to a standard solution: they recommended that a metropolitan planning commission be instituted, as it in fact was, the following year. The commission was always a compromise, though. It started as a purely advisory body and never, in its 45-year life, gained real authority over the metropolitan municipalities.

As soon as the commission was appointed, it began to develop a long-range plan, based on a broad vision of the city's future structure.[28] The commission's planners were also influenced, as planners in many places were at the time, by British experience with the construction of so-

called 'satellite towns' as a means of controlling population dispersal around large cities. Following this model,
Edmonton's first plan envisaged a compact, roughly circular
city of about 450,000 people, contained within a permanent green belt where no development of any kind was to
be permitted (Figure 3). This plan seemed to allow for generous growth, since it was roughly three times Edmonton's
existing size. Any further growth was then to be directed
into satellite communities well removed from the city.
Morinville, Stony Plain, and Leduc were suggested as possible locations.

This scheme quickly foundered on the rock of municipal opposition. The City of Edmonton, for one, was not
prepared to accept any restrictions on its long-term
growth, but the issue that sealed the plan's fate, and also
demonstrated how little power the commission had over
the location of new development, was a proposal to construct a new community on a 'greenfields' site in the
Municipal District of Strathcona. So began Sherwood
Park, the original purpose of which was to provide home-
sites for workers in 'refinery row,' the large new industrial
complex then taking shape to the east of Edmonton.[29] The
City of Edmonton, naturally enough, voiced strong objections to the Sherwood Park scheme, as did the metropolitan planners. Their concern was that it was too close to
Edmonton to be a genuine satellite on the English model,
so they suggested that an alternative site be sought farther
east.[30] That suggestion was of no interest to the developer,
however, or to the Municipal District, which favoured the
project. The planning dispute dragged on for several years,
but development went ahead anyway.[31] The first houses
were built in 1955, driving a large nail into the metropolitan plan's coffin.

The dispute had another consequence as well: it was one
of the principal factors that spurred the Government
of Alberta to set up a commission of inquiry into the
metropolitan government of Edmonton and Calgary. The
McNally Commission, as it was known, was chiefly intended to concern itself with fiscal and taxation issues, but its
terms of reference were so broad that it came to embrace
the whole structure of local government, including arrangements for physical planning.[32] The establishment of the
Commission then forced the City of Edmonton to adopt
an official position on long-term growth, which it has
effectively maintained ever since.[33] In a nutshell, the City
told the McNally Commission that it wanted all development to be concentrated under its own jurisdiction. The
corollary, of course, was that the city boundaries would
have to be extended in advance of growth, by annexing

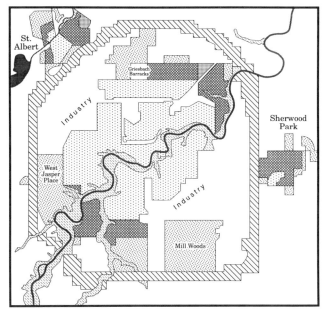

Figure 4. Residential expansion in Edmonton, 1961–95, illustrating
the influence of the second metropolitan plan on the subsequent
pattern of development. (MICHAEL FISHER)

territory from the surrounding municipalities, which would
remain forever rural. Nearby urban places, meaning St
Albert in particular, would also remain small. Thus were
the lines of battle drawn between Edmonton and its neighbours and the ground set for decades of political and planning conflict.[34] The McNally Commission's report served
to firm that ground as well, by endorsing the concept of a
consolidated, well-contained city.

Against this backdrop, a new metropolitan plan began
to take shape in the late 1950s. It had gained sufficient
acceptance by 1961 to be committed to a printed map that
showed Edmonton growing by compact extensions in two
directions: to the northeast, between Griesbach Barracks
and the river, and to the southwest, between the river and
the Calgary Trail (Figure 4). The city was starting to take
on a lineal form, oriented to the river, partly to economize
on physical infrastructure and partly to ensure convenient
access to major employment and service areas. The lineal
orientation was then repeated in Edmonton's main industrial zone, on the city's eastern and southeastern fringe,
and in a smaller way in the northwestern industrial zone.

Protecting land that is well located for industrial development, as determined by its access to major transport facilities, is always a prime planning concern. It was another important factor in the deliberate channelling of Edmonton's residential development into its own well-defined zones.

Such ideas were in clear deference to the City of Edmonton's wishes, although other interests were not ignored. For one thing, the plan designated a site of 4 square miles for residential development at Sherwood Park, an area adequate for about 40,000 people, its actual population in 1995. This decision was pragmatic in two respects: it included the land controlled by the development company, and it recognized that the project had secured the approval of the provincial government. The planners still thought Sherwood Park was too close to Edmonton—a 'tragedy' was how the McNally Commission had described it—but the most they could do in 1961 was zone a strip of agricultural land to maintain some separation from Edmonton. It was the last hangover from the original green belt proposal, along with a comparable strip between Edmonton and St Albert, which was also permitted to expand under the plan. Here, too, the provincial government was implicated, because St Albert had recently been designated a new town under the New Towns Act, 1956.[35] This statute was mostly used in the development of remote resource towns, such as Swan Hills and Fort McMurray, but it was also available to towns like St Albert that were experiencing unusual growth because of a metropolitan location.

Too much should not be read into the provincial government's involvement in either of these cases. Alberta governments have traditionally taken a hands-off approach to urban development issues, arguing that municipalities must resolve the issues for themselves, if they are truly self-governing.[36] Even the endorsement of the Sherwood Park and St Albert developments can be interpreted in this way, since it signified that the government had no intention of intervening in local planning conflicts to thwart the growth aspirations of autonomous communities. For the same reason, it made no move to implement the McNally Commission's central recommen-

Alberta governments have traditionally taken a hands-off approach to urban development issues, arguing that municipalities must resolve the issues for themselves, if they are truly self-governing.

dation, which was to consolidate the metropolitan area under Edmonton's jurisdiction. And again, in 1981, in response to Edmonton's bid to annex both St. Albert and Sherwood Park, the government ruled that independent, self-supporting communities could not be sacrificed to satisfy another community's desires.[37] Yet, in a separate part of the same annexation decision, the government did make an unprecedented intervention in Edmonton's development pattern, by ordering that at least 70 per cent of future metropolitan growth should be accommodated within the city. This 70-30 rule, as it became known, was highly unpopular with the suburban municipalities, as they made clear during the preparation of the new metropolitan plan a year or so later.[38] In the upshot, the rule, which was probably unenforceable anyway, was disregarded, leaving the municipalities free to attract whatever growth they could in open competition. The plan did continue a longstanding policy of restricting residential development to Sherwood Park and the existing urban centres, but otherwise location remained a market choice with the result demonstrated in Table 1.

Within Edmonton, the story has been quite different. When the city's residential development since 1960 is mapped, it is striking how concentrated it has been (Figure 4). With the great exception of Mill Woods, Edmonton has grown in well-contained, systematic extensions to the pattern first set by the 1961 plan. That plan was built on successively by the City's own plans of 1971, 1980, and 1990, all of which continued the general pattern of directing development into two broad sectors—a northern sector, which will eventually fill in to the inner margin of the 'restricted development area,'[39] and a southwestern sector, which is broken into three more or less separate zones by the valleys of the North Saskatchewan River and Whitemud Creek. The valleys are important locational features in their own right, attracting most of Edmonton's prime residential development; protecting them has been a deliberate planning goal since at least the 1961 plan.

In a perverse way, the 1961 plan was also a determining factor in the selection of Mill Woods as the location for Edmonton's venture into public land banking. The initial steps were taken in secret by the Government of Alberta—'in secret' because land prices would have escalated if the government's intentions had become known, thus defeating the whole purpose of the exercise.[40] But why choose the Mill Woods site? The answer lay in the fact that the land was zoned for agricultural use, and the plan gave no reason to suppose that it could ever be considered for residential development. For one thing, it was detached from other residential districts, in a sector of the metropolitan area that seemed most suitable for industrial development in the long term. For another, because it was not within an established expansion corridor, the Mill Woods site was not well connected to existing service networks. Road access was poor, for example, and special infrastructure had to be constructed, such as a deep trunk storm sewer leading directly to the river. The handicaps were overcome in time, but they were a direct consequence of the fact that Mill Woods represented a huge distortion of the planned development pattern. The advantage of cheap land was therefore undercut by the project's special costs—including 'opportunity costs,' an economist's term for opportunities forgone elsewhere. If the equivalent of Mill Woods had been built in the western and southwestern sectors of the city, for example, it is probable that their longstanding transportation problems, which erupted in the McKinnon Ravine and Keillor Road disputes, would have been resolved long since. Can we then say that Mill Woods was well located, from an urban planning perspective? The question is moot at best.

Apart from the Mill Woods experience, Edmonton's planning authorities have exercised a high degree of control over the location of residential development within the city and have been generally successful at directing it into the planned pattern. They have certainly had more effect on the location of development than its amount. Their strongest influence, however, with the greatest consequences for everyday life in Edmonton, has been expressed in the *physical character* of the residential environment, the third and final aspect of development that falls within the general scope of urban planning.

This last observation applies particularly to areas developed since 1950. Although plans have been devised for many of the city's older neighbourhoods (meaning those neighbourhoods subdivided on the grid street pattern before 1914), their purpose has been largely remedial and their impact on Edmonton's residential environment has been comparatively slight.[41] Zoning regulations have provided the main form of control in the older parts of the city, and zoning alone, although a powerful tool, does not produce environments that can reasonably be called planned, let alone well planned. This section of the review will therefore focus on areas of new development, with particular consideration for the planning principles that have given Edmonton's suburban districts their characteristic structure and form.

'Structure' is a technical term that refers to the composition and spatial organization of the essential components of the residential environment, meaning major land uses, circulation networks, and community facilities. Ensuring that new residential areas are adequately provided with schools, parks, shopping centres, and so on and that these facilities are conveniently located in relation to the populations they are intended to serve, are especially important planning responsibilities; they represent vital aspects of the community interest in residential development. A typical structure plan is also quite general. It sets out the broad outlines of the future development pattern for a prescribed area, leaving the details to be filled in later through plans for individual neighbourhoods and subdivisions.[42] At that time, each new residential area is given its specific form, though not all aspects of physical form come under effective planning control. Even architectural style, which is the most visible property of the residential environment, is normally excluded. What the planning system is mostly responsible for is the spatial or two-dimensional form of residential development, embracing such things as the layout of streets and walkways, the shapes and dimensions of building lots, and the precise location and arrangement of community facilities. These are all regulated through the subdivision control process, the exercise of which has permitted a strong public influence on the form of residential development in Edmonton—two-dimensional form, at all events. Three-dimensional form is more crudely regulated under the zoning system, which includes the power to control the size and spacing of buildings by setting height limits and minimum yard requirements. Such regulations impose a definite but unimaginative regularity on the typical residential scene, an outcome that is all too well demonstrated in Edmonton.

With respect to the spatial organization and detailed configuration of new residential areas, Edmonton's planning system has had much more success. This success can be traced back to Noel Dant, Edmonton's first full-time planning officer, whose greatest contribution to Edmonton was the introduction of a technique known as 'neighbourhood unit' planning. The basic concept was originally formulated in the 1920s by an American planner, Clarence Perry, but it did not come to be widely applied until the postwar period. Edmonton was actually a leader in this development, thanks to Dant, and his initial neighbourhood unit designs were publicized across Canada as examples for other cities to emulate.[43] In Edmonton itself, in the years since 1950, approximately 125 neighbourhoods have come under development, all of them following the same general principles that Perry laid down 70 years ago. These neighbourhoods do not all look alike; nor are they are all organized in exactly the same way. Perry's principles can take different forms and have also been subject to various modifications over the years. Most of the modifications reflect international developments in planning theory and practice, but some are unique to Edmonton.

To put these changes into historical perspective, it is useful to think of Edmonton as having progressed through four stages of residential planning and design, each stage giving rise to a characteristic neighbourhood form. These will be referred to, in chronological sequence, as modified-grid neighbourhoods, independent neighbourhood units, modified-Radburn neighbourhoods, and cluster-plan neighbourhoods.[44] The two last are further characterized by being organized into hierarchical structures. The approximate periods for which each type was representative are 1950–55, 1955 to the late 1960s, the late 1960s to the late 1970s, and the late 1970s to the present.

As originally conceived by Perry and his followers, neighbourhood units were intended to overcome the environmental deficiencies of the standard grid subdivisions of the day. Privacy, safety, and protection from traffic; security of investment for homeowners; access to amenities and essential services; and the residents' sense of community—these were the qualities that planners particularly sought to improve. They also believed, as Perry did, that the improvements would be best achieved by planning residential development on a neighbourhood basis in accordance with the following principles:[45]

1. Each neighbourhood should be large enough to support one elementary school (normally meaning a population of around three- to five-thousand people).

2. Each neighbourhood should form a definite, identifiable unit with clear boundaries. In most cases, these would be arterial streets designed to carry heavy loads of traffic past the neighbourhood but not into it.

3. The school and other 'neighbourhood institutions,' such as churches and meeting halls, should be grouped in a 'community centre,' near the geographical centre of the unit. This arrangement had a double value: it gave the neighbourhood a strong focus, in both a physical and a social sense, and it put the facilities within easy walking distance of all the neighbourhood residents.

4. Every neighbourhood should be generously provided with public open space, both for recreational purposes (including school playing fields) and as an amenity, to enhance the attractiveness of the residential environment.

5. Convenience shopping facilities should be provided as well, but not as part of the community centre. To avoid the risk of drawing external traffic into the neighbourhood, shopping centres should be located at neighbourhood entry points.

6. To provide further protection from external traffic, the neighbourhood street network should be designed to be impassable to through traffic, while directing local traffic in and out as efficiently and safely as possible. The favoured form of network was a curvilinear one organized as a hierarchy, in which 'collector streets' acted like streams, gathering traffic from a number of tributaries (the 'residential streets') and then feeding it out to join the arterial flow at carefully controlled intersections. Curving streets have other advantages as well. They are thought to create more attractive streetscapes than long, straight ones; they are safer because they carry less traffic, have fewer intersections, and discourage speeding; and they require less land. Pedestrians are safer, too, as a recent study of pedestrian accidents in Edmonton proved.[46]

These, then, were the theoretical considerations that influenced Noel Dant, when he came to apply the neighbourhood unit concept to Edmonton.[47] His ideas fell on unusually receptive ground through a fortuitous combination of circumstances. One, as mentioned, was the positive new attitude towards planning. Another was rapid growth, which meant that neighbourhoods could be built quickly as complete units. But the most favourable circumstance of all was the fact that the municipal government had become the principal owner of vacant land in Edmonton. In the years after the real estate boom collapsed in 1913, most undeveloped land was forfeited to the municipality because of tax delinquency.[48] This land was a liability for many years, but almost overnight it turned into an invaluable asset, not so much because of the revenue it earned as because of the power granted by public ownership. For most of the 1950s the City of Edmonton was able to control the whole residential development process, from initial planning and detailed design to eventual sale and construction.[49] Provided with a golden opportunity to create change, Dant took full advantage. Well before the supply of city-owned land was exhausted and the development process passed into private hands, the neighbourhood unit concept had become the established basis for residential planning and design in Edmonton.[50]

At first, however, as illustrated by neighbourhoods like Britannia and Parkallen (Figure 5A), the neighbourhood plans had to be modified from the theoretical principles, particularly with respect to their internal street networks. The explanation lay in a peculiarity of Edmonton's early development pattern—the extremely low density of development in its fringe areas, where isolated houses were widely scattered over the original grid subdivisions.[51] When these areas came to be resubdivided in the 1950s, using a legal technique known as 'replotting,'[52] the new plans had to accommodate the developed properties and the streets on which they were located. The result was a hybrid form, the modified-grid neighbourhood, in which neighbourhood unit features were grafted onto partially built-up areas.

This stage of neighbourhood planning did not last long. By the mid 1950s residential development was advancing onto land where there were no houses, no utilities, and no developed streets. Here, it was possible to use the replotting procedure to cancel the old subdivision plans entirely and replace them with neighbourhood unit plans. Over a period of 10 to 15 years, almost 40 such neighbourhoods were built in Edmonton. They differ appreciably in their detailed forms, but the imprint of Perry's principles is unmistakeable in every case. The Lendrum neighbourhood circa 1960 is a particularly good example (Figure 5B).

Meanwhile, even as the first generation of Edmonton's neighbourhood units was being built, new ideas were stirring in the planners' minds, ideas that would manifest themselves in plans for large new suburban districts, such as the West Jasper Place plan of 1967 and the Mill Woods plan of 1971.[53] These plans were the forerunners of today's area structure plans, and they introduced two key changes. The first, which is reflected in the term 'modified-Radburn neighbourhoods,' resulted in a new neighbourhood form. Its source was the new town of Radburn, New Jersey, which had been built in the late 1920s. Radburn incorporated all of Perry's neighbourhood unit principles, but in a radically different form, described by designers Clarence Stein and Henry Wright as 'realistically planned for the Motor Age.'[54] There were two chief innovations: a street network that was greatly simplified by clumping residential blocks into so-called 'superblocks,' with houses clustered around their margins on short culs-de-sac; and, in the inte-

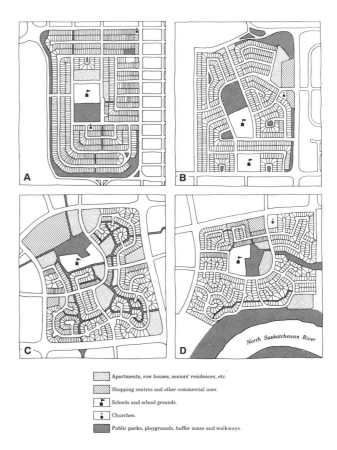

Figure 5. Examples of neighbourhood form in the four stages of residential planning and design in Edmonton: A) Parkallen, a modified-grid neighbourhood; B) Lendrum, an independent neighbourhood unit; C) Lee Ridge, a modified-Radburn neighbourhood; and D) Gariepy, a cluster-plan neighbourhood. (MICHAEL FISHER)

riors of the superblocks, common open space threaded with walkway networks that separated pedestrians from vehicular traffic. The Radburn model has long been touted as the ultimate in pedestrian safety, and that view appears to have been confirmed in Edmonton as well. Although Edmonton has no pure Radburn neighbourhoods, there are more than 30 with separate walkway networks; they are significantly safer on average than even the original neighbourhood units.[55] Neighbourhoods like Thorncliff and Aldergrove in West Jasper Place fall into this category, as do the first neighbourhoods in Mill Woods (Figure 5C).

The second critical change in planning approach grew out of the realization that individual neighbourhood units, no matter how carefully planned, could not provide for all the requirements of modern suburban life. Following Perry, Edmonton's first-generation neighbourhoods were designed as though they were independent, self-contained units— which they can never be. It takes several neighbourhoods to support a junior high school, for example, and even more for a senior high school. Edmonton also has the complication of two school systems of unequal size. The neighbourhood unit concept is admirably suited to Edmonton's public elementary schools, but it takes two neighbourhoods to form an adequate catchment area for a separate school. Other services, too, require population bases larger than a single neighbourhood—recreational services such as swimming pools and ice arenas, commercial services of the kinds found in regional shopping centres, health services, library services, and so on. How should suburban areas be structured to ensure that these higher-order services are adequately provided for at locations that are conveniently and safely accessible to the residents of their service areas? Edmonton's planners began to grapple with this general problem in the 1960s.

The theoretical solution was provided by one of Canada's most influential planners, Humphrey Carver, in a book entitled *Cities in the Suburbs*. Taking the British new towns as his model and Radburn and Don Mills in Toronto as the North American prototypes, Carver proposed that suburban districts should be planned like free-standing new towns.[56] Each district would form a distinct unit, large enough to be self-sufficient in service facilities and organized around a 'town centre' where the most specialized facilities would be concentrated. Neighbourhoods would still constitute the basic building blocks of these 'cities in the suburbs,' but they would be designed as integral components of the larger structure. Various technical considerations were entailed, the most visible of which was a major change in the form of street networks. Unlike the independent neighbourhood units, neighbourhoods in hierarchical structures are linked together by continuous through-streets that provide direct connections to town centres and other community facilities.[57] Walkway networks can similarly be designed to cover entire suburban districts, linking neighbourhood to neighbourhood as they did at Radburn itself. Mill Woods and West Jasper Place afford good examples of both features. Their effects at the neighbourhood scale are illustrated in Figure 5C, in the plan for Lee Ridge.

Then, in the next and (for the moment) final planning

Edmonton also has the complication of two school systems of unequal size. The neighbourhood unit concept is admirably suited to Edmonton's public elementary schools, but it takes two neighbourhoods to form an adequate catchment area for a separate school.

step, Edmonton's enthusiasm for separate walkways evaporated as quickly as it had been born. There were several reasons, including the cost to developers (who not only had to provide the land for walkways but were being asked to construct them), problems of maintenance and supervision (which were divided among several civic departments), and concerns about personal safety on secluded, lightly-used paths.[58] The abandonment of walkways does not mean that they were a failure, though. A recent study in West Jasper Place found them to be a popular feature of the residential environment, especially valued today as recreational facilities.[59] Nonetheless, from the late 1970s, walkways were no longer included in most neighbourhood plans, even in those districts where they had originally been proposed. In both West Jasper Place and Mill Woods, for example, the later neighbourhoods are of the 'cluster-plan' type, which is really the modified-Radburn type without full walkway networks. It is also the local variant of a form that has become standard across North America under the general term 'cluster development,' referring to the arrangement of houses in small, quiet, sheltered groups, with service access from culs-de-sac or short loop streets. Gariepy in West Jasper Place (Figure 5D) is just one of many Edmonton examples.

Despite their different appearance, cluster-plan neighbourhoods are underlain by essentially the same planning intentions and ideals that inspired Perry, Dant, and Stein and Wright, so long ago. The really significant difference, and the most important change in residential planning practice in Edmonton after the initial adoption of neighbourhood unit planning, is not in the design of neighbourhoods but in their organization into larger, more complex structures. Since this major innovation was made in the late 1960s, all of Edmonton's suburban areas have been arranged hierarchically, including those where development has barely started yet, such as Lewis Farms and The Meadows. The case *par excellence* is Mill Woods, in large part because the public land bank gave the City of Edmonton complete control over planning and development.[60] Mill Woods is also the largest of the new suburban communities, with an ultimate population of about 100,000. This size not only ensures a high degree of self-containment across a broad array of specialized services but also requires an unusually elaborate hierarchical system. At the bottom are 23 neighbourhoods that are grouped into 8 'communities,' the level at which junior high schools and district shopping centres are provided. The communities, in turn, are grouped around the large town centre complex that combines a regional shopping centre and other business outlets with special educational, recreational, and medical facilities (public and separate senior high schools, a campus of Grant MacEwan Community College, the Mill Woods recreation centre and district park, and the Grey Nuns Hospital). This is a complex unique in Edmonton, and by far the most successful expression yet of Carver's town centre concept. Elsewhere in the city, the concept has proved more difficult to realize, even allowing for the fact that town centre development is a long-term venture that cannot begin until a substantial population base has been built up.[61] In some cases (eg. Kaskitayo), the district is probably too small for a well-equipped town centre; in others (eg. Clareview), there has been no entrepreneurial interest in developing a shopping centre on the designated site; and in West Jasper Place, the developers preferred a different site altogether, the site that became West Edmonton Mall.[62] These circumstances have brought the whole notion of town centres into question, though the general municipal plan still presents them as desirable features of the residential environment.

Plans do not automatically result in development, of course. If development occurs, the planning system can do much to shape its structure and form; but it is the market that determines the need for development in the first place. To a large degree, too, plans depend on market acceptance for their success, as Edmonton's experience demonstrates in so many ways, both negatively and positively. Yet Edmonton's planning system has not been a mere handmaiden to the market or the development industry. Admittedly, planning has had to accommodate the market in certain respects, and the rare attempts to alter the pattern of market demand, or to shift it into new courses, were not particularly successful. But in those areas where the planning system has been allowed to act on behalf of the community interest, it has been a powerful force over the whole of the postwar period and has indeed had a major influence on the organization and appearance of the contemporary city. It has been less successful at the metropolitan scale, but that has always been a political matter as much as an economic one, as suburban municipalities have asserted their right to pursue their own

growth aspirations. Within the city proper, both the location of residential development and its physical character can be attributed primarily to planning. Nor should it be forgotten how quickly Edmonton's planning system took effect, or how early in the city's most sustained growth period. Almost from the outset, an effective planning system was in place, directing and controlling the residential development process and setting it on its modern track. In the long term, that is the most significant achievement of all—and in that sense, Edmonton can truly regard itself as a well-planned city. ❧

DAVID CHUENYAN LAI

THREE CHINATOWNS

Celebrating Chinese New Year in the streets of Edmonton's Chinatown, 1975.
(PAA J.2139/2)

*E*dmonton boasts many distinct neighbourhoods, each with its own lifestyle and flavour. Sometimes they are the result of careful civic planning, as P.J. Smith discusses; other times they emerge of their own momentum. One of Edmonton's oldest and most recognizable neighbourhoods is Chinatown, home or shopping centre for many Chinese as well as a popular source of Asian specialities for non-Chinese Edmontonians. In fact, as David Chuenyan Lai argues, Edmonton has had three Chinatowns. The Old (original) China-town, dating back to the pre-World War One mostly male Chinese immigrant community, was marginalized by white society. It was destroyed in the late 1970s. The nearby Replaced Chinatown developed in the 1980s through the co-operation of the City and the Chinese community, the latter augmented by large-scale Chinese immigration after 1967.

There are also two New Chinatowns, one in the traditional area of Chinese concentration near the downtown core and with a prominent Vietnamese Chinese presence, the other south of the river in trendy Old Strathcona.

A professor of geography at the University of Victoria, and named to the Order of Canada for his work in the Chinese community, David Chuenyan Lai is a recognized authority on Chinatowns throughout North America. He has worked as a consultant on many Chinatown development projects, from Victoria and Ottawa in Canada to Portland, Oregon. His interest in Edmonton's Chinatowns is also more than academic; in the 1980s he advised on the Chinatown Gateway project.

'CHINATOWN,' A TERM COMMONLY USED OUTSIDE China, refers to the Chinese quarter of a city. In 1973 I defined Chinatown in North America as 'a concentration of Chinese people and economic activities in one or more city blocks which forms a unique component of an urban fabric. It is basically an idiosyncratic, oriental community amidst an occidental urban environment.' Fifteen years later I proposed a three-model classification of Chinatowns—Old, Replaced, and New—and identified white racism, cultural barriers, and economic factors as important to the origins of the first type.[1] In her 1991 study of the role of the Canadian government in the social construction of Vancouver's Chinatown over the past hundred years, Kay Anderson concluded that Chinatown as both a label and a concept belonged to European society. Chinatowns, she said, were in large part created by Europeans who did not understand the Chinese residents and thus constructed a mental boundary between 'their' and 'our' territory.[2] A third authority on the Chinese-Canadian experience, sociologist Peter Li does not accept the notion of New Chinatown.[3] The interesting story of the development of Edmonton's three Chinatowns illustrates my point that Chinatown is not a European creation and that its characteristics have been changing since the end of the Second World War.

An Old Chinatown is a Chinese neighbourhood established before the Second World War and characterized by a great concentration of Chinese people, businesses, and institutions. In the late nineteenth century the white Canadian public had a very negative image of Chinatown. A reporter for the Victoria *Colonist*, for example, described Chinatown as an area '"alive" with human vermin . . . [where] no decent person now thinks of venturing.' A contemporary Vancouver newspaper claimed that Chinatown 'where the Celestials congregated was an eyesore to civilization.'[4] Less overtly prejudiced, a Methodist clergyman writing in 1913 described one Chinatown as 'a miniature Chinese town built by Chinese carpenters . . . [whose residents] were unloved and separated from their neighbours by an almost impassable gulf of race, colour, language and thought.'[5]

Since the 1950s many Old Chinatowns in Canada have been wholly or partially demolished through the relocation and replacement of residents during slum clearance, urban renewal, street-widening, and other projects. Some Old Chinatowns have been rehabilitated, or redeveloped, and contain many non-Chinese residents and business concerns as a result of gentrification. Today many cities try to preserve their Old Chinatowns as historic districts and to make them into tourist attractions. In spite of these changes, however, an existing Old Chinatown is still characterized by a great concentration of Chinese institutions such as clan society premises, district association buildings, schools, temples, and churches. Most of the structures were built in the late nineteenth and early twentieth centuries and still have typical Chinatown architectural features like recessed or projected balconies. Many residents are elderly or low-income people seeking companionship and cheap accommodation. Often former Chinatown residents, now living in the more affluent suburbs, retain an emotional bond and nostalgic attachment to the area. They look upon Old Chinatown as a socio-psychological well to which they can return and refresh themselves.

In Alberta, Edmonton's Old Chinatown was established much later than Calgary's, where the Canadian Pacific Railway influenced its origin and growth. In 1899 there were only thirteen Chinese men in Edmonton, working in the town's sole Chinese restaurant and two Chinese laundries.[6] A small Chinatown began to emerge around 1911, when the Chinese population stood at 154 (150 males, 4 females); by 1921 it had risen to 518 (501 males, 17 females).[7] Following the passage of the notorious Chinese Immigration Act of 1923, which prohibited further Chinese movement to Canada, the Chinese population in every town and city in the country began to decline. The number of Chinese in Edmonton dropped from 467 (440 males, 27 females) in 1931 to 384 in 1941. Chinese immigration resumed after 1947 with the repeal of the so-called exclusion act. Many new immigrants came to Edmonton, so that the city's Chinese population rose steadily from 782 (622 males, 160 females) in 1951 to 1,808 (1,092 males, 716 females) in 1961 and 4,940 (2,610 males, 2,330 females) in 1971.[8] Prior to the 1970s a highly unbalanced sex ratio virtually ruled out natural growth in the community.

The fortunes of Edmonton's Old Chinatown closely paralleled the increase and decrease in the local Chinese population. The first few Chinese in Edmonton came from Calgary, where, in June 1892, a Chinese laundry worker contracted smallpox. Officials immediately closed the laundry, burned the building and its contents, and placed its Chinese occupants under quarantine.[9] That summer, no doubt fearing that the white public would use this incident as an excuse to close all the Chinese laundries in Calgary, Chung Gee and his brother, Chung Yan, left for Edmonton and set up business in the newly incorporated town. Their existence was not well known until

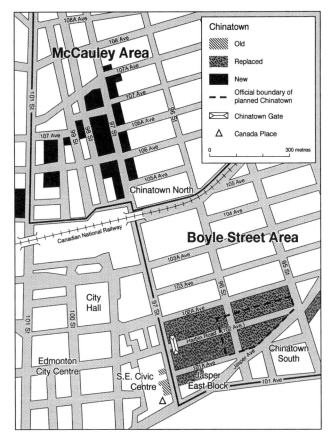

Figure 1. Locations of Edmonton's Chinatowns, 1995.
(DAVID CHUENYAN LAI)

It is estimated by the police and by the Chinese themselves . . . that there are between 250 and 275 Chinamen
resident in Edmonton.

Several of the stores hold every kind of Chinese merchandise, with restaurants and underground dives, where
the Chinamen spend their leisure time. In the back room
behind the stores the indolent ones roll and recline on
chairs and tables, smoking cigarettes and talking to one
another in their chop-stick sort of language. Here are also
tables where it is supposed the game of fan-tan is played
at night by those who indulge in the pastime of gambling.

In the Chinese stores queer wares are on sale; the long
strange pipes of the Celestials, strange looking masses of
Chinese foods, lacquer work, ivory carvings, silk clothing
and other curious and unknown articles. Down in the
basement of the building every foot is utilized and the
entire under part of the building is connected from end to
end with mysterious doors and passages.

The basement is fitted with bunks and beds. These
sleeping places are lined on each side of the walls as
thickly as possible and articles of clothing and Chinese
musical instruments hang over bunks. These bunks are
nothing but inch boards, nailed together and put on short
legs, the only covering or bedding being a couple of blankets of the kind that are in vogue in the lumber camp and
the shack of the homesteader.

In one room a half dozen Chinamen lay in various
stages of bliss induced by the smoking of opium, the acrid
fumes of which hung heavy in the air. One much-with-
ered and shrunken specimen of Chinese manhood lay
like dead with his flat chest barely moving.[12]

By 1921 Edmonton's Chinatown had expanded eastward along 101A Avenue from 98 Street as far as 95
Street. Most of its some 500 residents, who accounted
for only 1 per cent of the city's population, were single
labourers. Without any family life and amenities in
Chinatown, many men indulged in gambling, prostitution, and opium smoking to alleviate their loneliness
and while away their idle hours. Local Methodist and
Presbyterian missionaries, who organized English and religion classes, were eager to introduce Christianity and to
help the men spiritually and materially. The missionaries
succeeded in converting a few Chinese attendants,
although most of them were more interested in acquiring
English than the Christian faith.[13]

By far the most significant development in Chinatown
was the birth of formal, clan- or family-based organizations.
The community was dominated by people surnamed Mah,

March 1893 when Chung Yan was 'nearly mobbed' and
charged for depositing hot ashes near Hawey's stable,
causing a fire.[10]

Although the Chinese in Edmonton, like their compa-
triots in Vancouver and other Canadian cities, experienced discrimination, the local white public did not 'create' a Chinatown for them. For over a decade, Chinese
residents were so few and scattered that they did not need
a focal point for their socio-economic activities. A
Chinatown began to emerge on the eastern fringe of
downtown Edmonton around 1911 after a few Chinese
merchants established their businesses at the intersection
of Namayo Avenue (97 Street) and Rice Street (101A
Avenue) to cater to a growing Chinese population.[11]
Gradually, the small Chinese quarters expanded to cover
an area of about three city blocks bounded by Jasper
Avenue, Elizabeth Street (102 Avenue), Namayo Avenue,
and Fraser Street (98 Street) (Figure 1). An *Edmonton
Bulletin* reporter visited this Chinatown in 1908 and left
what is one of only a handful of known contemporary
accounts:

Wong, and Gee, giving rise to the Mah Association in 1913, the Wong Society in 1917, and the Gee Association in 1920. A Chinese Dramatic Club was formed in 1919. In the 1920s the Chinese Nationalist League (the Kuomintang), a political party, also established a local branch. All these groups provided services essential to their 'bachelor' members and organized social activities for them during the Chinese New Year and other festivals. The Chinese community did not have a community-wide organization to represent it until the Chinese Benevolent Association (CBA) was established in 1932.[14] It has since functioned as a voice for Chinese living not only in Edmonton but also throughout northern Alberta.

After the Second World War, Edmonton's Chinatown became a skid row in the Boyle Street area, where there were already many cheap hotels, rooming houses, shabby theatres, taverns, dance halls, and second-hand stores.[15] Most of the Chinese had moved to better residential neighbourhoods as they became better off economically and more accepted by white Edmontonians. Many Canadian-born Chinese children who were not brought up in Chinatown had integrated so well into the host society that they did not regard Chinatown as their home at all. The Chinese who remained in Chinatown were mostly elderly single males who could not afford better accommodation or newly arrived immigrants who could not speak English and did not have much money. To these new immigrants, Chinatown still functioned as a springboard for adaptation to the Canadian way of life and integration into the host society. As many newcomers were single or young couples with no children, natural increase could not make up the loss of population through death and departure. With steady depopulation, businesses in Chinatown continued to decline both in number and in variety. The traditional Chinese-speaking associations also found it difficult to recruit members since many locally born youths, unable to speak Chinese, did not bother to join; some rejected any type of affiliation at all. As a result, many community organizations in Chinatown closed or became defunct.

After Canada removed racial criteria for entering the country in 1967, new Chinese immigrants to Edmonton differed from their nineteenth-century predecessors with respect to place of origin, wealth, education, occupation, aspirations, and motives. Most were independent immigrants, admitted on points awarded for their educational background, occupational skills, knowledge of English, and related qualities. They came from many lands and cultures—chiefly Hong Kong, Taiwan, and southeast Asia—and

tended to settle in the suburbs or better downtown neighbourhoods. Hence, the post-1967 swell of Chinese immigrants did not help increase the population of Chinatown.[16]

Throughout the 1960s and 1970s the future of Edmonton's Old Chinatown was uncertain. A land use survey in 1973 found thirty-nine family households and seventy-six single-person households living in an area bound by Jasper and 102A avenues between 97 and 96 streets. About one-third of Chinatown's 260 residents were seniors; the remainder comprised mostly low-income people who worked as cooks, waiters, dishwashers, tailors, and store assistants in Chinatown itself. The twenty-seven Chinese businesses included ten grocery stores, seven restaurants, two barber shops, and two herbalist stores.[17] A large portion of Chinatown's commercial section, concentrated on the west side of 97 Street between Jasper and 102 avenues, faced demolition in autumn 1968 when the federal government proposed to consolidate its offices in the area known as the Southeast Civic Centre. Accordingly, in November of that year the CBA sent a brief to Ottawa requesting the preservation of Chinatown in any urban renewal project.[18] Partly because of the CBA's intervention and partly for financial reasons, the federal government shelved the consolidation project.

The threat to the survival of Old Chinatown re-emerged in July 1973 when the city considered widening the west side of 97 Street by 2.5 metres. Like the earlier federal government proposal, this project would have wiped out the remaining commercial strip of Chinatown. In August a Committee to 'Save Chinatown' was formed by representatives of the CBA, the Chinese Nationalist League, the Chinese Freemasons, and other Chinese asso-

The business section of Old Chinatown, 1977, destroyed in the 1980s to make way for redevelopment of the area. (DAVID CHUENYAN LAI)

ciations.[19] The Committee feared that the destruction of Chinatown would have a great impact on its Chinese residents, leading to a loss of social support networks, particularly for the elderly and those on low incomes, and producing feelings of isolation and depression. However, many Chinese people felt that Old Chinatown was going to die sooner or later. In response to widening apprehension, the Edmonton Chinese Community Development Committee (ECCDC), chaired by Bruce Yip, was formed in April 1975 and charged with looking for possible sites for a new Chinatown, a senior citizens' home, and a Chinese cultural centre. The following month City Council established a task force to determine the needs and commitments of the City as well as those of the Chinese community in the Chinatown issue. Council also decided in February 1976 to postpone the street-widening project until its impact was properly assessed.[20]

Throughout the late 1970s the city's Planning Department worked closely with the Chinese community to develop a new Chinatown. In April 1977 the ECCDC was replaced by the Edmonton Chinatown Planning Committee (ECPC), formed by representatives from the Chinese Merchants' Association, the Chinese Dramatic Club, the Chinese Freemasons, the Wong Society, and other Chinese associations. Chaired by Dick B. Wong, the ECPC worked with the Planning Department to prepare a Chinatown plan. Approved by City Council in September 1979, this plan called for the demolition of Old Chinatown and the creation of a Replaced Chinatown. Notices were sent to Chinese business owners telling them to vacate their premises before 30 April 1981: several operators

closed their doors permanently, while others relocated to the nearby Jasper East Block or moved to other parts of the city. By the end of 1981, its buildings razed, Old Chinatown was dead. Canada Place, the headquarters of the federal government's regional offices, eventually occupied the site.

A Replaced Chinatown is a post-1945 phenomenon in which at least 80 per cent of the buildings have been constructed to replace prewar structures. Like an Old Chinatown, a Replaced Chinatown combines residential, commercial, and institutional functions, but unlike an Old Chinatown, it is a newly-established or -renovated inner-city neighbourhood that can be either unplanned or planned. An unplanned Replaced Chinatown features a redeveloped Old Chinatown where most of the original structures have been demolished to make way for new buildings. Calgary's Old Chinatown, for example, has been redeveloped so extensively that its prewar characteristics are virtually invisible today. A planned Replaced Chinatown is built from scratch in another location, providing sites and buildings for residents, business concerns, and institutions displaced from a demolished Old Chinatown. Examples are found in Stockton and Sacramento, California, and in Edmonton.

In January 1978 the Planning Department of the City of Edmonton issued a report, entitled *Downtown Plan, Working Paper No. 1: The Future of Chinatown*, for the creation of a Replaced Chinatown. The report identified four alternative sites: the Southeast Civic Centre Complex, the City Market, the Jasper East Block, and city blocks at 102 Avenue between 96 and 95 streets.[21] The first area proved unsuitable because the development of a new Chinatown in the Complex depended on the interest and financial resources of the federal government as well as of the Old Chinatown merchants. The second alternative was more feasible because the City owned much of the land in the City Market, making land consolidation easier. Parking and future expansion would be restricted, however, due to the area's small size. The third alternative was also feasible because the Jasper East Block had many vacant premises into which dislocated Chinese businesses could be moved, but here, too, lack of space would limit any major future expansion. The last alternative offered the most possibilities. The site was only a block east of Old Chinatown (and close to the Chinese residents on 92 and 93 streets); it had open space for expansion; and a few Chinese stores and institutions had already located there. The Chinese Elders' Mansion, for example, was completed in September 1977 at 102

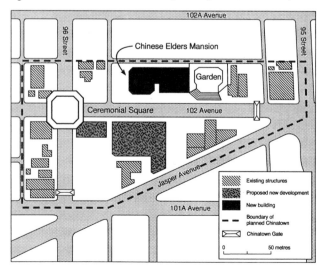

Figure 2. The Revised Chinatown Plan, 1980. (DAVID CHUENYAN LAI)

Avenue between 95 and 96 streets.[22] Not only would the availability of land around the Mansion provide sites for other Chinese institutions, like a cultural centre, but many Chinese people preferred to have the Replaced Chinatown near the senior citizens' home.

In June 1979 Stephen Iu, a consulting architect, was engaged to design a Chinatown plan based on the Planning Department report. Iu's plan, produced a month later, recommended the demolition of Old Chinatown and development of a Replaced Chinatown in a four-block area straddling 102 Avenue between 95 and 96 streets. It also recommended a ceremonial square at the intersection of 102 Avenue and 96 Street and a Chinese arch spanning 96 Street just north of Jasper Avenue.[23] Alex Szchechina, president of the Boyle Street Community League, and many other people in the neighbourhood supported the plan, which would help rejuvenate the Boyle Street area and increase police patrols. However, a few individuals voiced opposition. One was Pat O'Hara, owner of an auction house at 102 Avenue, who feared that the proposed Chinatown development 'could become a racial ghetto full of crime and vice' and claimed that 'Chinatown is not in the best interests of Edmonton. Every other North American city that has Chinatowns has found they've become the centre for crime and vice.'[24] O'Hara's views were not widely shared, for the proposed project received much support from the Edmonton public. City Council finally approved the Chinatown plan in principle in September 1979.

Edmonton's plan for a Replaced Chinatown was revised over the next year with respect to policy directives, land use proposals, and fiscal implementation. The revised plan suggested that the Chinatown area be designated for a mixture of high-density residential-cum-commercial and ancillary institutional uses and called for the construction of two Chinese arches as symbolic entrances (Figure 2).[25] The plan's authors advocated a design able to attract some of the existing scattered Chinese residential, commercial, and cultural functions as well as to provide a focal point for new Chinese initiatives. The envisaged development was also to complement the adjacent downtown core and reinforce the future revitalization of the lower Boyle Street area. Both the ECPC and the CBA supported the revised Chinatown plan.[26] City Council approved it in principle in August 1980 and engaged Joe Wai and Don Vaughan to prepare the preliminary designs of streetscape features, a Chinese garden, a parkade, and other cultural elements. These projects were included in the final report of the Mayor's Task Force on the Heart of the City, approved

The Chinese Elders' Mansion, 1977, in Replaced Chinatown. The adjacent Multicultural Centre is not visible. (PAA J.3658)

by Council in September 1984, which recommended the development of Edmonton's Replaced Chinatown in keeping with the revised Chinatown plan. Some developers began to purchase the old structures in the proposed area, expecting land values to rise.

Certain projects had started while the design of the Replaced Chinatown was still being reviewed. For example, construction of the $1.28-million Edmonton Chinatown Multicultural Centre, next to the Chinese Elders' Mansion, began in November 1983. The CBA raised nearly $1.6 million for the Centre: $953,000 from the provincial government, $585,000 from the Chinese community, and $60,000 from Dr and Mrs Dick Rice. Officially opened in February 1985, the Centre provides educational, cultural, and recreational resources to the people of the city; it also houses a Chinese-English bilingual daycare.[27] In 1991 the

Chinese Arch at 102 Avenue on the east side of 97 Street, officially opened by Edmonton mayor, Laurence Decore, and the vice mayor of Harbin, Hong Qiping, in 1987. (DAVID CHUENYAN LAI)

$7.2-million ten-storey Tower II of the Chinese Elders' Mansion, financed by the Alberta Mortgage and Housing Corporation, was completed. In 1989, in response to a promise by the Alberta government to fund a health care centre in Chinatown, the CBA launched a fund-raising campaign for the purchase of a property. However, in May 1990 financial constraints obliged the government to postpone its support of fifty-nine construction schemes, including the Chinatown health care centre. Today the CBA continues to try to obtain government funding since it has already bought the property for the project.

The two Chinese Elders' Mansions and the Multicultural Centre are located within the official boundaries of Edmonton's Chinatown, which may be considered 'Chinatown Proper' (see Figure 1). Yet many Chinese businesses and organizational buildings—such as the Hung Ying building owned by the Chinese Freemasons, the Gee Society building, the Mah Society building, and the CBA building—are outside this planned area. In reality, then, Edmonton's Replaced Chinatown covers a significantly larger area, bound by 95 and 97 streets to the east and west and by Jasper and 102A avenues to the south and north.

The revised Chinatown plan called for two Chinese gateways to mark the symbolic entrances to Replaced Chinatown. Accordingly, in February 1985 Mayor Laurence Decore wrote to Zhang Yongping, head of China's Architectural Arts Exhibition Delegation, soliciting technical assistance.[28] Zhang replied two months later and offered to design and construct the arches for Edmonton at a cost of $200,000, providing that all decorative materials and the necessary skilled labour could be sent at the same time as the crew scheduled to build the China Pavilion

for Expo 86 in Vancouver. Since Edmonton City Council could not make a decision before this deadline, the gateway project did not materialize.

In March 1986 I was invited by the Planning Department to lecture on the Chinese arch and Chinatown revitalization projects in Victoria.[29] I pointed out the ramifications of a Chinatown gate project, offering ideas on designs, materials, planning, engineering, and maintenance. Based on my suggestions, the Planning Department decided to construct one arch instead of two. In December 1986 City Council approved a capital budget of $350,000 for construction of a Chinese arch spanning Harbin Road (102 Avenue) on the east side of 97 Street. Yeung Zhi and Yang Ji Hong of Shenzhen Gardens Design and Decorative Engineering Company designed the gate; the cladding materials, valued at $98,000, were donated by Harbin, Edmonton's sister city in the People's Republic of China; and financial support came from the City of Edmonton ($366,000), the Alberta Cultural Heritage Foundation ($75,000), and the Alberta Department of Tourism ($25,000). In addition, the CBA organized a walkathon which raised $25,000 for the project. On 24 October 1987 the gate was officially dedicated by Edmonton's mayor, Laurence Decore, and the vice mayor of Harbin, Hong Qiping.[30]

Today Edmonton's Replaced Chinatown is officially known as Chinatown South. Since its development in 1981, business has not grown as rapidly or been as prosperous as expected mainly because the population base remains small and the area's elderly residents are not great consumers. In May 1995 Chinatown South had only thirty-three Chinese business concerns (of which six were located in New World Centre, formerly Chinatown Market Place Mall) (see Table 1). Shun Tak Restaurant, Mai Mai Restaurant, and a bakery had closed because of insufficient patrons. Many old buildings had been demolished and the sites either left vacant or used temporarily as parking lots (Figure 3). In spite of Chinatown South's proximity to Edmonton's city centre, it has so far failed either to achieve its development potential or to attract industry, commerce, and residents to the Boyle Street area. Nevertheless, it is the home of Chinese elderly people and the focal point of Chinese social activities. In May 1995 it had one Chinese church, two senior citizens' high-rise buildings, and six Chinese association buildings. Although not a great tourist attraction for the city, Chinatown South is still a vibrant spot in downtown Edmonton, especially when the city centre is deserted and virtually dead in late evenings.

TABLE 1:
Chinese Business Concerns in Chinatown South, May 1995

Type of Business	Number of Firms
Restaurant/barbecue	13
Barber	4
Office and service	4
Printing	2
Drug/gift	2
Grocery	1
Auto repair	1
Miscellaneous	6
Total	33

Source: Author survey, 10-15 May 1995

A New Chinatown, another post-Second World War phenomenon, can be planned or simply emerge. Unlike a Replaced Chinatown, it is neither established to replace an Old Chinatown nor developed as a Chinese residential and institutional area. It is a cluster of Chinese restaurants, grocery stores and supermarkets, bakeries, book stores, offices, and other commercial activities owned or operated by Chinese and catering mainly to Chinese customers. Unlike both Old and Replaced Chinatowns, a New Chinatown is usually not a tourist attraction. New Chinatowns in North America can be classified as plaza, mall, or linear.

Plaza Chinatowns consist of a single shopping plaza or a group of shopping plazas that house exclusively or predominantly Chinese businesses. For example, the Scarborough plaza Chinatown in Metro Toronto has two clusters of shopping plazas—one at the intersection of Glen Watford Drive and Sheppard Avenue, with three plazas (Cathay, Glen Watford, and Agincourt), and the second at the intersection of Brimley Road and Sheppard Avenue, with four plazas (Prince, Mandarin, Pearl, and Pun Chun).[31] Sometimes, a plaza Chinatown is designed not just to cater to the needs of its Chinese customers but to attract tourists as well. A good example is Mississauga's New Chinatown. Carefully planned and created by Chinese entrepreneurs, it features a single extensive plaza elaborately decorated with a Chinese gate, a Chinese gazebo, a nine-dragon wall, and a tiny Chinese garden. The mall Chinatown pattern can be observed in Richmond's New Chinatown in Metro Vancouver. It consists of a group of Chinese-operated shopping malls (Aberdeen Center, President Plaza, and Parker Place) in which virtually all businesses—such as restaurants, food stalls, supermarkets, barbecue shops, fresh fish markets, and theatres—are owned by Chinese. Finally, a linear Chinatown is denoted by a commercial strip of Chinese business concerns on sections of a street. This pattern can be seen in Ottawa's New Chinatown, which in 1987 consisted of about thirty Chinese businesses widely

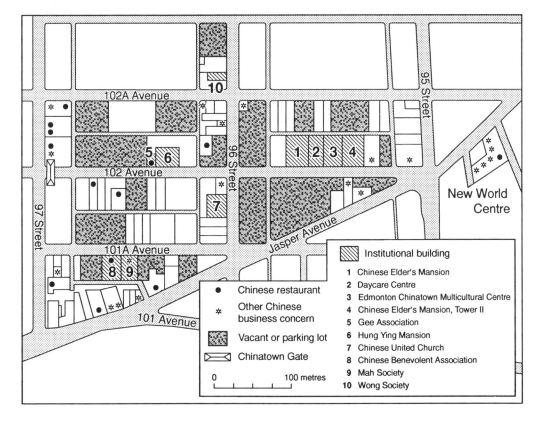

Figure 3. Edmonton's Replaced Chinatown, 1995.
(DAVID CHUENYAN LAI)

Chinese restaurant

Other Chinese business concern

Vacant or parking lot

Chinatown Gate

0   100 metres

Institutional building

1 Chinese Elder's Mansion
2 Daycare Centre
3 Edmonton Chinatown Multicultural Centre
4 Chinese Elder's Mansion, Tower II
5 Gee Association
6 Hung Ying Mansion
7 Chinese United Church
8 Chinese Benevolent Association
9 Mah Society
10 Wong Society

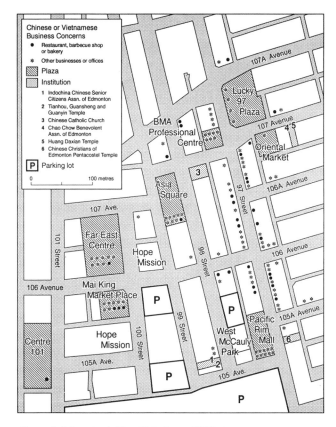

Figure 4. Edmonton's New Chinatown, 1995. (DAVID CHUENYAN LAI)

or the Vietnamese Chinese in the McCauley district.[33] Edmonton's Vietnamese and Vietnamese Chinese communities had mushroomed after July 1979 when Canada agreed to accept up to 50,000 Indochinese refugees over two years, through a partnership arrangement between the federal government and private sponsors.[34]

During the early 1990s several Vietnamese Chinese and Hong Kong Chinese developers acquired properties and constructed commercial plazas—including Asia Square, Far East Centre, Mai King Market Place, and Centre 101—between 97 and 101 streets. Strictly speaking, these developments are neither malls nor plazas but commercial complexes that occupy an entire or partial city block. Several entrepreneurs cited three main reasons for setting up business in New Chinatown instead of Replaced Chinatown. First, New Chinatown lies within walking distance for its customers, since many Vietnamese and Chinese Vietnamese live in its northern and eastern sections. Second, New Chinatown is easily accessible to car-driving customers from northern, western, and eastern suburbs because it lies near the intersection of 107 Avenue and 97 Street, both busy thoroughfares. Third, land prices are cheaper in New Chinatown than in Replaced Chinatown.[35]

Today Edmonton's New Chinatown—officially known as Chinatown North—exhibits a net-like pattern covering city blocks from 97 to 101 streets between 105 and 107A avenues. In May 1995 I conducted a survey of Chinatown North and found 126 business concerns—ranging from restaurants and supermarkets to florists, electrical suppliers, and pawn shops—operated by Vietnamese Chinese or Chinese from Hong Kong and other places (see Table 2).

TABLE 2:
Chinese Business Concerns in Chinatown North, May 1995

Type of Business	Number of Firms
Restaurant/barbecue	28
Office and service	17
Beauty salon/hairdresser	14
Grocery/supermarket	10
Book/gift	10
Fashion/clothing	7
Herbalist/pharmacy	7
Auto repair	6
Jewellery	5
Video and sound	4
Bakery	4
Miscellaneous	18
Total	126

Source: Author survey, 10–15 May 1995

spaced along Somerset Street West between Preston and Bank streets.[32] When a linear New Chinatown expands to other streets, it acquires a net-like pattern. This is the case with Edmonton's Chinatown North.

During the late 1970s, while the fate of Old Chinatown was still uncertain, an embryonic New Chinatown with a few Chinese stores (such as Tai Fat Grocery and Hing Lung Store, relocated from Old Chinatown) emerged on 97 Street north of the Canadian National Railway (CNR) overpass (see Figure 1). By the early 1980s New Chinatown comprised a commercial strip on 97 Street between 105 and 108 avenues (Figure 4). My survey in March 1986 revealed about twenty-five business concerns, including six restaurants, five grocery stores, and fourteen firms ranging from import companies and bakeries to book stores. Unlike Edmonton's Old and Replaced Chinatowns, New Chinatown had no Chinese organizational or residential buildings. The Chinese stores, widely spread out along the street, were operated by Vietnamese Chinese or Chinese people from Hong Kong. The reasons they gave for their choice of location were low rent, proximity to Old Chinatown, available space at the right time, and nearby low-rent residential areas favoured by the Vietnamese

Chinatown North's businesses and customers are quite different from those in Chinatown South. For example, while in spring 1995 Chinatown South had only four barbers, catering to elderly men, Chinatown North attracted family-oriented businesses like supermarkets, beauty salons, and women's and children's clothing stores, as well as enterprises serving a specifically Vietnamese clientele—restaurants specializing in Vietnamese cuisine, grocery stores stocked with Vietnamese foods and other commodities, and several goldsmith and jewellery shops. The popularity of the latter hinges in part on the legacy of the Vietnam War, when people tended to buy gold or jewellery as security.

Furthermore, unlike New Chinatowns in other Canadian cities, Edmonton's New Chinatown is next to Chinese or Vietnamese residential areas, which has given rise to two secular associations and four temples and churches: the Indo-Chinese Senior Citizens Association of Edmonton, the Edmonton Chao Chow Benevolent Association, the Chinese Catholic Church, the Chinese Pentecostal Temple, the Wong Tai Sin Temple, and the Temple of Tian Hou, Guan Sheng, and Guan Yin. If Edmonton's New Chinatown continues to expand, it might become a Chinese neighbourhood, like an Old Chinatown, characterized by a concentration of Chinese people, businesses, and institutions. The City Planning Department admits that Chinatown North 'represents the "real" Chinatown which has migrated northwards from its originally "planned" location near 102 Avenue and 96th Street . . . At times, the area is heavily congested with pedestrian as well as vehicular traffic . . . and has a high potential in terms of developing a unique cultural shopping experience for local and city residents and visitors to the city.'[36] I have suggested to the town planners and New Chinatown merchants that Chinatown North needs an identifying landmark that would act as the symbolic entrance to Edmonton's Chinatown North and make it more noticeable to visitors. For example, a mural with a dragon and a phoenix motif and a 'Chinatown North' signboard inscribed in three languages might be painted above the underpass on 97 Street below the CNR track.

A second New Chinatown is emerging south of the North Saskatchewan River in the former Prudham's Shoppers Park at the southeastern corner of the intersection of 104 Street and 80 Avenue in the revitalized Old Strathcona district. In 1994 the owners of Chinese Superstore leased Prudham's warehouse and converted it into Strathcona Chinatown Mall, which opened in March 1995. In May 1995 it housed ten Chinese businesses: a supermarket, kitchen wares, a video and book store, a bakery, a restaurant, a hobby store, a Japanese food store, a photo studio, a karaoke establishment, and a travel agent.[37] This mall Chinatown is still in embryo and might become the third Chinatown in the future.

In conclusion, it must be stressed that a Chinatown is a perceptual area, meaning different things to different peo-

Strathcona Chinatown Mall in Old Strathcona, south of the North Saskatchewan River, well outside traditional Chinese areas of the city, 1995.
(DAVID CHUENYAN LAI)

ple, at different times, and in different cities. Before the Second World War, the Chinese, mostly single males, were ostracized and discriminated against by the white community. In response, they congregated in what became Old Chinatown for mutual help and protection. Today Chinese Canadians are for the most part accepted and respected by the white community and no longer need to live inside a Chinese enclave. Nevertheless, there are also many new Chinese immigrants who cannot speak English and who, like the elderly old-timers, still rely on Old Chinatown for convenience and mutual assistance and use it as a springboard to assimilation. Many low-income people opt to live in Old Chinatown for reasons of proximity to work, cheaper accommodation, and nearness to facilities catering to Chinese-speaking people. To meet the needs of these groups, the City of Edmonton worked closely with Chinese organizations to establish a Replaced Chinatown after the Old Chinatown was demolished. The Replaced Chinatown, or Chinatown South, is significantly the only Canadian example of a Replaced Chinatown planned and created jointly by a city's urban planners and Chinese residents, with financial support from all three levels of government. Edmonton's New Chinatown, or Chinatown North, is also unique in Canada because it has emerged in the residential areas of Chinese from Hong Kong, Vietnam, and other southeast Asian countries. It is the only New Chinatown that has begun to acquire the characteristics of an Old Chinatown, encompassing a

Chinese or Vietnamese Chinese commercial, residential, and institutional area. Unlike Chinatown South, Chinatown North does not have institutional projects funded by the government, but it has developed much faster than Chinatown South mainly because of a larger market and more private investment.

Chinatown South, Chinatown North, and Strathcona Chinatown Mall attract not only Chinese customers but also non-Chinese patrons seeking authentic Chinese food, artwork, and other commodities with an Oriental flavour. Chinese community leaders and town planners should discourage the competition between Chinatown South and Chinatown North. Ideally, all three areas should complement each other. Chinatown South, for example, could concentrate on social and cultural development, while Chinatown North and Strathcona Chinatown Mall stressed commercial expansion. ∾

CYNTHIA DUNNIGAN

'DON'T EVER LET YOUR CREE DOWN'

Delia Gray, 1994. (COURTESY GRAY FAMILY)

*W*omen have helped define the nature of Edmonton. Many became well-known figures for the causes they championed and their work on behalf of the community. Others worked just as hard but received little recognition.

This is the story of Delia Gray: from childhood memories of her Métis grandmothers, through her work at the General Hospital and marriage to Bob Gray, to her ongoing volunteer leadership with groups like the Métis Nation of Alberta and the Canadian Native Friendship Centre. Throughout, she paid tribute to the advice given by her grandmother Sophie: 'Don't ever let your Cree down.'

Cynthia Dunnigan is a graduate student in anthropology at the University of Alberta. Her research interests include oral histories of Métis women and First Nations alternative dispute resolution. In 1994 she contributed a report to the Royal Commission on Aboriginal People. She interviewed Delia Gray for that report.

MRS DELIA GRAY (NÉE CUNNINGHAM) IS A MÉTIS woman who turned 78 in 1995.[1] Her family is a founding family of St Albert, Alberta. The Cunninghams trace their Métis heritage back to the Red River Settlement.[2] A leader in her community, Delia was one of the organizing members of both the Canadian Native Friendship Centre and the first Native mass in Edmonton, and she is a Senator on the Métis Nation of Alberta's Senate.[3]

Delia was the youngest child born into a Métis family on 17 March 1917. Both of her parents were Métis. Delia's paternal grandmother was Cree and Delia's paternal grandfather was of mixed Irish and Cree descent. It was Delia's paternal grandfather's parents who had lived at Red River. They were Patrick Cunningham and Nancy Bruce.[4] Patrick arrived at Red River with the Selkirk settlers on 27 October 1812.[5] Delia's paternal grandfather was John Patrick Cunningham an Irish, Cree man who ended up in Western Canada because he had travelled from Eastern Canada with the Hudson's Bay explorers. When John arrived in the West he met a Cree woman named Rosalie L'Hirondelle at Lac Ste Anne, Alberta. They were married 5 September 1846. Rosalie was his third wife.[6] John Patrick Cunningham and Rosalie L'Hirondelle began the western branch of the Cunninghams. They had eleven children. One of these children, Edward Cunningham, was the first Cree-speaking Oblate priest in Western Canada. Edward was educated in classical studies at the University of Ottawa and he was ordained by Bishop Grandin 19 March 1890.[7] A second brother, Samuel, was elected to the Northwest Territories legislative assembly in 1885; as well, he was an interpreter at the Treaty Eight negotiations in 1899 and first mayor of Grouard.[8] Finally, the youngest son of John and Rosalie was Delia's father, Henry Cunningham, born 1 January 1868. Henry and his twin brother, Alfred, married two sisters. Henry married Mary Rowland who was the mother of Delia while his twin married Mary's sister, Amelia Rowland. Henry was an educated man as he had studied accounting and business at Father Leduc's school in St Albert.

Delia's maternal grandmother was of French, Cree, and Blackfoot heritage while her maternal grandfather was Sioux and Scottish. Delia's maternal great-great grandfathers both had come from Europe and married Aboriginal women.

Delia's mother, Mary, was born around 1875 to John Rowland of Edmonton and Sophie Chatelain of Fort Pitt, Manitoba. Rowland road that runs from downtown Edmonton at Jasper Avenue into Riverdale community was named for John Rowland's father William Rowland, who lived at the top of the hill after he arrived from the Orkney Islands in 1820.[9] Mary Rowland was one of ten children. Her mother, Sophie, was born to a Cree-Blackfoot mother and a French father. Sophie's paternal grandparents were emigrants from France. Sophie was fluent in French, Cree, and Blackfoot.

Before Delia was born her family moved to Wabasca, Alberta, because her father had a job managing the local store. Their home was a log cabin next to the Desmarais reserve in Northern Alberta. Delia was born in the log cabin. Her grandmother Sophie was the mid-wife.

Many of Delia's childhood memories centre around her grandparents. Delia's grandparents looked after Delia and her siblings as their parents had to work all the time to keep the homestead running. The only items Grandma Rosalie ever bought from a store were tea, sugar, and flour. Everything else she made or processed herself. She snared rabbits and muskrats for meat, raised a garden for vegetables, and picked berries for fruits and jams. Delia's favourites were *nipiminanna*, the high bush cranberries, and the jam that was made from them. Chokecherries were never used for jam because they were mixed with dry meat and sugar and made into pemmican.

When Delia was four years old most of her family moved back to St Albert, but her father stayed in Wabasca a few more years running a trading post. When the family first moved back to St Albert they lived with Delia's grandmother, Sophie, for awhile. This was a pleasant time in Delia's life because she spent a lot of time with her grandmother. Sophie used to take Delia and some cousins to the muskeg. When they went on these visits all the children carried little shovels for digging up roots. Delia recalls that she usually looked for rat root and to find these roots she had to dig in among the cat tails:

> We used to go with her [Sophie], us children, to go and dig in the roots in the muskeg in St Albert, and she was a great believer. We sang in Cree and hopped, skipped and danced, four of us grandchildren. In these little trails we met, see, St Albert was quite a salamander country, and we met the salamander. We ran back screaming, we grabbed grandma, we pulled the sleeve right off her dress and she killed it. And the little shovels we carried, we dug a hole and she pushed it in there, and she wouldn't take that trail the rest of the summer, till next year.[10]

Whenever the children found a root or an herb that they were going to take they had to leave something behind. Sophie taught them that the earth has gifts to give but that these gifts cannot be taken randomly and without respect. She taught them to give something back to the earth to show respect for the earth's power and to show thanks for the gift. When they went to the muskeg Delia always carried a little bit of tea or sugar with her, which she left behind as her thanks to the earth. At that time tea and sugar were precious goods; they were expensive and were some of the few store bought items the family had.

To this day, Delia loves to tell stories about her grandmother Sophie because she did interesting things such as learning medicines from Big Bear. Sophie's family travelled much of the time and they often linked up with Big Bear or Poundmaker. Sophie watched and learned how to use roots and grasses and parts of the trees to cure different ailments. The things she learned she passed onto her granddaughter, Delia, who often says of Sophie 'that woman could cure anything.' Delia credits her grandmother Sophie for helping her to develop a strong Métis pride and identity. There were two important lessons that Sophie passed on; she would say to Delia '*Nosisim*, don't ever let your Cree down and don't ever try to hide who you are . . .' [11] Delia took this to mean that she was never to forget her language and that she was to be proud of her Métis heritage.

After about a year Delia's family moved from her Grandmother Sophie's house to the Cunningham estates which were west of the present city of St Albert. Originally there was one big section of land that belonged to Delia's grandfather; today the land is divided among various Cunningham descendants.

When they moved onto the estate, Delia's other grandmother, Rosalie Cunningham, moved in with the family. Delia and Rosalie had matching rocking chairs, a little one and a big one, so that they could sit on the porch and rock together. While Delia sat and rocked with her Grandma, she learned to sing Cree hymns. Rosalie would sit in her rocker, drinking endless cups of muskeg tea and smoking *kinnickkinnick* (leaves mixed with a certain type of willow). The porch was the place where a lot of things went on. On Sundays Delia's uncle Edward, the Catholic Priest, would come out to the farm to say mass in Cree for the family, and other family and friends would come from around the area. Those times Delia shared with Rosalie singing Cree hymns and listening to Mass instilled in her a religious nature which later in her life would lead her to organize the first Native mass in Edmonton.

When Delia was seven years old, she moved into St Albert to live with her Grandmother Sophie. She moved there because she had to start school and it was too far to travel from the farm every day. One of Delia's brothers and

one of her sisters also moved in with Sophie to attend school. It was at school that Delia learned to speak English as she spoke only Cree and some French when she started school. Delia attended the St Albert Catholic school for two years, but when she was in grade three the school was crowded and she was taken out and put in the residential school. Delia's memories of the residential school are pleasant because the nuns liked her and she liked the nuns. She attended the residential school for grade three but was not expected to reside at the school because her grandmother lived so close. When Delia was in grade five she contracted tuberculosis and had to stay home for five years.

It was not until she was about sixteen years old that the tuberculosis cleared up. In those years, between ages eleven and sixteen, Delia stayed at home and was cared for by her mother, her grandmothers, and one aunt who stayed at home because she had never married. She spent most of the summers sleeping outside in a teepee because

Father Edward Cunningham (right), circa late 1890s.
(MUSÉE HERITAGE MUSEUM ST ALBERT)

she needed fresh air and sunshine. Delia remembers that it was important for her to get enough sunshine: 'well I was a little girl then, but my head would be covered and [I would] lay on my stomach and let the sun see my back. And then lay on my back and cover up with an old towel, a skinny one, let the sun penetrate my chest.'[12] She had trouble adjusting to wearing leather shoes. The doctor told her that she could not wear moccasins anymore because she had to make sure that her feet were always warm and dry.

During the tuberculosis years Delia learned beadwork from her grandma and lots of Cree songs and furthered her reading and writing abilities. Delia's father and her brother Pat brought her books and comics to read. She remembers: 'The only books I had to read when I was sick, my brother would buy *True Detective, Master Detective, Inside Detective,* . . . That's why to this day I like that reading.'[13] Delia also remembers that her grandmothers would sneak Native medicines in to her because they did not trust the western medicines, but Delia's mother did not want them to interfere with the care Delia was receiving from the doctor. The family had already lost one child to tuberculosis and two to whooping cough.

When Delia recovered from tuberculosis at age sixteen in 1933 she was anxious to make up for lost time. Like many Métis children Delia had learned to dance jigs, waltzes, and reels as she learned to walk. While she had tuberculosis, she could not dance because it strained her lungs. Shortly after she recovered there was a dance in St Albert. She could not wait to get to a square dance so, heedless of her mother's warnings and requests that she stay home, she went to the dance. Her legs were not used to dancing as she had been unable to run or dance for five years. When she got home she became aware of a throbbing ache in her leg. Delia recalls what happened:

Mom used to rub my leg with Minard's liniment, they call it white liniment. And one time, you know how I love to dance, I came out of TB at 16 and I start going to dances . . . I got home, I couldn't sleep, I was just about in tears my leg. Oh my mother, she was mad, 'you should've stayed home.' She went in, she lit a match . . . she looked, she couldn't read eh. She took this bottle with white liniment, she rubbed my leg. The next morning there was white all over my leg, she used white shoe polish.[14]

In 1935 when Delia was eighteen years old she moved to Edmonton. She had known for years that as soon as she turned eighteen she would leave the farm and move to the city of Edmonton. She wanted to leave the crowded farmhouse which had fifteen people living in three bedrooms

and a living room. Her parents had their bed in the living room because all the bedrooms were taken up by children. Delia's brother, his wife, and their little girl had one bedroom. Delia shared her room with three of her sisters, and there was one more sister with five of her own children in the third bedroom. Delia had long wanted to get a job and experience comforts like indoor plumbing and electricity. She wanted to make money of her own, support herself, and make her own decisions about what to buy. As a Métis girl, Delia was always dressed in sombre browns and greys; she wanted to buy her own clothes that would be brand new, colourful, and storebought rather than handed down and homemade.

Delia's family was not happy about her decision to leave the farm at such a young age. She had three older sisters who all married in their late teens or early twenties. Delia was the only one to move to the city and support herself. Her oldest brother stayed on the farm as he was expected to take over its operations. Delia remembered the words of her grandmother and maintained her Métis identity, while in Edmonton. She did so by remaining close to other Cree speakers in the city and by using her Cree language. Delia also tried to remain close to her family as they always worried about her being single and living in the city, but there was not always a lot of communication with her family. There was no telephone at the farm so she could not phone and it was not easy to get back to the farm. She either had to hire someone to take her or take the train. Either way it cost more than she could afford so she and her family had to wait for messages from other people who went back and forth between St Albert and Edmonton.

Delia came to the city in March with about thirty dollars that she had saved from the money she was paid for milking cows for her cousin Mary Hodgson. They had paid her two dollars a week to milk the cows twice a day. The first place that Delia stayed when she arrived was at the Sisters of Service (order of nuns who provided lodging and meals for women in the city for a nominal fee) she stayed there because it was known to be a safe, clean place for single women.

Delia found a job at the General Hospital. She worked there for ten years and she had four different positions in the hospital. Delia found out about the first position when she arrived in the city and went to see a priest who was a friend of her family. He telephoned the Sister Superior at the General Hospital. The Sister hired Delia to work in the tuberculosis ward. While she was working in the tuberculosis ward, she moved out of the Sisters of Service and into the General Hospital. At that time there were dormitories in which the employees could live. As soon as an opening came up Delia moved into the dormitory. Dorm rent and meals were included in Delia's wage. There were usually fifteen women living in the dorm. There was a curfew of 9:30 p.m. for women living in the dorm unless they had a late leave which allowed them to stay out as late as midnight. Usually one could get a late leave only on Saturday.

After a few months in the tuberculosis ward Delia transferred to the dining room. She worked split shifts in the dining room from 6:00 a.m. until 1:30 p.m. and 3:30 until 7:00 p.m. six days per week. Her wage when she worked in the dining room was twelve dollars a month in addition to which her room and meals were provided.

When Delia was about twenty-two the war broke out and the hospital started building a cafeteria in the dormitory, so all the women had to find new homes. From the hospital Delia moved into the Rosary Hall which was close to the General and cost twelve dollars a month for a room and meals. Delia was able to afford this because her wages went up when the war began, from twelve dollars a month plus meals and a bed in the dormitory to fifty dollars a month plus the meals she ate during her shifts. Delia stayed at the Rosary Hall for a short time, and then she moved to a little suite in a house. The rent for a room in this house was twenty dollars a month. There was no curfew but single women could not have male visitors in the house.

After Delia moved out from the General Hospital dormitory she transferred from the dining room to a new position. She began running the elevator. She worked split shifts on the elevator and her wage stayed the same at fifty dollars per month. While Delia was running the elevator she was offered a chance to take a course in the pharmacy. One of the nuns was teaching a group how to work in the pharmacy. Delia took the course in the evenings and she learned how to measure out prescriptions and how to work with the pharmacist. After she finished the course she transferred to the pharmacy and she worked there until Spring 1946.

When Delia was about twenty-six years old she started to think about getting married. She had known Bob Gray, her future husband, since she was about twelve years old as both of their fathers had been raised in St Albert. Each year the families met at the Lac St Anne pilgrimage to visit, but Delia and Bob did not spend a lot of time together. Bob was the youngest child of Phillip Gray, a Scottish-Iroquois Métis whose parents were from Red River,[15] and Clarisse Karakonte, an Iroquois from Lac Ste Anne, Alberta.

When Delia moved to the city she did not see Bob very often for a few years until eventually she started to run

Delia Gray as young woman (right) with girlfriend, circa 1943.
(COURTESY GRAY FAMILY)

into him periodically because he played guitar in a band at dances and she used to go out dancing. These meetings were infrequent and inconsequential because they never really talked at the dances since he was busy playing. Then one day, when she went with some girlfriends to say goodbye to friends and relatives going out on the troop trains, Bob was leaving on one of the trains. About a year later he was injured in an airplane crash and ended up spending about three years in the hospital to recover from the injury. He was usually in the hospital in Calgary because Edmonton did not have a veteran's hospital, but he made trips to Edmonton to see his mother and when he was in town he and Delia dated.

On 22 June 1945 they were married at St Joseph's Cathedral in Edmonton. There were few family members in attendance. Delia and Bob wore matching chocolate brown gabardine suits and Delia carried a prayer book instead of flowers.

Bob Gray (second from right) with fellow airmen, circa 1945.
(COURTESY GRAY FAMILY)

Delia and Bob's first home was a housekeeping room on Jasper Avenue and 107 street in Edmonton. It was one room with a gas stove in it and there was no sink. The bathroom was down the hall. They had to share it with other boarders. They took turns paying the rent because they were both working at this time. Bob worked for Great West Saddlery as a credit manager for the first nine years that they were married. Delia worked in the General Hospital pharmacy for the first eight months of her marriage. She quit her job in March 1946 because she was five months pregnant with their first baby. She had four children between 1946 and 1951.

In 1948 the family moved to Camp 550, an old army barracks in the northwest part of Edmonton. In 1954 they moved to Rossdale community, down the hill from downtown Edmonton. In 1957 the family moved away from Edmonton when Bob took a job with the provincial government that required that the family move north to Paddle

Prairie, Alberta. The family lived on the Métis Settlement at Paddle Prairie while Bob ran the Métis Branch store that was owned by the provincial government.

The family returned to Edmonton six months later but only for a few months because Bob had been hired to open the first Métis Branch of Alberta Social Services in High Prairie, Alberta. Bob Gray was one of the few Cree speaking social workers employed by Alberta Social Services in the late 1950s. They lived in High Prairie for three years, moving back to Edmonton when Bob was given a job in the head office of Alberta Social Services. Between 1957 and 1962 Delia had three more children. She spent the next few years looking after her small children.

Once Delia was married almost all the work she did was on a volunteer basis rather than as a paid worker. Volunteer work became a priority for her when the family returned to Edmonton from High Prairie in 1962. She became a very active volunteer once all of the children were in school and she had the time and the energy to offer to the Aboriginal community.

The organization with which Delia has worked the longest is the Canadian Native Friendship Centre. She joined in the summer of 1962. At the time it was a brand new organization with little yet established. The organization's facility was an old brick house on 108 Street and 102 Avenue. There was a board of directors and Frank and Doris Paul, a couple who were on the board put forth Delia's name as a board member. She joined the board in 1962. Thirty-one years later she is still on the board of directors and is also a lifetime member of the Centre.

Some of the work Delia has done for the Friendship Centre includes establishing programs that appeal to the urban Aboriginal community and creating programs that benefit and empower people. The first program she helped to establish was the women's group, which generated funds for the centre. The women did this by having teas and bazaars throughout the year. Delia was the co-ordinator of events put on by the women's group.

The Canadian Native Friendship Centre Annual All-Native festival was one of Delia's favourite functions at the Centre. The festival is a display of Aboriginal talent and creativity. There are performers from all over Alberta and some from other parts of Canada. The festival is a showcase for the talents of jiggers, fiddlers, dancers, singers, and square dance callers; it is an inspiring event. It inspires personal pride in the performers because the community recognizes them for their talent, and it encourages cultural pride because it is a demonstration of the abundance of talent present in the community. At times there are huge crowds for the festival. Delia talks about one year when she saw thirty jiggers entered in the Red River Jig competition. Delia and Bob were part of the group that organized the first All Native Festival. They were the organizers until 1974 when Bob became terminally ill and could not continue with the organization.

For the ten years Delia had lived in the city as a single woman, she had made extra money by collecting at the door of dances. After her marriage, she continued as a volunteer because Bob played guitar in several bands during their marriage. In fact, he occasionally played with Gabby Haas on CFRN radio. Playing guitar was the way Bob made the extra money that enabled Bob and Delia to take their children on holidays. After Bob died, Delia continued collecting for the Canadian Native Friendship Centre until the building was condemned in the late 1980s. In 1993 the Centre attained a new space which is bigger and better than any previously occupied.

In 1964 Bob was asked to be Chairman of the board of the Centre. He was the first Aboriginal chair of the board. At the present time most board members are of Aboriginal ancestry but that was not the situation in 1964. Two months after Bob's death in 1975 Delia was presented with a painting of her husband to commemorate his position as chair of the board. The painting was hung in the Centre and it is still in the boardroom today.

Delia also did a limited amount of volunteer work for many years for the Catholic Women's League. As a long-time member of this organization Delia helped out at teas and bazaars. She was fifty years old when she, with the aid of Father Michael Troy and Gerry Amerongen, took on the responsibility of organizing a Native mass for the Aboriginal community. In 1967, Roman Catholic Archbishop Jordan, in Edmonton, was looking for people to organize a Native mass. A friend of the Grays gave their names to the Bishop as they were two people who were known to be practising Catholics, reliable, and a part of the Native community both in and outside of Edmonton.

The first Native mass was held in St Joseph's cathedral in downtown Edmonton in the fall of 1967. It was held in the main hall upstairs. A large crowd of people attended. The mass was a success. The good turnout led the Archbishop to approve continuation of the mass. Native Mass took place once a month. There was always a luncheon following the mass because many people came from out of town to attend and people wanted to visit before they returned home. Delia's whole family helped at the luncheon. All her children and her granddaughter pre-

pared and served the food and cleaned up the kitchen and the hall afterwards.

The Native mass continued for thirteen years until 1980 when Delia decided to build on the monthly Native mass by organizing a Native midnight mass for Christmas Eve. The midnight mass was well attended; there were always large crowds. The Native masses always had a relaxed atmosphere. People drank coffee or smoked through the service. Children could not make noise but they were free to roam from mother, to aunt, to grandmother. This kept them from getting bored. The Native mass was more than a church service as it was a gathering place for friends and relatives from the urban and rural First Nations communities. Delia ran the Native mass for seventeen years until 1984.

Delia recalls that people were glad to hear the news that there was to be a Native mass. People often gathered at each other's homes to sing Cree hymns but at that time there was no church in which one could sing Cree hymns. One of the first things she did was organize a Cree choir for the mass. That choir still exists today. They sing at Sacred Heart church located in Edmonton's inner city and there are still a few members of the original choir, including Mrs Eva Ladoceour.

Delia was involved with a number of other Native and non-Native organizations from the mid-1960s to the present. One of these was the John Howard Society. She was asked to join because of the disproportionate number of Natives on the receiving end of the justice system.[16] It was felt that a voice to represent Aboriginal people was needed in guiding the John Howard programs. Delia worked with the John Howard Society for about three years in the mid-1960s. Two more organizations with which Delia worked were the Native Society, from 1965 to 1973, and the Imperial Order of Daughters of the Empire. The Native Society held dances, dinners, and festivals to raise money for community development programs for the urban Aboriginal community. Delia's duties in the Imperial Order of Daughters of the Empire were attending meetings and working in the south side thrift shop owned by the Order.

About a year after Delia was widowed, she joined the Royal Canadian Legion because her husband was a veteran. She has been a member of the Legion for twenty years. She is currently on the executive of the ladies auxiliary and she is in charge of the cloakroom. In addition to her cloakroom duties she attends executive and members meetings, as well as working at teas, bazaars, and veterans' lunches.

In 1984 Delia was appointed a lifetime member of the National Association of Canadian Native Friendship Centres. As a lifetime member of the National Association she travels to the annual meeting of the National Association as a regional representative. It is her duty to report on the activities of the Edmonton Canadian Native Friendship Centre for the preceding year.

In 1990 Delia was appointed to the Elders Senate of the Métis Nation of Alberta. She had in the past been involved with the Métis Association but after her husband's death she devoted most of her time to the Legion and the Centre. The Métis Nation is the organization that now keeps her the busiest. As a Senator she travels frequently and attends many meetings, openings, and community functions. The Senate is the dispute resolution body for the Métis Nation of Alberta. It meets regularly to discuss and decide on membership and internal disputes. Senators are often called on for guidance and wisdom in resolving matters and planning the future for Métis people.

Periodically, Delia works with the Cree language instructors at the School of Native Studies, University of Alberta. She is an occasional guest speaker in Native Studies classes, and she has been a Cree language consultant for Cree textbooks. She is currently doing Cree language work for a professor at the University of Alberta, reviewing Cree vocabulary that will be used for a Cree language dictionary.

In addition to all her duties for various organizations, as an elder in Edmonton's Aboriginal communities Delia is often called on to pray in Cree at meetings, openings, and business and entertainment functions.

Mrs Delia Gray has been a leader in the Aboriginal community of Edmonton. She has donated a large part of her life to preserving the Cree language, to improving conditions for urban Aboriginal people, and to fostering Métis pride in people of all ages. She passes Métis pride to younger generations through her work and through her stories. When she is among her people she is called by many names, including Mrs Gray and Delia, but most often she is called Mom, Auntie, *Kokum* or *nicahkos*.[17] The use of these terms by many friends and relatives indicates the various relationships that she has with community members; these relationships with Aboriginal communities in and outside of Edmonton make her a leader. ❧

GORDON DREVER AND STEPHEN A. KENT

GODS FROM AFAR

Young Hare Krishnas— whose religion is based on Hinduism—on
Jasper Avenue, 1971. (PAA J.665)

*T*here is a close link between ethnicity and religious identity and activity. Whether through the
'Britishness' identified with the Anglican church,
the 'Frenchness' associated with the hospital work of the Grey
Nuns, or the 'Ukrainianness' tested in the Catholic-Orthodox
tensions surrounding the staging of Ukrainian-language plays,
ethnicity and religion have greatly enriched the city. Gordon
Drever, an independent researcher, and Stephen Kent, a sociologist at the University of Alberta, carry the discussion one
step further. Rather than look at the Judeo-Christian tradition
and European background of the majority of Edmontonians,
they focus on other great world religions—such as Islam,
Hinduism, and Buddhism—and the immigrant groups, particularly from Asia, that brought them to the city.

Edmonton has always been culturally diverse; its origins in
the Native-European partnership of the fur trade established
this fact at the outset. While the transition to an industrialized
urban community guaranteed the dominance of Europeans,
especially British values and settlers, the young city also attracted small numbers of immigrants from places like China, India,
and the Middle East. After the change to Canadian immigration laws in the 1960s, the number and variety of immigrants
from non-European sources multiplied, creating vibrant ethnic
communities where religious faith was often integral to their
identity. In an unprecedented and independent development,
many of these faiths simultaneously struck a chord among
segments of the larger Edmonton population, particularly the
restless youth of the sixties generation.

ITTLE RELIGIOUS DIVERSITY EXISTED IN EDMONTON during the city's first century. Gradually, the surrounding Native population was exposed (and often converted) to either the Roman Catholicism of French-speaking missionaries or the Protestantism of English-speaking Anglican, Methodist, and Presbyterian missionaries. By the beginning of the twentieth century, with growing European settlement, the spectrum of Christianity in the Edmonton area had expanded to include Baptists, Salvationists, Orthodox, and Lutherans. Likewise, Judaism's presence in the city was sufficiently strong to found the Edmonton Hebrew Association.[1] Now, over one hundred Christian denominations, as well as numerous independent congregations and a diversity of Jewish groups, operate in the city.

Our interest, however, is in the diversity of religions found in the city that lie outside of the Judeo-Christian and indigenous traditions.[2] At the beginning of Edmonton's third century, all of the world's major non-Christian and non-Jewish religious traditions are represented. A number of smaller religious movements from various parts of the world also exist in the city.[3] This religious diversity is the product of both immigration and conversion. Islam and Baha'i have had followers since the 1930s or 1940s; Hindu, Sikh, and Buddhist communities have operated in this part of Alberta since the 1960s; and today the city has small Zoroastrian, Jain, and Taoist communities as well. More recently, the migration of immigrant groups into the city accelerated rapidly during the boom years of the 1970s, and these new Edmontonians brought with them the faiths and cultures of their homelands.

ISLAM, DRUZE, AND BAHA'I

Islam[4] and Baha'i had a number of Edmonton adherents who preceded the influx of immigrants from Asia and other parts of the world. The origins of Edmonton's Muslim community date back to the early years of the twentieth century, when young entrepreneurs from Lebanon were drawn to the fur trade in northern Alberta. The twenty or so resident Muslim families had formed the Arabian Muslim Association by the 1930s and in 1938 built Al Rashid Mosque, the first mosque in Canada.[5] In 1989 city officials relocated and restored the original mosque (by then empty for several years) in Fort Edmonton Park.[6]

The history of this Sunni Muslim community exemplifies the changing ethnic composition of the city through the second half of the twentieth century. The small Arab community grew slowly through the forties and fifties, so that in 1960 there were some 500 Muslims, most of whom shared Lebanese ancestry. By the mid 1970s their number had grown to 5,000, boosted by the arrival of immigrants from India, Pakistan, and other parts of the Muslim world.[7] In 1981, when a large new Al Rashid Mosque opened as part of the Canadian Islamic Centre complex, the city had

Al Rashid Mosque, 1949. The origins of the Arab Muslim community in Alberta go back to the fur trade. (PAA A.8410)

an estimated 15,000 Muslims. Saleem Ganam, director of
the Centre, stated that approximately 80 per cent of this
population was not Arab[8]—a figure that provides some
indication of the current diversity of the community's
ethnic background. Today, the orthodox Sunni have two
additional places of worship: the Markaz-ul-Islam Mosque
opened in Millwoods in 1987[9] and a small mosque in the
university area opened in 1992 by the Muslim Community
of Edmonton.

The Shia branch of Islam differs from Sunni orthodoxy
primarily in giving greater weight to formalized leadership,
often in the context of sectarian divisions. Two Shia
groups operate in Edmonton, both made up largely of East
Indians forced to leave Africa in the early 1970s. The
smaller of these communities is the Islamic Shia Ithna-
Asheri Association; it opened a mosque, serving sixty-five
families, in 1982.[10] The larger and better known group is
the Shia Imami Ismaili community. By 1976 some 900
Ismailis had settled in the city and opened a mosque in
leased premises. Seven years later the community had
grown to 3,500. The hereditary spiritual leader of the
Ismailis, Prince Karim Aga Khan, the forty-ninth Imam,
visited Edmonton in 1978, 1983, and 1992.[11]

The Ahmadiyya movement in Islam, headquartered in
Pakistan, accepts Hazrat Mirza Ghulam Ahmad (1839-
1908) as the Mahdi and Messiah. This messianic belief sets
the Ahmadis apart from both Sunni and Shia Muslims
who accept the finality of Mohammed as Prophet. Indeed,
Pakistani religious officials declared Ahmadiyya to be non-

Muslim in 1984.[12] The Ahmadiyya Muslim Association of
Edmonton has met in rented premises since at least 1984
and in 1986 claimed a membership of about one hundred.[13] Considerable friction exists between Edmonton's
Amadis and orthodox Muslims over the state of affairs in
Pakistan. So heated did public tensions become, particularly in the letters column of the *Edmonton Journal*
between 1984 and 1986, that the Ahmadi leader, Hazrat
Mizra Tahir Ahmad, visited the city in 1986 and told his
followers to stop writing provocative letters directed at
orthodox Muslims. The feud resumed in 1988 when the
Ahmadis challenged the Sunni majority to a 'prayer duel,'
but the latter did not accept. Around that time the
Edmonton Ahmadi community claimed a membership of
250.[14] At present it is best known for its annual Religious
Founders Day, which is a symposium of the major faiths
held at the University of Alberta.

Sufism is a series of mystical movements in Islam whose
obscure history need not be discussed here.[15] As it has
spread to the West, a number of people who do not consider themselves Muslims, and, indeed, who do not follow the
accepted precepts of Islam, have undertaken some of its
practices. Over the past twenty years two Sufi convert
groups have emerged. The Edmonton branch of the Sufi
Order (Pir Vilayat Khan) was active for several years beginning in 1974, but it appears to have disbanded.[16] Another
group, best known as 'Dances of Universal Peace,' is a
branch of the Sufi Islamia Ruhaniat Society, which split
from the Sufi Order in 1977 under the leadership of Sam

Lewis. This group holds weekly dances and meditation sessions as well as an annual camp.[17]

Little agreement exists among scholars as to whether the Druze religion is a branch of Islam or a wholly separate religion.[18] A secretive, non-proselytizing, ethnically based faith that arose in the context of Islam around a thousand years ago, it has its own holy scriptures and a strong emphasis on reincarnation. A spokesperson for the Druze Association of Edmonton estimated the size of the local community at about 2,000 members in 1982.[19] The city's *Yellow Pages* telephone business directory carried a listing for the Association through the 1980s.

The Baha'i faith began in Persia in the middle of the last century. Although originating in an Islamic milieu, it considers itself a distinct religion based on a new prophetic revelation. The faith reached Edmonton in 1941, introduced by Mabel Pine, but the first five Edmonton converts to Baha'i did not join until the of fall 1942. Early converts held their meetings under the auspices of the Theosophical Society. By 1943 the nine converts (all women) were sufficient to constitute a local spiritual assembly.[20] When the group incorporated under the laws of Alberta in 1957, it had fifteen adult members. The Edmonton Baha'i Centre opened in 1990 in the former Orange Hall on 111 Avenue. In 1993, a spokesperson for the community indicated that local membership stood at approximately 400 people, about a quarter of whom were refugees who came from Iran in the 1980s.[21]

THE RELIGIONS OF INDIA

Changes to federal immigration laws in the 1960s made possible an influx of South Asians into Canada and Alberta. Early in the decade, the federal government began to eliminate racial and national criteria for entry into the country and in 1967 introduced the screening of prospective immigrants according to economic and social measures. Because many South Asians were highly skilled, their numbers grew, and by 1970 both Calgary and Edmonton had distinctive ethnic and religious communities.[22] The Hindu Society of Alberta, for example, was established in 1967 with a dozen members, under the leadership of Dr Ram Krishna Gupta. Ten years later there were some 3,000 Hindus in Edmonton and the Society acquired property for Canada's first Indian Cultural Centre. By 1976 Sushil Kalia was holding religious and social activities for the Society. Temple activities in the Centre began in 1981, although the building was not formally opened until September 1984.[23] By the mid 1990s some 15,000 Hindus resided in Edmonton.

A second Hindu group, comprising Tamils and others from south India, organized in the early 1980s as the Maha Ganapati Society and maintains a small temple in a rural setting in the southwest part of the city. There are plans to start construction of a new temple along traditional lines.[24] Another well-established group is the Sri Satya Sai Baba Centre of Edmonton. Indian holy man Sai Baba, who gained fame as a reputed miracle worker, enjoys a large following outside as well as within traditional Hindu communities. Edmonton devotees began to meet in the late 1970s and in 1983 organized the Centre. By 1992 it had some 200 members, all but five of East Indian origin, who met in the Aurora Waldorf School and were very active in community service. In 1995 the Centre moved to permanent premises in a former theatre on Whyte Avenue.[25]

Sikhism is a monotheistic faith that arose in India in the fifteenth century both as a protest against the Hindu caste system and as a response to the pressure of Islam. Although Sikhs were the first East Indians to immigrate to Canada in large numbers, only about forty families resided in Edmonton at the end of the 1960s.[26] The first Sikh temple in the city was the Nanaksar Gurdwara, which opened in a former church on 118 Avenue in 1976. In mid-1995 its members, who follow the teachings of Sant Muhair Singh Jee, were almost finished building a huge new temple on Edmonton's northern outskirts. The Nanaksar guru, Sant Jee, who died in British Columbia in 1994, led a movement numbering about 100,000 of the world's fifteen million or so Sikhs.[27] The mainstream Sikhs, under the auspices of the Sikh Society of Alberta, began raising money to build a temple in the mid-1970s and in the early 1980s opened the Sikh Centre next to the Hindu Temple off St Albert Trail. Another Sikh group, the Sri Guru Singh Sabha Society, opened a Gurdwara in north Edmonton in the late 1970s, moving to larger premises in the southwest in 1980[28] and to Mill Woods six years later. By 1983 as many as 10,000 Sikhs lived in Edmonton, mostly recent immigrants from Punjab, supporting three temples.[29]

An immigrant community committed to visible expressions of its faith, the Sikh community in Edmonton as elsewhere has experienced strife involving human rights issues. In 1982, for example, taxi drivers wearing turbans and beards became an issue with the Yellow Cab Company. The matter was eventually resolved in the Sikhs' favour.[30] The political struggles of Sikhs in India have also had ramifications in Edmonton, particularly following the storming of the Golden Temple in Amritsar in 1984. Local Sikhs withdrew from the National Association of Canadians of Origin in India, and, as a result, have since not participated in the annual August Heritage Days festival.[31] More serious-ly, government officials began avoiding contact with Sikh political organizations that called for Punjab independence.

At least four Edmonton groups derive directly or indi-rectly from Radhasoami—a movement (founded by Param Guru Shri Shiv Dayal Singh Sahab) that emerged from the Sikh tradition in 1861 but which orthodox Sikhs do not recognize since they do not believe in living gurus. In prac-tice the movement has Hindu overtones with beliefs somewhat resembling Gnosticism.[32] Guru Kirpal Singh was very successful in bringing the message to the west. On his death in 1974, the movement split among three leaders, each of whom claimed to be his spiritual heir. All three leaders have Edmonton followers. The largest group, and longest established, is Sant Rajinder Singh's Science of Spirituality. It was operating as early as 1972, well before the three-way division took place.[33] Some two dozen peo-ple continue to meet on a weekly basis for meditation in the Orange Hall in Strathcona. The Science of the Soul, led by Sant Thakar Singh, entered the city in 1993, with a missionary conducting home meetings. The third group, Sant Ajaib Singh Ji's Sant Mat organization, recently held an international convention in Rimbey.[34]

An unacknowledged part of the Radhasoami tradition, Eckankar is a larger and better known group. Paul Twitchell, its founder, drew heavily from his experience in Radasoami and the movement remains close in practice and belief, despite changes in terminology.[35] Former Kabalarians, Ross and Diane Banner, introduced Eckankar to Edmonton in 1971, holding meetings in their home until the organization opened a store-front centre down-town in 1975.[36] At that time the group claimed to have fifty members. Through the 1980s the centre was on 118 Avenue, but moved to larger premises on Whyte Avenue around 1990.

A small Zoroastrian community also exists in Edmonton, comprised mostly of Indian Parsis. Together with a corre-sponding group in Calgary, they formed the Zoroastrian Association of Alberta in 1980. The followers of this ancient Persian faith meet in homes, having neither a temple nor a full-time priest for their community.[37]

Apart from the immigrant communities that have brought Hinduism to Edmonton, a large number of religious organizations are derived in various ways from the Hindu tradition. (Along these lines, we will not even consider the dozens of organizations teaching yoga.) These convert groups themselves make varying claims about the extent to which Hinduism has influenced their doctrines and practices. On one end of the scale is a group such as the International Society for Krishna Consciousness (ISKCON), in which members undertake a life dedicated to devotional prayer, vegetarianism, and the study of the *Vedas* in Sanskrit. At the other end of the scale, Transcendental Meditation (TM) denies that it is a reli-gion, let alone a Hindu religion. While not wishing to debate the issue of TM's origins, we do wish to note that

Sod-turning for the Hindu Centre, 1976. East Indian settlement in Edmonton increased greatly following the change to Canadian immigration laws in the 1960s. (PAA J2621)

the content of the group's meditation practice as well as the 'unified field theory' are unquestionably of Hindu origin, despite the fact that TM uses the rhetoric of scientism.[38]

Followers of the Maharishi Mahesh Yogi, who organized a TM group in Calgary as early as 1964, brought the guru to Edmonton in 1966. At that time, TM emphasized teaching the meditation technique. Now the group offers an entire series of short courses—including architecture, business management, meditation, nutrition, and yogic flying—at the Maharishi Vedic College in Le Marchand Mansion. Courses cost from $1,000 to $3,000 each. The most surprising development in TM is the formation of the Natural Law Party, which in 1993 unsuccessfully ran candidates in Edmonton in both the federal and provincial elections. Apart from general issues concerning sound government, the political platform of the Natural Law Party seems to contend that a certain level of participation in TM will, by itself, resolve most social problems.[39]

ISKCON is the fruit of Swami Prabhupada's Hindu mission to New York in the 1960s.[40] The movement has had a controversial history, particularly with respect to power struggles and violent episodes following Prabhupada's death. Nothing of the kind appears to have occurred in the Edmonton Krishna community, although the group did find itself involved in considerable public controversy. In the early 1970s Krishna devotees from the Vancouver temple periodically solicited funds on the streets of Edmonton. By the end of the decade, this activity became a legal issue when police began charging Krishnas with unlicensed soliciting. The group challenged the Alberta Public Contributions Act, claiming it curtailed their religious freedom, but lost the case. By this time about twenty devotees lived in a west-end temple, and these orange-robed Krishnas were a regular presence on downtown streets. In the early 1980s the Krishnas were the focus of considerable controversy, even hostility, with accusations of mind control from the so-called 'anti-cult movement.' After that, the Hare Krishnas kept a low profile, no longer wearing saffron robes and chanting in public. The Edmonton group remains in existence, supporting itself by business activities, and members have recently built a temple.[41]

Another Hindu group that won numerous Edmonton converts in the 1970s was Guru Maharaj Ji's Divine Light Mission. The movement first entered the city in 1973 and one year later had some four dozen devotees. Late in the decade the core members lived in an ashram in a large house in Oliver. By 1978 the congregation had dropped to under thirty and early in the 1980s it broke up.[42] A Hindu

sect begun in the 1930s to promote a life of celibacy and prayer, Brahma Kumaris became international in scope in the 1970s and has functioned in Edmonton for the past ten years. The leader of the movement, Dadi Janki, visited the city in 1993. Brahma Kumaris actively advertises its services, including regular meditation under the pyramid at City Hall.[43]

Inclusion of the 'sex and Rolls Royce' guru, Bhagwan Shree Rajneesh, in the Hindu section of this survey in no way underplays the objections that many Hindus had towards him in India.[44] Pendants bearing the guru's picture were common in Edmonton during the late 1970s, when the movement's local star was the filmmaker, Anne Wheeler. Apart from introductory lectures, the group's focus for local activities at this time was the Samadhi Rajneesh Sannyas Ashram, located on a farm in the Tofield area. In 1985 a scandal erupted at the University of Alberta when a student complained that a professor who promoted the Rajneesh philosophy of 'letting go' in his classes had taken advantage of her sexually. Around the same time the ashram closed, and since 1986 no publicized Rajneesh activities have taken place in the city. Former Edmonton real estate investor, Michael O'Byrne (now known as Swami Prem Jayesh), directs the current Rajneesh empire from Poona, India.[45]

Jainism is the smallest and least known of the three ancient Indian religions. It differs from Hinduism and Buddhism in upholding even more rigourous standards of asceticism, non-violence, and vegetarianism. When Jain leader, Shri Chatrikirti Bhattarak, visited Edmonton in 1990, some fifteen families of the faith resided in the city. They worshipped at the Hindu Centre, where they installed an image of Lord Mahavir in 1989. When Bhattarak visited Edmonton again in 1993, he spoke at both Hindu temples.[46]

✿ BUDDHISM AND TAOISM

The striking feature of Buddhism in Edmonton is the diversity of this rather small community. Ethnically, the immigrant congregations of Edmonton Buddhists include people with Japanese, Chinese, Vietnamese, Sri Lankan, and Cambodian backgrounds.[47] Beyond immigrant congregations, however, are a bewildering assortment of convert groups and new sects.

The Theravada tradition is the most orthodox and conservative Buddhism of Sri Lanka and southeast Asia. Sri Lankan Buddhists in Edmonton formed the Buddhist Vihara Association of Alberta in the early 1980s. The

Alberta Buddhist Cultural Society, founded in 1983 with about 200 members, represents Buddhists from Thailand, Burma, Cambodia, and Laos.[48] For several years, the approximately 500 Cambodian Buddhists in the city had difficulty finding a monk because so few had survived their homeland's Communist purges, but the group eventually succeeded in establishing the Sum Nuk Song Temple.[49] Two small convert circles—Light of the Dhamma and the Theravadin Buddhist Group—have been active in the past few years.

Much more diverse in practice and belief than Theravada is Mahayana Buddhism, with its tradition of the *bodhisattvas*—the saints who forsake their own attainment of nirvana to help save others. Mahayana has been more open to the development of syncretism than its forerunner, so it is not surprising to see that Edmonton's Mahayana groups are quite diverse congregations. Mahayana also is rather more attractive to converts for the same reasons. Indeed, some of the convert groups in Edmonton have continuous histories going back to the early 1970s, thus predating the immigrant Buddhist communities. Vietnamese immigrants follow the Mahayana tradition and they comprise the largest of the Buddhist groups in Edmonton. The Phat Quang Pagoda, which is affiliated with the Vietnamese Unified Buddhist Congregation of Canada, opened in Mill Woods in July 1988. This group also operates the Truc Lam Monastery in Riverdale, in the premises of the former Rundle United Church. Another Vietnamese group is the Mui Kwok Temple on 96 Street in downtown Edmonton.

At least five groups in Edmonton follow different Tibetan traditions. They constitute by far the strongest element of the convert Buddhist community, since no immigrant Tibetan community exists in the city. Edmonton Dharmadhatu began in the early 1970s as the Edmonton Buddhist Society, organized by Thelma Habgood and Barb Schweger. Affiliating with Karma Dzong, founded by the late Chogyam Trungpa Rinpoche, it went by the name Dharma Study Group until fixing on the present name in 1980. Two other small groups affiliate with the Karma Kagyu lineage. One is Karma Tashi Ling, which follows the

For several years, the approximately 500 Cambodian Buddhists in the city had difficulty finding a monk because so few had survived their homeland's Communist purges, but the group eventually succeeded in establishing the Sum Nuk Song Temple.

teachings of the Venerable Trangu Rinpoche and has been active for about ten years. The other, established more recently, is the Kamtsang Choling Edmonton Buddhist Centre, begun by Lama Ole Nydahl in 1983.[50] The Novayana Society of Alberta follows the Venerable Namgyal Rinpoche, a Canadian sometimes confused with a Tibetan lama, who lived briefly in Edmonton when he first came to Canada in 1972.[51] This group operated as the Namgyal Group until adopting its present name in 1980. In 1974 one Edmonton and three British Columbia families sponsored the immigration of Geshe Ngawang Kaldan to Canada. He lived in Nelson, British Columbia, for seven months before moving to Edmonton, where he taught courses on Buddhism at both the University of Alberta and Grant MacEwan College. After several years at the University of Toronto, Kaldan returned to Edmonton in 1993 to become spiritual director of the Gaden Samten Ling Tibetan Buddhist Meditation Society.[52]

At least three groups in Edmonton follow new Chinese Buddhist movements. The largest, the True Buddha School of Master Shen-yen Lu (sometimes written Lu Sheng-Yen), which contains elements of Taoism, originated in Taiwan and now is centred in the state of Washington. The Edmonton chapter, the Chin Yin Tang Buddhist Society (also called the True Buddha School Chin Yin Buddhist Society), began in 1985 with three dozen members, and since has grown to around 800. The Jen Foo Chung Temple opened in 1991. While most members are Chinese or Vietnamese, many of them converted in Canada to this rapidly growing sect.[53] Buddha's Light International is another new sect from Taiwan, and in 1994 Venerable Master Hsing Yun attended the opening of the group's Edmonton centre.[54] The city also contains followers of a woman reputed to be a living Buddha, Supreme Master Ching Hai, and literature about her appeared downtown in the summer of 1994.

Japanese Buddhist traditions also have Edmonton followers. The Buddhist Church of Canada, established by Japanese immigrants early in the twentieth century, affiliates with the majority Jodo Shinshu denomination. A small group, comprising both Japanese and converts, meets monthly at the Japanese Community Association Centre under the direction of Sensei Fred Ulrich.[55] The Edmonton Buddhist Meditation Group, directed by the Reverend Dominic Lloyd, has its origins in Bill Jensen's course in Zen at Grant MacEwan College in the 1970s. By 1978 Jensen and others had founded the Edmonton Buddhist Priory, affiliated with the Soto Zen Church of Shasta Abbey in California. As a communal residence and business, the priory seems not to have survived after 1980.[56] Nichiren Shoshu is another Japanese sect whose lay arm, Soka Gakkai, experienced massive growth in the 1950s. Since then it has spread outside Japan, particularly among non-Japanese. The Soka Gakkai group in Edmonton that Paul Cake established in 1975 had attracted some three dozen Edmontonians by 1983.[57]

Probably Chinese immigrants have practiced Taoism in Edmonton throughout much of the twentieth century. Its first public manifestation, however, is the Fung Loy Kok Temple, which opened in 1990 as an adjunct to the Taoist Tai Chi Association.[58]

∾ CONCLUSION

Edmonton's growth in the twentieth century has included an increase in religious diversity. Some of this diversity occurred as a result of changes to Canada's immigration laws in the 1960s, allowing larger numbers of Asian and other non-European immigrants to enter the country. Political and social crises in various parts of the world have also helped create new immigrant sources. Evangelization has also been a factor in introducing religious groups outside the Judeo-Christian tradition to the city. For the most part, these processes—immigration and evangelization— are separate. Hinduism and Buddhism exemplify this separation, with immigrants and converts usually found in distinct organizations. An interesting exception is Baha'i, where refugees joined an established convert community. Frequently, immigrant groups coming from situations of persecution form tightly-knit communities in Edmonton (and elsewhere), even becoming more orthodox once in a social situation that permits religious freedom. Perhaps reflecting residues from the 1960s' counterculture movement, increasing numbers of Edmontonians from the 1970s onward have converted to non-Western religious faiths. As the number of faiths in the city rises, the likelihood of new, eclectic religions sprouting on home soil also increases. ∾

DOUG OWRAM

THE BABY BOOM AND THE TRANSFORMATION OF THE UNIVERSITY OF ALBERTA

University of Alberta campus, 1954-5, before the expansion of the 1960s and
1970s in response to escalating enrollments. (UAA 70-105-32)

*T*he 1950s were years of tremendous change. The relative isolation of the interwar years was gone. First Hiroshima and then the Russian A-bomb tests in September 1949 had seen to that. With the advent of television, Edmontonians were more and more aware of events elsewhere.

In the United States, McCarthy went on a witch hunt for communists, the McDonald brothers began selling hamburgers, the Cadillac acquired fins that kept growing and growing, and Blacks began demanding civil rights. In Canada, following the Pipeline debate, the businesslike government of Louis St Laurent gave way to the theatrics of Saskatchewan's John Diefenbaker. In Alberta, oil discovery followed oil discovery, from Leduc to Redwater to Pembina. Government expanded, new immigrant groups arrived, and women entered the business world in increasing numbers. Wealth and sustained growth seemed assured. In Edmonton, the local economy diversified from government, education, and agricultural supply to include oil field supply and refining. These were also the years of the baby boom.

Doug Owram is vice president academic of the University of Alberta and one of English Canada's most respected historians. He is currently working on a book on the baby boom generation. Here he tells us what happened when the baby boomers went to the University of Alberta. They arrived during a time of even greater change, when the nightly television news featured race riots, the war in Vietnam, student protests, and the rise of separatism in Quebec.

FROM DOWNTOWN, THE UNIVERSITY OF ALBERTA dominates much of Edmonton's southern skyline.[1] The campus sweeps from 109 Street on the east to Saskatchewan Drive and the Groat on the west, a visible, physical testimony to the role of higher education in the city. With between twenty-five and thirty-thousand students the University accounts for nearly 5 per cent of the city's population—it is by far the most common choice of Edmontonians seeking post-secondary education. Nationally, it is the second or third largest university in Canada, depending on how you measure such things. Comprised of more than seventy departments and a dozen faculties, it is the embodiment of the mega-university. In some ways, the University is even more important to Edmonton than these figures suggest. It may not be quite in the position of the true 'university town,' such as Oxford or Madison, Wisconsin. But relative to the University of Toronto, University of British Columbia, or McGill—other large institutions—the University of Alberta is a much more commanding presence for the simple reason that the city is smaller.

The progress of the University of Alberta towards this position of a mega-university has been far from even. Indeed, if you turn once again to the skyline across the river you quickly sense that much of the history of the University of Alberta's growth has come in short bursts, followed by years of stability or relative decline. Something of this pattern is revealed by the buildings. A few old structures dot the campus—Old Arts, Athabasca, Assiniboia, and so on. These are now refurbished and have appropriate plaques noting their connection to the first two decades of the university. Look, however, for the record of the 1930s and 1940s. There is nothing. The Great Depression and the Second World War effectively halted capital construction for almost two decades. After the war there was some return to construction; generally, however, the growth of the university in these years lagged behind that of a city fed by new oil revenue and a government that was growing in spite of itself.

Then, from the end of the 1950s to the beginning of the 1970s the modern campus was created. The Tory Building, Biological Sciences, Education, Clinical Sciences, Central Academic Building, Student Union, and others were constructed. On the drawing board was much of the remaining skyline—including Law and Humanities.[2] To further emphasize the importance of these years, construction slowed again. True, the oil boom of the 1970s brought some ongoing construction. In the 1980s that ground to a halt, however. So far in the 1990s the new Timms Centre,

built with private donations, remains an isolated monument in a financially troubled decade.

The stop and start pattern of construction has left a visible record suggestive of the changing role played by the University in the city through the years. Periods of stability and of being taken for granted have periodically been shattered by crises of growth and change. The period of greatest crisis and change came in the years from the end of the 1950s to the early 1970s. Both the size and the character of the university changed dramatically. So too did its relationship to the city that surrounded it.

∾ The University of Alberta was created in 1908 as, as one person idealistically put it, 'a sanctuary of truth' on a prairie frontier.[3] Yet 'sanctuary of truth' was only part of the role. From the beginning the University of Alberta was, as with most frontier universities, part of the larger booster campaign to sell Alberta to prospective immigrants. Both the University's first president, Henry Marshall Tory, and Alberta's first premier, Alexander Rutherford, saw the University as a community body—with the community being the province not just Edmonton. The University was to train and educate students and to show the outside world just how far Alberta had come.

Though aimed at the province and the outside world, the University was also vital to the city. Edmonton was the smaller of the two primary urban communities in Alberta. In 1911 its population was just over 30,000; Calgary's was closer to 45,000.[4] Edmonton had been chosen capital because of its Liberal affiliations. The University would be situated in nearby Strathcona (Premier Rutherford's home constituency), which was soon to be amalgamated with Edmonton. The University would thus provide legitimacy and money to an urban centre trying to assert a position of dominance over other prairie centres. 'Members of the Legislature,' wrote Tory's biographer, 'were inclined to be suspicious of each other, partly because in Alberta, at that time, every community of any size was anxious to assist real estate promotion by bringing public institutions to the home town.'[5] As Tory himself admitted, had Premier Rutherford been from Calgary, the University would likely have gone to the southern city.[6]

The University was indeed important to the city through its first twenty years. Tory became a well known national figure and the University asserted its predominant position in provincial education. Then the Great Depression hit. The city and the University lagged together. There was simply no money. The population grew only slowly and only the most affluent could afford to go to University. The war and post-war years were uneven. The returning veterans brought new pressures to the system but, in relative terms, the period 1945 to 1955 saw a decline in the University's importance to the city. Oil had been discovered at Leduc in 1947 and at Redwater in 1948. From 1951 to 1956 the city grew by more than 40 per cent—but the University, having dealt with the veterans, actually declined slightly in enrollment.

By the end of the 1950s, the University's relative influence may have been at an all time low since the First World War. In 1959 the University's budget was approximately $6 million, and there were fewer than 5,000 students, one for every 50 Edmontonians.[7] Only 5 per cent of Albertans had taken any post-secondary education, much less completed a university degree.[8] Thus the institution did not affect many lives directly. In an economy that was growing rapidly and oriented to blue collar jobs such as oil field supplies and agriculture, the University seemed less important both psychologically and in its financial contribution to the city. It was nice to have of course. It set Edmonton apart from that uneducated city to the south. It was convenient and an occasional source of expertise. Still, it did not seem vital to the existence or well-being of a growing city in a healthy economy based on oil and agriculture.

In the background—nationally and locally—were forces that were to change this picture. Canada was generally prosperous after the war and thus parents could afford to send their children to school longer. Already by the mid-fifties, high school was becoming a common experience where, only a couple of decades before, it had been for the minority. Attitudes were changing in response to the new realities of the job market. As late as 1954, 68 per cent of Canadians believed that boys should leave school at the age of 16.[9] By the later 1950s, however, various pressures emphasized the importance of advanced education. Best known of these was the crisis of confidence that the 1957 launch of the Soviet sputnik created in educational and political circles of the western world.[10] Reports issued through the later 1950s invariably talked about the desperate need for advanced research in engineering and science.

By the end of the 1950s, the University's relative influence may have been at an all time low since the First World War. In 1959 the University's budget was approximately $6 million, and there were fewer than 5,000 students, one for every 50 Edmontonians.

Yet, though best known, the sputnik scare may be less relevant than another trend. From the 1950s through the 1970s there was a tremendous expansion of white collar positions in administration, finance, and the public sector.[11] Society needed teachers, civil servants, nurses, doctors, and bankers. For example, from 1951 to 1971 the number of government workers in Canada increased from 318,000 to 710,000 and the number of teachers, from 153,000 to more than a quarter of a million. The list could go on but the point is that for those coming of age in the later 1950s and through the 1960s, high levels of education were needed to take advantage of the growth in the white collar sector. Moreover, in absolute terms, the bulk of new jobs were not in applied areas but required a general education in arts or science. There were thus very practical reasons why the middle class, for the first time, began to see post-secondary education as essential for the success of its offspring—and not just in engineering or science. Society, for its part, saw the production of increased numbers of sociologists, economists, and even historians as necessary to meet the tremendous demands of the robust white collar sector.[12]

The most potent force of all, though, was the baby boom. Historically birth rates follow certain tendencies so strong that they are often described as laws. Urbanization and industrialization bring lower fertility rates. Thus, as Figure 1 illustrates, both Canada and the United States had experienced a long term decline in fertility, beginning around 1870 or 1880. The patterns were uneven, with frontier and rural areas like Alberta beginning the decline later than settled and more urban areas like Ontario. Even in the West, however, fertility rates had gone into decline by the 1920s. Every sign indicated that North America was about to replicate the traditions of 'mature' societies such as France or Britain.

The decline was accentuated in the 1930s as the combination of long term trends and the GreatDepression pushed fertility rates to an all-time low. Predictions made at the beginning of the war stated that by 1971 the Canadian population would reach only 13.5 to 14 million. The longer term was even more bleak. A Dominion

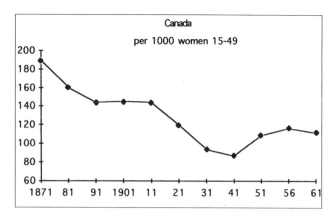

Figure 1. Birth Rate in Canada 1871–1961
Source: Derived from Jacques Henripin, *Trends and Factors of Fertility* (Ottawa: Queen's Printer, 1961).

Bureau of Statistics publication stated: 'A projection of the fertility and mortality trends of 1921–39 into the future indicates that the rate of natural increase will decline. If the trend towards smaller families continues, and no-large scale immigration occurs, the population will reach a maximum of about 15 million towards the end of the century, and thereafter will begin to decline.'[13]

Of course that scenario did not come to be. The return of prosperity during the war resulted in a steady increase in the number of births. The real explosion occurred after the war however. The number of babies born went up from just over 300,000 at war's end to 372,000 by 1947 and more than 400,000 by 1952. It would be 1966 before the number of children born again fell below 400,000. The

change in the birth rate was even more dramatic. From a figure of 24.3 per thousand population in 1945, it soared to 28.9 in 1947. Not until 1963 did it again fall to the 24 range. Throughout these years Alberta was slightly above the national average with a fertility rate of between 28 and 30 per thousand people.[14]

This then was the baby boom. The years when the birth rate went well above 24/1000 population (though only an inexact measurement) provide a convenient set of dates for the sake of defining the era. In Canada, therefore, the baby boom began in 1946, peaked in terms of absolute numbers in 1959, and ended by 1963. The births of those seventeen years have been among the most potent forces shaping Canadian cultural, political, and economic life ever since. The first half of this generation, born between 1947 and the mid-1950s, brought an especially turbulent time. After years in which Canada's population had aged, institutions were not prepared for the needs and demands this shock wave of children would create.

By the mid-1950s clear warnings existed that the baby boom was completely going to reshape Canadian universities. In 1955 a report commissioned by the National Conference of Canadian Universities (NCCU), the Sheffield Report, linked public school enrollments to the future higher education and warned that enrollment in Canada could double in the next decade. The NCCU reacted swiftly, sending the report to every daily newspaper in Canada.[15] The next year it sponsored a conference that, having taken the report to heart, talked of the 'crisis' in Canadian higher education and predicted post-secondary

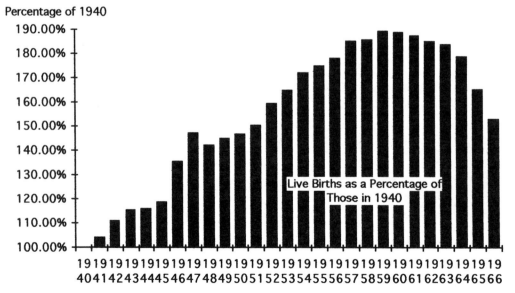

Figure 2. Live Births as a Percentage of 1940

The face of the campus changed dramatically from the sixties to the eighties, making it almost unrecognizable to alumni from an earlier era. Excavation for the Student's Union Building was begun in 1965 (foreground), while cranes on top of the nearly completed Tory Building are visible in the background. (UAA 79-149 3A)

enrollments could reach as high as 133,000 students by 1965. As it would turn out even that alarmist figure was far too low. In Ontario, universities reported to the Department of Education under J.G. Althouse. He also took the Sheffield numbers seriously and warned the government that the days of stability and quiet neglect were about to end: 'Can the universities and Provincial Government defy public opinion and deny to 10,000 to 20,000 young persons who could pass today's tests, the right to higher education?'[16]

The Sheffield report came just in time. Beginning in 1957 enrollment at the University of Alberta, as elsewhere, began to increase dramatically. From 1956 to 1961 enrollment doubled and operating expenditures more than doubled.[17] These increases, remember, were before the baby boom had even arrived. The real explosion came through the 1960s with full time student enrollment shooting up from 4,900 in 1959 to more than 15,000 a decade later.[18] New degrees were added. Graduate programs expanded dramatically, and really for the first time the University became a significant centre for PhD work. From 1911 to 1956 the University granted only 7 PhDs. From 1956 to 1982 it granted 2,753![19] The number of faculty more than tripled and the budget increased more than seven-fold.

Throughout the sixties the University expanded much faster than the city of Edmonton. Its impact on the city grew proportionately. Many construction firms owed their prosperity to university expansion. In 1968–69 alone some $25 million was spent in the construction of new buildings or the expansion and renovation of existing ones.[20] Well paid faculty members brought money into the community. The students, research grants, and supplies purchases all added to the city's economy.

More important than the expenditures, though, was the psychological impact of the University. As mentioned, for earlier generations the University was a remote thing. Only a small proportion of Albertans—let alone Edmontonians—went there. Symbolic, perhaps, was the fact that most of the Social Credit cabinets of the 1950s contained nobody with a university degree. All of this changed in a few years. Across Canada the participation rate of 18–24-year-olds in university and college education increased from 2 per cent in 1951 to 17 per cent by the end of the 1960s. In Alberta the post-secondary participation rate was at 20 per cent by the beginning of the 1970s, the highest in Canada.[21]

For the first time a significant percentage of Edmontonians had a direct stake in the University. It was where their children were educated. What went on there mattered to them. Public pressure to open the doors to the flood-tide of baby boomers explains much of the rapid growth in government grants. For the older generation, who themselves had never had a chance to go to university, the institution was a magic key for their children. Moreover, the key really did seem to work through the decade. Canada continued to prosper and Alberta, even more so. From the mid sixties through early 1970s unemployment barely existed, which, coupled with the continued growth of key sectors of the white collar world, provided something close to a guarantee of jobs for those who emerged with a degree in hand.

Yet the rapid transformation of the University also created friction. For the 1960s were years of upheaval. The large youth population and the affluence of the times created a climate that was particularly suitable for an assertion by the young of their own values and attitudes. These were the years of 'sex, drugs and rock and roll,' to quote a phrase of the era. It is no surprise that the so-called youth revolution caused shock and considerable debate in Edmonton, a relatively conservative community. Along the way the institution where youth congregated, the University, received more than its share of criticism as decadent, as fostering youth immorality, or simply as the home of weird people. At the very time, therefore, that the University was becoming more important to the community it was also becoming more foreign.

High school culture was a prelude to what happened in the universities in the 1960s, but it was also quite different. It was a prelude in that, for the first time since the 1920s, there was a distinct youth presence and youth culture. Between 1951 and 1961 the 10–19 age group in Canada increased by more than a million people. Each year more and more of the Canadian population were interested in adolescent fashions, issues, and identity. In the United States the adolescent population rose just as quickly, and on both sides of the border the pre-teens of the baby boom moved ever closer to adolescence. High school participation rates were also having an effect. In 1954 the percentage of 14- to 17-year-olds still in school went over 50 per cent for the first time in Canadian history. Within six years two thirds of the age group were still students.[22] Not only were there more adolescents but their activities were increasingly defined by an age-specific institution—the high school. The final ingredient was market-power. The continually rising standard of living in Canada made the adolescent market increasingly important.[23] In turn, the very existence of a special youth market reinforced the sense that youth were distinct from both children and adults.

Out of it all the cult of the teenager was born. In some ways the 'teenager' was just a more age-specific term for adolescence, but in one way it was a special word because, unlike adolescence, it implied a whole culture rather than merely a state of hormonal transition. 'Teenagers' were an American 'invention' but television, magazines, and the general pervasiveness of American culture quickly carried that invention north of the border. As others have noted, the baby boom did not invent modern youth culture, but the baby boomers did transform it.[24] The institutions, cultural forms, and economic power of the teenager were all put into place through the 1950s. Most important of all, so too was the conscious sense that youth had its own unique culture, not congenial to adults and therefore all the more special. By the time the baby boom reached adolescence the distinct world of the North American teenager was well entrenched.

The 1960s took modern youth culture and extended it in two ways. First, it was extended in age, increasingly centring not on high school but on the new magnet of education, the university. The focus was now on the early twenties and the most privileged and best educated of youth—the one in six or seven who went to university. Second, youth rebellion converted adolescent rebelliousness into a moral code. The 1960s can be interpreted as a reaction against the security conscious 1950s, and it was youth that most dramatically expressed that rebellion. Throughout the 1950s issues like 'respectability' or its negative counterpart 'conformity' had been a significant part of the social glue, allowing the adult world to subordinate the rebellious James Dean figure to the clean cut singer, Pat Boone. The clean teen image at the beginning of the 1960s implied that, whatever foibles teenagers might demonstrate, their ultimate goal was adult respectability. Then, during the 1960s adult society itself became less respectable. John Kennedy's death robbed that world of much of its magic. The senescent phase of the Cold War made traditional politics increasingly unattractive, especially once the catastrophic Vietnam venture escalated in 1964 and 1965. Emulation of adults became less desirable and what started as a fad soon began to take on political connotations. People who wore the uniform of mini-skirts, long hair, boots, and blue jeans were declaring themselves a part of the new youth sensibility. As American historian William O'Neill put it, 'aesthetics were exchanged for ethics' or, more appropriately perhaps, aesthetics became a statement of ethics.[25]

Once clothes assumed political significance people reacted accordingly. Indeed, in this post-sixties world it is difficult to conceive of the hostility and fear created by the rise of the new youth fashions of the 1960s. People with long hair were routinely threatened or harassed. In the United States students were sent to jail for 'disrupting the peace'—that is, wearing long hair to class.[26] Families broke up over the length of a boy's hair or his decision to comb his bangs down 'like the Beatles.' Girls were suspended for wearing blue jeans to school (not sufficiently feminine) or wearing dresses that were above the knee (too feminine?). The Principal of Baron Byng High School in Montreal summed up the rationale of the age: 'These eccentric habits are meant to distract the attention of other students and that's exactly what we don't want.'[27] A Vancouver restaurant owner threw a couple out of his establishment because the male had a beard and the girl had a 'beard like attitude.'[28] Such reactions accentuated the generation gap. 'Youths who tried the fashion of long hair found themselves on the other side of the great cultural divide. Many of them elected to stay.'[29]

These daily skirmishes had two related meanings. First, this hostility to the trappings of youth culture was the 1950s at its most repressed. North American society did not tolerate difference with any equanimity. The search for security had led to intolerance of diversity. Conformity in dress, manners, and outlook was a badge of social respectability.[30] Second, the battles over fashion were a struggle between generations for control of youth. Rejection of the outward symbols of respectability was threatening the tenuous balance that had been achieved in the post war years among family, work, and social demands.

The threat was particularly evident in the case of sexual identity. The increasingly androgynous styles of the 1960s directly assaulted the uncertainties about gender role, manliness, and Freudian sexual impulses that had shaped many of the values of the postwar generation. Old standards of gender behaviour clashed directly with new generationally directed styles. 'Get Your Hair Cut. You Look Like a Girl' was a potent insult in the hands of those who subscribed to 1950s standards of manliness. It meant nothing to an adolescent youth looking to a peer group for clues on behaviour and dress.

The conflict of values had special meaning when father, imbued with thousands of Freudian notions on child rearing and the ever present dangers of sexuality, watched his adolescent sons suddenly adopt 'non-manly' adolescent fashions. When John Lennon remarked flippantly that all he had to do to prove he was a man was have sex with a woman, he assaulted the sensibilities of a generation. For girls the analogous process was the increasingly open sexuality of the decade. The fear was that if boys were becoming girls, girls were ceasing to be ladies.

As one teenage girl complained in 1966, the belief that morality was breaking down was wrong, 'that because two people engage in sex they are not moral if they are not married. I take very great exception to this. I don't feel this is true at all.'[31]

Adult hostility further ingrained youth culture as a political statement, an effect perhaps most clearly demonstrated in the sub-culture of language. Throughout the 1960s language, as with clothes, was becoming a means of distinguishing young from old. Drug slang separated 'straights' from 'freaks' and drug words were converted into metaphors like 'trippy.' Other terms like 'far out,' 'cool,' and 'groovy' derived from the beat culture. Obscenity too played an important part as a symbol of youth's absence of inhibition and for the shock value it conveyed. Youth had always sworn but in the 1960s obscenity went up-scale and became co-educational. Words that would have been reserved for the locker room became a normal part of any university party or, in some cases, seminar.[32]

These changes shook some very fundamental principles in university society. From at least the 1920s college students had been forgiven a certain level of rowdiness. They were the elite, working hard to obtain grades, and being a 'college man' or 'college woman' implied an interest in style, the opposite sex, and breaking rules. Nevertheless, at most universities and certainly at the University of Alberta there was an assumption that the moral conduct of students was the responsibility of the University. In the time of Henry Marshal Tory this responsibility had been fulfilled through compulsory church attendance, a strict dress code, and considerable formality in the classroom.

By the 1950s the mood had relaxed, as had general standards of dress and behaviour throughout society. Nevertheless, even in the 1950s two principles shaped University of Alberta policy and student behaviour. First, society expected a degree of deference from young to old, from pupil to teacher. Such deference was part of a certain civil formality still in day to day life. A respectable man wore a tie and jacket for all but the most informal events. Certainly no respectable woman wore slacks in public, except maybe at the cottage. The fact that in an agricultural region like Alberta these rules were slightly less strictly observed than in, say, Toronto or Montreal, does not alter the general picture. Second, remember that the nature of the student body in the 1950s and 1960s was somewhat different than it is now. There was no significant graduate school and the majority of undergraduates had come directly from high school. The age of majority was 21 and therefore the vast majority of University of Alberta

students were minors. As well, as there was only one university in the entire province, a significant number of these students were living away from home for the first time.

Parents expected and the University of Alberta accepted that these students, therefore, would be under supervision during their time at school. The notion was summed up by the Latin phrase, *in loco parentis* (literally, in place of parents). Rules of behaviour and of protection—usually protection of morals and protection of time for the sake of study habits—were accepted by all sides. A handbook for all students entering the University's residence in 1958 had a careful description of everything from proper dress and table manners to dating etiquette. 'Wherever you go, whatever you do, does reflect directly on our university. Try to be an asset rather than a liability. Remember the campus is mecca for hundreds of visitors each term. Your uncontrolled, ridiculous or thoughtless actions may cause us unwarranted criticism.'[33] Complex rules reinforced the message. Visitors of the opposite sex weren't allowed past the lobbies; women were not allowed out past 11:30 pm except on Saturday night. Drinking was grounds for expulsion, though there was always a degree of benign neglect of that rule. Sexual conduct was regulated both by university rules and by social custom. As late as the mid-sixties a survey indicated that only a very small percentage of students had engaged in sex during their time in residence. They were busy in other ways. The majority indicated that they went to church.[34]

In a remarkably short period of time customs and regulations that had survived for decades were swept aside. If one looked, for example, at the nature of student life at the University in 1964-1965 it was little different than it had been in 1954, or 1949. Five years later everything had changed. *In loco parentis* was gone. Deference to authority had been replaced among elements of the students by angry protest. The Wauneita Society, to which every female undergraduate automatically belonged, stopped giving teas and started handing out birth control information.[35] Ties and jackets disappeared, replaced by jeans and long hair.

Activism appeared tentatively about 1965 and focussed on traditional issues of self-interest, such as student-fees.[36] Very quickly, though, the cause expanded into a more general critique of university education. 'The university is supposed to be a community of scholars,' lamented one *Gateway* column in 1966. 'Instead it is becoming a place where professors talk at—rather than to—huge classes and students learn to be stenographers quickly writing down lecture material without paying attention to what is being said.'[37] Soon everything was being questioned. The New Left appeared with its confrontational politics blended with an eclectic mixture of Marx, syndicalism, and romantic utopianism. Groups like the Student Union for Peace Action (SUPA) and later the Students for a Democratic University (SDU) had chapters on campus. Their critique pictured the university not as the opportunity of a lifetime but something approaching a prison camp. 'The university is a factory and treats its students as raw material to be processed into products.' Student government, that supposed bastion of student rights, was a sham. 'Where the "students union" at the present time is a lackey of the administration . . . a real Union of Students must be created which will fight for power—fight for the demands of its membership through negotiations and, if necessary, strike action, the power to control.'[38] At the extreme universities were called fascist or even as having an 'Auschwitz approach.'[39]

There are many aspects to the student radicalism of the years after 1965 that cannot be explored here. In general, though, three patterns are apparent. First, the critique moved very quickly from the specific and the moderate to the general and the radical. Second, along the way there was an almost complete collapse of deference to authority. The baby boomers, so numerous and so certain of their own place, were unwilling to accept any role that pushed them off centre stage. Third, and most important for a discussion of the University of Alberta, the students —or at least the activists—were increasingly tied into a continent-wide network of student values, student concerns, and youth rhetoric. Issues at Berkeley, Simon Fraser, or Columbia—to mention three very active centres of student protest—were a part of student culture across North America. Talk of 'the movement' and 'the revolution' circulated even among students who were only moderately reformist.

Over the next few years several incidents enlivened the campus. In 1968, for example, members of the SDU ran through the Faculty Club yelling 'thought police! thought police' at bemused or outraged faculty members.[40] In early 1969 there was a series of protests over the denial of tenure to two radical faculty members. Later that year attempts to bring a new disciplinary system into being led to yet more protests and claims of repression. Along the way campus radicals demanded that campus police be stripped of power.[41] Through the end of the decade and into the early 1970s, marches, protests, and a great deal of radical rhetoric were part of student political life.

None of the above is to portray the University of Alberta as an especially radical place. As with many other campuses, faculties such as Engineering and Medicine remained more or less aloof from the radicalism of the decade. Nor was the University of Alberta as radical as such strife torn United States schools as Berkeley or Wisconsin. Indeed, even by tamer Canadian standards the University was less radical than some. Instead, in a pattern also seen elsewhere, radical causes and issues contended with more conservative views. Radical student councils were elected only to be rebuffed in the next election cycle. Thus, for example, the mildly new left administration of Richard Price in 1965–66 led to a reaction by students and the next student President, Branny Shepanovich, rejected both the new left and the political activism of the Canadian Union of Students (CUS). Alberta withdrew from CUS, while CUS branded the University 'the home of student fascism in Canada.'[42]

Nor, in spite of some angry demonstrations and highly

'Establishment' events like the annual ball of the women's Wauneita Society, pictured here in 1965, were popular for several years. When radicalism swept the campus, however, the Wauneita Society began dispensing birth control information. (UAA 74-52-1)

publicized controversies toward the end of the decade, was the achievement of student and faculty participation in campus governance all that controversial here. The populist tradition of the prairies made such a presence seem much less radical than in other parts of the country. Even if less radical and less confrontational, though, the politics at the University did follow the patterns of the decade. As a result, by the early 1970s, as the great tide of student radicalism began to recede, the University curriculum and power structure had been altered dramatically.

Radical politics was paralleled by the small 'p' politics of culture. Casual clothes, long hair, and, by 1967 or so, drugs, began to be a part of campus life. Learned professors lectured against the dangers of LSD, and the RCMP drug squad moved its focus from 97 Street to the residences around campus. In Canada arrests under the Narcotics Act tripled between 1966 and 1968,[43] but to little avail. The use of drugs—usually marijuana and less usually LSD or speed—continued to spread through Canadian campuses, including the University of Alberta. Articles in the student newspaper called for the legalization of soft drugs and student culture condoned the use of drugs. Politicians condemned the apparent spread of drugs among the student population and some attempted to blame campus unrest on drug takers.[44] In 1968 the CUS called for the legaliza-

tion of marijuana.[45] By the early 1970s a University of Alberta study showed that more than a quarter of students in residents had used drugs during their time there. Only six years before the figure had been 1 per cent.[46] Remember, students in residence were predominantly in the first year of study. There were more than 1500 arrests in Alberta for cannabis possession alone, more than in all of Canada just four years before.

Even more controversial than drugs was sex. In the face of student demands, the administration at the University, as with administrations across the country, abandoned the notions of *in loco parentis* through the later 1960s.[47] By the beginning of the 1970s the curfew for women in residence was 3:00 am and there were regular visiting hours in the rooms of students of the opposite sex.[48] The University health services distributed the pill and both the student government and the rising women's movement made it clear that the sexual activity of students was not a matter for University interference.

Walter Johns, the University president through this turbulent decade, reminisced that provincial officials were 'happy to leave it [expansion] to the University because on examination of the way the university was going, they seemed to feel that the developments and the plans being followed at the university were satisfactory to

Enrollments at the University of Alberta skyrocketed as post-secondary education became affordable to larger numbers of Albertans. In 1971 more politicized students demanded a voice in university government. Here, they meet to seek parity on General Faculties Council. (UAA 74-51)

them.'[49] Such optimism was only partly justified. For even as the University was becoming more important to the province and the city, the changing nature of student life proved mystifying and shocking to many in and out of government.

By the later 1960s the Minister of Education regularly had to fend off questioners who would expel student radicals. [50] He also warned that the average student had to speak out if the campus wasn't to be hijacked by radicals. The 'silent and complacent majority are not living up to their responsibilities. They are not making sure that the voice being heard from the students, the student body, is representative of the cross section of that body.'[51] On another occasion the legislature erupted into applause when it was pointed out that high schools had rejected a radical pamphlet brought to them by University students.[52] The superintendent of Edmonton public school system praised the 'positive reactions' of the high school students. Praise of revolutionary leader Che Guevera by a philosophy professor caused a considerable flurry of letters to the editor of the *Journal*.[53]

All of this might seem extreme. Alberta did not have any riots. There were no strikes and, as I have argued, campus politics was dominated as much by liberals or even conservatives as it was by radicals. Remember, though, that Alberta in the 1960s still carried a strong tradition of rural values. The Social Credit Party, in power until 1971, had roots in Christian fundamentalism. In a way the two significant cities in the province remained dominated by the countryside. Only in the 1950s did Alberta finally become a province in which the majority of people lived in towns or cities. Even as late as the beginning of the 1960s the majority of citizens here lived in centres of fewer than 10,000 people.[54] The vast majority of people had not gone to University. For these small town, largely Christian, largely conservative Albertans, the whole tendency of students to reject adult mores was shocking even within the context of the relatively staid campus of the University.

There were thus two trends occurring simultaneously and they may have cancelled each other to a degree. Through the 1960s the University became economically and educationally much more important to the city. More and more Edmontonians depended on it for their education or the education of their children. Money from faculty, students, and all that construction poured into city businesses. The explosion of the University meant that many more cultural events, professional contracts, and research triumphs. All of this was positive and would seem to promise a new golden age between town and gown.

On the other side, however, the University was becoming a stranger in the midst of the city. Exploding internal demands meant that less priority was given to outreach. The activities of the Faculty of Extension, always an essential part of the University's place in the province, did not keep pace with development in other areas. Student values (and faculty values) often seemed at odds with those of Albertans. Politicians continued to see the faculty as a kind of bearded, bizarre group of eccentrics. The hundreds of new faculty members were often from elsewhere. Roots in the community would take time and, for at least a few, Edmonton was a primitive outpost with the University, a beleaguered island of civilization. Neither side made much effort to explain the increasingly vital research activities of this emerging mega-university.

By the mid seventies both the radicalism and the rapid growth had passed. The oil price shocks of 1973 diverted the city's attention elsewhere. Yet to this day there remains a degree of separation between the University of Alberta and the city. The University feels unloved and reads about itself most often in hostile terms in the local newspapers, particularly in *Alberta Report*. The City administration will make the appropriate comments when required but there is little sense that the community sees itself as closely dependent upon or connected to the progress of the University. Both sides seem to overlook or, at the very least, underestimate an intimate relationship that dates back to Henry Marshall Tory in 1908; a relationship that became crucial after the University was transformed into one of Canada's giant universities by the changes of the 1960s. ∾

TOMMY BANKS AND CENTURY II STUDIOS

Tommy Banks, entertainer, 1974.
(PAA 93.378/72)

According to the prevailing notion that Canadian cities are dominated commercially by Toronto and Montreal and politically by Ottawa, Edmonton occupies a middle tier in which it is important regionally but has little influence nationally or internationally. A person has only to look at the sense of western grievance tapped historically by Social Credit or, more recently, the Reform party to agree with this view. The West's subordinate role is particularly noticeable in the area of culture—where (national) news and entertainment programs on the CBC long originated only in Toronto, and where the shadow of Hollywood increasingly looms over all corners of the country. But every now and then the West nurtures a talent that challenges the received wisdom and turns the tables. One such talent is, of course, the country punk-turned-torch and twang singer, kd lang, who left her native Alberta for the music scene south of the border. Another is Edmonton's Tommy Banks, who stayed in the city to build a successful career as a jazz musician and recording studio manager. During the 1960s and 1970s Banks pulled much business into Edmonton—from regional performers cutting albums to international corporations seeking advertising jingles—and was as much a cultural booster for the city as men like Donald Ross and Alexander Taylor had been in their day.

As the chief audio-visual archivist at the Provincial Archives of Alberta, which recently acquired Tommy Banks's business papers and sound recordings, Brock Silversides has had a unique opportunity to come to know the musician and his career.

ENTURY II PRODUCTIONS (LATER CENTURY II STUDIOS) was an Edmonton-based music production company established by Tommy Banks in 1965. The next decade marked a golden era for the local musical community, not so much because of the establishment of new acts (although several notable ones emerged) but more because of the consolidation of a tight group of continuously employed musicians who turned out high-quality product in a world-class studio. Century II carved out a national reputation for creativity and technical excellence and was an important training ground for local musicians, songwriters, engineers, and producers. Much of the credit can be laid squarely at the feet of Tommy Banks. With his ambitious projects in television and radio, his encouragement and use of local musicians, and his unshakable conviction that 'we can do anything here in Edmonton,' Banks almost single-handedly made the city a potential competitor to Toronto or Vancouver in the quality (although obviously not quantity) of its production. That status has since receded, but this does not lessen the contribution that Banks made in that decade.

Tommy Banks was already a well-known figure on the Canadian and Edmonton music scenes by the mid 1960s. Son of musician Benjamin Banks and television program host Laura Lindsay, he initially earned a reputation as a teenage jazz prodigy. His introduction to the stage in 1950 came as a member of the Don Thompson band, which travelled Alberta for three years as part of the 'Jammin' the Blues' tours. Ten years later Banks led the orchestra, behind vocalist Mark Cohen, when London Records released his first commercial recording, 'A Summer Romance' (penned by Banks and musical cohort Phil Shragge). Banks increased his audience in 1960 with the formation of his own band —the Banknotes—with whom he performed in such Edmonton nightclubs as the Capri, the Paddock, and the Embers (in which he held part ownership). Banks was also an early member of both the Yardbird Suite, a club devoted to jazz, and the Orion Musical Theatre. And through one of his other companies, Associated Entertainment Services, he organized the musical entertainment for Edmonton's annual summer exhibition, Klondike Days. Banks expanded into television starting in 1959 when he co-hosted the CBC network program, *Keynotes*. A steadily increasing number of appearances finally resulted in the production of his own music and talk program, appropriately called the *Tommy Banks Show*. It opened in 1968 on CBC, moved to the new independent ITV station in 1974, and returned to CBC by the end of the decade. While it sounds like a busy period for Banks, his career was about to get even busier.

The beginning of what would become the Century II empire was quite humble. Simply put, while enjoying playing in clubs, Tommy Banks and members of his band wanted to make more money and they wanted to do so using their musical talent. For several years in the early 1960s Banks had worked as the radio-television director of the Edmonton-based McConnell-Eastman Company, Alberta's principal advertising agency. It had contracts with various provincial government departments, corporations such as Gainers Packers and GWG, and even that long-standing Alberta media institution, *Canada's Back to the Bible Hour*. The experience taught Banks that the role of music in electronic media advertising was paramount and that the use of music with taste, creativity, and thoughtfulness always resulted in a better product. He also learned that advertising could earn good money. It was with this knowledge of the business and his obvious musical talents that Banks founded Century II Productions in October 1965 to produce radio advertising.

The foundation of all radio advertising is the 'jingle.' Jingles are brief musical sound bites with a text that draws attention to a particular product or service. To be effective, they have to create a mood and be memorable in some way, whether by the musical hook, a clever combination of words, or a likeable, comfortable, and/or trustworthy voice. Banks never liked the term 'jingle'—he preferred 'sound concepts':

> We never used that term jingle. We didn't make 'jingles'—that was done by people who didn't know what they were talking about. We made broadcast advertising concepts in musical form. It sounds kind of funny, but we really did pride ourselves on the fact that we didn't make 'jingles.' What we did had a lot more marketing know-how and research and thought behind it. I would have to quickly say that a lot of mere jingles, that is to say, mindless things, were very effective. But in those days, we aspired to something grander than that. Oh, they were jingles; we just hated the word![1]

Although Banks was president and the driving force, Century II was much more than a one-man operation. Banks and Bob Miller, either together or individually, did most of the musical writing. The basic musical unit for the original company consisted of Banks on keyboards, Bob Miller on bass, Bob Cairns on guitar, and Tom Doran on drums. There was also a core group of vocalists, including Judy Singh, Evelyn Quaife, Cathy Christie, Lyn Levin, Buddy Victor, Dasha Goody, and Joe Vasos, as well as Banks and Cairns. The voice-overs for the commercials

The Banknotes, the band Tommy Banks formed in 1960, made its name in Edmonton performing in nightclubs like the Capri, the Paddock, and the Embers. This picture was taken in 1970. (PAA T.1983)

were done by local radio disc jockeys such as Bob McCord (CHED), Gordon Ross (CHQT), Maury Banks (CFRN), John Bohonos (CHQT), John Scrimshaw (CHED and CJCA), and Colin McLean (CBC). A few guest celebrity voices—like Leslie Neilson, the ex-Albertan Hollywood actor, and Stanley Burke, one-time anchor for the CBC National News—were also featured in the commercials. The Century II office, located in the basement of 10040 – 106 Street, had (at different times) three managers: Eddie Keen, Bill de Carteret, and Bert Shaw. Audio engineers Gordon Forbes, Mike Fawcett, Bob Miller, and, occasionally, film director and soundman Jim Tustian completed the list of personnel.

A production company without its own sound studio faced a major problem that had to be solved quickly if it was to get off the ground. In 1966 Banks approached two old friends—the manager of the local CHED radio station, Gerry Forbes, and his production assistant, Keith James—with an offer. In Banks's words:

We didn't have money for a studio—we didn't want to pay mortgages. CHED had a not bad little studio as far as radio stations go and a fairly good control room. So I went to Gerry and said, 'Look, we'll buy some equipment of the kind you normally can't have for production . . . and it would substantially enhance your capabilities in production for the station. Let's work out a deal where we'll put in microphones, upgrade the board a bit, and put in a multitrack tape recorder. You look after it, maintain it, build it into your system, and you use it all day. At six o'clock until eight the next morning we get to use it. Everybody wins—no one is out a whole lot of money— we get a studio parttime and you get an enhancement of your production capabilities.' So we made that deal and it worked out.[2]

The CHED studio period, lasting from 1966 to 1972, produced a dramatic upswing in both Century II's workload and reputation. Its list of corporate clients was huge, as the company had a virtual monopoly in Edmonton. A small company run by musician Dennis Ferbey provided its only competition in the late 1960s, although a larger firm, Dr Jingle and Mr Hype, managed by Garry McDonall and Gord Marriott, appeared in the 1970s.

Century II tapped into three main markets. The staple was the local Edmonton market, which included stores and malls, car dealerships, banks, realtors, restaurants, jewellers, moving companies, dry cleaners, manufacturers, car washes, utility companies, and the provincial government. Century II subcontracted much of this business from the McConnell-Eastman agency, which was still content to utilize Banks's talents. More profitable were the regional markets the company exploited either directly or in tandem with one of the local radio stations as a go-between. Century II did a great deal of commercial work in Winnipeg, Regina, Saskatoon, Calgary, Lethbridge, the Okanagan, and Vancouver.[3] A large amount of the British Columbia business was contracted through Vickers and Benson, James Advertising, and Gray Plus Gray Advertising, all of Vancouver. Finally, there were the big national accounts—clients such as the Bay, Simpsons, Eaton's, Woolworths, Woolco, Safeway, Imperial Oil, Molson Breweries, Colgate-Palmolive, Dad's Cookies, Burger King, and the federal government. These accounts brought in the really big money as the ads were heard on radio stations across the country. Century II even attracted a few international jobs such as Minnesota-based Standard Lager and Japan Airlines.[4] Clearly, the reputation of Century II spread well beyond Edmonton's city limits.

The company soon broadened its activities to encompass library production music and commercial audio-visual productions. Motion picture and television soundtracks also became a specialty. Some of the more notable film projects included *Badgerville* (1971), *A Choice of Futures* (1972), *Birds in Winter* (1974), *To Serve a City* (1975), and *Once a Wizard* (1975). A television special and series of short vignettes, *Alberta Together* (1971), featured Premier Harry Strom and the Social Credit party.[5] In addition, Century II moved into a new—and as it turned out very profitable—field, producing radio and television station ID packages. As a Canadian alternative to established American producers like Pepper-Tanner, Pamus, and TM, the company made IDs for many of the major Canadian stations and a significant number of smaller ones. They also completed IDs for broadcasters in Australia and New Zealand.

Century II also started to dabble in recording music not for jingles but for potential commercial release. Two albums were completed in 1970 in the CHED studio—*Reflections* by local folk singer Duane Davis (issued first on the CBC label and then on Capitol) and *Make Someone Happy* by Tom and Judy (Tommy Banks and Judy Singh), released by GRT Records. As well, the beginning of a Clarence (Big) Miller album was put to tape, although never completed. A few regionally prominent bands and individual singers also recorded demo tapes during this period, including Privilege and Manna from Edmonton, Wascana and the Miller Rovers from Regina, Gord Pendleton from Saskatoon, and Bob Lee.[6]

It seemed inevitable that Century II would try to market its music to a wider public. The decision ultimately meant the commercial release of recordings both by musicians who had done work for the firm and longed to put out full-length pieces of music and by other independent musicians Century II had started to sign to production contracts. Banks decided that until the company acquired the knowledge base and industry contacts so necessary to break in, Century II would enter into contractual arrangements with people already in the business to distribute its products. The first agreement, signed with GRT Records of Canada in December 1970, not only provided a record label and a distribution infrastructure for Century II artists but also made it obligatory for GRT to commit production dollars to help these musicians make top-quality recordings. The first single issued from the Century II stable was a seasonal novelty called 'Tiny Tony' with flipside 'Count Your Blessings' by Bob Bradburn (then an announcer for

Century II Recording session, CHED studio, circa 1967. From left to right, Tommy Banks, Gerry Forbes, and Dasha Goody. (PAA A.21275)

CJCA radio). The first album released was the previously mentioned *Make Someone Happy*.

With the end of the GRT contract in 1971, Century II started negotiations with another distributor, this time one of the major players, Capitol Records of Canada. The agreement signed in spring 1973 obliged Century II to deliver six LPs and twenty singles—fully finished and edited masters—on an annual basis. Of greater importance, these recordings would be released on the new Century II label, not on the label of the distributor, and Century II received a $5,000-advance on expected royalties.[7] Artists specifically identified in the contract as belonging to the Century II stable included Edmontonians Jack Hennig (formerly lead singer for the Breaking Point), Donna Warner (ex-lead singer of Three's a Crowd), and Tommy Banks, as well as Wascana and Gord Pendleton from Saskatchewan. Although all these artists would record, only Donna Warner's two songs, 'Irresistable You' and 'Make Your Day Brighter,' would see the light of day as the first single on the Century II label.

During 1973-74, Century II signed contracts with and released records by many more artists, such as Richard Adams, Valerie Hudson, Terry McManus, Bruce Innes (both a solo act and his well-known American band, the Original Caste), the British group K.J. and the Grand Band, Skipper, Sylvester Stretch (relocated from the Maritimes), and Russell Thornberry. The studio also tried to sign up Barry Allen (an ex-member of both the Rebels and Painter, a solo artist of considerable renown, and already working as an engineer with Century II) as well as Bob Ruzicka (the singing dentist who had had several hits for RCA), but both were tied up with other contractual obligations.

Commercial production increased again by 1970. 'Century II developed a very effective sales mechanism, philosophy and capability,' Banks says. 'We were very good at sales. We sold all over the country and we literally blanketed Western Canada. We almost owned that market. The point is we produced a very large volume of commercials in comparison with anybody else.'[8] The radio station ID market grew, and Century II even started producing short radio spots like announcer Bob Comfort's *Posters for Your Mind*, a daily three-to-five-minute commentary in which the host ruminated on society and the foibles of human nature. (Comfort would later move to Los Angeles where his show was syndicated across North America.)

Yet Century II still did not have sufficient access to recording facilities to keep up with its obligations. Success, in fact, hurt. Banks again:

The distribution contract signed with Capitol Records of Canada in 1973 allowed Century II to use its own label.
(PAA A.21301)

We found we couldn't do it in the time we had between six o'clock and the next morning. Some of us had other things to do as well in the evenings—like make a living and raise families. And the technology changed to eight-track, and then almost overnight to sixteen-track machines. So we knew we needed a sixteen track and that we couldn't continue at CHED.[9]

With Century II's productions needing greater technical sophistication to compete with production companies in bigger centres and its workload again becoming too heavy, Banks realized that two major issues had to be tackled—enlarging the organization and finding a real studio.

Although Banks was very much a hands-on manager, it was becoming clear that he could not possibly handle all the management chores and decision making that formed such a crucial part of any creative organization. As well, he was becoming more involved in other activities like the ongoing production of the *Tommy Banks Show* for which he was a co-producer, host, arranger, band leader, and pianist. Fortunately, three other people entered his professional life. One was Dale Partridge, an ex-disc jockey and open-line radio host with CJCA who had extensive experience in sales, promotion, and merchandising. When Banks met him, he was the advertising manager for the Edmonton Exhibition Association, but he soon left to set up his own firm. The second individual was Banks's chartered accountant, Wes Alexander, a partner in the successful firm, Alexander and Company. Finally, there was Keith James, his friend from CHED, who had untold numbers of contacts within the music, recording, and broadcast industries as well as his own company, Keith James Communications and Consulting. In July 1972 the trio pooled their resources with Banks' music publishing company (Banks Music Inc) and Century II Productions and entered into partnership as Century II Studios. All four became directors, with their working roles clearly defined: Banks as president and musical director, Partridge as vice-president sales and general manager, James as vice-president artists and repertoire (he would bow out before the end of the year), and Alexander as secretary treasurer and comptroller.[10] Additional staff quickly became necessary. Barry Harris (lured away from Doug Riley Music in Toronto) was hired as sales manager, Jim Vincent as creative director, Gordon Forbes (son of CHED's Gerry Forbes) as studio manager, and Maggie Maloney as office manager.

The second problem, the need for better studio access, also required a decision. There were five studios active in Edmonton by 1972. Park Lane was a small operation on

The first record on the Century II label, 1973. (PAA T. BANKS COLLECTION)

109 Street run by Wes Dakus and Barry Allen; it had four-track capability and attracted the patronage of local rock bands. Damon, managed by Garry McDonall, also had four-track machines and was utilized by rock, jazz, and polka musicians. Project 70 on 116 Street, another four-track operation, was run by Joe Kozak and handled most of the country and western artists. Finally, there were the three radio station studios—CBC, CJCA, and CHED. Banks came up with a solution designed to benefit both him and the local recording industry:

> I went to Wes [Dakus] and Garry [McDonall] and said, 'I need a sixteen-track studio. If you will upgrade and expand your studio, I will guarantee you so many hours of rental per month.' . . . I really did expect that, based on our demonstrable capacity to guarantee them that business . . . either one would take us up on it. Both said no for whatever reason, so we had no choice. We did not want to be in the studio business, to own a studio. But we either had to stop expanding our business or build our own studio. And so we built the studio.[11]

When the Century II management team first started searching for a suitable studio site in 1970, it sought a downtown location near the new company's luxurious offices in the Boardwalk. Unfortunately, no available building was suitable. Then, after two years of fruitless searching and negotiations, an acquaintance of Banks mentioned an old abandoned building on the edge of

The Second World War concrete bunker on the outskirts of Edmonton that became the permanent home of Century II Studios. Tommy Banks described the building as looking 'pretty awful' but 'wonderful' for his purposes. (PAA A.21263)

town. Banks recalls his meeting with the realtor handling the difficult account:

> The real estate guy said, 'I have a crazy building you may want to look at. It's off by itself—it used to be an army radio station'—so my ears perked up right away. And he said, 'It's isolated and hard to get at'—he was saying this apologetically as though it was a real disadvantage, when in fact it was wonderful. It was exactly what we wanted, but of course I didn't tell him that. So we went and looked. It was a derelict building then as it had been empty for years. It was not in much better shape than it is now. Actually, it looked pretty awful. But this weird ramshackle building had all of its partitions, floors, walls, ceilings, everything made of solid poured reinforced concrete. It was like a building carved out of a block of concrete. It can't be knocked down, although I know they would love to do that. When they finally get rid of it they are going to have to blow it up! It had two large rooms, completely soundproof, with high ceilings and no posts. I thought, 'This is heaven,' while I'm saying doubtfully to the guy, 'Well, I don't know about this . . .'[12]

The structure in question was the former Bissell Communications Centre on 184 Street several miles north of the CFRN studio. Built in 1941 by the Canadian army to house communications equipment required by the wartime regional command, it had been abandoned in 1945. The building subsequently found use as a grain storage shed and a summer residence for squatters and drifters.

Century II decided to lease the building in summer 1972, leaving the way open to an eventual purchase. In keeping with his high standards and in expectation of attracting major artists, Banks resolved to create the finest studio operation then possible. Accordingly, he contacted the foremost studio designers in North America, Auditronics of Memphis, Tennessee, which had recently completed two state-of-the-art recording studios for MGM in Hollywood (Burbank Sound) and New York. The president of Auditronics, Welton Jetton, described as 'North America's leading independent audio consultant,' flew to Edmonton, examined the layout and physical construction of the building, assessed the projected needs of the company, and assembled a set of design specifications and equipment recommendations. The latter were accepted by Banks and company, and, following two months of renovations, the studio officially opened on 15 December 1972. Production started immediately.

The cost of refurbishing the building and purchasing

and installing the equipment was estimated at $180,000. With several upgrades in equipment over the next five years, the final figure approached half a million dollars. Truly state of the art, the finished system boasted Scully sixteen-track recorders and a board with mix-down capabilities to either stereo or quadrophonic masters. It was also equipped with four-track and two-track recorders for demos and an early version of the Dolby Noise Reduction System.[13] In all Canada in 1972, there were only five sixteen-track studios (located in Toronto, Montreal, and Vancouver), and no other studio in the prairie provinces would acquire sixteen-track capability until 1974. The building itself, officially known as Stony Plain Studios but commonly called the Bunker, consisted of two studios. One was large enough to hold a 75-piece orchestra, while the other was more modest and used for individual musicians and small combinations. A control room, offices, a basement lounge, and rehearsal space completed the layout.

Booked studio time was split almost evenly between commercial/advertising activities (usually mornings and afternoons) and record production (evenings and all night). Not surprisingly, Century II acted as a magnet for skilled personnel throughout the prairie region and beyond. Its producers and engineers included Gordon Forbes, Barry Allen, Keith James, Vinnie Trauth, Les Bateman, Terry McManus, and the ever-present Banks. Century II was obviously a good training ground, for these individuals went on to operate their own studios or to teach music recording. The stable of session musicians included horn men Rick Tait, Harry Pinchin, P.J. Perry, Curt Watts, Gary Guthman, Earl Seymour, Ray Sikora, and Bob Stroup; guitarists Bob Cairns, Trevor Dunn, Gary Koliger, Terry Thomas, Roy Forbes, and Gaye Delorme; bassists Bob Miller, Bob Walker, and Rick Erickson; drummers Tom Doran and Bob Ego, and many members of the Edmonton Symphony Orchestra for strings. Most keyboards were played by Banks himself, Gerry Dere, or George Blondheim.[14]

The Century II record label caused immense problems with the rest of the firm's divisions. While it admittedly had the highest profile, generated the most press, and carried considerable prestige, it was also the most time-consuming and expensive and the least profit-generating part of the business. Banks is the first to admit that the financial cushion provided by the advertising work, the excitement and appeal of running a record label, and his own personal generosity all combined to open the door to unfortunate business decisions:

This is stupid—and it's all my fault—but we decided to be a record company in the true 1930s sense of the word. We were going to select artists, build their careers, bring them into the studio, and pay all the costs. I thought it was somehow morally wrong to make the artists pay, as I was once on the end of the stick. But what we did was quixotic, unrealistic, altruistic, and definitely not the way the way the music business did things.[15]

One musician who prefers anonymity confirms this attitude. 'We never had to deal with a studio manager or anything like that,' he says. 'The minute there was a break from the paying customers, we would go in, rehearse, and record demos with no inkling that we should be paying the fees. We didn't even pay for the tape reels, and nobody asked us to!'

Although busy, the Century II Studio was not constantly in use for the company's commercials or recording artists. Whenever possible during slow periods it was rented out to other musicians, either with or without a staff engineer or producer to handle the recording or mixing. Century II's growing reputation within the larger musical community also attracted a number of outside singers and bands whose studio rental fees helped to pay the company's bills. Artists who used the studio for demos or finished productions were Crowbar, Paul Horn, the Great Canadian River Race, Witness (with Kenny Shields), Brent Titcomb, Will Millar (of Irish Rover fame), Liam Clancy, Henry Evans, Paul Hann, Sunband, Buckeye (with Tim Feehan), Stash, Val Hudson, and Stratisfaction. Even the CBC utilized Century II: its recording of Banks's

State-of-the-art control room, Century II Studios, 1973. (PAA A.21262)

adaptation of *Gift of the Magi* in December 1972 marked the first time the corporation had ever used outside facilities in Edmonton.

Century II made a major contribution to the local music scene by participating in two rock band competitions sponsored by the Edmonton Kiwanis Club. Out of a host of Alberta bands, the one judged best for overall performance that year received a prize of three free hours of studio time at the Bunker. The 1972 winner was Spiney Norman's Whoopee Band (featuring the diverse talents of Holger Petersen, now owner of Stony Plain Records; Ross Harvey, currently leader of the Alberta New Democrats; Bob Edwards of Troyka; and Larry Reese of Manna). The two tunes they recorded were released as a single by GRT Records. The 1973 winner was the band Griffen. This type of tie-in, quite revolutionary in its day, became quite common as the winners of local competitions came to expect free studio time.

A natural outgrowth of all this musical activity was the establishment of a publishing wing, Century II Publishing. Associated with both national public performance rights associations, BMI (Broadcast Music Inc.) Canada and CAPAC (Composers, Authors and Publishers Association of Canada), it presumed to copyright, register, publish, and shop out the tunes of Century II's nest of writers to any artists, producers, managers, and record companies potentially interested in having these songs performed or recorded. Between 1973 and 1976, Century II signed almost twenty-five composers in the rock, jazz, and folk genres. Included were Paul Clarke, Tony Lewis, Billy Cunningham, John Duncan MacKenzie, Gaye Delorme, Gary Guthman, Paul Hann, Pete White, Doug Hutton, Bruce Innes, Don Johnston, Andy Krawchuk, Terry McManus, Bliss Mackie, Harry Pinchin, Beverly Ross, Russell Thornberry, Tony White, Robbie Campbell, Marc Jordan, Valerie Hudson, Gerald Hannah, and Barry Allen.[16] While none of the songs made Century II rich, they did earn a bit of money, ensured that Century II Records would not have to pay songwriting royalties to outside agencies very often, and in retrospect provided a representative selection of the type of material being composed in the first half of the 1970s.

What started as a small and humble, but successful, jingle company ended up as Edmonton's version of a tottering diversified entertainment giant that had lost sight of its original goals.

Ironically, Century II sowed the seeds of its own demise with the release of its first product, *Cantata Canada*, in September 1973. A full-length album performed by Privilege and produced by Doug Hutton, it interpreted the history of Canada in rock music, with songs contributed by composers from across the country like Marc Jordan, Bill Wuttunee, Rick Neufeld, Paul Hann, Graeme Card, Carol Zazula, and Bob Ruzicka. The record had luxurious packaging with an illustrated libretto. The comments Banks fed the press—'hugely important,' 'a milestone record,' 'a truly historical Canadian album'—underscored his faith in the recording. Century II also put its money where its mouth was and subsidized the promotional campaign to the tune of tens of thousands of dollars. To everyone's dismay and chagrin, the record failed to live up to expectations. 'We blew our brains out on that one!' Banks recalls. 'It was a noble undertaking which we had no hand in producing, but we distributed it and promoted it. We expected it to be a huge hit—but it never caught on with the record buying public.'[17]

For a new company, the record's poor showing was a major setback carrying distinct financial penalties. The situation was further exacerbated by an attractive (and extremely expensive), six-page spread advertising the start of the new label in the top-rated music industry magazine, *Billboard*, out of New York. Together, these unrealistic exercises made Century II feel like it was competing in a foot race after amputating one of its own feet. Despite brief moments when the company appeared to have recovered, its ongoing generosity to its artists continued to drag it down in a slow spiral. By 1974 Banks had spread himself too thinly and was ultimately paying more attention to his television concerns than to Century II. Day-to-day decisions were being made by competent record company people, but they had little to do with the original Century II Productions and no stake in seeing that the jingle part of the business remained healthy. That summer the partnership realized that Century II could not continue and pay its bills, so the directors, excluding Banks, recommended bankruptcy procedures. While Banks acknowledged the logic of this course of action, he could not accept it.

The stigma of bankruptcy was not one he wanted to carry with him.

Century II thus underwent an amicable reorganization—the partners walked away and Banks personally took over all liabilities. He immediately laid off the entire staff, shut down the executive offices in the Boardwalk, and shelved several almost complete album projects. Moving his centre of operations out to the studio, he rehired an office manager and an engineer/producer. He also changed the studio's booking system to allow for substantially more rental time for outside artists. At this much reduced level of activity, Century II continued and slowly Banks managed to pay off his creditors.

The end of Century II Studios came suddenly and quite painlessly for Banks. In summer 1976 his television show, Celebrity Revue (produced by a new company, Century III, headed by Banks and Wendel Wilks), decided to relocate to Vancouver for six months of shooting. Staging the show at the Cave Supper Club, Banks wanted to ensure that the audio was as good as at ITV when producing the Tommy Banks Show. When the facilities of the Vancouver affiliate, BCTV, did not measure up, Banks and Wilks decided to bring the gear from Century II to the coast. They purchased an eighteen-wheel semi-trailer, carefully loaded the key pieces of recording equipment, and had the truck driven to Vancouver along with engineer Les Bateman. The Bunker thus temporarily closed for half a year.

While in Vancouver, the company also decided to buy a four-camera colour mobile unit to complement its audio unit. Despite a bargain price (in broadcasting terms), the cost of both units put Banks deeply into debt—too far for his own comfort. After much reflection and many sleepless nights, he asked his partners in Celebrity Revue to buy him out of the camera mobile. They agreed immediately on condition that Banks also sell them the matching audio mobile. Banks remembers:

> I really did not want to be in the hardware business and mortgage my house again. Yet I had to think twice about selling the Century II equipment as I had put a lot of time and money into building it up. But I realized I never really wanted to be a studio proprietor in the first place. I had gone too far into the business end of music—I was doing little playing, almost no writing, and no conducting whatsoever by this point. This was a chance to almost be born again—to be an entertainer, a musician again. I really am a piano player more than anything else.[18]

Banks allowed the Century II equipment to be purchased, at which point Century II Studios effectively ceased to exist. The studio was never reconstituted and by the following year Banks had let the building's lease lapse. After the Celebrity Revue program wound up, the mobile units were sold to the CHUM corporation and relocated to Toronto where they remained in use for many years. The Bunker was abandoned, apparently suitable for no other purposes, and it still stands out in the country looking like it has gone through a hurricane. Century II Productions and Century II Publishing still exist, but Banks rarely uses the companies' names anymore.

So ended a golden age for Edmonton and indeed western Canadian music. What started as a small and humble, but successful, jingle company ended up as Edmonton's version of a tottering diversified entertainment giant that had lost sight of its original goals. If Century II had continued to concentrate on its strong points—the production and marketing of radio advertising—it undoubtedly would have prospered and grown. However, it chose to devote too much time and money to its weakest activity—the record label—and this ultimately led to the collapse of the whole structure. Century II Records was undoubtedly significant in that it was the first Edmonton-based label to have national distribution. Other labels had emerged in the 1960s (Pace, Fountain), but they were limited to local acts and local audiences. Century II aspired to a truly national (and in the occasional flight of fancy—an international) role, a role it could not play with its limited expertise and financing.

Whether the poor sales of its product are attributable to flawed artists and repertoire judgement on the part of Banks (and his successor in this position, Terry McManus), or whether the notoriously unpredictable vagaries of the marketplace just failed to overlap with the direction Century II headed will probably never be known. Banks's instincts were sound in theory. Signing Americans like the Original Caste (already enjoying huge success south of the border with 'Mr Monday' and 'One Tin Soldier') and Russell Thornberry (who likewise had domestic hits with 'Something To Believe' and 'Roseline'), as well as talented Canadian acts like Privilege and Donna Warner (both of whom had previous recording contracts and minor hits) was entirely defensible. In addition, the musicianship on the recordings was superb, the recording quality was second to none, and the marketing campaigns and distribution done in tandem with Capitol Records were similar in scope to those of other Capitol artists. Yet the records simply did not sell—the money Century II had put into acquiring and recording such artists was never returned in sales. A constantly negative balance book had to bring the venture to a close. There is, of course, always the chance that a venture like Century II could operate again in Edmonton, but it would need the vision, the leadership qualities, and the community pride of another Tommy Banks. ∾

∾ CENTURY II RECORDINGS

A. ALBUMS

1. Duane Davis—*Reflections* (1970)
   (CBC LM60, later Capitol ST-6320)
   Producer Duncan McKercher

2. Tom and Judy—*Make Someone Happy* (Dec. 1970)
   (GRT 9230-1000)
   Producer Keith James

3. Privilege—*Cantata Canada* (Sept. 1973)
   (Century II SPAL-17000)
   Producer Doug Hutton

4. Original Caste—*Back Home* (April 1974)
   (Century II ST-17001)
   Producer Bruce Innes

5. Bruce Innes—*Bruce Innes* (May 1974)
   (Century II ST-17002)
   Producer Bruce Innes

6. Privilege—*Enjoy* (Sept. 1974)
   (Century II LPC-1401)
   Producers Andy Krawchuk and Barry Allen

B. SINGLES

1. Tommy Banks and the Banknotes, featuring
   Evelyn Quaife (Sept. 1970)
   'We're All We've Got' (vocal) b/w 'We're All
   We've Got' (instrumental)
   (No label—produced for United Community Fund)
   No producer credited

2. Bob Bradburn (Dec. 1970)
   'Tiny Tony' b/w 'Count Your Blessings'
   (GRT 1230-01)
   Producer Garry McDonall

3. Tom and Judy (Dec. 1970)
   'It's Gonna Be Better' b/w 'Chelsea Morning'
   (GRT 1230-03)
   Producer Keith James

4. Male Chorus of Canada's Back To The Bible Hour
   (Feb. 1972)
   'Hold My Hand' EP
   (IRC no number)
   No producer credited

5. Privilege (July 1972)
   'Louie Louie' b/w 'When a Man Loves a Woman'
   (Capitol 72673)
   No producer credited

6. Skipper (June 1973)
   'Down on The Flat Rock' b/w 'Funny Thing'
   (Capitol 72705)
   Producer Gordon Forbes

7. Donna Warner (Sept. 1973)
   'Irresistable You' b/w 'Make Your Day Brighter'
   (Century II 1500)
   Producer Keith James

8. Original Caste (Oct. 1973)
   'Don't Stop Now' b/w 'Overdose of the Blues'
   (Century II 1501)
   Producer Bruce Innes

9. Skipper (Oct. 1973)
   Papa Sit Down' b/w 'That's Not Easy'
   (Century II 1502)
   Producer Terry McManus

10. Privilege (Oct. 1973)
    'Hired Man' b/w 'Hired Man'
    (Century II 1503)
    Producer Doug Hutton

11. Terry McManus (Oct. 1973)
    'A Girl on the Stage' b/w 'Leaky Old Boat'
    (Century II 1504)
    Producer Terry McManus

12. Russell Thornberry (March 1974)
    'Ramona' b/w 'Things I'll Never Be'
    (Century II 1505)
    Producer Russell Thornberry

13. Valerie Hudson (March 1974)
    'Big Green' b/w 'Stormy Grey'
    (Century II 1506)
    Producer Terry McManus

14. Original Caste (May 1974)
    'We Will Live Together' b/w 'Give Me the
    Good News'
    (Century II 1507)
    Producer Bruce Innes

15. K.J. and the Grand Band (May 1974)
    'Love Talk' b/w 'Whistlin' Man'
    (Century II 1508)
    Producers Merv Buchanan and Barry Greenfield

16. Richard Adams (May 1974)
    'Country People' b/w 'Took Away My Troubles'
    (Century II 1509)
    Producer Les Bateman

17. Sylvester Stretch (June 1974)
    'Aren't You Tired' b/w 'Turning Back'
    (Century II 1510)
    Producer Terry McManus

18. Skipper (June 1974)
    'Country Drive (Do You Wanna Go)' b/w
    'She's Gold'
    (Century II 1511)
    Producer Terry McManus

19. Bruce Innes (June 1974)
    'The Fat Girl and the Midget' b/w 'Woody Creek
    Lullabye'
    (Century II 1512)
    Producer Bruce Innes

20. K.J. and the Grand Band (Aug. 1974)
    'I Came to Borrow Some Sugar' b/w
    'Unemployed Dude'
    (Century II 1514)
    Producers Merv Buchanan and Barry Greenfield

21. Original Caste (Sept. 1974)
    'Slide Up under My Shoulder' b/w 'If He Don't Have
    No Love'
    (Century II 1515)
    Producer Bruce Innes

22. Privilege (Sept. 1974)
    'Rock and Roll' b/w 'Feel Good'
    (Century II 1516)
    No producer credited

DAVID MILLS

PETER POCKLINGTON AND THE BUSINESS OF HOCKEY

Peter Pocklington, 7 Sept. 1983. (PAA J.5268/1)

avid Mills is a historian at the University of Alberta. His current research interests include sports history, popular culture, and families during the Second World War. He is also a weekend hockey goalie. In the following pages, he examines the business dealings of the controversial owner of the Edmonton Oilers, Peter Pocklington.

Boosterism returned to Alberta and Edmonton in a big way in the flush days of the 1970s. Peter Lougheed promised to bring industry to Alberta, the Ghermezians built West Edmonton Mall, and Calgary and Edmonton bought their way into the National Hockey League. The seemingly endless prosperity came to a crashing halt, however, with the National Energy Policy and the economic downturn of the 1980s.

The boom and bust cycles Edmonton has experienced since the 1970s find a mirror in Pocklington's career. He has bounced from success to failure, from ownership of Westown Ford, the Oilers, Gainers, and Fidelity Trust (that allowed him to challenge for the leadership of the federal Progressive Conservative party) to political defeat and labour and financial trouble. In recent years Pocklington, like his hockey team, has been rebuilding.

THE NATIONAL HOCKEY LEAGUE (NHL) HAS BECOME part of the mass entertainment industry in the twentieth century; owners sell their product that just happens to be hockey. Peter Pocklington, the owner of the Edmonton Oilers, has bluntly concluded: 'Sports is too much of a business to be a sport.'[1] Although individual entrepreneurs like Pocklington remain, the NHL in expanding to twenty-six franchises has recently attracted ownership groups such as Molson in Montreal, Disney Corp. in Anaheim, Cablevision-ITT in New York, and Blockbuster Video and Kokusai Green of Japan in Florida. In the process it has acquired a corporate orientation. Like individual owners, corporate owners co-operate in order to maintain league control over both the game and its players so that profits can be maximized.[2] Corporate ownership, however, often has no long-term relationship with the game beyond the bottom line and threatens to push out the small businessman. Yet, for now, there is still room for the entrepreneur in professional sports. That is not to say that the patterns of entrepreneurial ownership in the NHL are the same, even for the two Alberta franchises.[3]

Edmonton is the home of the flamboyant Peter Pocklington, a dynamic businessman who has employed the profits from his NHL franchise for the betterment of his financial empire and the attainment of status and power. To some extent, Pocklington fits the classic definition of those entrepreneurs who gain from their creations 'the joys of ownership—the sense of having created an ongoing organization, of having built something useful, of having been one's own boss . . .'[4] Typically, such entrepreneurs maintain 'a close personal relationship with their managers, and . . . a say in top management decisions, particularly those concerning financial policies, allocation of resources, and the selection of senior managers.'[5] But Pocklington, a complex personality, cannot be portrayed so simply. He is the man who mouthed the platitudes of free enterprise while accepting grants and loans from the government, dumped failing companies before they collapsed and left the taxpayers to pick up the pieces, and traded 'the Great One,' Wayne Gretzky; but he also brought major-league hockey to the provincial capital and kept the team here in spite of lucrative offers to move elsewhere. As a result, he has been portrayed as both villain and hero.

In contrast, the owners of the Calgary Flames (originally Daryl K. and Byron Seaman, Norman Green, Harley Hotchkiss, Ralph Scurfield, and Norm Kwong), have not exploited the franchise for personal profits. They have kept hockey completely separate from their other business ventures. They have also kept a lower public profile than Pocklington. The nature of the ownership of the Flames is best explained in terms of boosterism. Traditionally, prairie boosters combined optimistic faith in the potential of their town or city with close cooperation between business and local government, community spirit, and constant competition with urban rivals for economic advantage and prestige. In this sense, the Flames have been a means to reflect and to promote Calgary's identity.[6] In recent years, however, the Flames owners, too, have had to respond to the pressures of doing business in the new corporate NHL.

Peter Hugh Pocklington was born on 18 November 1941 and grew up in London, Ontario; his father was a successful insurance agent. After leaving school at seventeen, Pocklington eventually went into the auto business; he came to Edmonton in 1971 when he acquired an auto dealership, renamed Westown Ford. He enjoyed great success; the seventies, as he has said, were 'great years.'[7] Not part of the corporate business world, he became wealthy through his own intuition, salesmanship, and enterprise at a time when the Alberta economy was booming.

Alberta's oil-induced prosperity in the 1970s stimulated rapid growth in real estate and property development. In 1974 the federal government created special tax shelters to encourage the construction of multiple unit residential buildings (MURBs). Investments in MURBs could be flipped quite quickly for large profits and thus attracted the attention of western Canadian entrepreneurs like Dr Charles Allard, until 1973 chief of surgery at the Edmonton General Hospital, Nelson Skalbania, a Vancouver real estate promoter whose hobby became buying and selling sports franchises (by 1981, he had purchased eight teams including the Flames[8]), and Peter Pocklington. Pocklington utilized the cash flow from his auto dealership to finance real estate investments. In 1978, for example, he and Skalbania swung a $51 million deal for some apartment buildings in Toronto, making a joint profit of about $20 million in the ensuing flip. With his share, Pocklington, through his Patrician Land Corporation, bought Gainers (a pork-packing company with annual sales of $70–80 million, mostly in markets across the Prairies), reportedly for about $7.5 million in Alberta mortgages and real estate.[9]

Access to mortgage money was essential to finance such deals. Entrepreneurs were often able to short-cut the normal arm's length borrowing from established financial institutions by buying their own money suppliers, often trust companies with broad deposit-taking and lending

Pocklington's 1978 acquisition of teenage phenomenon Wayne Gretzky would prove to be a coup for his hockey team and his business empire. Here, Gretzky signs a new contract, 27 Jan.1979. (PAA J.4853/10)

powers. (Canadian tax laws allowed trust companies to invest 10 per cent of their assets in real estate subsidiaries.) Allard, for example, bought North West Trust, and in 1979 Pocklington gained controlling interest in Fidelity Trust (with assets of $1.6 billion, Canada's twelfth largest trust company) for $15 million—$6.9 million in cash and the rest in preferred stock. He then bought the balance of the company for a reported $10 million and folded his real estate company, Patrician Land Corporation, into it.[10]

Pocklington has stated that his goal in such wheeling and dealing was to be rich: 'You become what you think about becoming. I wanted to become wealthy. So I did . . .' He was a vocal exponent of entrepreneurial capitalism: 'I prefer to own what I'm doing instead of getting the world in bed with me. Entrepreneurs are the salvation of business. Many companies are dying because they're looked after by caretakers who behave like bureaucrats.' Peter Pocklington, not managers, directed his business activities, while he built his financial empire on borrowed capital. 'To create wealth,' he said, 'you must utilize other people's money and other people's labour.' A federal tax judge was more blunt; Pocklington, the deal-maker, 'was ready to sell anything, except his wife.'[11]

In the late 1970s Pocklington became interested in the Edmonton Oilers, then just another money-losing franchise in the World Hockey Association (WHA). 'Wild Bill' Hunter, a junior hockey promoter, had acquired the franchise when the WHA was incorporated in 1971; he was chiefly bankrolled by Allard. The Oilers were not

very successful on the ice, and by 1976 the financial losses approached $3 million even though the team had moved into the new city-owned Northlands Coliseum and the average attendance had jumped from 4,423 to 10,722, the highest in the WHA. Allard wanted out and sold 80 per cent of the team to Skalbania. In March 1977 Skalbania sold a 40 per cent interest in the team, plus the assumption of half the debt, to Peter Pocklington, reportedly for a 1928 Rolls Royce, two oil paintings, a diamond ring, and a mortgage note for $500,000 worth of real estate.[12]

This change in ownership marked the beginnings of a turnaround for the Oilers, both on the ice and in the books. Pocklington appointed Glen Sather, then a player with the club, as coach and later put him in charge of all hockey operations. The Oilers made the playoffs in the 1977-8 season and finished first in the WHA in 1978–79, losing the Avco Cup to the Winnipeg Jets. The owner was not a 'meddler in the day-to-day operation but [was] always available for consultation,' according to then public relations director John Short. Pocklington's friendship with Skalbania, however, allowed him to acquire teenage phenomenon, Wayne Gretzky, from the Indianapolis Racers in November 1978.[13]

While the primary consideration for buying the Oilers was ego,[14] Pocklington saw the purchase as the first step towards gaining an NHL franchise. In 1979 the NHL expanded into Edmonton, and the Oilers faced a stiff entry fee of $6 million (about $4.6 million due immediately and the remainder to be covered by a letter of credit), while another $1.7 million had to be set aside to meet possible legal challenges from WHA teams left out of the expansion. Running an NHL rather than a WHA team also cost considerably more, during the 1979–80 season an estimated $2.5 million went for salaries, $500,000 for travel, $100,000 for training, $75,000 for supplies, $525,000 for hospital and medical, and $920,000 for rent. Moreover, the Oilers could not expect to share national television revenue for five years. But Edmonton fans were eager to see NHL hockey—the Oilers sold 14,000 season tickets and generated gross gate revenues of about $6.14 million. In addition, Pocklington was able to negotiate a local television deal with Molson Breweries, worth $2 million upfront and $75,000 annually for five years of exclusive advertising and promotional rights. As a result, the franchise was able to show a profit in its first year of operation in the NHL.[15] By 1981 the Oilers had become one of the most exciting teams in the NHL; Edmonton even knocked the Montreal Canadiens out of the playoffs before losing to the eventual Stanley Cup winners, the New York Islanders. By then the club brought in revenues totalling approximately $10 million, with profits of perhaps $1.6 million.[16]

Ownership of the Edmonton franchise had raised Pocklington's public profile, a factor in his decision to contest the leadership of the Progressive Conservative party, even though he was an outsider in politics. He commented: 'The Oilers are the rising star and I don't mind hitching myself to that star. The Oilers will mean a lot to the campaign. For starters, there's increased visibility. And name me a better marketing vehicle in this country than Gretzky and this hockey club.'[17] Pocklington campaigned as the voice of the 'new right' in this country, advocating free trade with the United States, a flat tax rate, deep cuts in government spending, a balanced budget, and deregulation and privatization of Crown corporations. His prescriptions were based on Ayn Rand's idea of creative selfishness, 'the belief that collective well-being can only be maximized if each individual is encouraged to pursue self-enrichment.' He finished well back in the race, which was won by Brian Mulroney who went on to become prime minister in 1984. The Tories, he said later, 'were still lodged in the past.'[18]

At the same time as Pocklington's political aspirations were dashed, his business empire began to crumble. He had borrowed heavily to campaign and even proposed to sell his companies to concentrate on politics. But events overtook him—the collapse of the Alberta economy in the early 1980s hit oil and real estate especially hard. Capri Drilling, which he had purchased in 1981, lost $8–10

million before going into receivership in April 1983. Between March and August of the same year the eastern divisions of Gainers were sold off, reducing a national company to one based almost exclusively in Alberta. Real estate was sold off and the assets of Patrician Land Corporation were written down. As a consequence, Fidelity Trust's asset base shrank and the company collapsed after running up huge losses. While Pocklington claimed that he personally lost $30 million, the failure of Fidelity Trust cost the Canadian taxpayer $359 million, the largest loss in the history of the Canadian Deposit Insurance Company.[19]

In 1986 Pocklington further tarnished his image by provoking a bitter strike at Gainers. The United Food and

By the early 1980s Edmontonians knew the Oilers would win a Stanley Cup—the only question was when. This sign gives an indication of the playoff fever that gripped the city in 1983, one year before the Oilers' first Stanley Cup. (PAA J.5206/2)

Commercial Workers, after a two-year salary freeze and reduction of benefits, sought a 27 per cent wage increase that would give them parity with workers in other food processing unions. Although the financial picture was improving in the pork-processing industry and Pocklington was making a profit, Gainers management countered with an offer of a 4 per cent raise and terminated the union's pension plan in order to claim the approximately $6 million surplus. Pocklington claimed he had to keep expenses low if the company was to compete in the North American market. On 1 June 1980 the workers went on strike. Pocklington bussed in replacement workers, leading to clashes, especially after the police were sent to maintain order. Almost 300 arrests were made; the rioting was seen on television, not just in Edmonton but across the country, and tensions remained high in the northeastern part of the city throughout the summer. A disputes inquiry board reported to the Alberta Government that Pocklington was 'insensitive' to his workers; it recommended a 5 per cent increase for the workers and the rehiring of all strikers. Both sides rejected the recommendations. In October the provincial government, fearing what it called 'a rift in our society' and the possibility of class warfare, exerted pres-

sure and by December an agreement had been reached. The workers accepted a four-year contract that froze their wages for another two years but guaranteed the strikers their jobs. From the government, Pocklington won the promise of loans and grants to upgrade the Gainers facilities. But the financial costs to each side—an estimated $10 million in lost wages for the workers and $10 million in lost sales for the company—and the social costs to the city of Edmonton were huge.[20]

If the Gainers strike brought public opprobrium for Pocklington, the Oilers brought public acclaim, especially because the team was winning. He said: 'The hockey team is sacred to me . . . [But] you don't own a professional sports franchise. You hold it in trust for the community.'[21] Hyperbole aside, the Oilers were to provide the foundation for Pocklington's economic recovery. Using the franchise and the players' contracts as security, he was able to borrow $31 million from the banks to finance new business deals.[22] Through a financially revitalized Gainers, he was able to reconstruct a North American meat-packing and food empire that included Magic Pantry, Z & W Foods, Marybank Foods, three American meat-processing plants (with annual sales of $500 million), Palm Dairies (purchased for $52.5 million in 1987), and Canbra Foods Ltd. (which produced edible oils for food processing to supply Gainers and Palm Dairies) for $13.5 million. The integration of these diversified companies produced a more efficient and large-scale conglomerate, co-ordinated by Pocklington. Gainers became the second largest food-processing company in Canada. It also acquired title to Cromwell Resources Inc., an oil and gas company that Pocklington had purchased in August 1984.[23] The hockey franchise was closely linked to these businesses. Gainers made a debt payment of almost $500,000 for the Oilers and signed loan guarantees for $8.7 million. In turn, the team made a $2 million payment in September 1989 on a debt owed by Kretschmar Foods Inc., a Gainer subsidiary, and guaranteed the company's $8-million debt.[24]

While resurrecting his financial empire, Pocklington continued to make money on the Oilers. To offset higher player salary demands and higher rents after the team won its first Stanley Cup in 1984, ticket prices were raised to among the highest in the league. Profits for the owner reportedly increased to $5.7 million for the period 15 December 1984 to 31 August 1985. Profits in fiscal 1986 amounted to another $3.2 million.[25]

More and more, Peter Pocklington came to see that running a hockey team was like running a business; the emphasis, he said, was on 'quality in what you sell. Sell it

Victory. *(EDMONTON JOURNAL)*

properly, present it properly, price it properly.' He believed that the business of hockey was 'simple, as long as you're winning and creating excitement. A winning team can make a lot of money.' Although Pocklington stated that he did not interfere in the running of the hockey team, he was consulted on management decisions by his best friend, president and general manager of the Oilers, Glen Sather. He also admitted that when players sought contracts over $300,000 (like Paul Coffey did before he was traded in October 1987) or when they sought to renegotiate their contracts (like Mark Messier did in September 1987), they 'deal with me.' When asked to elaborate on the reasons for the success of the Oilers, Pocklington replied: 'If I run the team like a business and don't get emotionally involved, it's very easy to run.'

Running the Oilers like a business led Pocklington to become personally involved in trading perhaps the greatest player in hockey, Wayne Gretzky, to the Los Angeles Kings in August 1988 for two players, three draft choices, and a reported $15 million (US) in cash.[26] A huge uproar ensued in Edmonton. Local citizens and businesses boycotted products from Gainers and Palm Dairies and Pocklington became a target on the cartoon page. The owner insisted, however, that there were valid reasons for the transaction—it made both business and hockey sense. A thirty-one-year-old Gretzky would become a free agent without compensation in 1992; he was 'an asset worth zero in four years.' (There were also tax advantages in shedding a large contract that could no longer be depreciated for two smaller ones that could.) Asserting 'my first love is to the team, not Wayne Gretzky,' Pocklington maintained that he was concerned the team's stars were getting older; younger players would provide the nucleus for 'a competitive club that can win more Stanley Cups . . . We're not going to be in last place in a couple of years.'[27]

The next year the Oilers had a disappointing season on the ice, being knocked out of the playoffs in the first round by the Gretzky-led Kings, but the franchise continued to make money for Pocklington. Even though average paid attendance to home games declined in the wake of the Gretzky trade, projected ticket sales yielded about $14.52 million dollars; in addition, broadcasting revenues were over $3 million. With total expenses of about $13.7 million, Pocklington admitted that 'our bottom line will be almost identical to last year'[28] (a profit of about $3–4 million).

Revenues from the Oilers continued to support Pocklington's other business ventures—the team has been his cash cow. After the Gretzky trade, Pocklington reorga-

For many Edmontonians, the trading of Gretzky made Pocklington a villain. It also turned him into a favourite target of cartoonists, including Delainey and Rasmussen, the creators of 'Bub Slug.'
(DELAINEY AND RASMUSSEN)

nized his empire, amalgamating Cromwell Resources Inc. and Edmonton Oilers Hockey Ltd. with his holding company, PFC Financial Ltd. The new company was to be the vehicle to organize his cash flow and business dealings. When asked if he needed the money from the Gretzky trade, Pocklington replied: 'I made a billion and a half in food sales. I have over 7000 people working for me and all my companies are very healthy financially.'[29] Importantly, Pocklington was relieved of any significant financial pressure because he had the backing of the Government of Alberta and its Treasury Branch.

This relationship, cemented by political donations to the provincial Conservative Party,[30] had disastrous consequences for the Alberta taxpayer. By July 1989, less than a year after Pocklington's assertion of the financial well-being of his companies, Gainers was in serious economic trouble because of a glut in the provincial pork market; the company was afloat 'in a sea of red ink,' according to a spokesman.[31] It had drawn $6 million of a $12 million loan

Edmontonians just did not seem to appreciate Peter Puck's business-like approach to the game they loved. (DELAINEY AND RASMUSSEN)

from the provincial government for upgrading facilities and building a new plant in southern Alberta; instead the money was used for operating expenses. (The Oilers' play-off failure that spring may have had a greater financial impact on Pocklington's businesses than first expected). By 1 October Gainers had not begun construction of the new plant, nor could it make an interest payment on its loan. As a consequence the Alberta Government took over control of the heavily mortgaged company and Pocklington walked away from over $100 million in debts, while still controlling Palm Dairies (purchased for $58.5 million in 1988, of which $55 was borrowed, and later sold for $100 million in 1990), Canbra Foods (with profits of $1.1 million on sales of $77.2 million), and, of course, the Oilers.[32] When the team won its fifth Stanley Cup in 1990, Pocklington is estimated to have profited by $3.25 million. Ticket prices were increased for the next season.[33]

By the early 1990s, though, the glory days of the Oilers both on and off the ice were over. After winning the Stanley Cup for the last time in 1990, the remaining stars from the 1980s, like Mark Messier, were traded away or

sold. Success in the playoffs came less often; the team had missed post-season play from 1993–5. Attendance fell— from 606,685 in 1992–3 to 552,569 in 1993–4—and gate receipts declined to about $12.7 million (Can), one-third below the league average; moreover, stadium revenues totalled only about $1 million (US), less than 10 per cent of that generated by the wealthiest franchise, the Detroit Red Wings. As a result, the Oilers lost about $2.3 million in 1993, after showing a profit of $1.3 million the year previous. The value of the franchise declined from $51 million to $46 million in the same period, prompting one analyst to suggest that the losses were directly related to the lease situation with Edmonton Northlands because the rent was the highest in the league and the team did not control revenues from concessions or parking.[34]

Threats to move the franchise to a more lucrative market, first Hamilton and then Minneapolis, prompted negotiations that saw Pocklington ultimately gain full control of the Coliseum; he was to pay $2.8 million annually to Northlands and put up $4 million for improvements to the facility. The City of Edmonton, on the other hand, was to contribute $15 million for renovations and build a new baseball park to house Pocklington's Triple-A club, the Trappers. It would be a good deal for the city, the Oilers' owner had said months earlier: 'First of all, the sports teams give the city international recognition . . . All the studies I've seen [suggest that] a major league franchise brings in roughly $100 million in economic activity.[35] For Peter Pocklington, Edmonton is 'a great spot' where 'I can get things done.' The city has 'a lot to offer' because of its 'heart and spirit,' but opportunities are being lost because of local attitudes. Edmonton seems to have an 'inferiority complex,' especially in comparison to its rival to the south, Calgary.[36]

While a dynamic entrepreneur like Peter Pocklington might seem more at home in Calgary, his pattern of team ownership has not been followed by the Flames, at least until recently. Early on, a group of owners, rather than an individual, owned the Flames, and they retained a low public profile. They also separated their outside entrepreneurial activities from the workings of the team. The Calgary ownership was not motivated only by the desire to maximize personal profits; rather, money was used to support amateur sports, mainly hockey. Moreover, there was a concern with raising the profile of the city of Calgary. As suggested, the owners of the Flames reflected old-fashioned Alberta boosterism.

Calgary's first brush with professional hockey came with the transfer of the WHA's Vancouver Blazers to the city in 1975. The Cowboys, as the team was called, were controlled by Vancouver entrepreneur Jimmy Pattison. But the franchise was badly run; there was no marketing because Pattison seemed to believe that 'the mere presence of a team of professional stature would bring out the fans in droves.'[37] He was wrong. The team averaged only 3000 fans in the 6,500-seat Corral. After losses totalling $6.5 million over two seasons, the Calgary Cowboys folded in August 1977.[38]

Calgary gained its NHL franchise in 1980 when Nelson Skalbania, the former owner of the WHA Oilers, bought the Atlanta Flames and shifted them to Alberta. The Flames' deal proved to be Skalbania's only major success in the sports world. The transaction illustrates the nature of entrepreneurship in hockey. Skalbania heard that the Atlanta Flames, having lost $8.6 million dollars since 1972, were for sale, but that a Calgary group led by the Seaman Brothers were also interested. He upped the bid and acquired the franchise, which could be shifted without permission of the other owners or financial penalty, for $16 million. The terms were a $1 million non-refundable deposit, a $6 million instalment in thirty days, and a final $9 million payment in the next sixty days. Believing that local involvement in the team was essential and needing money, Skalbania sold the Seaman brothers a 49 per cent interest in the team for $1.2 million (to cover his deposit and provide a 'finder's fee'); the Seaman brothers were to arrange financing for the final $9 million payment. To meet his other deadline, he negotiated a deal for broadcasting rights with Molsons for $6 million in advance. When he transferred the Flames to Calgary, he held a 50 per cent interest and was $200,000 ahead on the deal. There were also tax benefits, as he depreciated $12 million of the $16 million purchase price. By the end of 1981, however, Skalbania had to sell his remaining interest in the Flames, for a profit of $3 million, as his financial empire collapsed into bankruptcy.[39]

The new owners of the Flames' franchise were a close-knit group of Calgary entrepreneurs who were important members of the city's business community.[40] The group included the Seaman brothers, Daryl K. and Byron, who control Bow Valley Industries, an energy and environmental management group that by 1989 had profits of $25.7 million on revenues of $291.2 million;[41] Norman Green, chairman of Stewart, Green Properties Ltd. (specializing in the development, management, and ownership of major shopping centres in North America) and former president of the Chamber of Commerce (in 1992 Green sold his share of the franchise and purchased the Minnesota North Stars; he transferred the team to Dallas a year later); Harley Hotchkiss, an oil and gas developer and a director of Nova Corp., with interests in real estate and agriculture; Ralph Scurfield, the late president of the vast Nu-West Group that had assets of $3 billion before the collapse of the real estate market in the early 1980s; and Norman Kwong, former halfback with the Edmonton Eskimos and real estate businessman (now president of the Calgary Stampeders).[42] The owners soon showed a preference for remaining in the background. Green, who had been brought into the

For years the Battle of Alberta seemed inevitably to end in Oiler victories—here, a regular season game, 19 March 1982. When the Calgary Flames finally did beat Edmonton in the 1986 playoffs, the accomplishment seemed to dwarf the pursuit of the Stanley Cup. The Flames went on to lose to the Montreal Canadiens in the final. (PAA J.5256/3)

group because he had business dealings with Skalbania and could work out an arrangement to buy the franchise with the Seamans, noted the dangers of high profile ownership: 'It doesn't matter how successful you are in business, if you do something like [a bad trade] in sports all the public suddenly hates you . . . and who needs it?'[43] Within the franchise, the owners played a support role, setting policy and governing finances, notably ticket prices, while business and hockey decisions were largely delegated to the president of the team. The first president was Cliff Fletcher, a hockey man from the Montreal Canadiens' system (now President of the Toronto Maple Leafs), who had come over with the team from Atlanta.

The Flames organization proved successful on the ice. In the early years, the team might have faced financial problems because they were forced to utilize the small Calgary Corral, but the 6,500-seat facility was oversubscribed in the first week, even though ticket prices, at $21 per seat, were the highest in the NHL.[44] Leo Ornest, a marketing executive with the team, said, before the season had even started: 'Already, we're assured of an operating profit for our first year but, as far as we're concerned, the name of the game is to beat Edmonton.'[45] It was not until 1986 that the Flames were able to defeat their provincial rivals, winning the seventh game of the Smythe division final when Steve Smith, an Oiler defenceman, banked a pass into his own net to give the Flames a 3–2 victory. The reactions of the Calgary players and owners were the same; Mike Vernon, then the Flames' goalie, said: 'I'm glad to be part of beating Edmonton. I'm a Calgarian. There's nothing that I wanted more than to beat Edmonton, except to win the Stanley Cup.' Norm Green asserted: 'It's a pretty important goal to finally beat the Oilers after being humiliated for so many years.'[46] Calgary reached the Stanley Cup final that year, losing to Montreal. The Flames had the best record in the league over the regular 1987–8 and 1988–9 seasons, culminating in a Stanley Cup.

The Calgary organization was also successful off the ice. The team moved into the Olympic Saddledome in 1983 and has attracted sellout crowds ever since. With an average ticket price of $18 and crowds of over 20,000 per game during the 1988–9 season, the franchise could expect to generate about $14.4 million in gate revenues. Although exact figures are not made public, Clare Rhyasen, vice-president of business and finance, admitted that the team's profitability is probably comparable to the Oilers. The Flames franchise was estimated to have almost tripled in value by 1989, to about $45 million (by 1995, it was worth an estimated $50 million).[47]

Although the team's fortunes have steadily improved, the owners have not sought only to maximize personal profits; local boosters ,they have fostered civic pride and spirit. From the beginning, the idea of bringing an NHL team to Calgary was linked both to plans to celebrate Alberta's seventy-fifth anniversary and to the proposal to acquire the 1988 Winter Olympics. When the Flames arrived from Atlanta, the Calgary group convinced Skalbania that the owners should 'put their profits for ten years to a maximum of $5 million into amateur sports.' Daryl Seaman had been one of the first directors of Hockey Canada, and he was convinced that Canadians 'needed to spend more time and money on the development of the game at all levels.' He originally envisioned the establishment of a $5 million capital fund, providing revenue for hockey scholarships, research into the game, and a national hockey team. As a result, money would be directed towards Hockey Canada and its Centre of Excellence in Calgary and towards local amateur sports groups.[48]

The owners' plans soon ran into problems. High interest rates on the loans needed to purchase the franchise, the inability to generate large profits in the Corral, and higher-than-expected operating expenses meant that much of the profits was used to service the debt. According to Harley Hotchkiss, only $400,000 had been directly distributed by 1989. Realizing their philanthropic objectives might not be met from team profits, the owners set up a gas and oil operation and purchased properties that could produce revenue. They projected that as much as $500,000 annually would be directed into amateur hockey in the 1990s and that revenues over the life of the properties would substantially exceed the $5 million commitment. According to Seaman, 'the City of Calgary had been very good to a couple of boys from Saskatchewan and they wanted to do something to repay the city.' He had looked upon the acquisition of the Flames 'as a community project from the beginning.'[49]

Through their purchase of the Flames and their booster activities, the Flames owners reaped a tremendous amount of good will and support from the general public— but their success was also due in some measure to the co-operation of various levels of government. A new arena, the Saddledome, was built for the 1988 Olympics at a cost of $97 million, with the city, provincial, and federal governments footing the bill. The Government of Alberta, headed at that time by Peter Lougheed, reasoned that an NHL franchise would help the Olympic bid and that the Flames would later become the primary tenant of the new facility. The Saddledome was leased to the Olympic

Saddledome Foundation for fifty years at $1 per year; it is managed in turn by the Calgary Exhibition and Stampede. Concession revenues from the Saddledome (60 per cent of which have been generated by the Flames fans) are then divided in accordance with the management agreement, with the Foundation currently receiving 15 per cent. The Foundation also received a share of suite revenues during the first five years of the Saddledome's operation. The Foundation distributes funds to the City of Calgary Parks and Recreation, which funds local amateur groups; to the Calgary Olympic Development Association to maintain Olympic facilities; and to Hockey Canada. In 1988 each group received about $250,000, and it was estimated that $8.5 million would be available for distribution in the 1990s.[50]

୶ In the past, the boosterism approach of owners in Calgary differed markedly from the entrepreneurial approach of Peter Pocklington in Edmonton; but in the 1990s the new corporate mentality of the NHL is shaping the ownership of both franchises. Though not forsaking boosterism, recently the Calgary ownership has adopted more of a corporate orientation in its approach to the franchise. The Flames grossed approximately $17.5 million at the gate in 1992–3 (tenth in regular season box-office revenue) and earned $6 million in broadcasting revenue, for a profit of about $1.9 million. But with rising player salaries, the club's net income has been shrinking. As a consequence, the Flames' owners have been attempting to gain control of the Saddledome; they are seeking a larger share of the revenue from concessions, parking, and advertising. In addition they want $50-million renovations to the facility, especially the installation of more luxury boxes. In 1994 former team president Bill Hay announced that to remain competitive, the owners were 'aggressively looking at options,' including the construction of a new facility or a move to the United States.[51]

Pocklington has also had to adjust to the NHL's new corporate image. Following the amalgamation in August 1990 of Pocklington Financial Corporation with PFC Holdings, Pocklington Holdings Inc., and Pocklington Classics Inc., his portfolio was made up of the high profile sports franchises, the Edmonton Oilers and the Trappers; hobby assets like a vacation home in Kelowna and a condominium in Hawaii; operations in the food industry, notably Canbra Foods and chicken farming in the United States (Greenacre Farms and Greenacre Foods Ltd. are said to be worth between $50–60 million); Superior Furniture Manufacturing, with total sales of $15 million worth of office furniture in the 1990s; and a chain of fitness centres, Club Fit, in Edmonton and Calgary, worth about $11 million. It has been suggested that all these companies are profitable, except for the Oilers.

In response to the lower Canadian dollar, higher taxes compared to the United States, and escalating player salaries, Pocklington has had to focus on the bottom line rather than the blue line. Just when he needs greater revenues to compete in the new corporate NHL, however, fan disillusionment (a product of spiralling ticket prices, multi-million dollar contracts, declining quality of play because of over-expansion, lack of loyalty to either the team or the community exhibited by the players and the owners, the strike that produced an abbreviated forty-eight-game schedule in 1995, and, in Edmonton, the icing of a losing team) threatens the viability of the Oilers. Average attendance at Oiler home games in 1995 fell to 12,319, just 72 per cent of capacity, including the two smallest crowds in history, in spite of the renovations that have made the Coliseum a better venue for hockey. As a result, building another winning team, marketing the product, and pleasing the fans are all receiving more attention.[52]

In a curious twist, Pocklington has also become a vocal booster of Edmonton, the City of Champions. 'People,' he said, referring to himself, 'do grow up. Winning and losing are illusions. I have no interest in simply making another $100 million.' Increasingly he has contributed to the community and to charities. Recently he created a $400,000 scholarship program at the McCauley school in Edmonton's inner city.[53] Thus his contributions to the community are social and cultural, as well as economic. And Pocklington's true payoff might be in prestige and status, not just profit. ୶

PAUL VOISEY

UNSOLVED MYSTERIES OF EDMONTON'S GROWTH

Edmonton's skyline from the Macdonald Hotel, winter, 1948. The city was about to enjoy decades of sustained growth brought on by oil discoveries and government expansion. (PAA GS.305/1)

*A*s with any history, the preceding chapters broaden our understanding of how Edmonton came to be what it is today. They also raise unanswered questions and point out some of the gaps in our knowledge of the past. Paul Voisey of the Department of History and Classics at the University of Alberta is a specialist in western Canadian and Canadian urban history. He tackles the all-important issue of what is not known about Edmonton's growth. In other words, he identifies some of the 'unsolved mysteries' that hold the key to understanding the different stages of Edmonton's development better. Like Gilbert Stelter, Voisey situates Edmonton within a national and international context.

Voisey's original paper was the keynote address at the conference, Edmonton's Bicentennial: Historical Reflections, in May 1995.

*A*GOOD DEAL IS KNOWN ABOUT VARIOUS BITS AND parts in Edmonton's rise to Canada's fifth largest metropolitan area.[1] Many gaps in our understanding remain, however, and historians have been reluctant to consider important ideas about why cities grow and why some grow faster than others. There has also been a tendency to explain Edmonton's growth spurts solely in terms of the city itself or its region, instead of as part of a larger world, subject to a vast array of national and international influences. The result is a series of unsolved mysteries about the city's rise that defy easy explanations. The intention here is not to rectify the problem in any authoritative way, but merely to indicate some means of tackling these unsolved mysteries, and to hint at some possible answers.

Any discussion of Edmonton's emergence as a city must begin with the fur trade. In its days as a trading post, historians have not regarded Edmonton as a potential city, but as a strand in the fabric of fur trade society, a field of Canadian history intimately associated with the wilderness and its inhabitants. Indeed, the role of trading posts within this society has been de-emphasized over the past two decades, as fur trade historiography increasingly shifted attention from Europeans to Native peoples. Although beneficial for an analysis of fur trading as an economic and cultural system, this approach does the urban historian little good.[2]

Nonetheless, there is value in looking at the fur trade from the perspective of urban history. The spatial organization of the European side of the trade nicely demonstrates the metropolitan approach to urban development long favoured by Canadian historians. In J.M.S. Careless's refined definition of metropolitanism, some cities come to dominate not only their own countrysides, but also other cities and their countrysides.[3] For the fur trade empire of the Hudson's Bay Company (HBC), London, England, served as a grand metropolis of financial control with major overseas centres at places like York Factory, Upper Fort Garry, Victoria, and Edmonton. Below them in the command hierarchy, a myriad of lesser posts appeared, disappeared, and reappeared as the dictates of direct trade warranted.

Moreover, it is surely no coincidence that many fur trading posts later became important cities. Notable examples include Quebec, Montreal, Detroit, and Albany in the east, and Winnipeg, Victoria, and Portland, as well as Edmonton, in the west. To enquire about the extent to which such posts exhibited urban characteristics might seem foolish given their tiny populations, but if an urban place has regular and essential relationships with places outside of itself, including other urban places, then a major

post like Edmonton deserves scrutiny. Situated on the North Saskatchewan River, the great east-west highway of the fur trade, Edmonton assumed regional importance. It sat between the frozen north, which offered excellent furs but inadequate food supplies; and the open plains, which offered fewer furs, but abundant food. It received manufactured goods from Britain by way of York Factory and traded some of them to peoples from the south for buffalo meat and hides. It then sent manufactured goods, along with pemmican, to the north in exchange for furs that it shipped back to York Factory and London. It headquartered all posts within the HBC's vast Saskatchewan District and organized brigades across the Rockies. Thus, as the metropolitan model suggests, Edmonton had its own commercial hinterland and was itself part of the commercial hinterland of a great metropolis. That Edmonton would also occupy a middle position in subsequent metropolitan systems is probably no coincidence.

The rubric 'urban,' however, implies much more than participation in a metropolitan system, for urban places characteristically feature considerable diversity—in occupations, institutions, social groups, and social activities. Seemingly, a simple exchange point cannot offer the kind of heterogeneity that characterizes a genuine urban place. But a major post like Edmonton evolved beyond a simple store because it could not conveniently import all the goods and services necessary to carry out its exchange functions. Besides trading clerks and a chief factor to manage them, the post required a carpenter to construct and maintain its buildings and their furnishings, and to build and repair the York boats that carried cargoes on the river. It needed a blacksmith to make boat fittings and other simple hardware, and a cooper to make storage barrels. The fort needed less skilled workers for a variety of other tasks: to raise and attend the pack horses that supplemented water transportation; to cut timber, planks, and firewood; to gather coal for the blacksmith's forge; to make pemmican for the northern trade; to provide food for the post through local hunting, fishing, gathering, butchering, and gardening; to cook and clean; to repair and make some clothing. The fort also housed a preacher. All these specialized occupations appeared during the 1840s at the last-built Fort Edmonton, which featured separate buildings and rooms for most of its varied activities, and sustained an estimated population of 130 people.

Did Fort Edmonton exhibit enough occupational specialization to deserve the label urban? Probably not. Occupational specialization had certainly been greater at Quebec and Montreal during their fur trading days when the addition of political, legal, military, and church functions created more diversity and exerted greater 'multiplier effects.' Even so, Fort Edmonton more closely approximated an urban centre than a rural village, which might be described as a place that lacks diversity in almost everything, including occupations. In such places, specialization depends on the age and sex of household members, but each household lives much the same as every other. Moreover, specialization at Fort Edmonton led to a hierarchical social order, most sharply reflected in the difference between the spacious quarters of the factor's house and the cramped hall of the common labourers.

The existence of a specialized work force, rather than its minute size, provides the key to Edmonton's transformation from trading post to city because it offered trades and activities with the potential to serve functions beyond the fur trade itself. Agriculture presented one possibility, but only if the immediate hinterland of the post offered soils and climate amenable to marketable products that could be grown using prevailing technologies and techniques. These prerequisites prevented York Factory (in spite of greater occupational diversity than Fort Edmonton) and other far northern posts from shifting to agricultural service.

The transformation also required entrepreneurs independent of the HBC. In the parlance of urban history, Fort Edmonton was a company town and company towns generally fail to diversify or innovate. Their purposes are geared to the specific goals of a distant head office, and activities that are not directed towards those goals are discouraged. Headquarters is not interested in growth and diversification outside of its control. Nonetheless, independent frontiersmen commonly gravitated to Company forts. In a vast wilderness, only they offered goods and services useful to newcomers and established trade links to secure more. This attraction was particularly evident at Upper Fort Garry and Fort Victoria, both of which served as powerful magnets for independent newcomers. At Edmonton this process began in the 1860s when prospectors found it most convenient to pan for gold near the fort. Disheartened by low returns, a few of them tried farming, hoping to sustain themselves and perhaps to sell food to other miners and the fort.

Opportunities for newcomers really emerged after 1870 with the transfer of HBC territory to Canada accompanied by well-publicized plans to build railways and establish commercial agriculture in the West. Securing a railway represented another crucial element in the transformation from fort to city because prairie rivers could not adequately serve commercial agriculture. Too few in number, too shallow, too often encased in ice, and eventually spilling into Hudson Bay, they could move relatively small quantities of high-value goods for the fur trade, but not massive quantities of producer and consumer goods, nor bulky, low-value grain. A steamboat served Edmonton after 1875 but clearly played a transitory role until the arrival of steel rails.

Everyone in Canada knew that the promised railway would cut through the prairie park belt to the Yellowhead Pass, presumably through Edmonton. That knowledge brought more newcomers between 1870 and 1881. They established a host of retail outlets and services useful to an agricultural community. Their sudden appearance presumes knowledge of how the arrival of railways ignited urban growth elsewhere. To reap profits in trade and land speculation from an anticipated boom, one had to arrive ahead of the herd. It is hardly surprising, therefore, that bitter disappointment greeted the 1881 announcement by the Canadian Pacific Railway (CPR) that the Yellowhead route would be abandoned in favour of a more southerly path across the prairies.

Edmonton's growth faltered as Regina, Calgary, Vancouver, and other new towns on the transcontinental line sprang into being. But it is important to ask why the newcomers to Edmonton did not all leave. Some did, but others stayed, perhaps reluctant to abandon capital investments that could not be sold easily. More curiously, a trickle of newcomers continued to arrive. Expectations may again have brought them, particularly the assumption that the Edmonton region was an important enough market in the sparsely settled Northwest to warrant renewed railway interest. A branchline from Calgary finally arrived, but not until 1891, and even then it brought a new disappointment. Essentially a subsidiary of the CPR, the Calgary and Edmonton Railway refused to cross the river into Edmonton. Instead, the parent company proceeded to build the rival town of Strathcona, a trick the CPR had learned during construction of the transcontinental line in order to avoid real estate costs in established settlements.[4] Nonetheless, steel rails had finally reached the Edmonton area.

Some detail has been provided here because successful transitions from one urban function to another, in this case from fur trading to commercial agriculture, involve a chain reaction stemming from the interplay of events and expectations. Other places experienced a similar process. Although Edmonton's early history in the railway age has been compared in a cursory fashion with other emerging cities on the prairies, the transitional process suggested here requires more rigorous testing against the experience

Jim Little's brick yard, 1903. As agricultural settlement increased and Edmonton acquired more railway connections, it played the role of regional centre supplying hinterland customers with goods and forwarding their products to market.
(PAA B.1344)

of other fur trading posts, including those that failed to became agricultural centres. Moreover, Edmonton's history in this period warrants examination in light of studies that examine the origins of frontier cities generally.[5]

The arrival of steel rails in 1891 thrust Edmonton into the orbit of the industrial world. Membership did not require a city to sprout its own forest of black smokestacks, but merely to experience the vigorous impact of industrial technology and ideas. By themselves, railways produced much of that force as their insatiable appetite for labour, goods, and services exerted far-reaching multiplier effects. They provided the means not only for shipping out saleable commodities in bulk, but also for bringing in new products, people, and ideas quickly and in heavy volume. At first, the full magnitude of such changes eluded Edmonton because the railway did not immediately trigger the anticipated flood of settlers. A variety of well-known circumstances conspired against agricultural settlement in western Canada in the 1890s, but, as the century closed, conditions turned favourable, and the great settlement boom commenced. The city exploded. Edmonton- Strathcona had 4,000 people in 1901; 54,000 in 1916.[6] Viewed in isolation, such growth seems extraordinary and perhaps unprecedented, but in a comparative context it was hardly unusual. Over the same period, Winnipeg, Saskatoon, Regina, and Calgary also enjoyed wild rates of growth, and earlier so had Chicago, Minneapolis, Kansas City, and dozens of other frontier rail centres in the United States.

Many aspects of Edmonton's growth in this period are revealed in the general literature on prairie urbanization. Agriculture clearly provided the major stimulus. The modern settlers relied heavily on machinery and supplies for production, they made few consumer goods, and they generated large surpluses for sale. Much more than pioneers in earlier eras, they needed nearby distribution points to provide manufactured goods and a host of services, and nearby shipping points to collect, store, and transport grain. Hundreds of new towns appeared on the prairies to fulfill those functions. The scale of their activities called for regional metropolitan centres, places where long trains could be assembled for the shipment of grain east, and hence requiring major rail yards and shops. Such places could also order manufactured goods in bulk for distribution to small-town retailers. They could engage in manufacturing themselves, processing some western produce (giving rise to flour mills, meat packing houses, breweries, distilleries, and dairies), and making some of the bulkier, low-value goods required by the rural population (wagons and wheels, furniture, lumber and pre-fabricated housing

China department, Revillon Freres, 1903. The agricultural boom in the West brought prosperity and the demand for more luxury goods. (PAA B.4152)

materials, harness, machinery and hardware, and even clothing). The pursuit of these functions called for construction workers to build the necessary facilities, and for many retailers and services to supply the cities themselves.[7]

To serve these high order functions, only a few places could emerge as large regional centres and a titanic battle for urban supremacy erupted. The competition took the familiar form known as 'boosterism,' the attempt by boards of trade and city councils to promote urban growth by luring railways, factories, and government institutions with promises of free land, property tax exemptions, and cash bonuses. Often, too, governments acquired the ownership of utilities in order to offer free connections and cheap rates, a ploy especially common in Edmonton where municipal ownership proceeded more briskly than elsewhere.[8]

In assessing Edmonton's participation in this contest, perhaps too much has been made of its rivalry with Strathcona, particularly the fights over the location of the dominion land office and the continued refusal of the CPR to cross the river. Cross-river rivalries figure prominently in the early history of many cities, but competition faded once transportation links allowed two rivals to grow as one. From the founding of Strathcona, ferry service pro-

vided one connection with Edmonton, and in 1902 a bridge and the grandiosely named Edmonton, Yukon, and Pacific Railway provided another. In 1910 the CPR finally agreed to build a high level bridge after all three levels of government offered to shoulder much of the expense. Edmonton and Strathcona formally amalgamated in 1912, the first Canadian Pacific train rumbled across the bridge in 1913, and historical interest in the rivalry ends.[9] But these episodes are best regarded—not as rivalry between two cities—but as locational struggles within a single metropolitan area, both before and after the amalgamation.

Luring two new transcontinental railways proved far more significant to Edmonton's future than its bitter relationship with a Canadian Pacific branchline. Becoming a major distribution and shipping point called for the superior benefits that only transcontinental lines could deliver. The new entries, the Canadian Northern and the Grand Trunk Pacific, proved just as leery as the CPR about incurring the costs of plunging through existing settlements. In response, Edmonton showered them with gifts. They received free land, tax exemptions, and cash bonuses to enter the city in 1905 and 1909 respectively.

In return for such generosity, aspiring metropolitan centres always extracted favours. They wanted to become divisional points, places every hundred miles or so where trains switched running crews. Because railway employees would live in such centres and contribute to their growth, divisional points also became logical places to install maintenance shops, adding more railway employees to the town. Their various rail facilities then made divisional points logical centres for the construction of branch lines. These tentacles encouraged wholesaling and manufacturing, which might benefit from yet another blessing conferred by railways: special freight rates. They permitted favoured cities to receive and ship goods at lower per mile rates than nearby rivals. Such discrimination helped determine which towns became wholesaling and manufacturing centres and which remained retailers. While Edmonton's acquisition of transcontinental lines is well known, not enough is understood about the benefits they wrought.

Edmonton's success in acquiring government institutions is more widely celebrated, particularly in the contest to select a capital city for the new province of Alberta in 1905. Aspiring towns throughout North America have always fought over the location of capital cities, convinced that important economic benefits would follow. Calgary, Edmonton, and several smaller centres all sought the Alberta prize, and they blasted each other in a verbal duel over relative merits. Since dominion legislation created the province, Ottawa would determine the winner. Calgary's Member of Parliament sat with the opposition Conservatives, while long-time Edmonton booster and newspaperman, Frank Oliver, sat with the Liberal administration and became Minister of the Interior later that year. Not surprisingly, Edmonton won the capital, subject to the consent of the new Alberta government. Thanks to Oliver's gerrymandering of the new ridings, which greatly favoured Edmonton, and an election victory by fellow provincial Liberals led by A.C. Rutherford of Strathcona, Edmonton retained the capital. Political influence played a similar role in Edmonton's acquisition of the federal penitentiary in 1906. The following year the Premier's home riding won the right to house the provincial university.[10] Victory meant construction projects, government contracts, and employees, bolstering the local population and benefiting local merchants. As with railways, however, the acquisition of these institutions is studied more often than their subsequent impact.

On one level, Edmonton's aggressive boosterism seems to explain its lightning growth, but much remains unanswered. Did its victories in acquiring railway, manufacturing, wholesaling, and government functions employ enough people and generate sufficient economic spinoffs to account for the size of the city's population? While a few studies focus on specific economic activities in the city, the picture is very fragmentary and critical ideas about urban growth have not been considered. Eric Lampard, for instance, argues that urban growth in the industrial era stemmed from a rapid proliferation of inventions and innovations that bred increased specialization. Because the interdependent elements of proliferating specialization had to be brought together spatially, cities grew rapidly. And as invention and innovation raised the productivity of existing economic activities, they freed more people to develop newer specialties, especially in services. The process became self-perpetuating and so did urban growth.[11]

Much of Edmonton's rampant growth might be explained in this fashion. Everyone who writes about the city in the early twentieth century, for example, notes the building of utility systems for water, sewage, electricity, lighting, gas, and streetcars, but no one presents them as a major explanation for Edmonton's economic growth.

Sewer work, 1906. As Edmonton's population grew, new construction work on municipal utitlities benefited the entire community, creating jobs and a market for local goods and services. (PAA B.1306)

While their appearance was contingent on the success of Edmonton's functions in the larger agricultural economy, these systems served only the urban market and involved no direct exchanges with the agricultural hinterland. While no longer new inventions by the early twentieth century, they were new to Edmonton. They created their own specialized work forces and exerted their own multiplier effects on the construction, retail, and service sectors.

But studies of Edmonton's growth must also explain its limits. Why didn't the city become as large as Winnipeg or, for that matter, Chicago? Here one is tempted to turn to the locational theories favoured by many geographers and economists. They argue that new enterprises arise in centres that already possess an abundance of capital, labour, and markets, or else cheap and easy access to them. Allen Pred applies locational theory to history by discussing the compounding effect of initial advantages to explain why big cities kept getting bigger.[12] His argument helps explain Edmonton's size. In the mid nineteenth century Edmonton possessed initial advantages over other fur trading posts in the Saskatchewan District, helping it to attract new activities, which added to its locational advantages for still other new activities during the settlement boom. But within western Canada, Winnipeg possessed more initial advantages, which favoured it even more as a location for new activities. And within the industrial world at large, major locational advantages resided far from either centre.

Locational theory, however, does not help explain how huge cities can arise in frontier regions where such advantages do not prevail. Los Angeles provides a striking example. In the nineteenth century it was far removed from major centres of capital, labour, markets, and transportation. Indeed, it had no harbour, poor agricultural prospects, and a severe shortage of water. Yet in spite of handicaps that locational theory could only regard as crippling, Los Angeles became the great urban growth story of the twentieth century. Locational theory is only useful when considering certain economic activities, namely traditional ones. If a city tries to export the same sort of goods and services that a great many other cities provide, then it needs the advantages of location in order to succeed.

For an alternative model of urban growth that can account for the rise of poorly situated places, it is useful to consider the ideas of Jane Jacobs. She argues that cities can generate their own growth through innovations that create goods and services so unique that they overcome locational disadvantages. Indeed, all new urban places offer something special or they could not exist. They often begin by supplying a commodity that in type, quality, or price cannot be obtained elsewhere. Because the commodity is special in some respect, the goods and services that arise to procure, process, or transport it will often be special as well. Innovative diversification occurs when a use unrelated to the export commodity is discovered for one of those secondary activities. The secondary product is then exported on its own merits, often with modifications, to new markets.[13]

Jacobs's approach suggests studying entrepreneurs closely, but a trap awaits the unwary, who can easily slide into the 'men of outstanding vision and enterprise' explanation for urban growth. That uncritical assertion characterizes writings about cities during the booster era, but it confuses cause with effect.[14] It implies that Detroit, for example, became a great automobile manufacturing centre because Henry Ford happened to live there. The question that begs asking is why some cities produce, hold, and attract people of 'vision and enterprise.'

In rudimentary fashion, Edmonton advanced in the manner suggested by Jacobs when some of the services designed for the fur trade later found application in the agricultural trade, but the goods and services Edmonton provided for agriculture were seldom modified for wholly new purposes. The city tried to perform the same functions in an agricultural economy that many cities did, and thus made itself a prisoner of its locational handicaps even as it fattened on the locational advantages it did possess. In seeking reasons why Edmonton did not diversify through innovation, Jacobs is again instructive. She notes that cities that enjoy sudden and tremendous success in one activity tend to direct all their resources, energies, and attention towards that activity. Such cities do not vigorously explore alternative opportunities. Perhaps Edmonton grew so quickly and successfully from the agricultural settlement boom that it blinded itself to other possibilities.

Aside from questions about its own growth and size, Edmonton's place in the emerging urban network of the West and the nation is known in a general way. The metropolitan model suggests a commanding national presence for Montreal and Toronto, metropolitan status for Winnipeg in the West at large, and a dominating role for Edmonton in the northern half of Alberta's settled regions. (In the realm of provincial government jurisdiction, of course, Edmonton commanded all of Alberta).[15] But much is unknown about the nature, value, and extent of Edmonton's territorial market in terms of retailing, wholesaling, manufacturing, and services, to say nothing of any social or cultural influence it may have exerted beyond its city limits.

Dog team headed for the North, Feb. 1897, on the eve of the Klondike Gold Rush. Was Edmonton's reputation as 'Gateway to the North' more boosterism than economic boon to the city? (PAA B.5703)

A particularly murky aspect of Edmonton's metropolitan influence resides in the phrase 'Gateway to the North.' This popular slogan confers on the city a status that has never been seriously studied and is perhaps undeserved. Technically, gateway cities are places that can take advantage of their strategic locations to control exchanges on linear pathways. Edmonton does not qualify. Of course, the city has provided access to various parts of the north in various capacities at various times, but it is no more deserving of the title 'Gateway to the North' than many other cities. During the fur trade, boat brigades between York Factory and the fur-bearing territory directly north of Edmonton frequently connected with Cumberland House (near the present Saskatchewan-Manitoba border), bypassing Edmonton entirely. Similarly, Edmonton's role in the Klondike Gold Rush has been grossly exaggerated since the advent of Klondike Days celebrations in the 1960s. But no more than 1,500 souls passed through Edmonton on route to that historic boom, and the city was less significant as a gateway to the Yukon than San Francisco, Seattle, or even Victoria.[16]

Nonetheless, the vision of a northern commercial empire continued to fuel Edmonton's aspirations. City boosters persuaded the Alberta government to lend heavy support to the construction of two ill-fated railway pro-

jects: the Edmonton, Dunvegan and British Columbia to the Peace River country and the Alberta Great Waterways to Fort McMurray, completed in 1916 and 1925 respectively. But the geographical extent of a hinterland is less significant than its commercial value, and it is doubtful that the vast north contributed as much to Edmonton's growth as the more densely settled agrarian hinterland around the city.

If little is known about the exact extent and nature of Edmonton's relationship with its hinterland, even less is known about Edmonton's metropolitan relationship with larger units in the Canadian urban system. How and to what extent did it yield to Winnipeg, Toronto, and Montreal beyond the obvious fact that those cities owned most of Edmonton's railways, banks, and department stores?

Some scholars have protested that metropolitanism is no longer a suitable framework for the study of relationships among urban places, that it has become a tired cliche of Canadian urban history. The complaints have some validity, but the fact remains that while metropolitanism has long been discussed in Canadian scholarly circles, detailed work on its actual operation has often been lacking. A brilliant new book on Chicago, however, has demonstrated how revealing an intimate study can be.[17] Not only will a close examination of all these relationships promise to reveal more about Edmonton's role in the metropolitan hierarchy, but much about how metropolitanism functioned in general. Indeed, the study of a mid-tier city can reveal more about metropolitanism's operational aspects than a study of either the grand metropolis or the hinterland outpost.

No study of Edmonton's relationship with other places can ignore 'urban systems' analysis. In this schemata, cities tend to specialize in complementary ways rather than to compete. Minute advantages enjoyed by one city in carrying out a single function tend to increase over time, as the people who specialize in that function in the less favoured city relocate to improve their circumstances. The advantage therefore becomes magnified, giving the favoured city greater advantages still. Meanwhile, the losing rival attracts or develops a different set of specialists drawn to the minute advantages it offers in another function, creating what some geographers call an 'urban system.' Interlocking and complementary specialization, in which a change in one centre in the system ignites changes in the others, differs from the metropolitan model. Metropoli-tanism presumes the existence of many small places, each offering identical functions, ruled by a layer of larger competing places, each offering identical higher functions, and dominated at the top by a single metropolis that alone offers the highest level of functions. Both models are essential to understanding the reality of urban relationships, for direct competition in some functions and complementary specialization in others can readily be seen in the historical relationships between cities.[18]

Thus far, discussion of Edmonton's growth and place in the Canadian urban network has focused on the dynamic years before the First World War, but the same questions and possible approaches are applicable to its subsequent history. Scholars have even addressed some of them, but if cities diversify, grow, and assume new positions in an urban hierarchy from the possibilities inherent in an existing base of activities, then the prewar years demand more attention.

Edmonton's era of explosive growth ended in 1913 when the speculative bubble of rampant real estate speculation burst. Thousands fled the city and a general collapse seemed imminent, but the Great War sustained the urban economy. With rising wheat prices in Europe and good yields at home, agriculture boomed. Farmers acquired more land and machinery, almost doubling the acreage under production, and prairie cities and towns, including Edmonton, recovered by meeting the renewed demands of the hinterland. Nevertheless, Edmonton shared considerable bitterness with other western cities over war contracts for munitions, uniforms, and other supplies. The great majority went to eastern cities—largely, westerners

suspected, for political reasons. The Canadian government argued that western cities lacked the industrial base to supply war goods economically and faced much greater transportation costs to Europe, claims that probably carried considerable merit. These controversies, however, foreshadowed a new era in urban growth in which government decisions and spending would play an increasingly dominant role in the fate of cities.[19]

If the war entailed some economic disappointments, the postwar years brought more. Settlers had already claimed the better agricultural lands, and the river of newcomers shrivelled. Falling grain prices and a disastrous drought actually depopulated parts of southern Alberta and Saskatchewan. The main rail lines and facilities had already been built—or rather, overbuilt. The Canadian Northern and the Grand Trunk Pacific railways staggered towards bankruptcy, and in stages the Canadian government folded them into the new Canadian National Railways system. Excess capacity also troubled prairie coal mining as the demand for new locomotives, stoves, and furnaces declined.

All these developments meant that prairie cities and towns could not maintain the growth rates they enjoyed before the war. Booster campaigns no longer yielded results. The appetite of the war for capital made floating debentures for new promotional schemes difficult, and, in

any event, the big prizes had already been awarded. Meanwhile, the bills mounted from old campaigns and from the expansion of municipally owned utilities and services. Retiring those debts depended on continuous property development to expand the revenue base. Instead, the speculators who had ringed the cities with subdivisions could not sell their lots. They quit paying taxes. Municipalities seized their property, but, unable to market the lots themselves, acquired huge land banks that produced no revenue. No city suffered more from these calamities than Edmonton. No other had launched so many municipally owned utilities and expanded them so rapidly. As early as 1917 Edmonton's per capita debt soared beyond the level of any major city in Canada.[20]

The hinterland economy recovered in the mid 1920s, only to stumble again in the Great Depression. The collapse of international wheat prices reverberated through the economies of prairie cities, leaving bankruptcies and unemployment lines in its wake. In addition to old debt, municipalities now faced escalating demands for relief payments, and they collected even less revenue.

Much of the existing literature chronicles these problems in detail, but a mystery emerges. Edmonton's metropolitan population stood at 59,000 in 1921; by 1931 it reached 79,000, a gain of 20,000 people for a respectable 34 per cent increase over the decade. Equally remarkable,

The Hudson's Bay Company land sale, 13 May 1912. Edmonton's years of unbroken prosperity were coming to an end. Its real estate market was about to collapse and many of the lots that were already serviced would not see building activity until after the Second World War. (PAA B.4904A)

its population rose to 94,000 by 1941, an increase of 15,000 people and a growth rate of 19 per cent during the worst economic decade in prairie history. Except for stagnating Winnipeg, other large prairie cities also grew significantly, at rates that compared favourably with many cities across the country. How could this growth have happened, given the problems that plagued the interwar years?

Part of the explanation might lie in the fact that historians have exaggerated hinterland economic difficulties. The postwar troubles of the railways did not mean the actual end of construction, for many old projects limped forward. Four branchlines out of Edmonton were completed or extended between 1920 and 1927, expanding the city's trade territory. Some new construction even began during the burst of prosperity in the late 1920s. Moreover, the drought that depopulated parts of the southern prairies after the war and again in the Great Depression had little impact on cities in the park belt. Indeed, settlement continued along the northern fringe of the prairies between the wars, prompted by the brief revival of immigration after the Railways Agreement of 1925, and the steady drift of southerners into the Peace River country. These developments permitted a slow but steady expansion in Edmonton's wholesale trade, often at Winnipeg's expense.

But something else happened in the interwar years related to Lampard's idea about the self-sustaining nature of urban growth in an age of continuous invention. Many technological innovations appeared after the war, but none with more startling impact than the automobile. Although manufacturing began much earlier, the industry hit its stride after the war. In 1920 Canada boasted one car for every 22 people; by 1930, one for every 8.5. As a generator of urban growth, the automobile ignited assembly centres like Windsor and Oshawa, two of the fastest-growing cities of the decade. It also benefited cities that could provide parts or components like petroleum, sheet metal, glass windshields, rubber tires, asbestos brake-linings, or metal fixtures, all of which promoted vigorous growth in the urban network of southern Ontario.

Although manufacturing no cars or components for them, Edmonton and countless other urban places nonetheless received a notable (if largely ignored) stimulus from the automobile. It called for dealers to sell them, gas stations to service them, mechanic shops to repair them, and garages to house them. It created tire and parts shops, motels, and even the manufacture and sale of camping equipment. Everywhere, it called for highway and street building, rebuilding, and paving. And cars were only part of the transportation revolution. Buses that began replacing streetcars, and trucks that replaced horse-drawn delivery wagons, generated their own economic demands.[21]

The automobile also began to redefine Edmonton's relationship with its agricultural hinterland. The number of cars on Alberta farms almost doubled during the 1920s and by 1930 more than 40 per cent of all farmers owned one. Automobiles allowed them to patronize a wider variety of urban places. The small towns they bypassed began to decline, while those they favoured began to grow. Cars certainly brought more farmers and small townsfolk directly to Edmonton, particularly as improved roads and new highways radiated from the city. Edmonton's retail trade widened. Farmers also began buying farm trucks, tractors, and new machinery designed for tractor power. Too expensive for the great majority of farmers, mechanization proceeded slowly, but it still heightened demand for more urban goods and services. While vehicle and machinery sales fell precipitously in the 1930s, they did not disappear entirely, and the stock acquired in more prosperous times still required repair and servicing.[22]

Popular writers have lavished more attention on Edmonton's role in air transport, perhaps because it contributes to the city's cherished image as the 'Gateway to the North.' Edmonton bush pilots did supply many far northern communities with passenger service and light goods transport in the interwar years, including the new gold town of Yellowknife after 1934, but they held no monopoly. Vancouver and Winnipeg also launched flights into the north. Most certainly, air services contributed far less to Edmonton's growth or metropolitan stature than the much vaster transportation revolution on the ground.[23]

In addition to innovations in transportation, other elements of self-perpetuating growth in the interwar years await discovery and analysis. The increase in services, for example, included entertainment enterprises like motion picture theatres, radio, and professional sports. Their growth not only suggests a city large enough to support them, but also one registering gains in basic productivity, producing more people with discretionary income. Of course, many luxury expenditures declined during the Great Depression, and economic development cannot be assumed merely because the population continued to increase. Even so, economic refugees from the hinterland still spent some money. One must ask why Eaton's and the Hudson's Bay each opened new department stores in the city in 1938 after Woodward's had already done so in 1926.[24]

While unstudied, it is suggested here that the introduction of new technology and services can readily promote growth in a city even when its hinterland resource base experiences difficulties. Cities seemed to reach a threshold of population in the industrial age whereby it became very difficult, if not actually impossible, to stop growing entirely. Determining that threshold, which seems to have varied through time, presents numerous difficulties. All that can be noted here is that no Canadian city of Edmonton's size in 1921 ever lost population over a ten-year period until Sudbury and Windsor accomplished that remarkable feat during the 1970s.

If Edmonton's growth between the wars still poses an unexplored, and even largely unnoticed mystery, no one doubts the impact of the dramatic events of the Second World War. The Japanese attack on Pearl Harbor raised concerns about America's ability to defend Alaska. As a result, the United States sought a sheltered inland route to establish an alternate supply line to the northern state. Edmonton provided a base for three big projects: the Alaska Highway; the Northwest Staging Route, a series of airstrips used in part to ferry airplanes from the United States to Russia under Lend-Lease; and the Canol Pipeline, which supplied the necessary petroleum from a refinery at Fort Norman in the North West Territories. To build these facilities, American capital and manpower descended on Edmonton. The Canadian government contributed too, establishing an army base and a Commonwealth Air Training Centre, leading to frenzied airport activity and airplane assembly, repair, and servicing. As in the First World War (and largely for the same reasons), the city did not win major contracts for war goods, but it did supply some munitions and meat. Edmonton steamed out of the Great Depression. A shortage of warehouse, office, and residential space stirred construction. Retailing and services rebounded, and mobs of troops invigorated the entertainment business.[25]

The war economy invites speculation about Edmonton's subsequent development. The 'north' finally appeared to spearhead its growth and the city's gateway reputation acquired credibility. In that respect, Edmonton gained as much from accident as design. Political lobbying and manoeuvring ensured that many wartime projects benefited the city, but circumstances it did not control helped immensely: the particular course of military events in the Pacific, and Edmonton's existing base of goods and services in a strategic location. Thus, the economic gains seemed to be temporary and would end, presumably, with the war itself, even though Edmonton would retain some military importance in the Cold War. The phrase 'seemed to be temporary' is appropriate, however, because there may be a significant link between Edmonton's war econo-

Imperial Leduc No. 1, 13 Feb. 1947. (PAA P.2722)

my and its role in the petroleum boom ignited by the Leduc discovery of 1947. Did the war provide Edmonton with expertise in the sorts of engineering, construction, and camp supply functions that could service the oil boom? This possibility again introduces the idea that cities grow when the goods and services designed for one activity find applications in a new activity. If such occurred in this case, then the origins of Edmonton's new economy should not date from 1947, as tradition dictates, but rather from the war years.

Even so, 1947 must be regarded as a momentous year in Edmonton's history—not so much because of the scale of the Leduc discovery itself, but rather because it fired intensive exploration that led to other huge strikes in Alberta, most of them within a hundred-mile radius of the city. These successes led in turn to the establishment of three refineries in the city between 1948 and 1951, and to the subsequent development of petrochemical industries to produce a variety of products. Besides conventional oil, attention also focused on the Athabasca Tar Sands where a major extraction plant rose in 1964. Yet another trans-

Imperial Oil refinery, 1953. Edmonton became a major refinery centre for the oil industry, but most of the corporate head offices remained in Calgary, which enjoyed the 'initial advantage accruing from the 1914 Turner Valley discoveries.' (PAA GS.1032/2)

portation revolution ensued: pipelines. By 1952, a dense network of feeder roots connected well sites to main lines and finally to Edmonton, there trunk lines carried oil west to Vancouver and east through the United States to Ontario. Although Edmonton did not become a central hub for natural gas lines, the city profited from their construction. A cheap and abundant supply of natural gas also turned Fort Saskatchewan into an industrial satellite of Edmonton, beginning in 1952 when a plant opened to process nickel ore from Lynn Lake, Manitoba. A rail extension to Pine Point on Great Slave Lake in 1964 brought more minerals to Edmonton.[26]

Although these dazzling events presaged a great future in manufacturing for Edmonton, economists describe the petroleum industry as a highly capitalized activity, which is another way of saying that it is not very labour intensive. Like the imaged structures of science fiction, the petroleum refinery presents a surreal image of technology that seems to function without people. But if oil and gas did not employ many people directly, they spawned far-reaching linkages and exerted tremendous multiplier effects. Exploration involved a host of independent specialists in financial, technical, and legal services. Drilling demanded trucking, camp supply, earth-moving machinery, construction equipment, and materials like iron and

steel, pipe, wire, cement, and pumps, much of which could be manufactured in Edmonton. Refining and transporting petroleum raised a litany of further demands. They all rippled through the economy to the provisioners of still more producers' goods and services, as well as to general construction and retailing.[27]

The impact of petroleum is partly reflected in the raw statistics of population growth. Edmonton's metropolitan population rose from 94,000 in 1941 to 173,000 in 1951, to 338,000 in 1961, and to 496,000 in 1971, joining Calgary as one of the fastest-growing cities in Canada. As noted earlier, however, it is easy to become mesmerized by such rampant growth and to account for it so readily that one fails to note its limits. Edmonton's surge was not astonishing from an international perspective, and it remained a small city compared to the petroleum giants of Texas, Houston and Dallas, whose metropolitan areas bulged with two million and 1.5 million people respectively in 1970.

It must be remembered that in spite of the spiralling demand for petroleum products, the Alberta industry laboured under many restraints. Its oil was not particularly cheap or easy to find and drill compared to the shallow deposits around the Gulf of Mexico, in Venezuela, or in the Middle East. Situated near oceans, those places enjoyed much cheaper transportation rates to major markets, while Edmonton shipped over long distances through relatively expensive pipelines. Oil and gas were not rare commodities in the postwar world; prices remained low and generally stable. The result was that the products of Edmonton's petroleum industries seldom penetrated markets beyond western Canada, and did not even saturate that limited market. The same held true for Edmonton's non-petroleum manufactures. Its oil did reach Ontario, but not Quebec, where it became cheaper to import from elsewhere. Moreover, only crude oil reached Ontario. The great international companies that controlled the distribution of oil did not care whether Ontario obtained supplies from Alberta or elsewhere, but, since they had earlier built refining facilities at Sarnia, they did not wish to waste capacity there, and thus took only crude oil from Edmonton.

Moreover, not all of Edmonton's growth flowed from petroleum. Agriculture often disappears in the existing accounts of Edmonton's fortunes after the war, but it did not disappear in reality. The modest advances in farm mechanization, capitalization, and productivity noted in the 1920s stalled during the Great Depression and the war, but they surged forward thereafter, creating demand for more urban goods and services. Even in consumer spending, rising per capita prosperity compensated for the decline in the number of farmers, and a growing arsenal of

hinterland automobiles sped over newly paved roads into the city. As Edmonton itself became a more important market for foodstuffs, farmers raised a wider variety of crops and more livestock, dairy, and poultry products. In response, Edmonton manufactured a wider variety of food and beverage items. And although it became important only recently, a forest industry hinterland appeared with the development of pulp processing at Hinton in 1956.[28]

Once again, it must be emphasized that Edmonton's very inclusion in the modern industrial network also produced growth. The kind of analysis suggested for the interwar years must be employed again. If motor vehicles and airplanes helped sustain urban growth after the First World War, they did so with far greater fury after 1945. Meanwhile, the introduction of completely new technologies and products proceeded more rapidly than ever before. The postwar years witnessed huge productivity gains in basic enterprises, releasing more people and money to develop still more services. Activities as wide-ranging as pet grooming, golf lessons, and pizza delivery became viable businesses. And as Edmonton kept growing, it became an increasingly attractive market for goods and services that could not survive in a smaller place. All these developments would likely have occurred, albeit on a reduced scale, without the existence of oil. Note, for example, that Winnipeg, which did not have oil, or seem-

Stockyards, 1953. Small, mixed farm operations were particularly hard hit in the late 1940s and early 1950s, but agriculture itself remained a vibrant force and an important contributor to Edmonton's economy. (PAA GS.1067/3)

ingly much else in its favour, still managed to grow by more than 50 per cent between 1951 and 1971.[29]

The foregoing suggests that even though oil generated tremendous growth in Edmonton, its influence can still be exaggerated. Indeed, one can argue that scholars have placed too much emphasis on minerals, manufacturing, and transportation generally as the keys to urban growth in postwar Canada. By 1961 direct employment in those sectors, which could not account for even half the national work force, was declining rapidly. Many other traditional occupations also declined. Instead, more people worked at white collar jobs in expanding bureaucracies. Precisely at the time when industry became more important in Edmonton than ever before, the city lurched simultaneously into the post-industrial world.

Government expansion highlighted this shift. An adequate account of its postwar growth cannot be told here, and others have told it well, but it stemmed in large measure from the relief crisis of the Depression and the example of massive state intervention in wartime. Thereafter, huge increases in government functions, revenues, spending, and employees attended the acceptance of responsibility for the performance of the economy and for a plethora of social programs. Provincial governments shared fully

in this expansion, especially in the areas of health, welfare, education, highways, economic regulation, and the direct ownership of business enterprises. In spite of the reputation of the Social Credit administration that ruled Alberta from 1935 to 1971 as a parsimonious, laissez-faire operation, it was not immune to the forces propelling state intervention throughout the industrial world. Government growth under Social Credit only seems puny compared to the rapacious expansion of government under the Progressive Conservative administration that took control in 1971.[30]

While much about the growth of the state is well known, its relative contributions to bureaucratic proliferation in particular cities have been less closely scrutinized, but clearly provincial capitals like Edmonton reaped huge benefits. Education alone contributed enormously to the white-collar revolution. The new bureaucrats were themselves expected to have far more of it; some even required university training. Augmented by the baby boom, a bulging population surged through the school system and beyond to colleges, technical schools, and universities. Between 1959 and 1969, enrollments at the University of Alberta soared from 5,000 to 15,000, a growth rate notably faster than the city itself experienced. If the rise of

The Jell-O train arrives in Edmonton, 5 May 1951. After the poverty of the Great Depression and the rationing of the war years, Edmontonians rushed to buy the new consumer goods that were becoming available. (PAA BL.1890/3)

Edmonton after the Second World War seems unimaginable without the petroleum industry, imagine it without the provincial capital or the university.

In contributing to employment and population in Edmonton, the labour intensive nature of white-collar work should be noted. Unlike other activities, practically no technology reduced labour requirements. Until the 1960s, most offices featured no devices more complex than telephones, typewriters, and mechanical adding machines, but even when the electronic computer invaded the office, ample evidence indicates that it actually increased labour demands. Furthermore, the difficulty of measuring merit or productivity in white-collar work created problems in establishing rates of pay. The simplest solution was to reward white-collar workers according to the number of people under their supervision, which provided a powerful incentive for beaucracies to expand.[31]

Nor was government alone responsible for bureaucratic profligacy. Big corporations marched in that direction too, as desk work became increasingly important for a wide range of new and expanded functions.[32] Far more than most businesses, the petroleum industry relied on an astonishing array of specialized white-collar activities. But Calgary rather than Edmonton garnered most of those jobs. Since Alberta's first oil strike occurred at Turner

Valley in 1914 near Calgary, that city developed the financial and administrative expertise for the industry, and it retained control even after much bigger strikes later occurred near Edmonton. Calgary's ability to do so is testimony to the compounding effects of initial advantage. It continued to attract people involved in decision making, finance, and administration because of its existing base of services related to those functions. Edmonton could not overcome Calgary's early lead, as its ill-fated attempt to establish a stock exchange in the 1950s illustrates. Instead, the city attracted more people involved in drilling, manufacturing, and camp supply because it offered a greater abundance of services related to those activities. As a result, functional differences between Calgary and Edmonton sharpened.

Interlocking specialization between the two cities suggests that urban systems analysis becomes more important for understanding Edmonton's rise after the Second World War. Such an approach, it will be remembered, argues that growth and change in one city in an integrated network will ignite growth and change in other cities in the system. Thus, decisions about petroleum development originated in Calgary and flowed to Edmonton which did much of the actual work. Profits mainly flowed back to Calgary where new ventures took shape. But the movement of information, money, and people involved more than a simple feedback system between white-collar Calgary and blue-collar Edmonton. The capital had its own elaborate bureaucracies. The provincial government involved itself heavily in petroleum development; it formulated policies, administered crown lands and mineral rights, regulated the industry, and collected royalties and taxes, all of which generated messages and meetings between bureaucrats in both cities. And Edmonton remained the more important educational centre. Even after the University of Alberta's branch campus in Calgary acquired independence in 1964, the parent institution still offered a wider array of specialized programs and graduate studies that attracted the white-collar children of Calgary. Not only did the volume of every sort of exchange between the two cities far exceed that of any two other places in the province, it also figured prominently in national exchanges. When pairs of Canadian cities were ranked by the number of air passengers in 1965, for example, Edmonton-Calgary ranked third behind only Toronto-Montreal and Toronto-Ottawa.[33]

While both cities begrudgingly recognized their intimate relationship, they refused to accept its full implications. Instead, they persisted in rivalries reminiscent of early twentieth century boosterism. At that time, cities had perceived themselves to be engaged in what game theorists call a zero-sum contest. What one city won, the other lost. If one city dominated the trade of a hinterland town, then obviously the other did not. If one became capital of the province, then obviously the other could not. Much of this mentality persisted after the Second World War, except that it no longer made sense. Given the growing integration of the cities, big growth in one led to big growth in the other. A victory for one now became a victory for both.

This sketchy depiction of the new relationship between Edmonton and Calgary suggests the power of the urban systems approach, and hints that Edmonton's relations with other major Canadian cities also bear scrutiny. Not that metropolitanism loses its utility as a result. It remains an important, if still overly generalized, concept for studying postwar cities. Although uncharted in detail, Edmonton's position in the hierarchy of Canadian cities clearly gained ground. Indeed, given the growing economic intervention of all provincial governments, all provincial capitals gained something in metropolitan stature, curbing the intrusions of national centres. But as Edmonton and Calgary approached Winnipeg in size, they also began capturing more of its western wholesale trade. At the same time, chains of financial command that had once led to London, England, increasingly led to New York. Many Canadian industries had relied on American capital since the 1920s, but few more heavily than the Alberta petroleum industry after the Second World War. With many of its major companies headquartered in American cities, Calgary and Edmonton splintered the metropolitan control once wielded more exclusively by Montreal and Toronto.[34]

Within Canada, however, Edmonton's bid for national metropolitan influence flared most dramatically during the 1970s. More correctly, perhaps, it was a bid by a trio of fast-growing western cities with increasingly integrated functions: Edmonton, Calgary, and Vancouver. Given Montreal and Toronto's immensely greater financial status and corporate control, western ambitions seem somewhat preposterous in retrospect, but they did not seem so at the time. Flush with confidence from growth and prosperity, western cities had before them the dramatic example of American Sun Belt cities that had risen to metropolitan significance: Atlanta, Houston, Dallas, and Phoenix. The occasion for Edmonton's brash confidence stemmed from a sudden spike in oil prices. In 1973 oil sold for the modest price of $3 a barrel; the next year it hit $11; and by 1981, $40—a thirteen-fold increase in eight years. Old wells in Alberta produced immense wealth, and money poured into new exploration, leading to big new strikes. Known reserves not profitable enough to exploit in the 1960s suddenly became worthwhile: deep oil, heavy oil, tar sands oil. The monstrous Syncrude plant at Fort McMurray rose between 1975 and 1978. Vast sums poured into exploration in the far north and even to the shores of the Arctic. The effect on Edmonton was not unlike that of the preceding decades, but it now struck with amplified intensity. Greater Edmonton soared from 496,000 to 657,000 people between 1971 and 1981.

Major advances in metropolitan stature require large pools of concentrated capital. The acquisition of capital by western cities was marked by the rise of indigenous trust companies, banks, and other financial institutions. Edmonton shared in this growth, to which it added the provincial government's Heritage Trust Fund in 1974, a vast repository for the government's share of the petroleum bonanza, and into which hundreds of millions of dollars soon poured. The announced purpose of this money was to diversify the Alberta economy, transforming it into an industrial giant no longer dependent on petroleum.[35]

Several roadblocks stood in the way. From the beginning, petroleum development had been subject to dominion political policies, not all of them unfavourable to the West. The National Oil Policy of 1961, for example, reserved the Ontario market for Alberta crude, even though it cost slightly more than imported crude. Ontario grumbled, but the West maintained that long decades of tariff protection had forced it to buy eastern Canadian manufactures. When oil prices skyrocketed in the 1970s, eastern consumers were happy to take Alberta oil, but only at prices below world market. Beginning in 1973, Ottawa imposed a series of special taxes, price controls, and exploration initiatives that finally coalesced in the National Energy Policy of 1980. In conjunction with other federal initiatives, it sought a number of goals: to keep domestic oil prices below world levels, to tax and regulate the industry in a manner that deflected revenue from Edmonton to Ottawa, to divert exploration from Alberta to the North West Territories where Ottawa controlled natural resources, to concentrate greater petrochemical industrial development in Sarnia, and to rid the industry of foreign firms, largely through buy-outs by government-owned Petro-Canada.[36]

While the many ramifications of this complex policy cannot be explored here, Ottawa largely succeeded in meeting its goals. Historically, it is certain that the great energy controversy will be regarded as another episode in the West's long standing battle against eastern domination. From an urban perspective, however, it indicated that eastern metropolitan forces could and would use political power to crush the emergence of powerful rivals.

As the Alberta government fumed and contemplated drastic retaliation against Ottawa, a second calamity struck Edmonton's ambitions. Oil prices fell to $29 a barrel in 1983 and to $14 by 1986. The 'energy crisis,' as non-producing parts of the industrial world called it, had come about not because the world ran out of oil, but because the Arab-led Organization of Petroleum Exporting Countries had temporarily succeeded in controlling production and hence prices. But it drove prices so high that nations outside the cartel had a great incentive to find more oil, and they did. Much of the new oil in Alberta could not survive the ensuing price drop; exploration and drilling dwindled and many companies, including several financial institutions, went bankrupt. Ottawa bailed out those enterprises

From an urban perspective, however, the great energy controversy indicated that eastern metropolitan forces could and would use political power to crush the emergence of powerful rivals.

heavily indebted to eastern banks, but allowed the western banks to collapse.

A third calamity for Edmonton stemmed from the failure of the Alberta government's diversification program. Many of the companies it financed struggled for years before collapsing and the extent of public monies lost would not become apparent for more than a decade. In spite of the avowed goal of diversification, the province actually plowed most of its investment funds into petroleum-based enterprises—specifically those too risky and uneconomic to attract private capital. But non-petroleum investments fared no better, principally because the government tried to foster activities that cities outside the province performed more efficiently. As Jane Jacobs argues, successful diversification stems from innovations that spring naturally from trying to solve problems encountered in traditional work. The innovation designed for an existing activity is then exported on its own merits to serve wholly new purposes. It is important that the innovation spring from old work, because, if it fails, as the overwhelming majority of attempted innovations do, the old work still remains to sustain renewed efforts. But the Alberta government nurtured industries utterly divorced from this process: hazardous waste treatment, telephone equipment, magnesium.

The province's decentralization policy compounded these problems. Based on the hoary prejudice that cities must not become 'too big,' and nurtured by nostalgia for small town life (not to mention aggressive rural lobbying), decentralization would rescue the countryside from economic oblivion. But, as Jacobs demonstrates, the attempt to foster complex industries in small towns usually fails because they rely too heavily on goods and services readily available only in big cities.[37]

For its part, the municipal government continued to promote Edmonton in numerous ways, but a brash new element invaded traditional boosterism, overwhelming it sufficiently to warrant the description 'neo-boosterism.' In Canada, this phenomenon first emerged from the ambitions of Mayor Jean Drapeau of Montreal. Although annual fairs had always played a role in publicizing cities,

West Edmonton Mall.
(WEST EDMONTON MALL)

Drapeau envisioned big shows that would attract international attention. Montreal staged the World's Fair in 1967, acquired a major league baseball team in 1969, and hosted the Summer Olympics in 1976. Aside from immediate economic gains, the idea behind the big show was to generate 'free' publicity that would continue to attract investors, conventioners, and tourists; to erect striking monuments that would forever identify the city; and to acquire new infrastructure and other civic improvements at the expense of senior governments.

Many cities, including Edmonton, readily embraced neo-boosterism. The city acquired a World Hockey League franchise in 1971, followed by a move into the more prestigious National Hockey League in 1979. Additional publicity flowed from the Commonwealth Games in 1978 and the World University Games in 1983. Rival Calgary countered with its own National Hockey League franchise in 1980 and the Winter Olympics in 1988. Even a permanent retail fixture like the West Edmonton Mall could qualify as a publicity-generating big show, providing it was the largest and most spectacular shopping centre in the world, a feat accomplished with the completion of Phase III in 1985. Cities subsidized such ventures in various ways, justifying their actions on economic grounds, but perhaps the big show speaks more of a psychological need to fuse personal identity with place, a craving that professional sports seemed particularly adept at satisfying. Sports promoters everywhere shrewdly exploited this sentiment to receive all sorts of assistance from cities in much the same manner

as early twentieth-century manufacturers sought bonuses, and like them, frequently threatened to leave town if their demands were not met. But while neo-boosterism frequently cost cities dearly, its actual economic benefits, both short and long term, often proved disappointing.[38]

Thus, Edmonton's grand metropolitan ambitions faltered in the face of three major obstacles: political assaults from eastern metropolitan forces, collapsing oil prices, and inappropriate and ineffective government policies by both the province and the city. But Edmonton did not suffer alone. The energy boom of the 1970s masked major structural shifts in urban economies already apparent outside of Alberta by the middle of the decade. The era of cities that thrived on big resources, big manufacturing, and big transportation systems seemed to be ending. Big bureaucracies were in trouble too, as the advent of corporate 'downsizing' indicated, even though governments continued to fatten for another decade. These changes represented more than a cyclical downturn in the economy. New resource discoveries besides oil appeared throughout the world, and, like oil, often proved cheaper to extract, process, and transport than Canadian ones. Technological changes also lessened dependence on many traditional resources, and even eliminated the use of some of them. Others disappeared because of new health, safety, and environmental policies. Recycling cut the demand for new resources further. Much labour intensive manufacturing shifted to countries once known as the third world to take advantage of cheap labour costs, while managerial and technological leadership in complex manufacturing passed to Japan and Germany.

Those Canadian cities that thrived in the 1980s, particularly Toronto and Vancouver, did so on the strength of new ventures largely rooted in services and in the light, but sophisticated, manufacturing associated with them. Many activities involved complex information processing, but others sprang from such menial depths of the urban economy as cleaning and food preparation. Traditionally, such tertiary activities existed only to serve an urban population that lived from other means, but they became engines of growth in their own right when sales expanded to markets in other cities. While varying enormously in the products provided, from restaurant supplies to medical services to investment counselling, these new ventures shared a number of characteristics. They remained relatively small and agile enterprises, eschewing fully-integrated corporate structures in favour of franchising, contracting, and leasing, and the delivery of their products did not require massive transportation systems. Significantly, they did not rely on huge injections of public capital to survive and prosper.[39]

This new urban economy bears special attention in studying the recent past of any city, including Edmonton, for in spite of its many troubles in the 1980s, the city refused to shrink. It still grew, and at a respectable pace. A population of 657,000 in 1981 rose to 840,000 by 1991. While much of the analysis applied to other eras is useful in explaining this mystery, the key to unravelling Edmonton's continued growth probably lies in looking closely at services, especially those that first arose to meet the demands of petroleum, but then discovered new applications that could be sold in markets unrelated to oil. The most spectacular example, however, comes from Calgary where ATCO Industries discovered that the portable housing and office space it provided to petroleum camps had many other uses, leading to world-wide sales and overseas branch plants. Less dramatic examples in Edmonton no doubt await the alert scholar.

In conclusion, it should be evident that any understanding of Edmonton's development defies easy explanations, especially for the periods of relatively slow growth. The city must be seen within a broad historical context and mindful of many theories of urban growth, only some of which have been suggested here. The result of such an approach, however, promises to reveal as much about urban growth in general as it does about Edmonton specifically. ❧

NOTES

☙ ARCHIVES

CEA   City of Edmonton Archives
GAI   Glenbow Alberta Institute
HBCA   Hudson's Bay Company Archives
NAC   National Archives of Canada
PAA   Provincial Archives of Alberta
PAM   Provincial Archives of Manitoba
UAA   University of Alberta Archives

☙ JOURNALS

AG   Alberta Geographer
AH   Alberta History
AHR   Alberta Historical Review
ALN   Alberta Labor News
AR   Alberta Report
BH   Battleford Herald
CES   Canadian Ethnic Studies
CG   Canadian Geographer
CGJ   Canadian Geographical Journal
CH   Calgary Herald
CHR   Canadian Historical Review
CJS   Canadian Journal of Sociology
CN   Chinatown News (Vancouver)
CS   Calgary Sun
EB   Edmonton Bulletin
EFP   Edmonton Free Press
EJ   Edmonton Journal
ES   Edmonton Sun
G&M   Globe and Mail
GPH   Grande Prairie Herald
MB   Missionary Bulletin
PF   Prairie Forum
PC   Plan Canada
PRR   Peace River Record
PW   People's Weekly
SH   Social History
SJER   St John's Edmonton Report
SN   Saturday Night
UHR   Urban History Review
VN   Vancouver News
VS   Vancouver Sun
WC   Western Catholic
WCCR   Western Canadian Coal Review

☙ GILBERT A. STELTER, WHAT KIND OF CITY IS EDMONTON?

1. Claude Levi-Strauss, *Tristes Tropiques* (New York: Criterion Books, 1961), 127 [Fr. original, 1955].
2. I have commented on the quality of Canadian urban history in several places, including 'A Sense of Time and Place: The Historian's Approach to Canada's Urban Past,' in Carl Berger, ed., *Contemporary Approaches to Canadian History* (Toronto: Copp Clark Pitman, 1987), 165-80. The best recent evaluation is by Paul Voisey, 'Urban History,' in Doug Owram, ed., *Canadian History: A Reader's Guide*, vol. 2, *Confederation to the Present* (Toronto: University of Toronto Press, 1994), 228-45.
3. For a useful overview of the strengths and weaknesses of local history see Paul Voisey, 'Rural Local History and the Prairie West,' *PF* 10, no. 2 (1985): 327-38.
4. Fernand Braudel, *The Structures of Everyday Life* (New York: Fontana [1979], 1985), 481-3.
5. Henri Lefebvre, quoted by David Goldfield, 'The Urban South: A Regional Framework,' *American Historical Review* 86, no. 5 (1981): 1012.
6. I have outlined my views in some detail in 'A Regional Framework for Urban History,' *UHR* 13, no. 3 (1985): 193-205. The standard account is J.M.S. Careless, *Frontier and Metropolis: Regions, Cities and Identities in Canada before 1914* (Toronto: University of Toronto Press, 1989). For a criticism of the metropolitan thesis from the perspective of a class analysis see Donald Davis, 'The "Metropolitan Thesis" and the Writing of Canadian Urban History,' *UHR* 14, no. 2 (1985): 95-114.
7. *World Almanac*, (1995) (New York: Funk and Wagnalls, 1994), 675.
8. Michael Goldberg and John Mercer, *The Myth of the North American City: Continentalism Challenged* (Vancouver: University of British Columbia Press, 1986).
9. For a more detailed account of the impact of banking and industrial legislation on urban development see my 'The City-Building Process in Canada,' in Gilbert Stelter and Alan Artibise, eds., *Shaping the Urban Landscape: Aspects of the City-Building Process in Canada* (Ottawa: Carleton University Press, 1982), 1-29.
10. The West's urban history is more fully developed than that for any other region. Important overviews include Paul Voisey, 'The Urbanization of the Canadian Prairies, 1871-1916,' *SH* 15 (1975): 77-101; J.M.S. Careless, 'Aspects of Urban Life in the West, 1870-1914,' in A.W. Rasporich and H.C. Klassen, eds., *Prairie Perspectives 2: Selected Papers of the Western Canadian Studies Conferences, 1970 and 1971* (Toronto: Holt, Rinehart and Winston, 1973), 25-40; and the collection of articles in Alan Artibise, ed., *Town and City: Aspects of Western Canadian Urban Development* (Regina: Canadian Plains Research Center, 1981).
11. Alan Artibise, 'Exploring the North American West: A Comparative Urban Perspective,' in Gilbert Stelter, ed., *Cities and Urbanization: Canadian Historical Perspectives* (Toronto: Copp Clark Pitman, 1990), 246-67.
12. Recent events in this century-long rivalry are well described in *Maclean's*, 27 March 1995, 26.
13. The histories of Edmonton may not be as sophisticated as those of other Western cities, but the following are both useful outlines and very readable: James G. MacGregor, *Edmonton: A History*, 2d ed. (Edmonton: Hurtig, 1975); John Gilpin, *Edmonton: Gateway to the North, An Illustrated History* (Edmonton: Windsor Publications and Amisk Waskahegan Chapter, Historical Society of Alberta, 1984).; and Dennis Person and Carin Routledge, *Edmonton: Portrait of a City* (Edmonton: Reidmore Books, 1981).
14. Edmonton Board of Trade, *The Edmonton District of Northern Alberta* (Edmonton: Bulletin Office, 1890), 23.
15. Edmonton Board of Trade and Edmonton City Council, *The Edmonton District in Central Alberta* (Edmonton, n.p., 1923), 8.
16. Ibid., 4.
17. R.A. Cantelon, *Edmonton, Crossroads of the World* (Edmonton: Civic Enterprises, 1944), 11.
18. Ibid., 15.
19. John Gilpin, 'The Land Development Process in Edmonton, Alberta, 1881-1917,' in Gilbert Stelter and Alan Artibise, eds., *Power and Place: Canadian Urban Development in the North American Context* (Vancouver: University of British Columbia Press, 1986), 151-72.
20. P.J. Smith, 'The Principle of Utility and the Origins of Planning Legislation in

Alberta, 1912-1975,' in Alan Artibise and Gilbert Stelter, eds., *The Usable Urban Past: Planning and Politics in the Modern Canadian City* (Toronto: Macmillan, 1979), 196-225.

21. Susan Wagg, *Percy Erskine Nobbs, Architect, Artist, Craftsman* (Montreal: McGill-Queen's University Press, 1982), 50.

22. Ibid., 47-51.

23. Harold Kalman, *A History of Canadian Architecture*, vol. 2 (Toronto: Oxford University Press, 1994), 557, 718-20.

24. Spiro Kostoff, *The City Assembled: The Elements of Urban Form through History* (Boston: Little, Brown, 1992), 123-9.

25. Jac MacDonald, *Historic Edmonton, An Architectural and Pictorial Guide* (Edmonton: Lone Pine and the Edmonton Journal, 1987).

26. The best study of early Edmonton's culture is Carl Betke, 'The Original City of Edmonton: A Derivative Prairie Urban Community,' in Gilbert Stelter and Alan Artibise, eds., *The Canadian City: Essays in Urban and Social History* (Ottawa: Carleton University Press, 1984), 392-430.

27. Jan Morris, *City to City* (Toronto: Macfarlane Walter & Ross, 1990), 118-30.

28. P.J. Smith, ed., *Edmonton, The Emerging Metropolitan Pattern* (Victoria: University of Victoria, 1978).

29. Max Foran, *Calgary, An Illustrated History* (Toronto: Lorimer, 1978) is an example of the excellent urban history that has been produced on Calgary.

30. L.G. Thomas, comp., *Our Foothills* (Calgary: Millarville, Kew, Priddis and Bragg Creek Historical Society, 1975).

31. Earl Schultz, ed., *From Bush to Bushels, A History of Bruderheim and District* (Bruderheim: Bruderheim Historical Committee, 1983).

32. Morris, *City to City*, 120.

ᘧ JOHN FOSTER,
JAMES BIRD, FUR TRADER

1. John Foster, 'James Bird,' *Dictionary of Canadian Biography/Dictionnaire bibliographique du Canada (DCB/DbC)*, vol. 8 (Toronto: University of Toronto Press, 1985), 90.

2. For an appreciation of the Athabaska Country in terms of its importance in the fur trade see Marjorie Campbell, *The Northwest Company* (Toronto: MacMillan and Co., 1957), 27; and E.E. Rich, *The History of the Hudson's Bay Company, 1670-1870*, vol. 2 (London: Hudson's Bay Record Society, 1959), ch. 3 and 4.

3. A.J. Ray, *Indians in the Fur Trade: Their Role as Trappers, Hunters and Middlemen in the Lands Southwest of Hudson Bay, 1660-1870* (Toronto: University of

Toronto Press, 1974) remains the most useful work emphasizing Indian participation in the fur trade.

4. Controversy marks the question of whether the Cree expanded westward with the fur trade or whether they were already resident in the region when the fur trade arrived. For this latter view see Dale R. Russell, *Eighteenth Century Western Cree and their Neighbours* (Hull, PQ: Canadian Museum of Civilization, Mercury Series Paper No. 143, 1991); and James G.E. Smith, 'The Western Woods Cree: Anthropological Myth and Historical Reality,' *American Ethnologist* 14, no. 3 (1987): 434-48.

5. The importance of taking an appropriate Indian country wife was emphasized by George Simpson, later Governor of the Company's Overseas Territories, in his report to the Governor and Committee in London. See E.E. Rich, ed., *Journal of Occurences in the Athabasca Department, 1820 and 1821, and Report* (Toronto: Champlain Society, 1938), 395-6.

6. Martin Magne, 'Distributions of Native Groups in Western Canada, A.D. 1700 - A.D. 1850,' in Martin Magne, ed., *Archeology in Alberta 1986* (Edmonton: Archeological Survey of Alberta, Occasional Paper No. 31, 1987), 220-8.

7. Theodore Binnema, 'Conflict or Cooperation?: Blackfoot Trade Strategies, 1794-1815' (MA thesis, University of Alberta, 1992), ch. 3.

8. See John Nicks, 'William Tomison,' *DCB/DbC*, vol. 6, 775.

9. See John E. Foster, 'William Auld,' *DCB/DbC*, vol. 6, 17.

10. James G. MacGregor, *John Rowand: Czar of the Prairies* (Saskatoon: Western Producer, 1978), 22.

11. See John S. Milloy, *The Plains Cree* (Winnipeg: University of Manitoba Press, 1988), 110, for an example. Fur trade journals in this period record numerous incidents showing the vulnerability of horses belonging to fur traders.

12. The dimensions of this trade are reflected in the activities of the most famous of James Bird's sons. See David Smyth, 'Jimmy Jock Bird,' *DCB/DbC*, vol. 12, 110.

13. A number of studies touch upon the society of the fur trade with a decided emphasis on the Red River Settlement. See particularly Sylvia Van Kirk, *Many Tender Ties: Women in Fur Trade Society, 1670-1870* (Norman: University of Oklahoma Press, 1983); Jennifer S.H. Brown, *Strangers in Blood: Fur Trade Company Families in Indian Country* (Vancouver: University of British Columbia Press, 1980); and Frits Pannekoek, *A Smug Little Flock: The Social Origins of the Riel Resistance of 1869-70* (Winnipeg: Watson and Dwyer, 1991).

14. Alice Johnson, ed., *The Saskatchewan Journals and Correspondence, 1795-1802*, vol. 26 (London: Hudson's Bay Record Society, 1967).

15. Rich, *History of the Hudson's Bay Company*, 285, 293, 299.

16. Foster, 'William Auld'; and Foster, 'James Bird.'

17. W.L. Morton, *Manitoba, A History* (Toronto: University of Toronto Press, 1957), 54.

18. Great Britain, *Report of the Parliament Select Committee on the Hudson's Bay Company, 1857.* See particularly the testimony of Edward Ellice, 23 June 1857.

19. Foster, 'James Bird.'

ᘧ LEWIS G. THOMAS,
ESTABLISHING AN ANGLICAN PRESENCE

1. See Barry Ferguson, 'Secular History and Church History: An Introduction,' and Frits Pannekoek, '"Insidious" Sources and the Historical Interpretation of the Pre-1870 West,' in Barry Ferguson, ed., *The Anglican Church and the World of Western Canada, 1820-1970* (Regina: Canadian Plains Research Center, 1991), 1-15, 29-37.

2. For secondary accounts that discuss Newton's career see F.A. Peake, 'The Beginnings of the Diocese of Edmonton, 1875-1913' (MA thesis, University of Alberta, 1972); and T.C.B. Boon, *The Anglican Church from the Bay to the Rockies: A History of the Ecclesiastical Province of Rupert's Land and Its Dioceses from 1820 to 1950* (Toronto: Ryerson Press, 1962).

3. Robert Connell, 'Forty Years Ago: Recollections of Canon William Newton,' *Church Messenger, Diocese of Edmonton* 4, no. 65 (1936): 17.

4. William Newton, *Twenty Years on the Saskatchewan* (London: Elliot Stock, 1897), 6.

5. Ibid., 13-14.

6. For a sketch of the West's development before 1905 see Lewis G. Thomas, 'Introduction,' in Lewis G. Thomas, ed., *The Prairie West to 1905* (Toronto: Oxford University Press, 1975), 1-15.

7. Newton, *Twenty Years on the Saskatchewan*, 17.

8. Ibid., 26.

9. Ibid.

10. Ibid., 21.

11. Synod Office of the Anglican Diocese of Edmonton, Records (Synod Records), William Newton to the Bishop of Saskatchewan, 22 Oct. 1875. [After the original research for this paper was completed the records of the Anglican Diocese of Edmonton were

transferred to the Provincial Archives of Alberta - eds.]

12. Newton, *Twenty Years on the Saskatchewan*, 33.
13. Connell, 'Forty Years Ago,' 17.
14. Ibid.
15. Newton's itinerating work reached as far south as Red Deer, as far northeast as the Saddle Lake Reserve, and west for fifty miles along the survey line for the proposed transcontinental railway. He also visited Victoria (Pakan); Beaver Lake (Beaverhill Lake) where the parish of St James the Apostle, Newton (Logan), was formed; Fort Saskatchewan; Poplar Lake; and Sunnyside. See W. Leversedge, 'History of the Diocese of Edmonton,' in *Diocesan Annual, Diocese of Edmonton* (1934), 21.
16. See E. Pierce-Goulding, *The Cathedral Church of All Saints, Edmonton* (Edmonton: Anglican Diocese of Edmonton, 1935).
17. Synod Records, Newton to the Society for the Propagation of the Gospel, 26 June 1879, 25 June 1882.
18. See Pierce-Goulding, *Cathedral Church of All Saints*; and Synod Records, Newton to the Society for the Propagation of the Gospel, Christmas 1883, 29 Sept. 1884.
19. Synod Records, Newton to the Society for the Propagation of the Gospel, 25 June 1878.
20. Newton, *Twenty Years on the Saskatchewan*, 100.
21. *EB*, 7 Aug. 1886.
22. Ibid., 25 Sept. 1886.
23. Newton, *Twenty Years on the Saskatchewan*, 138.
24. Pierce-Goulding, *Cathedral Church of All Saints*, 38.
25. For a sketch of Alberta's development in its first seventy-five years as a province see Lewis G. Thomas, 'Alberta, 1905-1980: The Uneasy Society,' in Howard Palmer and Donald Smith, eds., *The New Provinces: Alberta and Saskatchewan, 1905-1980* (Vancouver: Tantalus Research, 1980), 23-41.
26. See Peake, 'Beginnings of the Diocese of Edmonton,' 63; and Boon, *Anglican Church from the Bay to the Rockies*, 364-5, 372-3.
27. Lewis G. Thomas, 'Mission Church in Edmonton: An Anglican Experiment in the Canadian West,' *Pacific Northwest Quarterly* 49, no. 2 (1958): 55-60.
28. Boon, *Anglican Church from the Bay to the Rockies*, 361.29. See J. Burgon Bickersteth, *Land of the Open Door*, 2d ed. (Toronto: University of Toronto Press, 1976) [originally published 1914].

◌ JOHN PATRICK DAY, DONALD ROSS, OLD-TIMER EXTRAORDINAIRE

1. *EB*, 19 Nov. 1881.
2. Ross's life prior to arrival in Edmonton is drawn from A.O. McRae, *History of Alberta*, vol. 1 (Np: Western Canadian Historical Publishing, 1912), 541-3; CEA, Reference File, 'Donald and Olive Ross,' and Olive (Dolly) Ross, interview with A.A. Campbell, 15 May 1951; *Census of Canada* (1881); *EB*, 25 July 1891, 1 Dec. 1895, 2, 20 Dec. 1901, 3 Jan., 1 Dec. 1903, 13 Sept. 1905, 21 Dec. 1915; and *EJ*, 21 Dec. 1915.
3. *EB*, 13 Sept. 1905; see also ibid., 18, 19 Aug. 1903; J.P. Day, *The Lamoureux Lumber Mill* (Edmonton: Fort Edmonton Park, 1976); and CEA, Records of the Northern Alberta Old-Timers' Association.
4. GAI, Richard Hardisty Papers, file 57, item 285, Lawrence Clarke to Richard Hardisty, 27 July 1873.
5. The best version of this ballad is found in *BH*, 13 Jan. 1879.
6. Olive Ross outlived her husband by seventeen years, dying in 1932. In her later years, she was frequently approached for interviews but reporters obtained little information. Dolly Ross never married. Deafness was blamed for the death of Donald Ross's brother, Alex, killed by a tram in Manchester (*EB*, 12 May 1892).
7. Ross's gold mining career in Edmonton is discussed widely in the *Edmonton Bulletin*, the *Edmonton Journal*, Edmonton Post Journals kept by HBC officers (PAM, HBCA, B 60/a series), and the HBC Trade Commissioner's Correspondence (PAM, HBCA, D 20 series); specifically, see *EB*, 28 Feb. 1881, 23 April 1896.
8. *EB*, 23 April 1896.
9. See CEA, Ross File, S.H. Smith, 'A Sketch of the Life of Charles Stevenson, Known in the Early Days of the West as "English Charlie"' (unpublished manuscript).
10. *EB*, 23 Nov. 1896, 24 Dec. 1928.
11. See ibid., 27 Jan., 27 Feb. 1883; *BH*, 29 Nov. 1880; and Department of the Interior, *Order in Council Books*, vol. 2 (Ottawa: Queen's Printer, 1874), 157.
12. *BH*, 8 Nov. 1880; *EB*, 7 Feb., 4 April 1881, 28 Jan. 1882, 23 Nov. 1896; and *Census of Canada* (1881).
13. *EB*, 6 Jan., 1 March, 10, 24 Nov. 1883, 15 March 1884, 25 Aug., 29 Sept. 1898.
14. See, for example, ibid., 16 Oct. 1905.
15. Hardisty Papers, file 98, item 561; this census of Edmonton and area, conducted in April 1874, was carried out by officers of the HBC at the request of the North West Territories Council.
16. *EB*, 26 April 1890; see also McRae, *History of Alberta*, 541-3, for a discus-

sion of the agreement between Ross and the HBC.
17. McRae, *History of Alberta*, 541-3.
18. Ross describes his crops in *EB*, 26 April 1890; information on Edmonton gardens and farms can also be found in the Edmonton Post Journals, the annual reports of the Department of Indian Affairs, and the *Census of Canada* (1881, 1885, 1891).
19. *EB*, 6 July 1889, 27 July 1895.
20. Ibid., 18 May 1892, 29 June, 10, 13 July 1893, 11 April, 13 June, 23 Sept. 1895.
21. Ibid., 25 Aug. 1904.
22. *BH*, 17 Nov. 1879.
23. Ibid., 13 Sept. 1880; *EB*, 30 Sept., 27 Dec. 1880, 21 Feb. 1881, 3, 17 April 1885.
24. *EB*, 8 June 1900, 29 April, 17 June 1901, 7 Nov. 1903, 8 June 1904, 23 Dec. 1905.
25. Cited in ibid., 27 Sept. 1905.
26. Ibid., 3 Aug., 14, 21 Sept. 1900, 12 Sept. 1902, 17 July, 13 Aug. 1903, 1, 6 Aug. 1904.
27. Ibid., 11 April, 29 Oct., 21 Nov. 1895, 27 Feb., 9, 19 Nov. 1896, 2 June 1898, 9 Oct. 1899. See also Ross File, Donald Ross Jr, interview, 21 May 1970; Town of Edmonton Assessment Rolls, 1892-6; and Edmonton Protestant Public School District No. 7 Assessment Rolls, 1886-91.
28. *EB*, 27 Sept. 1884; *BH*, 7 Oct. 1878; and *Census of Canada* (1881).
29. *BH*, 10 Feb. 1879, 26 Jan. 1880.
30. *EB*, 6 Jan. 1903.
31. *BH*, 27 Sept., 8 Nov. 1880; *EB*, 29 Oct. 1881, 12 Aug. 1882, 8 Sept. 1891, 27 June 1903, 10 Sept. 1887; on the Eureka saloon, see also Town Assessment Roll, 1892.
32. *EB*, 26 Nov. 1894, 12 Aug. 1895, 11 Oct., 22 Nov. 1901; and CEA, RG8 C4/2, C.A. Lowe, Census of Edmonton, 1899.
33. *EB*, 8 Oct., 24 Dec. 1887, 27 Feb. 1896, 18 Feb. 1901.
34. Ibid., 25 July 1891, 13 Feb. 1892.
35. Ibid., 4 May 1889, 15 Feb. 1894.
36. Ibid., 25 June, 26 Nov. 1894, 24 Oct., 1, 12 Dec. 1895.
37. Ross soon transferred the hotel's liquor licence and day-to-day management to Joseph Hostyn (ibid., 31 Jan., 23 May 1902).
38. Ibid., 3 Oct. 1892, 25 June 1900, 20 May 1901.
39. Ibid., 18 June 1900.
40. Ibid., 23 March 1892, 6 Aug. 1894, 29 April, 24 June 1895, 8, 15 Dec. 1898, 1 Dec. 1899, 9 May 1902.
41. Ibid., 20 May, 15 July 1901, 13 Aug. 1903.
42. Ibid., 1 Dec. 1892.
43. Ibid.
44. Ibid., 2 Aug. 1894, 11 Nov. 1895, 23 March, 16 July 1896.

45. Ibid., 19 Nov. 1896, 8 Feb., 12 April 1897.
46. Ibid., 11 Sept. 1897, 6 June 1898.
47. Ibid., 29 Oct. 1881, 28 Jan., 16 Dec. 1882, 27 Dec. 1884, 31 Jan., 28 March 1885, 8 Dec. 1888.
48. Ibid., 25 March 1882.
49. Ibid., 4, 11 April 1885. On the 1875 meeting see PAA, Oblates of Mary Immaculate Papers, diary of Vital Grandin, vol. 1, 13 March 1875.
50. EB, 4 Dec. 1905.

ᶜᵛ GERALD HILL,
LAURENT GARNEAU (POEMS)

The author wishes to acknowledge the Alberta Foundation for the Arts for its support of his work.

ᶜᵛ JANNE SWITZER,
'EDMONTON'S FORGOTTEN MAN'—ALEXANDER TAYLOR

1. *EJ*, 12 Feb. 1916.
2. CEA, Alexander Taylor Clipping Files.
3. See PAA, 70.174, Mrs James Taylor, interview with Naomi Radford, March 1970; and PAA, 69.258, George Sanderson, interview with Naomi Radford, 1969.
4. Mrs James Taylor, interview.
5. See *EB*, 11 Oct. 1884, for the testimony of 'Timber Tom' Anderson before an inquiry into Taylor's conduct as Edmonton's telegraph operator; and PAA, 70.170, Violet Wilson, interview with Naomi Radford, 1970.
6. Mrs Christina McKnight and Mrs Helen Learmonth to the author, 7 Oct. 1980.
7. *EB*, 6 Jan. 1880; and *Saskatchewan Herald*, 26 Jan., 27 April 1880.
8. *Saskatchewan Herald*, 21 June, 8 Nov.1880.
9. On the *Edmonton Bulletin* and its antecedents see Margaret Stinson, *The Wired City* (Edmonton: Edmonton Telephones, 1980), 3-4; *EB*, 6 Jan. 1903; and Taylor Clipping Files, Walker Taylor to G.D. Kinnard, 12 Dec. 1958. Walker claimed his father bought a small printing press by mail from Minneapolis and had it transported to Edmonton by Frank Oliver, whom he took on as a partner due to his past newspaper experience.
10. See Tony Cashman, *Singing Wires* (Edmonton: Alberta Government Telephones Commission, 1972), 20; and *EB*, 12 Jan. 1884.
11. *EB*, 8 March 1884.
12. Ibid., 19 Sept. 1885, 12 Oct. 1889.
13. Ibid., 10 Jan. 1885.
14. Cashman, *Singing Wires*, 48.
15. Ibid., 66.
16. There are two versions of this story, one by Jacques Hamilton in *Our Alberta Heritage* (Calgary: Calgary Power, 1978), 97, and the other by Charles Lewis Shaw in *Saturday News*, 19 May 1906. Shaw's is probably the more accurate account as he was living in Edmonton when the incident happened.
17. McKnight and Learmonth to the author.
18. *EB*, 30 Oct. 1886, reports a 12-foot by 20-foot telegraph office erected in Taylor's house.
19. Ibid., 14 May 1887.
20. Ibid., 18 Aug. 1893, 12 Nov. 1896. Other members of the elected board included J.A. McDougall, A.D. Osborne, and D.R. Frazer.
21. Ibid., 16 Oct. 1893.
22. Cashman, *Singing Wires*, 69, 120; and Mrs James Taylor, interview.
23. Mrs James Taylor, interview.
24. Ibid.
25. *EB*, 7 June 1913.
26. Ibid., 3 Oct. 1907; on Taylor's interest in grains see, for example, ibid., 2 Dec. 1882, 20 Jan. 1883.
27. McKnight and Learmonth to the author.
28. *EB*, 14 Feb. 1885.
29. On Taylor's personal life see Hamilton, *Our Alberta Heritage*, 95; *EB*, 8 Aug. 1885; and Mrs James Taylor, interview (including the suggestion that the second marriage was 'brought on' by Eleanor').
30. *EB*, 27 April 1896.
31. Mrs James Taylor, interview; McKnight and Learmonth to the author; and CEA, Northern Alberta Old-Timers' Association, Taylor File, 418-20.
32. Mrs James Taylor, interview; and Cashman, *Singing Wires*, 220.
33. See M.A. Kostek, *A Century and Ten* (Edmonton: Edmonton Public Schools, 1992), 256.
34. Mrs James Taylor, interview.
35. McKnight and Learmonth to the author.
36. Mrs James Taylor, interview.

ᶜᵛ WILLIAM C. WONDERS,
EDMONTON IN THE KLONDIKE GOLD RUSH

1. E.E. Rich, *The History of the Hudson's Bay Company 1670-1870*, vol. 2 (London: Hudson's Bay Record Society, 1959), 867-8.
2. Noteworthy books featuring Edmonton's role in the Klondike Rush include James G. MacGregor, *The Klondike Rush through Edmonton, 1897-1898* (Toronto: McClelland and Stewart, 1970); James Blower, *Gold Rush* (Toronto: McGraw-Hill Company of Canada, 1971); and Joan Weir, *Back Door to the Klondike* (Erin, ON. Boston Mills Press, 1988).
3. Rich, *History of the Hudson's Bay Company*, 445.
4. David Gregory, et al., *Athabasca Landing: An Illustrated History* (Athabasca: Athabasca Historical Society, 1986), 16-19.
5. Morris Zaslow, *The Opening of the Canadian North 1870-1914* (Toronto: McClelland and Stewart, 1971), 89.
6. *EB*, 31 Dec. 1900.
7. MacGregor, *Klondike Rush through Edmonton*, 153.
8. *EB*, 30 Jan. 1896.
9. CEA, Minutes of Edmonton Town Council Meeting 'Minutes), 9 Oct. 1896.
10. T.A. Rickard, 'The Klondike Gold Rush,' *Beaver*, 277 (Sept. 1946): 6-11; and Stuart R. Tomkins, 'The Klondike Gold Rush—A Great International Venture,' *British Columbia Historical Quarterly* 17, no. 2 (1953): 223-39.
11. *EB*, 6 May 1897.
12. Gordon Bennett, *Yukon Transportation: A History* (Ottawa: Indian and Northern Affairs, Canadian Historic Sites: Occasional Paper in Archaeology and History No. 19, 1978), 17.
13. Ken S. Coates and William R. Morrison, *Land of the Midnight Sun, A History of the Yukon* (Edmonton: Hurtig, 1988), 48-52; and William C. Wonders, *Alaska Highway Explorer* (Victoria: Horsdal and Schubart, 1984), 49.
14. *EB*, 27 Aug. 1896.
15. Jeanette Paddock Nichols, 'Advertising and the Klondike,' *Washington Historical Quarterly* 13, no. 1 (1922): 20-6.
16. Dianne Newell, 'The Importance of Information and Misinformation in the Making of the Klondike Gold Rush,' *JCS* 21, no. 4 (1986-7): 95-111.
17. William R. Hunt, *North of 53°* (New York: Macmillan Publishing Co., Inc., 1974), 58.
18. Wonders, *Alaska Highway Explorer*, 30.
19. Alfred Hulse Brooks, *Blazing Alaska's Trails* (Fairbanks: University of Alaska Press, 1973), 367.
20. Walter R. Hamilton, *The Yukon Story* (Vancouver: Mitchell Press), 7-8.
21. David Leonard, et al., *A Builder of the Northwest: The Life and Times of Richard Secord* (Edmonton: Richard Y. Secord, 1981), 60.
22. *EB*, 24 Jan. 1895.
23. Ibid., 19 March 1896.
24. Ibid., 25 Nov. 1895.
25. Zaslow, *Opening of the Canadian North*, 56.
26. *EB*, 17 Feb. 1896.
27. 'Minutes,' 27 Feb. 1897.
28. Gregory, *Athabasca Landing*, 40.
29. 'Minutes,' 27 Feb. 1897.
30. Gregory, *Athabasca Landing*, 64.
31. Ibid., 33.
32. The flat boat, really a large punt about 45 feet long, 8 feet wide at bottom, and 3 1/2 feet deep, could carry up to 10 tons of freight and was the cheapest of the three. It had the advantage of drawing

the least water, but the more expensive York boat was best on lakes where it could be sailed and it was considered the best general purpose boat. A full-sized York boat ordinarily could carry seven tons and had a crew of nine men. To cope with portages and a smaller crew, smaller, modified versions were constructed for the Klondikers. Still others preferred to use Peterborough canoes, locally costing $33 for a 15-foot model and $43 for an 18-foot (two men could handle the latter with 1,200-1,500 pounds of cargo). *EB*, 19 Aug. 1897.

33. Ibid., 5 Aug. 1897.
34. Ibid.
35. Ibid., 9 Aug. 1897.
36. Ibid., 12 Aug. 1897.
37. CEA, Letter Book of A.G. Randall, Edmonton Town Clerk, 7 Aug. 1897
38. *EB*, 30 Aug. 1897.
39. MacGregor, *Klondike Rush through Edmonton*, 39.
40. *EB*, 17 Feb. 1898.
41. MacGregor, *Klondike Rush through Edmonton*, 194.
42. *EB*, 9 Aug., 2 Sept. 1897.
43. Ibid., 14 Oct. 1897.
44. Ibid., 7 Oct. 1897.
45. *Alberta Plaindealer*, 12 Aug. 1897.
46. *EB*, 6 Sept. 1897.
47. Ibid., 14 Feb. 1898.
48. Ibid., 10 Feb. 1898.
49. 'Minutes,' 29 Dec. 1897.
50. *EB*, 19 Aug. 1897.
51. Ibid., 10 Feb. 1898.
52. Ibid., 3 March 1898.
53. Ibid., 16 Dec. 1897.
54. Ibid., 26 Aug. 1897.
55. J.W.G. MacEwan, 'Prairie Cattle to the Klondyke in the 90's,' *Canadian Cattlemen* 2, no. 1 (1939): 197, 200; and Anon., 'Suppliers of Beef to Dawson,' ibid., 3, no. 1 (1940): 373, 376.
56. Norman Lee, *Klondike Cattle Drive* (Vancouver: Mitchell Press, 1968).
57. MacGregor, *Klondike Rush through Edmonton*, 78.
58. *EB*, 14 Feb. 1898.
59. MacGregor, *Klondike Rush through Edmonton*, 221.
60. *EB*, 10 Nov. 1898.
61. Ibid., 19 Aug. 1897.
62. Ibid., 23 May 1898.
63. Ibid., 4 July 1898.
64. Ibid., 4 Aug. 1898.
65. Ibid., 10 Feb. 1898.
66. Ibid., 3 March 1898.
67. Ibid., 10 Feb. 1898.
68. Weir, *Back Door to the Klondike*.
69. *EB*, 30 Aug. 1897.
70. Ibid., 16 Dec. 1897, 23 June 1898.
71. MacGregor, *Klondike Rush through Edmonton*, 73.
72. 'Minutes,' 22 March 1898; and *EB*, 24 March, 18 April, 7 July 1898.
73. Gregory, *Athabasca Landing*, 82.
74. *EB*, 12 Sept. 1898.
75. Ibid., 15 Aug. 1898.

76. Ibid., 14 Oct. 1897.
77. Ibid., 8 Sept. 1898.
78. Frank Walker, 'Overland Trail to the Klondike,' *AHR* 7, no. 1 (1959): 2.
79. *EB*, 21 July 1898.
80. Wonders, *Alaska Highway Explorer*, 22-5.
81. Letter Book of A.G. Randall, 2 Sept. 1898.
82. MacGregor, *Klondike Rush through Edmonton*, 235.
83. Ibid., 1.
84. *EB*, 16 Dec. 1897.
85. Ibid., 4 Nov. 1897.
86. Hunt, *North of 53°*, 73.
87. William R. Morrison, *Showing the Flag* (Vancouver: University of British Columbia Press, 1985), 38-9.
88. Pierre Berton, *The Klondike Fever* (New York: Alfred A. Knopf, 1958), 231.
89. *EB*, 18 July 1898.
90. Coates and Morrison, *Land of the Midnight Sun*, 87.
91. 'Minutes,' 19 April 1898.
92. Ibid., 9 March 1898.

℃ R.G. MOYLES, COURTING SALLY ANN

1. Quoted in Robert Sandall, *The History of the Salvation Army*, vol. 2 (London, 1950), 1.
2. For a history of the Salvation Army's social work see Jenty Fairbank, *Booth's Boots: Social Service Beginnings in the Salvation Army* (London: The Salvation Army, 1983).
3. *Illustrated English Social History*, vol. 4 (Harmonsworth: Penguin, 1970), 109.
4. Booth's Darkest England Scheme with its book-length treatise, *In Darkest England and the Way Out*, is perhaps the better known of these two social experiments. Amid much controversy, it raised the money and paved the way for many of Booth's social schemes, including overseas farm colonies. The Maiden Tribute Affair, some years earlier, was an attempt to make the British Parliament raise the age of consent and thereby curb the white slave trade in which young girls were sold for sexual pleasure. A famous trial ensued in which some of the people involved in the agitation were sent to jail, though their efforts were successful in at least getting parliamentary action. See Charles Terrot, *The Maiden Tribute: A Study of the White Slave Traffic of the Nineteenth Century* (London: Muller, 1959).
5. John Gilpin, *Edmonton: Gateway to the North, An Illustrated History* (Edmonton: Windsor Publications and Amisk Waskahegan Chapter, Historical Society of Alberta, 1984), ch. 3.
6. Arnold Brown, *What Hath God Wrought?* (Toronto: Salvation Army, 1952), 31. For an overview of the Salvation Army

in Canada see R.G. Moyles, *The Blood and Fire in Canada* (Toronto: Peter Martin Associates, 1977).
7. This aspect of the Army's ministry—too complex to deal with in this chapter—has, of late, received deserved attention in such excellent articles as Lynne Marks's 'The "Hallelujah Lasses": Working-Class Women in the Salvation Army in English Canada, 1882-92,' in Franca Iacovetta amd Mariane Valverde, eds., *Gender Conflict: New Essays in Women's History* (Toronto: University of Toronto Press, 1992), 67-117.
8. *EB*, 25 Oct. 1894.
9. Ibid., 27 March 1894.
10. *EJ*, 26 April 1913.
11. Ibid.

℃ PÁDRAIG Ó SIADHAIL, KATHERINE HUGHES, IRISH POLITICAL ACTIVIST

1. For examples of biographical sketches of Hughes see Henry James Morgan, ed., *Canadian Men and Women of the Time*, 2d ed. (Toronto: William Briggs, 1912), 556-7; B. M. Green, ed., *Who's Who and Why 1921* (Toronto: International Press, n.d.), 598; *Canadian Who's Who* (London: The Times, 1910), 111; and W. Stewart Wallace, ed., *Macmillan Dictionary of Canadian Biography*, 4th ed., revised and updated by W.A. MacKay (Toronto: Macmillan of Canada, 1978), 372.
2. Quoted by Richard Davis in 'Irish Nationalism in Manitoba, 1870-1922' in Robert O'Driscoll and Lorna Reynolds, eds., *The Untold Story: The Irish in Canada*, vol. 1 (Toronto: Celtic Arts of Canada, 1988), 405.
3. National Library of Ireland, Dublin, 'Proceedings, Fifth Annual National Convention, American Association for the Recognition of the Irish Republic,' Terrace Garden, New York City, 18-19 July 1925, 41 (carbon copy of typescript).
4. *EB*, 27 April 1925.
5. *SN*, 20 Sept. 1913, 33.
6. Isabel Bassett, *The Parlour Rebellion. Profiles in the Struggle for Women's Rights* (Toronto: McClelland and Stewart, 1975), 158; and Carol Bacchi, 'Divided Loyalties: The Response of Farm and Labour Women to Suffrage,' in Linda Kealey, ed., *A Not Unreasonable Claim: Women and Reform in Canada, 1880s-1920s* (Toronto: Women's Press, 1979), 90.
7. While Hughes never stated why she opposed suffrage, it is worth noting that one source declares that interest in suffrage in Nova Scotia waned after 1895 'in the midst of a wave of anti-feminist propaganda, much of it emanating from the Roman Catholic archbishop

of Halifax [i.e., Hughes's uncle, Archbishop O'Brien]'; Alison Prentice et al., *Canadian Women: A History* (Toronto: Harcourt Brace Jovanovich, 1988), 186.

8. *1880 Illustrated Historical Atlas of the Province of Prince Edward Island* (Philadelphia: Meacham & Co., 1880).

9. Lauretta Hughes's career was as colourful as that of her sister. Having served as a nursing sister during the Spanish-American War of 1898, she became superintendent in the Ottawa General Hospital in 1899. Married in Oct. 1903 to Robert H. Kneil, an American businessman, Lauretta later was the first factories inspector in Alberta in 1917, worked on a federal government survey of women immigrants, and became the first organizing secretary of the Catholic Women's League of Canada in 1920. It was in her residence, a tenement dwelling at 2240 Grand Concourse, the Bronx, that Katherine died in 1925. Details of Lauretta's career are taken from an undated *curriculum vitae*, 'Short résumé of some former activities,' in NAC, Katherine Hughes Papers (KHP), vol. 4, file 21. As a founder and the first national secretary of the Catholic Women's League of Canada, Lauretta engaged in an organizational tour from Prince Edward Island to British Columbia that remarkably mirrored her sister's feats that same summer. It is noteworthy, however, that after Katherine's death, the *Irish World* of New York carried a report, quoting a New York clergyman as saying: 'There was a storm of objection against this lady [Hughes Kneil] being engaged on so important a work while her sister, Miss Hughes, was sowing the seeds of sedition throughout the Dominion' (18 July 1925).

10. *Ottawa Evening Journal*, 1 Aug. 1927.

11. *Island Guardian* (Charlottetown), 16 June 1892.

12. *Canadian Magazine of Politics, Science, Art and Literature*, Jan. 1918, 271.

13. NAC, Indian Affairs Letterbook, C-8448, Secretary, Indian Affairs, to Katherine Hughes, Ottawa, 6 July 1899.

14. 'More To Be Desired Than Gold,' *Catholic World* (New York), April 1897, 1-10; 'A New Year's Tale of the North,' ibid., Jan. 1900, 481-92; and 'The Member from Senarake,' *Prince Edward Island Magazine*, Aug. 1903, 200-207, Sept./Oct. 1903, 242-8.

15. KHP, vol. 4, file 19, 'Powerful Encouragement from High Ecclesiastical Dignitaries, Prominent Clergymen and representatives of the laity given to The Catholic Indian Association as may be seen from the following abstracts.'

16. Ibid., vol. 1, file 2, Lord Strathcona, London, to Miss Catherine [sic]

Hughes, Indian Reserve, St. Régis, Quebec, 25 March 1902.

17. Ibid., Father Francis J. (?) Schaefer, Secretary, Apostolic Delegation, Ottawa, to Hughes, 1 Sept. 1902.

18. Morgan, *Canadian Men and Women of the Time*, 556-7.

19. Katherine Hughes, *Archbishop O'Brien: Man and Churchman* (Ottawa: Rolla L. Crain Company, 1906), 13.

20. Barbara M. Freeman, *Kit's Kingdom: The Journalism of Kathleen Blake Coleman* (Ottawa: Carleton University Press, 1989), 138. There is some discrepancy about the number of women journalists on this trip as other accounts mention 13. See also 'Canada Women's Press Club,' *Western British America*, 25 June 1904.

21. Katherine described herself as a charter member of the CWPC in her 'Historian's Report' delivered at the June 1913 convention in Edmonton; *Canadian Women's Press Club: Triennial Report for 1910-1913* (Toronto: Bryant Press, n.d.), 14. A copy of this report to be found in NAC, Media Club of Canada Papers, vol. 46, file 8. For Hughes's appointment as recording secretary see *Winnipeg Telegram*, 9 June 1906. This account describes Katherine as representing the *Ottawa Citizen* while another account calls her a 'Syndicate Writer' (*Manitoba Free Press*, 9 June 1902). These suggest that Hughes may have left the *Montreal Star* by this stage, which may well explain her willingness to move to Edmonton.

22. *Winnipeg Telegram*, 11 June 1906.

23. Ibid. Although one party of journalists visited Edmonton, Katherine did not travel with that group (*EB*, 12 June 1906).

24. Ibid., 3 Nov. 1906. The *Bulletin* stated that Katherine was to spend 'the next year or two' in Edmonton.

25. 'Travel and Talk,' *SN*, 20 Sept. 1913, 33.

26. *EB*, 29 May 1908.

27. *Canadian Who's Who*, 111.

28. PAA, O.C. 325/08, 11 June 1908. Although the salary was backdated to 26 May 1908, Katherine would edit the Christmas 1908 number of the *Bulletin*.

29. *EB*, 29 May 1908.

30. For copies of the letter dated 21 Sept. 1908 see PAA, Katherine Hughes Papers (KHP), 74.340/81.

31. Ibid., 'Preliminary Report in connection with the recently established Bureau of Archives for the Province of Alberta, submitted to The Honourable Alexander C. Rutherford, L.L.D., Premier of Alberta, by Katherine Hughes, Provincial Archivist, Edmonton, February 15, 1909.'

32. For examples of Hughes's work see ibid., file 12, 'Memoirs of John Francis Grant, One of Edmonton's Old Timers'; 'John

Norris, Pioneer,' *AHR* 9, no. 4 (1961): 10-13; and 'The Last Great Roundup,' *AHR* 11, no. 2 (1963): 1-7. This article was published originally in the *EB* on 22 June 1907.

33. Katherine Hughes, *Father Lacombe, The Black-Robe Voyageur* (Toronto: William Briggs, 1911), 439.

34. Hughes's letters to Lacombe close with Katherine using an indecipherable Indian pet name. See PAA, Albert Lacombe Papers, 71. 220, file 6548, Correspondence, Letters received, 1908-1909.

35. *Canadian Magazine*, Jan. 1918, 271-2; and *SN*, 20 Sept. 1913. Katherine compiled an account ('Notes of a Trip made into the Northern Half of Alberta in the summer of 1909—the journey comprising a tour of the Peace River and Athabasca Districts') based on notes she had made during part of this trip. PAA/KHP, file 83 (which covers the period until 2 July 1909); and PAA, 74.1, file 32-5 (3 July–28 Aug. 1909).

36. *Canadian Women's Press Club Annual Report for 1909-1910* (Toronto: Bryant Press, n.d.), 4, in Media Club of Canada Papers, vol. 46, file 7.

37. Susan Jackel, 'First Days, Fighting Days: Prairie Presswomen and Suffrage Activism, 1906-1916,' in Mary Kinnear, ed., *First Days, Fighting Days: Women in Manitoba History* (Regina: Canadian Plains Research Center, 1987), 68. See also occasional references to Hughes in the PAA, 78.32, Papers of the Women's Canadian Club of Edmonton.

38. *Saint John Globe*, 12 July 1920.

39. Lacombe Papers, file 6548, Hughes to Lacombe, 26 April [1909?].

40. For examples of reviews see *New York Times*, 31 Dec. 1911; and *Book Review Digest* (Minneapolis: H. W. Wilson Company, 1912), 229. Hughes's biography of Lacombe was well received by the Catholic establishment as well (GAI, M2685, 'A Letter From The Most Reverend John Ireland, Archbishop of St. Paul to Miss Katherine Hughes . . .,' 7 April 1911). French and German translations of *Father Lacombe, The Black-Robe Voyageur* were subsequently published. In 1920 McClelland and Stewart published a new Canadian edition of the book, with an additional chapter, penned by Hughes, covering the final years of an extraordinary life.

41. Lacombe Papers, file 6548, Hughes to Lacombe, 6 July [1909?].

42. The spiritual fate of the Ruthenians, approximately 170,000 of whom had recently arrived in Canada, posed a major challenge for the 'Church militant' (George Thomas Daly, *Catholic Problems in Western Canada* [Toronto: Macmillan Company of Canada, 1921], 75-6).

43. 'A Short History of the Catholic Women's League in Alberta and the Northwest Territories,' unsigned and undated notes made available to the author by Valerie J. Fall, Executive Director, the Catholic Women's League of Canada, Winnipeg; and 'Early Memories of the Catholic Women's League of Edmonton,' text prepared by Katherine Hughes for the National Convention of the Catholic Women's League of Canada in Edmonton, July 1924 (copy provided to the author by Fall).

44. As regards Hughes's relationship with the Press Club, she seems to have withdrawn from active participation in its activities by 1913. Even though the Edmonton branch hosted the 1913 Convention of the CWPC, she appears not to have figured prominently in either the preparations or the events associated with it, although she did read the 'Historian's Report.' Her name is not to be found in subsequent membership lists of the CWPC. Her involvement with the Club was not mentioned in Miriam Green Ellis's pamphlet, *Pathfinders* (Np.: Canadian Women's Press Club, n.p.,. n.d.) or in Effie Laurie Storer's typescript, 'Charter Members of C.W.P.C. Whom I have known' (copies of these documents in Media Club of Canada Papers, vol. 11, files 28 and 16). One can speculate that Hughes's strong stand against suffrage in 1913 or in favour of Irish political independence may have contributed to her neglect by chroniclers of the CWPC.

45. This was Katherine's description of the relationship between the Edmonton League and the national organization ('Early Memories of the Catholic Women's League of Edmonton').

46. KHP, vol. 1, file 2, Paul A. von Aueberg to Hughes, 1 May 1913, von Aueberg to Hughes, 25 Oct. 1912.

47. Quoted in Morgan, *Canadian Men and Women of the Time*, 557.

48. J. Castell Hopkins, ed., *Canadian Annual Review of Public Affairs 1913* (Toronto: Annual Review Publishing Company, 1914), 625. The official government order transferring Hughes to the Office of the Agent General for Alberta in London stipulated a salary of $1,500 per annum, to date from 1 Sept. 1913 (PAA, O.C. 759/13, 8 Aug. 1913).

49. In Philadelphia in Feb. 1919 at the Irish Race Convention Hughes is quoted as stating: 'For we are here not to talk, but to practice the Sinn Fein doctrines of self-sacrifice and unceasing activity, to pledge ourselves before the Living God to stand by and support the people of Ireland until they have attained their full freedom'; *Gaelic American* (New York), 15 March 1919.

50. Ibid., 1 June 1918.

51. Lacombe Papers, file 6549, Hughes to Lacombe, 6 Aug. [1914].

52. Caitlín Ní Aodha [= Katherine Hughes], 'How the Wild Geese can Help,' *Saothar na hÉireann* (Being an Occasional Bi-lingual Magazine, published by the Gaelic League of London, and containing the Programme and full particulars of the Aonach, 1914. The Twelfth Annual Irish Industrial Exhibition Held at the Royal Horticultural Hall, London, November 7th to 14th [1914]), 24-5.

53. NAC, Roderick MacFarlane Papers, vol. 1, 2213-4, Hughes to Roderick MacFarlane, 13 May [1914]. She stated: 'Politics have been interesting here this year. I of course am a Home Ruler, but quite looking away from that issue it seems to me that England is passing through a bloodless revolution—a contest between the democratic forces of the Twentieth Century and the remaining grip of earlier limited rule and aristocratic privilege.'

54. *Gaelic American*, 1 June 1918.

55. *Dramatic Compositions Copyrighted in the United States 1870 to 1916*, vol. 2 (Washington: Government Printing Office, 1918).

56. Lacombe Papers, file 6549, Hughes to Lacombe, 6 Aug. [1914].

57. KHP, vol. 1, file 2, Van Horne to Hughes, 15 Dec. 1911; and Lacombe Papers, file 6549, Van Horne to Lacombe, 28 Dec. 1911.

58. KHP, vol. 1, file 2, Hughes to Van Horne, 17 Aug. 1915, Hughes to Van Horne, 20 Aug. 1915.

59. Ibid., Van Horne to Hughes, 19 Sept. 1915.

60. New York Public Library, Joseph Cyrillus Walsh Papers, Letters, box 1, Hughes to Joseph Cyrillus Walsh, 31 Oct. [1916].

61. Katherine Hughes, *Ireland* (Kingston: Canadian Freeman, 1917).

62. SN, 30 March 1918, 22.

63. *Gaelic American*, 1 June 1918; and *Irish Press* (Philadelphia), 25 May 1918.

64. American Irish Historical Society, New York, Daniel F. Cohalan Papers, Correspondence: Katherine Hughes File, Hughes to Judge Daniel F. Cohalan, 10 June 1919.

65. *Gaelic American*, 21 Dec. 1918.

66. Katherine Hughes, *English Atrocities in Ireland* (New York: Friends of Irish Freedom, Inc., n.d.).

67. *Gaelic American*, 12 July 1919.

68. Cohalan Papers, Hughes to Cohalan, 14 May 1920.

69. *Morning Leader* (Regina), 4 Aug. 1920.

70. CH, 10 Aug. 1920.

71. Ibid., 4 Aug. 1920.

72. NAC, Arthur Sifton Papers, vol. 9, Royal Canadian Mounted Police, 'Memorandum,' 26 Aug. 1920. Irish activists in Canada were aware that the Criminal Investigation Bureau of the RCMP was monitoring their activities. See *Irish Press*, 13 Aug. 1921. Agent Bell, who apparently committed suicide, allegedly had been spying on the Self-Determination for Ireland League in Vancouver on behalf of the CIB.

73. See reports on 'Sinn Fein' and 'Sinn Fein Movement' in NAC, RG 24, vol. 4471, file 20-1-43, Department of National Defence, Military District No. 4; and occasional references to League and League members in file 20-1-44, 'Bolsheviki & O.B.U. Movement.'

74. *EB*, 16 Aug. 1920.

75. Ibid., 17 Aug. 1920.

76. Archives of the Catholic Archdiocese of Edmonton, Archbishop Henry J. O'Leary Papers, Correspondence, undated anonymous hand-written letter.

77. *Ottawa Morning Journal*, 18 Oct. 1920.

78. KHP, vol. 1, file 2, Hughes to R. B. Van Horne, 4 Nov. 1920.

79. Ibid., draft of letter from Hughes to Mr Walsh, Attorney, 4 Nov. 1920.

80. Ibid., vol. 2, file 9, 'My understanding of the arrangement with Sir William Van Horne.'

81. Walter Vaughan, *Life and Work of Sir William Van Horne* (New York: Century Co., 1920), vi; and KHP, vol. 2, file 9, 'My understanding of the arrangement with Sir William Van Horne.'

82. A copy of her draft of the biography can be found in KHP, vol. 2.

83. *The Advocate* (Melbourne), 24 Feb. 1921.

84. Ibid., 3 March 1921.

85. Ibid., 5 Jan. 1922.

86. *New Zealand Tablet*, 12 May 1921.

87. Richard P. Davis, *Irish Issues in New Zealand Politics 1868-1922* (Dunedin: University of Otago Press, 1974), 202.

88. For background see Richard Davis, ' The Self-Determination for Ireland Leagues and the Irish Race Convention in Paris, 1921-22,' in *Tasmanian Historical Research Association: Papers and Proceedings* 24, no. 3 (1977): 91; and *Imtheachta Aonaighe na n-Gaedheal ib-Páris, Eanair, 1922. Proceedings of the Irish Race Congress in Paris, January 1922* (Dublin: Fine Ghaedheal Central Secretariat, n.d.).

89. Most biographical sketches note that Hughes died on 27 April 1925. Date of death on the Certificate of Death issued by the Bureau of Records of the Department of Health of the City of New York is given as 26 April 1925 at 7:15 p.m. Copy of Certificate provided to the author by Peter R. Hughes, Ottawa.

90. *Irish World*, 9 May 1925.

91. *Catholic Bulletin* (Dublin), Oct. 1925.

92. *EB*, 27 April 1925.

93. Quoted by Christopher Lasch in *The New Radicalism in America (1889-1963)* (New York: Vintage Books, 1967), 8.

JARS BALAN,
UKRAINIAN THEATRE: SHOWTIME
ON THE NORTH SASKATCHEWAN

1. In a letter to the editor published in an Edmonton newspaper sometime in the 1930s, Gowda identified himself as the 'First Ukrainian Citizen in Edmonton, Alta., May 18, '98'(PAA, Michael Gowda Papers [MGP], undated clipping). For an early biographical sketch see *Ukrains'kyi holos*, 20 Aug. 1924.

2. The exact origins of Edmonton's first *chytalnia* are a matter of some debate. In 'Svidok velykykh zmin i postupy,' *Ukrains'kyi pioner* 3, no. 6 (1958): 13, Tom Tomashevsky (a pioneer member) indicates that the association obtained its library from the failed Taras Shevchenko Reading Society of Beaver Creek, which disbanded sometime after summer 1901. Gowda arranged to have its books (which most likely included playscripts) transferred to the recently-purchased home of Ivan (John) Kiliar just east of the corner of 96 Street and 101A Avenue. It was there that in the autumn Gowda and a fellow immigrant, Ivan Letavsky, established an Edmonton *chytalnia*, also called Taras Shevchenko. In *Recollections about the Life of Ukrainian Settlers in Canada*, trans. Louis T. Laychuk (Edmonton: Canadian Institute of Ukrainian Studies, 1981), 81-2, William Czumer claims that the society came into existence in 1903 and suggests that there were different opinions as to who initiated it. Since Czumer emigrated to Canada in 1904 and lived in Manitoba for nine years before taking a teaching position in Alberta, his account was obviously based on second-hand sources rather than personal experience. Tomashewsky had emigrated to Edmonton as a sixteen-year-old in 1900, moving the following year with his parents to a homestead near Chipman.

3. The only reference to the production is Czumer, *Recollections*, 82; Czumer likely got his information from Gowda, who was still alive when the Ukrainian edition of Czumer's memoirs (*Spomyny*) was published in 1942. Tomashevsky, 'Svidok,' 13, was describing the character of Edmonton's Ukrainian population at the founding of the Taras Shevchenko Chytalnia.

4. The only information about the 1909 Edmonton production is a photograph in Mykhailo Marunchak, *Istoriia ukraintsiv Kanady*, vol. 1 (Winnipeg: Ukrainian Free Academy of Sciences, 1968), 395, 430. Confusingly, in Michael Marunchak, *The Ukrainian Canadians: A History* (Winnipeg and Ottawa: Ukrainian Free Academy of Sciences, 1970), 197, the same picture is captioned, 'Actors of the Drama Group of Vegreville after staging "Natalka

Poltavka" in Edmonton, 1909.' It is highly unlikely that the performers were from Vegreville, where the first documented theatrical presentation took place on 28 Feb. 1910, when the Young Ruthenian Club put on Sigmund Bychinsky's moralistic drama, *V starim i novim kraiu* (In the old and the new country) (*VO*, 23 Feb., 2 March 1910). None of the players identified in the 2 March article correspond to the actors in *Natalka Poltavka*. Furthermore, there is no record of *Natalka Poltavka* having been mounted in 1909 anywhere in rural Alberta.

5. Mykhailo Khom'iak, ed., *Propamiatna knyha—Ukrains'kyi narodnyi dim* (Edmonton: Ukrainian Catholic Council-Ukrainian National Home, [1966]), 52. Research by Orest Martynowych identifies these plays as *Znimchenyi Yurko* (Germanized George) by Ivan Naumovych, *Seme ne krady* by Hieronim Ya. Lutsyk, and *Hostyna Sviatoho Nykolaia* (The visit by Saint Nicholas) by E. Kalytovsky.

6. The birth of Ukrainian theatre in Vegreville was especially remarkable because all the plays staged between 1910 and 1912 were written by immigrant authors.

7. MGP, unidentified clipping. Although the article was published the day after the event, it does not appear in the existing microfilm of either the *Edmonton Journal* (late edition) or the *Edmonton Bulletin* (morning edition); judging from the layout and type, the article was probably published in the *Bulletin*.

8. *Novyny*, 4 Nov. 1913.

9. Undeterred by this scandal, Boian staged a repeat performance of the play eleven days later, with the proceeds once again earmarked for the National Home; *Novyny*, 13 Nov. 1913.

10. *Russkii golos*, 6/19 June 1913. Little is known about Vasyl Dmytrenko other than that he was a nineteenth-century actor and author of several one-act plays. *Kum-miroshnyk, abo satana v bochtsi* was first staged in 1850 from a manuscript and first published in Kiev in 1884.

11. See *Russkii golos*, 26 June, 5 July 1913; and *VO*, 16 July 1913. The second play put on by the group was *Itsko svat* (Izzy the matchmaker) by Isydor Trembitsky; it was likely also performed at some time in Edmonton, although to date there is no documented proof.

12. *Novyny*, 27 Dec. 1913.

13. Ibid., 13 June 1913.

14. See the cryptic and cynical remarks by Vasyl' Kushnir of Edmonton in *Robochyi narod*, 29 Jan. 1913; the group is not named.

15. *Kanadyiets'*, 15 Oct. 1913.

16. Khom'iak, *Propamiatna knyha*, 52. The other plays were *Nevol'nyk* (The cap-

tive) by Marko Kropyvnytsky, on 11 June; *Pidhiriany* (The people of the Piedmont), also by Kropyvnytsky, with music by Mykhailo Verbytsky, on 25 July; and *Kara sovisty* (Punishment of the conscience) by Hryhorii Tsehlynsky, on 4 Oct. The last play was presented at the Separate School Hall before more than three hundred people at a reception honouring Bishop Budka.

17. One actor, with the mysterious initials N.N., had dual roles; *Novyny*, 6 Jan. 1914. Bodrug wrote the play in 1909 while working as a minister in Newark, New Jersey; three Canadian editions were eventually published, and between 1910 and 1954 it was staged more than fifty times in Ukrainian communities across the country.

18. See ibid., 5, 15, 17, 22 Dec. 1914. Unlike some plays in the pioneer repertoire (including Bodrug's *Ubiinyky*), *Zhydivka vykhrestka* portrayed Jews sympathetically while showing many peasant Ukrainians to be ignorant and prejudiced. The Franko group's other productions were Boris Hrinchenko's Cossack-era drama, *Stepovyi hist'* (The visitor from the steppes), on 17 Jan., and *Ukradene shchastia* (Stolen happiness) by Ivan Franko, on 28 April.

19. *Novyny*, 26 March, 22 Dec. 1914.

20. I.K. Dorosh was the pen name of Ivan Kvasniak, a talented and energetic pioneer-era theatre activist.

21. See *EJ*, 1, 2, 6 Jan. 1915.

22. Ibid., 5 Jan. 1915.

23. Ibid.

24. A repeat performance of *Oi, ne khody, Hrytsiu!* was also staged at this venue on 9 Jan. 1915.

25. *Novyny*, 9 Jan. 1915.

26. *Russkii golos*, 11 Jan. 1915.

27. Presented at the Separate School Hall on 20 Feb. 1915. Other documented Boian shows in 1915 included a re-mount of *Kara sovisty* on 28 Jan.; *Uchetyl'* (The teacher) by Ivan Franko, on 20 April; and *Pravda vse horoiu* (The truth is always distressing), on 2 Oct.

28. The only documented performance attributable to the Franko players was Kropyvnytsky's adaptation of Shevchenko's *Nazar Stodolia*, staged on 16 Jan. 1915. However, given the collapse of *Novyny* in the middle of the year, information on Ukrainian theatre becomes extremely limited.

29. In 1907 Strutynski briefly visited Manitoba on behalf of Soter Ortynski, the newly-appointed Greek Catholic bishop for the United States. However, when he began urging local Catholics to retain ownership of their church property and to petition Rome for Ortynski's jurisdiction to be extended to Canada, he was swiftly recalled; see Orest Martynowych, *Ukrainians in Canada: The Formative Period, 1891-*

1924 (Edmonton: Canadian Institute of Ukrainian Studies Press, 1991), 201, 295-6.

30. See *Almanakh Tovarystva ukrains'kyi robitnycho-farmers'kyi dim v Kanadi i bratnikh orhanizatsii, 1918-1929* (Winnipeg: Labour-Farmer Publishing Association, 1930), 187.

31. Korzeniowski's 1843 Polish-language drama, *Karpaccy gorale* (Carpathian highlanders), underwent several renderings into Ukrainian. The one most likely used for the Edmonton production was V. Derzhyruka's 1909 translation.

32. Hrinchenko's work was completed in 1897, Nykolyshyn's in 1911.

33. The only documented performances were of *Bludnyi syn* (Prodigal son) by Sydir Vorobkevych, on 17 Feb., and *Lykholittia* (Troubled times) by Hnat Khodkevych, on 30 Nov.

34. The former staged Kvitka-Osnovianenko's *Shchyra liubov* (True love) in Feb., the latter Ivan Tobilevych's *Martyn Borulia* (Martin Borulia) in March.

35. These plays included two performances of S. Makar's *Amerykans'kyi shliakhtych* (The American lord), and one each of David Edelstadt's *Amerykans'kyi robitnyk* (The American worker), Trembitsky's *Itsko svat*, and *Striliai na smert* (Shoot to kill) by an unknown author.

36. See Khom'iak, *Propamiatna knyha*, 67.

CHRISTOPHER SPENCER, THE SQUIRE OF SYLVANCROFT

1. Peggy O'Connor Farnell, *Old Glenora* (Edmonton: Old Glenora Historical Society, 1984), 17.

2. Lines, a local architect who died during the First World War, was responsible for the Edwardian design of several homes in the Glenora district.

3. Farnell, *Old Glenora*, 31.

4. Sylvia Evans, interview with the author, 21 Sept. 1994.

5. Ibid.

6. In the 1960s at his wife's request, H.M.E. Evans wrote a brief history of his early life. A copy of the history, mainly a list of the famous people he had encountered (including Sir John A. Macdonald and Sir Winston Churchill), has been retained in a family scrapbook.

7. 'Harry Marshall Erskine Evans,' in *Alberta, Past and Present*, vol. 3 (Chicago: Pioneer Historical Publishing Company, 1924), 21.

8. Tony Cashman, *The Edmonton Story* (Edmonton: Institute of Applied Art, 1956), 156.

9. James G. MacGregor, *Edmonton: A History* (Edmonton: Hurtig Publishers, 1967), 89.

10. Ibid., 178.

11. *EB*, 12 Sept. 1912.

12. Ibid., 13 Sept. 1912.

13. *EJ*, 8 June 1914.

14. *South Edmonton Sun*, 5 Oct. 1968. The article, 'Biography, H. M. E. Evans,' is taken from an unpublished essay written by Jenny Macleod.

15. CEA, H.M.E. Evans Special Collection, Class 3, Evans to Sir William Plender, 16 June 1914.

16. CEA, H.M.E. Evans Personal File, Evans to Sir Robert Nivison, 27 Nov. 1917.

17. John F. Gilpin, *Century of Enterprise* (Edmonton: Edmonton Chamber of Commerce, 1988), 62.

18. Virginia Byfield, 'As the boom becomes a bust Edmonton politics turn violent,' in Ted Byfield, ed., *Alberta in the Twentieth Century*, vol. 3, *The Boom and the Bust* (Edmonton: United Western Communications, 1994), 355.

19. *EB*, 28 Nov. 1917.

20. Ibid., 8 Dec. 1917.

21. Byfield, 'As the boom becomes a bust,' 351.

22. Ibid., 354.

23. Ibid., 351; included in this unwanted booty was the last home of Malcolm Groat.

24. David G. Bettison, John K. Kenward, and Larrie Taylor, *Urban Affairs in Alberta* (Edmonton: University of Alberta Press, 1975), 23.

25. *EJ*, 2 Feb. 1918.

26. Byfield, 'As the boom becomes a bust,' 354.

27. MacGregor, *Edmonton*, 224.

28. Byfield, 'As the boom becomes a bust,' 355.

29. Ibid.

30. Eric Hanson, *Local Government in Alberta* (Toronto: McClelland and Stewart, 1956), 34.

31. Evans, interview.

32. Cicely Louise Evans-Melson, interview with the author, 21 Sept. 1994.

33. Evans, interview; H.M.E. Evans contributed to the city's social life as chairman of the ground committee of the Edmonton Country Club in 1935 and as treasurer of Memorial Hall beginning in 1922.

34. Hanson, *Local Government*, 34.

35. Farnell, *Old Glenora*, 51.

36. *EJ*, 11 July 1940.

37. *Canadian Encyclopedia*, 2d ed., s.v. 'Victory Loans.'

38. *EJ*, 17 Aug. 1966.

39. Evans, interview.

40. *EJ*, 17. Aug. 1966.

BOB IRWIN, WHOSE RAILWAY WAS IT?

1. Lewis G. Thomas, *The Liberal Party in Alberta* (Toronto: University of Toronto Press, 1951); and Jay Heard, 'The Alberta and Great Waterways Railway Dispute, 1909-13' (MA thesis, University of Alberta, 1990).

2. *EJ*, 18 Nov. 1911.

3. *EB*, 28 April, 4 Jan. 1911.

4. Ibid., 24 Jan. 1911.

5. Morris Zaslow, 'Transportation and Development of the Mackenzie Basin, 1870-1921' (MA thesis, University of Toronto, 1948), 216-17.

6. *Canadian Finance*, 21 June 1911, cited in Morris Zaslow, *Opening of the Canadian North, 1870-1914* (Toronto: McClelland and Stewart, 1971), 214.

7. Zaslow, *Opening of the Canadian North*, 214. See also Patricia Roy, 'Railways, Politics, and the Development of the City of Vancouver as a Metropolitan Centre, 1886-1929' (MA thesis, University of Toronto, 1963), 169-84.

8. *Statutes of Canada*, 1907, ch. 85; and *Statutes of Alberta*, 1912, ch. 16.

9. *Statutes of Alberta*, 1912, ch. 19.

10. *Statutes of British Columbia*, 1912, ch. 34 and ch. 36.

11. John Williams, 'A History of the Edmonton Dunvegan and British Columbia, 1911-29' (MA thesis, University of Alberta, 1956), 32.

12. *Statutes of Alberta*, 1913, First Session, ch. 46; and ibid., 1913, Second Session, ch. 7.

13. Along the branch line between Rycroft and Grande Prairie, McArthur used no ballast at all and simply laid the ties and rails on the earthen grade.

14. GPH, 15 Aug., 3 Sept. 1918; and R.G. Moyles, ed., *Challenge of the Homestead: Peace River Letters of Clyde and Isabel Campbell* (Calgary: Historical Society of Alberta, 1988), 2.

15. PRR, 18 May 1920.

16. The Dominion government estimated McArthur made a $1,132,400 profit as contractor on the ED&BC. NAC, Dept. of Railways, RG 43, vol. 556, file 17773, part I, Alex Ferguson to Maj. G.A. Bell, 26 April 1920.

17. For all the charges made against McArthur see Williams, 'History of the Edmonton Dunvegan,' 61-2, 69, 80-7.

18. Ibid., 83-94; and Dept. of Railways, v. 555, file 17773, Alex Ferguson to W.A. Bowden, 1 Aug. 1919.

19. PRR, 28 Nov., 5, 12 Dec. 1919, 30 Jan., 4, 21 May, 4, 18 June 1920; and Williams, 'History of the Edmonton and Dunvegan,' 100.

20. GPH, 29 June 1920.

21. PRR, 10 Oct. 1919.

22. The estimate for maintenance was raised to $2,432,000 in 1920. Dept. of Railways, vol. 556, file 17773A, part 1, Alex Ferguson to Maj. G.A. Bell, 26 April 1920.

23. Stewart had become premier following Sifton's decision to join the Union government under Robert Borden in 1917.

24. *PRR*, 12 Sept. 1919, 28 July 1920; and Dept. of Railways, vol. 556, file 17773A, part 1, George Foster to McArthur, 24 Jan. 1920, McArthur to J.A. Calder, 10 Feb. 1920, McArthur to Calder, 27 Feb. 1920, Memo Maj. G.A. Bell to Minister, 2 March 1920.

25. *Statutes of Alberta*, 1920, ch. 56.

26. *EB*, 22 July 1920.

27. *PRR*, 15 Sept. 1920. See also *EJ*, 21 July 1920.

28. Alberta, *Annual Report of the Department of Railways, 1922*, 5-10.

29. PAA, Alta. Railways, 84.388, file 1100.101.1, Calculation of Profit accruing to the CPR in 1924.

30. PAA, Premiers' Papers (PP), 69.289, file 389, Report of J. Kennedy and C. Cartwright, 23 Aug. 1923.

31. His first request in 1915 resulted in an intermediate tariff (*PRR*, 10 June 1915). He then obtained higher rates in 1917 (Zaslow, 'Transportation and Development,' 67-9). He requested even higher rates in 1920 (*PRR*, 4 June, 16 July 1920).

32. Alta. Railways, file 1100.150.1, United Farmers of the Peace River Block to Alberta Government, 14 Feb. 1922, and 'Application to the Board of Railway Commissioners for reduced freight rates on the ED & BC and the CCR by Grande Prairie Board of Trade, 30 May 1923'; file 400, R.P. Butler (High Prairie Board of Trade) to A. Chard, 6 July 1932; NAC, Bennett Papers, 380299, George Slaney (Peace River Board of Trade) to Bennett, 13 July 1932; *PRR*, 2 April, 3 Sept. 1925, 17 March 1933; *GPH*, 8 June 1925; and Morris Zaslow, 'The Development of the Mackenzie, 1920-40' (PhD diss., University of Toronto, 1957), 68-70.

33. Dept. of Railways, vol. 534, file 16860, Lake Saskatoon Board of Trade to Arthur Meighen, 7 Jan. 1918; Alta. Railways, file 1100.102.1, Charles Stewart to E.W. Beatty, 22 April 1921; file 1100.61.1, Norman Soars to V.W. Smith, 12 Feb. 1924; file 200, V.W. Smith to Greenfield, 30 April 1923; PP, file 374A, Oliver to Greenfield, 27 Sept. 1922; file 388, H.A. Robson to Greenfield, 28 June 1923, R.B. Bennett to Greenfield, 4 July 1925, R.B. Bennett to Brownlee, 9 Jan. 1926; and *EJ*, 21 May 1926.

34. PABC, Premiers' Papers, GR 1222, box 248, file 4, J.G. Sullivan, 'Report on the Engineering and Economic Features of the Pacific Great Eastern Railway.'

35. Grande Prairie had suggested the Brulé route in 1915 (*GPH*, 5 Jan., 3 Feb. 1915). The first note in the CNR Files on the Peace River outlet is a memo dated 5 Feb. 1920 on the Hoppe Coal field. The first reference in Sir Henry Thornton's personal files is a memo dated 26 Feb. 1923 regarding the completion of the CNR line from Whitecourt to the Peace (NAC, CNR, RG 30, vol. 3059 and vol. 7327). For a survey of the coast outlet issue see Morris Zaslow, 'The Peace River Outlet,' in Carl Berger and Ramsay Cook, eds., *The West and The Nation* (Toronto: McClelland and Stewart, 1976), 273-99.

36. CNR, vol. 3059, Thornton to Graham, 18 April 1923.

37. Ibid., Norman Soars (Peace River Board of Trade) to Thornton, 16 March 1923; NAC, William Lyon Mackenzie King Papers (WLMK), MG26J1, vol. 104, 80802, J. Sutherland (Grande Prairie Liberal Assoc.) to King, 1 April 1923; vol. 92, 73008-9, Frank Matheson (Grande Prairie) to Robert Forke, 5 April 1923; vol. 89, 70936, Resolution of the Edmonton Board of Trade, 16 May 1923; and PP, file 376, Greenfield to King, 24 April 1923.

38. CNR, vol. 7337, Envelope 1, 'Report of E.M.M. Hill, Nov. 1923'; and vol. 3059, Gzowski to George Graham, 20 Dec. 1923.

39. PP, file 376, Greenfield to King, 24 April 1923; WLMK, vol. 100, 77778-82, John Oliver to King, 13 Feb. 1923; CNR, vol. 3059, N. Soars (Peace River Board of Trade) to Thornton, 14 March 1924, John Blue (Edmonton Board of Trade) to Thornton, 18 March 1924, R.J Cromie (editor of *VS*) to Thornton, 23 June 1924; and vol. 7327, H.F. Kellner (Edmonton City Council) to Thornton, 19 March 1924. See also *EB*, 23 June 1924.

40. The Beaverlodge farmers wrote the *PRR* 24 April, 30 Oct. 1924, and Thornton (CNR, vol. 3059). Their criticism was echoed in the towns of Peace River, Pouce Coupé, and Fort St. John. The *PRR* 2 Oct. 1924 front page editorial was especially important and provided a detailed critique of the project. It appears in PABC, Pattullo Papers, Add.MSS 3, box 17, file 2; and CNR, vol. 7377, envelope 2.

41. PAA, NAR, 86.587, file 265a, Memo to File, 8 Dec. 1938.

42. E.W. Beatty to Standing Committee on Railways Canals and Telegraphs, 17 Nov. 1932, cited in PP, file 370; and Zaslow, 'The Development of the Mackenzie Basin,' 88.

43. *PRR*, 17 May, 21 June, 6 Sept. 1923, 2 Oct., 27 Nov., 11 Dec. 1924.

44. PP, file 376, Premier's notes for statement made to conference; House of Commons, Debates, 306; *PRR*, 15 Jan. 1925; *VS*, 24 Feb. 1925; and Zaslow, 'Peace River Outlet,' 282.

45. CNR, vol. 7327, Memorandum to File regarding Meeting of CNR and CPR Engineers, 16 Jan. 1925; and NAR, file 265a, 'Report of Various Routes for a Western Outlet to the Pacific from the Peace River District,' 26 Feb. 1925. The Minister presented it to the House on 10 June 1926 (Canada, *Sessional Papers*, 1926, no. 237, 'Joint Report of engineers of the Canadian National Railways and the Canadian Pacific Railway regarding construction of a railway from the Peace River Country to the Pacific Coast').

46. CNR, vol. 3059, Thornton to Maj. G.A. Bell, 10 March 1925, Bureau of Economics to Thornton, 11 March 1925.

47. Williams, 'History of the Edmonton and Dunvegan,' 177-8.

48. Thornton sent two letters to Greenfield on the same day. In one he offered to lease the Dunvegan lines, and in the other he made it clear that he would build into the region if the CPR gained control of the ED&BC system. CNR, vol. 3059, Thornton to Greenfield, 4 Aug. 1925.

49. Dept. of Railways, vol. 556, file 17773A, part II, Brownlee to Dunning, 3, 6 May 1926, Thornton to Dunning, 11, 21 May 1926. The Provincial valuation of the line can be found in Alta. Railways, file 1100.101.1, Callaghan to Smith, 11 Sept. 1925.

50. Alta. Railways, file 1100.142.1, Agreement between the National Railways and Alberta Government, 11 Nov. 1926; and file 1100.103.3, Estimates of Profit to CNR. The CNR estimated their profits at $350,000. Dept. of Railways, vol. 556, file 17773A, part II, Dominion Bureau of Statistics to Dunning, 9 Nov. 1927, Hungerford to Maj. Bell, 9 Dec. 1927.

51. People in the northern districts supported the CPR. PP, file 376, E.L. Lamont (M.D. of Peace) to Greenfield, 15 April 1926, N. Soars (Peace River Board of Trade) to Greenfield, 6 Aug. 1925; and *PRR*, 19 March 1926. In the Grande Prairie district, the people backed the CNR. Alta. Railways, file 1100.150.1, L. Alward (Clairmont) to V. Smith, 7 Sept. 1925; CNR, vol. 3060, Anson Wager to Brownlee, 30 March 1926 (copy to Thornton), L.C. Porteous (Grande Prairie) to Thornton, 15 April 1926; and Dept. of Railways, vol. 556, file 17773A, part II, J. Thompson to Dunning, 15 April 1926.

52. PP, file 374A, Beatty to Greenfield, 22 Aug. 1925; file 395A, Beatty to Brownlee, 19 Oct. 1927; file 374B, Brownlee to Dunning, 12 Nov. 1927, Dunning to Brownlee, 12 Nov. 1927; and Canada, *Sessional Papers*, 1929, no. 226, Hungerford to Brownlee, 11 Nov. 1927, Brownlee to Dunning, 13 Nov. 1927.

53. *EJ*, 12 Nov. 1927.

54. PP, file 377B, P.R. Gauvreau to Brownlee, 22 Dec. 1927; file 374A, J.W. Sawyer to Brownlee, 4 Jan. 1928; file 374B, I.V. Macklin to Brownlee, 20

March 1928; CNR, vol. 3060, J.F. McMillan (Edmonton) to Chas. Stewart, 19 Dec. 1927 (copy to Thornton), Anson Wager to Thornton, 2 Jan. 1928; NAC, WLMK, vol. 172, 123802, J.F. McMillan to Dunning, 21 Dec. 1927; vol. 189, 134528, J.H. Sissons to King, 3 Jan. 1928; vol. 189, 134440-2, J.T. Shaw to Chas. Stewart, 10 Feb. 1928; and PRR, 30 Dec. 1927.

55. PAA, Hugh Allen Papers, 75.188, file 62, Anson Wager to Allen, 16 Feb. 1928, J. Floey (Buffalo Lakes) to Allen, 22 Feb. 1928; PP, file 374B, Edmonton Board of Trade to Brownlee, 15 Feb. 1928, J.E. Thompson (Grande Prairie Board of Trade) to Brownlee, 9 March 1928; EB, 29 March 1928; and PRR, 16 Nov. 1928.

56. PRR, 11 Nov., 23 Dec. 1927.

57. PP, file 374B, Brownlee to Thornton, 27 Dec. 1927.

58. Alta. Railways, file 1100.103.3, 'Offer to Purchase the ED & BC, 16 Jan. 1928'; and PP, file 395B, Thornton to Brownlee, 30 Jan. 1928.

59. EJ, 3, 6, 16 Feb., 3 March 1928.

60. PP, file 395B, Brownlee to Thornton and Beatty, 5 June 1928, V.W. Smith to Beatty, 13 June 1928, Smith to Thornton, 13 June 1928.

61. Alta. Railways, file 1100.103.3, Beatty to Brownlee, 17 Sept. 1928, Brownlee to Beatty, 19 Sept. 1928. Beatty had correctly assessed Thornton's reaction. He desired to build into the country after the CPR purchase but probably reassessed his position following an economic study that questioned this action. Canada, Sessional Papers, 1929, no. 278, Thornton to Dunning, 20 Sept. 1928; and CNR, vol. 7327, Bureau of Statistics to Hungerford, 20 Oct. 1928.

62. EJ, 22 Nov. 1928.

63. WLMK, vol. 180, 128928-33, Grande Prairie Liberal Association to King, 23 Nov. 1928; PP, file 395A, D.M. Kennedy (MP Peace River) to Brownlee, 2 March 1929; and Page Rideout in PRR, 15 Feb. 1929.

64. PP, file 395A, Office of the Provincial Auditor to Brownlee, 22 Sept. 1928.

ᦓ PAULINE PAUL AND JANET ROSS KERR, A PHILOSOPHY OF CARE: THE GREY NUNS OF MONTREAL

1. Edmonton Hôpital Historique, Archives des Soeurs Grises de Montréal, Edmonton (ASGME), doc. 6, Drs H.C. Wilson, H.L. McInnis, P.S. Royal, J.H. Tofield, J.D. Harrison, and E.A. Braithwaite to Bishop Grandin, 25 April 1894.

2. This chapter is based in large part on the work of Pauline Paul, 'A History of the Edmonton General Hospital, 1895-

1970: "Be faithful to the duties of your calling"' (PhD diss., University of Alberta, 1994).

3. Emile Legal, Règlements concernant couvents et hôpitaux. Extraits des règlements, usages, et disciplines de l'Archidiocèse d'Edmonton (Quebec: n.p., 1916), 10-11. Unless otherwise specified, all translations are by Pauline Paul.

4. ASGME, Edmonton General School of Nursing File (EGSN), Sister St Augustine, Première réunion des soeurs missionnaires dans nos hôpitaux de l'ouest, compte rendu des réunions de juillet 1917.

5. Alvine Cyr Gahagan, Yes Father, Pioneer Nursing in Alberta (Manchester NH: Hammer Publications, 1979), 72.

6. ASGME, Edmonton General Hospital (EGH), Nursing Procedures Manual (1957), ii.

7. See Vaticana, Canonizzazione Della Beata Marie Marguerite d'Youville (Rome: Tipographia Poliglotta, 1970), 7.

8. EB, 10 Jan. 1896.

9. Ibid., 30 Jan. 1899.

10. Ibid., 2 Feb. 1899. A French version of this article appeared in the weekly, L'Ouest Canadien, 6 Feb. 1899.

11. EB and L'Ouest Canadien, 9 Feb. 1899.

12. CEA, Edmonton Public Hospital Board (EPHB), minutes, 1899-1939, 1BT.E24h, meeting at the home of the Reverend H.A. Gray, 2 Feb. 1899.

13. ASGME, doc 4.

14. EPHB, 1BT.E24h.

15. EB, 10 April 1899.

16. Drs Tofield and Whitelaw also stayed. Although their religious affiliation is unknown, they were likely Catholics.

17. In 1898 the EGH was exempted from paying property taxes; see ASGME, 'Chroniques' (1897, 1900).

18. ASGME, Hôpital Edmonton visites canoniques, 1896-1953, canonical visit of Mother Filiatrault, 15 April 1901; and 'Chroniques,' 1901.

19. 'Chroniques,' 1901.

20. Ibid., 1897, enclosed letter from Mother Deschamps, Superior General, 17 June 1897.

21. Edmonton General Hospital, Annual Report (1913-67).

22. The hospital's annual income cited in its operating budget is a good indicator of the financial problems of the era. In 1925-6 the hospital's income was $196,933; in 1930-3 it was $115,879; and by 1935 it had been reduced to $90,071; similarly, the surplus represented by subtracting liabilities from assets dropped from $504,280 in 1931 to $202,343 in 1936 (ibid., 1925-6, 1930-1, 1935-6).

23. ASGME, doc. 101.

24. George Wherret, The Miracle of Empty Beds: A History of Tuberculosis in Canada (Toronto: Toronto University Press, 1977), 253.

25. ASGME, Département des tuberculeux 1932-1946, doc. 1, Sister Laberge, Superior of the EGH, to Dr M.R. Bow, Deputy Minister of Health, 1 March 1932; also ibid., doc. 3, Bow to Laberge, 19 April 1932.

26. 'Chroniques,' July 1936.

27. Ibid., July 1937.

28. Ibid., 11-13 Nov. 1943.

29. ASGME, Ecole des infirmières—registre des infirmières graduées, 1911-1973, School of Nursing Files.

30. Paul, 'History of the Edmonton General Hospital,' 251-354.

31. ASGME, Youville Memorial Hospital Files, sod turning and opening, 1978-82.

32. ASGME, Sisters Files; and ibid., Liste des Soeurs qui ont missionnées à l'Hôpital Général d'Edmonton.

33. Jean-Claude Dupont and Jacques Mathieu, Héritage de la francophonie canadienne, traditions orales (Sainte Foy: Presses de l'Université Laval, 1986), 26.

34. 'Chroniques,' 1895-1970.

35. Sister Fernande Champagne, SGM, ASGME archivist.

36. The 1830s were marked by political agitation in both Lower and Upper Canada, where men like Louis Joseph Papineau and William Lyon Mackenzie claimed that Britain should grant its North American colonies greater autonomy. Unrest peaked during the rebellions of 1837, which to some degree contributed to Confederation in 1867.

37. Edward S. Hart, Ambitions et Réalités, la Communauté Francophone d'Edmonton, trans. Guy Lacombe and Gratien Allaire (Edmonton: University of Alberta Press, 1981), 33. Later L'Association Canadienne Française de l'Alberta became more important; the Grey Nuns regularly attended the meetings of both associations ('Chroniques,' 1895-1988).

38. 'Chroniques,' 1915-28.

39. Ibid., 24 June 1928.

40. ASGME, Medical Executive Committee, minutes, 1933-70; 'Chroniques,' 1895-1970; and ASGME, Collective Bargaining Files.

41. These individuals were identified by surname (which might have excluded French women with non-French husbands); married women with French surnames were not included because their own nationality could not be determined. See ibid., Board of Directors Papers, 1969.

42. See ASGME, 'Chroniques,' correspondence, and other documents.

43. See Hart, Ambitions et Réalités, 45, 70, 80, 146. In 1995, 22,000 Edmontonians spoke French on a regular basis (personal communication with the Régionale d'Edmonton de l'Association Canadienne Française de l'Alberta);

probably a majority were Franco-Albertans.

44. See Robert Choquette, *Language and Religion: A History of English-French Conflict in Ontario* (Ottawa: University of Ottawa Press, 1975). Although focusing on the Ontario schools question, Choquette demonstrates the extent to which the problem assumed national proportions and how the Irish and French hierarchies of the Roman Catholic church competed for power.

45. Raymond Huel, 'Gestae Dei Per Franco: The French Canadian Experience in Western Canada,' in Benjamin Smillie, ed., *Visions of the New Jerusalem: Religious Settlement on the Prairies* (Edmonton: NeWest Press, 1983), 38-53; André Lalonde, 'Les Canadiens Français dans l'Ouest: Espoirs, Tragédies, Incertitudes,' in R. Louder and Eric Waddell, eds., *Du Continent Perdu à l'Archipel Retrouvé—le Québec et l'Amérique Française* (Sainte Foy: Presses de l'Université Laval), 92-3; and Robert Choquette, 'Problèmes de Moeurs et de Discipline Ecclésiastique: les Catholiques des Prairies Canadiennes de 1900 à 1930,' *SH* 8 (1950): 108-13.

46. See ASGME, EGH School of Nursing, Correspondence doc. 6, letter and petition of the Alumnae to the Provincial Superior, 3 March 1929; ibid., doc. 10, Sr Gallant to Archbishop O'Leary, 28 July 1929; and *EJ*, 27 Sept. 1929.

47. ASGME, doc. 119, Sr Duckett to the Assistant General of Montreal, 3 Oct. 1929.

48. *La Survivance*, 2 Oct. 1929.

49. ASGME, doc. 121, Reverends McGuigan, O'Neil, and Retchen to Mother Gallant, Provincial Superior, 28 Oct. 1929.

50. Ibid., doc. 122, Mother Dugas, Superior General, to Sister Gallant, Provincial Superior, 11 Nov. 1929; see also ibid., doc. 123, Decisions of the General Council.

51. PAA, Records of the Oblates of Mary Immaculate, 72.220/1132, Mother Gallant, Superior General, to Father Langlois, OMI Provincial Superior, 4 Nov. 1937.

52. Ibid., Father A. Boucher, OMI Provincial Superior, St Albert, to Mother Gallant, Superior General, 31 March 1945.

53. 'No one here tonight should be astonished by the fact that I chose to speak in French, the opposite would be strange, as the name of incorporation shows Les Soeurs de la Charité des Territoires du Nord Ouest is a French-Canadian accomplishment' (ASGME, doc. 252A, unpublished paper).

∞ SHARON RICHARDSON, **STAFFING THE HOSPITALS: EDMONTON'S NURSE TRAINING PROGRAMS**

This chapter is based on a larger program of research that is ongoing. The author would like to acknowledge funding received from the Alberta Foundation for Nursing Research, the Alberta Association of Registered Nurses, and the Hannah Institute for the History of Medicine.

1. Pauline Paul, 'A History of the Edmonton General Hospital, 1895-1970: "Be faithful to the duties of your calling"' (PhD diss., University of Alberta, 1994), 82.

2. Betty Wilson, *To Teach This Art: The History of the Schools of Nursing at the University of Alberta 1924-1974* (Edmonton: Hallamshire Publishers, 1977), 1-5.

3. CEA, MS 12, Edmonton Hospital Board Minutes, 1899-1939 (EHBM), box 1, 'Edmonton Hospital Association Minute Book, 18 Jan. 1910 - 30 Dec. 1926,' 8 May 1913.

4. Ibid., 'Edmonton Public Hospital Minute Book'; and Minutes of the Board of Directors of the Strathcona Hospital. For example, Miss Jessie Turnbull, first matron of the Edmonton Public Hospital, came to Edmonton from the Galt Hospital, to which she returned after one year as Lady Superintendent at the Edmonton Public.

5. Ibid., 'Edmonton Public Hospital Minute Book'; 'Edmonton Public Hospital Annual Report of the Board of Directors for the Year Ending Dec. 31, 1905'; Wilson, *To Teach This Art*, 7, 22 ; John Gilpin, *The Misericordia Hospital: 85 Years of Service in Edmonton* (Edmonton: Plains Publishing, 1986), 51; and Paul, 'History of the Edmonton General', 84, 295. The programs at the Misericordia, Royal Alexandra, and University of Alberta closed in June 1995. The Edmonton General program was transferred in 1968 to Collège Saint-Jean and then in 1972 to Grant MacEwan Community College, where it continues today as a two-year diploma program.

6. Little is known about the nature of hospital nurse training programs in Canada prior to the First World War. There has been no systematic analysis of the experiences of pupil nurses or of the work they performed. For example, John M. Gibbon and Mary S. Mathewson (*Three Centuries of Canadian Nursing* [Toronto: Macmillan Company, 1947]) provide a basic chronology of early Canadian nurse training programs, with minimal factual information on only three of the 70 schools in operation by 1909. Tony Cashman (*Heritage of Service: The*

History of Nursing in Alberta [Edmonton: Alberta Association of Registered Nurses, 1966]) gives a popular account of Alberta nurse training programs but is not factually accurate. Further complicating historical analysis of early Alberta programs, archival sources are minimal. For example, although eleven programs were begun in Alberta between 1894 and 1915, no individual student records currently exist, and only a fragmentary record of what was taught in two of these programs (Medicine Hat General and Calgary General) has survived. Minimal secondary data on the Medicine Hat program can be found in the Medicine Hat Museum and Art Gallery Archives, Medicine Hat General Hospital School of Nursing Collection. Some information about the Calgary General program can be gleaned from the Moody Family and the Calgary General Hospital School of Nursing collections in the GAI. There are no extant records detailing the pre-1918 nurse training programs of the Edmonton Public, Strathcona Municipal, Holy Cross (Calgary), Misericordia, Edmonton General, Galt, Lamont Public, and St Joseph's (Vegreville) hospitals. The evidence for this chapter has been culled from board of management meeting minutes and annual reports of the public hospitals. It is hoped that this chapter advances the analysis of Alberta's nurse training programs.

7. Christina Dorward and Olive Tookey, *Below the Flight Path* (Edmonton: Alumnae Association of the Royal Alexandra Hospital School of Nursing, 1968), 5; and EHBM, box 1, Minutes of the Board of Directors of the Strathcona Hospital Dec. 18, 1911-July 29, 1915.

8. These were the criteria common to the Misericordia and Royal Alexandra schools of nursing after 1920 and to those in Medicine Hat, Calgary, and Lethbridge prior to 1920.

9. This conclusion is derived from the educational level of pupil nurses (in several cases, only grade eight or nine) enrolled in both the Misericordia and Royal Alexandra programs after 1919.

10. Wilson, *To Teach This Art*, 10.

11. Dorward and Tookey, *Below the Flight Path*, 5, 10, 15; Wilson, *To Teach This Art*, 9; and Paul, 'History of the Edmonton General,' 296-7.

12. EHBM, box 1, 'Edmonton Public Hospital Minute Book'; 'Edmonton Public Hospital Annual Report of the Board of Directors, 1905'; 'Annual Report of the City Hospital,' 1910; and 'Annual Report of the Royal Alexandra Hospital,' 1912.

13. See the annual reports of the Medicine Hat General Hospital published in the *Medicine Hat Times* and *Medicine Hat*

News from 1891 to 1919; Medicine Hat General Hospital Collection; and GAI, Calgary General Hospital Board Papers, Annual Reports of the Calgary General Hospital, 1905-1970. Comparable pre-First World War data for other Canadian hospitals has not been published.

14. Dorward and Tookey, *Below the Flight Path*, 5; Wilson, *To Teach This Art*, 9-11; Paul, 'History of the Edmonton General,' 302-303; EHBM, box 1, 'Annual Report of the Edmonton Public Hospital,' 1905; 'Annual Report of the City Hospital,' 1910; and 'Annual Report of the Royal Alexandra Hospital,' 1912.

15. EHBM, box 1, 'Edmonton Hospital Association Minute Book 18 Jan. 1910 - 30 Dec. 1926'; 'Annual Report of the Royal Alexandra Hospital,' 1912; Dorward and Tookey, *Below the Flight Path*, 5; Paul, 'History of the Edmonton General,' 302; and Wilson, *To Teach This Art*, 10.

16. Gibbon and Mathewson, *Three Centuries of Canadian Nursing*, 143-65.

17. This conclusion is derived from patient census information for the Edmonton Public and Strathcona from 1901 to 1916 contained in EHBM, boxes 1 and 2, 'Edmonton Public Hospital Minute Book 2 Feb. 1899 - 19 Dec. 1909'; 'Edmonton Hospital Association Minute Book 18 Jan. 1910 - 30 Dec. 1926'; Minutes of the Board of Directors of the Strathcona Hospital 18 Dec. 1911 - 29 July 1915; 'Minutes of the Edmonton Hospital Board and of the RAH Committee from 26 June 1913 - 13 June 1916'; 'Minutes of the Edmonton Hospital Board 26 June 1916 - 19 Dec. 1924'; and Paul, 'History of the Edmonton General,' 310.

18. Following completion of the new Royal Alexandra building in 1912 and the new Strathcona building in 1913, the number of operations more than doubled at each institution. EHBM, box 1, 'Edmonton Hospital Association Minute Book 18 Jan. 1910 - 30 Dec. 1926'; and 'Minutes of the Board of Directors of the Strathcona Hospital 18 Dec. 1911- 29 July 1915.'

19. Ibid., box 1, 'Edmonton Public Hospital Minute Book 2 Feb. 1899 - 19 Dec. 1909,' 10 Oct. 1907.

20. Ibid., 'Annual Report of the City Hospital,' 1910, 5-6; and 'Edmonton Hospital Association Minute Book 18 Jan. 1910 - 30 Dec. 1926.

21. Dorward and Tookey, *Below the Flight Path*, 5, 14; and Wilson, *To Teach This Art*, 9.

22. EHBM, box 1, 'Minutes of the Edmonton Hospital Board and the RAH Committee,' 16 Dec. 1918.

23. Wilson, *To Teach This Art*, 7; EHBM, box 1, 'Minutes of the Strathcona

Hospital Committee, 1915'; and 'Minutes of the Board of Directors of the Strathcona Hospital 18 Dec. 1911 - 29 July 1915.'

24. EHBM, box 2, 'Minutes of the Edmonton Hospital Board 26 June 1916 - 19 Dec. 1924,' 18 Jan. 1917.

25. Gilpin, *Misericordia Hospital*, 42-4; Paul, 'History of the Edmonton General,' 85; and EHBM, box 1, 'Edmonton Hospital Association Minute Book 18 Jan. 1910 - 30 Dec. 1926,' April and Aug. 1911.

26. Dorward and Tookey, *Below the Flight Path*, 11-12. The exact date of completion is uncertain, since in 1913 the Edmonton Hospital Association transferred its ownership of the Royal Alexandra to the City and records for the first six months of 1913 are sketchy.

27. This interpretation is based on a comparison of numbers of pupil nurses reported as probationary, first, second, and third years in EHBM, box 1, 'Edmonton Hospital Board Minutes, 1899-1939'; and the number of graduates from 1908 to 1912, as reported in Royal Alexandra Hospital, School of Nursing, Office of the Director, 'Graduating Classes 1908-53.'

28. For example, there is no mention of either pupil nurse attrition or the reasons for it in the annual reports of the Royal Alexandra Hospital prior to the First World War. Individual pupil nurse records retained by the Misericordia Hospital School of Nursing for graduates prior to 1924 contain no demographic or health and little academic information. There are no extant pupil nurse records at the Royal Alexandra Hospital School of Nursing for years 1908 to 1921. Detailed information about reasons for pupil nurse attrition in the University of Alberta diploma nursing program is located in UAA, University of Alberta Hospital School of Nursing Collection, Minutes of the Council of the School of Nursing.

29. Paul, 'History of the Edmonton General,' 273; Royal Alexandra Hospital, 'Graduating Classes 1908-53'; Misericordia Hospital, School of Nursing, Office of the Director, 'Number of Graduates from the Misericordia Hospital School of Nursing'; and Wilson, *To Teach This Art*, 8.

30. The Edmonton General did not begin paying pupil nurses a stipend until 1943, according to Paul, 'History of the Edmonton General ,' 301; however, both the Royal Alexandra and Strathcona paid stipends, as did the University of Alberta diploma program when it began in 1923. It is not known whether the Misericordia paid stipends in the early years.

31. See note 29. The exact number of diploma graduates at the University of

Alberta is not known, since the names of baccalaureate students completing their final hospital year are mixed with those of diploma students completing their third and final hospital year. University of Alberta Hospital School of Nursing Collection, Minutes of the Council of the School of Nursing.

32. George Weir, *Survey of Nursing Education in Canada* (Toronto: University of Toronto Press, 1932), 191.

33. For example, see Dorward and Tookey, *Below the Flight Path*, 9-19; and Wilson, *To Teach This Art*, 9-12.

34. Cashman, *Heritage of Service*, 208-9. See also Dorward and Tookey, *Below the Flight Path*, 31-3.

35. Kathryn McPherson, 'Skilled Service and Women's Work: Canadian Nursing, 1920-1939' (PhD diss., Simon Fraser University, 1989), 9.

36. Weir, *Survey of Nursing Education In Canada*, 75.

∾ FAYE REINEBERG HOLT, MAGISTRATE EMILY FERGUSON MURPHY

1. Having the first woman judge was a bragging point for the capital; however, Calgary claimed the same honour. On 21 April 1915 two of its citizens, Alice Jamieson and Annie Elizabeth Langford, were appointed Justices of the Peace in and for the Province of Alberta and Commissioners under the Children's Protection Act. The *Calgary Herald* of 15 March 1920 claimed that Mrs Jamieson was the first woman judge in the world. True, in 1915, she had been made Commissioner of the Juvenile Court, an appointment held under both the dominion and provincial governments. This appointment meant she enforced the Alberta Child Protection Act and the Dominion Children's Act. According to Alberta's Act Respecting Juvenile Courts of 25 Oct. 1913, commissioners did become judges of the juvenile courts for the city, town, village, rural municipality, or district to which they were appointed. However, such positions did not grant these Calgary women equal power to that of magistrate, whose job was to rule on criminal charges against adults. By Order in Council, on 13 June 1916 Emily Murphy received her magisterial appointment. Alice Jamieson's appointment as magistrate was by Order in Council on 27 Dec. 1916. As a result, although Jamieson was called *judge* prior to Murphy's appointment, Murphy was first woman magistrate in Canada and the British Empire.

2. Emily Ferguson, *Janey Canuck in the West*, 4th ed. (London, New York,

Toronto & Melbourne: Cassell and Company), 280-1.

3. Elsie Schneider, 'Addressing the Issues: Two Women's Groups in Edmonton, 1905 - 16,' *Alberta History* 36, no. 3 (1988): 15-22; and Rebecca Coulter, 'The Working Young of Edmonton 1921-1931,' in Joy Parr, ed., *Childhood and Family in Canadian History* (Toronto: McClelland and Stewart, 1988), 143-59.

4. Veronica Strong-Boag, *The Parliament of Women: The National Council of Women of Canada 1893-1929* (Ottawa: National Museum of Man, Mercury Series, 1976), 440. Edmonton Local Councils are listed for the periods 1895-6 and 1908-29.

5. PAA, 74.1, Murphy, Convenor of Committee on Laws for the Better Protection of Women and Children, to the Chairman, Legal Bills Committee, Legislature of Alberta, 27 Feb. 1910.

6. CEA, EMP (EMP), Emily Murphy, Report as Convenor of the Committee on Laws for the Better Protection of Women and Children, Edmonton Local Council [of Women], January 1911.

7. PAA, 74.1/192, Ella C. Timbres, Report as Convenor for the Standing Committee on Equal Moral Standards and Prevention of Traffic in Women [for the Local Council of Women], 23 March 1916.

8. Ibid.

9. CEA, Emily Murphy Scrapbooks (EMS), 724, Murphy to Hon. C.W. Cross, Attorney General, 23 March 1916.

10. EMP, Emily Murphy, Report as Convenor of the Committee on Laws for the Better Protection of Women and Children.

11. Byrne Hope Sanders, *Emily Murphy, Crusader* (Toronto: Macmillan, [1945] 1975), 345-7.

12. *EB*, 14 June 1916.

13. PAA, 79.105/92.9, memo Mr E.R. Hughes to Mr Henwood, 11 June 1935; also Justice J.W. McClung to the author, 28 May 1992.

14. *Star Weekly*, April 1926.

15. Ibid.

16. Magistrate Emily F. Murphy, 'A Straight Talk on Courts,' *Maclean's*, 1 Oct. 1920.

17. Helen Melnyk, 'Outrageous Emily finally won her biggest battle,' *EJ* clipping.

18. EMS, Emily F. Murphy, 'The Woman's Court,' *Maclean's* 1919.

19. *Star Weekly*, April, 1926.

20. Ibid.

21. CEA, EMS, clipping 'Sterilization of All Insane Persons Urged,' *EJ*, June 1926; and clipping 'Alberta's Mental Deficient Problem Most Serious Declares Mrs. Murphy,' *Lethbridge Herald*, 1926. Murphy claimed 75 per cent of the causes of feeble-mindedness and insanity were due to heredity, and she suggested the enacting of laws requiring sterilization—laws also recommended by eminent British physicians. Murphy's popularity as a speaker regarding these issues is evident from EMS, clippings, *Medicine Hat News*, 1926, which indicate that citizens thronged to City Hall to hear her.

22. Pierre Burton, *The Promised Land* (Toronto: McClelland and Stewart, 1984), 59.

23. Emily Murphy, *The Black Candle* (Toronto: Thomas Allen Publishers, 1922), 44.

24. EMS, clipping 'Woman to Try Two Chinese,' 1924.

25. Murphy, *Black Candle*, 82.

26. EMS, clipping.

27. Murphy, *Black Candle*, 300-01.

28. EMP, Magistrate's Notebook, vol. 2, case no. 265, 3 June 1918. Quoted in 'Maternal Feminism in Action—Emily Murphy, Police Magistrate,' by John McLaren in *The Windsor Yearbook of Access to Justice*, vol. 8 (1988), 339.

29. EMP, Margaret Garrison [McKee] to Murphy, 5 June 1921.

30. Ibid., Murphy to Margaret Garrison, Provincial Gaol, Fort Saskatchewan, 16 June 1921.

31. Ibid., Murphy to Mrs Clye Macdonald, Edmonton, 3 March 1920.

32. Ibid., Murphy to A.G. Browning, Secretary, Board of Provincial Police Commissioners, 17 April 1918.

33. Murphy, 'Women's Court.'

34. Sanders, *Emily Murphy*, 345-7.

35. Ibid.

36. PABC, McClung Papers, Murphy to Nellie McClung; and Sanders, *Emily Murphy*, 309-10.

37. Sanders, *Emily Murphy*, 305.

REBECCA PRIEGERT COULTER, **PATROLLING THE PASSIONS OF YOUTH**

1. Edmonton Public School Board (EPSB), minutes, 9 Feb. 1922, 3408.

2. Ibid., 3407-9.

3. Joseph F. Kett, *Rites of Passage: Adolescence in America, 1790 to the Present* (New York: Basic Books, 1977), 258. See also, for example, John R. Gillis, *Youth and History: Tradition and Change in European Age Relations, 1770-Present* (New York and London: Academic Press, 1974); and John Davis, *Youth and the Condition of Britain: Images of Adolescent Conflict* (London: Athlone Press, 1990).

4. Mike Brake, *The Sociology of Youth Culture and Youth Subcultures: Sex and Drugs and Rock 'n' Roll* (London: Routledge and Kegan Paul, 1980).

5. The classic works on the invention and discovery of adolescence are Gillis's *Youth and History* and Kett's *Rites of Passage*. Useful summaries of the literature can be found in Davis, *Youth and the Condition of Britain*; and John Springhall, *Coming of Age: Adolescence in Britain 1860-1960* (Dublin: Gill and Macmillan, 1986).

6. For discussion of social reformers and child savers in Canada see, for example, Neil Sutherland, *Children in English-Canadian Society: Framing the Twentieth-Century Consensus* (Toronto: University of Toronto Press, 1976); and Patricia T. Rooke and R.L. Schnell, *Discarding the Asylum: From Child Rescue to the Welfare State in English-Canada, 1800-1950* (Lanham: University Press of America, 1983). On international influences see, for example, Tamara Hareven, 'An Ambiguous Alliance: Some Aspects of American Influences on Canadian Social Welfare,' *SH* 3 (1969): 82-98.

7. See Rebecca Coulter, 'Alberta's Department of Neglected Children, 1909-1929: A Case Study in Child Saving' (MEd thesis, University of Alberta, 1977), 31-2.

8. Ibid., 32-3.

9. Alberta, Department of Neglected Children, *Annual Report* (1909, 1911-29).

10. G. Stanley Hall, *Adolescence: Its Psychology and Its Relations to Physiology, Anthropology, Sociology, Sex, Crime, Religion and Education*, 2 vols. (New York: D. Appleton, 1904); and the shortened, more popular version, *Youth: Its Education, Regimen and Hygiene* (New York: D. Appleton, 1904). Hall's importance in shaping twentieth-century understandings of adolescence is discussed in Davis, *Youth and the Condition of Britain*.

11. *Annual Report* (1911), 8.

12. Ibid. (1912), 22.

13. Ibid. (1913), 30.

14. Ibid. (1912), 39.

15. See Carol Dyhouse, *Girls Growing Up in Late Victorian and Edwardian England* (London: Routledge and Kegan Paul, 1981), 115-38, for an interesting discussion of ideas about the differences in male and female adolescence.

16. For a discussion of gender and the psychology of adolescence see Barbara Hudson, 'Femininity and Adolescence,' in Angela McRobbie and Mica Nava, eds., *Gender and Generation* (London: Macmillan, 1984), 31-53.

17. Differences over technique, as opposed to content and arguments, in 'getting things done' were common among child welfare practitioners and classroom teachers; *Annual Report* (1909, 1911-19).

18. A brief summary of youth groups can be found in Carl Betke, 'The Development of an Urban Community in Prairie Canada: Edmonton, 1898-1921' (PhD diss., University of Alberta, 1981).

19. The following represent only a fraction of the relevant scholarly literature: John Springhall, *Youth, Empire and Society* (London: Croom Helm, 1977); Dominick Cavallo, *Muscles and Morals: Organized Playgrounds and Urban Reform, 1880-1920* (Philadelphia: University of Pennsylvania Press, 1981); David I. Macleod, *Building Character in the American Boy: The Boy Scouts, Y.M.C.A., and Their Forerunners, 1870-1920* (Madison: University of Wisconsin Press, 1983); Harry Hendrick, *Images of Youth: Age, Class, and the Male Youth Problem, 1880-1920* (Oxford: Clarendon Press, 1990); Diana Pedersen, '"Keeping Our Good Girls Good": The Young Women's Christian Association of Canada, 1870-1920' (MA thesis, Carleton University, 1981); and Margaret Prang, '"The Girl God Would Have Me Be": The Canadian Girls in Training, 1915-39,' *CHR* 66, no. 3 (1985): 154-84.

20. See *WC*, editorials and syndicated articles, 1920s.

21. *WC*, 16 Oct., 25 June 1924.

22. Ibid., 25 June 1925.

23. Ibid.

24. Ibid., 15 July 1926.

25. Ibid., 31 July 1924.

26. See, for example, ibid., 9 April 1925.

27. Ibid., 20 Oct. 1927.

28. Veronica Strong-Boag, *The New Day Recalled: Lives of Girls and Women in English Canada, 1919-1939* (Toronto: Copp Clark Pitman, 1988).

29. NAC, Girl Guides Records, MG I 290, box 1, 'Organization and Rules of the Canadian Council, Girl Guides Association.'

30. PAA, Sisters, Faithful Companions of Jesus Papers, GA, M1395, file 31, 'Annals' (1923).

31. *WC*, 10 July 1920, 24 March 1927.

32. Ibid., 24 March 1927.

33. NAC, YWCA Records, MG 28, I 198, vol. 40, 'Citizenship.'

34. National Girls' Work Board, *Canadian Girls in Training: A Book for Leaders* (Toronto: Ryerson Press, 1922), 39.

35. Ibid., 18.

36. PAA, United Church Records (UCR), 75.387, box UC100, 657/108, minutes, Edmonton McDougall WMS CGIT Alberta Vistas, 1921-3.

37. For example, see PAA, Anglican Church-All Saints Pro-Cathedral, 76.48, Ed. 15/68, 'Annual Report'(1931), which notes that for the first time in eight years the Parents' Association of the Guides, Rovers, Scouts, Brownies, and Cubs was able to elect 'a real live Executive.' Also

UCR, box UC100, 656/16, 'Thirty-fifth Annual Report, Knox Presbyterian Church, 1928,' which comments that leaders of youth groups did not get the cooperation of many parents or church members and officers as a whole.

38. UCR, box UC95, file 657/12; there are several examples of youth workers being employed for six-month or one-year terms.

39. PAA, Edmonton District Girl Guides Records (EDGG), 68.73, file 68, 'Report 1929'; and *Census of Canada* (1931), 28.

40. NAC, Boy Scout Records, MG 28, I 73 (Microfilm #C-13940), 'Annual Reports,' 1915-45.

41. NAC, YMCA Records, MG 28, I 95, vol. 245, yearbooks.

42. See, for example, Stephen Humphries, *Hooligans or Rebels? An Oral History of Working-Class Childhood and Youth, 1889-1939* (Oxford: Basil Blackwell, 1981); and Michael J. Childs, *Labour's Apprentices: Working-Class Lads in Late Victorian and Edwardian England* (Montreal and Kingston: McGill-Queen's University Press, 1992).

43. UCR, box UC100, 657/100, McDougall Methodist Church Sunday School, minutes (annual meeting), May 1921.

44. YMCA Records, yearbooks.

45. YWCA Records, vol. 40.

46. Prang, '"The Girl God Would Have Me Be"'; Leila McKee, 'Voluntary Youth Organizations in Toronto, 1880-1930' (PhD diss., York University, 1982); and Kett, *Rites of Passage* all claim that youth groups had growing memberships.

47. E.S., interview with the author, 12 Nov. 1981; EPSB, minutes, 18 Nov. 1920, 2474, 17 Nov. 1921, 3266-7, 18 Jan. 1923, 4969-70, 20 Jan. 1927, 6321, illustrate community league use of schools to provide physical training and gymnastics classes for teenagers.

48. EPSB, minutes, 19 Feb. 1925, 5265.

49. Ibid.

50. J.C., interview with the author, 2 Nov. 1981.

51. Elliott Henry Birdsall, 'A Questionnaire Investigation of the Reactions of School Children to Moving Picture Shows' (MA thesis, University of Alberta, 1933).

52. David C. Jones, 'The Reflective Value of Movies and Censorship on Interwar Prairie Society,' *PF* 10, no. 2 (1985): 383-98.

53. ESPB, minutes, 5 Feb. 1921, 2654.

54. Ibid., 2655-6.

55. Ibid., 15 Feb. 1921, 2684.

56. PAA, Premiers' Papers (PP), 69.289, file 364, Standards of the Association of Provincial Moving Picture Censors.

57. Ibid., Pictures Condemned by Alberta Censor Board, 1 Jan.—1 Sept. 1922.

58. Jones, 'The Reflective Value.'

59. ESPB, minutes, 5, 12 Jan. 1922, 3353-4, 3360-1, 18 Sept. 1924, 5042, 5050-1, 18 Sept. 1928, 7029, 30 June 1931, 8477-8.

60. J.C., interview; see also *WC*, 6 Oct. 1921.

61. Examples of the ambivalence adults felt can be seen by comparing the report on the Social Services conference in *WC*, 17 Feb. 1927, with the 6 Nov. 1930 clipping, 'Edmonton Crime,' in CEA, Newspaper Clipping Collection, A77/18, box 17.

62. Carl Betke, 'Sports Promotion in the Western Canadian City: The Example of Early Edmonton,' *UHR* 12, no.1 (1983): 47-56.63. *WC*, 8 Aug. 1929.

∾ CATHERINE COLE, GARMENT MANUFACTURING IN EDMONTON

1. Canadian labour and business historiography has focused on garment manufacturing in Ontario, Quebec, and Manitoba; see Jacques Rouillard, *Les travailleurs du coton du Quebec, 1900-1915* (Quebec: Presses de l'Université du Quebec, 1974); Gail Cuthbert Brandt, 'Weaving it Together: Life Cycle and the Industrial Experience of Female Cotton Workers in Quebec, 1910-1950,' *Labour/Le Travail* 7 (1981): 113-35; Jacques Ferland, 'When the cotton mills' "girls" struck for the first time: a study of female militancy in the cotton and shoe factories of Quebec (1880-1910),' (unpublished paper presented to the Canadian Historical Association, 1986); N.M. Davidson, 'Montreal's Dominance of the Canadian Men's Fine Clothing Industry' (MA thesis, University of Western Ontario, 1969); and Laura C. Johnson with Robert E. Johnson, *The Seam Allowance: Industrial Home Sewing in Canada* (Toronto: Women's Educational Press, 1982). On Edmonton see Cole, 'Garment Manufacturing in Edmonton, 1911-1939' (MA thesis, University of Alberta, 1988); and Catherine C. Cole, *The Great Western Garment Company, 1911-1939* (Edmonton: Alberta Museums Association Occasional Paper No. 1, 1989).

2. I would like to acknowledge the support of the Alberta Historical Resources Foundation and the Alberta Museums Association, through moneys provided by the Alberta Lotteries, while researching this project for my MA. This chapter has been written with the support of the Provincial Museum of Alberta. I would also like to acknowledge the co-operation of Anne Ozipko of Local 120 of UGWA and the many former employees of garment manufacturing firms who gave freely of their time and allowed me to interview them

in 1987-8, including: Dan Starko, Emery Manufacturing; Roberta Watson and Arthur McIntyre, Courtney Manufacturing and General Whitewear and Uniform Manufacturers; Anne Ozipko, Lillian Morris, Max Bedard, Georgina Graff, Elizabeth Shinbine, and Louis Kabesh, Great Western Garment; and LeRoy LaFleche Sr and Ivy Grimstead, LaFleche Bros. Lillian Morris and Max Bedard worked for GWG from about 1915 until their retirement; others started in the 1920s or 1930s.

3. Doug Smith, *Let Us Rise! A History of the Manitoba Labour Movement* (Vancouver: New Star Books, 1985), 61; see also John Hample, 'Workplace Conflict in Winnipeg's Custom Tailoring Trade, c1887-1921,' *Manitoba History* 22 (Autumn, 1991); and James D. Mochoruk and Donna Webber, 'Women in the Winnipeg Garment Trade, 1929-45,' in Mary Kinnear, ed., *First Days, Fighting Days: Women in Manitoba History* (Regina: Canadian Plains Research Center, 1987), 134-48.

4. See *Henderson's* directories for the period.

5. Mercedes Steedman, 'Skill and Gender in the Canadian Clothing Industry, 1890—1910,' in Craig Heron and Robert Storey, eds., *On the Job: Confronting the Labour Process in Canada* (Kingston and Montreal: McGill-Queen's University Press, 1986), 154.

6. *EJ*, 28 March 1911. In his only reference to garment manufacturing, Warren Carragata erroneously notes that GWG was one of many plants organized during the war (*Alberta Labour: A Heritage Untold* [Toronto, James Lorimer, 1979], 82).

7. *EJ*, 28 Nov. 1914.

8. *ALN*, 17 Sept. 1927.

9. *EFP*, 31 May 1919. The *EFP* (after 1920 the *ALN*) was the official organ of the Edmonton Trades and Labour Council and the Alberta Federation of Labor. Alvin Finkel argues that the establishment of a Labour church, Labour education classes, and Labour Day picnics and parades were signs of a growing labour sense of forming a distinct social class ('The Rise and Fall of the Labour Party in Alberta, 1917-42,' *Labour/Le Travail* 16 [1985]: 90). GWG advertised regularly in the paper, but its editorial pages contained few references to UGWA beyond periodic notices of raises or new executive members.

10. Steedman, 'Skill and Gender in the Clothing Industry,' 167; see also Veronica Strong-Boag, 'The Girl of the New Day: Canadian Working Women in the 1920s,' *Labour/Le Travail* 4 (1979): 140.

11. Steedman, 'Skill and Gender in the Clothing Industry,' 152; see also Eliane Leslau Silverman, *The Last Best West: Women on the Alberta Frontier, 1880-1930* (Montreal: Eden Press, 1984).

12. *EJ*, 12 Dec. 1931.

13. Ibid., 4 Feb. 1913.

14. *ALN*, 26 March 1921.

15. Interviews with Graff and Grimstead, both of whom started working as teenagers to help support their parents and siblings.

16. Interview with Shinbine.

17. Interviews with Bedard, Graff, and Morris.

18. *Statutes of Alberta*, 1917, ch. 20; and *EJ*, 6 April 1917.

19. Manitoba, British Columbia, and Saskatchewan all introduced distinct minimum wage legislation in 1917 (Robert McIntosh, 'Sweated Labour: Female Needleworkers in Industrializing Canada,' *Labour/Le Travail* 32 [1993]: 105-38). Bob Russell argues that a minimum wage was not a fair wage. In Manitoba the passage of the minimum wage bill in 1918 followed well-publicized strikes by women workers, the birth of the Women's Labour League (WLL), and women's gaining the right to vote ('A Fair or a Minimum Wage? Women Workers, the State, and the Origins of Wage Regulation in Western Canada,' *Labour/Le Travail* 28 [1991]: 70,77).

20. Research Division, Alberta Department of Labour, *A History of Labour and Social Welfare Legislation in Alberta* (Edmonton, 1973), 16; and Michael J. Piva, *The Condition of the Working Class of Montreal, 1897-1929* (Toronto, 1974), 18-20. Dianne Smith notes the regular appearance of advertising for homeworkers to work for the National Manufacturing Company of Montreal. She concludes, however, that homework or outworking was not significant in the garment industry in Edmonton ('Dressmaking Occupations in Edmonton: 1900-1930' [MSc thesis, University of Alberta, 1987], 74).

21. The clause in the Alberta legislation was 25. Alice Klein and Wayne Roberts, 'Besieged Innocence: The "Problem" and Problems of Working Women—Toronto, 1896-1914,' in Janice Acton et al., eds., *Women at Work: Ontario 1850-1930* (Toronto: Canadian Women's Educational Press, 1974), 215; and *EFP*, 8 Nov. 1919.

22. PAA, 70.414, file 436, *Sessional Papers*, no. 54, 'Report of the Advisory Committee under Factories Act, January 6, 1921.' Alberta was the first province with minimum wage legislation but was among the last to establish a minimum wage board; see Margaret E. McCallum, 'Keeping Women in Their Place: The Minimum Wage in Canada, 1910-25,' *Labour/Le Travail* 17 (1986): 29-56 for a discussion of the development of minimum wage legislation in Canada. *Statutes of Alberta*, 1922, 'An Act to Provide a Minimum Wage for Women'; *ALN*, 6 Jan. 1923; and PAA, Records of the Minimum Wage Board, 75.490, 'Proceedings of the Eleventh Convention of the Alberta Federation of Labour,' 22-4 Nov. 1926, Calgary, 11.

23. *ALN*, 7 Oct. 1922; Records of the Minimum Wage Board; and Morris, interview

24. Interview with Graff.

25. Records of the Minimum Wage Board, Minimum Wage Act, Suggested amendments to the Act, J.J. Franley to M.A. Hamilton, 20 Dec. 1935.

26. Ibid., Great Western Garment, written brief to the Minimum Wage Board, 27 April 1933.

27. Ibid., Minutes of the Minimum Wage Board, 15 Dec. 1923.

28. A change to the Act in 1928 allowed companies to apply to the Minimum Wage Board to pay a worker less on transfer from one department to another. GWG then had its staff perform a primary function and have one or two alternate operations in which they were trained. GWG informants frequently mentioned consideration on the part of the firm; and Bedard, Kabesh, interviews.

29. PAA, Records of the Minimum Wage Board , Walter Smitten, Commissioner of Labour to Judge A.A. Carpenter, Chairman, Minimum Wage Board, 23 Feb. 1932.

30. Records of the Minimum Wage Board, Morris to Smitten, 2 March 1932. Employee lists of over one hundred people handicapped for one reason or another are on file.

31. Interviews with Bedard, who started in 1919, and Shinbine, who started in 1921. Kabesh noted that this was no longer possible when he joined the firm in 1938. See also Grimstead.

32. *EJ*, 5 April 1917.

33. *ALN*, 9, 16 Oct. 1920.

34. Records of the Minimum Wage Board, Minutes of the Minimum Wage Board, 8 April, 5 March 1925, 2 Nov. 1926. The Edmonton Knitting Company was founded in 1919. In 1921 it branched out as a wholesale concern and in 1922 went public under the name of the Edmonton Knitting Mills Ltd. The company struggled between 1925 and 1927 and eventually went bankrupt. See Alberta, Consumer and Corporate Affairs, Edmonton Knitting Mills Ltd., Articles of Association, 8 March 1922; Prospectus, 9 March 1922; and Report by A.G. Aldridge prepared for Messrs Slaters Ltd., April 1927.

35. *Statutes of Alberta*, 1926, 'An Act for the Protection of Persons Employed in Factories, Shops and Office Buildings,'

clause 23. J.A. LaFleche was joined by the Calgary Knitting Company, manufacturers of pure wool and worsted sweaters, and twelve other firms in forwarding petitions signed by employees. PAA, 414.560, file 23, J.A. LaFleche to the Canadian Manufacturers Association, 1 March 1926; and *EB*, 20 March 1926.

36. PAA, 414.560, file 23, *Sessional Papers*, no. 47, 'Majority Report of the Commission re: 48 hour working week,' 8 Feb. 1927. A minority report, submitted by Elmer E. Roper, is included.

37. Interview with Morris.

∿ ANNE NOTHOF,
**MAKING COMMUNITY HISTORY:
THE RADIO PLAYS OF RINGWOOD
AND GOWAN**

1. University of Calgary Special Collections, Gwen Pharis Ringwood Papers (RP), Ringwood to Gowan, 30 Jan. 1975.

2. UAA, Elsie Park Gowan Scrapbooks, Gowan to Ringwood, 5 Feb. 1975.

3. Biographical information is taken from Geraldine Anthony, *Gwen Pharis Ringwood* (New York: Twayne, 1981).

4. RP, Gwen Pharis Ringwood, 'Speech to the Association of Canadian Theatre History,' University of Saskatchewan, 24 May 1979, 1.

5. Moira Day, ed., *The Hungry Spirit: Selected Plays and Prose by Elsie Park Gowan* (Edmonton: NeWest Press, 1992).

6. Howard Fink, 'The Sponsor's v. the Nation's Choice: North American Radio Drama,' in *Peter Lewis*, ed., *Radio Drama* (London and New York: Longman, 1981), 87.

7. RP, Gwen Pharis Ringwood, 'Speech for Association of Radio and Television History,' Saskatoon, 23 May 1979, 1.

8. Sheila Marryat grew up on a farm in southern Alberta, attended Olds School of Agriculture, and then pursued a degree in agriculture at the University of Alberta, where she was the first woman graduate in that field in 1923. During her holidays she studied at the London School of Speech and Drama, and attended rehearsals of BBC plays. Her initial contribution to CKUA was in the form of nature talks during a 'children's hour.' On 17 Jan. 1939, the *Edmonton Journal* wrote that since 1928 'her name has been synonymous with radio in this province.'

9. *EJ*, 17 Jan 1939.

10. Howard Fink, 'CKUA: Radio Drama and Regional Theatre,' *Theatre History in Canada* 8, no. 2 (1987): 224.

11. RP, Gowan to Ringwood, 30 April 1979.

12. Ibid., Dick MacDonald to Ringwood, 4 May 1979.

13. Ringwood, 'Speech to Association of Canadian Theatre History,' 3.

14. Ringwood, 'Speech for Association of Radio and Television History,' 3.

15. Ibid., 4.

16. Ibid., 6.

17. UAA, Elsie Park Gowan Radio Plays, Elsie Park Gowan, 'Mary Wollstonecraft,' 19.

18. Ibid., Elsie Park Gowan, 'The Coming of Power,' 6.

19. RP.

20. Gwen Pharis Ringwood, 'The Rainmaker,' in Enid Delgatty Rutland, ed., *The Collected Plays* (Ottawa: Borealis, 1982), 191.

21. Ibid., Gwen Pharis Ringwood, 'Stampede,' 253.

22. Ringwood to Dr Robert Gard, quoted in Geraldine Anthony, *Gwen Pharis Ringwood* (New York: Twayne, 1981), 27-8.

23. Quoted in ibid., 164.

24. Gowan Scrapbooks, clipping, *EJ*, n.d.

25. Moira Day 'Elsie Park Gowan's (re)-*Building of Canada* (1937-1938): Revisioning the Historical Radio Series through Feminist Eyes,' *Theatre Research in Canada* 14, no. 1 (1993): 3, interprets 'The Building of Canada' as 'a complex attempt to reconcile her [Gowan's] vision as a trained historian, concerned with the objective chronicling and analysis of the male-dominated world of wars, economy, politics and public life, with her vision as a social activist playwright committed to interpreting the human world through the focus of her socialistic, pacifistic [sic] and feminist convictions.'

26. Day, *Hungry Spirit*, 18.

27. Gowan Radio Plays, Elsie Park Gowan, 'Who Builds a City?,' part 9: 'A Time of Testing.'

28. Ibid., part 11: 'Drillers on our Doorstep.'

29. RP, Gowan to Ringwood, 31 Jan. 1979, Ringwood to Gowan, 16 April 1979.

30. See the articles by drama critics Howard Fink ('The Sponsor's v. the Nation's Choice'; 'CKUA: Radio Drama'), Anton Wagner ('Elsie Park Gowan: "Distinctively Canadian,"' *Theatre History in Canada* 8, no. 1 [1987]: 68-72), and Moira Day ('Elsie Park Gowan's (re)-*Building of Canada*'); and the MA thesis by Steve Olsen ('The Function of Radio Drama: An Alberta Perspective,' [MA thesis, University of Alberta, 1991]). Also see CKUA's drama series, 'Theatre of the Air,' for which two of Gowan's early stage plays were adapted for radio production— 'Homestead' (1933) and 'The Hungry Spirit' (1935).

31. Quoted in Day, *Hungry Spirit*, 31.

32. RP, Elsie Park Gowan, 'On Growing Old.'

∿ JOHN GRIGSBY GEIGER,
**'WRONG TIME, WRONG PLACE,
WRONG COLOUR'**

1. Biographical data on Brion Gysin can be found in Colin Naylor, ed., *Contemporary Artists*, 3d ed. (London: St James Press, 1988), 386-7; Jaques Cattell Press, ed., *Who's Who in American Art* (New York: R.R. Bowker Company, 1980), 285-6; and *International Herald Tribune*, 26-7 July 1986.

2. Cited in Terry Wilson, *Here to Go: Planet R-101* (San Francisco: Re/Search Publications, 1982), xv.

3. Brion Gysin, 'Family Album' (unpublished manuscript, n.d.), William Burroughs Communications, Lawrence, Kansas; this work appeared in France as *Légendes de Brion Gysin* (Paris: Gris banal, editeur, 1983).

4. Gysin, 'Family Album.'

5. William S. Burroughs, interview with the author, Lawrence, Kansas, 6 March 1992.

6. Paul Bowles, 'Brion,' Gysin exhibition catalogue (1957), Sagittarius Gallery, New York.

7. Brion Gysin, 'FIRE: Words by Day— Images by Night,' *Soft Need* 17 (1977): 44-5.

8. For an analysis of Gysin's literary approach in *The Process* see Robert Palmer's 'Foreword' in the 1987 Overlook Press (Woodstock NY) edition of the novel.

9. Gysin, 'Family Album.'

10. Gysin wrote various accounts of this incident, the most detailed appearing in *Beat Museum-Bardo Hotel Ch. 2* (Los Angeles: Inkblot Publications, 1982), 21. The scene was removed when the complete manuscript was published as *The Last Museum* (London: Faber and Faber, 1986).

11. Michael Zwerin, 'Brion Gysin: The Dreamer and His Dream Machine,' *Paris Metro*, 16 Aug. 1979, 20.

12. Gysin, 'Family Album.'

13. Gysin, 'FIRE,' 45.

14. William Burroughs Communication, Stella Gysin to Father Trafford, Headmaster, Downside (England), 31 Jan. 1932.

15. Brion Gysin, *The Process* (London: Quartet Books, 1985), 236. All subsequent references are from this edition of the novel.

16. PAM, Homestead Records, reel 1178.

17. Gysin, *Beat Museum-Bardo Hotel*, 21.

18. Gysin, 'Family Album.'

19. Ibid.

20. Stella Gysin to Trafford.

21. Wilson, *Here to Go: Planet R-101*.

22. Ted Morgan, *Literary Outlaw* (New York: Avon Books, 1988), 371.

23. Marion Wilson, interview with the author, Edmonton, 9 April 1992; and

Brion Gysin, 'Excerpt from an Empty Tape,' *Soft Need* 17 (1977): 22.

24. CEA, Edmonton Public Library Records, payroll, 1932-8.
25. Wilson, interview.
26. *SN*, 21 June 1908.
27. PAA, 85.412/1, Westward Ho!
28. Gysin, 'Family Album.'
29. Ibid.
30. Ibid.
31. Ibid.
32. Gerard Amerongen, interview with the author, Edmonton, 17 March 1992.
33. William Burroughs Communications, Stella Gysin to Trafford, 2, 9 Sept. 1932.
34. Gysin, 'Family Album.'
35. Wilson, interview.
36. Gysin, 'Family Album.'
37. Burroughs, interview.
38. Gysin, *Beat Museum-Bardo Hotel.*
39. Gysin, 'Excerpt from Empty Tape,' 22.
40. Gysin, *The Process*, 235.
41. Ibid., 237; and Alberta Education, Student Records, official transcript of academic achievement for Brion Gysin.
42. Gysin, *The Process*, 248.

RODNEY PIKE,
FRANK PIKE, BANKER AND POET

1. I have turned my father's papers over to the PAA; Frank Pike Papers, 88.480.
2. Dinning's memoirs of early banking adventures with my father are on video tape in the PAA.
3. See the copies of the yearly inspection reports in my father's scrap book.
4. There are many letters to head office in my father's papers asking for special consideration for farm customers in trouble.

GEOFF IRONSIDE,
SLOPES AND SHAFTS

1. I owe a debt of gratitude to my former graduate student, Sally Hamilton, for her hard and conscientious scholarship represented in her masters thesis. I would also like to thank Michael Fisher for the cartographic work, the CEA and the PAA for permission to publish historical photographs, and the Edmonton Geological Society for permission to publish Figures 2 and 3.
2. See Umfreville's comments in John Warkentin, ed., *The Western Interior of Canada, a Record of Geographical Discovery, 1612-1917* (Toronto: McClelland and Stewart, 1964), 72-3.
3. Alice M. Johnson, ed., *Saskatchewan Journals and Correspondence; Edmonton House 1795-1800; Chesterfield House 1800-1802* (London: Hudson's Bay Record Society, 1967).

4. G.H. MacDonald, *Edmonton, Fort-House Factory* (Edmonton: Douglas Printing, 1959).
5. *EB*, 6 Dec. 1880.
6. The source for Fig. 1 is Sally Hamilton, 'Coal Mining in the Edmonton Area' (MA thesis, University of Alberta, 1971); and R.G. Ironside and Sally Hamilton, 'Historical Geography of Coal Mining in the Edmonton District,' *AHR* 20, no. 3 (1972): 6-16.
7. Hamilton, 'Coal Mining,' 14. See Edgar Stansfield and W.A. Lang, 'Coals of Alberta: Their Occurrence, Analysis and Utilization' (Edmonton: Alberta Research Council, 1944), 35.
8. *EB*, 7 Jan. 1887.
9. Hamilton, 'Coal Mining,' 43.
10. CEA, Ross, Donald, and Olive File, Edmonton Hotel Fire, History of the Province of Alberta clipping, 543-44.
11. CEA, Coal File #1, clipping from the *Edmontonian*, May 1964. See also *EB*, 21 Dec. 1915.
12. CEA, Donald Ross File, clipping from the *Alberta Hotelman*, June 1965, 17, 18.
13. Coal File #1; *EB*, 10 June 1907; and *EJ*, 21 Nov. 1978.
14. The North West Mounted Police census of Edmonton's population in 1893 was 1,331. *EB*, 13 July 1893.
15. *WCCR*, Aug. 1923, 59.
16. John D. Campbell, 'Black Diamonds,' in John D. Godfrey, ed., *Edmonton Beneath our Feet: A Guide to the Geology of the Edmonton Region* (Edmonton: Edmonton Geological Society, 1993), 60.
17. *WCCR*, April 1921, 30.
18. UAA, 69-76, Coal General, vol. 2, 'Alberta Coal Shipped to Ontario during Season of 1928,' Vide P.C. 439.
19. Hamilton, 'Coal Mining,' 12; and Stansfield and Lang, 'Coals of Alberta,' 51.
20. Hamilton, 'Coal Mining,' 14; and *EJ*, May and Sept. 1942.
21. *EB*, 12 Aug. 1882.
22. Ibid., 10 July 1886.
23. 'Alberta Coal Shipped to Ontario,' 69-76.
24. Ironside and Hamilton, 'Historical Geography of Coal Mining,' 11.
25. *WCCR*, Aug. 1927, 34.
26. Hamilton, 'Coal Mining,' 102, Table III, 103.
27. Campbell, 'Black Diamonds.'
28. Alberta, Department of Mines and Minerals, Mines Branch Annual Report (1937), 7.
29. See Hamilton, 'Coal Mining,' 18; and Mr W. Worthington to Hamilton, 3 Aug. 1971.
30. Reported in David Cruden and Stanley Thompson, 'Engineering Geology,' in Godfrey, *Edmonton Beneath our Feet*. See Palliser Papers, Hector, 9 Jan. 1887.
31. Cruden and Thompson, 'Engineering Geology.'

32. Hamilton, 'Coal Mining,' 120; and R.S. Taylor, 'Atlas: Coal-Mine Workings of the Edmonton Area' (Edmonton: Spence Taylor and Associates, 1971), 1.
33. *WCCR*, Jan. 1923, 34; and Hamilton, 'Coal Mining,' 126.
34. *WCCR*, June 1925, 6; and Hamilton, 'Coal Mining,' 128.
35. CEA, Minutes of City Council 1927, 36-37.
36. Hamilton, 'Coal Mining,' 130.
37. Coal File #1, Ronald Hannan Watson, Mining Engineer, 'Report to City Commissioner, June 1930, Report upon coal mining within the City of Edmonton by the Penn Coal Co. and Penn Mines Ltd. and the effect thereof upon the surface of the land and in particular upon the property and public services of the Corporation of the City of Edmonton and the Common Good,' 2.
38. Ibid., clipping of *Edmontonian*, May 1964; see also City of Edmonton Engineering Dept, RG 11, Class 90, file 90, J.B. Poppitt, 'Historical Summary—Grierson Hill Stabilization Project.'
39. Coal File #1; see also Alex Mair, 'The Story of the School that Sank,' *Edmonton Real Estate Weekly*, 22 Dec. 1988.
40. Cruden and Thompson, 'Engineering Geology,' 87.
41. K.C. Er, Construction Branch, Public Works Department, City of Edmonton, to Ironside, 20 March 1995.
42. Edmund H. Dale, 'The Role of Successive Town and City Councils in the Evolution of Edmonton' (PhD diss., University of Alberta, 1969), 358; and Hamilton, 'Coal Mining,' 124.
43 Hamilton, 'Coal Mining,' 125.
44. *EJ*, 3 June 1971.
45. *WCCR*, Aug. 1929, 20; and Hamilton, 'Coal Mining,' 104.
46. *WCCR*, 25 April, 4, 15; and Hamilton, 'Coal Mining,' 104.
47. *EB*, 10 Nov. 1922; *WCCR*, Feb. 1923, 24; and Hamilton, 'Coal Mining,' 106-07.
48. The mines included the Edmonton city group (Dawson, Chinook, Standard, Penn, Pioneer); the Clover Bar group (Humberstone, Black Diamond, Bush, Clover Bar, Marcus, Fraser-Mackay, Ottewell, Keith and Fulton, Ferndale); west of the city on the Grand Trunk (Lakeside, Pembina); north of the city on CN (Cardiff group—Great Northern, Cardiff, Banner); north of the City on the Edmonton and BC line (Sturgeon Valley, Kelly No. 1 and No. 2); east of Edmonton on the GTP line (Dobell Co., Tofield Co., J.J. McDevitt strip mine at Tofield). *EB*, 10 Nov. 1922.
49. Hamilton, 'Coal Mining,' 107.
50. *EB*, 17 July 1912; and CEA, William Humberstone File, Pioneer Coal Miner.

51. CEA, Jack Starky File, clipping, *Edmontonian*, n.d.

52. Rick March, Energy, Resources Conservation Board, Calgary, to Ironside, 25 April 1995.

53. Ironside and Hamilton, 'Historical Geography of Coal Mining,' 15; and Dr J.D. Campbell, Alberta Research Council, to Hamilton, Summer 1971.

54. Hamilton, 'Coal Mining,' 94.

55. Ibid., Table VI, 162.

✺ KATHRYN CHASE MERRETT, THE CITY MARKET

1. The archival sources consulted in the preparation of this chapter all come from the City Market Papers (catalogued and uncatalogued) at the CEA. Most of the collection is uncatalogued. The research for this project is still in process. Histories of specific farmers' markets have been written, but they are descriptive rather than analytical in approach. The Edmonton City Market is one of the markets discussed in Linda Biesenthal's *The Public Market Tradition in Canada* (Toronto: Peter Martin Associates, 1980). The author wishes to acknowledge the assistance of the Alberta Historical Resources Foundation during her research.

2. The site acquisition process was both long and complicated, revealing an ongoing ambivalence on the part of successive Councils to commit to maintaining the Market in the so-called 'heart' of the city. In an unpublished paper I have argued that the changing stance taken by City Councils to locating the City Market on the Rice Street site provides insights into civic cultural values.

3. CEA, Minutes, Edmonton Town Council meeting, 13 Nov. 1900.

4. On 10 July 1946 Commissioner J. Hodgson of Edmonton wrote to Commissioner R.S. Gillespie with advice about starting a market: '[The] producer marketers' operating overhead, must be kept low [so] that they can stay in business. Revenue from this section, while important, would not keep our market solvent as their operations are confined mostly to Saturdays; therefore, it has been necessary to install fruit and vegetable stalls, meat and fish markets, who operate continuously on a weekly rental basis and supply the greater amount of our revenue' (CEA, RG 11, Class 44, file 11). This strategy for ensuring stable operating costs is currently employed by both European and North American markets, including weather-protected facilities.

5. Joseph Bre-Win, interviews with the author, 7 Oct., 9 Dec. 1993, 15 Feb. 1994.

6. The role of the City Market in horticultural innovation and development requires further research. There are indications that for several decades there was ongoing dialogue between several of the Market vendors and the University of Alberta regarding the development of both flowers and vegetables.

7. According to Kathrine Granstrom, Marius Granstrom's widow, Marius and Pete bought Virginia Park Greenhouse in fall 1928 from a Mr Chris Johnson, a Greek who owned and ran the Johnson Cafe in the city.

8. Kathrine Granstrom, interviews with the author, 3, 29 Dec. 1993; Rita Arends (née Granstrom), interviews with the author, 3, 29 Dec. 1993; and Ray Granstrom, interview with the author, 3 Dec. 1993.

9. Mary (Chipil) Sernowski, interviews with the author, 3 Dec. 1992, 20 Jan. 1993.

10. Flore (Bilodeau) Hinse, interviews with the author, 20, 26 April 1993.

11. The Report is attached to a letter dated 21 Nov. 1962 from J. R. Warner (City Market Papers [uncatalogued]), Superintendent and intended for the information of the City Council.

12. The City attempted to contract the management of the City Market to the private firm of Kelly and Ennes at the beginning of 1911. The motive appears to have been financial: the City had been losing a small amount each year. The experiment, however, was not popular and within a few months the City had resumed control.

13. The position of Market Superintendent was created by the Commissioners when Edmonton amalgamated with Strathcona. By-law #601, passed by Council on 13 Nov. 1914, made the Superintendent responsible for the three markets administered by the City. In addition to the Rice Street Market, which was by far the largest and the only one to return significant revenue to the City, there was a South Side Market which had been taken over from Strathcona after the amalgamation and the 'North Side' Market on 101 Street and 107 Avenue.

14. Financial records for the City Market were not systematically preserved and the methods of reporting were not consistent. The records suggest that, for the first ten years of the Market's existence, it lost a small amount of money each year. The reason for the losses, and the solution, are given in a letter from the City Clerk to the Secretary of the Stettler Board of Trade, 11 July 1910. The City had calculated that weigh fees would generate enough income to pay the operating expenses of the Market. This assumption proved to be false and the City Clerk recommended that if Stettler were to establish a market, it should consider charging fees. Shortly after, the City of Edmonton implemented a fee-charging policy that was vigorously protested by farmers. Thereafter, the City ran operating surpluses except for the year it tried to move the Market to 101 Street and 107 Avenue.

15. *EB*, 4 Aug. 1888.

16. *EJ*, 25, 28 Aug., 4, 19, 27 Sept. 1962.

17. Hinse, interviews.

18. This story is conveyed in a series of letters in City Market Papers (uncatalogued). On 27 Oct. 1927 the legal firm of Robertson, Winkler & Hawe wrote to the Edmonton City Commissioners on behalf of their unnamed Chinese client who had been informed that 'no Chinamen would be rented space on the market for the sale of produce.' The victim of discrimination must have complained to the Chinese Consul in Ottawa, for on 16 Nov. 1927 Mayor Bury received a letter from Chow Kwo-Hsien, Consul General for China, requesting 'information as to why Chinese market gardeners are not allowed to sell their produce on the Edmonton City markets.'

19. Betty (Oppelt) Bre-Win, interviews with the author, 7 Oct., 9 Dec. 1993, 16 Feb. 1994.

20. Peter Lupul, interviews with the author, 9, 22 Sept. 1993, 4 Oct. 1993.

✺ ERNA DOMINEY, 'LES GIRLS'

1. McGill University, for example, did not admit women to the Faculty of Applied Science until 1939; see Blanche Lemco van Ginkel, 'Slowly and Surely, (and Somewhat Painfully) More or Less the History of Women in Architecture in Canada,' Society for the Study of Architecture in Canada *Bulletin* 17, no. 1 (1992): 5-11.

2. Alexandra Birukova and Elma Laird were registered as architects in Ontario in 1931, but after 1934 the former worked as a nurse and the latter as a secretary; see Geoffrey Simmins, *Ontario Association of Architects: A Centennial History, 1889-1989* (Toronto: University of Toronto Press, 1989), 110, 112.

3. Veronica Strong-Boag, *The New Day Recalled: Lives of Girls and Women in English Canada, 1919-1939* (Toronto: Copp Clark Pittman, 1988), 53.

4. *EB*, 25 Sept. 1936.

5. See the Register of the AAA, 10515 Saskatchewan Drive, Edmonton, Alberta.

6. *EJ*, 29 June 1953.

7. Lynne Walker, 'Concrete Proof: Women, Architecture and Modernism,' *FAN* 3, no. 4 (1990): 6-8.

8. Wallbridge and Imrie's business papers and over 2,000 architectural drawings are housed in the PAA; the UAA holds some of Wallbridge's student drawings.

9. See Don Wetherell and Irene Kmet, *Homes in Alberta: Building, Trends, and Design, 1870-1967* (Edmonton: University of Alberta Press et al., 1991), 219.

10. PAA, 95.16, interview with the author, Edmonton, June 1991; correspondence with the author; both informants requested anonymity. There are historical precedents in the seventeenth to the nineteenth centuries in England, where an amateur architectural tradition developed of upper-class women designing buildings for their own use and for the poor. See Lynne Walker, 'Women Architects,' in Judy Attfield and Pat Kirham, eds., *A View from the Interior: Feminism, Women and Design* (London: Women's Press, 1989).

11. *EJ*, 28 Feb. 1942.

12. See Frank Burlington Fawcett, ed., *Their Majesties' Courts Held at Buckingham Palace, 1932* (London: Grayson and Grayson, 1932), 115, 138.

13. Appointed Superintending Architect and Professor of Architecture at the new University of Alberta in 1913, Burgess (1870-1971) played a significant role in Alberta's architectural development; see C.S. Burgess, 'Recollections of a Half Century,' *RAIC Journal* (July 1957): 241-5.

14. Tony Cashman and Norman H. Croll, *50 Years of Architecture* (Edmonton: Schmidt Feldberg Croll Henderson, 1988), 30.

15. *EJ*, 19 June 1942.

16. Harold Kalman, *A History of Canadian Architecture*, vol. 2 (Toronto: Oxford University Press, 1994), 785.

17. CEA, City Commissioners' Papers (CCP), RG 11, Cl.207, files 11 and 13, D.B. Menzies to M.C. Dewar, 23 July 1947.

18. The diaries and photographs from Wallbridge and Imrie's European trip can be found in PAA, Jean Wallbridge and Mary Imrie Papers (WIP), 88.290. For articles emerging from later trips see, for example, the Feb. 1958 ('Les Girls en Voyage'), May 1958 ('Hong Kong to Chandigarh'), and July 1958 ('Khyber Pass to Canada') issues of the RAIC Journal.

19. *EJ* clipping (July 1947), in WIP.

20. Sandy MacTaggart, telephone conversation with the author, June 1991.

21. CCP, files 17 and 21, especially M.C. Dewar to D.B. Menzies, 31 Jan. 1949.

22. Ibid., specifically Dewar to Menzies, 8 Feb. 1949.

23. Mary Clark, 'Architectural Scrapbook,' prepared for the 1986 exhibition, For the Record, documenting women graduates in architecture from the

University of Toronto (the scrapbook is now in the university's archives).

24. Ibid., 280.

25. PAA, 95.16, Roy Gordon (Gordon Mangold Hamilton Architects), interview with the author, Edmonton, 28 June 1991.

26. Ibid., Gordon Wynn (Rule Wynn and Rule), interview with the author, Edmonton, 27 June 1991.

27. Ibid., Sanford T. Fitch, interview with the author, Edmonton, 21 June 1991. The Fitch family took occupancy of their home in April 1967.

28. Ibid., Bernie Wood (Wood Gardener O'Neill O'Neill), interview with the author, Edmonton, 12 July 1991.

29. Ibid., Mickie Holland, interview with the author, Edmonton, 24 June 1991.

30. Letter, Jock Bell to the author, 27 June 1991.

31. WIP, Mary Imrie to Eric Arthur, 3 June 1954.

32. Mary Imrie, 'Viewpoint,' RAIC *Journal* (March 1955): 95.

33. PAA, 95.16, Marnie Fitch, interview with the author, Edmonton, 21 June 1991.

34. Ibid., Jean Ward, interview with the author, 20 June 1991. Mrs Ward and her late husband, Henry, moved into their house in Oct. 1968.

35. WIP, Mary Imrie to Paul and Dale, 1 May 1977.

ALVIN FINKEL, ELMER ROPER: SOCIALIST, BUSINESSMAN, MAYOR

1. Biographical information regarding Elmer Roper is found in Joseph Rek, *Municipal Elections in Edmonton, 1892-1989: Summary of Results with Short Mayoral and Aldermanic Biographies* (Edmonton: City of Edmonton, 1990); *PW*, 18 July 1942, 17 Jan. 1948; and *ALN*, 3 Jan. 1931.

2. Roper was foreman of the *CH* press room by day and the *Albertan* press room at night. *EJ*, 15 June 1984.

3. GAI, Calgary Labour Council Papers, box 1, file 5, Trades and Labour Council Minutes, 16 March 1917.

4. PAA, Edmonton Trades and Labour Council Papers, Minutes, 4 May 1917.

5. On the history of labour parties in Alberta see Alvin Finkel, 'The Rise and Fall of the Labour Party in Alberta, 1917-1942,' *Labour/Le Travail* 16 (1985): 61-96.

6. The first issue appeared 12 April 1919 and identified the newspaper as the 'Official Organ of the Edmonton Trades and Labour Council.' *EFP*, 12 April 1919. A complete set of the *EFP* and its successor newspapers is found in the PAA.

7. Finkel, 'Rise and Fall of the Labour Party,' 67.

8. *ALN*, 4 Sept. 1920.

9. Ibid., 6 Nov. 1920.

10. *PW*, 17 Jan. 1948.

11. Elmer Roper, interview with the author, Victoria, British Columbia, 21 Feb. 1984.

12. *PW*, 25 Jan. 1936.

13. Ibid., 25 Nov. 1944, announced the change to become effective in Jan. 1945.

14. *ALN*, 8 Aug. 1931.

15. So, for example, in an editorial on 13 June 1931 Roper wrote in the *ALN*: It seems to the *Labor News* that the Bennett Budget but further serves to emphasize the fact that the interests of eastern Canada are not by any means identical with those of the west. The farmers of the west must sell the greater share of their product to the industrialized countries. People to whom we sell wheat want to sell us something in return. They cannot do so because eastern Canada demands a tariff that will keep the products of other industrial countries out of this country . . . Canadian unity is paid for with a high price by western Canada, and it is going to be increasingly difficult to maintain it unless the east shows a greater disposition to consider western needs than it has done so far.

16. This was the essence of the CCF position that Roper championed tirelessly. In one editorial he attempted to reconcile the two positions by arguing that it was the combination of the capitalist marketplace with central Canadian business domination of the old-line parties that created the grievances of western Canadians: 'Under a planned social economy in Canada any talk of secession on the part of the West would be foolish and unscientific. Under our present system secession would be the lesser of two evils' (*ALN*, 12 May 1934).

17. There is general agreement among historians that western farmers, chafing under the 'national' polices of railways and tariffs established by John A. Macdonald and continued by his successors, Conservative and Liberal, felt that their region was victimized by Ottawa. There is, however, much debate among historians of western labour regarding the extent to which a sense of regional antagonism motivated worker radicalism. The view that it was an important factor is defended in Paul A. Phillips, 'The National Policy and the Development of the Western Canadian Labour Movement,' in A.W. Rasporich and H.C. Klassen, eds., *Prairie Perspectives 2: Selected Papers of the Western Canadian Studies Conferences, 1970*

and 1971 (Toronto: Holt Rinehart and Winston, 1973), 41-62.

The opposing view regards class antagonisms as far more important than regional antagonism in explaining western labour radicalism. David Bercuson, for example, in a refutation of Phillips, focuses on the expectations of immigrant workers and on the ideological baggage that British immigrants in particular brought with them to explain western labour perspectives. See David Jay Bercuson, 'Labour Radicalism and the Western Industrial Frontier, 1897-1919,' *CHR* 58, no. 2 (1977): 154-75. Roper, while not an immigrant, was active in a milieu in both Calgary and Edmonton where British labourite ideas were more important than western populist views.

18. *ALN*, 17 April 1926.
19. *EFP*, 6 March 1920.
20. For example, on 15 Sept. 1923, a page one headline in *ALN* read 'Dominion Trades Congress Demands Total Exclusion of Orientals from Canada.' Page one on 19 Jan. 1924 carried a story indicating that Calgary Labour aldermen were protesting the employment of Orientals in city hospitals.
21. One editorial called the Klan members 'cowards who hide their faces in white hoods' and who 'are parading our streets with their threat to take the law in their own hands.' Roper called for state suppression of the Klan and added: 'In the meantime Labor should keep its eye on the Klan. The people who join such an organization are the kind of tools that Mussolini uses to carry out his policy of suppression. The Klan means enmity to the Labor movement. It should be suppressed' (*ALN*, 26 Dec. 1925).
22. Ibid., 29 Jan. 1921.
23. So, for example, Roper ran a two-part front-page series called 'A Socialist View of Russia' in 1930 which stressed the determination of the Russian people to industrialize and rid the country of dependence on outsiders (ibid., 11, 18 Oct. 1930).
24. Ibid., 3 July 1926; and *Canadian Parliamentary Guide* (1927), 360.
25. *EJ*, 10 Jan. 1931; *ALN*, 17 Jan. 1931; and *Canadian Parliamentary Guide* (1932).
26. *EJ*, 3 July 1962.
27. *EB*, 21 Oct. 1943, for example, gave much of its social page over to the marriage of Frances Roper to a Warrant officer, describing the bride's outfit in detail as well as that of her sister, who was her attendant.
28. *ALN*, 21 March 1931.
29. *EJ*, 24 July 1994.
30. *ALN*, 15 May 1920.
31. The anti-collaborationist view was summarized by Communist Jan Lakeman in ibid., 6 March 1926. Roper's defence

of Farmer-Labor cooperation and the record of the United Farmers government appeared in the same issue.
32. Ibid., 6 March 1926.
33. Roper, interview.
34. *ALN*, 3 Jan. 1931.
35. On the travails of the CCF and the Labour Party in this period, see Alvin Finkel, 'Obscure Origins: The Confused Early History of the Alberta CCF,' in J. William Brennan, ed., *'Building the Cooperative Commonwealth:' Essays on the Democratic Socialist Tradition in Canada* (Regina: Canadian Plains Research Center, 1984), 99-122; and Myron Johnson, 'The Failure of the CCF in Alberta: An Accident of History,' in Carlo Caldarola, ed., *Society and Politics in Alberta: Research Papers* (Toronto: Methuen, 1979), 87-107.
36. Roper's first two editorials regarding the Social Credit upsurge suggested naively that the CCF would be the beneficiary of the demand for social change embodied in the monetary-reform movement (*PW*, 7, 14 April 1934).
37. From early March 1935 onwards *ALN* featured strident attacks against Social Credit in almost every issue.
38. *PW*, 25 Jan. 1936.
39. See Finkel, 'Obscure Origins,' 109-11.
40. *PW*, 1 May 1937. Roper's arguments for considering such a coalition were rather hazy. Attacking the Social Credit administration's unwillingness to borrow, he noted that the proponents of a multi-party united front to oust Social Credit argued to the CCF: 'You have a program that calls for the socialization of various industrial and commercial activities. In order to carry out such a program you must first re-establish the credit of the province. That can best be done by a non-partizan government representing a majority of all sections of the population.' Roper, however, had more serious concerns about Social Credit than its impact on the province's credit rating. The *PW* often suggested similarities between fascism and Social Credit. And in one particularly intemperate editorial, Roper, incensed at the government's plans to limit press freedom, compared Aberhart with Hitler (4 Sept. 1937).
41. Roper's campaign promises included public ownership of natural resources and the major manufacturing and service industries in the province to be achieved by a program of gradual nationalization, free medical and hos-pital services, and a revolving fund to build homes to be rented at reasonable rates or sold on 'easy terms with low interest rates' (ibid., 15 Aug. 1942).
42. *Canadian Parliamentary Guide* (1944), 389; and *PW*, 26 Sept. 1942. The latter reported that Roper received 2,026 of

the Socred candidate's seconds against 1,107 for the Independent candidate.
43. *PW*, 12 Dec. 1942.
44. GAI, CCF Records, box 5, file 42, William Irvine to David Lewis, 28 June 1944; and Alberta Provincial Office to Margaret Telford, CCF National Office, 4 Nov. 1944.
45. So, for example, Roper moved a resolution in the Alberta legislature in early 1944 that read:
    Whereas all wealth comes into being as the property of those who own the means by which it is produced;
    Whereas the exploitation of the natural resources of the nation for private profit, and the private ownership of the principal means of wealth production, distribution and exchange, has resulted in gross inequalities and inefficiencies in the economy of Alberta and Canada, be it therefore
    Resolved, that this legislature is of the opinion that future development of the natural resources of the province should be by public ownership and that the whole future economic development of the province should, as far as practicable, be on the basis of social ownership of the principal means of production and distribution (*Today and Tomorrow*, 9 March 1944).
46. The CCF failed to become the Official Opposition even though its popular vote was almost twice as large as that of the Independents. The latter, however, had three seats. Four years later, with the CCF popular vote down to 19 per cent, the party still had two seats but this time the other opposition party, the Liberals, also had only two seats and a popular vote almost identical to the CCF vote. The government recognized no Leader of the Opposition and the leader's allowance was split between Roper and Liberal leader J. Harper Prowse. So Elmer Roper was never recognized as Leader of the Opposition. See David Byron, 'The Recognition of Leaders of the Opposition in Alberta, 1905-1983,' *PF* 9, no. 1 (1984): 45-55.
47. One prominent attack on the Alberta CCF strategy was Morris Shumiatcher, 'Alberta Election,' *Canadian Forum*, Sept. 1944, 127-9.
48. Ibid., Oct. 1944, 161-2.
49. *PW*, 6 Sept. 1947.
50. Judging by his resolutions in the legislature as reported in Legislative Assembly of Alberta, *Journals* (1945-55); and his speeches in PAA, Premiers' Papers, boxes 1853, 1856, 1857.
51. Legislative Assembly of Alberta, *Journals*, 27 Feb. 1947.
52. On Alberta labour during the Manning period see Alvin Finkel, 'Labour, Social Credit and the Cold War,' *Labour/Le Travail* 21 (1988): 123-52.

53. Larry Pratt, 'Grant Notley: Politics as a Calling,' in Larry Pratt, ed., *Socialism and Democracy in Alberta: Essays in Honour of Grant Notley* (Edmonton: NeWest Press, 1986), 4-12.

54. Roper, interview. Roper's financial contributions, it should be noted, allowed the CCF to continue to have some institutional existence during a period when its membership was falling along with its support. Jack King, the provincial secretary, noted in 1949: 'The office is in Roper's building. We have never paid rent, heat or light. In addition he has regularly made contributions up to $500 per year and other donations on special occasions' (CCF Papers, box 5, file 43, Jack King, Secretary, Alberta CCF, to Lloyd Shaw, Provincial Secretary, Nova Scotia CCF, 10 March 1949).

55. The most thorough examination of the charges is Bob Hesketh, 'The Company A, Company B Charges: The Manning Government, the Treasury Branches and Highway Contracts' (MA thesis, University of Alberta, 1989).

56. When he announced that he was not seeking re-election to the school board in 1929, Roper added that he would not seek elected office again: 'From now on I'm going to golf, and curl, attend to my own business, and have a good time generally' (*EJ*, 19 Oct. 1929).

57. Jack Masson and Peter Blaikie, 'Labour Politics in Alberta,' in Caldarola, *Society and Politics in Alberta*, 274; and Pratt, 'Grant Notley,' 12-13.

58. Various articles in *EJ* in 1959 trace the evolution of the CRA and its attempts to win Roper as its candidate for mayor.

59. The official vote count was: Roper, 25,465 votes; Prowse, 19,318; W. Pasternak, 6,624; J. Bennett, 542 (Rek, *Municipal Elections*, 44).

60. *EJ*, 12 Dec. 1959.

61. CEA, Elmer Roper File, 'Address by Mayor E. Roper,' 22 June 1960.

62. The official count was Roper, 37,600 votes; Leger, 13,106; and R. Simmins, 8,234 (Rek, *Municipal Elections*, 44).

63. *EJ*, 30 Sept. 1963.

64. Ibid., 15 June 1984.

65. Ibid., 24 July 1994.

∾ P.J. SMITH,
PLANNING FOR RESIDENTIAL GROWTH SINCE THE 1940S

1. The only departure from this trend, the decade 1961-71, was due to Edmonton's amalgamation with the Town of Jasper Place in 1964.

2. P.J. Smith, 'Community Aspirations, Territorial Justice and the Metropolitan Form of Edmonton and Calgary,' in Guy M. Robinson, ed., *A Social Geography of Canada* (Toronto: Dundurn Press, 1991), 245-66.

3. Thomas L. Burton, *A Strathcona County Residents Survey* (Edmonton: Makale and Kyllo Planning Associates, 1979); Earl Berger, *St. Albert Community Attitude Survey* (Edmonton: Alberta Local Authorities Board, 1980); and Thomas J. Plunkett and James Lightbody, 'Tribunals, Politics and the Public Interest: The Edmonton Annexation Case,' *Canadian Public Policy* 8 (1982): 207-21.

4. P.J. Smith, 'The Principle of Utility and the Origins of Planning Legislation in Alberta, 1912-1975,' in Alan Artibise and Gilbert Stelter, eds., *The Usable Urban Past: Planning and Politics in the Modern Canadian City* (Toronto: Macmillan, 1979), 196-225; and P.J. Smith, 'Land Development in Edmonton,' in Donald Kerr and Deryck W. Holdsworth, eds., *Historical Atlas of Canada*, vol. 3 (Toronto: University of Toronto Press, 1990), plate 20.

5. P.J. Smith, 'American Influences and Local Needs: Adaptations to the Alberta Planning System in 1928-1929,' in Gilbert Stelter and Alan Artibise, eds., *Power and Place: Canadian Urban Development in the North American Context* (Vancouver: University of British Columbia Press, 1986), 109-32.

6. Edmund H. Dale, 'Decision-making at Edmonton, 1913-1945: Town Planning without a Plan,' *PC* 11 (1971): 134-47.

7. K.C. Mackenzie, 'Noel Dant, FCIP—A Pioneer and Pillar of Professional Planning in Alberta,' *PC* (Nov. 1993): 41; and Wayne Jackson, 'Noel Dant 1913-1993,' *Newsletter*, AACIP (Fall 1993), 5.

8. For interpretations of these developments, particularly with reference to housing and community planning, see Dennis Guest, *The Emergence of Social Security in Canada* (Vancouver: University of British Columbia Press, 1980); Albert Rose, *Canadian Housing Policies 1935-1980* (Scarborough: Butterworth, 1980); John C. Bacher, *Keeping to the Marketplace: The Evolution of Canadian Housing Policy* (Montreal and Kingston: McGill-Queen's University Press, 1993); and John Sewell, *House and Home: Housing for Canadians* (Toronto: James Lorimer, 1994).

9. Colin K. Hatcher and Tom Schwarzkopf, *Edmonton's Electric Transit: The Story of Edmonton's Streetcars and Trolley Buses* (Toronto: Railfare Enterprises, 1983).

10. In 1995 the Alberta Planning Act was repealed and incorporated, with numerous amendments, into the Municipal Government Act. The change of greatest importance in respect to this chapter was that the Edmonton Metropolitan Regional Planning Commission ceased to exist on 31 March 1995. It was replaced by an advisory body, the Capital Region Forum, that effectively returned metropolitan planning to the situation prevailing in the early 1950s.

11. Edward J. Kaiser, David R. Godschalk, and F. Stuart Chapin Jr, *Urban Land Use Planning*, 4th ed. (Urbana: University of Illinois Press, 1995).

12. For a more general Alberta perspective on residential planning and design in the early postwar period see Donald Wetherell and Irene Kmet, *Homes in Alberta: Building, Trends, and Design, 1870-1967* (Edmonton: University of Alberta Press, et al., 1991), 249-59.

13. *Guidelines for the Distribution and Design of Neighbourhood Density* (Edmonton: City of Edmonton Planning Department, 1978); and Mark A. Sorenson, 'Density as an Issue in Suburban Development: The Case of West Jasper Place' (MA thesis, University of Alberta, 1982).

14. For recent examples see Peter Calthorpe, *The Next American Metropolis* (Princeton: Princeton Architectural Press, 1993); Anthony Downs, *New Visions for Metropolitan America* (Washington DC: Brookings Institution, 1994); and Philip Langdon, *A Better Place to Live* (Amherst: University of Massachusetts Press, 1994).

15. Michael Dennis and Susan Fish, *Programs in Search of a Policy: Low Income Housing in Canada* (Toronto: Hakkert, 1972).

16. Peter Spurr, *Land and Urban Development: A Preliminary Study* (Toronto: James Lorimer, 1976).

17. For a Canadian review of the public land banking concept see S.W. Hamilton, 'Public Land Banking—Real or Illusionary Benefits?' (unpublished report to the Urban Development Institute of Ontario, 1974).

18. Ed Flood, 'Mill Woods and the Edmonton Land Supply,' *Living Places* 12, no. 4 (1976): 26-37; and Jean-Pierre Le Bourgeois, 'The Effects of the Mill Woods Land Bank on Land and Housing Prices in Edmonton' (MA thesis, University of Alberta, 1981).

19. *Edmonton General Municipal Plan*, City of Edmonton, Bylaw #6000, 1980.

20. John Steil and Richard Powell, 'The Design and Distribution of Increased Density in Suburban Neighbourhoods in Edmonton,' *Alberta Journal of Planning Practice* 1 (1982): 23-43. For an example see Fig. 5c later in this chapter, the Lee Ridge neighbourhood in Mill Woods.

21. L.D. McCann, *Neighbourhoods in Transition: Processes of Land Use and Physical Change in Edmonton's Residential Areas* (Edmonton: University of Alberta, Studies in Geography, Occasional Paper No. 2, 1975); L.D. McCann and P.J. Smith, 'The Residential Development Cycle in Space and Time,' in P.J. Smith, ed., *Edmonton: The Emerging Metropolitan Pattern* (Victoria: University of Victoria, Western Geographical Series 15, 1978), 119-59; and P.J. Smith and L.D. McCann, 'Residential Land Use Change in Inner Edmonton,' *Annals of the Association of American Geographers* 71 (1981): 536-51.

22. P.J. Smith and Michael J. McGibbon, *Effects of Neighbourhood Planning on Housing Quality in Edmonton* (Ottawa: Canada Mortgage and Housing Corporation, 1991).

23. *Housing Intensification: Policies, Constraints and Options* (Toronto: Canadian Urban Institute, Urban Focus Series, 1991), 90-6; and Ralph Perkins, 'What's Happening in the Suburbs of Greater Vancouver?,' *City Magazine* 14, no. 3 (1993): 19-24.

24. *Edmonton General Municipal Plan*, City of Edmonton, Bylaw #9076, 1990, 13.

25. P.J. Smith and Elizabeth Woodman, 'Geographical Overview of Housing Renovation in Edmonton,' in Eileen Badiuk, ed., *Issues in Housing and Neighbourhood Rehabilitation* (Winnipeg: University of Winnipeg, Institute of Urban Studies, Occasional Paper No. 19, 1990), 29-86.

26. *Edmonton General Municipal Plan*, 1990, 11.

27. John Bland and Harold Spence Sales, 'A Report on the City of Edmonton Concerning the State of Physical Development and Administration under the Provisions of the Town Planning Act 1929' (unpublished report to Edmonton City Council, Sept. 1949).

28. *Second Annual Report 1951-1952* (Edmonton: Edmonton District Planning Commission, 1952).

29. Gary A. Gahr, 'Sherwood Park: Residents' Attitudes towards a Dormitory Satellite of Edmonton' (MA thesis, University of Alberta, 1979).

30. The essence of the satellite town concept is that satellites should be far enough away from their parent city to discourage commuting. They must also have their own employment bases, rather than being mere dormitories for the parent cities. See *Fourth Annual Report 1953-1954* (Edmonton: Edmonton District Planning Commission, 1954).

31. The dispute is described at length in Gahr, 'Sherwood Park,' 39-59.

32. *Report of the Royal Commission on the Metropolitan Development of Calgary and Edmonton* (Edmonton: Queen's Printer, 1956). See also David G. Bettison, John K. Kenward, and Larrie Taylor, *Urban Affairs in Alberta* (Edmonton: University of Alberta Press, 1975).

33. For a typical example see 'A Statement on the Future of This City,' a submission to the Minister of Municipal Affairs approved by Edmonton City Council on 1 Oct. 1973.

34. P.J. Smith and H.L. Diemer, 'Equity and the annexation process—Edmonton's bid for the Strathcona Industrial Corridor,' in P.J. Smith, ed., *Edmonton: The Emerging Metropolitan Pattern*, 263-89; W.L. Batey and P.J. Smith, 'The Role of Territory in Political Conflict in Metropolitan Fringe Areas,' in Ken B. Beesley and Lorne H. Russwurm, eds., *The Rural-Urban Fringe: Canadian Perspectives* (Downsview: York University-Atkinson College, Geographical Monographs No. 10, 1981), 199-217; and P.J. Smith, 'Municipal Conflicts over Territory and the Effectiveness of the Regional Planning System in the Edmonton Metropolitan Area,' in Hans Becker, ed., *Kulturgeographische Prozessforschung in Kanada* (Bamberg: Fach Geographie an der Universitat Bamberg, Bamberger Geographische Schriften 4, 1982), 207-33.

35. *Eighth Annual Report 1957-1958* (Edmonton: Edmonton District Planning Commission, 1958).

36. For an exhaustive account of provincial government attitudes towards municipal government up to 1970 see Bettison, Kenward, and Taylor, *Urban Affairs in Alberta*.

37. 'Report and Decision Concerning the Edmonton Annexation Application,' issued by the Government of Alberta, June 1981.

38. P.J. Smith and Patricia E. Bayne, 'The Issue of Local Autonomy in Edmonton's Regional Plan Process: Metropolitan Planning in a Changing Political Climate,' in Frances Frisken, ed., *The Changing Canadian Metropolis: A Public Policy Perspective* (Berkeley and Toronto: Institute of Governmental Studies Press, University of California, and Canadian Urban Institute, 1994), 725-50. Under the 1977 Planning Act, regional planning commissions were required to adopt regional plans by 31 Dec. 1982, though Edmonton's plan did not actually take effect until 22 Aug. 1984—the first (and only) time in Edmonton's history that it had an official metropolitan plan.

39. The restricted development area was established by the Government of Alberta in 1974. It is being developed as a pipeline and transportation corri-

dor, including an eventual ring road around Edmonton.

40. LeBourgeois, 'Effects of Mill Woods Land Bank,'6-11; and Patricia E. Bayne, 'Generation of Alternatives in the Planning Process—Theoretical Discourse and a Practical Test' (PhD diss., University of Alberta, 1992), 247-53.

41. Emma C. Sicoli, 'An Evaluation of the Canora Neighbourhood Improvement Project' (MA thesis, University of Alberta, 1984); and Smith and McGibbon, *Effects of Neighbourhood Planning*.

42. 'Step by Step: Edmonton's Land Development Process,' *City Trends: A Review of Planning and Building Issues and Activities in Edmonton* (Oct. 1989), 3-6.

43. Several Edmonton neighbourhoods were featured in 'Housing Design Supplement Two,' a technical bulletin produced by the Community Planning Association of Canada in 1952 or 1953. An information sheet on the Sherbrooke neighbourhood, that was prepared at about the same time, was widely distributed as well.

44. This classification of neighbourhoods follows Shuguang Wang, 'Evaluation of Planned Residential Environments with Regard to Pedestrian Safety: A Case Study of Edmonton' (PhD diss., University of Alberta, 1994).

45. Clarence A. Perry, *Housing in the Machine Age* (New York: Russell Sage Foundation, 1939), 50-76.

46. Wang, 'Evaluation of Planned Residential Environments.'

47. Noel Dant, 'Edmonton: Practical Results of Planning Measures since 1950,' *Community Planning Review* 4 (1954): 31-40.

48. Edmund H. Dale, 'The Role of Successive Town and City Councils in the Evolution of Edmonton, Alberta, 1892-1966' (PhD diss., University of Alberta, 1969), 153-81.

49. M.W. Winnie Chan, 'The Impact of the Technical Planning Board on the Morphology of Edmonton 1950-1963' (MA thesis, University of Alberta, 1969).

50. Robert F. Graden, 'The Planning of New Residential Areas in Edmonton, 1950-1976' (MA thesis, University of Alberta, 1979).

51. Smith, 'Land Development in Edmonton.'

52. As a legal procedure and as long as a majority of owners are agreed, replotting permits all existing titles to be extinguished. The new land parcels created under the resubdivision plan are then allocated to the previous owners, in the original proportions.

53. *West Jasper Place Review Area: Outline Plan* (Edmonton: City Planning

Department, 1967); and Mill Woods (Edmonton: A Development Concept Report Prepared on Behalf of the Civic Administration by the City Planning Department, 1971). The introduction of large-area structure planning is discussed in many secondary sources, including Dale, 'Role of Successive Town and City Councils,' 343-7; Graden, 'Planning of New Residential Areas,' 49-129; Wetherell and Kmet, *Homes in Alberta*, 257-9; and Wang, 'Evaluation of Planned Residential Environments,' 101-13.

54. Clarence S. Stein, *Toward New Towns for America* (New York: Reinhold, 1957), 19.

55. Wang, 'Evaluation of Planned Residential Environments,' 182-97.

56. Humphrey Carver, *Cities in the Suburbs* (Toronto: University of Toronto Press, 1962). On Don Mills see John Sewell, *The Shape of the City: Toronto Struggles with Modern Planning* (Toronto: University of Toronto Press, 1993), 79-96.

57. R. Jean Frost, 'Public Transportation and Neighbourhood Design: An Edmonton Example' (MA thesis, University of Alberta, 1985).

58. These problems were first identified in a report entitled 'Walkway Systems' which was prepared by Edmonton's City Planning Department in 1977.

59. Alyce Z.C. Wickert, 'Evaluation of Planned Walkway Networks in Two Edmonton Neighbourhoods' (MA thesis, University of Alberta, 1993).

60. For a detailed explanation of the Mill Woods design process and plan see Bayne, 'Generation of Alternatives in the Planning Process,' 224-300.

61. Hazel Christy, *Town Centre Development in Edmonton* (Edmonton: Planning and Development Department, Research Paper 17, 1987).

62. P.J. Smith, 'Coping with mega-mall development: an urban planning perspective on West Edmonton Mall,' CG 35, no. 3 (1991): 295-305.

DAVID CHUENYAN LAI, THREE CHINATOWNS

1. Chuen-yan Lai, 'Socio-economic Structures and Viability of Chinatown,' in Charles Forward, ed., *Residential and Neighbourhood Studies in Victoria* (Victoria: University of Victoria, 1973), 101; and David Chuenyan Lai, *Chinatowns: Towns within Cities in Canada* (Vancouver: University of British Columbia Press, 1988), 4, 34-5.

2. Kay J. Anderson, *Vancouver's Chinatown: Racial Discourse in Canada, 1875-1980* (Montreal and Kingston: McGill-Queen's University Press, 1991), 9, 30.

3. For example, Peter Li does not use the term Chinatown or examine the geographical concentration of Chinese-operated firms in his 'Ethnic Enterprise in Transition: Chinese Business in Richmond, B.C., 1980-1990,' CES 24, no. 1 (1992): 120-38.

4. *Colonist* (Victoria), 15 Sept. 1881; and VN, 13 Jan. 1887.

5. George E. Hartwell, 'Our Work among the Japanese and Chinese in British Columbia,' MB 9 (1913): 518.

6. J. Brian Dawson, *Moon Cakes in Gold Mountain: From China to the Canadian Plains* (Calgary: Detselig Enterprises, 1991), 40. The two laundries were Chung Gee and Ning Lee; the restaurant was first Ah Sing and then To-Chu-Loo (see *Henderson Directory*, 1886-1900).

7. John Patrick Day, *Wong Sing Fuen and the Sing Lee Laundry* (Edmonton: Edmonton Parks and Recreation, 1978), 7.

8. Ibid. Sex was not identified in the 1941 census. In 1971 there were 5,110 Chinese in the metro area (Edmonton City, St Albert, Bon Accord, Sturgeon and Strathcona counties, Fort Saskatchewan, Gibbons, Morinville, and Legal).

9. Gunter Baureiss, 'The Chinese Community in Calgary,' AHR 22, no. 2 (1974): 3.

10. EB, 23 May 1908.

11. Lai, *Chinatowns*, 92-3.

12. EB, 23 May 1908.

13. See, for example, S.S. Osterhout, *Orientals in Canada* (Toronto: United Church of Canada, 1929), 102; and EB, 23 May 1908.

14. *Sing Tao Daily News* (Vancouver), 28 Jan. 1984.

15. See Beng Seng Hoe, *Structural Changes of Two Chinese Communities in Alberta* (Ottawa: Canadian Centre for Folk Culture Studies, 1976), 113.

16. According to the 1991 census, Alberta's Chinese population was about 80,000. Metro Edmonton (36,280) had the largest number, followed by Metro Calgary (36,140).

17. Hoe, *Structural Changes*, 113, 118.

18. City of Edmonton, Planning Department, *Downtown Plan, Working Paper No. 1: The Future of Chinatown* (1978), 2, 35.

19. CN, 3 Oct. 1973.

20. See EJ, 4. Aug. 1976; and City of Edmonton, *Downtown Plan*, 30, 36-7.

21. EJ, 14 April 1977; and City of Edmonton, *Downtown Plan*, 31-7.

22. Bing K. Mah, 'Reminiscences of My Past Fifty Years,' *Chinese Benevolent Association and Edmonton Chinatown Multi-Cultural Centre Special Issue* (Edmonton: Chinese Benevolent Association, 1986).

23. EJ, 21 June 1979.

24. Ibid., 19 July 1979.

25. City of Edmonton, Planning Department, *Revised Chinatown Plan* (1980), 2, 11.

26. Dick B. Wong, Chairman, ECPC, to Mayor Cec J. Purves, 11 Aug. 1980; and Tommy Mack, President, CBA, to Mayor Cec J. Purves, 11 Aug. 1980.

27. See CN, 18 Nov. 1983; and Frank Gee, Kim Hung, and Dong Wong, 'The Chinese Benevolent Association of Edmonton: Then and Now,' *Edmonton Chinese Benevolent Association Special Issue* (Edmonton: Chinese Benevolent Association, 1991).

28. CN, 18 May 1986.

29. Armin Preiksaitis, Manager, Area Planning Branch, City of Edmonton, to David Chuenyan Lai, Chairman, Chinatown Redevelopment Committee, Victoria, 17 March, 7 April 1986.

30. On the financing and construction of the gate see CN, 4 April, 18 May 1986; Yeung Zhi and Yang Ji Hong, 'Edmonton's New Chinatown Chinese Entrance Gate Plan' (unpublished plan, 5 April 1987); Kulbir Singh, Senior Planner, Planning and Building Department, City of Edmonton, interview with the author, July 1987; and EJ, 25 Oct. 1987. In 1968-9 the Alberta Chinese Cultural Society, founded by Kim Mah, arranged the twinning of Heilongjiang and Alberta (CN, 18 Oct. 1983), making the two provincial capitals, Harbin and Edmonton, sister cities.

31. Lai, *Chinatowns*, 170.

32. Survey conducted by the author, April 1987. A linear New Chinatown can also been found in San Francisco's New Chinatown in Richmond, which in 1991 had over ninety Chinese businesses on both sides of Clement Street between Park Presidio and Arguello boulevards (survey by the author, May 1991).

33. Owners of Tai Fat Grocery and Hing Lung Store, interview with the author, March 1986.

34. *Canada Year Book* (1980-1), 125.

35. Pak Chi Ming (owner, Asia Square and Centre 101), Helena Lee (manager, Sakura Japanese Restaurant), Van Dien Lam (manager, Grace Willow Blinds), and others, interviews with the author, May 1995.

36. City of Edmonton, *Boyle Street/McCauley Planning Coordinating Committee, Boyle Street/McCauley Area Redevelopment Plan* (1994), 63.

37. Survey by the author, May 1995.

CVCYNTHIA DUNNIGAN,
**'DON'T EVER LET YOUR CREE
DOWN'**

1. The information that follows is from a life history study I conducted between April 1993 and Aug. 1994. This research was funded by the Royal Commission on Aboriginal Peoples. Information was gathered using oral history methods. Interviews with Mrs Gray took place between 21 May and 25 Aug. 1993 in Edmonton, Alberta.
2. D.N. Sprague and R.P. Frye, *The Genealogy of the First Metis Nation: The Development and Dispersal of the Red River Settlement 1820-1900* (Winnipeg: Pemmican Publications, 1983), Table 1.
3. The material presented here is not about general Metis history and culture so much as it is a sampling of the life experiences of one Metis woman. Mrs Gray's experiences are not to be taken as representative of all Metis women or Metis culture in general. For information about Metis history and culture see Jacqueline Peterson and Jennifer Brown, eds., *The New Peoples: Being and Becoming Metis in North America* (Winnipeg: University of Manitoba Press, 1983); and Anne Anderson, *The First Metis: A New Nation* (Edmonton: Plains Publishing, 1985). On First Nation women's experiences see H.C. Wolfart and Freda Ahenakew, eds., *Kohkominawak Otacimowiniwawa: Our Grandmothers' Lives As Told in their Own Words* (Saskatoon: Fifth House Publishers, 1992); Maria Campbell, *Halfbreed* (Halifax: Goodread Biographies, 1983); and Jeanne Perreault and Sylvia Vance, eds., *Writing the Circle: Native Women of Western Canada* (Edmonton: NeWest, 1990). For information about the writing of life history, particularly life histories of First Nation peoples, see Arnold Krupat, ed., *Native American Autobiography: An Anthology* (Madison: University of Wisconsin Press, 1994); and Julie Cruikshank in collaboration with Angela Sidney, Kitty Smith, and Annie Ned, *Life Lived Like a Story: Life Stories of Three Yukon Native Elders* (Vancouver: University of British Columbia Press, 1990).
4. According to Gray, Patrick was married to a woman named Anne Bruce. According to PAA, Cunningham File, 75.582, Patrick's wife was named Nancy Bruce. I discussed the difference with Mrs Gray who pointed out that the name Nancy occurs several times in the generations after Patrick and Anne/Nancy. It may be that Nancy is the correct name or it may be a nickname.
5. PAA, 75.582.
6. Elzaide Cunningham, 'Cunningham Story,' in Arlene Borgstede, ed., *Black Robe's Vision: A History of St. Albert and District* (St Albert Historical Society, 1993), 48.
7. Father A. Tetreault, 'Historic St. Albert: Transformation and Highlights (1890-1954),' *AHR* 5, no. 1 (1955): 25.
8. Samuel is listed in *Canadian Parliamentary Companion Northwest Territories Assembly* (Ottawa: J. Durie & Son, 1887) and is noted as an interpreter at Treaty Eight in Richard Price, *Legacy: Indian Treaty Relationships* (Edmonton: Plains Publishing, 1991), 142. Samuel is listed as the first mayor of Grouard in St Albert Archives, St Albert File, 1885.
9. Borgstede, *Black Robe's Vision*, 246.
10. Gray, interview, 21 May 1993.
11. Cree term meaning My Grandchild; and Gray, interview, 21 May 1993.
12. Gray, interview.
13. Ibid.
14. Ibid.
15. Eddie Gray, 'Ambrose and Mary Gray,' in Elizabeth Turnbull and Jean Payne, eds., *The Pathfinders: A History of Onoway, Bilby, Brookdale, Glenford, Goldthorpe, Heatherdown, Hillcrest, Nakamun, Rich Valley, Speldhurst, Stettin, and Sturgeon River* (Winnipeg: Intercollegiate Press, 1978), 351.
16. For more information on the subject of Aboriginal people and the justice system see Therese Lajeunesse, 'Cross Cultural Issues in the Justice System: The Case of Aboriginal People in Canada,' in *Program on Conflict Resolution* (Honolulu: University of Hawaii at Manoa, 1991); and Marianne O. Nielsen and Robert A. Silverman, eds., *Aboriginal Peoples and Canadian Criminal Justice* (Vancouver: Butterworths, 1992).
17. Cree terms for Grandmother and My Sister-in-Law.

CVGORDON DREVER
AND STEPHEN A. KENT,
GODS FROM AFAR

1. *Edmonton Jewish Life*, 31 Jan. 1992.
2. This chapter draws upon material from both the City of Edmonton Archives and Gordon Drever's private archives. Stephen Kent also utilizes material collected with the assistance of a grant from the Social Sciences and Humanities Research Council of Canada.
3. On religious groups in Edmonton during the 1950s see William E. Mann, *Sect, Cult and Church in Alberta* (Toronto: University of Toronto Press, 1955). Also useful for background information is J. Gordon Melton, *Encyclopedia of American Religions*, vol. 2 (Wilmington NC: McGrath Publishing Company, 1978).
4. A very useful study of Islamic and Hindu religions in the United States is Raymond Brady Williams, *Religions of Immigrants from India and Pakistan* (Cambridge: Cambridge University Press, 1988).
5. Baha Abu-Laban, 'The Canadian Muslim Community: The Need for a New Survival Strategy,' in Earle Waugh et al., eds., *The Muslim Community in North America* (Edmonton: University of Alberta Press, 1983), 80-1; and Abu-Laban, *An Olive Branch on the Family Tree: The Arabs in Canada* (Toronto: McClelland and Stewart, 1985), 139.
6. *EJ*, 30 May 1992.
7. Ibid., 12 Aug. 1976.
8. Ibid., 27 Feb. 1981; and *The New Canadian*, Dec. 1984, 1-2.
9. *EJ*, 24 Jan. 1987.
10. *The Prairie Link*, Jan. 1983, 16-17.
11. *EJ*, 17 Aug. 1976, 24 April 1983, 15 Aug. 1992.
12. See the pamphlet by Louis J. Hammann, *Ahmadiyyat: An Introduction* (London: Al Shirkatul-Islamiyyah [The London Mosque], 1985); and *EJ*, 21 Nov. 1987.
13. See *EJ*, 22 July, 7 Aug. 1984, 30 Aug. 1986.
14. Ibid., 4 Oct. 1986, 19 Aug., 8 Oct., 19 Nov. 1988.
15. For a partial discussion of Sufism see Moojan Momen, *An Introduction to Shi'i Islam* (New Haven: Yale University Press, 1985), 208-16; and Annemarie Schimmel, *Mystical Dimensions of Islam* (Chapel Hill: University of North Carolina Press, 1975).
16. *Edmonton Access Catalogue* (1978), 99.
17. *EJ*, 16 Jan. 1988; and Judy Evaski-Mclean, 'Dances of Universal Peace,' *Life Rhythms* (Summer 1994): 6-7.
18. For example, Robert Brenton Betts argues in *The Druze* (New Haven: Yale University Press, 1988), that 'even in its earliest stages Druzism was not merely a sect of Islam but a new religion, which aimed at establishing a new world order' (3).
19. *EJ*, 14 Aug. 1982.
20. Andrew Pemberton-Pigott, 'The Baha'i Faith in Alberta, 1942-1992: The Ethic of Dispersion' (MA thesis, University of Alberta, 1992), 25-6; and *EJ*, 23 Sept., 15 Oct. 1941, 29 April 1972, 15 Dec. 1990.
21. *EJ*, 18 Sept. 1993.
22. See Norman Buchignani, 'South Asians in Alberta,' in Howard Palmer and Tamara Palmer, eds., *Peoples of Alberta: Portraits of Cultural Diversity* (Saskatoon: Western Producer Prairie Books, 1985), 419; and David Goa et al., 'Hindus in Alberta: A Study in Religious Continuity and Change,' *CES* 16, no. 1 (1984): 96-113.
23. Hindu Society of Alberta, *Silver Jubilee Souvenir* (1992), 1; *EJ*, 17 Aug. 1976, 16 Sept. 1984; and *Times of India*, May 1984.

24. Maha Ganapati Society of Alberta, *Annual Report* (1992, 1993).

25. *AR*, 3 Sept. 1984, 40; and *EJ*, 28 March 1992, 22 April 1995.

26. *EJ*, 15 Nov. 1969.

27. On the Nanaksar see ibid., 28 Aug. 1976, 19 July 1993; *Edmonton's Weekly News*, 1 July 1994; and *VS*, 2 Sept. 1994.

28. *EJ*, 23 Aug. 1980.

29. Ibid., 21 May 1983.

30. Ibid., 26 June 1982, 16 Dec. 1983, 25 Feb. 1984.

31. Ibid., 24 July 1984.

32. Melton, *Encyclopedia of American Religions*, 389.

33. Advertisement, *Gateway* (University of Alberta student newspaper), 5 Oct. 1972.

34. *EJ*, 20 June 1992.

35. Melton, *Encyclopedia of American Religions*, 231-2; see also the Sept. 1979 issue of the *Spiritual Counterfeits Project Journal* from Berkeley, California, which discusses Twitchell's Scientology connection.

36. *SJER*, 25 Nov. 1974, 20; and *EJ*, 18 March 1975.

37. Zoroastrian Association of Alberta, Minutes of the Thirteenth Annual General Meeting, Calgary, 25 Sept. 1993; and *Fourteenth Annual General Body Meeting Programme*, Edmonton, 27 Aug. 1994.

38. On TM's use of scientific language and denial of its religious base see, for example, the exchange between Earl Legate, a former follower, and Bob Chelmick, a current practitioner, in *EJ*, 26 Sept., 3 Oct. 1986. See also Stephen A. Kent, 'Deviance Labelling and Normative Strategies in the Canadian "New Religions/Countercult" Debate,' *CJS* 15, no. 4 (1990): 399-400.

39. See *EJ*, 11 Nov. 1966; the Maharishi Vedic College's 1992 brochure, *Dawn of a New Era in Education and Health Care*; and the 1993 campaign brochure, *The Natural Law Party of Alberta: Bringing the Light of Science to Politics*.

40. For the swami's religious biography see the six-volume *Srila Prabhupada-lilamrta* (Los Angeles: Bhaktivedanta Book Trust, 1980-3) by Satsvarupa Gosvami Dasa.

41. On the Hare Krishnas in Edmonton see *SJER*, 5. Aug. 1974, 21; and *EJ*, 14 Sept., 14 Dec. 1978, 21 Sept. 1979, 25 Sept. 1981, 17 Oct. 1982, 12 Jan. 1985, 8 Feb. 1985.

42. See James V. Downton Jr, *Sacred Journeys: The Conversion of Young Americans to Divine Light Mission* (New York: Columbia University Press, 1979); *SJER*, 2 June 1973; *Gateway*, 19 Nov. 1974; and *Edmonton Access Catalogue*, 98.

43. See, for example, *Times of India*, 28 June 1981; and *EJ*, 4 June 1993.

44. See W.E. Mann, *The Quest for Total Bliss: A Psycho-Sociological Perspective on the Rajneesh Movement* (Toronto: Canadian Scholars' Press, 1991), 81-104; and Win McCormack, ed., *The Rajneesh Chronicles: An 'Oregon Magazine' Book* (Portland: New Oregon Publishers, 1987), 25-34.

45. See *EJ*, 25 Feb. 1978, 4, 6, 12 Aug. 1985; and *G&M*, 12 March 1994.

46. *EJ*, 11 March 1989, 3 Nov. 1990, 28 Aug. 1993.

47. For an overview of some of these groups in the province see Doreen Indra, 'Khmer, Lao, Vietnamese, and Vietnamese-Chinese in Alberta,' in Palmer and Palmer, *Peoples of Alberta*, 437-63.

48. *EJ*, 30 Oct. 1983.

49. *ES*, 11 Nov. 1985.

50. *EJ*, 15 March 1986.

51. *Daily Colonist*, 16 Oct. 1974.

52. *EJ*, 10 July 1993.

53. Ibid., 7 Sept. 1991, 25, 27 June 1994.

54. *Canadian Chinese Times*, 15 Sept. 1994.

55. *Moshi Moshi* (newsletter of the Japanese Community Association of Edmonton), 12 May 1992; see also *EJ*, 1 Dec. 1991, 28 Aug. 1993.

56. See *SJER*, 24 Nov. 1975, 27; and *EJ*, 19 Aug., 4 Nov. 1978, 14 July 1979.

57. *EJ*, 16 July 1983. On Soka Gakkai and Nichiren Shoshu see Richard Causton, *Nichiren Shoshu Buddhism: An Introduction* (London: Rider, 1988); H. Neill McFarland, *The Rush Hour of the Gods: A Study of New Religious Movements in Japan*, 1970 ed. (New York: Harper Colophon Books, 1967), 194-220; and Daniel Metraux, *The History and Theology of Soka Gakkai: A Japanese New Religion* (Queenston ON: Edwin Mellon Press, 1988).

58. *EJ*, 9 June 1990.

DOUG OWRAM, THE BABY BOOM AND THE TRANSFORMATION OF THE UNIVERSITY OF ALBERTA

1. My thanks to Heather Rollason who assisted with the research for this chapter.

2. *EJ*, 26 March 1969.

3. T.C. Byrne, 'Forward,' in Duncan Campbell, *Those Tumultuous Years: The Goals of the President of the University of Alberta during the Decade of the 1960s* (Edmonton: University of Alberta, 1977).

4. *Canada Year Book* (1930), 119.

5. E.A. Corbett, *Henry Marshall Tory. A Biography* (Edmonton: University of Alberta press, 1992) , 104[originally published 1954].

6. Ibid., 93.

7. University of Alberta, *Report of the Board of Governors*, 1968-1969, 18.

8. *Census of Canada* (1951), Table 59-4.

9. Canadian Institute of Pubic Opinion, 29 June 1963. By 1963 the figure had shifted dramatically.

10. M. Long, 'Competing with Russia in the Schools,' *Canadian Comment*, Nov. 1957.

11. Economic Council of Canada, *The Challenge of Growth and Change, Fifth Annual Review* (Ottawa: Queen's Printer, 1968), 68.

12. Gordon Bertram, *The Contribution of Education to Economic Growth* (Ottawa: Economic Council of Canada, Staff Study no. 12, 1966), 55-63. See also David Dodge, *Returns to investment in university training, the case of Canadian accountants, engineers and scientists* (Kingston: Queen's University, Industrial Relations Centre, 1972).

13. Enid Charles, *The Changing Size of the Family in Canada* (Ottawa: Dominion Bureau of Statistics, Census Monograph no. 1, 1948), 33.

14. *Canada Year Book* (1961), 204.

15. E.F. Sheffield, 'Canadian University and College Enrolment,' *Proceedings of the National Conference of Canadian Universities for 1955*; George Croskery and Gerald Nason, eds. *Canadian Conference on Education. Addresses and Proceedings* (Ottawa: Mutual Press, 1958), 210; see also *Financial Post*, 22 Jan. 1955. On the efforts of the NCUU to generate publicity see Robin Harris, *A History of Higher Education in Canada* (Toronto: University of Toronto Press, 1976), 460.

16. Cited in Paul Axelrod, *Scholars and Dollars: Politics, Economics and the Universities of Ontario, 1945-1980* (Toronto: University of Toronto Press, 1982), 85.

17. Eric J. Hanson, *Projections of Enrolment and Operating Expenditure, University of Alberta Fiscal Years 1964-1972* (Edmonton: University of Alberta, 1964), Table 1.

18. University of Alberta, *Annual Report of the Board of Governors*, 1968-1969, 18.

19. Arthur G. McCalla, 'The Development of Graduate Studies at the University of Alberta' (Edmonton: University of Alberta, 1983), ix.

20. Ibid., Table 2b, 'Schedule of capital account expenditures for the year ended March 31, 1939. See for the next year *EJ*, 26 March 1969.

21. Province of Alberta, *Alberta Statistical Review 1980*, Table 12.

22. Wolfgang M. Illing and Zoltan E. Zsigmond, *Enrolment in Schools and Universities 1951-2 to 1975-6* (Ottawa: Economic Council of Canada, 1967), Appendix, Table B-2.

23. See, for example, *Financial Post*, 10 Sept., 2 July 1960. By 1959 *Life* estimated the United States teenage market to be almost $10 billion a year. See Wini

Breneis, *Young, White and Miserable: Growing Up Female in the Fifties* (Boston: Beacon Press, 1992), 92.

24. Thomas Patrick Doherty, *Teenagers and Teenpics: The Juvenilization of American Movies in the 1950s*, (Boston: Unwin Hyman, 1988), 45; and Breneis, *Young, White and Miserable*, 94. For a discussion of the nature of culture in the United States in these years see T.J. Jackson Lears, 'The Concept of Cultural Hegemony' *American Historical Review* 90, no. 3 (1985): 567-93.

25. William O'Neill, *Coming Apart*, 249.

26. Ibid., 259; and 'What the Beatles Have Done to Hair,' *Look Magazine*, 29 Dec. 1964.

27. Jon Ruddy, 'Where Did You Go? School? What Did You Learn? Don't!' *Maclean's*, 19 Nov. 1966, 9-11.

28. Jon Ruddy, 'Stop the World They Want to Get Off,' *Maclean's*, 1 Nov. 1965, 51.

29. Helen Horowitz, *Campus Life. Undergraduate Cultures from the Eighteenth Century to the Present* (Chicago: University of Chicago Press, 1988), 228.

30. Paul A. Carter, *Another Part of the Fifties* (New York: Columbia University Press, 1983), 96-8.

31. Female teenager calling a Vancouver talk show in 1966. Cited in Simma Holt, *Sex and the Teenage Revolution* (Toronto: McClelland and Stewart, 1967), 17.

32. Peter Gzowski, 'How You Going to Keep Them Down on the Farm after They've Said F**** You,' *SN*, May, 1969, 29-31.

33. UAA, 84-54, box 2, 'This is the Way, a Handbook for University Residences,' 1958-1959, 18.

34. W. Keith Wilkinson, 'Residence Culture: A Descriptive Study' (PhD diss., University of Alberta, 1966), 164, 171.

35. *Gateway* (University of Alberta student newspaper), 12 Sept. 1969. The information on the Wauneita Society comes from Elaine H. Chalus, 'From Friedan to Feminism: Gender and Change at the University of Alberta 1960-1970,' in Catherine Cavanaugh and Randi R. Warne, eds., *Standing on New Ground: Women in Alberta* (Edmonton: University of Alberta Press, 1993), 119-44.

36. *Gateway*, 2 March 1965.

37. Ibid., 2 Nov. 1966.

38. See John Thompson, John Bordo (members of Students for a Democratic Society), 'A memorandum for the administration,' in *Gateway*, 20 Sept. 1968.

39. See Jerry Farber, 'The Student as Nigger,' in *Gateway*, 26 March 1969. This article, originating in California, was reprinted in several Canadian student newspapers.

40. Myrna Kostash, *Long Way from Home* (Toronto: James Lorimer and Co., 1980), 92.

41. *EJ*, 27 March 1969.

42. On the background see 'Left Fights Right on CUS Policy,' *Ubyssey*, 13 Sept. 1966, 1. On the withdrawal see *Gateway*, 22 Nov. 1968.

43. *Canada Year Book* (1969), 428; and ibid. (1970-1), 513.

44. PAA, taped debates of the Legislative Assembly of Alberta, 70.397, tape 19, 24 Feb. 1969.

45. *Gateway*, 26 Oct., 29 Nov. 1968.

46. N. Mehra, *The Residence Student: A Study of Opinions and Reactions* (Edmonton: University of Alberta, Office of Institutional Research and Planning, 1971), 68.

47. *Gateway*, 16 Oct. 1968. Note that even by this time the primary decisions on rules were being made by students, not the administration.

48. Ibid., 105. See for a comment on the potential danger of drugs, ibid., 19 Sept. 1968. Note as well the CUS resolution to legalize marijuana in ibid., 29 Nov. 1968.

49. 'Private Interview 1972,' in Campbell, *Those Tumultuous Years*, 2.

50. Taped debates of the Legislative Assembly of Alberta, tape 30, 26 Feb. 1969, tape 221, 25 April 1969.

51. Ibid., tape 44, 24 Feb. 1969.

52. Ibid., tape 124, 31 March 1969.

53. *EJ*, 28 March, 27 Oct., 2 Nov. 1969.

54. *Canada Year Book* (1946), 111; and ibid. (1961), 148.

BROCK SILVERSIDES, TOMMY BANKS AND CENTURY II STUDIOS

1. Tommy Banks, interview with the author, 4 March 1993.

2. Ibid.

3. PAA, Tommy Banks Papers (TBP), 93.378, production files 486-717. The Tommy Banks collection, which is still in the process of being organized, documents not only Banks's personal career but also the activities of Century II Productions and Century II Studio.

4. See ibid., production files 489, 494, 497-8, 502, 513, 536, 547, 550, 569, 578.

5. Ibid., production files 237-53, 603, 670.

6. Ibid., production files 720-25.

7. Ibid., file 410, Agreement between Capital Records of Canada and Century II Productions, 20 June 1972.

8. Banks, interview.

9. Ibid.

10. TBP, file 377, Century II Partnership Agreement, 1 Aug. 1972.

11. Banks, interview.

12. Ibid. On Century II's initial announcement of its intention to expand see *EJ*,

26 Nov. 1970; and *Edmonton Examiner*, 3 Dec. 1970.

13. TBP, file 378, W. Jetton, 'Recording Studio Design and Equipment Proposal' (unpublished manuscript), 11 Nov. 1971; and file 379, correspondence—Auditronics, 1971-3. See also *EJ*, 15 Dec. 1972.

14. TBP, files 391-3, Century II Index (Musicians and Payments), 1972-5; and file 390, Century II Musician Contracts, 1973-7.

15. Banks, interview.

16. TBP, file 732, Century II publishing index (names and addresses of songwriters), 1973-4; files 733-54, Century II songwriters, 1973-4; and files 755-811, Century II songs, 1973-4.

17. Banks, interview. See also *EJ*, 7 Sept. 1973.

18. Banks interview. Media coverage of Banks's career and his contribution to the cultural life of Canada and Edmonton has been extensive. See, for example, *Edmonton TV Calendar*, Dec. 1971 ('Tommy Banks: Music and More'); *Canadian Composer*, Feb. 1985 ('Tommy Banks: Making a Musical Living in Edmonton'); and *EJ*, 29 Jan. 1973 ('Century II Puts City in Big Times').

DAVID MILLS, PETER POCKLINGTON AND THE BUSINESS OF HOCKEY

1. *EJ*, 10 Aug. 1988.

2. Rob B. Beamish, 'The Impact of Corporate Ownership in Labor-Management Relations in Hockey,' in Paul D. Staudohar and James A. Mangan, eds., *The Business of Professional Sports* (Urbana: University of Illinois Press, 1991), 202-21; and Richard S. Gruneau and David Whitson, *Hockey Night in Canada: Sport, Identities and Cultural Politics* (Toronto: Garamond Press, 1983), 223-46.

3. Because private owners do not reveal their books and accounting practices to the public, data must be pieced together from newspapers, records in the Corporate Registry, and interviews. Popular writing elevates hockey to a metaphor—the Canadian experience that explains us—and tends to portray team owners as folk heroes. See William F. Dowbiggin, ed., *Positive Power: The Story of the Edmonton Oilers* (Edmonton: Executive Sport Publications, 1982); Peter Gzowski, *The Game of Our Lives* (Toronto: McClelland and Stewart, 1981); and Peter C. Newman, *The Acquisitors: The Canadian Establishment*, vol. 2 (Toronto: McClelland and Stewart, 1981). Exceptions include Bruce Kidd and

John Macfarlane, *The Death of Hockey* (Toronto: New Press, 1972); and David Cruise and Alison Griffiths, *Net Worth: Exploding the Myths of Pro Hockey* (Toronto: Viking, 1991). Serious academic works too often evoke an equally simple image—the businessman as 'robber baron,' maximizing profits by eliminating competition, manipulating governments, exploiting the workers, extracting bucks from the rest of us, and translating economic wealth into political power and social status, at the expense of the community. James Quirk and Rodney D. Fort, *Pay Dirt: The Business of Professional Team Sports* (Princeton: Princeton University Press, 1992), 15-16. See also J.C.H. Jones, 'The Economics of the National Hockey League,' in Richard S. Gruneau and John G. Albinson, eds., *Canadian Sport: Sociological Perspectives* (Don Mills: Wesley Addison, 1976), 225-48; and Rob Beamish, 'The Political Economy of Professional Sport,' in Jean Harvey and Hart Cantelon, eds., *Not Just a Game: Essays in Canadian Sport Sociology* (Ottawa: University of Ottawa Press, 1988), 141-57. Sport thus becomes a microcosm of the larger society and sports owners tend to be discussed in moral rather than analytical terms.

4. Michael Bliss, *Northern Enterprise: Five Centuries of Canadian Business* (Toronto: McClelland and Stewart, 1987), 569.

5. Alfred D. Chandler, *The Visible Hand: The Managerial Revolution in American Business* (Cambridge MA: Belknap Press, 1977), 9.

6. Alan Artibise, 'Boosterism and the Development of Prairie Cities, 1871-1913,' in Alan Artibise, ed., *Town and City: Aspects of Western Canadian Urban Development* (Regina: Canadian Plains Research Center, 1981), 211-14; Paul Voisey, 'Boosting the Small Prairie Town, 1904-1931: An Example from Southern Alberta,' in ibid., 171; and Voisey, 'In Search of Wealth and Status: An Economic and Social Study of Entrepreneurs in Early Calgary,' in A.W. Rasporich and H.C. Klassen, eds., *Frontier Calgary: Town, City and Region, 1875-1914* (Calgary: University of Calgary, 1975), 221-41.

7. Peter Pocklington, interview with the author, Edmonton, 8 May 1995.

8. For more detail on Skalbania's business and sports deals see Newman, *Acquisitors*, 127-43; and *G&M*, 20 Nov. 1981.

9. Newman, *Acquisitors*, 292; *ES*, 24 Dec. 1980; and *EJ*, 6 May 1978.

10. *ES*, 18 April 1982.

11. Ibid., 10 Sept. 1978; Newman, *Acquisitors*, 293; *ES*, 1 April 1979; and *EJ*, 13 Aug. 1987.

12. John Short, 'The Edmonton Oilers: A History,' in Dowbiggin, *Positive Power*, 83; and *EJ*, 10 Aug. 1988.

13. *ES*, 14 Jan. 1979.

14. Pocklington, interview. The *Journal* (9 Dec. 1990) reported that Pocklington looked into the mirror every morning and said: 'I am a god, I am a god.'

15. *ES*, 4 April, 28 Nov. 1979. Estimated profits of $1.4 million for the Oilers compared quite favourably to losses of $2 million suffered by Colorado, Washington, and Pittsburgh and $1 million in Chicago, St Louis, Los Angeles, and Atlanta.

16. *EJ*, 18 Aug. 1988.

17. *ES*, 6 May 1983.

18. Patrick Martin, Allan Gregg, and George Perlin, *Contenders: The Tory Quest for Power* (Scarborough: Prentice-Hall Canada, 1983), 147; and Pocklington, interview.

19. *G&M*, 19 April 1983; and *EJ*, 9 Dec. 1990.

20. *SN*, Aug. 1987, 34-40. Labour relations are not Pocklington's strong suit. During the lockout preceding the shortened 1995 hockey season, he was a hard-liner, even though he said he was losing as much as $100,000 a night because no games were being played. Frustrated with the demands of the NHL Players' Association, he claimed that his players were being 'brainwashed' by their leader, Bob Goodenow, and 'maybe they should get out of the union.' *EJ*, 17 Nov. 1994.

21. *ES*, 28, 31 July 1983.

22. On 30 Dec. 1982 Pocklington Amalgamated Sports Corporation secured a $20 million debenture from the Canadian Commercial Bank, that was transferred to the Province of Alberta's Treasury Branch on 29 July 1984. Another $11 million debenture was taken with the Treasury Branch on 29 June 1983. When a new corporation, Edmonton Oilers Hockey Ltd. (the result of an amalgamation between Pocklington Amalgamated Sports Corporation and Edmonton Oilers Hockey Ltd.) was registered on 11 Feb. 1985, corporate records show that the $31 million in debentures was still held by the Treasury Branch. Government of Alberta, Department of Consumer and Corporate Affairs, Corporate Registry, Edmonton Oilers Hockey Ltd. #21324671. See also Edmonton Oilers Hockey Ltd. #20336285 and Pocklington Amalgamated Sports Corp. #21271927.

23. See *G&M*, 8 Feb. 1986; and *ES*, 13 June 1986, 28 April 1987. Pocklington has come to rely upon government subsidies to finance expansion; in Dec. 1985 he received a $21 million loan from the Province of Saskatchewan to build a meat-packing plant. In March

1988 he obtained a $12 million loan plus $55 million in loan guarantees from the Government of Alberta (*ES*, 10 Dec. 1985; and *G&M*, 7 March 1988). Pocklington has argued that 'individuals should be free to create wealth by operating for their own gain within a system of private property and unencumbered by rules or confiscatory taxation by the state.' But in 'an imperfect world, where the state demands taxes from its corporate citizens, then the state must be willing to offer offsetting grants to help these corporations prosper' (*EJ*, 7 Dec. 1988).

24. *EJ*, 25 Nov. 1989.

25. Prices ranged from $15 to $23; only the Calgary Flames had higher prices (*ES*, 6 June 1984). Player salaries in the NHL had increased significantly; in 1979 the average salary was $101,000 and by 1983 it was $125,000 (Staudohar, *Sports Industry and Collective Bargaining*, 123). *ES*, 8 Oct. 1987.

26. Pocklington was reported to have said that he received enough cash 'to buy another company or two' (*EJ*, 10 Aug. 1988).

27. Pocklington, interview with the author, Edmonton, 11 Oct. 1988; and *ES*, 11 Aug. 1988, 27 Jan. 1989.

28. *ES*, 28 Feb. 1989; and *G&M*, 3 March 1989.

29. Government of Alberta, Corporate Registry, PFC Financial Ltd. #20344214 and #20388319. The Treasury Branch, which then held $42 million worth of debentures, also agreed to discharge any of its claims against Wayne Gretzky's contract which was held as security. *EJ*, 11 Aug. 1988.

30. According to the *EJ*, 17 July 1989, he donated $12,200 in 1988.

31. Ibid., 13 July 1989.

32. The Government of Alberta paid $32 million to Lloyd's Bank to reduce the company's debt and was left with a debenture held against assets by a Crown-owned company, 354713 Alberta Ltd., that manages real estate obtained through bailouts (*ES*, 5 Oct. 1989; and *G&M*, 7 Oct. 1989).

33. *EJ*, 9 June 1990. It was also estimated that Pocklington's assets totalled around $175 million (*G&M*, 19 Oct. 1989).

34. Financial World Magazine, 10 May 1994. While the Oilers were losing money, the franchise was still worth considerably more than the $6.5 million that Pocklington had paid for the team.

35. *EJ*, 27 July, 12 April 1994.

36. Pocklington, interview, 8 May 1995.

37. *CH*, 16 May 1980.

38. Jimmy Pattison with Paul Grescoe, *Jimmy: An Autobiography* (Toronto: McClelland and Stewart, 1987), 148; and Newman, *Acquisitors*, 61-2.

39. Newman, *Acquisitors*, 141-2; also *CH*, 15 Jan. 1980; *ES*, 8 Dec. 1982; and *CS*, 4 May 1986.

40. See J.D. House, *The Last of the Free Enterprisers: The Oilmen of Calgary* (Toronto: Macmillan Company of Canada, 1980.) Only Norm Kwong is a Calgarian. The Seamans and Ralph Scurfield were born in Saskatchewan, Green in Manitoba, and Hotchkiss in Ontario. The owners' anxiety to boost Calgary, their new home, may reveal a desire to strengthen local status and identity through expressions of community spirit.

41. *G&M*, 15 Feb. 1990. For more details on their business activities see Peter Foster, *From Rigs to Riches: The Story of Bow Valley Industries Ltd.* (Calgary: Bow Valley Industries, 1985). The Seamans keep their activities in the oil industry quite separate from the hockey business. The only reference to the Calgary Flames in Foster's book is on page 11.

42. Each of the partners, now including Sonia Scurfield who assumed her husband's share after his death in 1985, controlled 18 per cent of the franchise, except for Kwong who held 10 per cent. (*G&M*, 2 March 1989; also Newman, *Acquisitors*, 367; and Calgary Flames, *Media Guide and Record Book* (Calgary: Calgary Flames Hockey Club, 1988), 4-5.

43. Clare Rhyasen, vice-president of business and finance, interview with the author, 21 Feb. 1989. Peter Pocklington said that the Seaman brothers were 'not just buying a team to make money. They are not on an ego trip' (*CH*, 9 May 1980). Green is quoted in biographical material from the Calgary Flames magazine provided during the Rhyasen interview.

44. *CH*, 22 May 1980. The franchise is estimated to have grossed about $6 million in its first season in Calgary, from season ticket sales, the sale of broadcasting rights, and playoffs.

45. Ibid., 5 Aug. 1980.

46. Eric Duhatschek and Steve Simmons, *On Fire: The Dramatic Rise of the Calgary Flames* (Winlaw: Polestar Press, 1986), 19; and *CS*, 4 May 1986.

47. *Hockey News*, 28 Oct. 1988; Rhyasen, interview; *G&M*, 2 March 1989; and *EJ*, 20 April 1994.

48. Rhyasen, interview; *G&M*, 2 March 1989; and Seaman, quoted in the biographical material provided during the Rhyasen interview.

49. In the first year of operation, it was apparent that sufficient profits could not be generated in the old Corral. The owners stated that $10,000 from each home playoff game would be directed to the hockey fund; $80,000 was raised as a result. *G&M*, 2 March 1989; and *CS*, 4 May 1986. The same

sentiments were expressed by Green and Hotchkiss in the biographical material provided during the Rhyasen interview.

50. Rhyasen, interview; and Olympic Saddledome Foundation, *The First Five Years, 1983-1988* (Calgary: Olympic Saddledome Foundation, 1988), 1-16.

51. *G&M*, 7 Jan. 1994. There was also an infusion of new capital into the franchise when a national corporation, Tim Horton Donuts, became a minority shareholder in 1994.

52. Ibid., 23 Feb. 1995; *Hockey News*, 24 March 1995; *EJ*, 12, 22 March, 23 June 1995; and *ES*, 21 April 1995.

53. Pocklington, interview, 8 May 1995; and *EJ*, 16, 2 March 1995. His companies, especially the Oilers, have given over $4.7 million to local charities and other endeavours over the past 15 years. He is also promoting a concert at the Coliseum by internationally-renowned tenor, Luciano Pavarotti, in the fall of 1995. The event should not only make money but also raise Edmonton's international profile (*EJ*, 20 May 1995).

PAUL VOISEY, UNSOLVED MYSTERIES OF EDMONTON'S GROWTH

1. Broad surveys that trace aspects of Edmonton's growth include A.W. Cashman, *The Edmonton Story* (Edmonton: Institute of Applied Art, 1956); James G. MacGregor, *Edmonton: A History*, 2d ed. (Edmonton: Hurtig, 1975); and John Gilpin, *Edmonton: Gateway to the North, An Illustrated History* (Edmonton: Windsor Publications and Amisk Waskahegan Chapter, Historical Society of Alberta, 1984).

2. For Fort Edmonton in the fur trade see A.S. Morton, *A History of the Canadian West to 1870-71* (Toronto: University of Toronto Press 1973); E.E. Rich, *The History of the Hudson's Bay Company, 1670-1870*, 2 vols. (London: Hudson's Bay Record Society, 1959); Janice E. MacDonald, *The Northwest Fort: Fort Edmonton* (Edmonton: Lone Pine Publishing, 1983); and MacGregor, *Edmonton*, 17-62.

3. J.M.S. Careless, 'Frontierism, Metropolitanism, and Canadian History,' *CHR* 35, no. 1 (1954): 1-21; and, for his latest views, *Frontier and Metropolis: Regions, Cities, and Identities in Canada before 1914* (Toronto: University of Toronto Press, 1989).

4. The most comprehensive history of early Strathcona is John Gilpin, 'The City of Strathcona, 1891-1912: "We see just ahead the glory of the sun in his might"' (MA thesis, University of Alberta, 1978). See also John Gilpin,

'Failed Metropolis: The City of Strathcona, 1891-1912,' in Alan Artibise, ed., *Town and City: Aspects of Western Canadian Urban Development* (Regina: Canadian Plains Research Center, 1981), 259-88.

5. Edmonton's transition to an agricultural service centre after 1880 can be closely followed in the *Edmonton Bulletin*; see also MacGregor, *Edmonton*, 89-120. For early comparisons with other prairie cities see Paul Voisey, 'The Urbanization of the Canadian Prairies, 1871-1916,' *SH* 15 (1975): 77-83; Alan Artibise, *Prairie Urban Development, 1870-1930* (Ottawa: Canadian Historical Association, 1981); and J.M.S. Careless, 'Aspects of Urban Life in the West, 1870-1914,' in A.W. Rasporich and H.C. Klassen, eds., *Prairie Perspectives 2: Selected Papers of the Western Canadian Studies Conferences, 1970 and 1971* (Toronto: Holt, Rinehart and Winston, 1973), 25-40. For the development of frontier cities generally see Christopher J. Schell and Patrick E. McLear, 'Why the Cities Grew: A Historiographical Essay on Western Urban Growth, 1850-1880,' *Missouri Historical Society Bulletin* 28 (1972): 162-77. Particularly useful ideas are presented in Richard C. Wade, *The Urban Frontier, 1790-1830* (Cambridge MA: Harvard University Press, 1959); and James E. Vance, *The Merchant's World: The Geography of Wholesaling* (Englewood Cliffs NJ: Prentice-Hall, 1970).

6. All population statistics are taken or calculated from *Census of Canada* (1901-91); or *Census of the Prairie Provinces* (1906-36).

7. Voisey, 'Urbanization of the Prairies'; Artibise, *Prairie Urban Development*; and Careless, 'Aspects of Urban Life.'

8. Ibid. See also Alan Artibise, 'In Pursuit of Growth: Municipal Boosterism and Urban Development in the Canadian Prairie West, 1871-1913,' in Gilbert Stelter and Alan Artibise, eds., *Shaping the Urban Landscape: Aspects of the Canadian City-Building Process* (Ottawa: Carleton University Press, 1982), 116-47; John C. Weaver, 'Edmonton's Perilous Course, 1904-1929,' *UHR* 2-77 (1977): 20-32; and Edmund H. Dale, 'The Role of Successive Town and City Councils in the Evolution of Edmonton, Alberta, 1892-1966' (PhD diss., University of Alberta, 1969), 2-151.

9. Gilpin, 'City of Strathcona.'

10. See especially, Alexander Bruce Kilpatrick, 'A Lesson in Boosterism: The Contest for the Alberta Provincial Capital, 1904-1906,' *UHR* 8, no. 3 (1980): 47-109.

11. Eric Lampard, 'History of Cities in the Economically Advanced Areas,'

Economic Development and Cultural Change 3 (1954-5): 81-136; and his 'Historical Aspects of Urbanization,' in Philip M. Hauser and Leo F. Schnore, eds., *The Study of Urbanization* (New York: John Wiley and Sons, 1965), 519-54. Scattered studies on new economic activities in Edmonton include James G. MacGregor, *Edmonton Trader: The Story of John A. McDougall* (Toronto: McClelland and Stewart, 1963); Catherine Cole, 'The Garment Manufacturing Industry in Edmonton, 1911-1939' (MA thesis, University of Alberta, 1988); Sally Hamilton, 'An Historical Geography of Coal Mining in the Edmonton Area' (MA thesis, University of Alberta, 1971); R.G. Ironside and Sally Hamilton, 'Historical Geography of Coal Mining in the Edmonton District,' *AHR* 20, no. 3 (1972): 6-16; and Michael A. Crowston, 'The Growth of the Metal Industries in Edmonton' (MA thesis, University of Alberta, 1971).

12. F.E. Ian Hamilton, 'Models in Industrial Location,' in R.J. Chorley and Peter Haggett, eds., *Models in Geography* (London: Methuen, 1967), 361-424; Allan Pred, 'Some Locational Relationships Between Industrial Inventions, Industrial Innovations, and Urban Growth,' *The East Lakes Geographer* 2 (1966): 45-70; and Pred, 'Industrialization, Initial Advantage, and American Metropolitan Growth,' *Geographical Review* 55, no. 2 (1965): 158-85.

13. Jane Jacobs, *The Economy of Cities* (New York: Random House, 1969).

14. See, for example, John Blue, *Alberta Past and Present: Historical and Biographical*, 3 vols. (Chicago: Pioneer Historical Publishing, 1924).

15. Voisey, 'Urbanization of the Prairies'; Careless, 'Aspects of Urban Life'; and Artibise, *Prairie Urban Development*.

16. Andrew F. Burghardt, 'A Hypothesis About Gateway Cities,' *Annals, Association of American Geographers* 61, no. 2 (1971): 269-85; and James G. MacGregor, *The Klondike Rush through Edmonton, 1897-1898* (Toronto: McClelland and Stewart, 1970).

17. L.D. McCann, 'The Myth of the Metropolis: The Role of the City in Canadian Regionalism,' *UHR* 9, no. 3 (1981): 52-8; Donald F. Davis, 'The "Metropolitan Thesis" and the Writing of Canadian Urban History,' ibid., 14, no. 2 (1985): 95-114; and William Cronon, *Nature's Metropolis: Chicago and the Great West* (New York: W.W. Norton, 1991). One useful approach to the mechanics of metropolitanism in western Canada is found in Donald Kerr, 'Wholesale Trade on the Canadian Plains in the Late Nineteenth Century: Winnipeg and

its Competition,' in Howard Palmer, ed., *The Settlement of the West* (Calgary: Comprint, 1977), 130-52. European historians often equate what Canadian scholars call metropolitanism with central place theory; see Paul M. Hohenberg and Lynn Hollen Lees, *The Making of Urban Europe, 1000-1950* (Cambridge MA: Harvard University Press, 1985), 47-73.

18. Allan Pred, *Urban Growth and the Circulation of Information: The United States System of Cities, 1790-1840* (Cambridge MA: Harvard University Press, 1973). For an application to Canada, albeit largely non-historical, see James W. Simmons, *Canada as an Urban System: A Conceptual Framework* (Toronto: University of Toronto Centre for Urban and Community Studies, 1974).

19. The problems of prairie cities between the wars are charted in Alan Artibise, 'Patterns of Prairie Urban Development, 1871-1950,' in David J. Bercuson and Phillip A. Buckner, eds., *Eastern and Western Perspectives: Papers from the Joint Atlantic Canada/Western Canadian Studies Conference* (Toronto: University of Toronto Press, 1981), 124-37; Artibise, 'City-Building in the Canadian West: From Boosterism to Corporatism,' *JCS* 17, no. 3 (1982): 35-44; and Paul Phillips, 'The Prairie Urban System, 1911-1961: Specialization and Change,' in Artibise, *Town and City*, 7-30.

20. Artibise, 'Patterns of Prairie Urban Development,' 126; Weaver, 'Edmonton's Perilous Course'; and Dale, 'Role of Successive Councils,' 253-91. For the scale of prewar speculation see John Gilpin, 'Urban Land Speculation in the Development of Strathcona (South Edmonton), 1891-1912,' in John E. Foster, ed., *The Developing West: Essays on Canadian History in Honour of Lewis H. Thomas* (Edmonton: University of Alberta Press, 1983), 179-99; and Gilpin, 'The Land Development Process in Edmonton, Alberta, 1881-1917,' in Gilbert Stelter and Alan Artibise, eds., *Power and Place: Canadian Urban Development in the North American Context* (Vancouver: University of British Columbia Press, 1986), 151-72.

21. Almost nothing has been published on these economic aspects of the automobile, but some information was culled from Timothy C. Losey, 'History of the Automobile in Alberta' (unpublished manuscript, Reynolds-Alberta Museum, 1984); and David van Leenen, 'Paving the Way: Edmonton and the Impact of the Automobile, 1919-1930' (unpublished manuscript, n.d.).

22. Many aspects of farm mechanization in interwar Alberta are discussed in Paul

Voisey, *Vulcan: The Making of a Prairie Community* (Toronto: University of Toronto Press, 1988), 140-54.

23. See, for example, Stan McMillan and Mike Finland, eds., *Uncharted Skies: Canadian Bush Pilot Stories* (Edmonton: Reidmore, 1988); and Louise Eugenie Myles, *Airborne from Edmonton* (Toronto: Ryerson, 1959).

24. For the growth of entertainment enterprises see Donald G. Wetherell with Irene Kmet, *Useful Pleasures: The Shaping of Leisure in Alberta, 1896-1945* (Regina: Canadian Plains Research Center and Alberta Culture and Multiculturalism, 1990); and MacGregor, *Edmonton*.

25. The works that discuss Edmonton's role in the war and northern development most fully include William C. Wonders, 'Repercussions of War and Oil on Edmonton, Alberta,' *Cahiers de géographie de Québec* 6 (1959): 343-51; Ken Coates, *North to Alaska* (Toronto: McClelland and Stewart, 1992); and articles in Ken Tingley, ed., *For King and Country: Alberta in the Second World War* (Edmonton: Provincial Museum of Alberta, 1995); and Bob Hesketh, ed., *Three Northern Wartime Projects: The Alaska Highway, The Northwest Staging Route, and Canol* (Edmonton: Canadian Circumpolar Institute, forthcoming).

26. Developments in the petroleum economy are described in Ed Gould, *Oil: The History of Canada's Oil and Gas Industry* (Victoria: Hancock House, 1977); Eric J. Hanson, *Dynamic Decade: the Evolution and Effects of the Oil Industry in Alberta* (Toronto: McClelland and Stewart, 1958); David H. Breen, *Alberta's Petroleum Industry and the Conservation Board* (Edmonton: University of Alberta Press, 1993); Wonders, 'Repercussions of War and Oil'; and P.J. Smith, 'Fort Saskatchewan: An Industrial Satellite of Edmonton,' *PC* 3, no. 1 (1962): 4-16.

27. Paul J. Curtis, 'Some Aspects of Industrial Linkages in Edmonton's Oil Industry with Special Reference to the Tertiary Sector' (MA thesis, University of Alberta, 1972); Crowston, 'Growth of the Metal Industries'; and Neil R.M. Seifried, 'The Changing Economy of Edmonton, 1961-1971,' in P.J. Smith, ed., *Edmonton: The Emerging Metropolitan Pattern* (Victoria: Department of Geography, University of Victoria, 1978), 1-27.

28. Changes in the rural economy are traced in many essays in P.J. Smith, ed., *Studies in Canadian Geography: The Prairie Provinces* (Toronto: University of Toronto Press, 1972); A.W. Rasporich, ed., *The Making of the Modern West: Western Canada since 1945* (Calgary: University of Calgary Press, 1984); and B.M. Barr and P.J. Smith, eds., *Environment and Economy: Essays on*

the *Human Geography of Alberta* (Edmonton: Pica Pica, 1984).

29. Aspects of these developments are suggested in Neil R.M. Seifried, 'The Expanding Urban Economy of a Spontaneous Growth Centre: Edmonton, Alberta,' *AG* 14 (1978): 105-21; and J. Anderson, 'Economic Base Measurement and Changes in the Base of Metropolitan Edmonton, 1951-1961,' ibid., 4 (1967-8): 4-9.

30. For the advent of white-collar work generally see Daniel Bell, *The Coming of Post Industrial Society* (New York: Basic Books, 1976). For the revolution in thought that led to government expansion in Canada see Doug Owram, *The Government Generation: Canadian Intellectuals and the State, 1900-1945* (Toronto: University of Toronto Press, 1986). Works that trace the growth of Alberta's provincial government most explicitly include John J. Barr, *The Dynasty: The Rise and Fall of Social Credit in Alberta* (Toronto: McClelland and Stewart, 1974); John Richards and Larry Pratt, *Prairie Capitalism: Power and Influence in the New West* (Toronto: McClelland and Stewart, 1979); and Breen, *Alberta's Petroleum Industry*. For the general impact on Canadian cities see James W. Simmons, 'The Impact of the Public Sector on the Canadian Urban System,' in Stelter and Artibise, *Power and Place*, 21-50. Limited applications to prairie cities include Walter G. Hardwick, 'Transformation of the West From Industrial to Post-Industrial Society,' in Rasporich, *Making of the Modern West*, 89-96; Patrick G. Cadden, 'The Economic Role of Public Employees in the Urban Communities,' in Barr and Smith, *Environment and Economy*, 154-66; and Elizabeth S. Szplett, 'The Transactional Environment: Quaternary and Quinary Industry,' in Barr and Smith, *Environment and Economy*, 167-80.

31. Michel Crozier, *The World of the Office Worker* (Chicago: University of Chicago Press, 1971). The most complete history of office work in Canada is Graham S. Lowe, *Women in the Administrative Revolution: The Feminization of Clerical Work* (Toronto: University of Toronto Press, 1987).

32. The growth of bureaucracy in private business is charted in Alfred Chandler, *Strategy and Structure: The History of the American Industrial Enterprise* (Cambridge MA: Harvard University Press, 1962). White-collar activities stemmed from the growing importance of planning, financing, marketing, advertising, taxation, accounting, labour negotiations, public relations, personnel administration, legal services, training programs, pensions, and benefits.

33. Some aspects of specialization and interaction between the cities can be seen in George H. Zieber, 'Inter- and Intra-city Location Patterns of Oil Offices for Calgary and Edmonton, 1950-1970' (PhD diss., University of Alberta, 1971); Zieber, 'The Dispersed City Hypothesis with Reference to Calgary and Edmonton,' *AG* 9 (1973): 4-13; P.J. Smith and Denis B. Johnson, *The Edmonton-Calgary Corridor* (Edmonton: Department of Geography, University of Alberta, 1978); P.J. Smith, 'Edmonton and Calgary: Growing Together,' *CGJ* 92, no. 3 (1976): 26-33; David H. Breen, 'Calgary: The City and the Petroleum Industry Since World War Two,' *UHR* 2-77 (1977): 55-71; and Brent Johner, 'Too Little, Too Late: The Rise and Fall of the Edmonton Stock Exchange, 1952-1957,' *AH* 42, no. 4 (1994): 2-10.

34. Shifting metropolitan relations on the prairies are discussed in Donald P. Kerr, 'Metropolitan Dominance in Canada,' in John Warkentin, ed., *Canada: A Geographical Interpretation* (Toronto: Methuen, 1968), 531-55; Phillips, 'Prairie Urban System'; P.J. Smith, 'Urban Development Trends in the Prairie Provinces,' in Rasporich, *Making of the Modern West*, 133-43; and Neil R. Seifried, 'Growth and Change in Prairie Metropolitan Centres after 1951,' *PF* 7, no. 1 (1982): 49-68. By the 1970s Edmonton had firmly displaced Winnipeg as a wholesale supplier for the entire western portion of northern Canada but faced a new challenge from Vancouver; see R.G. Ironside and Dale D. Peterson, 'Edmonton's Wholesale Relationships with Northwest Canada,' *CG* 26, no. 3 (1982): 207-44.

35. On the question of growing metropolitan status in the 1970s see McCann, 'Myth of the Metropolis'; and the debate, 'Power Shift West: Myth or Reality?' *CJS* 6, no. 2 (1981): 165-83.

36. For petroleum development and related political conflict after 1970 see Michael Bliss, *Northern Enterprise: Five Centuries of Canadian Business* (Toronto: McClelland and Stewart, 1987), 515-47; Richards and Pratt, *Prairie Capitalism*; Larry Pratt, 'The Political Economy of Province-Building: Alberta's Development Strategy, 1971-1981,' in David Leadbeater, ed., *Essays on the Political Economy of Alberta* (Toronto: New Hogtown, 1984), 194-222; and Bruce G. Doern and Glen Toner, *The Politics of Energy: The Development and Implementation of the NEP* (Toronto: Methuen, 1985).

37. Aspects of recent economic history are discussed in Andrew Nikiforuk et al., eds., *Running on Empty: Alberta after the Boom* (Edmonton: NeWest, 1987), but most of it must be pieced together from journalistic sources like the *Financial Post* and *Alberta Report*.

38. Dane Lanken, 'Drapeau's Montreal: Great Moments, Great Monuments,' *CGJ* 106, no. 4 (1986): 10-23; and David Mills, 'The Battle of Alberta: Entrepreneurs and the Business of Hockey in Edmonton and Calgary,' *Alberta Studies in the Arts and Sciences* 2, no. 2 (1990): 1-26. West Edmonton Mall is examined in a special issue of the *CG* 35, no. 3 (1991).

39. For the growing shift from resources to a service economy see Bliss, *Northern Enterprise*, 547-84. H. Craig Davis and Thomas A. Hutton, 'The Two Economies of British Columbia,' *BC Studies* 82 (1989): 3-15, argue that the urban complex of British Columbia's southern coast began to develop a self-driven service economy increasingly divorced from the old resource economy of the interior.